Information Technology Management

Information Technology Management

Edited by **May Sanders**

New York

Published by Willford Press,
118-35 Queens Blvd., Suite 400,
Forest Hills, NY 11375, USA
www.willfordpress.com

Information Technology Management
Edited by May Sanders

International Standard Book Number: 978-1-68285-258-3 (Hardback)

Printed in the United States of America.

Contents

Preface

Every book is initially just a concept; it takes months of research and hard work to give it the final shape in which the readers receive it. In its early stages, this book also went through rigorous reviewing. The notable contributions made by experts from across the globe were first molded into patterned chapters and then arranged in a sensibly sequential manner to bring out the best results.

Information technology management is the discipline that aims to study and analyse the management and allocation of an organisation's information technology resources and techniques. It focuses on both broader as well as specific functions of information technology and management. This book provides comprehensive insights into the fields of database management, IT configuration management and IT infrastructure. It emphasizes on understanding of information systems planning, facilitating information technology management, etc. This book includes contributions of experts and scientists which will provide innovative insights into this field and provide comprehensive knowledge to students, academicians and professionals.

It has been my immense pleasure to be a part of this project and to contribute my years of learning in such a meaningful form. I would like to take this opportunity to thank all the people who have been associated with the completion of this book at any step.

Editor

EPQ models for deteriorating items with linearly discounted backordering under limited utilization of facility

Hui-Ming Teng

Department of Business Administration, Chihlee Institute of Technology, No. 313, Sec. 1, Wunhua Road, Banciao City, Taipei County 220, Taiwan.

This study presents an economic production quantity model for deteriorating items in which backorder is allowed. The selling price of backorder depends on the customers that are willing to purchase the items under the condition that they receive their orders after a certain fraction of waiting time. The utilization of facility is an important index of production efficiency in the opportunity cost perspectives. This model considers both the impact of discounted selling price of backorder and the utilization rate of facility during the production process. Numerical examples and sensitivity analysis are given to illustrate the model.

Key words: Deterioration, linearly discounted backordering, utilization of facility, opportunity cost.

INTRODUCTION

Shortage backorder issues had received much attention from researchers. Many kinds of backordering were assumed. Wee (1999) had studied that the fraction of stockout demand backordered was constant. Abad (1996) suggested that customers do not like to wait, and therefore the fraction of customers who choose to place backorders is a decreasing function of waiting time such as $B(t) = k_0 e^{-k_1 t}$ or $B(t) = k_0 /(1 + k_1 t)$, while t being waiting time and k_0, k_1 being parameters. You (2005) had studied the optimal replenishment policy in which the probability of customers backordered is assumed to be linearly decreasing with waiting time t and is assumed to be $\theta(t) = 1 - t/T$, $0 \le t < T$. However, they did not consider the suitable selling price which depended on the waiting time. In practice, the selling price always depends on the customers that are willing to purchase the items under the condition that they receive their orders after a certain

fraction of waiting time. In this study, the linear fraction of waiting time for selling price is assumed. In the past, many researchers had developed inventory models (Wee, 1999; Kang and Kim, 1983; Raafat et al., 1991; Hsu et al., 2007). Goyal and Gunasekaran (1995) developed an integrated deteriorating production – inventory -marketing model for determining the economic production quantity (EPQ) and economic order quantity for raw materials in a multi-stage production system. Luo (1998) extended the model proposed by Goyal and Gunasekaran (1995) to include backorder as a decision variable. In his model, any shortages were satisfied at the beginning of the cycle, and all shortage costs were known. Teng and Chang (2005) established an EPQ model for deteriorating items when the demand rate depends not only on the on-display stock level but also on the selling price per unit. In addition, they imposed a ceiling on the number of on-display stocks because

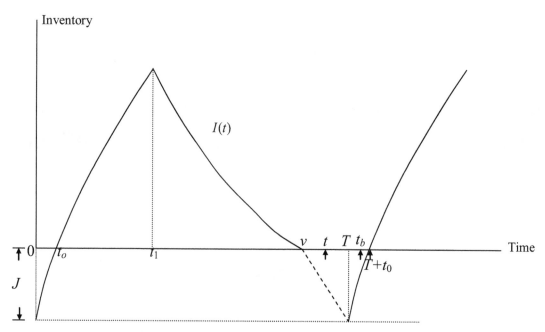

Figure 1. Inventory system of deteriorating items with backordering.

having too much stock left a negative impression on the buyer and the amount of display space was limited. Huang (2010) investigated that if an item is out of stock in an inventory system in which shortage is allowed, the supper may offer a negotiable price discount to the loyal, tolerant and obliged customers to pay off the inconvenience of backordering. Hung (2011) developed a ramp type demand rate and Weibull deterioration rate to arbitrary demand rate and arbitrary deterioration rate in the consideration of partial backorder. Hou et al. (2011) developed an inventory model for deteriorating items that the shortages are allowed and the unsatisfied demand is partially backlogged at the exponential rate with respect to the waiting time. Lin (2012) investigated the impact of setup cost reduction on an inventory policy for a continuous review mixture inventory model involving controllable backorder rate and variable lead time with a service level constraint. However, the inventory model with linear discounted backordering (that is, the backordered selling price of customer is assumed to be linearly decreasing with waiting time) has received little attention in past years.

The utilization of facility is an important issue in recent literature (Einhorn, 1987; Hou, 2007; Chakraborty et al., 2008). Many managers treat the utilization of facility as an index of production efficiency or expect the industries will run their production facility at an optimum level (Sharma, 2008).

Opportunity cost is the cost incurred by choosing one option over the other best alternative. Clark and Easaw (2007) studied optimal access pricing for natural monopoly networks with large sunk costs and uncertain

revenues when considering the opportunity cost. Azaiez (2002) integrated opportunity costs for the unsatisfied demand to develop a multi-stage decision model for the conjunctive use of ground and surface water with an artificial recharge. In this paper, an EPQ model for deteriorating items with backordering is developed. This model considers linearly discounted selling price of backordered items and the constraint on the utilization rate. The aim of this model is to determine the production run time and shortage demand so that the average profit per unit time is maximized.

MATHEMATICAL MODEL AND ANALYSIS

A constant production rate K starts at $t=0$ to both finish the last backorder and the demand, then continues up to $t=t_1$ where the inventory level reaches the top. Production then stops at $t=t_1$, and the inventory gradually depletes to v (with $t_1 < v \leq T$) due to deterioration and consumption. A graphical representation of this inventory system is depicted in Figure 1. The objective is to determine the optimal values for the shortage demand, J, and the production run time, t_1, such that the average profit per unit time is maximized. From the above assumptions and notation, we know that the inventory level $I(t)$ at time t satisfies the following two differential equations:

$$dI(t)/dt + \theta I(t) = K - (d+rt), \quad 0 \leq t \leq t_1 \qquad (1)$$

with initial condition $I(0) = -J$, and

$dI(t)/dt + \theta I(t) = -(d+rt), \quad t_1 < t \le v$. (2)

with initial conditions $\lim_{t \to t_1^+} I(t) = I(t_1)$ and $I(v) = 0$.

Solving the equations gives

$$I(t) = \frac{K-d-rt}{\theta} + \frac{r}{\theta^2} + \frac{e^{-\theta t}(-K\theta + d\theta - r - J\theta^2)}{\theta^2} ,$$

$0 \le t \le t_1$. (3)

$$I(t) = \frac{-d-rt}{\theta} + \frac{r}{\theta^2} + e^{-\theta(t-t_1)}\left[\frac{d+rt_1}{\theta} - \frac{r}{\theta^2} + I(t_1) \right],$$

$t_1 < t \le v.$ (4)

Solving $I(t_0) = 0$ and $I(v) = 0$, with $e^x \approx 1 + x + x^2/2$, using software Maple, one has

$$t_0(J) = \frac{K - d + J\theta - \sqrt{K^2 - 2Kd + d^2 - 2Jr - J^2\theta^2}}{r + (K-d)\theta + J\theta^2} .$$ (5)

$$v(t_1, J) = \frac{d + \left[t_1 d + t_1^2 r + I(t_1)\right]\theta + t_1 I(t_1)\theta^2 - \sqrt{d^2 + t_1^2 r^2 + 2rI(t_1) + 2rt_1 d - I(t_1)^2 \theta^2}}{-r + (d + rt_1)\theta + I(t_1)\theta^2} .$$ (6)

The shortage backordered quantity is

$$J = \int_v^T d \, dt = d(T - v) .$$ (7)

One has

$$T(t_1, J) = v + \frac{J}{d} .$$ (8)

When the customer agrees to place backorder at time t, the backorder satisfied time, t_b, can be approximated as follows:

Using linear interpolation, $\dfrac{T-t}{T-v} \approx \dfrac{T+t_o-t_b}{T+t_o-T}$, one has

$$t_b = T + t_o - \frac{(T-t)t_o}{T-v} .$$ (9)

From the definition of $p_b(\eta)$, the backordered revenue is

$$\int_v^T d(t_b - t)p_b \, dt = dp \int_v^T 1 - \frac{\delta(t_b - t)}{T - v} dt.$$ (10)

From the analysis above, the average profit per unit time, AP, is

$AP = \dfrac{1}{T}$ [normal revenue + backordered revenue − production cost − inventory holding cost − ordering cost]

$$= \frac{1}{T}\left[\int_0^v (d+rt)p\,dt + \int_v^T d(t_b-t)p_b\,dt - \int_0^{t_1} Kc_p\,dt - \int_{t_o}^v I(t)c_h\,dt - c_o \right].$$ (11)

Where

$$\int_0^v (d+rt)p\,dt = (dv + rv^2/2)p .$$ (12)

$$\int_v^T dp_b(t_b - t)dt = \{J/d - \delta(T + t_o - Tt_o d/J) - \delta(t_o d/J - 1)(T + v)/2\}dp.$$ (13)

$$\int_0^{t_1} Kc_p\,dt = Kt_1 c_p .$$ (14)

$$\int_{t_o}^v I(t)c_h\,dt \approx I(t_1)(v - t_o)c_h/2 .$$ (15)

Since t_o is a function of J, and v is a function of t_1 and J, therefore, AP is a function of t_1 and J. When the backordering quantity is J, the production run time t_1 needs to satisfy the production quantity which meets the customer's demand, the backordering quantity and

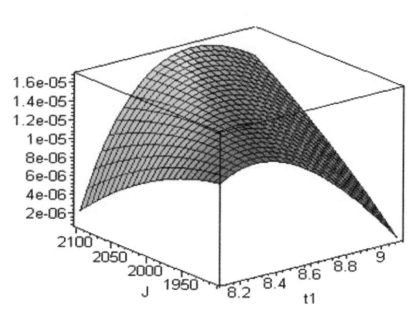

Figure 2a. Graph of the Hessian matrix function of AP(t1, J) on [8.1, 9.1] [1900,2100].

deterioration. That is, the following inequality is satisfied:

$$t_1 \ge t_o = \frac{K - d + J\theta - \sqrt{K^2 - 2Kd + d^2 - 2Jr - J^2\theta^2}}{r + (K-d)\theta + J\theta^2} \quad . \quad (16)$$

If the idle time of facility is limited and the utilization rate, $\dfrac{t_1}{T}$, is more than a fraction of ω, then the problem can be formulated as follows:

Max: $AP(t_1, J)$

Subject to: (a) $t_1 \ge t_o$, (b) $1 \ge \dfrac{t_1}{T} \ge \omega$, $0 < \omega < 1$ (17)

From Equation 17(a) and (b), the domain of the problem is closed and bounded, which means the optimum of the problem occurs at either relative maximum of $AP(t_1, J)$ in the interior of the domain or at the boundary of the domain [20,21]. Since the complexity of $AP(t_1, J)$, the closed form of the solution is hard to find, the following solution procedure is used.

Solution procedure

Step 1. Check the concavity of $AP(t_1, J)$.(Hessian matrix function of $AP(t_1, J)$ is positive)

Step 2. Find both the relative maximum of $AP(t_1, J)$ in the interior of the domain and at the boundary of the domain.

Step 3. Find the maximal value of Step 2, the optimum is obtained.

Stop.

NUMERICAL EXAMPLE

The proposed model can be illustrated with the following numerical example.

Example 1

Let K=300, θ=0.05, d=75, r=0.5, c_o=100, c_p=1.5, c_h=0.65, p=4, δ =0.9 and ω =0.1.

Figure 2a (Using software Maple) shows the graph of the Hessian matrix function of $AP(t_1, J)$ on [8.1, 9.1]×[1900, 2100]. That means Hessian matrix of $AP(t_1, J)$ on [8.1, 9.1]×[1900, 2100] is positive. A graphical representation showing the concave function AP is given in Figure 2b. With the given data, the optimal decision for the retailer is obtained by using software MATHCAD. The optimal shortage demand J=2018, the optimal production run time t_1=8.325, the total cycle time T=37.445, the facility utilization rate t_1/T=0.222, and the average profit per unit

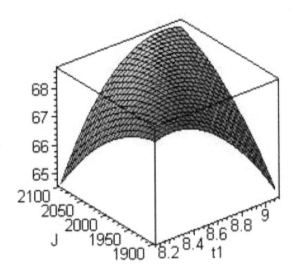

Figure 2b. Graph of the average profit AP(t1, J) on [8.1, 9.1] [1900,2100].

$K=290, c_o=100, d=75, c_p=1.5, \theta=0.05, \delta=0.9, r=0.5$						
c_h	ω	J	t_1	T	t_1/T	AP
0.6	0.1	1737	7.716	33.055	0.233	61.272
0.6	0.25	3631	20.30	81.202	0.25	32.785
0.65	0.1	1857	8.104	35.008	0.231	61.083
0.65	0.25	3705	20.708	82.832	0.25	32.106
0.7	0.1	1933	8.339	36.219	0.23	60.931
0.7	0.25	3758	21	83.998	0.25	31.553

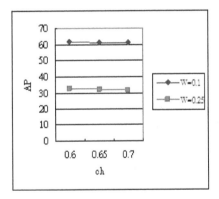

Figure 3. The effect of constant production rate K=290 on the average profit AP.

time AP=\$61.25.

SENSITIVITY ANALYSIS

Sensitivity analysis is carried out and shows the changes in J, t_1, T, t_1/T, and AP for variables K, c_h, and ω.

Figures 3, 4 and 5 show that as the production rate K increases, the average profit AP increases. However, as ω increases, the average profit AP decreases. It is shown that as the holding cost c_h increases, the production run time t_1 increases, the utilization rate of facility t_1/T and the average profit AP decreases.

CONSIDERING THE OPPORTUNITY COST

Other than the limited utilization rate of production facility discussed earlier, we consider the opportunity cost of the production facility as a linear function of utilization rate in the current section. That is, the opportunity cost of production facility is assumed to be $(1-\frac{t_1}{T})c_u$, where c_u is the unit opportunity cost. Then, the average profit of considering opportunity cost per unit time, APU, is

$APU = \frac{1}{T}$ [normal revenue + backordered revenue - production cost - inventory holding cost-ordering cost - opportunity cost]

$$= \frac{1}{T} [\int_0^v [d+rt]p\,dt + \int_v^T dp_b(t_b - t)dt - \int_0^{t_1} Kc_p\,dt -$$

$$\int_{t_o}^v I(t)c_h\,dt - c_o - (1-\frac{t_1}{T})c_u] \quad (14)$$

$K=300, c_o=100, d=75, c_p=1.5, \theta=0.05, \delta=0.9, r=0.5$						
c_h	ω	J	t_1	T	t_1/T	AP
0.6	0.1	1927	8.056	36.007	0.224	61.414
0.6	0.25	3840	22.214	88.855	0.25	23.716
0.65	0.1	2018	8.325	37.445	0.222	61.25
0.65	0.25	3884	22.477	89.909	0.25	22.982
0.7	0.1	2082	8.51	38.45	0.221	61.115
0.7	0.25	3919	22.687	90.748	0.25	22.346

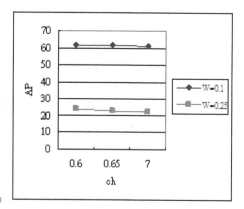

Figure 4. The effect of constant production rate K=300 on the average profit AP.

$K=310, c_o=100, d=75, c_p=1.5, \theta=0.05, \delta=0.9, r=0.5$						
c_h	ω	J	t_1	T	t_1/T	AP
0.6	0.1	2093	8.285	38.516	0.215	61.565
0.6	0.25	3564	21.76	87.041	0.25	7.446
0.65	0.1	2169	8.496	39.698	0.214	61.418
0.65	0.25	3574	21.856	87.424	0.25	5.181
0.7	0.1	2226	8.649	40.573	0.213	61.296
0.7	0.25	3.581	21.925	87.702	0.25	2.947

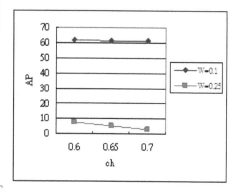

Figure 5. The effect of constant production rate K=310 on the average profit AP.

Then the problem can be formulated as follows:

Max: $APU(t_1, J)$
Subject to: $t_1 \geq t_o$.

Example 2

Let $K=300$, $\theta=0.05$, $d=75$, $r=0.5$, $c_o=100$, $c_p=1.5$, $c_h=0.65$, $p=4$, $\delta=0.9$ and $c_u=500$.

Figure 6a (Using software Maple) shows the graph of the Hessian matrix function of $APU(t_1, J)$ on [9, 12]× [2700,3000]. That means Hessian matrix of $APU(t_1, J)$ on [9, 12]×[2700,3000] is positive. A graphical represent-tation showing the concave function APU is given in Figure 6b. With the given data, the optimal decision for the retailer is obtained by using software MATHCAD. The optimal shortage demand $J=2842$, the optimal production run time $t_1=11.213$, the total cycle time $T=52.321$, the

facility utilization rate $t_1/T=0.214$, and the average profit per unit time $APU=\$52.792$.

(15)
CONCLUSION

This study develops a deteriorating EPQ model. We develop the model by considering the linearly discounted selling price of backorder and the utilization rate of facility. In practice, the selling price usually depends on the customers that are willing to purchase the item under the condition that they receive their orders after a certain fraction of waiting time.

The utilization of facility issue has drawn attentions in the recent years. Many managers treat the utilization of facility as an index of production efficiency. In this study, sensitivity analysis shows that as the holding cost c_h increases, the production run time t_1 increases, however, the utilization rate of facility t_1/T and the average profit AP decreases. This can be used as a reference for the decision-makers.

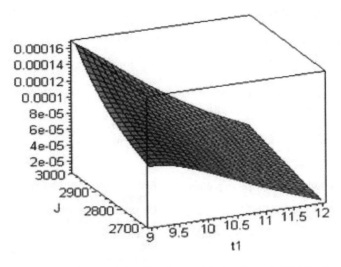

Figure 6a. Graph of the Hessian matrix function of APU(t1, J) on [9, 12] [2700,3000].

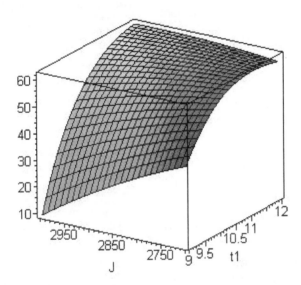

Figure 6b. Graph of the average profit APU(t1, J) on [9, 12] [2700,3000].

ASSUMPTIONS AND NOTATION

The following notations were used throughout this paper.

T total cycle time

t_1 the production run time ; t_1 is a decision variable

t_0 a production time to make up shortage from the previous cycle, $0 < t_0 \leq t_1$

v a critical time at which inventory level reaches zero after t_1, $t_1 < v \leq T$

t_b the backorder satisfied time when the customer agrees to place backorder at time t

$I(t)$ the inventory level at time t

K the constant production rate

θ the constant deterioration rate, where $0 < \theta \leq 1$

c_o the set-up cost per cycle

c_p the production cost per unit

c_h	the holding cost per unit per unit time
c_u	the unit opportunity cost
p	the constant selling price per unit
p_b	the backordered selling price during shortages
δ	the discount factor
ω	the lower bound of facility utilization rate
J	the shortage demand; J is a decision variable
AP	the average profit per unit time
APU	the average profit of considering opportunity cost per unit time

In developing the model, the following assumptions were made:

1. The demand rate $D(t)$ for the product follows a deterministic function of time t such that:

$$D(t)= \begin{cases} d + rt, & 0 \leq t < v, \\ d, & v \leq t \leq T, \end{cases}$$

where d, $r{>}0$ are constants. That means the customers' demand increases before time v for the advertisement effect, and the demand is constant during v and T since the customers are willing to be backordered due to discount and new items.

2. Backorder is allowed, and the backlogged demand is satisfied sequentially at the beginning of each cycle which depends on the customer's waiting time.

3. The product deteriorates with time, and there is no replacement or repair of deteriorated items during a given cycle.

4. The backordered selling price of customer is assumed to be linearly decreasing with waiting time η such that:

$$p_b(\eta) = (1 - \frac{\delta\eta}{T-v})p, \quad t_o \leq \eta < T\text{-}v,$$ where the discount factor, δ, is a constant with, $0 < \delta \leq 1$.

5. The capacity of the warehouse is unlimited.

6. The production rate is higher than the consumption and deterioration rate combination.

7. The opportunity cost of production facility is a decreasing function of utilization rate which is assumed to

be $(1 - \frac{t_1}{T})c_u$, where $\frac{t_1}{T}$ is the utilization rate, c_u is the unit opportunity cost.

REFERENCES

Abad PL (1996) Optimal pricing and lot-sizing under conditions of perishability and partial backordering. Manage. SCI. 42: 1093-1104.

Azaiez MN (2002). A model for conjunctive use of ground and surface water with opportunity costs. Eur. J. Oper. Res.143(3): 611-624.

Chakraborty T, Giri BC, Chaudhuri KS (2008). Production lot sizing with process deterioration and machine breakdown, Eur. J. Oper. Res. 185(2): 606-618.

Clark E, Easaw JZ (2007). Optimal access pricing for natural monopoly networks when costs are sunk and revenues are uncertain. Eur. J. Oper. Res.178 (2): 595-602.

Einhorn MA(1987). Optimal pricing of utility power purchases from qualifying facilities. Resour. Energy Econ. 9(3): 301-308.

Goyal SK, Gunasekaran A. (1995). An integrated production– inventory - marketing model for deteriorating items. Comput. Ind. Eng. 28(4): 755-762.

Hou KL (2007). An EPQ model with setup cost and process quality as functions
of capital expenditure. Appl. Math. Model. 31(1):10-17.

Hou KL, Huang YF, Lin LC (2011). An inventory model for deteriorating items with stock-dependent selling rate and partial backlogging under inflation. Afr. J. Bus. Manag. 5 (10): 3834-3843.

Hsu PH, Wee HM, Teng HM (2007). Optimal Ordering Decision for Deteriorating
Items with Expiration Date and Uncertain Lead Time. Comput. Ind. Eng. 52:448-458.

Huang SP (2010). Using simple and efficient algorithm involving ordering cost reduction and backorder price discount on inventory system under variable lead time. Information Technology Journal: 1-7.

Hung KC (2011). An inventory model with generalized type demand, deterioration and backorder rates. Eur. J. Oper. Res. 208(3): 239–242.

Kang s, Kim I (1983). A study on the price and production level of the deteriorating inventory system. Int. J. Prod. Res. 21: 449–460.

Lin HJ (2012). Effective investment to reduce setup cost in a mixture inventory model involving controllable backorder rate and variable lead time with a service level constraint. Math. Probl. Eng. 2012: Article ID 689061, 15 pages, doi:10.1155/2012/689061.

Luo W (1998). An integrated inventory system for perishable goods with backordering. Comput. Ind. Eng.: 34(3): 685-693.

Raafat F, Wolfe PM, Eldin HK (1991). An inventory model for deteriorating items. COMPUT. IND. ENG. 20: 89–94.

Sharma s (2008). Theory of exchange. Eur. J. Oper. Res.186(1):128-136.

Teng JT, Chang CT (2005). Economic production quantity models for deteriorating items with price- and stock-dependent demand. Comput. Oper. Res. 32: 297–308.

Wee HM (1999). Deteriorating inventory model with quantity discount, pricing and partial backordering. Int. J. Prod. Econ. 59: 511-518.

You PS (2005). Optimal replenishment policy for product with season pattern demand. Oper. Res. Lett. 33(1): 90-96.

2

Accounting information systems: An intelligent agents approach

Marcelo Seido Nagano* and Marcelo Botelho da Costa Moraes

Department of Production Engineering, School of Engineering, São Carlos, University of São Paulo
Av. Trabalhador Sãocarlense, 400, São Carlos – SP, 13566-590, Brazil.

The purpose of this paper is to present new approaches in the development of accounting information systems to enable better data management and information creation. The objective is achieved by applying an object-oriented modeling with the use of intelligent agents, according to the needs of users of accounting information. In development of this work, it was observed that a structure based on objects and using intelligent agents enables the development of reports for different users, with gains in the quality of information developed. The major limitation of this work is that it was done on a theoretical basis; however, the practical aspect is yet to be carried out due to the extent of its development. The great advantage of working is to use an object-oriented modeling with simultaneous application of intelligent agents, who carry on the development and analysis of accounting. Thus, the accounting information system is able to meet fully the qualities needed to users, without loss of comprehensibility, relevance, reliability and comparability, even with changes in business model or in accounting standards used. Furthermore, the development of new intelligent agents enables a retrospect on previous year's analysis.

Key words: Accounting information systems, DCA (debit-credit accounting) model, resource, events and agents (REA) model; intelligent agents, object-oriented.

INTRODUCTION

Accounting is a science which can be defined as an information and evaluation system. The aim is to provide to its users demonstrations and analyses of an economic, financial, physical and productivity nature in relation to the entity.

Accounting information is quantitative and qualitative which meets the needs of internal and external users. According to the Financial Accounting Standards Board (FASB) in the Statement of Financial Accounting Concepts (SFAC) No. 1, 1978, the information from financial reporting is subject to limitations. Moreover, according to the SFAC No. 2, 1980, information should

be comprehensible to those who have a reasonable amount of knowledge about business and economics (FASB, 1980), but it does not indicate to which level of depth this knowledge is.

These characteristics and needs intrinsic to accounting should be observed in its information system. Therefore, these results in the importance of modeling an accounting information system which can meet all the ways and visions needed to make decisions.

The most classic way of registering economic transacttions was made formal by the friar Luca Pacioli, who showed merchants at that time how to register commercial transactions, emphasizing the doubling of each transaction in relation to "cost vs. benefit", known as the double entry system (Fisher, 1997).

Another way of retaining information is the REA model (*economic Resources, economic Events, economic Agents*), based on the modeling of databases. This

---

*Corresponding author. E-mail: drnagano@usp.br, drnagano@sc.usp.br.

approach is used in integrated system environments whereby each economic transaction is associated to (Entity-Relationship) a series of economic resources and economic agents (Fisher, 1997).

There are various modeling techniques in the literature on information systems (e.g. entity-relationship diagrams and data flow charts), but the REA model is preferred due to a specific technique in accounting information systems (Rom and Rohde, 2007).

Aims

The aim of this work is to propose a way of modeling accounting information systems oriented towards the objectives using support from intelligent agent tools to help take decisions according to various possibilities of formatting among different types of users and decisions. The following specific aims are presented:

1. Present the accounting information system models;
2. Check how they can be made suitable regarding the needs of different types of information;
3. Develop oriented modeling to objects using the support of intelligent agents, which are flexible in terms of dealing with information;
4. Compare the proposed system with the current model according to the qualitative characteristics of accounting information.

Motivation

Studying ways of information modeling has become a relevant subject in accounting as it includes the way that data and information are registered. It is worth mentioning that data is a source which does not add value as the information consists of the data in the structuring and relationship used in decision making process.

Therefore, the work in this article can help improve accounting information systems so that they can provide assistance to a wide range of information users who have different levels of knowledge and distinct needs concerning accounting.

Taking this into account, the way in which databases save information, provide access, search for data and proceed in formalization are fundamental for the user to use them efficiently. Therefore, the REA model can be highlighted in this sense.

However, one of the characteristics of the REA model is its limitation at a transactional level. Most of the literature on the subject ignores the supply of information to take decisions (Rom and Rohde, 2007), thus the need to use intelligent agents to overcome this limitation.

Artificial intelligence has been applied successfully in

structured, programmable and repetitive tasks whereby the human knowledge obtained is not extremely difficult (Baldwin et al., 2006). Considering this, the use of specialist systems is justified by problem structuring and the possibility of obtaining current knowledge from accountants and auditors.

Research problem

Considering the aspects mentioned earlier, as well as the importance of accounting information systems and the constant need of improvement, this work describes and analyses the following question: How can accounting information systems be developed in order to perform better considering the users´ needs based on modern information technology?

METHODOLOGY

This work is of a theoretical nature and is strongly based on bibliographical research. It presents a methodology to develop information systems which use object-oriented modeling together with intelligent agent applications to deal with information.

Therefore, from the existing theories of accounting information systems, as well as technological tools of information and intelligent systems, this work uses deductive methods to present how these theories can be applied by developing accounting information systems which are more suitable for organizational needs.

ACCOUNTING INFORMATION SYSTEMS

Progress in information technology and the increase in the use of the Internet requires administrators, accountants, auditors and academics to become cleverer and more knowledgeable in terms of design, operations and accounting information systems control (Beard and Wen, 2007) having direct implications in the security and reliability of the system.

Considering this, it has become more important to define how economic events can be classified:

1. Transactions, where something with measurable value is passed voluntarily from one part to another, or simultaneously between both parts; and
2. Inter-actions, whereby there is a measurable effect on the value in the entity without there being the participation of another part (Birkett, 1968).

The transactions normally refer to the negotiation process, while the inter-actions are related to the process of aggregating value. In both cases, measuring is relevant in terms of registering information regardless of the model and the way they are used. The measurement methodology establishes criteria checked for accounting, meeting the needs of consistency and comparability. In spite of this, there are some difficulties in devising measurement techniques and the current systems can reflect incorrect metrics without having the capacity to alter them later (Chambers, 1998). Measuring cannot be confused with quantification. The former derives from an estimate technique of evaluation, usually in monetary terms, while the latter, quantification, is related to physical counting, and is easily checked.

Therefore, it is important to observe the reduction of information throughout the registration process in accounting information systems. This synthesizing process (in terms of the economic transaction) is used to make understanding easier for users. Thus, there is a need to summarize information, grouping it in a small number of account balances to increase the utility of the statement in its understanding (Babich, 1975).

Currently, accounting information systems can be found isolated or inserted into ERP systems (Enterprise Resource Planning). In dedicated systems, as well as integrated systems (ERP), performance is usually based on databases. To understand the existing accounting information systems better, the DCA and REA models are described in detail as follows.

The DCA model

The double entry method consists of the most classic way of accounting. Part of the presupposition of each economic event must be registered by debit and credit, hence the name double entry. This happens due to the duality of each event having a resource origin and an application on the same date and for the same amount of money.

To better understand the DCA model (debit-credit accounting), the way in which accounting deals with these origins and resource applications should be observed. Each event, whether it be a transaction (negotiation) or inter-action (production) happens from an origin, that is, a financial loss in terms of reducing assets or generating liabilities.

After information technology was introduced and computers, as well as data processing systems became more widespread, information systems of large corporations began to be developed within available computational language to use on a large scale.

The current ERP systems work with related databases, where each event automatically generates debits and credits according to its configuration. This has made the accounting process easier. Moreover, standardized reports show the total amount of the accounts balances analytically or synthetically, producing the main financial statements.

However, accounting information systems based on the DCA model are not very malleable as any change in the structure of a company that needs alterations in its chart of accounts would need a total restructuring of configuretions and system parameters. This would cause problems of losing uniformity and consistency of accounting information hindering its comparability and quality of information which enables users to identify similarities and differences between two economic phenomena (Hendriksen and Van Breda, 1999).

This makes it impossible for users to compare the results of the organization before and after changing accounting decisions as these results reflect different measurement methodologies. Therefore, changes in accounting end up eliminating historical comparison data which help to check the efficiency and efficacy of the processes.

The REA model

The REA accounting model is based on the principle of each economical event being in an entity carried out by internal and external economical agents bringing about changes in economic resources. This is why it is called REA: to relate aspects of economic Resources, economic Events and economic Agents.

Developed in the 1980s, this model came from applying the events theory proposed by Sorter, according to whom accounting must be oriented to register the event which took place, and not just the financial amounts involved (Sorter, 1969).

Therefore, as well as the usual information of dates and amounts involved in the event, data that can describe the event in detail and make its future forecasting possible is aggregated. The system's user can make his own model only decides which information is significant or not, given the function loss when only monetary values are observed (Sorter, 1969).

The REA model can reduce the problems inherent to the traditional model, which limits the monetary measurement, without multidimensional information and often classified inappropriately, storing too much aggregated information without integrating other areas of the company (McCarthy, 1982).

The model defines the economic resources as the patrimony of the entity. The economic agents are responsible for patrimonial changes (Figure 1).

The economic events are transactions by negotiating (buying and selling) economic resources, or inter-actions in aggregating value to the resources, carried out by internal economic agents or together with external agents in the entity (Figure 2).

As each event involves an origin and an application of resources (the main idea of double entry) there is a double event in this model. This relationship is called

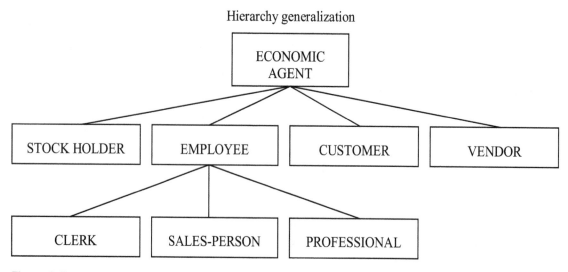

Figure 1. Example of generalization (McCarthy, 1982).

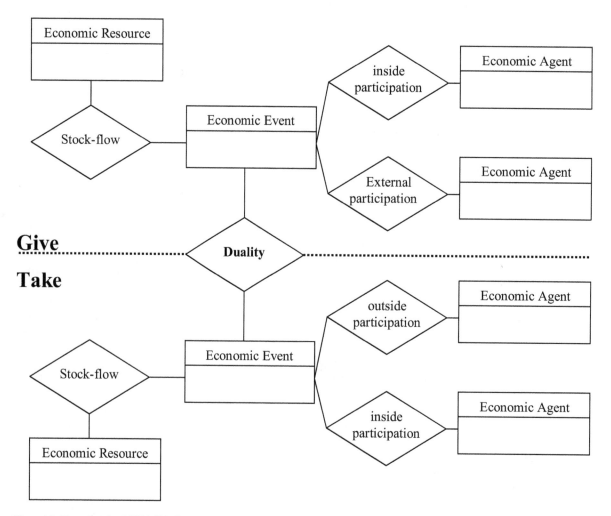

Figure 2. The standard REA (McCarthy, 2003).

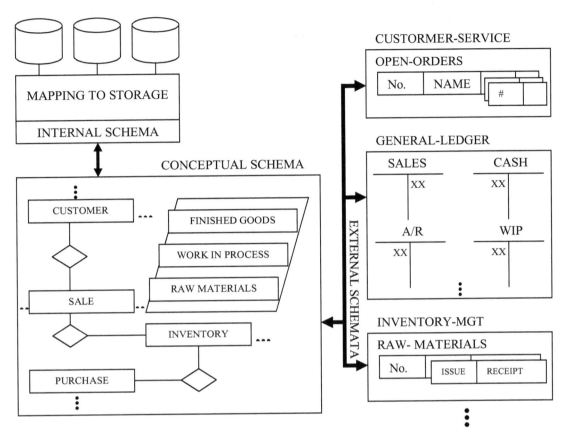

Figure 3. Schema specification for databases (McCarthy, 1982).

duality and binds economic events because every increment economic event must be related by a duality to a decrement economic event (Kasik and Hunka, 2011).

This shows two types of relationship of each entity. At this point, the term entity is interpreted according to database theories referring to events, resources and agents: The first is the association, which determines how the different entities interact among themselves; the second is the generalization, in which each entity is a generalization of various different factors, but having the same characteristics (McCarthy, 1982).

Where the database program (language) refers to internal schema, the conceptual schema which the REA model is applied can be determined. Exiting the system can be presented in various ways using formatted reports by the external schema (Figure 3).

Currently, the ERP systems which met the needs of company resources attend to the REA model as each process cycle needs to be modeled in the system by databases based on entity-relationship (McCarthy, 2003).

In practice, the ERP systems do not use this technique completely. The aim of accounting in systems is usually to record debits and credits. This would not be necessary when the REA model is used.

When comparing the REA and SAP model, one of the main ERP systems on the market, significant similarities are found, although there are situations whereby the REA model is less detailed (O'Leary, 2004).

Moreover, companies which implant ERP systems cannot use the whole capacity of the capturing system, processing and delivering financial and non-financial information to the decision makers in time (Wier et al., 2007).

REA based system can capture a comprehensive set of business information more efficiently than traditional business reporting systems, allowing organizations to make more efficient and better business decisions, but the REA model needs a technological language to help take advantage of its benefits (Amrhein et al., 2009).

INTELLIGENT AGENTS

Intelligent agents are a field of artificial intelligence based on computing, highlighting perception, reasoning and action. Reasoning is particularly essential for higher intelligence to function (Wachsmuth, 2000).

The agent does some activity for another, known as the

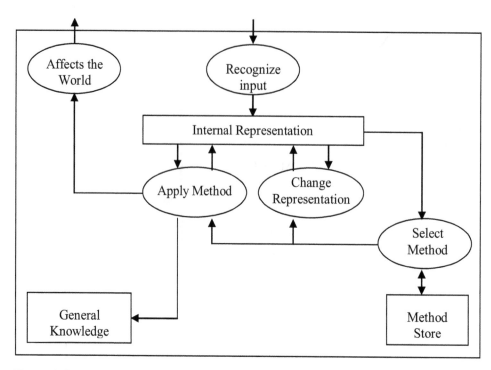

Figure 4. Functional diagram of general intelligent agent (Wachsmuth, 2000).

main one, having autonomy when developing its functions. The idea of intelligent agents was introduced in the mid-1950s, and they have been defined in many different ways (Liu, 2011).

Due to the inexistence of a universally accepted definition, concepts of "weak-notion" and "strong-notion" of the agency are used. The weak notion of the agency consists of the vision of an agent corresponding to an element of *hardware* and *software* based on the computational system having characteristics of (1) autonomy, operating without human intervention; (2) social ability, interacting with other agents (human or not); (3) reactivity, noticing its environment and responding; and (4) pro-activity where initiatives are taken (Wooldridge and Jennings, 1995).

The strong notion of the agency consists of an agent being a computational system having the characteristics described previously, as well as being developed and implemented using concepts that are usually applied to humans (Wooldridge and Jennings, 1995), as the reasoning, belief, intention and others.

The intelligent agent notices the input of the environment (Figure 4) and acts to change the environment, but before it uses an internal representation to observe the possible effects of alternative methods. These methods are observed from an internal method store and its exploration is guided by general world knowledge also internally (Wachsmuth, 2000).

Observing the characteristics given by the notions from the agency, two aspects are extreme important in determining an intelligent agent (Figure 5).

1. Agency/autonomy: The agency determines the level of autonomy invested in the agent being able to be evaluated from an asynchronous application, passing to the representation of the user, to the interactivity with other agents in handling data, applications and services;
2. Intelligence/capacity of reasoning: Intelligence is the level of learning and reasoning related to the agent's skills to incorporate the determined objectives by the user and fulfill the tasks which are delegated to it. Varying from instructions on preferences, normally rules, progressing to reasoning from inference models to planning and learning (Vasarhelyi et al., 2005).

Therefore, the relationship between the agent's autonomy and the capacity of reasoning (intelligence) determines an intelligent agent.

Among the various existing models in the area of artificial intelligence, expert systems are used in this work. Despite this, in accordance with the usefulness of the intelligent agent, other techniques can be used.

The expert systems are computational programs which do tasks for human specialists, although they do not substitute a human being as a decision maker (Barbera, 1987) because they do not have autonomy characteristics. The expert systems grew out of the data mining studies in the 1990s because of increasing amount of

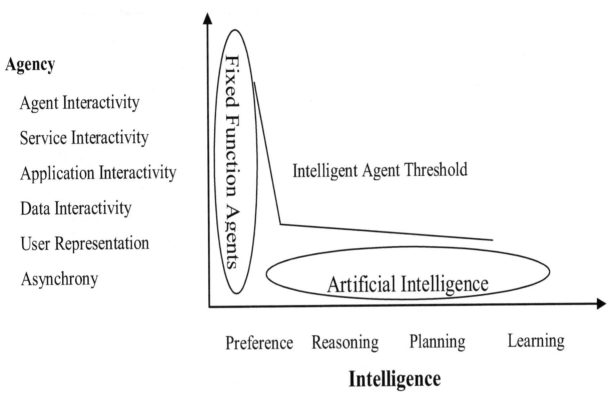

Agency

Agent Interactivity

Service Interactivity

Application Interactivity

Data Interactivity

User Representation

Asynchrony

Figure 5. Intelligent agent scope (Adapted from Vasarhelyi et al., 2005).

data stored in relatively easily accessible databases (Kilpatrick, 2011).

Furthermore, the expert systems differ as far as the computational programs are concerned in terms of function and structure. Regarding function, by doing activities normally designated to humans and in its structure in the way in which these functions are carried out –artificial intelligence tools and methodologies (Brown and Phillips, 1995).

Expert knowledge about the process can be expressed in linguistic rules by words of spoken or even artificial language (Pamucar et al., 2011). To use intelligent agents in accounting, expert systems were selected as an artificial intelligence tool because the application in accounting information systems is well-structured, having specialists and documented knowledge on accounting operations to obtain rules.

By using rules such as "If...., Then.......", these systems are developed with the help of specialists who by themselves find ways of condensing their experience to simple rules (Foltin and Smith, 1994). This system of rules follows logic of how a human being takes decisions, called heuristics. In case the task is structured and advanced calculations are not needed and heuristics are used, the system specialist will be ideal in helping with the decision making (Shim and Rice, 1988).

OBJECT-ORIENTED INFORMATION SYSTEMS USING INTELLLIGENT AGENTS

The presented model is based on applying the technology of intelligent agents to accounting information systems attempting to improve the way the systems make information available to the users, providing variations of format and giving information in detail.

Even though, the REA model is the most accepted in terms of structuring the accounting phenomena; it is efficient in storing data, but not in handling information (Verdaasdonk, 2003). Taking this into account, developing a system to deal with data is needed, which provides relevant, reliable and comparable information. These are all characteristics that determine the usefulness of accounting information (FASB, 1980).

Developing this model is done by language databases oriented to objects. Using the oriented modeling to objects was introduced by Knaus (2001) in accounting information systems developing. However, his proposal uses the DCA model as a base and each account is a distinct class (Knaus, 2001).

Modeling databases oriented to objects came from the limitations of the relational databases. Their basic objective is to manage large amounts of information, making handling data easier and meeting the current

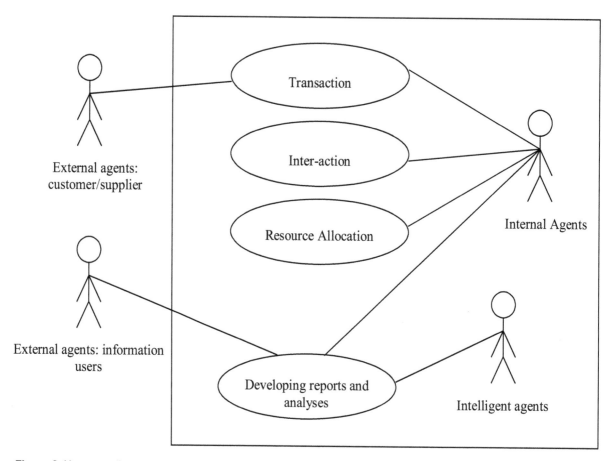

Figure 6. Use case diagram – general model for REA applying intelligent agents.

requirements of the systems with other types of databases, such as hypertexts, which are in constant use (Silberschatz et al., 1999).

Within this characteristic, the UML language (Unified Modeling Language) can be applied, mainly as it is an appropriate tool for modeling intelligent agents (Heinze, 2004) and is based on object-oriented databases. This approach differs from the traditional accounting information systems because it separates data from information modeling operations the same time it uses an approach oriented to objects.

Aiming to have a better performance in the proposed modeling, the UML developing is used to make visualization easier and integrate among the different objectives.

In traditional systems, reports are developed in database itself while in the REA model object-oriented (REAOO), the reports and their analyses are developed using intelligent agents based on expert systems. The biggest difference is separating application from accounting databases, which does not normally happen.

Therefore, in terms of this development, the use of UML language to model the system is of great help. It is important to mention that the model is a simplification of reality presenting a general case of an information system for any activity that needs to be done. Taking this into account, while Entity-Relationship modeling in the REA model has 3 entities (Resource, Events and Agents) to develop the modeling Object-Oriented, these resources, events and agents are the classes to be implemented.

Therefore, by using intelligent agents to develop information for different types of users, the external scheme (according to the REA model) can be developed by intelligent agents, where this agent is a new actor in this diagram (Figure 6).

While the external agents can take part in transaction events as clients and suppliers, the internal agents act in the transaction and they are responsible for interaction and resource allocation; furthermore, inserting intelligent agents in the development and report analyses of information.

Normally, there are many similar objects in a database, that is, they respond to the same messages, use the same methods and have variables of the same name and

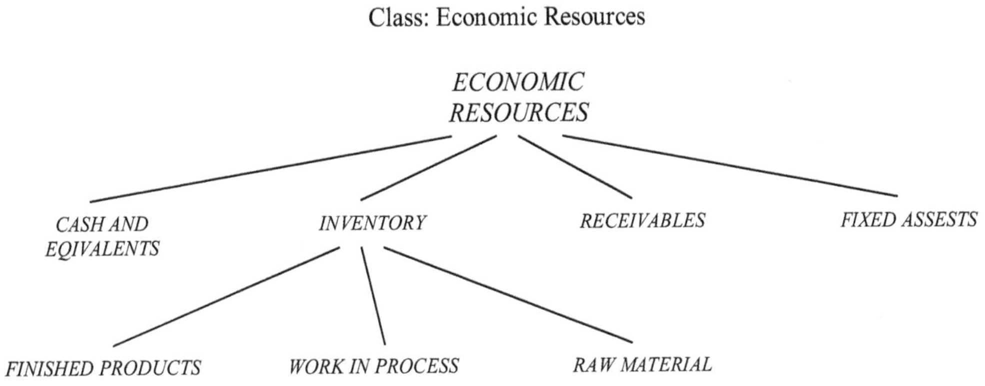

Class: Economic Resources

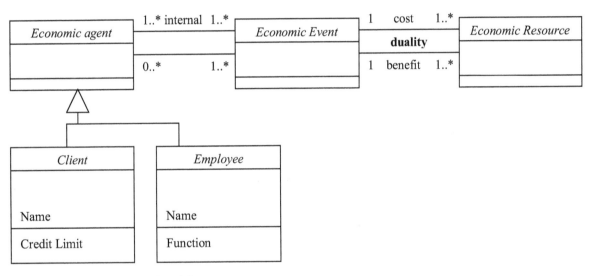

ECONOMIC
RESOURCES

CASH AND   INVENTORY   RECEIVABLES   FIXED ASSESTS
EQIVALENTS

FINISHED PRODUCTS   WORK IN PROCESS   RAW MATERIAL

Figure 7. Hierarchy of classes.

Economic agent   1..* internal 1..*   Economic Event   1   cost   1..*   Economic Resource

duality

0..*   1..*   1   benefit   1..*

Client   Employee

Name   Name

Credit Limit   Function

Figure 8. REA object-oriented model.

type. Considering this , grouping these similar objects is done by these classes (Silberschatz et al., 1999).

Taking this into account, the entities used in the REA model can be considered as classes. In object-oriented modeling for databases, a class can have a specialization hierarchy, that is, the ISA relationship, which shows a class as being specialized from another (Silberschatz et al., 1999).

Therefore, as in the generalization of the REA model, specialization of Resource, Event and Agent classes can be determined. An example is shown in Figure 7.

Determining the classes and their specializations, the general model of the class diagram can be made in the presented proposal of the REA model (Figure 8).

In the REA object-oriented model (REAOO), an economic agent, which can be internal or external, carries out one or more economic events and the economic event itself brings about the duality in relation to the resources,

providing consumption (cost) and generation (benefit) of one or more resources simultaneously.

In the general case of commercializing, a product manufactured in the entity itself, a client (external economic agent) can acquire one or more products with a seller (internal economic agent), bringing about an economic event (sale) which will have an impact on the economic resources, whether it be from the cost of one or more units or the benefit of a cash receipt or account receivable.

This model, similar to the original format of the REA model, can be applied to any situation within the various types of organizations that carry out economic activities.

An intelligent agent is autonomous, that is, the intelligent agent is a software program separate from the data-bases, which accesses it remotely and makes searches, obtaining data which is needed to develop and/or analyze the information.

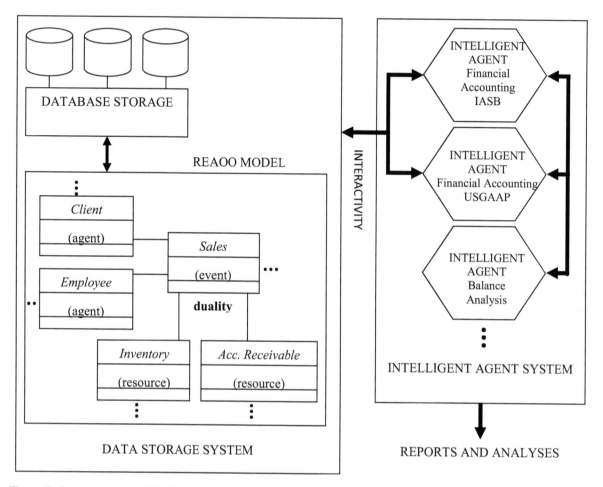

Figure 9. General model - REA object-oriented with intelligent agents.

Considering this, the accounting information system consists of two separate environments. The first one is an environment to store data, where the REA object-oriented model acts. The second environment consists of an intelligent agent system which accesses the database by software interactivity and carries out its interpretation function (Figure 9).

As an example of the expert system technique, the different ways of accounting a determined can be compared.

Observing the between international accounting standards from the IASB (International Accounting Standards Board) and United States Generally Accepted Accounting Principles (USGAAP) by FASB, the accountant can increasingly make inferences about the economic aspect of the events to determine the most suitable way of accounting.

Generating knowledge from the expert system which will make the inference within each intelligent agent (Figure 9) must be made by obtaining knowledge from the specialist, that is, an accountant and/or auditor who can establish the knowledge in a formal way essentially using rules and heuristics to take decisions.

Taking this into account, in accordance with the need of the information system's user, the intelligent agent system will develop the financial statements according to the desired standards, only altering its knowledge base, that is, the rules of the expert system.

After developing traditional accounting reports (Balance Sheet and Income Statement, for example), the intelligent agent can proceed to analyze traditional financial indicators using an expert system developed for this. This agent will base its analysis on the other intelligent agent's responses by the interactivity of agents.

Therefore, these intelligent agents can continuously monitor the situation and financial/operational performance of the entity in terms of returning recommendations to the internal users of the system, helping or even taking decisions.

It is worth mentioning that the preference to use expert systems as an artificial intelligent tool of intelligent agents is due to the easiness of structuring knowledge from human accounting specialists (accountants), but other ways of artificial intelligence could be used. An example would be to use neural networks to forecast results.

ANALYSIS OF THE MODEL

Based on the needs of the stakeholders, the proposed accounting information system evaluation can be made from four qualities of accounting information determined by FASB.

Comprehensibility

According to this analysis, the proposed system has advantages regarding the current systems because the REAOO model with intelligent agents provides the development of intelligent agents which can develop more specific reports to different types of users according to their capacity of understanding and level of knowledge about accounting. Greater information is necessary to a higher level of detail in making a specific decision (Cohen and Kaimenaki, 2011).

Relevance

The REAOO and intelligent agents are based on providing relevant information to take decisions at the right time, that is, when necessary. However, the predicttive value and feedback can be highlighted as important.

While the DCA and REA models essentially focus on storing past information, the REAOO model can use intelligent agents to develop forecasts and future projects, adding the predictive value that current systems cannot.

Another factor is the value as feedback. In this case, it is worth mentioning that previous expectations are fulfilled in case they happen, or corrected otherwise. Essentially, this quality is applied in forecast and realized comparison. Once again, the current systems cannot make these applications, but the REAOO model can develop specific intelligent agents to develop and control, even for budgeting and cash flow development and analysis.

Reliability

Reliability of information is closely linked to the definitions of the rules of business. In the traditional systems, reliability is developed by the storing data system. In the REAOO model, reliability should at least be observed in the intelligent agent.

Therefore, applying intelligent agents in financial accounting eliminates the need of having computational routines to convert accounting standards. In the REAOO model, accounting register according to different accounting standards is direct, without the need for conversion, avoiding problems of reliability in this process and making it easier to check auditory processes.

Comparability

This quality shows the capacity of comparing accounting information over time in the same organization or between different organizations at the same moment the REAOO model can be highlighted.

From the time in which the data analysis is disassociated from its storage, the comparison only depends on developing a new intelligent agent for the required objective. Therefore, from the time when the company starts using the REAOO model, it will be storing data in the model. If the company needs to change the way of accounting or even the way of analyzing some years afterwards, they just need to change the responsible intelligent agent and the past data will be available from the original REAOO system.

In the case where this same organization decides to implant a budget system or even develop its accounting according to accounting standard from another country, they just need to develop specific intelligent agents for this work and the organization will have past information and analyses since the REAOO system was implanted.

By doing this, possibilities of comparing become limited only from start storing the data in the REAOO system, the analysis provided by the intelligent agents can be replied to original data, without bias or adjustments. This is a characteristic of the proposed system which makes it possible not to lose past comparison parameters in case of changes in accounting standards or calculus methodologies. In other words, theoretically it will never lose consistency.

Normally, after having changes in standards, or even new analysis needs (using new costing methodologies, for example), entities end up being adopted to make adjustments in previous periods (restricted to few periods) for comparison.

In the proposed model, REAOO, any alteration in the standards implies that making a specific intelligent agent is suitable. Thus, when it is created, it can recalculate the past, without having to be adjusted prone to errors.

Conclusion

As shown, accounting information systems are fundamental for taking decisions in entities. In spite of this, most of the modeling and development of the systems do not observe the users´ needs or a way of accounting work.

Alles et al. (2008) discussed accounting separating it between research in accounting information systems

(AIS) and research which is not focused on accounting information systems. They show the need to aggregate value in AIS research as this area of research shows difficulties in methodologies when presenting the results as they depend on application and rarely possible practical tests.

Therefore, it is common to see problems between the needs shown by the accountants and the existing specifications in the systems which make suitable replies impossible, as shown by Sayed (2006).

Analyzing the progress of information technology and its application in accounting information systems, it can be observed that there were practically no improvements in the way of working. The DCA model, which is still the standard model, did not progress after the computer age.

Currently, most systems simply automatically replicate double entry in accounting general ledger. It was only when the REA model came about that accounting began to see computing as a way of improving processes. However, these initiatives are still specifics, perhaps because accountants do not know about the existing technology and developers unknown the accounting needs.

The concept of new models, as in this work, has become pertinent, but at the same time complex as multidisciplinary knowledge is needed in distinct areas. There are also difficulties in applying it. Because of this, the present work has as the major limitation a non practical development of the model REAOO. Moreover, the definition of intelligent agent based on expert system requires a more complex modeling, identifying practical problems observed in companies.

Despite all this, by creating conditions to apply an object-oriented model using intelligent agent support, this work makes it possible to study the development of new applications of intelligent agents in more perspectives areas such as costs, forecasting, budgets and simulations among others in practically all the objectives involved in accounting and using other artificial intelligence techniques.

So, there are future perspectives as the practical application of the model, with a further development of artificial intelligence techniques in reporting and decision making is associated.

REFERENCES

Alles MG, Kogan A, Vasarhelyi MA (2008). Exploiting comparative advantage: a paradigm for value added research in accounting information systems Int. J. Account. Inform. Syst. 9(4):202-215.

Amrhein DG, Farewell S, Pinsker, R (2009). REA and XBRL GL: Synergies for the 21st Century Business Reporting System Int. J. Dig. Account. Res. 9:127-152.

Babich G (1975). The application of information theory to accounting reports: an appraisal ABACUS 11(2):172-181.

Baldwin AA, Brown CE, Trinkle BS (2006). Opportunities for artificial intelligence development in accounting domain: the case for auditing Intell. Syst. Account. Finan. Manag. 14:77-86.

Barbera AT (1987). Artificial intelligence in accounting: the future has arrived Rev. Bus. 9(2):17-21.

Beard D, Wen J (2007). Reducing the threat levels for accounting information systems CPA J. 77:34-42.

Birkett WP (1968). Accounting inputs ABACUS 4(2):164-173.

Brown CE, Phillips ME (1995). Expert systems for management accounting tasks Montvale: The IMA Foundation for Applied Research Inc. p.204.

Chambers RJ (1998). Wanted: foundations of accounting measurement ABACUS 34(1): 36-47.

Cohen S, Kaimenaki E (2011). Cost accounting systems structure and information quality properties: an empirical analysis J. Appl. Account. Res. 12(1):5-25.

Financial Accounting Standards Board (1978). SFAC/01: objectives of financial reporting by business enterprises Norwalk: FASB. p.8.

Financial Accounting Standards Board (1980). SFAC/02: qualitative characteristics of accounting information Norwalk: FASB. p.60.

Fisher SA (1997). In defense of double entry accounting Nat. Pub. Account. 42(3): 33-34.

Foltin LC, Smith LM (1994). Accounting expert systems CPA J. 64(11):46-53.

Heinze C (2004). Modeling intention recognition for intelligent agent systems Edinburgh: DSTO Systems Sciences Laboratory p.249.

Hendriksen ES, Van Breda MF (1999). Accounting theory São Paulo: Atlas p.550.

Kasik J, Hunka F (2011). Business process modelling using REA Ontology. Econ. Manag. 16:1047-1063.

Kilpatrick J (2011). Expert systems and mass appraisal J. Prop. Invest. Finan. 29(4/5):529-550.

Knaus M (2001). Object-oriented accounting – a Framework for a modern accounting information systems Zurich: PhD Thesis in Economic Sciences, University of Zurich p.409.

Liu G (2011). The application of intelligent agents in libraries: A survey. Program 45(1):78-97.

McCarthy WE (1982). The REA accounting model: a generalized framework for accounting systems in a shared data environment Account. Rev. 57(3): 554-578.

McCarthy WE (2003). The REA modeling approach to teaching accounting information systems Issue Account. Educ. 18(4):427-441.

O'leary DE (2004). On the relationship between REA and SAP Int. J. Account. Inform. Syst. 5:65-81.

Pamucar D, Bozanic D, Dorovic B, Milic A (2011). Modelling of the fuzzy logical system for offering support in making decisions within the engineering units of the Serbian Army. Int. J. Phys. Sci. 6(3): 592-609.

Rom A, Rohdes C (2007). Management accounting and integrated information systems: a literature review Int. J. Account. Inform. Syst. 8:40-68.

Sayed HE (2006). ERPs and accountant's expertise: the construction of relevance J. Enter. Inform. Manag. 19(1):83-96.

Shim JK, Rice JS (1988). Expert systems applications to managerial accounting J. Syst. Manag. 39(6):6-13.

Silberschatz A, Korth HF, Sudarshan S (1999). Database systems São Paulo: Makron Books., p. 808.

Sorter GH (1969). An "events" approach to basic accounting theory Accout. Rev. 44(1):12-19.

Vasarhelyi MA, Bonson E, Hoitash R (2005). Artificial intelligence in accounting and auditing: international perspectives - Vol. 6 Princeton: Markus Wiener Publishers p.257.

Verdaasdonk P (2003). An object-oriented model for ex ante accounting information. J. Inf. Syst. 17(1):43-61.

Wachsmuth I (2000). The concept of intelligence in AI In: Cruse H, Dean J and Ritter H, eds. Prerational Intelligence–Adaptive Behavior and Intelligent Systems without Symbols and Logic (Vol. 1). Dordrecht: Kluwer Academic Publishers, pp.43-55.

Wier B, Hunton J, Hassabelnaby HR (2007). Enterprise resource planning systems and non-financial performance incentives: the join impact on corporate performance Int. J. Account. Inform. Syst. 8:165-190.

Wooldridge M, Jennings NR (1995). Intelligent agents: theory and practice Knowl. Eng. Rev. 10(2):115-152.

3

Using AHP and ANP approaches for selecting improvement projects of Iranian Excellence Model in healthcare sector

Elahe Shariatmadari Serkani[1], Mostafa Mardi[2], Esmaeel Najafi[3], Khadijeh Jahanian[3] and Ali Taghizadeh Herat[3]

[1]Department of Industrial Engineering, Science and Research Branch, Islamic Azad University, Tehran, Iran.
[2]Department of Management, Islamic Azad University, Tehran Central Branch, Iran.
[3]Department of Management and Economics, Islamic Azad University, Science and Research Branch, Tehran, Iran.

Healthcare has a long tradition in developed methods and models to assess the quality of work. There have been several models presented for deployment and assessment of quality management which much more attention is paid to organization excellence models due to their being total and complete. The European Foundation for Quality Management (EFQM) excellence model can be used for continuous improvement of activities and performance of organizations from both private and public sector by establishing a Total Quality Management (TQM) philosophy. Iran national productivity and excellence award in collaboration with Azad University – Science and Research campus and ministry of health, treatment and medical training, designed a model for healthcare organizations and this model was used in 23 hospitals. The study was based on experience gained in hospitals, to rank the improvement projects using Analytic Network Process (ANP) and Analytic Hierarchy Process (AHP) methods. The objective of this paper is to present the results of the application of AHP and ANP to select a project within the field of healthcare in Iran. Project number nine "Leadership Development and Succession Planning" got the highest score, and it is the most appropriate choice.

Key words: European Foundation for Quality Management, multi-criteria decision methods, analytic hierarchy process, analytic network process, health sector.

INTRODUCTION

Nowadays many Iranian organizations have realized the need for regular and systematic self-assessment on improving projects. It has realized that on-time detection and management of change is a competitive advantage. Improvement projects help the organization achieve higher level of excellence. A self-assessment process clearly identifies the strength and improvement potentials of the organization (Najmi and Hosseini, 2009). Today, many countries around the world encourage organiza-

tions and companies to follow the models of excellence such as EFQM, Deming and Baldrige. They award prizes, such as Human Resource (HR) excellence awards of HR management association of America, standard of investment in Human Resources and developer standard in Singapore, through institutions and professional associations of human resource development and management to companies and organizations that have accomplished significant achievements in the field of human resources.

The EFQM model is a generic model for quality management, which is used in all types of organizations as a multidimensional framework. One of the most positive aspects of EFQM is the use of self-assessment (Tutuncu and Kucukusta, 2009). In order to achieve excellence; companies need to be aware of the impact of criteria on each other and also the analysis of relations between enablers and results. Since the EFQM excellence model does not show the relationships clearly, companies are not able to accurately analyze the effects of the projects on the criteria after implementing self-assessment and identifying areas that have to be improved. Understanding the relationships between the criteria makes it possible for companies to analyze the projects' effects on model criteria and to apply appropriate tools for improvement while planning and setting goals for the future direction of organizational excellence. Accordingly, in 2002, following the model of the EFQM Excellence Award (EEA), Iran has lunched Iran National Productivity and Excellence Award (INPE). Also due to the needs of various sectors for an exclusive and customized model, the plan for the recreation of the EFQM excellence model in accordance with the healthcare sector was proposed in 2010.

MCDM applications in healthcare settings have spread into various areas, including allocation of health resource (Earnshaw and Dennett, 2003), health policy (Epstein et al., 2007), medical assessment (Oddoye et al., 2006), medical decision (Liberatore and Nydick, 2008), regional resource (Wilson and Gibbard, 1990), resource allocation (Flessa, 2003), surgical case (Cardoen et al., 2009), and surgical waiting lines (Arenas et al., 2002). AHP has been widely used in the multiple criteria decision making in various fields such as the assessment of medical implementation plan (Dolan, 1989), the planning of healthcare human resources (Kwak et al., 1997), health care assessment and policies (Hannan et al., 1981), the assessment of medical institutions' performance care (Ahsan and Bartema, 2004); healthcare (Javalgi et al., 1991), business process reengineering (Kwak and Lee, 2002), etc. Recently, there has been increased interest in its application for evaluating health care facilities. The analytic hierarchy (AHP) and analytic network process (ANP) are two Multi-Criteria Decision Methods (MCDM), originally developed by Prof. Thomas L. Saaty. ANP is a generalization of the AHP. A hierarchy is comprised of a goal, levels of elements and connections between the elements. These connections are oriented only to elements in lower levels. Many decision regarding problems cannot be structured hierarchically because they involve the interaction and dependence of higher-level elements in a hierarchy on lower-level elements. Not only does the importance of the criteria determine the importance of the alternatives as in a hierarchy, but also the importance of the alternatives themselves determines the importance of the criteria. A network has clusters of elements, with the elements in one cluster being connected to elements in another cluster (outer dependence) or the same cluster (inner dependence). A hierarchy is a special case of a network with connections going only in one direction. An example of the format of a network is shown in Figure 1(b).

Therefore, ANP is represented by a network, rather than a hierarchy. The ANP consist of the clusters, elements, interrelationship between elements in the cluster and interrelationships between clusters, while AHP does not include interrelationship and feedback within the elements in the model.

Mashhad University of medical sciences which, in the form of MUMS[1] Evaluation and Excellence Award (MEEA), uses the EFQM excellence model in order to assess performance of its affiliate branches, in 2011, used the re-conceptualized model for health sector in 23 of hospitals controlled by this university. While using the model, Hospitals noticed a large number of areas for improvement, and in order to grow they had to cover them by implementing improvement projects. But it was not possible to implement the entire project simultaneously and they needed to prioritize and chose the most effective ones. Therefore in this paper ANP and AHP methods will be applied to prioritize 10 improvement projects. The opinions of 15 experts are collected by means of a matrix based questionnaire and the analysis is performed based on the responses.

Beneath there will be a literature review and criteria of healthcare organization excellence model, the process of deploying the excellence model, description of AHP and ANP methods, and a review on background of the study. The research methodology is given in the following section. Also, deployment of these methods in 23 treatment centers (hospitals) in Mashhad is described. And finally, conclusion of the whole discussion is drawn.

LITERATURE REVIEW

In this section, EFQM and AHP, ANP will be described.

EFQM excellence

The European Foundation for Quality Management (EFQM) based in Brussels was founded in 1988 by 14 leading corporations. The aim is to induce and secure a systematic and incremental increase in quality in European organizations in order to strengthen their position in the global market (Herget and Hierl, 2007). There are some researches that have pointed out that the EFQM Excellence Model constitutes an appropriate framework to guide the systematic implementation of Total Quality Management (TQM) (Bou-Llusar et al., 2005; Calvo-Mora et al., 2005; Martinez-Lorente et al., 2009; Vijende and Gonzalez, 2007; Westlund, 2001).

---

[1] Mashhad University of Medical Sciences

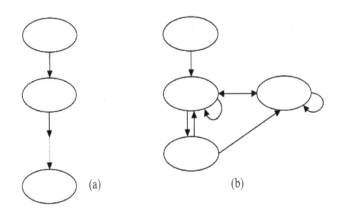

Figure 1. Structural difference between a hierarchy and a network. (a) A Hierarchy (b) a Network.

After reviewing the literature, it turned out that many researchers have considered excellence model as a systematic mechanism to improve organizational performance (Bergquist et al., 2005; Dahlgaard-Park, 2008).

The EFQM excellence model is a non-prescriptive framework that establishes nine criteria, which any organization can use to assess the progress towards excellence. These nine criteria are divided between enablers and results (Calvo-Mora et al., 2006). The model includes five "enabler" criteria: leadership, strategy, people, partnership and resources; and processes, products and services. It also comprises four "results" criteria: customer results, people results, society results, and key results (European Foundation for Quality Management, 2010). The enablers represent the way the organization operates, and the results concentrate on achievements relating to organizational stakeholders (Bou-Llusar et al., 2009). According to EFQM (2010) organizations that aim at achieving excellence focus on improvement in some concepts of TQM theory such as achieving balanced Results, adding value for customers, leading with vision, inspiration and integrity, managing by processes, succeeding through people, nurturing creativity and innovation, building partnerships and taking responsibility for a sustainable future. The specific purpose of the EFQM excellence model is to provide a systems perspective for understanding performance management. With their acceptance nationally and internationally as the model for performance excellence, the criteria represent a common language for communicating and sharing best practices among organizations (Wongrassamee et al., 2003).

EFQM Model has been comprised of two parts: One part entitled "Enablers" while the other part is entitled "Results". Of total nine criteria, five of which have been used as "Enablers" while four of these criteria are related to the "results" part. Leadership, strategy, policy, staff and personnel, trade partners, resources and processes are considered of the criteria which are posed at "Enablers" part. Moreover, results of customers, results of staff and personnel, results of sample society, and key results of performance are of the criteria which are discussed at "results" sector.

The structure of EFQM Model has been shown in Figure 2.

The process of using organizational excellence model in the health sector

Based on the method defined by EFQM, the organizational excellence model is used through an eight-stage process, as shown in Figure 3.

Stage 1 - The first stage of this process is establishing and maintenance of organizational leaders' commitment to organizational excellence. In this stage, using educational plans and culture building, leaders become familiar with the concepts and models of organizational excellence and the necessity of self-assessment and improvement planning based on excellence model.

Stage 2 - The aim of this stage is establishing organizational excellence relationships. The speeches and messages of the leaders, using panels and newsletters, and creating websites are among tools which are used to implement excellence relationships strategy.

Stage 3 - In the self-assessment planning stage, the manager of organizational excellence is appointed and organizing excellence is performed (appointing excellence teams). Besides, the technique used for self-assessment is specified and a schedule for implementing self-assessment is prepared.

Stage 4 - Implementing self-assessment begins with selecting individuals and appointing them to excellence teams as well as familiarizing them with the model and self-assessment based on excellence model.

Stage 5 - In the self-assessment stage, using techniques selected for self-assessment, excellence team members perform different stages of self-assessment. Self-assessment will have three major results for the organization; strong points, improvable areas, and score. The obtained improvable areas are the input of the sixth stage.

Stage 6 - At this stage, organization leaders discuss the improvements which have priority for the organization and prioritize them and eventually, select some of them.

Stages 7 - For the selected improvable areas, improvement projects are defined, trustees are selected, resources are allocated to them and their implementation begins.

Stage 8 - In the last stage, the progress of improvement projects is periodically monitored and by revising the process of self-assessment in the previous stages, a new self-assessment is performed at the organization. In fact, using excellence model is a continuous improvement cycle which lasts forever.

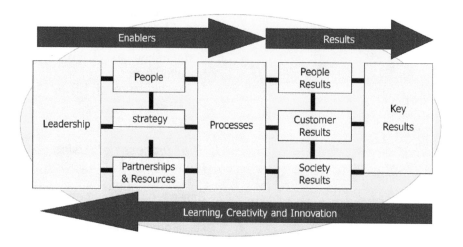

Figure 2. EFQM excellence framework.

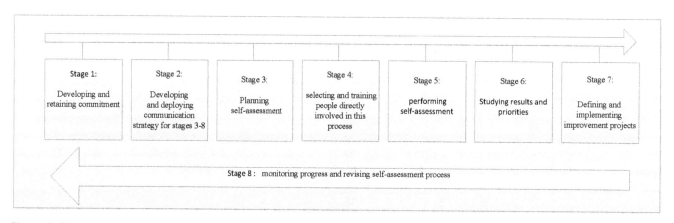

Figure 3. Stages for using organizational excellence model.

AHP technique

The AHP is a structured practice for representing the elements of a problem, hierarchically. The AHP method was developed by Saaty (2005). It can enable decision makers to represent the interaction of multiple factors in complex, unstructured situations. The procedure is based on the pair-wise comparison of decision elements with respect to attributes or alternatives.

Structuring the hierarchy for evaluation

In general, the AHP method divides the problem into three levels:

• Define a goal for resolving the problem
• Define objectives for achieving the goal
• Determine evaluation criteria for each objective.

After structuring a hierarchy, the pair-wise comparison matrix for each level is constructed. During the pair-wise comparison, a nominal scale is used for the evaluation. The scale used in AHP for preparing the pair-wise comparison matrix is a discrete scale from 1 to 9, as presented in Table 1.

A reciprocal value is assigned to the inverse comparison; that is, $a_{ij} = \frac{1}{a_{ji}}$, where a_{ij} (a_{ji}) denotes the importance of the ith (jth) element. The values of pair-wise comparisons are allocated in comparison matrix and local priority vector is obtained from eigenvector which is calculated from this equation:

$$A \times w = \lambda_{max} \times w$$

Where A is the matrix of pair-wise comparison, w is the eigenvector, and λ_{max} is the largest Eigen value of A.

Consistency of pair-wise matrix is checked by consistency index (CI). For accepted consistency, CI must be smaller than 0.10.

$$CI = \frac{\lambda max - n}{n-1} \qquad CR = \frac{CI}{RI}$$

Table 1. Scale of relative importance.

Intensity of importance	Definition
1	Equal importance
3	Moderate importance
5	Essential or strong importance
7	Very strong importance
9	Extreme importance
2,4,6,8	Intermediate value between adjacent scale values

In the equations above, CI, RI and CR represent consistency indicator, random indicator and consistency ratio, respectively.

Analytic Network Process (ANP) method

The ANP, a new theory extending from the AHP, is proposed by Saaty (1996). The ANP is composed of four major steps (Saaty, 1996):

Step 1: Forming the network structure.

The problem should be stated clearly and decomposed into a rational system like a network. The structure can be obtained by the opinion of decision-makers through brainstorming or other appropriate methods. Firstly, criteria, sub criteria and alternatives are defined. Then, the clusters of elements are determined. The network is formed based on relationship among clusters and within elements in each cluster.

Step 2: Forming pair-wise comparison matrices and obtaining priority vector.

Pair-wise comparisons are performed on the elements within the clusters as they influence each cluster and on those that it influences, with respect to that criterion. The pair-wise comparisons are made with respect to a criterion or sub-criterion of the control hierarchy. Thus, importance weight of factors is determined. In pair-wise comparison, decision makers compare two elements.

Then, they determine the contribution of factors to the result (Saaty, 2001). In ANP, like AHP, it is formed pair-wise comparison matrices to use a 1 to 9 scale of relative importance proposed by the Saaty. 1 to 9 scale of relative importance is given at Table 1. Using superdecision software the pair-wise comparisons were provided for dependencies among the clusters and decision elements. The superdecision software reports an inconsistency ratio for every pair-wise comparison matrix. A comparison matrix is considered to be consistent when its inconsistency ratio is less than 0.10. Inconsistency ratios of all our comparison matrices turned out to be less than 0.10, therefore, accepted as consistent.

Step 3: Super-matrix formation.

For evaluating the weights of the elements, the AHP uses the principal eigenvector of comparison matrix, while the ANP employs the limiting process method of the powers of the super-matrix. The super-matrix concept is similar to the Markov chain process (Saaty, 2005). To obtain global priorities in a system with interdependent influences, the local priority vectors are entered in the appropriate columns of a matrix. As a result, a super-matrix is actually a partitioned matrix, where each sub-matrix represents a relationship between two nodes (components or clusters) in a system.

Step 4: Selection of best alternatives.

It is able to determine importance weights of alternatives, factors and sub-factors from limited super-matrix. The highest importance weight shows the best alternative.

Research background

Table 2 shows some researches around using AHP and ANP methods in healthcare sector.

METHODOLOGY

The research methodology consisted of three main phases the process is presented in Figure 4.

Phase 1: Defining problem and Theoretical framework of research. Review on fundamental of Organization excellence model and healthcare excellence model and Process of using organization excellence model.

Phase 2: Deployment of AHP and ANP for ranking the projects. In the final phase AHP and ANP method was used for prioritizing 10 improvement projects.

SOLUTION APPROACH

In this paper, ANP and AHP methods was applied to prioritize 10 improvement projects. The names of these projects are provided in Table 3 (a and b).

Project selection using AHP technique

The application of the AHP to the study case has been performed with reference to the three phases described earlier, the model has been developed through the use of the specific Expert choice software. Figure 5 shows the

Table 2. Some researches around using AHP and ANP methods in healthcare sector.

	Year	Authors	Methodology and Results
AHP and Healthcare	2006	Chan	This paper proposes to apply the AHP to hospital scorecards in performance assessment. Although AHP could be a time-consuming exercise, it allows participative input in determining a comprehensive measure for comparing performance of healthcare organizations. The objective of this paper is to examine the value of balanced scorecard in the management of healthcare organizations and to describe an analytic hierarchy framework that can be used to evaluate scorecards of departments and programs within healthcare organizations and the performance of healthcare organizations as a whole.
	2007	Brent et al.	This paper focuses on the application of the AHP technique in the context of sustainable development to establish and optimize health care waste management (HCWM) systems in rural areas of developing countries. This is achieved by evaluating the way in which the AHP can best be combined with a life cycle management (LCM) approach, and addressing a main objective of HCWM systems, that is to minimize infection of patients and workers within the system. The modified approach was applied to two case studies: the sub-Saharan African countries of South Africa and Lesotho. Quantitative weightings from the AHP are used to identify alternative systems that have similar outcomes in meeting the systems objective, but may have different cost structures and infection risks. The two case studies illustrate how the AHP can be used (with strengths and weaknesses) in environmental engineering decision support in developing countries.
	2010	Chung-Hsiung et al.	This study conducts AHP method to develop a managerial competency framework for middle managers in the medical industry. The data collection is from nursing supervisors and top-level executives in medical institutions. Participants are required to make a comparison in importance between two competencies and then comparison results are processed and analyzed. Factors at the first level for selecting middle managers in the medical industry are sorted by importance as follows: personality, plan, manage, professional ability and interpersonal ability, indicating that experts believe that personality and plan are very important to middle managers in the medical industry, most of which are responsible for administrative management. We establish a core competency model for reserve middle-level managers in the medical industry. Reserve cadres can take training courses for administrative management arranged by the Nursing Department and the hospital, in which they can establish their career plans and improve their abilities and the human resource department can also find and train excellent talents.
	1997	Hokey et al.	This paper proposes an AHP that can help medical clinics formulate viable service improvement strategies in the increasingly competitive healthcare industry. This paper also illustrates the usefulness of the proposed health care quality measures using the case of prominent Korean cancer clinics.
	2011	Hummel et al.	The objective of this study is to review the past applications of the AHP in supporting health care decision making, and to make recommendations for its future use. We conducted a systematic review of AHP applications in health care, as described in the relevant medical, health-economical, psycho-sociological, managerial, and applied mathematical literature. They found 62 distinctive AHP applications in health care. Of the retrieved applications, 13% focus on shared decision-making between patient and clinician, 27% on the development of clinical practice guidelines, 5% on the development of medical devices and pharmaceuticals, 40% on management decisions in health care organizations, and 15% on the development of national health care policy. From the review it is concluded that the AHP is suitable to apply in case of complex health care decision problems, a need to improve decision making instead of explain decision outcomes, a need to share information among experts or between clinicians and patients, and in case of a limited availability of informed respondents.

Table 2. Cond.

ANP and Healthcare	2009	Liao et al.	This study describes the use of ANP in Taiwanese hospital public relations personnel selection process. In this article, they interview 48 practitioners and executives to collect the selecting criteria. Then, they retained the 12 critical criteria that was mentioned 40 times by theses respondents, including: interpersonal skill, experience, negotiation, language, ability to follow orders, cognitive ability, adaptation to environment, adaptation to company, emotion, loyalty, attitude, and response. Following a discussion with 20 executives, we took 12 criteria into account in three perspectives to construct the hierarchy. In another research, they found that most of the contributors applied AHP concept to facilitate the personnel selection process. Because of the interrelated relation among the selecting criteria, they apply a more accurate approach, ANP, to solve this selection problem.
EFQM and AHP	2010	Iranzadeh et al.	Designing and formulating a comprehensive organization performance evaluation model based on EFQM in AHP method is the main aim of the present research study. Evaluation is considered as one of the most important activities in each organization in a way that reformation of processes and procedures of doing activity without evaluation of results will be impossible. At the present research activity, AHP has been used as one of MADM (Multi-Attribute Decision Making) methods for the evaluation of performance of organizations through the application of EFQM excellence model criteria. Also, Municipality of City of Tabriz has been selected as subjects for testing the presented model. In the same direction, seven districts of this municipality were selected as sample model. Necessary and required information were accumulated through questionnaire, interview and also taking advantage of data and library resources, details of which were analyzed and studied through the application of advanced Excel and Expert Choice 11.5 software package system.

Table 3a. Comparisons of AHP and ANP.

Projects	Ranking by ANP	Ranking by AHP
1	7	6
2	3	3
3	9	9
4	10	10
5	4	4
6	5	7
7	8	8
8	2	2
9	1	1
10	6	5

hierarchical structure which could correctly represent the decision-making problem. During the analysis, the elements at each level of the hierarchy have been compared pair-wise with respect to the upper-level element. Mention should be made to fact that the judgments that have been used to fill the comparison matrixes have been derived from expert opinions. Both AHP and ANP derive ratio scale priorities by generating pair-wise comparisons of elements based on a common property or criterion. Table 4 presents an example pair-wise comparison. A final ranking of the projects is presented in Figure 6.

It can be clearly seen that project number nine "Leadership Development and Succession Planning" has the best score and can be said that it is most suitable project and followed by projects 8,2,5,10,1,6,7,3,4.

Project selection using ANP technique

The ANP method allows dependence relations between elements and clusters. Such relations are represented by arrows, when the dependence occurs between a cluster over another cluster, or through a loop, when there is dependence among elements of a same cluster. In order to exist an arrow from a cluster to another, it is enough that at least one element of the original cluster is connected to an element of the destination cluster (Saaty, 2005).

This way, with the possibility to analyze dependences among criteria and influences among alternatives, ANP method was applied to rank the improvement projects with the help of the superdecisions software. Priorities obtained from the pair-wise comparison matrix (Table 4), as the shown in Figure 8.

The un-weighted super-matrix is constructed after weighting that matrix with the component matrix, and finally, we obtain the limit super-matrix, represented as follows: The un-weighted, weighted and limit super-matrix for this model is shown in Tables 5, 6 and 7 respectively.

Table 3b. Name of alternatives (Projects).

Projects	Name of alternative
1	Design and implementation of employee performance management system
2	Design and implementation of macro-level performance management system
3	Design and implementation of mechanisms for periodic monitoring of aberrations to improve its budgeting and planning
4	Design and implementation of systems and equipment maintenance and calibration of measuring instruments
5	Designing and implementing a patient relationship management System
6	Designing and implementing a process management system (identification, formulation, implementation, measuring, improve)
7	Designing and Implementing a promotion and marketing system to increase bed occupancy rate
8	Formulation, implementation and evaluation of current strategies
9	Leadership Development and Succession Planning
10	Staff surveys and improvement planning in human resources

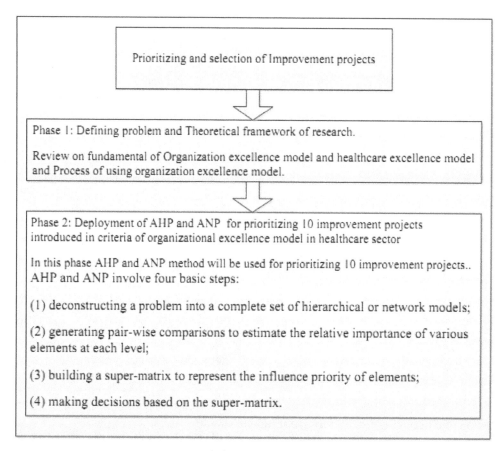

Figure 4. Research methodology.

Limit super matrix shown in Table 7 is obtained from the weighted super matrix by raising it to power until it converges and shows the importance weights of sub-factors, factors and alternatives. All columns in this limiting super matrix are identical.

Finally, we obtained scores of projects, which are represented by raw values, from limit super-matrix table.

To get normal values, raw values are summed up and every row in the raw column is divided by the sum. To obtain ideal values, every value in raw values column is divided by the greatest value of the column. The final ranking of the projects is presented in Figure 9.

It can be clearly seen that project number nine "Leadership Development and Succession Planning" has

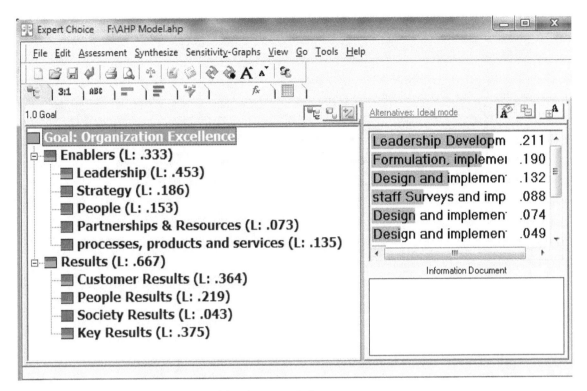

Figure 5. Hierarchical approach of the problem in expert choice.

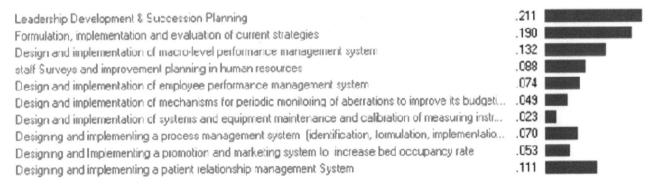

Figure 6. AHP results and ranking.

the best score and can be said that it is the most suitable project and followed by projects 8,2,5,6,10,1,7,3,4.

Conclusion

The analysis of selecting improvement projects was carried out by comparison of two methods, AHP and ANP. The definition of network structure is based on the inter- dependencies between elements or sub criteria and the criteria themselves. ANP is characterized for including qualitative and quantitative criteria, structured in a network, where the dependence relations among elements are allowed. Calculating the super-matrix and limit matrix shows that the priorities in ANP technique are different with AHP. Both decision metrics ANP and AHP, for the 10 improvement project alternatives evaluated.

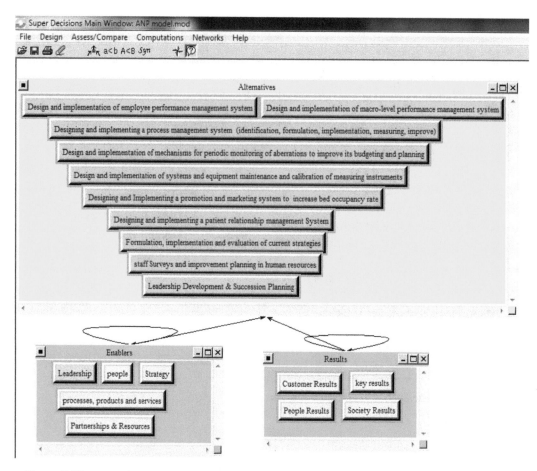

Figure 7. The network structure of the proposed model.

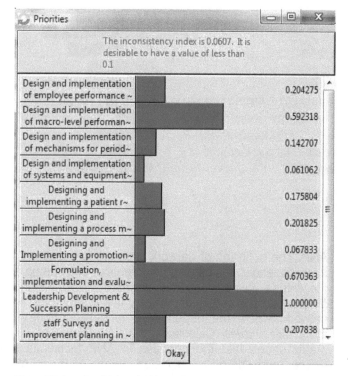

Figure 8. Leadership's priorities relative to alternatives.

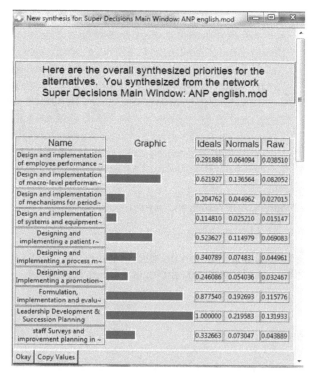

Figure 9. The results of the proposed model.

Table 4. Pair-wise comparison matrix improvement projects respect to the leadership.

Leadership	1	2	3	4	5	6	7	8	9	10
1		1/5	2	4	1	2	5	1/5	1/5	1/2
2			5	7	3	3	7	1	1/3	5
3				3	1	1/2	5	1/5	1/7	1/2
4					1/5	1/5	1/2	1/6	1/7	1/4
5						1	3	1/7	1/6	1
6							5	1/4	1/5	1
7								1/7	1/7	1/4
8									1/7	5
9									1/3	5
10										

Table 5. Un-weighted super-matrix.

	Design~	Design~	Design~	Design~	Designi~	Design~	Formula~	Leaders~	StaffS~	Leaders~	Partner~	People~	Process~	Strategy	Custome~	Key res~	People~	Society~
Design~	0	0	0	0	0	0	0	0	0	0.06145	0.10655	0.1991	0.02515	0.04104	0.04317	0.07515	0.13639	0.04142
Design~	0	0	0	0	0	0	0	0	0	0.17819	0.18338	0.09396	0.11483	0.21853	0.08772	0.16692	0.07383	0.10002
Design~	0	0	0	0	0	0	0	0	0	0.04293	0.06759	0.03767	0.02464	0.07935	0.03146	0.07493	0.02764	0.02471
Design~	0	0	0	0	0	0	0	0	0	0.01837	0.05341	0.01748	0.05169	0.02126	0.02708	0.01529	0.01799	0.01785
Designi~	0	0	0	0	0	0	0	0	0	0.05289	0.02379	0.02447	0.15351	0.04287	0.20239	0.11438	0.03226	0.13108
Designi~	0	0	0	0	0	0	0	0	0	0.06072	0.06449	0.06637	0.10855	0.09001	0.10405	0.03618	0.05663	0.07125
Designi~	0	0	0	0	0	0	0	0	0	0.02041	0.03089	0.01957	0.09617	0.03136	0.07683	0.05747	0.02119	0.09359
Formula~	0	0	0	0	0	0	0	0	0	0.20167	0.2116	0.11822	0.19888	0.21853	0.19839	0.18183	0.18079	0.20397
Leaders~	0	0	0	0	0	0	0	0	0	0.30084	0.1718	0.15009	0.19911	0.20637	0.18524	0.194	0.25285	0.25085
Staff S~	0	0	0	0	0	0	0	0	0	0.06253	0.0865	0.27308	0.02748	0.05068	0.04368	0.08387	0.20043	0.06525
Leaders~	0	0	0	0	0	0	0	0	0	0	0	0	0	0	0	0	0	0
Partner~	0	0	0	0	0	0	0	0	0	0.09821	0	0.25	0	0.14286	0	0	0	0
People~	0	0	0	0	0	0	0	0	0	0.29464	0	0	0	0.42857	0	0	0	0
Process~	0	0	0	0	0	0	0	0	0	0.25075	1	0.75	0	0.42857	0	0	0	0
Strategy	0	0	0	0	0	0	0	0	0	0.3564	0	0	0	0	0	0	0	0
Custome~	0	0	0	0	0	0	0	0	0	0	0	0	0	0	0	0	0	1
Key res~	0	0	0	0	0	0	0	0	0	0	0	0	0	0	0.58608	0	0.88889	0
People~	0	0	0	0	0	0	0	0	0	0	0	0	0	0	0.35313	0	0	0
Society~	0	0	0	0	0	0	0	0	0	0	0	0	0	0	0.06079	0	0.11111	0

As shown in Table 3a, projects number 2, 3, 4, 5, 7, 8, 9 have the same ranking by AHP and ANP methods and these are different only in the ranking of 3 projects. Finally, ANP method resulted more suitable than the AHP method because it enhances the function of the AHP to develop a complete model that can incorporate interdependent relationships between elements from different levels or within levels, which are

Table 6. Weighted super-matrix.

	Design~	Design~	Design~	Design~	Designi~	Designi~	Designi~	Formula~	Leaders~	StaffS~	Leaders~	Partner~	People	Process~	Strategy	Custome~	Key res~	People~	Society~
Design~	0	0	0	0	0	0	0	0	0	0	0.03073	0.05327	0.09955	0.02515	0.02052	0.02159	0.07515	0.06820	0.02071
Design~	0	0	0	0	0	0	0	0	0	0	0.08910	0.09169	0.04698	0.11483	0.10926	0.04386	0.16692	0.03692	0.05001
Design~	0	0	0	0	0	0	0	0	0	0	0.02147	0.03380	0.01884	0.02464	0.03968	0.01573	0.07493	0.01382	0.01236
Design~	0	0	0	0	0	0	0	0	0	0	0.00919	0.02670	0.00874	0.05169	0.01063	0.01354	0.01529	0.00899	0.00893
Designi~	0	0	0	0	0	0	0	0	0	0	0.02645	0.01189	0.01223	0.15351	0.02144	0.10119	0.11438	0.01613	0.06554
Designi~	0	0	0	0	0	0	0	0	0	0	0.03036	0.03225	0.03319	0.10855	0.045	0.05202	0.03618	0.02831	0.03563
Designi~	0	0	0	0	0	0	0	0	0	0	0.01020	0.01545	0.00979	0.09617	0.01568	0.03841	0.05747	0.01060	0.04679
Formula~	0	0	0	0	0	0	0	0	0	0	0.10084	0.10580	0.05911	0.19888	0.10926	0.09919	0.18183	0.09039	0.10198
Leaders~	0	0	0	0	0	0	0	0	0	0	0.15042	0.08590	0.07504	0.19911	0.10319	0.09262	0.194	0.12643	0.12543
Staff S~	0	0	0	0	0	0	0	0	0	0	0.03126	0.04325	0.13654	0.02748	0.02534	0.02184	0.08387	0.10022	0.03263
Leaders~	0	0	0	0	0	0	0	0	0	0	0	0	0	0	0	0	0	0	0
Partner~	0	0	0	0	0	0	0	0	0	0	0.04911	0	0.125	0	0.07143	0	0	0	0
People	0	0	0	0	0	0	0	0	0	0	0.14732	0	0	0	0.21429	0	0	0	0
Process~	0	0	0	0	0	0	0	0	0	0	0.12538	0.5	0.375	0	0.21429	0	0	0	0
Strategy	0	0	0	0	0	0	0	0	0	0	0.17820	0	0	0	0	0	0	0	0
Custome~	0	0	0	0	0	0	0	0	0	0	0	0	0	0	0	0	0	0	0
Key res~	0	0	0	0	0	0	0	0	0	0	0	0	0	0	0	0.29304	0	0.44444	0.5
People~	0	0	0	0	0	0	0	0	0	0	0	0	0	0	0	0.17657	0	0	0
Society~	0	0	0	0	0	0	0	0	0	0	0	0	0	0	0	0.03040	0	0.05556	0

Table 7. Limit super-matrix.

	Design~	Design~	Design~	Design~	Designi~	Designi~	Designi~	Formula~	Leaders~	StaffS~	Leaders~	Partner~	People	Process~	Strategy	Custome~	Key res~	People~	Society~
Design~	0	0	0	0	0	0	0	0	0	0	0.03730	0.04390	0.07501	0.02515	0.03365	0.03972	0.07515	0.06862	0.03886
Design~	0	0	0	0	0	0	0	0	0	0	0.09089	0.09940	0.06955	0.11483	0.10132	0.07321	0.16692	0.07758	0.08898
Design~	0	0	0	0	0	0	0	0	0	0	0.02418	0.03074	0.02166	0.02464	0.03351	0.02985	0.07493	0.03265	0.03321
Design~	0	0	0	0	0	0	0	0	0	0	0.01694	0.03503	0.02220	0.05169	0.01986	0.01335	0.01529	0.01094	0.01105
Designi~	0	0	0	0	0	0	0	0	0	0	0.04399	0.05910	0.05176	0.15351	0.04709	0.09418	0.11438	0.04829	0.08182
Designi~	0	0	0	0	0	0	0	0	0	0	0.04477	0.05768	0.05421	0.10855	0.05591	0.04515	0.03618	0.03101	0.03581
Designi~	0	0	0	0	0	0	0	0	0	0	0.02473	0.04235	0.03443	0.09617	0.03161	0.04021	0.05747	0.02640	0.05035
Formula~	0	0	0	0	0	0	0	0	0	0	0.11314	0.13683	0.10198	0.19888	0.12117	0.11842	0.18183	0.11908	0.12860
Leaders~	0	0	0	0	0	0	0	0	0	0	0.14203	0.12364	0.11065	0.19911	0.11843	0.12183	0.194	0.14727	0.14828
Staff S~	0	0	0	0	0	0	0	0	0	0	0.04196	0.03799	0.09854	0.02748	0.04123	0.04582	0.08387	0.09271	0.04971
Leaders~	0	0	0	0	0	0	0	0	0	0	0	0	0	0	0	0	0	0	0
Partner~	0	0	0	0	0	0	0	0	0	0	0.04931	0	0.08	0	0.05930	0	0	0	0
People	0	0	0	0	0	0	0	0	0	0	0.10758	0	0	0	0.12938	0	0	0	0
Process~	0	0	0	0	0	0	0	0	0	0	0.15985	0.33333	0.28	0	0.20755	0	0	0	0
Strategy	0	0	0	0	0	0	0	0	0	0	0.10334	0	0	0	0	0	0	0	0
Custome~	0	0	0	0	0	0	0	0	0	0	0	0	0	0	0	0	0	0	0
Key res~	0	0	0	0	0	0	0	0	0	0	0	0	0	0	0	0.24348	0	0.30909	0
People~	0	0	0	0	0	0	0	0	0	0	0	0	0	0	0	0.10978	0	0	0.33333
Society~	0	0	0	0	0	0	0	0	0	0	0	0	0	0	0	0.025	0	0.03636	0

assumed to be uncorrelated in AHP. Liao and Chang (2009) research showed similar results.

There were some limitations in this research project. For example, Iranian Excellence Model in healthcare Sector has been implemented in 23 hospitals and therefore the number of Improvement Projects was limited. If the model were implemented in most hospitals, the results were probably more accurate. Another limitation was Pair-wise comparison matrix improvement projects respect to the Criteria built based on the thoughts, comments, and suggestions of 15 experts. If these matrixes were built using more experts, the results were probably more accurate.

REFERENCES

Ahsan MK, Bartema J (2004). Monitoring healthcare performance by analytic hierarchy process: A developing country perspective. Int. Trans. Oper. Res.11:465-478.

Arenas M, Bilbao A, Caballero R, Gómez T, Rodríguez MV, Ruiz F (2002). Analysis via goal programming of the minimum achievable stay in surgical waiting lists. J. Oper. Res. Soc.53 (4):387-396.

Bergquist B, Fredriksson M, Svensson M (2005). TQM – terrific quality marvel or tragic quality malpractice. TQM Mag. 17(4):309-321.

Bou-Llusar JC, Escrig-Tena AB, Roca-Puig V, Beltra-n-Marti-n I (2005). To what extent do enablers explain results in the EFQM excellence model? Int. J. Qual. Reliab. Manage. 22(4):337-353.

Bou-Llusar JC, Escrig-Tena AB, Roca-Puig V, Beltra-n-Marti-n I (2009). An empirical assessment of the EFQM Excellence Model: Evaluation as a TQM framework relative to the MBNQA Model. J. Oper. Manage. 27(1):1-22.

Brent AC, Rogers DEC, Ramabitsa-Siimane TSM, Rohwer MB (2007). Application of the analytical hierarchy process to establish health care waste management systems that minimize infection risks in developing countries. Eur. J. Oper. Res. 181:403-424.

Calvo-Mora A, Leal A, Rolda´n JL (2005). Relationships between the EFQM Model Criteria: a study in Spanish universities. Total Qual. Manage. 16 (6):741-770.

Calvo-Mora A, Leal A, Rolda´n JL (2006). Using enablers of the EFQM model to manage institutions of higher education. Qual. Assur. Educ. 14(2):99-122.

Cardoen B, Demeulemeester E, Belien J (2009). Sequencing surgical cases in a day-care environment: An exact branch-and-price approach. Comput. Oper. Res. 36(9):2660-2669.

Chan Y-Ch Lilian (2006). An Analytic Hierarchy Framework for Evaluating Balanced Scorecards of Healthcare Organizations. Can. J. Adm. Sci. 23(2):85-104.

Dahlgaard-Park SM (2008). Reviewing the European excellence model from a management control view. TQM Mag. 20(2).

Dolan JG (1989). Medical decision making using the analytic hierarchy process: Choice of initial antimicrobial therapy for acute pyelonephritis. Med. Decis. Mak. 9(1):51-56.

Earnshaw SR, Dennett SL (2003). Integer/linear mathematical programming models: A tool for allocating healthcare resources. Pharmacol. Econ. 21(12):839-851.

Epstein DM, Chalabi Z, Claxton K, Sculpher M (2007). Efficiency, equity, and budgetary policies: Informing decisions using mathematical programming. Med. Decis. Mak. 27(2):128-137.

European Foundation for Quality Management (2010). The EFQM Excellence Model. EFQM, Brussels.

Flessa S (2003). Priorities and allocation of health care resources in developing countries: A case-study from the Mtwara region-Tanzana. Eur. J. Oper. Res. 150(1):67-80.

Hannan EL, O'Donnell J, Freedland T (1981). A priority assignment model for standards and conditions in a long term care survey. S-Econ. Plann. Sci. 15(6):277-289.

Herget J, Hierl S (2007). Excellence in libraries: a systematic and integrated approach. New Lib. World 108(11/12):526-544.

Hokey M, Amitava M, Sharon O (1997). Competitive Benchmarking of Healthcare Quality Using the Analytic Hierarchy Process: an Example from Korean Cancer Clinics Socio-Econ. Plann. Sci. 31(2):147-159.

Hummel M, IJzerman M (2011). The past and future of the AHP in health care decision making. Proceedings of the International Symposium on the Analytic Hierarchy Process.

Iranzadeh S, Chakherlouy F (2010). Designing and formulating organization performance evaluation model in AHP method based on EFQM criteria (case study), ICAMS 2010- Proceedings of 2010 IEEE International Conference on Advanced Management Science 1:606-609.

Javalgi R, Rao SR, Thomas E (1991). Choosing a Hospital: Analysis of Consumer Tradeoffs. J. Health Care Market. 11(1):12-23.

Kwak N.K, Lee C.W (2002). Business process reengineering for healthcare system using multicriteria mathematical programming. Eur. J. Oper. Res. 140(2):447-458.

Kwak NK, McCarthy KJ, Parker GE (1997). A human resource planning model for hospital/medical technologists: An analytic hierarchy process approach. J. Med. Syst. 21(3):173-187.

Liao SK, Chang KL (2009). Selecting Public Relations Personnel of Hospitals by Analytic Network Process. J. Hosp. Market. Public Relat. 19:52-63.

Liberatore MJ, Nydick RL (2008). The analytic hierarchy process in medical and health care decision making: A literature review. Eur. J. Oper. Res. 189(1):194-207.

Martinez-Lorente A, G_omez-Go_mez J, Martinez-Costa M (2009). An evaluation of the EFQM excellence model. proceeding of 16th International annual EUROMA conference.

Najmi M, Hosseini S (2009). The EFQM Excellence Model: From idea to practice. Saramad Puplication, Tehran, Iran.

Oddoye JP, Yaghoobi MA, Tamiz M, Jones DF, Schmidt P (2006). A multi-objective model to determine efficient resource levels in a medical assessment unit. J. Oper. Res. Soc. 57(10):1173-1179.

Saaty TL (1996). Decision Making with Dependence and Feedback: The Analytic Network Process. Pittsburgh, PA: RWS Publications.

Saaty TL (2001). Making with Dependence and Feedback. 2nd ed., RWS Publication.

Saaty TL (2005). Theory and Applications of the Analytic Network Process: Decision Making with Benefits, Opportunities, Costs, and Risks. RWS Publications, Pittsburg, PA, USA.

Tutuncu O, Kucukusta D (2009). Canonical correlation between job satisfaction and EFQM organization excellence model. Springer Science and Organization Media B.V, DOI: 10.1007/s11135-009-9269-0.

Vijende M, Gonzalez L (2007). TQM and firms performance: An EFQM excellence model research based survey. Int. J. Organ. Sci. Appl. Manage. 2(2):22-41.

Westlund AH (2001). Measuring environmental impact on society in the EFQM system. Total Qual. Manage. 12(1):125-135.

Wilson RM, Gibberd RW (1990). Combining multiple criteria for regional resource allocation in health care systems. Math. Comput. Model. 13(8):15-27.

Wongrassamee S, Gardiner PD, Simmons JEL (2003). Performance measurement tools: the Balanced Scorecard and the EFQM Excellence Model. Meas. Organ. Excell. 7(1):14-29.

4

A heuristic algorithm for determining the production batch size and the idle time for minimizing makespan

Taghizadeh Houshang[1] and Honarpour Amir[2]

[1]Islamic Azad University - Tabriz Branch, - Yaghchian- Tohid Street- Mosque Square- Saba Alley- West Sixth alley- No. 229- Second Floor, Tabriz, Iran.
[2]University Teknology Malaysia, 33c-30-1, Villa Puteri Condo, Jalan Tun Ismail, Kuala Lumpur, Malaysia.

In this paper, a heuristic algorithm has been presented with the aim of determining the quantity of the best batch size for minimizing the makespan of a production system in order to meet the demands of a specified period for a product. This algorithm calculates the time required for fulfilling each of the requisite operations for producing a batch size by taking into account the standard time for fulfilling the operations, the number of similar parts used in one unit of a product, the machinery setup time, the scrap proportion of each operation on the relevant machinery and the quantity of that batch size. This algorithm allots the requisite operations to the machinery for producing the total demand of a specified period by making use of the calculated information, shortest processing time (SPT) rule, the specified conditions in the algorithm and the quantity of the production in each batch size. Then, with respect to the quantity of this batch size, the aggregate of the setup and idle times of machinery is calculated for the whole period. Afterwards, the quantity of the optimum batch size, which minimizes the aggregate of these times, is obtained by calculating the aggregate of these times for the different quantities of the batch sizes and comparing them. Some examples have been presented to compare this algorithm with the algorithms of Ho and Chang, Johnson, and Palmer.

Key words: Flow-shop, batch size, makespan, setup time, idle time.

INTRODUCTION

Production as a major element of human social life, needs planning. The elimination of idle time and using this time will lead to a quicker response to a customer's order and many similar consequences. Assume that there are m different machines and n jobs that should be done on the machines, $m_1, m_2, ..., m_m$ are the index numbers of the machines and n is the number of jobs. Each job has to be processed first on m_1, then on m_2, and so on, until it is processed on the last machine m_m.

The processing time of each job on each machine is known. Backward flow is not allowed. Each machine processes one job at a time at most and each job is processed on one machine at a timeat most.

This algorithm, regarding the standard time of each operation, number of similar parts used in one unit of product, time for setup of machines, scrap proportion of each operation on the relevant machine and quantity of batch size, is going to calculate the necessary time to do each of the needed operations to produce the same batch size.

To meet the demand of the determined algorithm, first, one unit batches are allocated to the machines; then the total setup and idle times of the machines for the demand for the period were computed. In the next step, by changing the batch sizes the total setup and idle times of the machines were calculated. Finally, the best batch size, which minimizes the total time, is attained. The aim of this algorithm is to specify the timing programme of an demand. To test the offered algorithm, its results are compared to the attained results for the algorithms of Ho and Chang, Johnson and Palmer and it is shown that this algorithm can present better results.

Problem specification

a. There are n jobs at time zero (production start time) in the factory.
b. Any machine is reachable continuously and is not idle as long as there is a job in operation.
c. Process direction will always be observed (This means that every time the first stage of each job is done before the second stage).
d. Setup times for an operation are independent from their sequence.
e. The specifications of any job and machine and the standard time of jobs are determined from the beginning.
f. Once the operation is started on a machine, it will be continued on the same machine until the end (a job cannot be stopped and be redone).
g. The setup time is determined from the start and according to the sort of operation.
h. Every machine is independent from others and can function with its maximum capacity.
i. The production method is discontinuous.
j. The specifications of the problem are static and definite.
k. Any machine can only execute one job at a time.
l. The scrap proportion in every operation on every machine is known from the beginning.

REVIEW OF LITERATURE

As Bayat et al. (2010) mentioned, most of the scheduling problems in industry and the real world are NP-hard. Different methods and techniques have been studied in the product programming literature to determine the operation sequence of n jobs on m machines. The GANT chart is the most popular method to represent loading jobs on the equipment during the time (Quinn and Novels, 2001).

The matrix method for timing activities is another method to calculate timing schedules for jobs and machines, which was presented by Wright (Wild, 1989). In that study, an approximate method was presented for timing by using the index of machines for determining the sequence of job delivery on machinery that has many functions and is relatively simple. This method is based on determining the index number of machines (Wild, 1989).

Palmer introduced a slope order index to the jab's sequence that is based on the processing time. He gave the priority to jobs from short times to long times in the sequence of operation (Widmar and Hertz, 1989). A new heuristic for solving the flow-shop scheduling problem introduced by Ho and Chang (1991), this new method minimizes gaps between successive operations in

solutions generated by other heuristics. Allahverdi and Aldowaisan (2002) considered the m-machine no-wait flow shop scheduling problem with the objective of minimizing a weighted sum of makespan and total completion time.

Koulamas and Kyparisis (2007) showed that the derived bound can be used to improve the best available worst-case ratio bound for the flexible flow shop makespan minimization problem with an arbitrary odd number of stages.

Shabtay et al. (2007) extended the classical no-wait two-machine flow shop scheduling problem to the case where job-processing times are controllable through the allocation of a common, limited and non-renewable resource. They showed that the problem reduces to a new special case of the TSP and this newly defined class of the TSP is strongly NP-hard even though the problem is NP-hard.

Tahar et al. (2006) considered the problem of scheduling as a set of independent jobs with sequence-dependent setup times and job splitting on a set of identical parallel machines such that the maximum completion time (makespan) is minimized. Zhang et al. (2008) proposed a heuristic search approach by combining the simulated annealing (SA) and Taboo search (TS) strategy. The main principle of this approach is that SA is used to find the elite solutions inside big valley (BV) so that TS can re-intensify the search from the promising solutions. Yilmaz et al. (2007) presented a novel approach for realizing group setup strategies. This approach has been detailed for the case of a single collect-and-place assembly machine.

In considering the previous mentioned methods and investigating their strengths and weaknesses, we suggest another algorithm. The difference between the proposed algorithm and the other algorithms for scheduling n jobs on m machines is that it uses inventory control. In inventory control models the economic order quantity is obtained when the sum of annual costs of the inventory system, which contains annual ordering costs, annual holding costs, purchasing costs, is minimized. In this algorithm, the previous mentioned topic has been used as the pattern of the study.

INPUT INFORMATION OF ALGORITHM

The input information for this algorithm is as follows:

A. Number of each operation.
B. Standard time to execute each of the operations on the relevant machines.
C. The number of the similar operations used in producing one unit of the product.
D. Machinery code.
E. Time of setup for each operation.
F. Quantity of needed product in a particular process.
G. Scrap proportion in each operation on the related

machine.

Notations

This paper uses these notations: C_i = scrap proportion of operation i on the relevant machine, K = quantity of production batch size, n = number of operations to produce one unit of a product, m = number of machines, D = demands of period, V = number of production batches, S_i = standard time of operation I, P_i = number of operations i used on one unit of product (number of the same operations), t_i = standard time for total operation I $(t_i = S_i \times P_i)$, A_i = setup time for operation i in one product batch, T_i = standard time for total operation i in K unit product batch $(T_i = K \times t_i)$, U_i = needed time for fulfilling operation i in K unit product batch (aggregate of total standard time and setup time of operation i in K unit product batch), ($U_i = T_i + A_i$), F_i = required time for fulfilling operation i in a K unit product batch by considering the scrap proportion $(F_i = \dfrac{U_i}{1-C_i})$, r = represents the specific number of the machine, F_{rq} = required time for fulfilling q'th operation on r'th machine, T_{rq} = idle time after q'th operation on r'th machine, R = number of parts, Q = number of operations on a machine, H_K = total time to setup machines in order to meet the demands for k unit product batch, W_K = totalidle times of machinery in order to meet the demands for k unit product batch, Z_K = total aggregate of the setup and idle times of machinery for k unit production batch size ($Zk = Hk + Wk$), M_K = period demand makespan quantity.

THE PROPOSED ALGORITHM

The schematic algorithm is shown in Figure 1. In executing the algorithm, the number of production batches throughout the process for the situation in which the quantity of batch size is K, will be calculated from the relation as follows:

$$V = \left[\frac{D}{K}\right] + \delta \ \& \ \delta = \begin{cases} 0 & \left[\ if \ \ \overline{\dfrac{D}{K}} \right. \\ 1 & \left[\ if \ \ \dfrac{D}{K} \right. \end{cases}$$

(1)

The necessary steps in executing the algorithm systematically are:

1. Multiply the number of operations i used in one product by its standard time, called "total standard time", as follows:

$$t_i = S_i \times P_i$$
$$i = 1, 2, ..., n \tag{2}$$

2. Total standard time of operation i with batch size K should be calculated as follows:

$$T_i = K \times t_i$$
$$i = 1, 2, ..., n \tag{3}$$

3. Time needed to fulfil operation i in K unit product batch is equal to:

$$U_i = T_i + A_i$$
$$I = 1, 2, ..., n \tag{4}$$

4. Required time for fulfilling operation i in a K unit product batch considering the scrap percentage is calculated as follows:

$$F_i = \frac{U_i}{1-C_i}$$
$$i = 1, 2, ..., n \tag{5}$$

5. Allocate operation on machines by using F_i according to these steps:

5 i. Set K equal to "one" and then calculate steps 1 to 4.
5 ii. Allocated the first operation to machines in time zero (start time of production) considering these points:

a. In case of simultaneous reference of some operations to one machine, allocate activities according to the order of shortest processing time (SPT) to the machines.
b. In allocating operations to the machines, in cases where more than one machine can execute the operations, allocate the operation to a machine that could execute it in a shorter time.

5 iii. Allocate next operation (second, third ...) relating to each part, to the machines considering the conditions mentioned in step (5 ii). In allocating the next operation of the parts to machines these cases may happen:

a. If the machine is unemployed the referring operation will be computed immediately.
b. If the machine is executing one of the operations, the referring operation will join the queue of other expecting

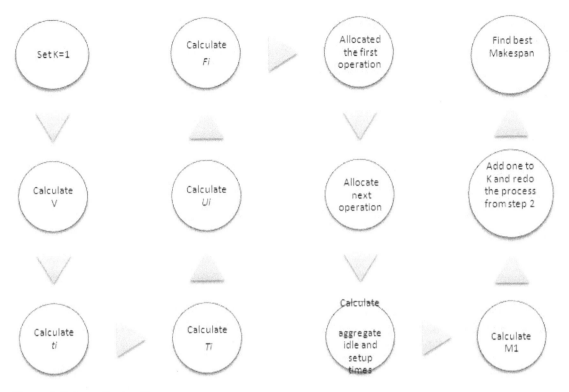

Figure 1. Schematic algorithm.

operations to this machine.

c. When the machine finishes the operation, it uses the SPT rule to determine the next job; that is, it chooses the task that has the shortest time of processing.

5 iv. After allocating the total operation of first batch size (k = 1) on machines, the allocation of the next sets (second, third ...) for k = 1 will be done. This process will be continued for the complete timing plan of the period of demand.

In allocating other batches (second, third, ..., and V) to proper machines (where the amount of V is obtained from formula (1), consider these points :

a. In case of simultaneous referring of the parts with the same set numbers, observe SPT rule in allocating part operation to the machine.

b. In case of simultaneous referring of the parts with different set numbers, operation of sets that have lower numbers should be allocated (without respecting SPT rule).

5 v. After allocating all operations of the parts of total sets related to k = 1 to machines, the quantities related to "aggregate idle and setup times" during timing schedule of defined process demands will be computed and called Z_1.

In calculating Z_k, the aggregate of the idle and setup

times to meet the period demand will be gained from the operation sequence and the following relations (H_k is aggregate of setup times and W_k is aggregate of idle times):

$$Z_k = H_k + W_k \ , $$
$$k = 1,2,...,n \tag{6}$$

$$W_k = \sum_{r=1}^{m} \sum_{q=1}^{Q} T_{r,q} \tag{7}$$

$$H_k = V \times \sum_{i=1}^{n} A_i \quad k = 1,2,...,D \tag{8}$$

Where F_{rq} is the required time for fulfilling q'th operation on r'th machine and $T_{r,q}$ is the idle time after q'th operation on r'th machine gained from the recursive relation.

$$T_{r,q} = \sum_{s=1}^{q} F_{r-1,s+1} + \sum_{s=0}^{q} T_{r-1,s} - \sum_{s=1}^{q} F_{r,s} - \sum_{s=0}^{q} T_{r,s} \text{ if } \quad q \le Q-1$$

(9)

If the above sum is not positive ($T_{r,q} \leq 0$) we replace its value with zero.

$$T_{r,Q} = M_k - \sum_{q=0}^{Q} F_{r,q} - \sum_{r=0}^{Q-1} T_{r,q} = M_k - M_r \qquad (10)$$

Where M_k is makespan. It can be defined as follows:

$$M_r = \sum_{q=1}^{Q} F_{r,q} + \sum_{r=0}^{Q-1} T_{r,q} \qquad (11)$$

And

$$M_k = \max\{M_r\}_{r=1}^{m} \qquad (12)$$

For obtaining the idle time after every operation, we define idle time and setup time matrices that have m rows and Q columns, and the idle time matrix after the last operation has m rows and *one* column. We define the entities of the matrices as follow:

k = Quantity of batch size that belongs to $\{K_1, K_2\}$, q = Specific number of operation on r'th machine, s = Represents the specific number of the part, $T_{r,0}$ = Idle time before first operation on machine r that is equal to aggregate of setup and idle times on machine r' before prerequisite operation of $F_{r,1}^{k,s}$.

$$T = \begin{bmatrix} T_{1,0} & T_{1,1} & \cdots & T_{1,Q-1} \\ T_{2,0} & T_{2,1} & \cdots & T_{2,Q-1} \\ \cdot & & \cdot & \cdot \\ \cdot & & & \cdot \\ \cdot & & \cdot & \cdot \\ T_{m,0} & T_{m,1} & \cdots & T_{m,Q-1} \end{bmatrix}$$

$$F = \begin{bmatrix} F_{1,1}^{k,s} & F_{1,2}^{k,s} & \cdots & F_{1,Q}^{k,s} \\ F_{2,1}^{k,s} & F_{2,2}^{k,s} & \cdots & F_{2,Q}^{k,s} \\ \cdot & & \cdot & \cdot \\ \cdot & & & \cdot \\ \cdot & & \cdot & \cdot \\ F_{m,1}^{k,s} & F_{m,2}^{k,s} & \cdots & F_{m,Q}^{k,s} \end{bmatrix} \qquad T_Q = \begin{bmatrix} T_{1,Q} \\ T_{2,Q} \\ \cdot \\ \cdot \\ \cdot \\ T_{m,Q} \end{bmatrix}$$

Operations on machinery are as the matrix shown as follow:

$$FT = \begin{bmatrix} T_{1,0} & F_{1,1}^{k,s} & T_{1,1} & F_{1,2}^{k,s} & \cdots & T_{1,Q-1} & F_{1,Q}^{k,s} & T_{1,Q} \\ T_{2,0} & F_{2,1}^{k,s} & T_{2,1} & F_{2,2}^{k,s} & & T_{2,Q-1} & F_{2,Q}^{k,s} & T_{2,Q} \\ \cdot & \cdot & \cdot & \cdot & \cdot & \cdot & \cdot & \\ \cdot & \cdot & \cdot & \cdot & & \cdot & \cdot & \\ \cdot & \cdot & \cdot & \cdot & & \cdot & & \cdot \\ T_{m,0} & F_{m,1}^{k,s} & T_{m,1} & F_{m,2}^{k,s} & \cdots & T_{m,Q-1} & F_{m,Q}^{k,s} & T_{m,Q} \end{bmatrix}$$

We assume these conditions:

i. Each operation has a situation on every machine. If it does not work its $F_{r,q}^{k,s}$ is equal to zero.

ii. After every situation is idle time, which could be zero.

iii. Concerning the operation sequence on machine 1, first we take the elements of the first row of F.

iv. Denotes operations that do not work on machine r, then let their $F_{r,q}^{k,s} = 0$ on the same column as they were on machine r-1. Then write the F elements from sequence of operation on machine r, respectively.

v. The first row of T is always zero. For obtaining other elements of T we use relation 4.

Proof of relation 9:

Two states will happen for the relation (9).

The first state shows that

$$\sum_{s=1}^{q} F_{r-1,s+1} + \sum_{s=0}^{q} T_{r-1,s} \geq \sum_{s=1}^{q} F_{r,s} + \sum_{s=0}^{q} T_{r,s}$$

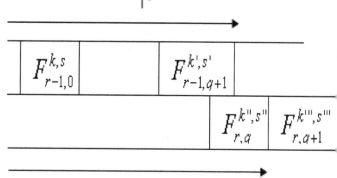

Because T** is larger than T*, it does not matter what operation is $F_{r,q+1}^{k''',s'''}$ and relation gives true quantity.

The second state is the reverse of the first:

Table 1. Needed time for producing parts (example 1).

Machine part	M_1	M_2	M_3	M_4
A	3	3	5	3
B	4	2	4	2.5
C	1.5	2.5	3.5	1.5
D	1.5	2.5	3.5	3.5

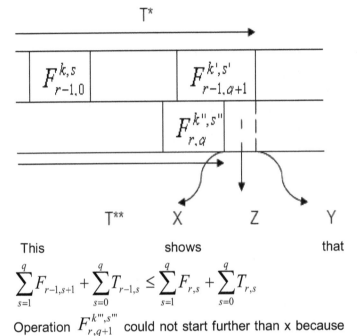

This shows that

$$\sum_{s=1}^{q} F_{r-1,s+1} + \sum_{s=0}^{q} T_{r-1,s} \leq \sum_{s=1}^{q} F_{r,s} + \sum_{s=0}^{q} T_{r,s}$$

Operation $F_{r,q+1}^{k''',s'''}$ could not start further than x because

at least $F_{r,q+1}^{k',s'}$ is there. Now assume that the relation is not true, therefore, there should be an operation like $F_{r,q+1}^{k''',s'''}$ on machine r that starts between y and x on point z. Therefore, its prerequisite should be on the machine whose number is less than r-1 like r'. This operation does not work on machines between r' and r-1.From assumption (v) on machine r-1 and column q+1 it should be $F_{r-1,q+1}^{k''',s'''}$ instead of $F_{r-1,q+1}^{k',s'}$, which is a contradiction, therefore, our first assumption is false and the relation is true.

5 vi. Set K equal to 2 and then repeat the mentioned stages. In this allocation, first calculate V from formula (1) and then consider this point in allocating to machines.

a. if $V = \left[\dfrac{D}{K} \right]$ then allocate K set in number of V .

b. if $V = \left[\dfrac{D}{K} \right]$ +1 then allocate in number of (V-1), K unit batch, then V'th batch quantity will be equal to (D-VK).

Considering the accomplished allocation, calculate the aggregate of setup and idle times from (2) and show it with Z_2.

5 vii. If D>2, then set k equal to 3, 4, 5,..., D and according to stage 5 iv execute each K allocations. For each K, calculate the aggregate of the setup and idle times from (6) and show them respectively with Z_3, Z_4, Z_D. 5 viii. Calculate the quantity of minimum Z_k and show it with Z*; namely:

$$Z^* = \min (Z_1, Z_2, ..., Z_D)$$

5 ix. Show the quantity of K corresponding to Z* with K* and let K* bethe quantity of the best batch size.
5 x. Allocation related to K*, will be the best sequence to allocate the operation to the machines, and the time duration of its total operation will form the makespan of the production system.

Performance evaluation

The presented algorithm is compared with the algorithms of "Ho and chang", "Johnson" and "palmer". Different examples show that the presented algorithm gives better makespan. To compare, the subsequent examples are completely solved initially with the offered algorithm and then the final answers of the algorithms of "HO and Chang", "Johnson" and "palmer" are calculated for these examples.

Example 1. Suppose there is a product that demand of it in a defined process is 7 units and this product is consisted of a 4 parts. Every part needs 4 operations. The number of machines is 4. The characteristics of the machine and parts are presented in Table 1. Other necessary information such as number of same parts in one product unit, quantity of batch size, special setup time of each operation in one batch size and scrap proportion of each machine is given in columns 5, 8, 9, 12 of Table 2. Regarding this information, the timing schedule of the operation on machines is calculated and the best batch size that minimizes the makespan is shown.

a. Solving with the offered algorithm: (1) for k = 1, Table 2 is computed using step 1 to 4 of the offered algorithm. By using F_i (last column of Table 2), according to 5iv through 5v steps of the algorithm, we completed the sequence of the operation (Figure 2).

Then according to this sequence of operation, we calculated the aggregate of operation and idle times as a comparing index. To reach this purpose, at first consider matrix T_1.

Table 2. Required time for fulfilling operation i in a k unit product batch by considering the scrap proportion (k=1) (example 1).

Part	Operation number	Prerequisite	Standard time of Operation i (Si)	Number of operation i on a product (Pi)	Total standard time of operation I (ti=Si×Pi)	Machine's code	Quantity of batch size (K)	Specific setup time for operation i in one product batch (Ai)	Standard time for total operation i in k unit product batch (Ti=k×ti)	Aggregate of total standard time and setup time of operation i in k unit product batch (Ai+Ui= Ti)	Scrap proportion of operation i on the relevant machinery (Ci)	Required time for fulfilling operation i, in k product batch by considering the scrap percentage [Fi=Ui÷(1- Ci)]
A	A10	-	3	1	3	M1	1	4	3	7	0/03	7/22
	A20	A10	3	1	3	M2	1	4	3	7	0/03	7/22
	A30	A20	5	1	5	M3	1	4	5	9	0/03	9/28
	A40	A30	3	1	3	M4	1	4	3	7	0/03	7/22
B	B10	-	4	1	4	M1	1	3	4	7	0/04	7/29
	B20	B10	2	1	2	M2	1	3	2	5	0/03	5/15
	B30	B20	4	1	4	M3	1	3	4	7	0/03	7/22
	B40	B30	2/5	1	2/5	M4	1	3	2/5	5/5	0/03	5/67
C	C10	-	1/5	2	3	M1	1	3	3	6	0/05	6/32
	C20	C10	2/5	2	5	M2	1	3	5	8	0/04	8/33
	C30	C20	3/5	2	7	M3	1	3	7	10	0/06	10/64
	C40	C30	1/5	2	3	M4	1	3	3	6	0/03	6/19
D	D10	-	1/5	2	3	M1	1	3	3	6	0/04	6/25
	D20	D10	2/5	2	5	M2	1	3	5	8	0/04	8/33
	D30	D20	3/5	2	7	M3	1	3	7	10	0/06	10/64
	D40	D30	3/5	2	7	M4	1	3	7	10	0/06	10/64
Sum									52			

$$F_1^{'} = \begin{bmatrix} 6.25 & 6.32 & 7.22 & 7.29 & 6.25 & 6.32 & 7.22 & 7.29 & 6.25 & 6.32 & 7.22 & 7.29 \\ 8.33 & 8.33 & 7.22 & 5.15 & 8.33 & 8.33 & 7.22 & 5.15 & 8.33 & 8.33 & 7.22 & 5.15 \\ 10.64 & 10.64 & 9.28 & 7.22 & 10.64 & 10.64 & 9.28 & 7.22 & 10.64 & 10.64 & 9.28 & 7.22 \\ 10.64 & 6.19 & 7.22 & 5.67 & 10.64 & 6.19 & 7.22 & 567 & 10.64 & 6.19 & 7.22 & 5.67 \end{bmatrix}$$

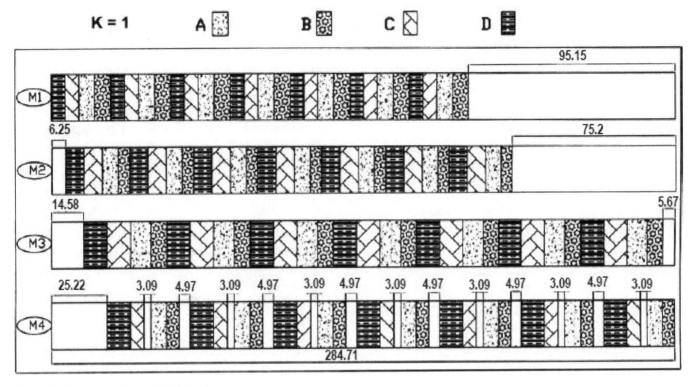

Figure 2. Sequence of operation for k=1.

$$T_1 = \begin{bmatrix} 0 & 0 & 0 & 0 & 0 & 0 & 0 & 0 & 0 & 0 & 0 & 0 & 0 & 0 & 0 & 0 & 0 & 0 & 0 & 0 & 0 & 0 & 0 & 0 & 0 & 0 & 0 & 0 & 0 \\ 6.25 & 0 & 0 & 0 & 0 & 0 & 0 & 0 & 0 & 0 & 0 & 0 & 0 & 0 & 0 & 0 & 0 & 0 & 0 & 0 & 0 & 0 & 0 & 0 & 0 & 0 & 0 & 0 & 0 \\ 14.58 & 0 & 0 & 0 & 0 & 0 & 0 & 0 & 0 & 0 & 0 & 0 & 0 & 0 & 0 & 0 & 0 & 0 & 0 & 0 & 0 & 0 & 0 & 0 & 0 & 0 & 0 & 0 & 0 \\ 25.22 & 0 & 3.09 & 0 & 4.97 & 0 & 3.09 & 0 & 4.97 & 0 & 3.09 & 0 & 4.97 & 0 & 3.09 & 0 & 4.97 & 0 & 3.09 & 0 & 4.97 & 0 & 3.09 & 0 & 4.97 & 0 & 3.09 & 0 \end{bmatrix}$$

$T_{r,q}$'s are presented in T_1. Idle times of each machine and the total idle times of all the machines are calculated according to relation (3) through (8).

$T_{2,0} = F_{1,1} + T_{1,0} = 6.25 + 0 = 6.25$

$T_{2,1} = T_{1,0} + T_{1,1} + F_{1,1} + F_{1,2} - T_{2,0} - F_{2,1} =$
$0 + 0 + 6.25 + 6.32 - 6.25 - 8.33 = -2.01 \Rightarrow T_{2,1} = 0$

$T_{4,0} = F_{3,1} + T_{3,0} = 10.64 + 14.58 = 25.22$

$T_{4,1} = F_{3,1} + F_{3,2} + T_{3,0} + T_{3,1} - F_{4,1} - T_{4,0} =$
$10.64 + 10.64 + 14.58 + 0 - 10.64 - 25.22 = 0$

$T_{4,2} = T_{3,0} + T_{3,1} + T_{3,2} + F_{3,1} + F_{3,2} + F_{3,3} - T_{4,0} - T_{4,1} - F_{4,1} - F_{4,2}$
$= 14.58 + 0 + 0 + 10.64 + 10.64 + 9.28 - 25.22$
$- 0 - 10.64 - 6.19 = 3.09$

$M_1 = \sum_{q=1}^{Q} F_{1,q} + \sum_{r=0}^{Q-1} T_{1,q} = F_{1,1} + F_{1,2} + ... + F_{1,28} + T_{0,1} + T_{1,1} + ... + T_{1,27}$

$= 6.25 + 6.32 + 7.22 + 7.29 + 6.25 - 6.32$

$+ 7.22 + 7.29 + 6.25 + 6.32 + 7.22 + 7.29 + 6.25 - 6.32$

$+ 7.22 + 7.29 + 6.25 + 6.32 + 7.22 + 7.29 + 6.25 + 6.32$

$+ 7.22 + 7.29 + 6.25 + 6.32 + 7.22 + 7.29 = 189.56$

$M_1 = 189.56$, $\qquad M_2 = 209.46$, $\qquad M_3 = 279.04$,

$M_4 = 284.71$

$M_k = \max\{189.56, 209.46, 279.04, 284.71\} = 284.71$

$T_{r,Q} = M_k - \sum_{q=0}^{Q} F_{r,q} - \sum_{q=0}^{Q-1} T_{r,q}$

$$T_{1,Q} = T_{1,28} = M_k - F_{1,1} - F_{1,2} - \ldots - F_{1,28} - T_{0,1} - T_{1,1} - \ldots - T_{1,27} = 284.71 - 6.25 - 6.32 - 7.22 - 7.29 - 6.25 - 6.32$$
$$- 7.22 - 7.29 - 6.25 - 6.32 - 7.22 - 7.29 - 6.25 - 6.32 - 7.22 - 7.29 - 6.25 - 6.32 - 7.22 - 7.29 - 6.25 - 6.32 - 7.22$$
$$- 7.29 - 6.25 - 6.32 - 7.22 - 7.29 = 95.15$$

$$T_{2,Q} = T_{2,28} = 75.25 \qquad , \qquad T_{3,Q} = T_{3,28} = 5.67,$$
$$T_{4,Q} = T_{4,28} = 0$$

$$W_1 = \sum_{r=1}^{m} \sum_{q=1}^{Q} T_{r,q} = 0 + 0 + \ldots + 95.15 = 273.57$$

From Table 2, the aggregate of the operation setup times for a batch size in case k = 1 is equal to:

$$\sum_{i=1}^{16} A_i = 52$$

Now with respect to values K = 1 and D = 7, V is equal to seven. Therefore the aggregate of setup times in total period is equal to:

$$H_1 = V \times \sum_{i=1}^{n} A_i = 7 \times 52 = 364$$

As a result, the aggregate of setup and idle times in the period is equal to:

Z_1 = W_1 + H_1 = 273.57 + 364 = 637.57, Z_3 = 514.81.

For other K values, K = 4, K = 6, K = 6 and K = 7 we computed setup and idle times. This information along with makespan of each K is shown in Table 3.

Compare gained idle and setup times for different K values, from table 3, it could be seen that this aggregate in state K = 4 has minimum value, therefore, Makespan process for K = 4 is 248.36 min.
b. Solving the problem with the existing algorithms: For comparing the suggested algorithm and the existing algorithms, we also used F_i values (the needed time for doing operation i for producing seven products with respect to scrap percentage) for K = 7 and the calculated and obtained makespan is compared with the makespan obtained from the suggested algorithm. For doing this, with the use of winQSB "Ho and chang" ,"Johnson" and "palmer" algorithms the makespans were computed. The makespan obtained from the foregoing algorithms and the suggested algorithm to produce 7 products is given in Table 4.

Example 2. Suppose a product demand during a specified period is 6 units and this product consists of three parts. Each part needs 3 operations and there are 3 machines. Machines and parts specifications are inserted in Table 5. Other necessary information is presented in

Table 6. The aggregate of idle times, the aggregate of setup times, the aggregate of idle and the setup times and makespan for each batch size is presented in Table 7.

By comparing the aggregate of idle and setup times in producing K unit production, it is clear that K = 2 has minimum makespan. It means that the best sequencing of operation algorithm in operation allocation state in producing classes is two units. In Table 8, the makespan obtained from the existing algorithms with the use of "needed time of producing every operation for six unit product considering the scrap percentage" and suggested algorithm is presented. It could be seen that that the suggested algorithm has lower makespan.

Conclusion

By comparing the results of the suggested algorithm and the mentioned algorithms, it is clear that the makespan of the suggested algorithm is the minimum value for all of the foregoing. We can consider that the suggested algorithm has lower makespan. Other examples also solved with this algorithm show that: (a) Increasing the quantity of batch size also increases the idle times. (b) By increasing the quantity of production, the aggregate of setup times decreases because of the decrease in the amount of batch sizes. When the setup times for each operation is longer, the decreasing in the amount of batch sizes speeds up. (C) For K > 1, in the beginning the aggregate of the setup and idle times decreases and for the value of K, K*, it reaches minimum point. Then the decrease in the quantity of batch size leads to an increase. This algorithm is efficient for planning and timing operations and its advantages are:

(a) Specifying the best quantity of a production batch is one of the main goals of the algorithm. By using the best batch sizes in allocating operations to machines, the setup and idle time sets will be minimized. Minimizing the aggregate of the setup and idle times in production leads to minimizing the production system makespan.
(b) Considering the scrap proportion of the production machines in loom timing: this issue helps the timing calculation. Because of the existence of a defective product among the products of a machine, in order to produce a specific number of intact products, we should add the number of the defective products to the number of the programmed products. The existing algorithms regarding the calculating of operation timing do not consider this major factor and the machines are considered with zero percent of defective products.

Table 3. Identifier of best production batch size (example 1).

Quantity of batch size (K)	Aggregate of setup times in state k unit production(min)	Aggregate of idle times in state k unit production (min)	Aggregate of idle and setup times in state k unit production (min)	Makespan (min)
1	364	273.57	637.57	284.71
2	208	306.9	514.9	252.74
3	156	335.8	514.81	251.89
4	104	398.8	502.8	248.36*
5	104	416.97	520.96	252.59
6	104	467.97	517.97	264.37
7	52	552	604.09	273.16

Table 4. Ho and chang, Johnson, palmer and suggested algorithm makespans (example 1).

Algorithm	Makespan (min)
Ho and Chang	255.48
Johnson	268.52
Palmer	268.52
Presented	248.36

Table 5. Needed time for producing parts (example 2).

Machine part	M_1	M_2	M_3
A	2	2.5	4
B	3	2	3
C	1.5	2	3

Table 6. Required time for fulfilling operation i in a k unit product batch by considering the scrap proportion (k=1) (example 2).

Part	Operation number	prerequisite	Standard time	Number of operation on a product	Total standard time	Machine code	Specific setup time for an operation in one product batch	Scrap percentage
	A10	-	2	1	2	M1	1	0.03
A	A20	A10	2.5	1	2.5	M2	2	0.05
	A30	A20	4	1	4	M3	1	0.02
	B10	-	3	2	6	M1	2	0.04
B	B20	B10	2	2	4	M2	1	0.01
	B30	B20	3	2	6	M3	1.5	0.03
	C10	-	1.5	1	1.5	M1	1	0.04
C	C20	C10	2	1	2	M2	1	0.01
	C30	C20	3	1	3	M3	1	0.03

In addition to the mentioned advantages, one of the outputs of the suggested algorithm (like other existing algorithms) is the time interval during which the machines are idle and could be programmed to be utilized. Some of these jobs are:

(1) Receiving job order from the market.
(2) Implementing re-creative plans for production personnel.
(3) Implementing training plans for improving production personnel abilities.

Table 7. Identifier of best production batch size (example 2).

Quantity of batch size (K)	Aggregate of setup times in state k unit production (min)	Aggregate of idle times in state k unit production (min)	Aggregate of idle and setup times in state k unit production (min)	Makespan (min)
1	69	63.12	132.12	108.62
2	34.5	95.46	129.96	107.55*
3	23	116.75	139.75	110.69
4	23	136.98	159.98	117.43
5	23	157.17	180.17	124.15
6	1.51	180.34	191.84	128.23

Table 8. Ho and chang, Johnson, palmer and suggested algorithm makespans (example 2).

Algorithm	Makespan (min)
Ho and Chang	127.31
Johnson	127.31
Palmer	127.31
suggested	107.55

(4) Doing preventive repairs on machines.

REFERENCES

Allahverdi A, Aldowaisan T (2002). No-Wait Flowshops with Bicriteria of Makespan and Total Completion Time. J. Opl. Res. Soc. 53:1004-1015.

Bayat H, Akbari H, Davoudpour H (2010). A metaheuristic and PTAS approach for NP-hard scheduling problem with controllable processing times. Afr. J. Math. Comput. Sci. Res. 3(12):307-314.

Ho JC, Chen Y (1991). A new heuristic for the n-job, M-machine flow-shop problem. Eur. J. Oper. Res. 52(2):194-202

Koulamas C, Kyparisis GJ (2007). A note on performance guarantees for sequencing three-stage flexible flowshops with identical machines to minimize makespan. IIE Trans. 39:559-563.

Quinn G, Novels M (2001). Analyzing production schedules A selection of IIE Solutions. Iran Inst. Ind. Eng. 9:25.

Shabtay D, Kaspi M, Steiner G (2007). The no-wait two-machine flow shop scheduling problem with convex resource-dependent processing times. IIE Trans. 39:539-557.

Tahar D, Yalaoui F, Chu C, Amodeo L (2006). A linear programming approach for identical parallel machine scheduling with job splitting and sequence-dependent setup times. Int. J. Prod. Econ. 99:63-73.

Widmar M, Hertz A (1989). A new heuristic method for the flow shop sequencing problem. Eur. J. Oper. Res. 41:186-193.

Wild R (1989). Production and operation Management. Cassel Educational limited: London.

Yilmaz IO, Grunow M, Gunther HO, Yapan C (2007). Development of group setup strategies for makespan minimisation in PCB assembly. Int. J. Prod. Res. 45:871-897.

Zhang CYP, Li Y, Rao ZG (2008). A very fast TS/SA algorithm for the job shop scheduling problem. Comput. Oper. Res. 35:282-294.

5

Role of marketing information system (MkIS) for the organizational culture and its effectiveness

Rahul Hakhu[1] , Ravi Kiran[2] and D. P. Goyal[3]

[1]Rayat Institute of Management, Rayat Technology Centre of Excellence, RailMajra, District. S.B.S. Nagar, Punjab, INDIA-144 533.
[2]School of Management and Social Sciences, Thapar University, Patiala, Punjab, INDIA – 147 004
[3]Management Development Institute, Gurgaon, INDIA - 122 007.

In this paper, an attempt has been made to illustrate the role of marketing information system (MkIS) for organizational culture and its effectiveness. This study investigates the success factors of MkIS model. The study uses a survey analysis for 140 SMEs (Small and medium enterprise) of manufacturing sector of Punjab in India to understand the level of MkIS by firms. However, the development of MkIS depends largely on the organizational, technical, managerial and technical cultures/environments of a company. These cultures are to be nurtured and made developed in order to improve and install a sustainable MkIS for accomplishing the corporate objectives in the highly competitive world economy in the long run. The study uses Step-wise Regression technique to find the important variables of the MkIS model for enhancing the effectiveness of an organizational culture. These are MkIS sophistication, design characteristics of MkIS, capabilities of MkIS, primary characteristics of MkIS and hindrance factors of MkIS. The results depict that coefficient of determination is 0.508 and adjusted coefficient of determination is 0 .490. These predictors explain 49% of the variation.

Key words: Marketing information system (MkIS), organizational culture and small and medium enterprises.

INTRODUCTION

To understand the proper role of information systems one must examine what managers do and what information they need for decision making. We must also understand how decisions are made and what kinds of decision problems can be supported by formal information systems. One can then determine whether information systems will be valuable tools and how they should be designed. Since time immemorial the evolution of human civilization has been enriched, and developed by the proper and effective sharing of information carried out by different generations. The modern civilization is the outcome of that persistent information sharing system and perennially taking its logical and scientific shape from it. However, in economic literature, the assets are classified into two types: Tangible and intangible assets. The tangible assets are those, which are visible and having their material existence. These are, for instance, land, gold, cash, diamond, goods etc., whereas intangible assets are those, which are invisible. In simple sense "information is about experience, values, contextual information, and expert insight". Since time immemorial the use of information or intellect of human being has been playing a very crucial role in shaping the evolution process of civilizations on earth. The creation and dissemination of information have been carried out through various institutions for the promotion of human welfare from generation to generation. These institutions are family, society, various organizations, groups, etc.

MkIS can be best understood in terms of a discipline rather than a "silver bullet" or a technological solution. To some researchers MkIS is: Getting the right information to the right person at the right time.

However, in a world of radical discontinuous change, there are no programmable systems that can predict in advance what the right information, right person or the right time will be at any given point in the future. This can

---

*Corresponding author. E-mail: rahul.hakhu@yahoo.co.in.

also help understand the key distinction between "doing the right thing" and "doing things right". The relatively stable and unchanging environment of the past allowed the luxury of predicting, pre-defining and pre-determining the future based on past data.

Generally speaking, MkIS is a process through which organizations generate value from their intellectual property and knowledge-based assets. MkIS involves in the creation, dissemination, and effective utilization of information to its optimal level. Moreover, MkIS could be effective in creating various benefits such as, revenue growth, production innovation, profit growth, enhancing customer focus, improving competitive and marketing both in short term and long term for a company when the information sharing culture is deeply rooted in the organizational structure of the entire company. In the present competitive business world order, establishing and developing an effective MkIS is one of the tough challenges faced by the mangers of a company. However, the mangers are trying hard and investing huge funds to nurture and build up a sound and sustainable MkIS in order to mitigate risk involved in the increasing agency and transaction cost problems arising out of improper and ineffective organizational culture.

As it is known that the corporate structure basically consists of three important agents: Namely, managers, stakeholders or employees and owners. The harmony among these agents is required for the attainment of broad cooperate objectives such as, profit making and higher growth. However, these objectives of a company only could be fulfilled if there is proper knowledge sharing culture in place.

Significance of culture in an organization

Culture is a term, which comprises of set of formal and informal rules, norms, values, attitude and behaviour of an organization. As we know that corporate organizations are group of individuals, stakeholders, shareholders, owners and communities who share some kind of common values, norms and rules to accomplish certain objectives. Each organization has a very distinct culture of its own, which clearly outlines how member of the organization relate to one another while working together in order to accomplish certain stipulated objectives, which would enrich the participation of each members (Goffee and Jones, 1996).

It exerts its influence in numerous invisible ways -- from the kinds of people who get hired, to the types of questions and comments that are tolerated, the formal and informal expectations made of staff, the focus of reward systems, how people interact and when they ask for help (Gupta and Govindarajan, 2000). The influence of culture in a corporate organization can be understood as shown in Figure 1.

It is apparent in Figure 1 that culture is an overarching

mechanism in any kind of organization whether it is corporate or any other organization, which constrains all other aspects of organizational life and limits what is considered desirable, possible and practical to do. Needless to say, an organization's culture will therefore, affect its knowledge management initiatives and will predispose employees towards particular forms of behavior in knowledge sharing. Therefore, it plays very pivotal role in enhancing the performance of the organization in numerous ways and means by influencing different aspects.

Furthermore, organizational culture does not exist in a vacuum. Basically, it is shaped by the social culture in which the corporate organization lives. This is explained in Figures 1 and 2.

Therefore, a multinational corporate organization's culture may vary somewhat from country to country. It is known fact that before a cultural change such as information sharing, can be effected, an organization's present cultural sphere and state must be taken into consideration while implementing any strategies pertaining to MkIS.

Moreover, culture plays a very special role in organizations because it can powerfully influence human behavior in the right directions to maximize an objectives of an organization, and because it is extremely hard to change (Kotter, 1996).

All organizational cultures tend to vary along two dimensions: sociability and solidarity. These two dimensions capture much of what we know about organizational culture (Goffee and Jones, 1996).

Solidarity refers to the emotional and non-instrumental relations, which exist within an organization that is the friendliness and among members of the corporation. In fact, sociability makes work enjoyable, enhances spirit of teamwork, promotes information sharing and creates openness to new ideas and relieves stress factor on the part of the members. However, solidarity refers to the degree to which members of an organization share goals, plans, strategies, problems and tasks. It makes easy for the members or a worker to pursue shared objectives quickly and effectively regardless of personal identities and generates strategic focus, quick response and a strong sense of trust. Thus, these two dimensions of organizational culture should be well understood when a manager wishes to change it for implementing or adopting a new kind of cultural dimension such as MkIS.

As per Singh and Jain (2006) in the present scenario, there is a need of change felt to adapt cost cutting, technological up-gradation, lean structure and supportive systems to add to the competitiveness in the context to the culture of manufacturing small scale industry of Punjab. According to Talvinen (1995) in addition to the management perspective, MkIS can be an essential tool for the entire marketing organization. Bakos (1991) says that MkIS reduces buyers search costs and increase the efficiency of business culture, and therefore create

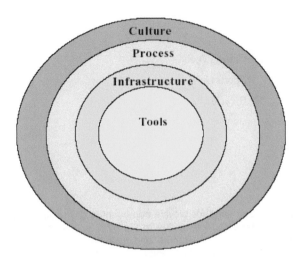

Figure 1. Culture influences activities in all spheres of the organization.
Source: Smith and McKeen (2003).

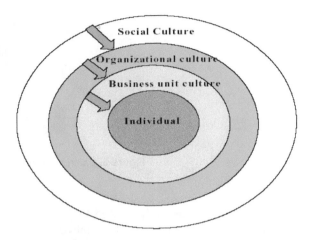

Figure 2. Culture operates in many different spheres of an organization.
Source: Smith and McKeen (2003).

numerous possibilities for the strategic uses of these systems. The study by Lynne (1983) identified an emerging trend from single-source sales channels to electronic markets, lowering coordination costs for producers and retailers and resulting in fewer distribution costs and further enhancing the effectiveness of an organizational culture.

On the basis of literature, the following five predictors have been identified as variables of MkIS for enhancing the effectiveness of an organizational culture.

These are:

(1) Design characteristics of MkIS (Piercy and Evans, 1983; Little, 1979; Milis, 2008) deals with information. It covers the following: a. Broad scope information; b. Timely information; c. Accurate information; d. Current information; e. Aggregated information.
(2) Capabilities of MkIS: According to Knuckles (1987) and Fleisher et al. (2008), the broad capabilities of MkIS range from providing data to decision support system for sophisticated analysis of data. These capabilities are highlighted as: a. It simply provides data on which decisions are made; b. It has the capability to undertake simple analysis of the data and from this provides information on which decisions are made; c. It provides sophisticated analysis of data, and therefore provides invaluable decision support information; d. It provides sophisticated analysis of data and has the ability to make recommendations, if so required, as an aid to decision making.
(3) Primary characteristics of MkIS: According to Bhagwat and Sharma (2007), the primary characteristics of MkIS are considered as a major tool to help companies provide a competitive edge in the era of globalization. According to Murray et al. (2004), it covers the basic tools for MkIS, and it's highlighted as: a. Windows 98 and

Windows XP as Operating system; b. E-Mails and Search Engines as Internet; c. Word, Excel and PowerPoint as Applications; d. Timely information of marketing needs; e. Stores marketing information; f. Processed information maintained in the data-base.
(4) Hindrance factors of MkIS: For success of MkIS, it is essential to identify the factors that can deter its progress. It is essential to deal with them properly, so that they cannot act as impediment. As per tackling hindrance factors of MkIS is in fact very important (Sisodia, 1992). Infact, system implementation success factors is not just the use of technology. According to Thatcher and Oliver (2001) problems are the result of the interaction between characteristics of the people being asked to adopt the system and characteristics of the system itself. The hindrance factors covered are: a. Not as an information processing system; b. Can solve all management problems; c. Lack of training; d. Adequate attention not given; e. Impersonal system; f. Does not give perfect information; g. Under estimating.
(5) MkIS sophistication: According to Van Nievelt (1984) and Martin (2004), sophistication covers the marketing needs for meeting customer requirements and also for formulating of the strategic plan for effective marketing decision. The MkIS sophistication covered in the study are: a. Strategic perspective; b. Meeting customer needs; c. Threat; d. Strategic planning; e. IT budget; f. Marketing decision.

ROLE OF MkIS IN AN ORGANIZATION

Today, MkIS is widely–held view that it is indispensable for achieving and improving the performance of any corporate enterprises in the light of fast changing information technology across the globe.

Recently, some scholars suggest that willingness to

Figure 3. Category of industry.

share knowledge is positively related to profitability and productivity, competitiveness and negatively related to labour cost (Jarvenpaa and Staples, 2000; Desai, 2002). In the same line of arguments, scholars of some focus groups believe that MkIS is positively linked to growth and innovation, increased customers satisfaction, increased shareholders value and learning.

The role of the MkIS in an organization can be compared to the role of heart in the body, the information is the blood and MkIS is the heart. In the body the heart plays the role of supplying pure blood to all the elements of the body including the brain. The MkIS plays exactly the same role in the organization. The MkIS helps the middle management in short them planning, target setting and controlling the business functions. It is supported by the use of the management tools of planning and control. The MkIS plays the role of information generation, communication, problem identification and helps in the process of decision making.

In order for MkIS, individuals must adhere to the norms, values, attitudes and beliefs established by the organization. Participants described a organization culture as one where people share openly, there is a willingness to teach and mentor others, where ideas can freely challenged ad where knowledge gained form other sources is used.

In MkIS, marketing is considered to be power, so information hoarding is the norm. Management operates on a need-to-know basis and actively promotes a culture of secrecy. The "not-invented-here" syndrome is rife and rewards are based on individual contributions. The challenge for today's leaders is therefore to evolve from such a culture to one, which actively encourages and facilitates MkIS and discourages industrial age thinking and behaviors.

RESEARCH METHODOLOGY

The present study has been based on a survey analysis conducted for enhancing the effectiveness of an organizational culture in the state of Punjab, one of the growing states of Indian economy. Data has been collected through a self-structured questionnaire from 140 manufacturing industries which include 124 small and 16 medium enterprises respectively of Punjab from the following districts: Patiala for cutting tools (30 units), Jalandhar for sports goods (50

units) and Ludhiana for bicycle components (60 units). Reason for selecting these districts is due to the 82% exports of total exports from these districts of Punjab and they have prominent range of product. Cutting tools from Patiala, sports goods from Jalandhar and bicycle components from Ludhiana compromises nearly 15% of total exports from Punjab and provides 75% of the country's requirement. These districts contribute to about 43% of the total small units and about 34% medium units respectively in Punjab. The random samples were drawn from the population of enterprises in the Punjab state with 4000 bicycle components units in district Ludhiana, 1000 sports goods units in district Jalandhar and 30 cutting tools units in district Patiala respectively. By using Table 1, we get 140 manufacturing units as the sample size.

The survey was tested for reliability and overall reliability score (Cronbach Alpha) of the questionnaire has been 0.902. Face and content validity have been done. The questionnaire had been validated by the peers and has a validation score 3.75 on a scale of five. Some questions were reframed. Table 2 describes the details of the reliability statistics. The data so gathered analysed using SPSS ver.19. The reliability score of all the four sections ranged between 0.710 and 0. 829.

Regarding the nature of industry in the sample out of total 140 firms there are 30 firms producing cutting tools, 50 are producing sports goods and 60 are producing bicycle components. Categories of firms within these sectors have been depicted in Figure 3.

Size-wise sample has 124 small enterprises and 16 medium enterprises respectively as depicted in Figure 4.

Further to validate the success of MkIS model for SMEs, a case study has been developed from six firms of which 2 firms produce cutting tools from district Patiala, 2 firms producing sports goods from district Jalandhar and 2 firms producing bicycle components from district Ludhiana respectively have been included.

ANALYSIS

The regression model results are highlighted through Table 3 for which is highlighted the effectiveness of an organizational culture. The value of co-relation is .713, co-efficient of determination is 0 .508 and adjusted co-efficient of determination is 0.490, these variables explain 49% of the variation and Durbin-Watson index is 2.102, which is acceptable for the model. The ANOVA results are also significant, which depict the overall significance of the model. Moreover the results of step wise regression depict that value of R^2 has improved from 0.331 to 0.508 with the introduction of all variables. That means the model can include all these factors as the predicting power has improved from 32.6 to 49%. Thus the results verify that success factors of MkIS are

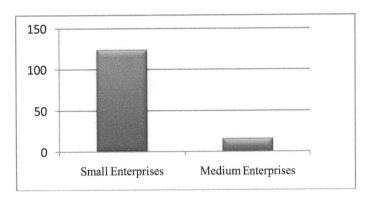

Figure 4. Type of enterprises.

Table 1. Sample size with segmentation.

S/No.	Manufacturing units	Percentage of sample
1.	< 50	100
2.	≥50<100	50
3.	≥100<300	30
4.	≥300<500	20
5.	≥500<1000	10
6.	≥1000<3000	5
7.	≥3000<4000	2.5
8.	≥4000	1.5

Table 2. Reliability statistics.

Item	No of items	Cronbach alpha
Primary characteristics (Usage of computers)	11	.829
Design characteristics/capabilities/marketing Mix/ sophistication of MkIS	19	.792
Success factors of MkIS	07	.710
Hindrance factors of MkIS	07	.807
Organizations performance	06	.729
Overall	50	.902

positively associated with design characteristics, capabilities, primary characteristics and sophistication. Regarding predicting power primary characteristics and sophistication have higher value of 'B' and are relatively more important than other predictors.

Concluding remarks

Today, installing a MkIS is a challenge for even the most knowledge savvy organizations in spite of having best information technology. Because technology is not the only one thing by a manger could build up a sustainable MkIS in the corporate structure. Rather it is corporate culture, which plays very significant role in installing a MkIS. And it not that easy for the managers to develop a

MkIS overnight without developing its internal culture which embodies social, organizational, managerial and technical cultures of a firm, which generally takes very long period to get maturity for the sustainable information in an organization. Because culture is difficult to pin down, it is often underestimated in efforts to change how firms work. Developing a culture which values and practices MkIS is a long term /multi-year effort involving attention to the social, organizational, managerial, and technical components of this behavior. Until organizations make a concerted effort to refocus their efforts, they will find it extremely difficult, if not impossible to grow a true MkIS. Therefore, the factors motivating a successful MkIS along with technology should be given equal priority and thrust while outlining the strategies for installing a successful and sustainable MkIS in a corporate structure.

Table 3. MkIS (Marketing Information System) Regression Model for enhancing the effectiveness of an organizational culture.

Model	R	R square	Adjusted R square	Std. error of the estimate	Change statistic					Durbin-Watson
					R square change	F-change	df1	df2	Sig. F change	
1	.575a	0.33	0.32	0.25	0.33	68.33	1	138	-	
2	.641b	0.41	0.40	0.23	0.07	18.43	1	137	0.000	
3	.676c	0.45	0.44	0.23	0.04	11.47	1	136	0.001	2.102
4	.702d	0.49	0.47	0.22	0.03	9.68	1	135	0.002	
5	.713e	0.50	0.49	0.22	0.01	4.25	1	134	0.041	

*** $p<.001$; ** $p<.01$; and * $p < .05$

Design characteristics[a], Capabilities[b], Primary characteristics[c], Hindrance factors[d], Sophistications[e].

Successful MkIS in any firm is a means rather than ends to increase its performance in the highly competitive world business compared to its counterpart.

REFERENCES

Bakos J (1991). "A Strategic Analysis of Electronic Marketplaces", Manag. Inform. Syst. Quart. 15(3):295-310.

Bhagwat R, Sharma MK (2007). "Information system architecture: a framework for a cluster of small and medium-sized enterprises (SMEs)", Production Planning & Control: The Management of Operations 18(4):283-296.

Desai P (2002). "Knowledge Management: Research Report", available at http://www.knowledgepoint.com.au/knowledge_management/Articles/KM-Indi-2002.pdf.

Fleisher CS, Wright S, Allard HT (2008) "The role of insight teams in integrating diverse marketing information management techniques", Eur. J. Market. 42(7):836-851.

Goffee R, Jones G (1996). "What holds the modern company together?", Harvard Business Review, November-December, pp.133-148.

Gupta A, Govindarajan V (2000). "Knowledge management's social dimension: lessons from Nucor Steel", Sloan Manag. Rev. 42(1):71-80.

Jarvenpaa S, Staples D (2000). "The use of collaborative electronic media for information sharing: an exploratory study of determinants", J. Strateg. Inform. Syst. 9:129-154.

Knuckles BM (1987) "Plan based decision support systems", J. Advert. Res. 27(3):10-11.

Kotter J (1996). "Leading Change", Harvard Business School Press, Boston.

Little JDC (1979) "Decision support systems for marketing managers", J. Market. 43(3):9-27.

Lynne M (1983). "Power, Politics and MIS Implementation", Commun. ACD 26(6):430-444.

Martin L (2004). "E-innovation: Internet Impacts on Small UK Hospitality Firms", Int. J. Contemporary Hosp. Manag. 16(2):82-90.

Milis K (2008). "Critical Analysis of Policy Measures for the Advancement of the Level of Computerization of SMEs", Inform. Technol. Dev. 14(3):253-258.

Murray E, Don A, Olayele A (2004). "E-Commerce Infrastructure Success Factors for Small Companies in Developing Economies", Electronic Commerce Research, 4(3):263-286.

Piercy P, Evans M (1983). "Managing Marketing Information", Croom Helm Ltd, Billing & Sons Ltd, Worcester.

Singh L, Jain V (2006). "Unorganised Manufacturing Industry in the Era of Globalization: A Study of Punjab" available at http://mpra.ub.uni-muenchen.de/197/1/MPRA_paper_197.pdf (Assessed September 25, 2011).

Sisodia RS (1992). "Marketing information and decision support systems for services", J. Serv. Market. 6(1):51-64.

Smith A, MaKeen J (2003). "Installing Knowledge -sharing Culture," available at http://business.queensu.ca/kbe/docs/Smith-McKeen%2003-11.pdf.

Talvinen JM (1995). "Information systems in marketing: Identifying opportunities for new applications", Eur. J. Market. 29(1):8-26.

Thatcher ME, Oliver JR (2001). "The impact of technology investments on a firm's production efficiency, product quality, and productivity", J. MIS 18(2):17-46.

Uhl KP (1974). "Marketing information systems", In: Ferber R (Ed.), Handbook of Marketing Research, McGraw-Hill, New York, NY.

6

Social vices associated with the use of Information Communication Technologies (ICTs) in a Private Christian Mission University, Southern Nigeria

Omonijo, Dare Ojo[1], Nnedum, Obiajulu Anthony Ugochukwu[2], Fadugba, Akinrole Olumuyiwa[3], Uche, Onyekwere Chizaram Oliver[4] and Biereenu-Nnabugwu, Makodi[5]

[1]Department of Student Affairs, Covenant University, P. M. B. 1023 Ota, Nigeria.
[2]Department of Psychology, Nnamdi Azikiwe University, P. M. B. 5025 Awka, Nigeria.
[3]Department of Business Management, Covenant University, P. M. B. 1023 Ota, Nigeria.
[4]Department of Religion and Human Relations, Nnamdi Azikiwe University, P. M. B. 5025, Awka, Nigeria.
[5]Department of Political Science, Nnamdi Azikiwe University, P. M. B. 5025, Awka, Nigeria.

This study is designed to address social problems associated with Information Communication Technologies (ICTs) and implications they portend on studentship in a Private Christian Mission University, Southern Nigeria. It tries to find out how the engagement of ICT devices results in social vices on campus. Drawing from recorded data between 2006 and 2012 academic year, the study reported six ICT tools associated with eight social-ills. Relying on raw data of 900 students disciplined within this period, the study reported that 187 students were expelled while 46 were advised to withdraw due to their involvement in ICT-related vices. Moreover, the study shows that 78 students served 1 year suspension while 589 students were suspended for one month. Findings of the study also revealed loss of all student rights infinitely for expelled students, nearly all rights for those advised-to-withdraw and all for a specified period for the suspended students. Practical implications of these disciplinary actions are discussed and potential future directions on this subject are proposed.

Key words: Social vices, ICTs, students', private mission university.

INTRODUCTION

The rapid aculturation arising from globalisation has been identified as an important factor responsible for increase social vices in modern societies (Udebhulu, 2009). Individuals have to contend with these vices because they violate societal norms and values. In other words, they could be regarded as 'a thorn in the flesh' of human peace and tranquility. Although Jones et al. (1985) noted that the rate of vices in the developed economy is very high as indicated by its increasing occurrence, but it could be observed that it has minimal impact on national development because of a robust structure to fund security systems that are committed to protecting lives and properties and bringing perpetrators to book. However, the problem is a major issue of concern in most developing countries, where complex vices are alien to their culture (Omonijo and Nnedum, 2012b). Moreover, powerful security network and committed security personnel to combat social-ills, mostly ICT related ones are relatively lacking in this aspect of the world, and most especially in their Universities.

Nigeria is a classic case in point, where large quantity of literature on social vices are found. Prominent among them being the works by Jumaat (2001), Kuna (2008), Atabong et al., 2010; Fasasi, 2006; Kayuni, 2009; Olasehinde-Williams (2009), Okafor and Duru (2010), Jekayinfa et al. (2011), Osakwe (2011) and Omonijo et al. (2013b). Other studies focused on vices hindering the peace and smooth running of academic calender on many campuses. Some examples include, investigations on the escalation of cultism, which has claimed lives of many young promising students (Ajayi et al., 2010; Arijesuyo and Olusanya, 2011); dynamics of Gang Criminality and Corruption in Nigeria Universities (Kingston, 2011); cultism or gangsterism and its effect on moral development of learners in Nigerian tertiary institution (Pemede and Viavonu, 2010).

Another frequently studied topic is on ICT-related social problems prevailing among underdraduates. These challenges have been threatening academic achievement of many students in these institutions (Okwu, 2006; Utulu et al., 2010; Abdulkareem and Oyeniran, 2011; Folorunso et al., 2006; Omonijo et al., 2011a; Omonijo and Nnedum 2012b). Global revolution in ICTs, in spite of its usefulness, has lucid problems it creates to diverse areas of human endeavours (Okonigene and Adekanle, 2010; Omonijo and Nnedum, 2012b). It is also evident from these studies that the educational sector seems to have failed in rendering quality education that is much needed for personal and national development, hence the birth of private Universities in Nigeria (Obasi, 2006; Ajadi, 2010; Aina, 2010) as cited by Anugwom et al. (2010); suggesting that the high level of discipline which has continued to decline in the public sector educational systems, is one of the core issues being addressed in the Private sector. Hence, social vices, mostly, ICT-related types, which students indulge in with impunity in the public sector is regarded as grievous misconducts and treated as such in the private sector driven educational system. Consequently, this study is focused on a Private Christian Mission University, where many students have been sanctioned based on ICT-related social vices. Implications of these sanctions for studentship are vital issues that have been hitherto ignored in the literature. Thus, to achieve the goal of this study the following research questions are raised.

1. What are the diverse disciplinary actions taken against students for involving in ICTs related -social vices on campus?
2. What are the ICTs associated with social vices and implications for studentship?
3. What programmes could be used to rehabilitate students engaged in ICT associated vices?

Findings of this work, as planned reveal how the use of ICT devices could result in social vices on campus. Apart from the academic value of this article, the study is expected to come out with programme to inform policy makers on how to rehabilitate the affected students. The fact that many existing studies in the area of education in Nigeria fell short of these efforts, suggests that this study could be significant. The quest for national development and its attendant successes is largely dependent on these youths (Enueme and Onyene, 2010). Therefore, the view of these young students as future leaders as suggested by Omonijo et al. (2011a) should inform the design and development of a transformation programme to assist in reclaiming them from the consequences of these vices and reposition them to be of immense value to a nation (Nigeria) in dire need of advancement.

STATEMENT OF THE PROBLEM

Numerous studies on ICTs related problems have been conducted within the Nigerian context (Folorunso et al., 2006; Lenhart and Madden, 2007; Abdulkareem and Oyeniran, 2011; Omonijo et al., 2011a; Adeoye, 2010; Arinola et al., 2012; Abdullahi, 2012). The flagrancy of the problem keeps on debasing measures put in place to curtail its escalation, and worsening general safety of the entire citenzenry (Adeyemi, 2012; Fasan, 2012). The involvement of regional vigilante groups such as Oodua Peoples Congress (OPC), Ijaw National Congress (INC), Arewa People`s Congress (APC), The Movement for the Actualization of the Biafra (MASSOB), "Bakassi Boys" (BB), Egbesu Boys of Africa (EBA) etcetera amplified the problem Fatai (2012), by creating more tension for the nation (Adebanwi, 2004; Akinwunmi, 2005).

Scholarly endeavours on the possible solutions in recent times have so far concentrated on the need to have regular seminars, symposium, lectures and resear-ches. The study of Adeoye, (2010) on various ways in which students employ mobile phones to perpetuate examination misconduct is one of such efforts. Findings of this study revealed four ways through which students indulge in examination misconduct with mobile phones and resolutions on how to curb them. Nevertheless, the study failed to examine "e-cheating" habit of students within academia. "E-cheating" according to Omonijo et al. (2011a), is the habit of students employing ICT gadgets to indulge in examination misconduct. Although mobile phone is one of these devices, but other ICT materials such as I-pods, I-pads, desktop computer, galaxy tabs etcetera were conspicuously omitted in Adeoye (2010) study. This gap in knowledge was addressed by Omonijo and Nnedum (2012b), in three selected Universities in Nigeria. Using data of 199 students, five ICT devices were identified with examination misconduct. However, the work recommended 10 ways of getting rid of this social problem among the nation's undergraduates. Nonetheless, the study limits its scope to public citadel of learning and ignored private institutions, which are not only more ICT compliant, but effectively and efficiently managed than public sector institutions (Aina, 2010). Moreover, the study focused on only one social vice (examination misconduct) and thereby excluded other social-ills associated with ICTs, diverse disciplinary actions taken against students as well as implications of such actions on their studentship. Hence, the need to make up for these gaps in knowledge on this subject matter from the Nigerian perspective.

AN EXPOSITION OF RESEARCH ON SOCIAL VICES IN NIGERIA

Social vices arise from behaviours of maladjusted people in the society Okwu (2006), but this ailment does not constitute much problem to humanity because movement of affected persons is seriously restricted to a defined location. The bulk of social vices escalating in the society recently has to do with high level of illiteracy, mass unemployment Omonijo and Nnedum (2012a); abject poverty Omonijo et al. (2011b), prevalence of general indiscipline at all levels of the society, incomplete sociali- sation (Nwosu, 2009; Anho, 2011) and globalisation, which touches on economic, political, social, cultural, technological and environmental facets of human life (Jike and Esiri, 2005). The socio-cultural and technological aspects according to Jike and Esiri (2005) are crucial to this discourse, as it has resulted in the acculturation of countries worldwide. It has also prompted developing nations to embrace ICTs, which is partly responsible the current challenges confronting modern nations (Udebhulu, 2009).

In the Nigerian, Omonijo and Nnedum (2012b) obser- ved that exposure of children to ICTs has been instrumental to the raising wave of social vices such as examination misconduct, criminal behaviours, Srivastava (2005) among others. In many homes in Nigeria, parents are not available to train their children due to their engagement in white collar jobs, businesses and other economic activities (Nwosu, 2009). As a result, the activities of children are not checked by their parents at home. This is an indication that deviation from the traditional role of women in home keeping, caring for the children and aged as emphasized by Murdock (1949), has created a vacuum, which most parents filled with ICTs. The time spent on child training in the traditional settings is now being spent in work settings and busines- ses for salaries, remunerations and profit making ventures. The over pursuance of wealth syndrome by most parents has produced wards who do not know and comprehend their parents. Consequently, most children reflect what they watch in television programmes, videos and internet web pages (Aggarwal, 2010). Some of them equally learn from nannies, housemaids and relations

(Nwosu, 2009). Such children are at risk of developing dysfunctional and psychopathic behaviours, due to ineffective parenting, poor supervision and unchecked access to ICTs (Ajiboye et al., 2012).

On the other hand, in homes, where parents are available, children are often led into dysfunctional behaviours like cheating, dishonesty, cultism, smuggling, prostitution, probably for financial gain and other reasons best known to them (Nwosu, 2009). In fact, the study by Omonijo and Fadugba (2011) identified ten ways in which parents influence their wards to indulge in examination misconduct. The danger of this as Nwosu (2009) noted is that children first learn ways of coping with the society through socialization in the family before proceeding to institutions of learning. The implication of this is that if children are not brought up properly at home, it would definitely affect their behaviours in the school environment, this scenario seems to exhibit true situation of most children in various institutions of higher learning in Nigeria today.

THEORETICAL INSIGHTS

Over the years, studies have shown that man's society translates from a primitive form to a more complex state in the process of time (Marx and Engels, 1848; Darwin, 1861; Spencer, 1887; Durkhiem, 1893; Marx, 1894; Tonnies, 1925; Sorokin, 1937; Toynbee, 1946; Rostow, 1960; Lerner, 1958; Levy, 1966; (Comte, 1856) as cited by Coser 1977). Of all these works none to a large extent gives credence to this article than (Rostow, 1960). The paradigm emphasises the process of change towards social, economic, and political systems developed in Western Europe and North America from the 17th to 19th century and spread to other parts of the world (Eisenstadt, 1966). It claims that developing societies must pass through five stages before attaining development, engaging the efficacy of capitalism. The instrumentality of capitalism as a weapon of achieving development makes this view different from the standpoint of classical Marxism, which opts for socialism that seriously abhors private accumulation of wealth and exploitation of the working class that capitalism stands for (Rodeny, 1972). On this note, Frank (1971), condemns Rostow (1960), and presents 'development of underdevelopment' as the radical counterpart of his take off stage. Frank (1971), advances by scornfully describes the entire thesis as an uneven structure, tagged: "metropolis-satellite relations". The nature of this relationship is a gigantic and systematic rip-off, because 'surplus is continuously appropriated and expropriated upwards and outwards to the detriment of under- developed societies (Frank, 1971). Scholars such as (Lenin, 1919; Fanon, 1965; Rodney, 1972) share the same view with Frank (1971) mostly on the ground of slavery and colonialism, and conclude that development is not possible within capitalist relations. Hence, their advice for developing countries to de-link radically from the world system.

Examining these approaches in development context, dependency scholars could be commended for observing the implications of slavery and colonialism in the process of development of underdeveloped societies, which Modernization scholars fail to recognise. Certainly, there is wide agreement among critics that the conceptual weakness inherents in modernization theories consists in failing to emphasize both internal and external connections or relationship between and within societies. Nevertheless, dependecy scholars should not have been employing this experience to justify the continuous underdevelopment of Africa in the comity of nations. Thinking and acting in that direction is what Omonijo et al. (2011b) called an 'escapist approach' in order to shift the blame to the extrinsic others.

Dependency scholars have also been questioned for maintaining that development is not possible within metropolis-satellite relations. Although this suggestion justifies South-South underdevelopment experience within capitalist powers, but it negates the spectacular growth of many East- Asian economies-Japan, Hong Kong, Singapore, Taiwan and South Korea and the late developers like China, Thailand, Malaysia and Indonesia within metropolis-satellite relations (Pereira, 1993). Besides, dependency approach fails to recognize the role of internal factors in the backwardness of Africa. Factors such as inter-tribal war, religious riots, communal clashes Omonijo et al. (2011b), ethnicity and tribalism Nnoli (1980), prevalence and persistence of endemic corrupttion across the Nation (Akani, 2001; Offiong, 2001; Omonijo et al., 2013a) have played more cogent roles in her backwardness than imperialism (Warren, 1980). Moreover, radical de-link from the world system is a policy problem limiting the application of dependency paradigm. It is practically impossible and thus, very useless to any development planner worldwide. Therefore, it may never be an antidote to African development. No matter the situation, no country will ever be an Island on its own. Nations will continue to interact with one another in order to enforce the law of comparative advantage (Smith, 2003). In the process, acculturation, which introduces a new way of life including latest technologies to the existing culture Mishra (2010), is enforced. The leadership of each society determines how the change will be managed and sustained for the betterment of the entire citizenry. Therefore, underdeveloped nations' contact with the West was a positive development as posited by Warren (1980), but poorly managed largely by the elite of underdeveloped societies as indicated in Rostow's thesis.

The first stage, that is traditional, is akin to Pre-Colonial era of underdeveloped societies, when there were no formal education, industrialization and white collar jobs. Traditional African religious worshiping was prevalent in traditional settings. Human beings were being used to make sacrifice to gods. Giving birth to twins and albinos was a taboo that warranted death. People's means of livelihood were subsistence agriculture, petty trading, fishing etc (Omonijo and Nnedum, 2012b). Obnoxious cultural practices such as widowhood, preference for male child, female genital mutilations etc were in vogue. The second stage, *that is precondition for take-off,* could be considered as colonial era, which introduced underdeveloped societies to western culture. The period marked establishment of formal education, paid jobs, modern means of communication, trade and commerce. Another form of government that brought about the commencement of the rudiment of democracy emerged (Omonijo, 2008). In the same manner, a new form of religion known as Christianity was introduced to traditional people. This development marked the commencement of destruction of barbaric cultural practices and worshipping of idols or gods. Education and politics brought about the emergence of elite as a social class. The third stage, that is *take off* could be considered as independence era, but it failed to capture Rostow's prescriptions in social, political and economic terms.

Socially, our institutions could not be properly reshaped to permit the pursuit of growth. Elite elites are squandering resources by marrying many wives, taking chieftancy titles, organising unnecessary parties (obituaries, naming ceremonies, birthday parties etc.). Politically, the reign of power was handed over to mediocre in 1959 general election. 1965 elections were mercilessly rigged. Chaos and anarchy that characterised the 1965 general elections was greater than that of 1959 (Akani, 2001). It resulted in military incursion into politics and later aggravated to civil war that cost the nation 2 million persons and valuable properties (Omonijo et al., 2011b). Economically, investment, which should have been a proportion of national income, suffered a serious setback due to corruption and other internal problems. These adversely affected strategies such as Exportation of Primary Produce (EPP), Import Substitution Industrialization (ISI) and Export Oriented Industrialization (EOI) put in place to ensure the growth of manufacturing industries (Ake, 1986; 1996). Consequently, per capital output failed to outstrip population growth. Hence, continuous progress that would have ushered in Nigeria to industrialization and the last two stages of development, *Stage of maturity and age of mass consumption*, was nipped in the bud. Haralambos et al. (2000) believe that a country is considered to be industrialized when her industrial sector contributes at least 25% of GDP, consists of 60% or more of manufacturing and employs more than 10% of the population. These conditions failed to materialize in Nigeria because elites, mostly the rulling class, siphoned financial resources meant for their actualisation Omonijo (2008), which invariably affected the nation's human capital, in term of brain drain (Omonijo et al., 2011b).

In every developed nation, elites played an active role in her take off stage. Such includes Bismarck of Germany, Meiji of Japan, Lenin of USSR, Ataturk of Turkey, Bonaparte of France and Chamberlain of Britain (Aboribo, 2009). Thus, the stage is an actively pursued project in which the state plays crucial economic roles. Instead of taking a clue from these societies, as well as Paraguay, which refused satellization and permitted self-generating development, African elites, either in the military or politics, being 'a class in itself', (Wright 2006; Borland, 2008) have failed woefully to act decisively. They mercilessly embezzled resources meant for national development (Omonijo et al., 2013a) in their countries and stockpiled the loot in foreign banks. It is not evident in the literature that a white man loots the resources of his country and stockpiles the loot in Africa. Ironically, the loot of African elites is being used to boost economies of Western nations. What a shame! Consequently, the structure of Nigeria could not make adequate provision for employment for classes of people interested, leading to high rate of joblessness (Omonijo and Nnedum, 2012b) that aggravates abject poverty among the citizenry (Omonijo et al., 2013c). Hence, the nation retrogressed from one of the richest 50 nations in early 60s to become one of the poorest in the world in recent times (Omonijo et al., 2013c). Going by Merton, (1968), inability to secure means of livelihood legitimately can prompt escalation of social-ills among youths. Untrained, unfed and uncared for children may likely resort to stealing, child prostitution, thuggery, kidnapping, Advance-Fee-Fraud "419", secret cult, examination misconduct, in order to fend for themselves. With proliferation of ICTs, such social-ills could be facilitated easily than before through "almajiri" and "omole" or "agboro" or "omoonile" and "boko haram" syndrome in Nigeria.

Although, underdeveloped countries began to embrace modernization in early 60s as a tool of achieving development, but the process was largely derailed by the elites of these countries as noted earlier. Global revolution in ICTs is an aspect of modernization meant for effective and efficient computer systems for processing information for the betterment of humanity in underdeveloped societies (Olaniyi, 2009; Ramjit and Singh, 2004 as cited by Omonijo and Nnedum, 2012b). E-learning, e-administration, e-banking or commerce are all parts of ICT, which modernity originally designed for human comfort, but hoodlums in Nigeria seem to have hijacked the initial good intention of introducing ICT through modernity to the detriment of the nation's advancement. While developed nations are advancing in science and technology many Nigerians are advancing in

using the same to perpetrate social-vices (cyber scam, e-cheating, hijacked e-mails, fake websites and all sort of computer fraud) through the aid of the internet online business transactions (Chawki, 2009) as cited by (Igwe, 2011). This could be corrected by instituting sound education at all level, through discipline, not only in the Private Christian Mission Institutions but also in the public sector.

METHODOLOGICAL ISSUES

Research design

This study employs ex-posit descriptive design because events that led to it took place in the past. Moreover, cross-sectional design was used to complement the former. This is because opinions of different sections of the university community were sought for the study.

Research instruments

Primary and secondary means of data collection was adopted. It involved excursion into literature and retrieving of information from registers. Information concerning the number of students penalized for ICTs related social vices in the last seven years and their penalties were retrieved from written documents produced by the Chairman of Disciplinary Committee (CDC) in the institution under study. Moreover, in-depth interview was used to complement retrieved information.

Population of study and sample size

Students and staff constitute the population of study. The total population in figure is 8, 322. Out of this figure, the student body represents 7, 840 academic staff constitutes 402 while staff of Student Affairs represent 80. Out of this number - 8, 322, 60 interviewees were randomly selected, that is, 45 from the student body, 10 from the academic staff and 5 from student affairs unit.

Sample techniques

Opinions of staff acquainted with students' activities as regard ICTs on campus were of paramount importance to the study rather than general opinions of people that may not reflect reality. Thus, purposeful sampling method was used to select interviewees from the population. Proportional sample method was first of all applied to the population. Therefore, the University was divided into 22 departments. Each of them produced interviewees according to its population. The same method was applied to academic and student affairs' staff. Simple random method was later used to select each interviewee from their departments and sub-units.

Data analysis

The data was analyzed using frequency tables and percentages.

RESULTS

Table 1 presents the descriptive statistics on diverse

Table 1. Descriptive statistics on diverse disciplinary actions taken against perpetrators' of ICTs related social vices.

S/n	Diverse Disciplinary Action Taken Against Perpetrators of ICT related social vices	No. of students involved	%
1	Expulsion	187	20.7
2	Withdrawal	46	5.1
3	1 year	78	8.7
4	4 weeks	589	65.5
	Total	900	100

Source: Field survey data, 2013.

disciplinary actions taken against perpetrators' of ICTs related social vices on campus between 2006 and 2012 academic year. Statistics indicate that 900 students were penalized for indulging in ICTs-related social vices. Out of this figure, 187 (20.7%) were expelled, 46 (5.1%) were advised to withdraw, 78 (8.7%) were placed on one year suspension and 589 (65.5%) were placed on 4 weeks suspension.

Table 2 shows descriptive statistics on ICTs which students used to indulge in social vices and its implications. Around 18.7% of them used their laptops to indulge in pornography while 15% used their I-Pod. Also 4.8% used their mobile phones while 2.7% used their modems. This was followed by 28.3% students that were involved in the act of stealing ICT tools. The result shows that 24.6% of them were identified with laptops, 3.2% were linked with I-Pods while 0.5% associated with mobile phone. Similarly, 10.2% of the students involved in indecent behaviour relating to storing pictures, where they were smoking cigarette and Indian hemp as well as drinking of alcohol on the following ICT materials: I-Pods 5.9% and laptops 4.3%. Students caught in possession of cult-related materials on their laptops represent 9.1% while those caught for examination misconduct with ICT devices represent 8.5%. 3.2% of them used their desktops to cheat, 2.7% used their I-pod and 2.1% used their calculators. 1.6% students involved in computer related fraud i.e. hacking into data base and bank fraud. Finally, 1.1% students used their laptops to store indecent pictures. The first implication of the above on studentship is expulsion from the University, which is the ultimate penalty. This is followed by advised-to-withdraw from the institution.

Data in Table 2 also show that greater proportion, 8.7% of the students served 1 year suspension for using their ICT devices to engage in indecent behaviour. About 17.9% of them used laptops while the same number used I-pods to store indecent movies. Also 38.6% used the following ICT devices in storing pornographic pictures and browsing restricted websites. These include 19.2% that used modem, 18.1% I-pod and 1.3% mobile phones. In the same vein, 10.5% of the affected students used the

following devices to store indecent movies: 12.8% I-pods, 6.4% mobile phone and 1.3% laptop. 52 of them involved in possession of indecent pictures on their ICT tools: 25.8% used mobile phones, 24.2% used modem, 17.7% used laptops and 14.5% used I-pods. 6.4% students were caught for indecent music and video with I-pods. 1.3% student each was caught for examination misconduct with mobile phone and I-pod while 1.3% was caught with cult-related materials with an I-Pod. In addition, 76.4% of the students used their mobile phones to engage in immoral sexual communication with the opposite sex, followed by 9.2% students who used the following ICT tools for indecent movies: laptops 5.1% and mobile phones 4.1%. However, 3.6% of the students used their modem to browse pornographic web sites, 3.1% used their I-pods to store indecent music and video materials, 2.6% students used their laptops to store indecent pictures and finally 0.2% used his Galaxy tab to store indecent music and video. These students served 4 weeks suspension.

Note: 5 students did not agree with counselling and advise. 1 academic staff did not subscribe to referral to youth development and leadership institute. Finally, 3 academic staff, 2 staff of student affairs and 15 students did not agree with Bible school attendance.

Examination of the result in Table 3 will, reveal that, three programmes for rehabilitation of affected students were suggested by 59 interviewees among the staff. The first on the list is compulsory counselling and advice. It was found that 16.7% of the interviewees were academic staff, 8.3% were members of staff in Student Affairs and 75% were students. The remaining 8.3% did not subscribe to this program. This was followed by Referral to Youth Development and Leadership Institute in which 15% academic staff subscribed to. 8.33% members of student affairs subscribed to it and 75% students suggested the same thing. Meanwhile, 1.7% academic staff did not agree with this programme. Lastly, Bible school attendance is the third program. 11.7%, 5% and 50% of academic staff, members of Student Affairs Department and students subscribed to this respectively. Meanwhile 5% academic staff, 3.3% members of Student

Table 2. Descriptive statistics on ICTs associated with social vices and implications on studentship.

S/n	ICTs	Social vices	Expulsion	Advised to withdraw	Suspension		Total
					1 year	4 weeks	
			F	F	F	F	
1	Mobile Phone	Possession of pornographic materials.	9 (4.8%)	-	1 (1.3%)	-	10
		Examination misconduct	1 (.5%)	-	-	-	1
		Stealing	1 (.5%)	-	-	-	1
		Illegal possession and immoral sexual communication with the opposite sex	-	-	-	450 (76.4%)	450
		Possession of indecent movie	-	-	14(17.9%)	24 (4.1%)	38
		Possession of indecent pictures	-	-	5(6.4%)	10 (1.7%)	15
2	Laptops / Desk-tops	Possession of pornographic materials	35 (18.7%)	23 (50%)	-	-	58
		Examination misconduct	6 (3.2%)	-	-	-	6
		Stealing	46 (24.6%)	14 (30.4%)	-	-	60
		Display of indecent pictures	-	-	1(1.3%)	20 (3.3%)	21
		Possession of indecent movie	-	-	14(17.9%)	30 (5.1%)	44
		Possession of cult-related materials	17 (9.1%)	3 (6.5%)	-	-	20
		Lesbianism	2 (1.1%)	-	-	-	2
		Indecent behaviour-smoking of cigarette & Indian hemp and drinking of alcohol	8 (4.3%)	-	4 (5.1%)	-	12
		Bank and internet fraud/hacking	3 (1.6%)	-	-	-	3
3	I-Pods	Possession of pornographic materials	28 (15%)	6 (13.1%)	8 (10.4%)	-	42
		Examination misconduct	5 (2.7%)	-	1(1.3%)	-	6
		Stealing	6 (3.2%)	-	-	-	6
		Possession of indecent pictures	-	-	10 (12.8%)	15 (2.4%)	25
		Possession of cult-related materials	-	-	1(1.3%)	-	1
		Possession of indecent music and video	-	-	5 (6.4%)	18 (3.1%)	23
		Indecent behaviour-smoking of cigarette & Indian hemp and drinking of alcohol	11 (5.9%)	-	-	-	11
4	Calculator	Examination misconduct	4 (2.1%)	-	-	-	4
5	Galaxy tap	Possession of indecent music and video	-	-	-	1 (0.2%)	1
6	Modem	Browsing of pornographic web site	5 (2.7%)	-	14(17.9%)	21 (3.7%)	40
	Total		187 (100%)	46 (100%)	78 (100%)	589 (100%)	900 (100%)

Source: Field survey data, 2013

Affairs and 25% students did not agree with this programme.

Note: 4 academic staff and 1 member of student affairs unit did not subcribe to referral to youth development and leadership institute.

From Table 4, it is evident that three programs were suggested by 60 interviewees. The first on the list is compulsory counselling and psychotherapy for students slated for suspension. 16.7% of them were academic staff, 8.3% were members of staff in Student Affairs and 75% of them were students. This is followed by Referral to Youth Development and Leadership Institute during holidays in which 14.3% academic staff subscribed to. 9.5% members of student affairs subscribed to it while

Table 3. Descriptive statistics on suggested programmes to rehabilitate expelled and advised-to-withdraw students.

S/n	Suggested programmes	Respondents			Total
		Academic staff	Staff of Student Affairs	Students	
1	Counselling and advice	10(16.66%)	5(8.33%)	40(66.66%)	55
2	Referral to youth development and leadership institute	9(15%)	5(8.33%)	45(75%)	59
3	Bible school attendance up to 3 stages	7(11.66%)	3(5%)	30(50%)	40

Source: Field survey data

Table 4. Descriptive statistics on suggested programmes to rehabilitate suspended students.

S/n	Suggested programmes	Respondents			Total
		Academic staff	Staff of Student Affairs	Students	
1	Compulsory counselling and advice	10 (16.66%)	5 (8.33%)	45 (75%)	60(100%)
2	Referral to youth development and leadership institute during holidays	6 (14.28%)	4 (9.52%)	50(83.33%)	60(100%)
3	Bible school attendance on campus.	10 (16.66%)	5 (8.33%)	45 (75%)	60(100%)

Source: Field survey data

83.3% students suggested the same thing. Lastly, Bible school attendance is the third programme. Academic staff, members of Student Affairs and students, who subscribed to this programme are 16.7%, 8.3% and 75% respectively.

OTHER IMPLICATIONS OF INVOLVING IN ICT-RELATED VICES ON STUDENTSHIP.

Implications of involving in ICT related vices are diverse, therefore, they are stated in categories below:

Category A, Expulsion: Expulsion is the ultimate penalty an erring student can obtain. Such a student would vacate campus as soon as he collects his/her letters of expulsion. They are no longer students of the institution ad infinitum, except by a decision of the highest level of management reversing the expulsion. Privileges of registration, class attendance, residence in the hall of residence are withdrawn. It equally connotes withdrawal of privileges of the use of university facilities like sport complex, cyber cafe, library etcetera. All the money spent from admission to the point of expulsion is wasted. They do not have any right to academic transcript. Instead, they will start their academic career afresh by sitting for another Univertsities Matriculation Examination.

Category B, Advised-to-withdraw: Advised-to-withdraw is next to expulsion. Under this category, students involved are expected to vacate campus as soon as they collect their letters of withdrawal. They are no longer students of the university ad infinitum, except by a decision of the

highest level of management reversing the withdrawal. Privileges of registration, class attendance, residence in the hall of residence are withdrawn. It equally connotes withdrawal of privileges of the use of university facilities like sport complex, cyber cafe, library etc. All the money spent from the day of admission up to the point of expulsion is wasted. However, students involved are allowed to collect thier academic transcript at the point of withdrawal and continue their study in another university.

Category C, 1 year Suspension: This is next to withdrawal. Students involved are expected to vacate campus as soon as they collect their letter of suspension. With this development, they are no longer students of the university for one solid year, except by a decision of the highest level of management reversing the suspension. Privileges of registration, class attendance, residence in the hall of residence are suspended. It equally connotes suspension of privileges of the use of university facilities like sport complex, cyber cafe, library etcetera. Such students will forfit one year and they will not be able to graduate with their set.

Category D, 4 weeks suspension: This is the least penalty that can be giving to students. Such students will vacate campus as soon as they collect their letters of suspension. With this development, they are no longer students of the university for a month, except by a decision of the highest level of management reversing the suspension. Privileges of registration, class attendance, residence in the hall of residence are suspended. It equally connotes suspension of privileges of the use of university facilities like sport complex, cyber cafe, library etcetera for this period. However, if this period falls within examination, such students may not sit for all examination slated for that period. This will prevent them from registering for the next academic semester. In that wise, such students will loose one academic session.

Apart from the above, a copy of disciplinary letters received by students is always kept in their files for future reference. That serves as a negative implication on their studentship. Moreover, such students are not allowed to take part in any excursion outside the University. Furthermore, they are not allowed to hold any leadership position throughout their studentship on campus.

RELATIONSHIP BETWEEN ICT AND SOCIAL VICES

A-Mobile phone: Students employed this device to store relevant materials in courses being examined prior to examination. Such students were caught while copying these materials from their phone to answers scripts in the examination hall. Moreover, the same device was used to store pornographic materials and indecent movies. Such students (male and female) used to watch these materials at night in order to learn, secretly how to engage in fornication with the opposite sex. Moreover, students engaged mobile phone to indulge in indecent sexual communication with the opposite sex in and outside campus. Discussion on how to meet with the opposite sex in club houses and hotels were being made with this device. Finally on this device, those who cannot afford expensive mobile phones used to steal from other careless colleagues.

B-Laptops/Desktops: These devices were used to store pornographic materials, indecent movies, cult-related materials and pictures such as nudity. Since laptops are being used to browse for academic materials, they copy these materials from the internet and watch them secretly on campus. More often than not, they store them in hidden places where they can only be discovered by ICT-knowledgeable persons. Secret cult materials such as songs, pictures, logos etcetera are stored on their laptops. Furthermore, students use this device in hacking into data base with the aim of committing fraud. Also, pictures where students were drinking alcohol, smoking cigarette and Indian hemp in parties outside the campus were stored on laptops. Where computer desktops are very essential for examination, students used to copy answers from other students through internet in the examination hall. The use of laptop led to high rate of stealing on campus. Students who need money for other things such as school fees, secret cult initiation and material things stole the laptops of thier colleagues who were careless and sold them outside the University.

C, I-Pods: I-Pods were also used to store pornographic materials, indecent movies and pictures. Moreover, cult-related materials such as logo, songs and pictures are stored in it directly. Also, pictures where students were drinking alcohol, cigarette and Indian hemp in parties outside the campus are taken and transferred to their I-Pods. Since I-pods are used to store lecture notes, students also use it to store materials relevant to subjects being examined during examination. The aim of such attempt is to copy answers from the device. Also, it has led to stealing on campus. Students who cannot afford it steal from their friends or roommates.

D-Calculator: This was used to perpetrate examination misconduct. Relevant materials such as formula etcetera were inscribed on calculators prior to examination. Students were caught in the process of coyping them to their answer scripts.

E-Galaxy tap: This device was used to store indecent music and video. Students used to listen and watch them at their private time.

F-Modem: This device was used to browse web sites for pornographic materials, indecent movies and music etcetera. They stored these materials on their ICTs.

DISCUSSION

Apparently, it could be deduced from this study that the citadel of learning under study operates by strigent rules and regulations. Moreover, it is observed that justice is administered without fear or favour. No matter whose ward is involved, the wrath of law is applied as indicated in Tables 1 and 2, and the seriousness of vices committed determined penalties meted out. This is largely appreciated and commendable because these are very rear not only in the management of public sector education, but other institutions in Nigeria and their implementation of justice (Omonijo and Nnedum 2012b). Nigeria is a country where justice is denied. Thus, evil peoples hold sway in every affairs of life. This may be associated with the escalation of social-ills in her tertiary institutions as well as moral decadence in the country at large. Being caught and punished may deter offenders from committing a crime again, as well as deter future offend-ers who contemplate committing crimes (Saridakisa and Spenglerb 2012).

However, the financial cost of these disciplinary actions on parents is grevious. It costs a parent .6 million naira to finance a ward in a year, if such a child is expelled after two or three or five years, it means, such a parent has lost a substantial amount in cash as well as in human capital to ICT related vices. Its psychological trauma, mostly to parents who borrowed money to pay school fees could lead to high blood presssure, hypertention and sudden death. The sociological implication is that such a child may lose proper parenting that is needed at that point in life. Psychologically, such a child will have to grapple with self enacted stigma that trails a university drop-out in Nigerian society. In term of time, if a child is rusticated after four years on campus, it means starting his or her higher education afresh. Four years lost may prevent a student from catching up with his mates in life. In order not to inflict permanent stigma on such students, disciplinary actions could be complement with spiritual exercise such as counselling, psychotherapy and spiritual transformation as presented in Tables 3 and 4. These measures could enable them to be transformed, as Jesus is not interested in the death of any sinner, but his repentance and acceptance to iternal glory. Therefore, such programme could go a long way in destroying and reconditioning the dysfunctional habit in the lives of affected students.

CONCLUSION

As long as human society exists, occurrence of social-vices may not be altered. More importantly, the more human society advances in science and techonology, the more likely humanity experiences more complex vices which are the vicious fallout of postmodernism. However, the rate of its escalation in Nigeria, previously known for moral decency and decorum is beyond the writers imagination. In other word, the way Nigeria suddenly emerged as a purveyor of cultural and structural vices due to the alarming level of social decadence arising from ICTs is an issue of concern to academia, which public institutions seem to have failed in addressing. Therefore, the hope of restoring sanity in the citadel of learning in Nigeria lies in Private Christian Mission Institutions. Elites who lack discipline would definitely be void of ingredients for effective and effecient administration. This may not be unconnected with bad government, resulting in the backwardness of Nigeria. When the righteous are in positions of authority, the people may likely rejoice, but when the wicked are in power, the people may lament, mourn and regret. Nigeria has degenerated to this level because graduates recruiting to work settings from the public tertiary institutions lack the moral, spiritual, psychological and sociological competence required for constructive engagement in postmodern workplace.

Also, it is observed with keen interest that most students enroling in Private Christain Mission institutions do not realise the essentials of discipline that the institution is out to enforce. They must have conceived out of their ignorance that social vices being displayed with impunity in the public sector are part and parcel of life, which should be left unchanged. This must have ocassioned the large number of victims recorded in the last 7 years. However, programs of action should be instituted to rehabilitate them, as a faith based citadel of learning, to ensure their usefulness in the nation's building at this crucial time that the nation needs a crop of regenerated leaders to bail the nation out of oblivion.

RECOMMENDATIONS

Based on the above conclusion this study makes the following recommendations.

1. The use of ICT devices should be strictly monitored by the school management on campus and parents at home.
2. Parents should equally make themselves available at home to train their children and stop leaving them in the hands of nannies, house boys and maids.
3. Parents should stop exposing their wards to ICT without adequate check. The use of ICTs should not be used to replace their non-availability at home.
4. Manifestations of social-ills should be reviled in the formal sector and disparaged in informal in Nigeria.
5. Faith based organizations should commence emphazising on holiness and righteousness, mostly among children instead of much trouncing on prosperity.
6. Good conducts among children should be commended and rewarded in the family, school and church environments.
7. Acculturation is good, but things that add value to the existing culture should be copied while bad habits should be left in the lurch.

ACKNOWLEDGEMENTS

We have benefited from the librality of the editor of this journal, academic prowess of Professor, E. E. Anugwom, University of Nigeria, Nnsukka campus. The corresponding author equally expresses his gratitude to Mrs C. A. Okafor for her strong support. We thank them very much.

REFERENCES

Abdulkareem AY, Oyeniran O (2011). Managing the performance of Nigerian universities for sustainable development using data envelopment analysis. Int. J. Acad. Res. Bus. Soc. Sci. 1:1-7

Abdullahi B (2012). Nigeria: Mubi Massacre -Students Cautioned Against Social Vices. Vanguard, Daily October 10, 2012, p.7.

Aboribo (2009). The military and its impact on Nigerian state and society. Interdisciplinary J. Nig. Sociol. Soc. 1(1):167-184.

Adebanwi W (2004). Violence and the Materiality of Power: Oodua People's Congress. Ritual and the Reinvention of Culture. Master Thesis, Unpublished. Oxford: University of Oxford.

Adebayo SO (2011). Common Cheating Behaviour Among Nigerian University Students: A Case Study of University of Ado-Ekiti, Nigeria. World J. Educ. 1(1):144-149.

Adeoye OS (2010). Emerging Communication Technology and Examination Malpractices in Nigeria Educational Sector. Int. J. Educ. Technol. 5(4):59-64.

Adeyemi DO (2012). Security Challenges: FG, don't drag feet on the issue. Tribune, Online. From <http://www.tribune.com.ng/index.php/letters/ 47845-security-challenges-fg-dont-drag-feet-on- the-issue> (Retrieved November 12).

Aggarwal R (2010). Patterns of Domestic Injuries in Rural India. Internet J. Health 11(2):4.

Aina TA (2010). The Role of the private University in Driving Social and economic Change: Challenges and Opportunities. 5th Convocation Ceremony's Distinguished Lecture at Covenant University, Ota p.2.

Ajadi TO (2010). Private Universities in Nigeria – the Challenges

Social vices associated with the use of Information Communication Technologies (ICTs) in a Private Christian...

61

Ahead. Am. J. Sci. Res. 10(7):15-24.

Ajayi IA, Haastrup TE, Osalusi FM (2010). Menace of cultism in Nigerian tertiary institutions: The way out. J. Soc. Sci. Kamla-Raj 12(3):155-160.

Ajiboye OE, Atere AA, Olufunmi AN (2012). Changing patterns of child rearing practice in Badagry area of Lagos state: Implication for delinquent behaviour. Eur. Sci. J. 8(12):33-59

Akani C (2001). The Nigerian state as an instrument of corruption, in C. Akani (ed.) Corruption in Nigeria-The Niger-Delta Experience. Enugu: 4th Dimension Limited.

Ake C (1986). Political Economy of Nigeria. Ibadan: Spectrum Books.

Ake C (1996). Democracy and development in Africa. Ibadan: LongmanNigeria Limited.

Akinwunmi O (2005). Ethnicization of Violence in Nigeria under Democratization Rule, 1999-2003 (ed.) Hassan Saliu. Ibadan: University Press.

Anho RO (2011). Moral Conducts of Students in Secondary Schools in Delta State: An Assessment of the Effects of Native Culture on Discipline, Order and Control. Afr. J. Educ. Technol. 1(1):45-52.

Anugwom EE, Omonijo DO, Fadugba OA (2010). A Review of Gender Performance of Graduating Students in a Private Christian Mission University in Nigeria Between 2008 and 2010. Nigeria Journal of Gender and Development: An International Interdisciplinary J. 10(1& 2):44-54.

Arijesuyo AE, Olusanya OO (2011). Theoretical Perspectives on Campus Cultism and Violence in Nigeria Universities: A Review and Conceptual Approach. Int. J. Psychol. Stud. 3(1):1-7.

Arinola AA, Adigun GO, Oladeji BO, Adekunjo OA (2012). Impact of Ict on Cataloguing & Classification of Library Materials; Case Study of Some Selected University Libraries in South-West Nigeria. Am. Int. J. Contemp. Res. 2(6):1-6.

Atabong TA, Okpala MC, Abondem AL, Essombe CE (2010). Eliminating Examination Malpractice in Africa with Automated Test Taking, Marking and Result Printing. Trop. J. Biomed. Appl. Sci. Res. 4(1):452-469.

Borland E (2008). Class consciousness. In: Parrillo Vincent N. Encyclopedia of social problems, Volume 1. London: Sage.

Coser L (1977). Masters of Sociological Thought (2nd ed.). New York: Harcourt Brace Jovanovich, Inc.

Darwin C (1861). On the Origin of Species by Means of Natural Selection, or the Preservation of Favoured Races in the Struggle of Life, 3rd edition. London: John Murray.

Durkhiem E (1893). The Division of Social Labour. New York: Free Press.

Eisenstadt SN (1966). Modernization: Protest and Change. Englewood Cliffs, N.J.: Prentice-Hall.

Enueme CP, Onyene V (2010). Youth Restiveness in the Niger Delta of Nigeria: Implication for education and Leadership. Eur. J. Soc. Sci. 182:286-296.

Fasan R (2012). Issues of insecurity: How complicit are the security agencies? Vanguard online. From <http://www.vanguardngr.com/2012/06/issues-of- insecurity-how-complicit-are-the-security-agencies> (Retrieved November 12).

Fanon F (1965). The Wretched of the Earth. United Kingdom: Macgibbon and Kee.

Fasasi YA (2006). Quality Asurance: A Practical Solution To Examination Malpractices In Nigerian Secondary Schools. Int. J. Afr. Am. Stud. 5(2):1-7.

Fatai B (2012). Democracy and National Identities: The Travails of National National Security in Nigeria. British Journal of Arts and Social Sciences,9, II:126-140

Folorunso O, Ogunseye OS, Sharma SK (2006). An exploratory study of the critical factors affecting the acceptability of e-learning in Nigerian universities. Inform. Manage. Comput. Security 14(5):496-505.

Frank AG (1971). The Sociology of Development and Underdevelopment of Sociology. London: Plato Press.

Haralambos M, Head R, Holborn M (2000). Sociology: Themes and Perspectives. New York, Harper Collins.

Igwe CN (2011). Socio-economic Developments and the Rise of 419 Advanced-Fee Fraud in Nigeria. Eur. J. Soc. Sci. 20(1):184-193.

Jekayinfa AA, Omosewo EO, Yusuf AA, Ajidagba UA (2011). Curbing Examination Dishonesty in Nigeria Through Value Education. Educ. Res. Rev. 6(2):161-167.

Jike VT, Esiri M (2005). "Globalization and the Social Sciences In: Mordi AA and Jike V (eds.), Philosophy of the Social Sciences. Benin-City: Justice Jeco Press and Publishers pp.129-136

Jones EF, Forrest JD, Goldman N, Henshaw SK, Lincoln R, Rosoff JI, Westoff CF, Wulf D (1985). Teenage Pregnancy in Developed Countries: Determinants and Policy Implications. Fam. Plann. Perspect. 17(2):53-63.

Jumaat B (2001). Social Vices Associated with Information Communication Techniques. Retrieved from Goggle search <http://www.socialvices/informationcommunicationtechnologies/statistics.htm>. May 3, 2012.

Kuna M (2008). The root of cultism and other forms of violence in Nigeria. Gombe Studies. Journal of Gombe State University, 1 (1), 141-168

Kayuni HM (2009). The challenge of studying sexual harassment in higher education: An experience from the University of Malawi's chancellor college. J. Int. Women's Stud. 11(2):83-99.

Kingston KG (2011). The Dynamics of Gang Criminality and Corruption in Nigeria Universities: A Time Series Analysis. Afr. J. Law Criminol. 1(1):58-68.

Lenin VI (1919). Imperialism, the Highest Stage of Capitalism. New Delhi: Leftwoods Books.

Lenhart A, Madden M (2007). Social networking websites and teens: an overview. The pew internet and American life project. Retrieved from http://www.pewinternet. org/pdfs /PIP_SNS_Data_Memo (Accessed on January 19th 2011).

Lerner D (1958). The passing of traditional society: Modernizing the Middle East. New York: Free Press.

Levy M Jr. (1966). Modernization and the Structures of Societies. Princeton: Princeton University.

Marx K (1894). Das Kapital. Germany: Verlag von Otto Meisner.

Marx K, Engels F (1848). The Communist Manifesto. Chicago: Henry Reginery Company.

Merton RK (1968). Social theory and social structure. New York: Free Press.

Mishra P (2010). Economics of development and planning-theory and practice. Delhi: Himalaya Publishing House.

Murdock GP (1949). Social Structure. New York: Macmillan.

Nnoli O (1980). Ethnic Politics in Nigeria. Enugu: Fourth Dimension Publication coy. Limited.

Nwosu NP (2009). The family, society and the menace of examination malpractices: A critical overview. State and Society: Interdisciplinary J. Nig. Sociol. Soc. 1(1):87-102.

Obasi NI (2006). New Private Universities in Nigeria. Int. Higher Educ. 45:14-26.

Okafor HC, Duru NE (2010). Sexual promiscuity among female undergraduates in tertiary institutions in Imo State: An issue for healthy living. Edo J. Couns. 3(1):15-21.

Okonigene RE, Adekanle B (2010). Cyber crime. Bus. Intell. J. 3(1):1-4.

Okwu OJ (2006). A Critique of Students' Vices and the Effect on Quality of Graduates of Nigerian Tertiary Institutions. J. Soc. Sci. 12(3):193-198.

Olaniyi S (2009). The potential of using information and communication technology for poverty alleviation and economic empowerment in Osun State, Nigeria. Int. J. Educ. Dev. Inform. Commun. Technol. 5(3):131-140.

Offiong DA (2001). Globalization: Post-neo dependency and poverty in Africa. Enugu: Fourth Dimension Publishing Company Ltd.

Olasehinde-Williams O (2009). Measures of consistency in lecturer and student sensitivity to academic dishonesty intervention approaches in the University of Ilorin, Nigeria. Educ. Res. Rev. 4(2):1-6.

Omonijo DO (2008). Patterns of corruption in power holding company of Nigeria (PHCN). An Unpublished Main M. Sc thesis, Department of Sociology/Anthropology, Faculty of Social Sciences, Nnamdi Azikiwe University, Awka, Nigeria.

Omonijo DO, Nndeum OOU, Ezeokana JO (2011a). Understanding the escalation of brain drain in Nigeria from poor leadership point of view.

Mediterr. J. Soc. Sci. 2(3):487-510.

Omonijo DO, Nndeum OU, Ezeokana JO (2011b). The relationship between youthful lust and violation of GSM rule in a private Christian Mission University, South-West Nigeria. World J. Educ. 2(2):49-61.

Omonijo DO, Fadugba OA (2011). Parental influence in escalation of examination malpractices in Nigeria. Eur. J. Soc. Sci. 19(2):297-307

Omonijo DO, Nnedum OOU (2012a). Impacts of societal prejudice on attainment of life/personal goals of physically challenged persons in Nigeria. Int. Res. J. Human. 4(5):12-35.

Omonijo DO, Nnedum OOU (2012b). A Study of E-Cheating Habits of Students in three selected Universities in Nigeria. Wufenia J. 8(4):37-60.

Omonijo DO, Nnedum OOU, Uche OCO, Biereenu-Nnabugwu (2013a). Social Perspectives in the Pervasiveness of Endemic Corruption in Nigeria. J. Sociol. Soc. Anthropol. Kamal Raj Enterprices, India. In press.

Omonijo DO, Nnedum OOU, Uche OCO, Kanayo (2013b). A Study of Sexual Harassment in Three Selected Private Mission Universities, Ogun-State, Western Nigeria. J. Soc. Sci., Kamal Raj Enterprices, India. In press.

Omonijo DO, Nnedum OOU, Uche OCO, Kanayo (2013c). An Assessment of Work-Study Programme in a Private Christian Mission University, Ogun-State, Western Nigeria. Work in Progress.

Osakwe E (2011). A Re-Appraisal of Attitudes and Reactions towards Repentant Examination Cheats. Arts Soc. Sci. J. 25(1):1-5.

Pemede O, Viavonu B (2010). Cultism or Gangsterism and Its Effect on Moral Development of Learners in Nigerian Tertiary Institutions. J. Emerging Trend Educ. Res. Policy Stud. 1(2):61-64.

Pereira AW (1993). Economic Underdevelopment, Democracy and Civil Society: The North-east Brazilian case. Third World Q. 14(2):365-380.

Rostow WW (1960). The stages of economic growth: A non-communist manifesto. Cambridge: Cambridge University Press.

Rodney W (1972). How Europe underdeveloped Africa. Free Press: Moscow.

Saridakisa G, Spenglerb H (2012). Crime, Deterrence and Unemployment in Greece: A Panel Data Approach. Soc. Sci. J. 49:167-174.

Spencer H (1887). The Factors of Organic Evolution. London: Williams and Norgate.

Srivastava L (2005). Mobile Phone and the Evolution of Social Behaviour, Pro Quest J. 15(7):111-129.

Sorokin PA (1937). Social and Cultural Dynamics. 4(1-3), 1941 (vol.4); Rev. 1957 (reprinted: Transaction Publishers, 1985).   [SCD].

Smith A (2003). The Wealth of Nations. New York: bantam dell Books.

Tonnies F (1925). The Concept of Gemeinschaft, In: Cahnman WJ & Heberle R (Eds), Ferdinand Tonnies on Sociology: Pure, applied and empirical. Selected writings. Chicago: University of Chicago Press.

Toynbee AJ (1946). A Study of History: Abridgement of Volumes 1-6. Oxford: Oxford University Press.

Udebhulu M (2009). Globalisation and social change: A sociological viewpoint. State and society: Interdisciplinary J. Nig. Sociol. Soc. 1(1):233-242.

Utulu SCA, Alonge AJ, Emmanuel OS (2010). Use of mobile phones for project based learning by undergraduate students of Nigerian private universities. Proceedings of Informing Science & IT Education Conference (InSITE).

Warren B (1980). Imperialism: Pioneer of capitalism. London: NIB &Verso.

Wright EO (2006). Class. In: Beckert J and Zafirovski M. International encyclopedia of economic sociology. Psychology Press p.62.

7

Metrics for data accuracy improvement in a production scheduling software: An application in the Brazilian Meat Industry

Eduardo Scherer Rücker[1], Luis Henrique Rodrigues[1], Daniel Pacheco Lacerda[1]* and Ricardo Augusto Cassel[2]

[1]Production and System Engineering Program – UNISINOS, Research Group on Modeling for Learning – GMAP, Av. Unisinos, 950 – São Leopoldo – Rio Grande do Sul – Brasil.
[2]Production Engineering Program – UFRGS, Av. Osvaldo Aranha, 99 – 5°. Andar – Porto Alegre – Rio Grande do Sul – Brasil.

This study aims to develop a method for improving the data accuracy of a specific production scheduling software for the meat industry. The proposed method was based on the results obtained in the implementation phase of the scheduling tool in Empresa Alfa, that produces food based on chickens, turkeys and porks. The research method used was a case study, by means of which the influence of data accuracy on the information generated by the system during the project is reported and analysed. The development of the proposed method was based on the theoretical framework on production scheduling, data quality and information quality, the author's perceptions about the project which was applied in the case study and the contributions of experts in the subject of the work. The method was structured in processes and subprocesses, hierarchy that enabled the implementation of the objectives of each process regarding the data accuracy in stages (subprocesses).

Key words: Data accuracy, meat industry, production scheduling, data quality.

INTRODUCTION

The competitive context of the business environment demands quality on decision-making. Given this situation, the data and consequently the information represent a significant input in the decision-making process. Investments in information systems are an attempt to make the choice of the alternative actions (decision-making) fast and qualified. Thus, in order to meet the increasingly demanding consumer markets, manufacturing industries depend on qualified data. These data will be used in the decisions related to the production scheduling process. Therefore, the quality of the production scheduling will be a result of the quality of the database and consequently of the information used. In organizations, the operationalization of information systems for this purpose depends on the availability of data whose accuracy faithfully reflects the reality of the company.

The accuracy of the data collected, particularly in manufacturing environments, is important due to the impacts that its quality can have on the decision-making process and on production planning and scheduling. This perspective is analogous to the input-transformation-output model of processes shown in Figure 1. In a production system, the raw materials go through a manufacturing process in which they ultimately acquire form and economic value. In the same way, the data are processed for generating information. Thus, if the data (raw materials) are not properly collected and fed into the system (by inaccuracy or by differing of the nature from the expected data), the results generated (end product) will differ from reality. It is noteworthy that the nature of the expected data refers to the pattern established for the input of data into the system.

These divergences have a significant set of implications for the organization as a whole, such as: i) the information on costs can be questioned; ii) the stock levels may not be adequate; iii) delivery deadlines may not be met; and; iv) the best use of the company's capacity may be compromised. Goldratt (1991, p. 3)

---

*Corresponding author. E-mail: dlacerda@unisinos.br.

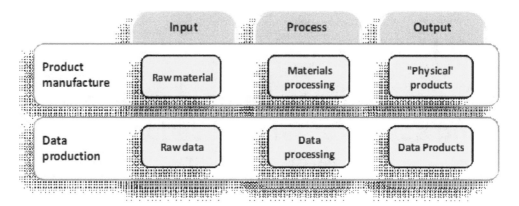

Figure 1. Analogy between product manufacturing and data generation.
Source: Constructed from Wang et al. (1995).

states that "we are drowning in oceans of data; however, it seems that we rarely have enough information." In turn, Olson (2003, p. 3) says that "data is the fuel we use to make decisions." These authors confirm the evidences that data influence decisions, being accuracy an important factor to be considered. Yet, Wang et al. (1995, p. 637) discuss what they consider to be essential for the improvement of data accuracy: "it is necessary to study the link between the poor quality of data and the procedures used to detect and eliminate problems." The research in the data quality area motivated the creation of the Total Data Quality Management (TDQM) at the Massachusetts Institute of Technology (MIT), a project that had its origin in the need of the industry for better indexes of data quality (Tdqm, 2008).

Seeking to contribute in the construction of "procedures to detect and eliminate problems in data quality" (Wang et al., 1995 p. 637), this paper proposes an approach for the improvement of data quality. This approach consists of processes of identification and correction of data, and is supported by indicators and control indexes. To support the research, a case study on the implementation of a production scheduling system in a meat company was used, through the measurement of the input and output data (information or results of the system).

The Brazilian meat-based food companies have led the country to the position of world leader in the export of this kind of product in the 2004 to 2007 period (Abef, 2008). The implementation of production scheduling systems in this type of companies allows the analyses of impact of the peculiarities inherent to the production environment of the meat-based food companies on the decisions on orders scheduling.

The developed approach and the results of its application were derived from a single case study. The study occurred in one of the largest Brazilian meat-based food companies, whose project for implementing the production scheduling and control system presented pitfalls, in part due to the lack of data quality.

The next section presents the theoretical framework necessary for the development of this work. Later, the methodological approach that led the study and supported its findings will be shown. Then, the case study and the proposed approach are discussed. Finally, conclusions, limitations and suggestions for further studies are presented.

THEORETICAL FRAMEWORK

Data quality has a close connection with the information quality. The concept of data quality is widespread in the literature according to its suitability for use, that is, the quality of the data is bound to answer a need (Tayi and Ballou, 1998; Helfert, 2001; Lee et al., 2006). Redman (2004) argues that data quality relates to "obtaining the right and proper data, in the right place and at the right time to accomplish a task" (Redman, 2004, p. 2).

Different methodologies were developed due to the need to treat data with the proper focus. Wang et al. (1995) highlight the importance of having methods that assist in the qualification of data as a way to prevent them from damaging the information generated for the decision-making process. In the scope of these methods, there are identification, analysis and data correction procedures. In addition, there are also the data measurement procedures.

Each one of the studies about data quality developed by Wang et al. (1995) proposes different dimensions (or categorizations) to analyse the quality of the data. Among the terms used, the *accuracy*, the *completeness*, the *consistency* and the degree of data updating (*timeliness*) stood out, and are detailed in Table 1.

The accuracy dimension is intertwined with data quality in terms of representing the level of conformity of the data in relation to its value in the real world. If a data is correct, it will be reliable for decision-making; therefore, its quality, which could be evaluated under other dimensions

Table 1. Dimensions of data quality.

Dimension	Description
Accuracy	It is the level of conformity of a data in relation to its value in the real world. An example of inaccuracy would be the ability of a machine in a database registered as 1,000 parts per hour, but which in reality can process up to 1,500 pieces per hour.
Completeness	It refers to the ratio between the existing and the necessary data. For example, the table of stocks in a database. If storage units lack in the database registration, the data will be incomplete; therefore, the completeness is low.
Consistency	It occurs when the representation of the data is the same in different sources. An example of consistent data is the ZIP (Postal Code) of a correspondence referring to the ZIP code of the destination of the same correspondence.
Updating degree	It refers to how much the data reflects its current value at the source where it was collected in relation to the moment when it should have been updated. An outdated data, for example, is a production batch of a product that is listed in the inventory system, but that in fact was dispatched to the final customer.

Source: Authors (2010).

sions, is evaluated according to its accuracy.

Olson (2002) adds the shape and the content of a data to the concept of accuracy, also pointing out some of the causes of inaccuracy: i) wrong values inserted into a database or on a report; ii) errors made by people who do not pay attention to the handling of the data; iii) confusing or contradictory screens or forms; iv) procedures that allow data not to be inserted or not registered within the deadline; v) procedures that promote the inclusion of erroneous data; and; vi) databases structured mistakenly.

According to Barchard and Pace (2011), to err is human. And human data entry can result in errors that ruin statistical results and conclusions. When humans do data entry, errors are therefore expected. Unfortunately, data entry errors can have devastating effects on research results. Simple data entry errors – such as typing an incorrect number, typing a number twice, or skipping a line – can ruin the results. Data entry errors can have serious effects on the results of a statistical analysis.

The incorrect input of data in a system has effects extremely harmful to the corporation. One such effect is the difference between the values of physical (reality) and system (virtual) stocks of a corporation. This ends up generating missing values and balances of finished products, raw materials, information, among others. These values have direct implications in the moment of decision-making in companies, as well as in corporate balance sheets.

An approach used in the attempt to improve the quality of the data is the TDQM (Total Data Quality Management).

The TDQM was developed with the aim of constructing theoretical foundations and methods that would contribute to the improvement of data quality (Tdqm, 2008).

This is a mixed approach, which combines the application of statistical (control charts, standard deviation, among others), technological (automatic validations of data errors identification, for example) and managerial methods (analysis techniques and data problem solution). The scope of the TDQM researches is divided into three components, which are detailed in Table 2.

In Table 2, it is possible to understand how the TDQM addresses the data quality issue, because the components proposed lead to a systematic view of the problem. The TDQM methodology is inspired in the Deming's Cycle of the Total Quality Management. Similar to the PDCA, instead of the known stages of *Plan*, *Do*, *Check* and *Act*, the TDQM cycle analogously contemplates the Set, Measure, Analyse, and Improve activities, respectively. TDQM's proposal, based on Wang (1998), is shown in Figure 2.

The "Set" stage of the TDQM cycle refers to the identification of data quality dimensions and the respective requirements that will be considered in a project. Later, in the "Measure" phase, metrics for the evaluation of data quality are developed. Based on the results of the measurements, the causes of errors in data are identified in the "Analyse" component. Finally, the "Improve" stage is characterized by data correction. In Figure 2, one can verify that the process must be continuous. This means that after the last improvement stage, it proceeds again to the set stage, resuming the cycle. Thus, a process of continuous data improvement is pursued. The methodological approach that guided the work is highlighted next.

METHODOLOGICAL APPROACH

In terms of its nature (Silva and Menezes, 2001), the present study is characterized as an applied research. It is so characterized

Table 2. Data quality research components.

Component	Characteristics
Definition of data quality	The theme research sustains itself in the study of the concept dimensions. Aspects such as the measurement of data quality and the support of algorithms for the identification of errors are studied in this component.
Analysis of the impact of data quality in organizations	The activities involve the comparison between the data quality and some key parameters identified in a company, such as customer satisfaction.
Improvement of data quality	The third component comprises methods for the improvement of data, which are divided into 4 categories: – Processes redesign: simplification and processes rationalization, in order to minimize the chances of data errors occurrence; – Motivation for the data quality: deals with rewards and benefits to employees for the purpose of sensitizing them on the handling of data; – Use of new technologies: automated techniques for data capturing and communication among systems; – Data interpretation technologies: assist employees in data capturing and imply the redesign of processes.

Source: Constructed from TDQM (2008).

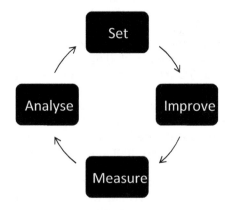

Figure 2. TDQM cycle. Source: constructed from Wang (1998).

considering the objective of generating knowledge for practical application aimed at solving specific problems. In terms of goals, several authors (Gil, 2007; Yin, 2004; Silva and Menezes, 2001; Vargas and Maldonado, 2001) classify researches as: i) descriptive; ii) exploratory; and; iii) explanatory. This research is characterized by an exploratory objective, since it aims to empirically construct and verify an approach to the improvement of data quality. Describing the nature of the existing problems in data quality, as well as the causal relations that imply the quality of the data, does not make part of the objective of this paper.

In this sense, according to the objective to which it was set, this study is characterized by the need of a qualitative approach. The objective is related to the specific environment where the construction and the implementation of the proposed approach occur. In situations with this configuration, several authors (Srivastava and Teo, 2006, Sobh and Perry, 2006; Amaratunga et al., 2002; Mangan et al., 2004; Neves, 1996; Godoy, 1995a, 1995b, 1995c) recommend the use of a qualitative approach.

Within the qualitative approach, there are different research methods, among which are the case studies (Godoy, 1995b). Case Study is a research method that is characterized by a thorough analysis of a given reality. According to Dubé and Paré (2003), Case Studies are appropriate when the object of research is complex, when it requires a vision of the whole and when the phenomenon in question cannot be analysed outside the context where it occurs. This research method is also appropriate in cases where a deeper study is necessary (Dubé and Paré, 2003; Einsenhardt, 1989). In addition, according to Ellram (1996), the Case Study can be used to: (1) explore a particular issue or problem, understanding it deeply; (2) explain a phenomenon; (3) describe a phenomenon; and; (4) predict its characteristics. Some of the purposes for using the Case Study described by Ellram (1996) justify the use of this method for this research.

Some procedures were established for conducting this work. These procedures are summarized in Figure 3. However, it is noteworthy to report that the present study covered the project design stage (pre-implementation) until the early months of the effective use of the developed production scheduling tool.

Initially, a wide review about production planning and scheduling concepts was carried out, since the system, which is the object of this research, consisted of the features of this area of knowledge. At the same time, the different existing methods for data qualification were analysed. After this review, the main methods, their characteristics and possible weaknesses were summarized. After that, it was possible to empirically verify how the data quailfication issue was being dealt with in the system being implemented. In addition, the implications of data quality on the information generated by the system under analysis was sought to be verified.

The first data collection instrument was made viable through the personal observation of the project team members of the production scheduling system. These observations had an open characteristic, since the researcher had permission to carry out the research inside the Alfa Company. On the Alfa Company's side, among the project team members, there were managers, professionals of the industrial, commercial and Information Technology areas, besides the key users of the production sequencing tool. In the implantation team, there were business consultants and systems analysts of the company that developed the production scheduling system.

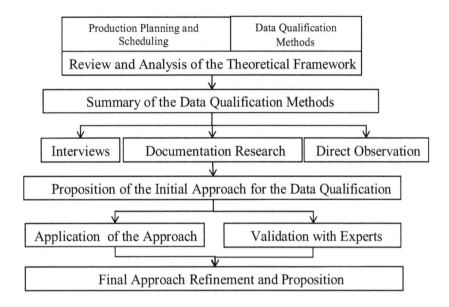

Figure 3. Work Method. Source: Authors (2010).

The second source of evidence (documents) was used to retrieve the information that was stored in printed or electronic media. Examples of this source are the electronic messages (emails), records of meetings, reports of the company that developed the system, tool guides (interface and operationalization) and the guides, prepared by the implementation team, of the procedures for identifying and solving data problems. Another instrument used to collect data during the application of the case study was the retrieval of diaries of the project. With them, it was possible to analyse the history of the system implementation, which enabled to identify, for example, the events that influenced the behavior of the indicators created for the information generated by the tool.

After collecting the information, it was possible to establish an initial approach to the data qualification. Two parallel procedures were adopted in order to allow a greater robustness of the approach. The first one was the implementation of the approach in a real situation during the tests of the system under development. The second procedure consisted of the explanation and validation of the proposed approach with different experts. It is noteworthy that, prior to the validation meetings, the project, strategies, critical success factors and flowcharts of the approach stages were sent to the experts. Table 3 briefly describes the experts who validated the research.

Finally, the initial approach was revised in light of the observation of the behavior that was presented in the application and of the contributions provided by the experts. Next, the case study and its results are presented.

CASE STUDY

In this section, the necessary information for understanding the case study is presented. Initially, the production system of the company is detailed; then, the structure of the data in the scheduling system researched is presented. Finally, an indicator used in the case study, as well as an analysis of the results will be shown.

The study was conducted in the Production Scheduling

and Control (PSC) area of one of the largest organizations of the meat industry in Brazil. This organization slaughters poultry, pigs and turkeys, and exports approximately 80% of its production. The company owns nearly a dozen slaughterhouses and factories of Industrialized meat-based products, in addition to other units of a verticalized structure (feed mills, hatcheries, farms, among others). Next, its production system is detailed.

Production scheduling systems

The company where the study was conducted has two types of productive systems in its factories. To facilitate the understanding, the V-A-T analysis of the Theory of Constraints (Cox III and Spencer, 2002) will be used. One of the productive systems is characterized by the divergence of the production processes (plants of the "V" type). This kind of organization has a small number of raw materials if compared to the number of end products generated (Cox III and Spencer, 2002). A slaughterhouse has a divergent manufacturing system, where poultry and pigs go through cutting processes until they are transformed into end products.

The other productive system is represented by the convergence of the manufacturing operations (plants of the "A" type), where a small number of end products is produced from a larger number of raw materials (Cox III and Spencer, 2002). The meat-based products (sausage, bologna, among others) are produced based on the formulation defined by the Research and Development (R&D) area, and are composed by raw meat and condiments.

The production scheduling system implemented was

Table 3. Experts and their qualifications.

S/N	Qualification
1	Bachelor's Degree in Marketing by Universidade Anhembi Morumbi and Graduate Degree in IT Governance by Instituto Mauá de Tecnologia. Experience as a consultant and in management and directorship positions in IT companies. Currently, is the Director of Data Quality Products in a Brazilian company that develops systems for this purpose.
2	Bachelor's Degree in Business Administration by Universidade de Caxias do Sul and 9-year experience in the PSC (Production Scheduling and Control) areas of two companies of the meat industry, having held the position of corporate management in both. Coordinated the implementation of an aggregated and optimized system for production and sales planning, and of a production scheduling tool, both for the meat industry.
3	Bachelor's Degree in Production Engineering by Universidade do Vale do Rio dos Sinos (UNISINOS) and Master's Degree student of the Graduate Program in Production Engineering and Systems at the same institution. Since the year 2003, works in the area of production and sales scheduling in the meat area, having worked at three companies of the industry in Brazil. During this period, participated in the implementation of an aggregated and optimized system for production and sales planning, and currently coordinates the demand management team of a Brazilian company in the area of meat-based foods. In that position, uses a system of production and sales planning.
4	Bachelor's Degree in Production Engineering by Universidade do Vale do Rio dos Sinos (UNISINOS) and Master's Degree in Production Engineering and Systems by the same institution. Professor in the Undergraduate Programs of Business Administration, Accounting, Production Management and in Graduate Programs at Feevale. Professor in the Logistics Technological Program at UNISINOS. Business and consultancy experience in the Management of Productive and Quality Systems, implantation of Production Planning and Scheduling systems and in projects of Modeling, Optimization and Systemic Thinking in companies of the poultry, metal-mechanic, oil and automotive industries.
5	Bachelor's Degree in Mechanical-Aeronautical Engineering by ITA and Master's Degree in Electrical Engineering by UNICAMP. Has 15 years of experience in the development of decision support systems for the optimization of decision-making processes of Supply Chains (Supply Chain Management). Is Partner-Stockholder of a company in Brazil that is reference in the development and implantation of production scheduling systems for the meat industry.
6	Bachelor's Degree in Business Administration by Instituição Educacional São Judas Tadeu, Master's Degree in Business Administration by University of Vale do Rio dos Sinos (UNISINOS) and Ph.D. in Production Engineering by COPPE/UFRJ. Has experience in the Management area, with emphasis in Production Management, working especially on the following topics: Business Process Engineering, Theory of Constraints, Costs, Strategy.

Source: Authors (2010).

endowed of its own heuristic sequencing; therefore, not optimizing. This heuristic was defined together with the representatives of the Production Planning area of the company. The structuring of the system, from the information need point of view, included the development of three modules: planning, order tracking and scheduling. The planning module encompasses the production plans for the factories, the raw material requirements, the purchase and consumption of material, the transfers between units and the occupation of productive resources.

9The order tracking module consists on the display of: i) the stage at which the orders are (approved or not by the corporative PSC area); ii) the backlog; and; iii) the adherences (comparison between the delivery date requested by the customer and the dispatch date of the order).

Finally, the scheduling module is characterized by allowing the quotation of the delivery date for the customers, as a "Promise to Order" system. This process is performed prior to the confirmation (or not) of the order, since the date suggested by the system is submitted to the evaluation of the corporative Production Planning area and the customer.

In order for the production scheduling system to work properly, there is a dependency of the data input. In this sense, a global and integrated view of the data used for the operation of the production scheduling system will be presented next.

The structuring of data in the system

Table 4 presents the groups of data that were collected to be updated in the database of the production scheduling

Table 4. Description of the data groups in the production scheduling system.

	Description
Registration	It aggregates the data used for the structuring or modeling of other data groups; therefore, it is basic for the system to function. Example: an order may be composed by the registration data of a country, customer and product.
Slaughters	It comprises the data related to the animals that generate the end products or raw materials through the product structures (the bill of materials, also called cutting trees, which represent the "dismantling" of animals). Among these data, the slaughter scales inform the type of animal to be slaughtered (chicken, turkey or pig), its weight band, the factory where the slaughter will be done, the date, the shift and the number of animals.
Industrial	It represents the data that are collected in the productive area of the company and which are related to the products and raw materials. Examples: cutting trees, productive resources (bottlenecks and other constraints) and work schedules.
Commercial	It comprises the data related to the volumes of confirmed orders and to the demand forecast by market and product. The function of these data is to direct the decisions of the PSC system for the programming of the end products in the factories, as well as of the raw materials, as they are demanded according to the need of the formulated production (sausages, for example).
Logistic	It is composed of the data related to product transportation and storage of supplies and products. In the transportation case, times and permissions of product transfers between factories are considered, as well as storage facilities and boarding points (dry port, seaport and airport). Meanwhile, the data related to the storage include product and supply stocks in the factories, as well as storage capabilities.

Source: Authors (2010).

tool. The registration data, in addition to being inserted into the system, have a relationship with the other groups of data. The insertion of the data from the other groups depends on the availability of the registration data. Once all these data are populated in the database, the system uses them in the processing, which generates information for decision-making (production plans).

The approach applied in the case

After researching the population of the production scheduling system database in a project environment, the tests of the tool began. The project team concluded that it was necessary to adopt analysis, identification and data error correction procedures. This need was due to the existing inconsistencies between the information generated by the system and the real data of a particular selected period. The adoption of indicators and a checklist were proposed to identify data errors in the case the results did not achieve the goals set, which were determined by the high management of the company.

One of the indicators used was the planned slaughter (Figure 4), which represented the percentage of the total volume of poultry and pig (kg) planned by the system in relation to the volume (kg) actually produced by the company. The indicator covered the planning horizon

(three months) of all factories. The main idea was to visualize the metric behavior in a global dimension, instead of using it separated for each production plant or in a short term (days or weeks, for example). This indicator was established for representing the beginning of the process of generating the end products; therefore, basic for further analyses (such as orders planning, for example).

In Figure 4, it can be verified that in most part of the period in which the indicator was measured, the results did not reach the goal and remained unstable. Throughout the whole period, a checklist (Table 5) was proposed for the identification and correction of data errors if the results did not reach the goal. With the support of this checklist, errors were identified according to the results of the total global slaughter indicator shown in Figure 4.

The checklist was created based on the problems encountered in the data migrated from the legacy systems of the company, as well as on the data registered by the team that worked on the project. In the case of data, there were cases where the wrong data was collected at source (e. g the measurement capacities of machines in the factory) and situations in which, after collecting the data correctly, wrong data were registered in the system during the typing process. Therefore, the team concluded that an approach to improve the accuracy of data should begin with these issues. Four focus points were chosen

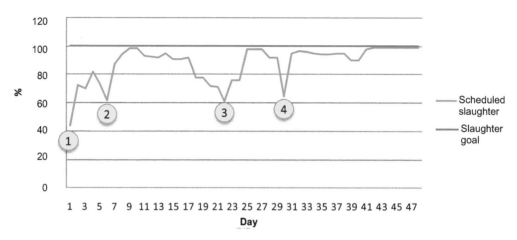

Figure 4. Indicator of the total global slaughter. Source: Authors (2010).

Table 5. Checklist for the identification and correction of data errors.

S/N	What to analyse
1	- Check if there are resources (machines, for example) without a calendar, which makes it unviable for the system to generate the production plans. The calendar sets the net available time of the resource in each day and shift of the week.
2	- Check if the orders (clients' needs) were loaded without any error in the part numbers, quantities, delivery dates, etc.
3	- Check if the unit weights registered for the animals are correct.
4	- Check if there are resources with an occupancy greater than or equal to 99%. In this case, the resource should be identified, as well as the day and the shift in which the problem occurs. - Check if the available times in the shifts are correct (calendar registration). - Analyse the products that are consuming the resource. - Check the bill of material of the product.

Source: Authors (2010).

to analyse the metric.

At point 1 in Figure 4, it was identified that there were productive resources saturated or close to this level (occupancy of 95 to 100%). Data errors were found in the registration of shifts of some resources calendars, which were corrected. At points 2 and 3, it was verified that there were errors in the bill of materials. Finally, at point 4, a malfunction in the production scheduling system was identified. Unlike the initial perception, in fact, there were data errors that took the software to a bug. It was identified an error in the bill of materials where the same product was registered in the system with a convergent and a divergent structures, which made the system go into loop and thus the output data differed from reality.

Based on the knowledge acquired during the measurement, it was diagnosed that the analysis should be improved by detailing the steps, focusing on the input data that most influenced the output data (slaughter planning); also, the analysis should be done in a

sequence that could optimize the analysis and correction of the data.

In other words, after applying the checklist shown in Table 5, it was realized that a deepen detailing of the items to be checked was necessary (analyzing the planning of the production plants, for example). Furthermore, it was concluded that the analysis should be done in a sequence, starting from the analysis of the output data and going through the accuracy of the groups of data (those on Table 4). This expanded list is shown in Table 6.

Next, the proposed approach for data accuracy is presented.

Proposal of an approach for the improvement of data accuracy

Given the learning acquired in the case and the

Table 6. Expanded checklist for the identification and correction of data errors.

S/N	What to analyse
1	Generate a listing of the planned volumes and of the slaughter goals, by type of animal and factory.
2	Sort the list in a descending order of the absolute differences between the projected and the planned volumes, prioritizing the analysis of the major differences.
3	For each selected difference, identify in which factory, animal and cutting tree the difference occurred.
4	Check if the cutting tree in analysis is habilitated for the factory.
5	Check if the unit weight of the animal in analysis is correct.
6	Check if there are resources without a calendar, which makes it unviable for the system to generate the production plans.
7	Analyse the product "dismantling" structure (cutting trees).
8	Check if the orders have been loaded from the legacy system which stores that information.
9	Generate a list of all orders, in which it is possible to visualize the amount requested in the order and the order volume programmed by the system.
10	Sort the list in a descending order of the absolute differences between the allocated and the requested amount in orders, prioritizing the analysis of the major differences.
11	For every selected order, analyse the following situations: • Check if the amounts requested for the products of the order are consistent with the reality. • Check if the products of the order are habilitated in the factories that can produce them in reality.
12	Analyse the resources occupancy: • Check if there are resources with an occupancy greater than or equal to 99%. In this case, the resource should be identified, as well as the day and the shift in which the problem occurs. • Check if the available hours in the shift are correct (calendar registration). • Analyse the products that are consuming the resource.

Source: Authors (2010).

knowledge gained through the theoretical framework, the conditions for proposing an approach for the improvement of the data accuracy in the system studied were established. A preview of this model was then submitted to the evaluation of the experts, whose skills were displayed in Table 3. The final version of the approach, presented in Figure 5, was prepared based on the experts' contributions and their validation of the proposal.

In addition to the use of checklists and a metric to measure the quality of the slaughter data, other points must be listed as learnings during the case study. First of all, there must be a premise that data must be entered in the tool with accuracy – the software should not run until it is guaranteed a minimum data quality, with the previous identification of outliers, for example. The model proposes the application of metrics in the input data, and not only

for the output data, as done in the case study. On the other hand, the results after the run of the software (output data) should also be submitted to the measurement to make sure that the information will be in accordance with reality.

In Figure 5, it is verified the use of the control indexes. These correspond to the metrics that are applied to the data before the system's processing, unlike the indicators, which are verified based on the information (output data) generated by the tool's processing. It is noteworthy that a premise of the approach is that there will be no errors when importing data into the system.

Another learning, which is not shown in Figure 5, but facilitates the analysis of the results of the software, is the load of the input data gradually. These data were presented as mentioned earlier in the previous section

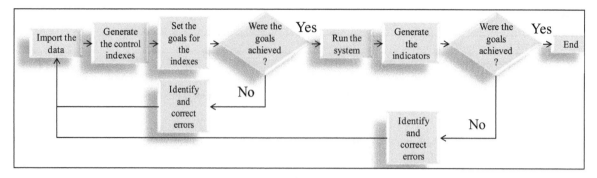

Figure 5. Approach for the improvement of the data accuracy of a production scheduling system for the meat industry. Source: Authors (2010).

Table 7. Detailing of the identification and correction of errors based on the results of the stock average occupancy indicator.

S/N	What to analyse
1	Create a list in which it is possible to visualize the products and the respective volumes planned for the stock over the horizon.
2	Select the planned stocks in the last day of the planning horizon.
3	Sort the list in a descending order of the differences between the stock planned volumes and the maximum level considered consistent with the reality of the company.
4	For each product selected for analysis, the following situations should be verified: - Verify if the initial stock of the product is correct. - Verify if the data of the firm orders and of the demand forecast are correct. - Verify if the orders and the demand forecasts are being properly planned by the system. If not, analyse the product structures and the manufacturing routings. - Verify the permissions and the transportation times for the boarding points.

Source: Authors (2010).

and should be loaded in a predetermined sequence and in different cycles, cumulatively. The sequence was defined based on the dependency relationship among the data, which is linked to the architecture of the software database.

The stages in Figure 5 represent the generic model of the proposal, since all the flow should be applied to each data grouping in the following order: i) registration data; ii) logistical data; iii) commercial data; iv) product structures; and; v) manufacturing routes. It is important to highlight that the data should not be tested individually, but cumulatively – in other words, the commercial data will be validated while the registration and logistics data will remain populated in the database system after having been submitted to their specific control indexes

In the scope of the proposal, there are also a number of sub-processes for each data group (shown in Table 4), which in turn contain the details of the necessary steps to implement each stage of the flow. An example of a sub-process is shown in Table 7.

Next, the conclusions and recommendations for future studies are presented.

CONCLUSIONS AND RECOMMENDATIONS FOR FUTURE STUDIES

Based on the research carried out, this article pointed out the data quality problem and the advantages obtained by adopting a methodological approach to improve the quality of the data used in a production scheduling system of a meat product company. The results achieved in the case presented, despite of being a direct consequence of the use of a checklist for the identification of data errors, were also supported by the indicators generated on the information of the system. Therefore, the contribution of the indicators is not only in regards to the improvement of the data accuracy, but also on the understanding of the status of a systems implementation project. They point out the possible discrepancies or anomalies – and if there were no indicators, all data should be checked at all times, activity which would be expensive in any situation.

The application of indicators and the use of the control indexes refer the proposed approach to the flow of the input-transformation-output model. Thus, both ends of the process are contemplated. Furthermore, the logic of the database population in an orderly manner, differently from all data groups at the same time, leads to the use of the Parsimony Principle, contributing for certain factors that impact the results of the system to be better identified and corrected.

The measurement of data complements the subjective analysis that is always needed in any situation. It also helps to show how close or far we are from the desired state (that is consistent in terms of scheduling).

The checklist provides a guide for the analysis, but it should be flexible in face of the variables of planning and control. It is important to know when a control index verifies the resources capacities; one should consider all the issues that surround them, in a broad sense, being open to the possibility of finding different results in the reality. Sometimes, it may be possible that they are consistent and the reference metrics used by the company in fact have some divergence of measurement and analysis.

The challenge is to identify the cause of an error and take preventive measures so that the problem does not recur, as well as opportunities for improvement arising from the analysis to avoid the appearance of other errors not occurred so far. In other words, the search for the cause of data errors can enable to identify opportunities to improve the accuracy of data.

The operationalization of this challenge is to adopt techniques of analysis, identification and correction of data errors, which in this study pointed to the metrics as the central point, and beside the checklist for error checking and sequential data loads, among other techniques presented in this study.

In terms of future studies on this article's theme, the implementation of the proposal could be made at another company in the same area in which the research was conducted, so that the robustness of the approach could be evaluated. Another study possibility would be the development of an array of metrics for the data and information considered important in the meat industry, initiative that would not be limited to localized issues, but would provide a global view of the data accuracy.

REFERENCES

Abef (2008). Exportação mundial de carne de frango – principais países. União Brasileira de Avicultura. Available at: <http://www.abef.com.br/noticias_portal/exibenoticia.php?notcodigo=74>. Accessed: 23 feb.

Amaratunga D, Baldry D, Sarshar M, Newton R (2002). Quatitative and Qualitative Research in the built environment: application of "mixed" research approach, Work Study, Emerald 51(1):17-31.

Barchard KA, Pace AL (2011). Preventing human error: The impact of data entry methodson data accuracy and statistical results. Comput. Hum. Behav. pp.1834-1839.

Cox III JF, Spencer MS (2002). Manual da Teoria das Restrições. Porto Alegre: Bookman.

Dubé L, Paré G (2003). Rigor in Information Systems Positivist Case Research: Current Practices, Trends and Recommendations, MIS Quart. 27(4):597-635.

Einsenhardt KM (1989). Building theories from case study research. Academy of Management Review. Stanford 14:532-550.

Ellram LM (1996). The use of the case study method in logistics research. Journal of Business Logistics. Arizona 17(2):93-138.

Gil AC (2007). Métodos e técnicas de pesquisa social. São Paulo: Atlas.

Godoy AS (1995a). Introdução à Pesquisa Qualitativa e suas possibilidades, RAE–Revista de Administração de Empresas 35(2):65-71.

Godoy AS (1995b). Pesquisa Qualitativa – Tipos Fundamentais, RAE – Revista de Administração de Empresas 35(3):20-29.

Godoy AS (1995c). A Pesquisa Qualitativa e seu uso em Administração de Empresas, RAE – Revista de Administração de Empresas 35(4):65-71.

Goldratt EM (1991). A síndrome do palheiro: garimpando informações num oceano de dados. São Paulo: IMAM.

Helfert M (2001). Managing and measuring data quality in data warehousing. Proceedings of the World Multiconference on Systemics, Cybernetics and Informatics.

Lee YW, Pipino LI, Funk JD, Wang RY (2006). Journey to Data Quality. Boston: MIT Press.

Mangan J, Chandra L, Bernanrd G (2004). Combining quantitative and qualitative methodologies in logistics research, Int. J. Phys. Distrib. Logist. Manage., Emerald 34(7):565-578.

Neves JL (1996). Características, usos e possibilidades. Caderno de Pesquisas em Administração, Pesquisa Qualitativa 1(3):1-5.

Olson J (2003). Data quality: the accuracy dimension. San Francisco: Morgan Kaufmann.

Olson J (2002). Data accuracy: the challenge, DM Review Magazine. Available at: <http://www.dmreview.com/dmdirect/20021108/6019-1.html> Accessed: 20 may 2008.

Redman TC (2004). Data: an unfolding quality disaster. DM Review Magazine. Available at: <http://www.dmreview.com/issues/20040801/1007211-1.html> Accessed: 20 may 2008.

Silva E, Menezes EM (2001) Metodologia da Pesquisa e Elaboração de Dissertação. 3. ed., Florianópolis: UFSC Distance Learning Laboratory.

Sobh R, Perry C (2006). Research design and data analysis in realism research, Eur. J. Mark. Emerald 40(11/12):1194-1209.

Srivastava SC, Teo TSH (2006). Understanding, Assessing and Conducing Interpretative Management Research. IIMB Management Review, Bangalore, June.

Tayi GK, Ballou DP (1998) Examining Data Quality. Commun. ACM 41(2):54-57, February.

Tdqm (2008). What is Tdqm. Total Data Quality Management. Available at: <http://web.mit.edu/tdqm/www/about.shtml>. Accessed: 12 apr 2008.

Vargas L, Maldonado G (2001). Guia para apresentação de trabalhos científicos. 3. ed., Porto Alegre: Business Administration Graduate Program – PPGA/UFRGS.

Wang RY (1998). A product perspective on Total Data Quality Management. Commun. ACM 41(2):58-65.

Wang RY, Storey VC, Firth CP (1995). A framework for analysis of data quality research. IEEE Trans. Knowl. Data Eng. 7(4):623-640.

8

Benefits of internet financial reporting in a developing countries: Evidence from Malaysia

Mohd Noor Azli Ali Khan[1] , Noor Azizi Ismail[2] and Norhayati Zakuan[1]

[1]Department of Management, Faculty of Management and Human Resource Development, Universiti Teknologi Malaysia, Johor Bahru, Johor, Malaysia.
[2]College of Business, Universiti Utara Malaysia, Sintok, Kedah, Malaysia.

The use of the internet as a new platform for dissemination of corporate information is a recent, fast growing phenomenon and is expanding rapidly. Corporate information includes records of historical and financial data, descriptions of activities, information of the company, exposition of current situation and future plans, etc., that can be in multiple formats via website. Most early Internet Financial Reporting (IFR) research are either descriptive studies and exploratory in nature, or association studies addressing the determinants of IFR. IFR is known as new medium and technology which has been introduced in the area of financial reporting or disclosure. However, little attention has been given to investigate the attitudes and preferences of preparers of financial information especially in the Malaysian context. Therefore, this paper focuses on investigating the perceptions of preparers of financial information by using a survey mailed questionnaire. The findings of this study suggested three main benefits to companies that engage in IFR: attract foreign investors, promote company to the public, and attract local investors. The findings also revealed that three main benefits to the users who collect financial information of companies via their website are: increases timeliness and efficiency in obtaining financial information, helps users in the decision making process and provides another medium of disclosure. In conclusion, this study makes a positive contribution to enhancing our knowledge of IFR and disclosure practices in emerging capital markets, and provides a basis for the conduct of future research.

Key words: Benefit, preparers, financial statements, internet financial reporting, Malaysia.

INTRODUCTION

Accounting disclosure, financial reporting and information plays an important role in individual and corporate decision making. In particular, a fundamental use of accounting information is to help investors make an effective decision concerning their investment portfolios (Elsayed and Hoque, 2010). Otherwise, the internet has become one of investors' most frequently used sources of information and many companies are now reporting all or part of their financial information on their websites (Hindi and Rich, 2010). In the internet era, many listed companies have decided to use internet as a communication tool for investors' relations (Pervan and Sabljic, 2011). The internet is a technology with the power to revolutionise external reporting and is becoming increasingly important for financial reporting (Jones and Xiao, 2004). The internet provides a unique form of corporate voluntary disclosure that enables companies to provide information instantaneously to global audience (Abdelsalam et al., 2007). The internet also enables organizations to disclose information on real-time basis and increase the accessibility of both financial and non-financial information (Bollen et al., 2008). The internet revolution has altered the traditional flow of accounting, auditing and accountability information to various interest groups (Khadaroo, 2005).

The practice of disseminating business information in a digital format is spreading around the world (Bonson et

*Corresponding author. E-mail: m-nazli@utm.my.

al., 2006) and becoming a very important part of business information services (Liu, 2000). It is a unique information disclosure tool that encourages flexible forms of presentation and allows immediate, broad, and inexpensive communication to investors (Kelton and Yang, 2008). Technological advancement has made the internet a useful, timely and cost-effective tool for communication of financial information to stakeholders (Mohamed et al., 2009).

Many studies investigate the potential effect of using the internet in disclosing information on the corporate website (Ezat and El-Masry, 2008). Despite the growing usage of the internet in financial markets by companies, academic research into the use of the internet in financial disclosure is still in its infancy stage in developing countries such as Malaysia (Hassan et al., 1999; Ismail and Tayib, 2000; Khadaroo, 2005; Al Arussi et al., 2009). While considerable attentions has been given to internet financial reporting (IFR), research over the last decade, little attention has been given by researchers to investigate the relationship between corporate behaviour and the attitudes and preferences of preparers of IFR, especially in the context of Malaysia (Khan and Ismail, 2009). Lack of studies on factors influencing perceptions on IFR prompted the need for such a study, especially in a non-Anglo-American environment. Therefore, this study attempts to fill the gap in our knowledge of this subject by investigating the perceptions of preparers of financial information and to elicit their views about the benefits, advantages and disadvantages of IFR.

PREVIOUS RESEARCH

A comprehensive review of existing literature on IFR indicates a significant evolution of IFR research. IFR is a new technology which has been introduced in the area of financial reporting or disclosure (Moradi et al., 2011). The evolution of IFR research can be categorized into four research themes; classification of IFR, descriptive studies, association studies and dimension of IFR (Ali Khan and Ismail, 2008). Otherwise, on top of the statement produced by professional bodies, there were also numerous empirical studies that serve as evidence to the phenomena.

There have been a growing number of empirical studies on IFR since 1995 reflecting the growth in this form of information dissemination (Davey and Homkajohn, 2004). IFR is an attractive and fast growing research topic (Oyelere et al., 2003; Xiao et al., 2005). IFR is a new and wide research area (Moradi et al., 2011), become a focus of urgent investigation at international level (Al-Htaybat, 2011) and important and interesting agenda to be investigated (Ali Khan and Ismail, 2011).

A lot of IFR researches have emerged over the last decade. The earliest studies were produced in 1996 and

1997, only a year after the global and corporate interest in Internet as an advertising medium began (Allam and Lymer, 2003). In general, the IFR literature can be classified into two themes; (1) the practices of companies using the internet for financial reporting purposes and as an investor relations communication strategy, and (2) the determinants of web-based disclosure policy choice (Joshi and Al-Modhahki, 2003). Furthermore, IFR research can be divided into several themes: descriptive research, comparative research and explanatory research (Pervan, 2006; Abdelsalam et al., 2007).

In contrast to traditional printed reports, the internet offers many more opportunities to communicate financial information and its importance in this respect is rapidly increasing (Pirchegger and Wagenhofer, 1999). Corporate websites are designed for multiple reasons, to advertise firms' products, to facilitate electronic commerce, to promote brand identification, to attract potential employees, and to enhance corporate image (Lybaert, 2002). The advantages of the internet for financial reporting are its cost, speed, dynamism, and flexibility (Lymer, 1999). IFR can be cost effective, fast, flexible in format and accessible to all users within and beyond national boundaries (Haniffa and Rashid, 2004). The last five years have witnessed a growth in the number of companies adopting IFR. Indeed, IFR is one of the fast growing phenomenon (Ashbaugh et al., 1999; Oyelere et al., 2003; Mohamed et al., 2009). IFR has become a focus of urgent investigation at the international level (Al-Htaybat, 2011). The development of IFR practice has been rapid, largely mirroring, and motivated by, the development of the World Wide Web (WWW) since 1994, being the primary internet medium for IFR (Allam and Lymer, 2003).

The disclosure of corporate information via the Internet is attracting the attention not only of various accounting bodies but also researchers. In recent years, the principal accountancy bodies have conducted several studies analysing the possible repercussions of corporate reporting practices on the accounting profession (Bonson and Escobar, 2006). Several professional studies in the US, UK and Canada have also examined the status of IFR. These include the Institute of Chartered Accountants in England and Wales (ICAEW) (Spaul, 1997), the International Accounting Standard Committee (IASC), now the International Accounting Standards Board (IASB) (Lymer et al., 1999), Canadian Institute of Chartered Accountants (CICA) (Trites, 1999), and the U.S. Financial Accounting Standards Board (FASB) (FASB, 2000, 2001).

Furthermore, the digital distribution of accounting information has also been studied intensively by researchers in recent years (Bonson and Escobar, 2006). IFR practices have been the focus of a number of academic studies in many countries, for example US (Petravick and Gillett, 1996; Ashbaugh et al., 1999; Ettredge et al., 2001), UK (Lymer, 1997; Marston and Leow, 1998; Craven and Marston, 1999; Abdelsalam et al., 2007), Japan (Marston, 2003), New Zealand (McDonald and Lont, 2001; Oyelere et al., 2003) and Ireland (Brennan and Hourigan, 1998; Abdelsalam and El-Masry, 2008). Several studies have also examined the relationship between the specific characteristics of firms and IFR (Ashbaugh et al., 1999; Craven and Marston, 1999; Hassan et al., 1999; Pirchegger and Wagenhofer, 1999; Bonson and Escobar, 2002; Debreceny et al., 2002; Allam and Lymer, 2003; Joshi and Al-Modhahki, 2003; Oyelere et al., 2003; Marston and Polei, 2004; Xiao et al., 2004; Chan and Wickramasinghe, 2006; Barako et al., 2008; Kelton and Yang, 2008; Ezat and El-Masry, 2008; Al Arussi et al., 2009). The growing use of the internet for corporate dissemination, including providing annual reports on the internet, and the extent and sophistication of IFR practices, vary across countries (Mohamed et al., 2009).

While numerous studies have examined the status and determinants of IFR, only a few have focused on the timeliness issue which is an important part of IFR (Pirchegger and Wagenhofer, 1999; Ettredge et al., 2002; Abdelsalam and Street, 2007). Timeliness is crucial as users are demanding more timely information (Fisher et al., 2004). It is even more important as shorter delays are often associated with greater profitability. Unfortunately, many companies tend to focus more on the user support and information content than timeliness and technology (Davey and Homkajohn, 2004).

More importantly, studies on the perceptions of IFR from the preparers' perspectives are very limited compared to those of traditional reporting. One exception is a study by Joshi and Al-Modhahki (2003). They found 'global reach and mass communication', 'timeliness and updateability' and 'interaction and feedback' as important advantages of IFR, while 'security problems' and 'authentication, attestation and legal impediments' as important disadvantages of IFR.

Although, interest in this topic has clearly increased in recent years, little attention has been given by researcher to study IFR and companies in the developing countries. For example, in Malaysia, perception studies on the benefits of IFR are still lacking. To the best of our knowledge, only a few studies have examined the perception and attitudes of interested parties especially preparers of financial information in relation to IFR.

RESEARCH DESIGN

The aim of this study is to examine and document the perception of preparers of financial information towards the benefits, advantages and disadvantages of IFR. For this purpose, data were collected via survey questionnaire. In designing the questionnaire, comments and feedback from postgraduate students and academics were elicited in an endeavour to ensure that questions were clear and precise. Early draft of the questionnaire was pre-tested by two PhD accounting students, six accounting lecturers at Universiti Teknologi Malaysia and Universiti Utara Malaysia. Based on their feedback, some modifications were made to the wording of some questions

and some less important questions were deleted to reduce the length of the questionnaire.

The target preparers of IFR are chief financial officer (CFO), finance manager and accountants. CFO, finance managers or accountants of the public companies listed on the main board represented the preparers. CFOs were chosen because they are the senior executives who are responsible for both accounting and financial operations (Jiambalvo, 2004). CFO possesses an edge because of their financial acumen and their ability to dissect and explain the business's financials (Izma, 2010). CFO is the member of a management team that would typically be associated with the development of the corporate annual report and be in a position to comment on what influence the decision to disclose (Wilmshurst and Frost, 2000). CFO has a good knowledge regarding the disclosure practice in their companies and actively involved in preparing financial statements or annual reports (Ho and Wong, 2003). These individuals also have the necessary knowledge and competency regarding IFR matters (Ho and Wong, 2003; Mohd Isa, 2006). CFO and accountants are selected because they have the knowledge, competency and understanding of such preparation (Ku Ismail and Chandler, 2007). Accountants have been instrumental in imposing an increasingly rigid and pervasive structure of regulation (Gowthorpe, 2000). Accountants' roles as gatekeepers, interpreters and beneficiaries of the accounting process have significant influence in shaping reality (Morgan, 1988). The respondents were asked to indicate their opinions on a five-point scale in terms of strongly disagree to strongly agree.

Since this paper is exploratory in nature, a preliminary study is conducted to preliminary determine the respondent perceptions. A sample of this study consists of 450 respondents (preparers of public listed companies in Bursa Malaysia). The sample size satisfies the rule of thumb proposed by Roscoe (1975) as noted by Sekaran (2003). Sekaran noted Roscoe as suggesting that, among others, a sample size larger than 30 and less than 500 is appropriate for most research, with a minimum number of sub-sample sizes of 30 for each category is necessary.

The data were collected during the month of July to October 2008. Each respondent received a marked questionnaire (for tracking purposes) together with a letter outlining the objective of the research, respondent confidentiality, and availability of survey result upon request, as well as a stamped addressed enveloped. The questionnaire was sent to elicit their opinion on benefits, advantages and disadvantages of reporting financial information on the Internet. A total of 68 completed questionnaires were returned, representing 15.11% response rate. CFOs and accountants are busy people and are generally unwilling to participate in survey studies (Ho and Wong, 2001); the low response rates (between 10 and 20%) were in line with the expectation of this study. PricewaterhouseCoopers (2002) reported that the average response rate for postal surveys in Malaysia is around 16% and the ample response rate for a questionnaire survey is 15 to 20% (Staden, 1998).

The questionnaire consists of two parts. Part one covers the demographic profile of the respondents pertaining to general background information such as gender, age, education level and position. Part two consists of the respondent's perceptions toward benefits, advantages and disadvantages of IFR. The properties of the questionnaires have been thoroughly tested for its content and validity. The data collected are then analysed and summarised. The results of the analysis are presented and discussed further.

RESULTS

Table 1 presents a brief profile of the respondents. A total of 68 respondents participated in this study. The results

Table 1. Profile of respondent.

Demographic	Item	Frequency	%
Gender	Male	46	67.6
	Female	22	32.4
Race	Bumiputera	24	35.3
	Non-bumiputera	44	64.7
Academic certification	Diploma	3	4.4
	Degree / Professional	49	72.1
	Masters/PhD	16	23.5
Occupation	Chief financial officer	36	52.9
	Finance manager	21	30.9
	Accountants	11	16.2

show that about 53% of the respondents are CFOs while the remaining are finance managers and accountants. Two-third of the respondents were male. Majority of the respondents are non-bumiputera. Almost all respondents have at least a degree or a professional qualification.

As presented in Table 2, the results indicate that 'attract foreign investors', 'promote company more widely to the public', 'attract local investors', 'provide wider coverage compared to the traditional form of annual reports', 'promote transparency' 'attract potential customers', 'discharge accountability' and 'enhance managerial efficiency' as the main benefits of IFR to the company (mean > 3.50). Almost all items can be categorized as the main benefits of IFR to the company. Table 2 show that over 75% of the respondents either agree or strongly agree that such policy benefits the companies because they are able to attract foreign investors, promote company more widely to the public, attract local investors, provide wider coverage compared to the traditional form of annual reports and promote transparency compared to the traditional form of annual reports. Thus, it can be deduced, from the perspective of preparers of financial information in companies, disclosure of financial information via the website is an alternative medium for communicating with their major stakeholders, namely customers and investors.

As shown in Table 3, the results show 'increase timeliness and efficiency in obtaining financial information', 'helps users in the decision making process', 'provides another medium of disclosure', 'provides information for company inexpensively', 'provides accessibility to the users' and 'makes investment decision process easier and faster' as the main benefits of IFR to the company (mean > 3.50). Table 3 show that over 75% of the respondents either agree or strongly disagree that such policy benefits the users because they are able to increase timeliness and efficiency in obtaining financial information, help users in the decision making process,

provide another medium of disclosure, provide information for company inexpensively and provide accessibility to the users. In general, the respondents' perception shows that all the items are the benefits of IFR to the company (mean > 3.50).

A further analysis was carried out to investigate the perceptions of preparers of financial information toward the advantages and disadvantages of IFR. These items were extracted from various literatures (Wallman, 1995; Green and Spaul, 1997; Lymer and Tallberg, 1997; Joshi and Al-Modhahki, 2003). The perceptions were elicited using a Likert scale ranging from 1 (Strongly disagreed) to 5 (Strongly agreed). The results in Table 4 show that respondents perceived 'global reach and mass communication', and 'timeliness and updateability' as the two most important advantages from financial reporting on the Internet. This finding is consistent with others works (Joshi and Al-Modhahki, 2003). In general, the respondents' perception shows that all the items are the advantages of IFR (mean > 3.50). As can be seen, the results in Table 4 show that respondents perceived 'security problems' as the most important disadvantages of placing financial information on the Internet. This result is similar to the findings of Joshi and Al-Modhahki (2003).

Additional finding

We also gave open ended question to the respondent to obtain their opinion on IFR in Malaysia. The result can be classified into four main themes which are expressed by the respondents:

General

"It is easy to get the annual report but the information should be more complete" CFO 1.
"The IFR practices in Malaysia are focusing more on the

Table 2. Benefits to the company.

Item	Strongly disagree		Disagree		Neutral		Agree		Strongly agree		Total		Mean	Std. Dev.
	No.	%	No.	%	No.	%	No.	%	No.	%	No.	%		
Attract foreign investors					13	19.1	29	42.6	26	38.2	68	100	4.19 (1)	0.738
Promote company more wider to the public			3	4.4	8	11.8	33	48.5	24	35.3	68	100	4.15 (2)	0.797
Attract local investors					10	14.7	42	61.8	16	23.5	68	100	4.09 (3)	0.617
Provide wider coverage	1	1.5			12	17.6	34	50.0	21	30.9	68	100	4.09 (3)	0.787
Promote transparency			2	2.9	15	22.1	32	47.1	19	27.9	68	100	4.00 (5)	0.792
Attract potential customers			1	1.5	19	27.9	36	52.9	12	17.6	68	100	3.87 (6)	0.710
Discharge accountability	1	1.5	5	7.4	15	22.1	33	48.5	14	20.6	68	100	3.79 (7)	0.907
Enhance managerial efficiency	1	1.5	7	10.3	21	30.9	28	41.2	11	16.2	68	100	3.60 (8)	0.933
Improve financial performance	2	2.9	8	11.8	27	39.7	21	30.9	10	14.7	68	100	3.43 (9)	0.982

Table 3. Benefits to users.

Item	Disagree		Neutral		Agree		Strongly agree		Total		Mean	Std. Dev.
	No.	%	No.	%	No.	%	No.	%	No.	%		
Increase timeliness and efficiency in obtaining financial information			14	20.6	33	48.5	21	30.9	68	100	4.10 (1)	0.715
Helps users in the decision making process			15	22.1	33	48.5	20	29.4	68	100	4.07 (2)	0.719
Provides another medium of disclosure	1	1.5	11	16.2	41	60.3	15	22.1	68	100	4.03 (3)	0.668
Provides information for company, inexpensively	4	5.9	14	20.6	28	41.2	22	34.4	68	100	4.00 (4)	0.881
Provides accessibility to the users	1	1.5	16	23.5	35	51.5	16	23.5	68	100	3.97 (5)	0.732
Makes investment decision process easier and faster			23	33.8	25	36.8	20	29.4	68	100	3.96 (6)	0.800

annual report" CFO 4.

"In my opinion, IFR is just a medium to disseminate the information through the internet" CFO 8.

"IFR in Malaysia just focuses on Bursa Malaysia performance" CFO 9.

"IFR in Malaysia is developing" CFO 10.

"The level of IFR practice in Malaysia is still at the infancy stage. Company do not fully explore the facilities on the Internet" CFO 15.

"For me, IFR is just a medium. The most important thing is the content. If the content is similar to the hardcopy, with no value added, it makes little difference" CFO 16.

Advantage

"It is easy to get the financial information from interested parties. Some advantages of IFR are: information can easily access and download, can make a comparison between their ratio and more useful to the potential investor" CFO 2.

"The IFR practice in Malaysia is easily accessed through Bursa Malaysia website" CFO 6.

"The big companies in Malaysia engage in IFR practice. The information is easy to access. It saves time and cost" CFO 13.

"The practice of IFR in Malaysia is useful for investor and financial analyst but the content should be accurate and comprehensive" CFO 14.

Disadvantage

"IFR in Malaysia is not widely implemented" CFO

Table 4. Advantages and disadvantages of IFR.

Item	Mean	Standard deviation	Rank
Advantages			
Global reach and mass communication	4.26	0.683	1
Timeliness and up-date ability	4.10	0.694	2
Increased information (downloadable) and analysis	4.01	0.723	3
Navigational ease	3.94	0.689	4
Interaction and feedback	3.87	0.751	5
Cost beneficial	3.72	0.789	6
Presentation flexibility and visibility	3.65	0.768	7
Disadvantages			
Security problems	3.94	0.896	1
Cost and expertise	3.84	0.874	2
Poor website design and advertising	3.53	0.954	3
Authentication, attestation and legal impediments	3.50	0.889	4
Information overload	3.44	0.920	5
Developed and developing country digital divide	3.34	0.874	6

3.
"The IFR practice in Malaysia is hard to access. If you can access, the information is too limited" CFO 5.
"IFR in Malaysia is not a popular practice, not too many companies report their information through the internet" CFO 7.

Suggestion

"The level of IFR practice in Malaysia is satisfactory but still it needs improvement" CFO 11.
"IFR in Malaysia can be improved in term of their quality and content" CFO 12.

It can be concluded that almost all the respondents agree on the importance of IFR to be implemented in Malaysia. Otherwise, there are advantages and disadvantages of IFR; the rapid growth of the internet technology has created the ability for firms to directly and instantly disclose their financial and non-financial information to worldwide users. Owing to its capacity in providing information at high speed, internet technology can be accessed at almost anytime and from everywhere, although low costs dissemination and wide coverage that are considered by the companies to be important are disclosed on the Internet. In addition, the internet technology can become a perfect medium for information disclosure and communication.

Conclusion

This paper has investigated and reported on the preparer's perceptions of the benefits, advantages and disadvantages of IFR. Given that there is hardly any piece of empirical study on the benefits, advantages and disadvantages of IFR in Malaysia, this paper is an important contribution to filling the gap in our knowledge of this subject. Two important findings emerged from this study that can be used as a basis for future research. First, the respondents ranked that IFR implementation benefits the companies because they are able to attract foreign investors, promote the company to the public, attract local investors, provide wider coverage compared to the traditional form of annual reports and is better at promoting transparency compared to the traditional form of annual reports. Furthermore, IFR implementation benefits the users because IFR increases timeliness and efficiency in obtaining financial information, helps users in the decision making process, provides another medium of disclosure, provides information for company, in-expensively and provides accessibility to the users. Second, respondents perceived 'global reach and mass communication' as the most important advantage of IFR, while 'security problems' as the most important disadvantage of IFR.

In summary, this paper provides important insights into the benefits, advantages and disadvantages of IFR from the perspectives of preparers of financial information which has been neglected by prior research. However, this study has several limitations. The first is the small sample size. As the Internet continues to evolve, we expect more companies to create websites and adopt IFR within the next few years. Therefore, it would be interesting for researchers to further investigate this issue with a larger sample size. Secondly, studies may also survey various corporate stakeholder groups, including shareholders, management, users, relevant governmental agencies, managers, bank officers, tax officers, auditors etc. to ascertain their perceptions of the nature and extent of IFR practices in Malaysia. Thirdly, questionnaire may not be the best way of collecting data about IFR. Further research could try other approaches, such as interviewing companies, prepares and users. Fourth, this study only focuses on Malaysia. The generalisability of the current study to other countries may contingent upon the results of future studies on companies in those countries. Future research may investigate and compare the issue between countries, especially between developed and developing countries to shed light on benefits affecting disclosure that are not captured by the model used here. Furthermore, users' view on IFR should be further investigated, in order to develop an overall viewpoint of IFR. Replications of IFR practice in other national settings warrant potential research extensions of this paper. Finally, it is hoped that this study will be interest to those the investing community (preparers, users, regulators, stakeholders and researchers) towards IFR. Perhaps the findings should enhance the quality of IFR practices in Malaysia.

ACKNOWLEDGEMENTS

The financial support for the authors' research from Ministry of Higher Education (MOHE), Malaysia and Research Management Center (RMC), Universiti Teknologi Malaysia, Johor Bahru, Johor, Malaysia vote no. Q.130000.2629.02J80 by Research University Grant (RUG) are appreciated.

REFERENCES

Abdelsalam OH, Bryant SM, Street DL (2007). An Examination of Comprehensiveness of Corporate Internet Reporting Provided by London-Listed Companies. J. Int. Account. Res. 6(2):1-33.

Abdelsalam OH, El-Masry A (2008). The impact of board independence and ownership structure on the timeliness of corporate internet reporting of Irish-listed companies. Manager. Finan. 34(12):907-918.

Abdelsalam OH, Street DL (2007). Corporate governance and the timeliness of corporate internet reporting by U.K. listed companies. J. Int. Account, Audit. Tax. 16:111-130.

Al-Htaybat K (2011). Corporate online reporting in 2010: a case study in Jordan. J. Financ. Report. Account. 9(1):5-26.

Al Arussi AS, Selamat MH, Mohd Hanefah M (2009). Determinants of financial and environmental disclosures through the internet by Malaysian companies. Asian Rev. Account. 17(1):59-76.

Ali Khan MNA, Ismail NA (2008). An Evolution of Internet Financial Reporting Research. Paper presented at International Accounting and Business Conference (IABC) 2008, Puteri Pan Pacific, Johor Bahru, Johor, August 18-19.

Ali Khan MNA, Ismail NA (2009). Internet Financial Reporting in Malaysia: Factors, Pros and Cons. Accountants Today 22(2):28-31.

Ali Khan MNA, Ismail NA (2011). A Review of e-Financial Reporting Research. Journal of Internet and e-Business Studies. Forthcoming.

Allam A, Lymer A (2003). Development in Internet Financial Reporting: Review and Analysis Across Five Developed Countries. Int. J. Digital Account. Res. 3(6):165-199.

Ashbaugh H, Johnstone KM, Warfield TD (1999). Corporate Reporting on the Internet. Accounting Horizons 13(3):241-257.

Barako DG, Rusmin R, Tower G (2008). Web communication: An Indonesian perspective. Afr. J. Bus. Manage. 2(3):53-58.

Bollen LH, Hassink HF, Lange RKD, Buijl SD (2008). Best Practices in Managing Investor Relations Websites: Directions for Future Research. J. Inform. Syst. 22(2):171-194.

Bonson E, Escobar T (2002). A Survey on Voluntary Disclosure on the Internet: Empirical Evidence from 300 European Union Companies. Int. J. Digital Account. Res. 2(1):27-51.

Bonson E, Escobar T (2006). Digital reporting in Eastern Europe: An empirical study. Int. J. Account. Inform. Syst. 7:299-318.

Bonson E, Escobar T, Flores F (2006). Online transparency of banking sector. Online Inform. Rev. 30(6):714-730.

Brennan N, Hourigan D (1998). Corporate Reporting on the Internet by Irish Companies. Accountancy Ireland. 30(6):18-21.

Chan WK, Wickramasinghe N (2006). Using the internet for financial disclosure: the Australian experience. Int. J. Electro. Finan. 2(1):118-150.

Craven BM, Marston CL (1999). Financial reporting on the Internet by leading UK companies. Eur. Account. Rev. 8(2):321-333.

Davey H, Homkajohn K (2004). Corporate Internet Reporting: An Asian Example. Malaysian Account. Rev. 3(1):61-79.

Debreceny R, Gray GL, Rahman A (2002). The determinants of internet financial reporting. J. Account. Publ. Pol. 21(4-5):371-394.

Deller D, Stubenrath M, Weber C (1999). A Survey on the Use of the Internet for Investor Relations in the USA, the UK and Germany. Eur. Account. Rev. 8(2):351-364.

Elsayed MO, Hoque Z (2010). Perceived international environmental factors and corporate voluntary disclosure practices: An empirical study. Br. Account. Rev. 42:17-35.

Ettredge M, Richardson VJ, Scholz S (2001). The presentation of financial information at corporate Web sites. Int. J. Account. Inform. Syst. 2:149-168.

Ettredge M, Richardson VJ, Scholz S (2002). Dissemination of information for investors at corporate Web sites. J. Account. Publ. Pol. 21:357-369.

Ezat A, El-Masry A (2008). The impact of corporate governance on the timeliness of corporate internet reporting by Egyptian listed companies. Manager. Finan. 34(12):848-867.

FASB (2000). Business reporting research project: Electronic distribution of business reporting information. Steering Committee Report Series, Financial Accounting Standards Board.

FASB (2001). Improving business reporting: Insights into enhancing voluntary disclosures. Financial Accounting Standards Board.

Fisher R, Oyelere P, Laswad F (2004). Corporate reporting on the Internet Audit issues and content analysis of practices. Manager. Audit. J. 19(3):412-439.

Gowthorpe C (2000). Corporate reporting on the Internet: developing opportunities for research. J. Appl. Account. Res. 5(3):3-29.

Green G, Spaul B (1997, May). Digital Accountability. Accountancy, International Edition pp.49-50.

Haniffa MH, Ab Rashid H (2004). The determinants of voluntary disclosures in Malaysia: The case of internet financial reporting. Paper presented at International Business Management Conference 2004, Kuantan, Pahang, December 6-7.

Hassan S, Jaaffar N, Johl SK, Mat Zain M/N (1999). Financial reporting on the internet by Malaysian companies: Perceptions and practices. Asia-Pacific J. Account. 6(2):299-319.

Hindi NM, Rich J (2010). Financial Reporting on the Internet: Evidence from the Fortune 100. Manage. Account. Q. 11(2):11-21.

Ho SSM, Wong KS (2001). A study of the relationship between corporate governance structures and the extent of voluntary disclosure. J. Int. Account., Audit. Tax., 10: 139-156.

Ho SSM, Wong KS (2003). Preparers' perceptions of corporate reporting and disclosure. Int. J. Disclos. Govern. 1(1):71-81.

ICAEW (2004). Digital reporting: a progress report. London: The Institute of Chartered Accountants in England and Wales.

IFAC (2001). Financial reporting on the internet. International Federation of Accountants.

Ismail NA, Tayib M (2000, November/December). Financial Reporting Disclosure on the Internet by Malaysian Public Listed Companies. Akauntan Nasional 13(10):28-33.

Jiambalvo J (2004). Managerial Accounting (2nd ed.). USA: John Wiley & Sons, Inc.

Jones MJ, Xiao JZ (2004). Financial reporting on the Internet by 2010: a consensus view. Accounting Forum. 28(3):237-263.

Joshi PL, Al-Modhahki J (2003). Financial reporting on the internet: Empirical evidence from Bahrain and Kuwait. Asia-Pacific J. Account. 11(1):88-101.

Kelton AS, Yang Y (2008). The impact of corporate governance on Internet financial reporting. J. Account. Publ. Pol. 27(1): 62-87.

Khadaroo I (2005). Corporate reporting on the internet: some implications for the auditing profession. Manager. Audit. J. 20(6): 578-591.

Ku Ismail KNI, Chandler R (2007). Quarterly financial reporting: a survey of Malaysian preparers and users. Res. Account. Emerg. Econ. 7:53-67.

Liu LG (2000). The emergence of business information resources and services on the Internet and its impact on business librarianship. Online Inform. Rev. 24(3):234-255.

Lybaert N (2002). On-Line Financial Reporting: An Analysis of the Dutch Listed Firms. Int. J. Digital Account. Res. 2(4):195-234.

Lymer A (1997). The Use of the Internet in Company Reporting: A Survey and Commentary on the Use WWW in Corporate Reporting in UK. Paper presented at the British Accounting Association Annual Conference, Birmingham.

Lymer A (1999). The Internet and the future of corporate reporting in Europe. Eur. Account. Rev. 2(2):289-301.

Lymer A, Tallberg A (1997). Corporate Reporting and the Internet - a survey and commentary on the use of the WWW in corporate reporting in the UK and Finland. Paper presented at the Annual Congress of the European Accounting Congress, Graz, Austria, April.

Lymer A, Debreceny R, Gray GL, Rahman A (1999). Business Reporting on the Internet. IASC Research Report.

Marston C (2003). Financial reporting on the internet by leading Japanese companies. Corporate Communication: Int. J., 8(1): 23-34.

Marston C, Leow CY (1998). Financial reporting on the Internet by leading UK companies. Paper presented at the 21st Annual Congress of the European Accounting Association, Antwerp, Belgium.

Marston C, Polei A (2004). Corporate reporting on the Internet by German companies. Int. J. Account. Inform. Syst. 5:285-311.

McDonald R, Lont D (2001). Financial Reporting on the Web – A 2001 Review. Chartered Account. J. pp.64-68.

Mohamed EKA, Oyelere P, Al-Busaidi M (2009). A survey of internet financial reporting in Oman. Int. J. Emerg. Mark. 4(1):56-71.

Mohd IR (2006). Graphical Information in Corporate Annual Report: A Survey of Users and Preparers Perception. J. Financ. Report. Account. 4(1):39-60.

Moradi M, Salehi M, Arianpoor A (2011). A study of the reasons for shortcomings in establishment of internet financial reporting in Iran. Afr. J. Bus. Manage. 5(8):3312-3321.

Morgan G (1988). Accounting as a reality construction: towards a new epistemology for accounting practice. Account. Organ. Soc. 13(5):477-485.

Nazatul I (2010). From Finance to Corporate Leader. Accountants Today 23(6):6-8.

Petravick S, Gillett J (1996). Financial reporting on the World Wide Web. Management Accounting. July: 26-29.

PricewaterhouseCoopers (2002). Market Readiness for Disclosure-Based Regulation, Highlights from the survey on the readiness of the Malaysian Capital Market participants for DBR. Kuala Lumpur: Securities Commission.

Oyelere P, Laswad F, Fisher R (2003). Determinants of Internet Financial Reporting by New Zealand Companies. J. Int. Financ. Manage. Account. 14(1):26-61.

Pervan I (2006). Voluntary Financial Reporting on the Internet- Analysis of the Practice of Stock-Market listed Croatian and Slovene Joint Stock Companies. Financ. Theory Practice 30(1):1-27.

Pervan I, Sabljic M (2011). Voluntary Internet Financial Reporting in Croatia – Analysis of Trends and Influential Factors. Bus. Rev. 17(2):213-219.

Pirchegger B, Wagenhofer A (1999). Financial information on the Internet: a survey of the homepages of Austrian companies. Eur. Account. Rev. 8(2):383-395.

Sekaran U (2003). Research Methods For Business A Skill Building Approach (4th ed.). USA: John Wiley & Sons, Inc.

Spaul B (1997). Corporate dialogue in the digital age. London. The Institute of Chartered Accountants in England and Wales.

Staden CJV (1998). The usefulness of the value added statement in South Africa. Manager. Finan. 24(11):44-59.

Trites G (1999). The impact of technology on financial and business reporting. Canadian Institute of Chartered Accountants.

Wallman S (1995). The Future of Accounting and Disclosure in Evolving World: The Need for Dramatic Change. Account. Horizon 9(3):81-91.

Wilmshurst TD, Frost GR (2000). Corporate environmental reporting A test of legitimacy theory. Accounting, Audit. Account. J. 13(1):10-25.

Xiao JZ, Jones MJ, Lymer A (2005). A Conceptual Framework for Investigating the Impact of the Internet on Corporate Financial Reporting. Int. J. Digital Account. Res. 5(10):131-169.

Xiao JZ, Yang H, Chow CW (2004). The determinants and characteristics of voluntary Internet-based disclosures by listed Chinese companies. J. Account. Publ. Pol. 23:191-225.

9

Technological innovation implementation: A proposed model on organizational learning capability with moderating effect of knowledge complexity

Adam Mat[1] and Razli Che Razak[2]

[1]Faculty of Business Management, Universiti Teknologi MARA (UiTM), Malaysia.
[2]Centre for International Affairs and Cooperation (CIAC), Universiti Utara Malaysia (UUM), Sintok, Kedah, Malaysia.

The purpose of this paper is to explore the relationship between organizational learning capability, knowledge complexity and their impact on technological innovation implementation success. The rapidly rising rate of technological change in manufacturing process presents a lot of challenges and opportunities for organizations. Research has fairly established that technological innovation implementation is associated with organizational learning. However, few studies have investigated on the roles of knowledge complexity on the established relationship. This paper focuses at implementation phase of innovation process, where innovation has been fully developed, then it must be implemented. The issue of implementation is crucial in innovation research. Identification of success or failure of innovation can be done through implementation phase. Furthermore, the success of the technology implementation will determine whether any innovation has achieved its objective or not.

Key words: Technological innovation, knowledge complexity, organizational learning capability.

INTRODUCTION

In competition-based economic system, the role of innovation as a part of management practice is an important factor for survival within the firm and to be effective, managers need to accept this requirement to accelerate the rates of innovation (Lipsey, 1996; Johannessen et al., 1997). Ravichandran (2000) has mentioned that organization has a single choice in today's environment; innovating or creating technological and managerial innovation. Bessant and Francis (1998) and McAdam (2000) argue that the role of innovation in organization must flow through every discipline, process and level to produce effective result. Innovation induces organizational growth, leads future success, and is the important factor that allows businesses to sustain their viability in a global economy (Gaynor, 2002). Cottam et al. (2001) agree that innovation is one of the ways to maintain growth and to achieve desirable organizational performance. Therefore, it is important to link technology

to innovation in sustaining competitiveness (Humphrey et al., 2005). Through competitive market, firms need to develop and exploit new technology as an essential element to succeed (Leonard-Barton, 1995). Cooper and Schendel (1976) argue that technological innovation creates new industry and destroys or transforms existing firms.

The main factor for organization to succeed in inno-vation is organizational learning (Mabey and Salaman, 1995). In fact, organizational learning and innovation can be viewed as "intangible" resources because they are hardly imitated (Edmondson and Moingeon, 1998). Lukas (1996) acknowledged "organizational learning is consi-dered by many scholars as a key to future organizational success". Therefore, organizational learning is recognized as a critical factor to innovation success. Furthermore, Stata (1989) mentioned that organizational learning leads to innovation especially in knowledge-intensive of the industry which individual and organizational learning lead to further innovation and creates sustainable competitive advantage. Sinkula et al. (2002) highlighted that the important role of organizational learning capabilities is generating innovation. Organizations that posses a superior learning are able to coordinate and combine their traditional capabilities and resources in new and distinctive methods, providing more value for their customers and, in general, stakeholders compared to their competitors (Teece et al., 1997).

Technological innovation is the incorporation of a new technology into the production process, producing new products that have a propensity to change the profitability or the market share of the innovatory firms (Rosenthal, 1995). Compatibility of a new technology with existing technology provides a firm with an easier way to accept new technology (Rebentisch and Ferretti, 1995). Through competitive market, firms need to develop and exploit new technology as an essential element to succeed (Leonard-Barton, 1995). Study at organizational level has recommended that a process of individuals concentrating to learn new technologies is the answer to implementation success (Aiman-Smith and Green, 2002). The management must prepare to establish appropriate incentive and reward to encourage employee involved in learning especially in life-long learning. Successful exploitation of opportunities from new technology requires integration of those technology with the firm's existing skills and technologies (Saban et al., 2000). Importantly, organizational learning can take effect not only at the initial phase of innovation but also at the implementation phase (Glynn, 1996).

As expressed by Tidd et al. (2001), implementation is the heart of the innovation process; when a problem at implementation phase occurs, an innovation cannot be utilised to the fullest, and the concentration to the related activities will be low (Rogers, 1995). Evidence showed that most failures occurred at this phase. Day (1999) claimed that the failure rate for innovation implementation process is around 75%. A study conducted by Tidd et al. (2001) revealed that a higher failure rate of more than 50 percent were experienced by organization in implementing advanced manufacturing technology (AMT) in 1990s. Arokiasamy (2004) who conducted a research in manufacturing sector found that 59.42% of organi-zation experienced interruption in ERP implementation. Accordingly, the estimated failure rate of 47% for technological innovation took place at this phase (Beatty, 1992; Galbraith, 1990; Majchrzak, 1988). On the other hand, only 30 to 50% success rate of new technology implementation is recorded (Tang, 2000). Instead of high failure rate, innovation implementation remains a main priority to the organization. A new technology implementation is influenced by performance gaps because of the management priority to change the existing technology (managerial pull) or new technology that has a big potential to the organization (technology push) (Zmund, 1984).

Problem statement

The phenomenon of success of technological innovation in manufacturing sector is rather discouraging. However, technology-related innovativeness shows the readiness of firms to encourage new technologies as business prospects (Kimberly, 1981; Kitchell, 1995) despite success or failure in implementing the new technology. The main factor for organization to succeed in innovation is organizational learning (Mabey and Salaman, 1995). Nonaka and Takeuchi (1995) explained that companies innovate through a constant learning process through which they generate new technological knowledge. Ju et al. (2006) argued that when knowledge complexity exists, organizations have difficulties in acquiring, integrating and using the knowledge in organization to achieve objectives. Therefore, knowledge complexity influences organization in pursuing its activities especially in learning and innovation. The alignment between organizational learning capability and knowledge complexity needs to be explored further because it might impact the success of technological innovation implementation.

Objective of the study

In line with the problem afore stated, the objectives of this research are as follows:

1. To identify the level of success of technological innovation implementation among manufacturing firms.
2. To identify the influence of organizational learning capability (OLC) on success of the technological innovation implementation
3. To investigate the extent to which knowledge complexity moderates the relationship between organizational learning capability (OLC) and success of the technological innovation implementation.

THEORETICAL FRAMEWORK

Goh and Richards (1997) define organizational learning capability (OLC) as the managerial and organizational characteristic or element that facilitate the organizational learning process or encourage an organisation to learn. Organisational learning facilitating factors were grouped through a comprehensive analysis so that a simplified essential set of dimensions for organisational learning was obtained (Gatignon et al., 2002). Chiva et al. (2007) identify five underlying dimensions of organizational learning capability: experimentation, risk taking, interaction with the external environment, dialogue, and participative decision making. These dimensions were considered as the most underlined facilitating factors in the literature (Chiva, 2007). Figure 1 present a conceptual model concerning the relationship between

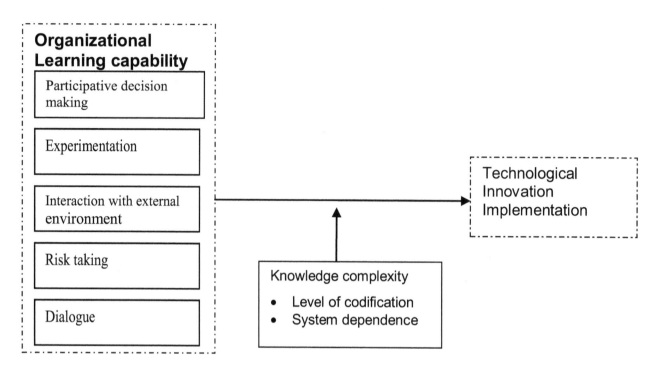

Figure 1. Conceptual model.

constructs of the proposed conceptual model.

According to Gorton and Schmid (2000), organisational learning and competitiveness will be increased through defining the underpinning theory of innovation implementation more consistently and applying supportive measures. Technology innovation implementation provides a good perspective in which to investigate how organizational routines can be changed. For example, Klein and Sorra (1996) and Tyre (1991) argue that researchers' and managers' values of new technology implementation are crucial in the United State manufacturing firms. Implementation phase is the least understood phase of the innovation process (Van de Ven, 1993). Therefore, when technological innovation is adopted (decision was made), the innovation must be implemented, employees need to know how to use it and integrate it into their daily routines or the expected efficiencies will not be accomplished (Rogers, 1995).

The measurement of innovation implementation success remains unclear. Linton (2002) states that, there is no specific measurement to measure innovation implementation success; it is difficult to measure successful innovation because of the difficulty in generalizing the outcomes of different studies (Wolfe, 1994). The most suitable definition of measurement of innovation success was provided by Cozijnsen et al. (2000), where "innovation success is measured through the degrees to which the innovation goals are achieved". Successful technological innovation projects can be assessed by isolating their contribution to improvement in a firm performance (Narveka and Jain, 2006). Cozijnsen et al.

(2000) state that the indirect results of an innovation project, relates to profits and competitive position of the organization. Most common measurement of innovation outcomes involves efficiency and effectiveness. Efficiency involves the extent to which customer requirements are met meanwhile, effectiveness is determined through how firm's resources are utilized (Neely et al., 2005). Therefore, innovation implementation success measurement is through effectiveness and efficiency of new technology.

Theoretical construct

Theoretical foundation of this framework is mainly derived from resource-base view (RBV). Newbert (2007) argues that a current review of empirical RBV literature in management related firm's competitive position depends essentially on its organizing context and on its valuable, rare and inimitable capabilities and core compentencies rather than on its static resources. However, resources are inadequate for gaining a sustained competitive advantage and a high performance as well (Teece et al., 2007; Newbert, 2007). Through the capability-based theory (CBT), it is suggested that firms can achieve sustained competitive advantage by distinctive capabilities owned by the firm (Grant, 1991; Hayes et al., 1996). Being so, firms must be capable to change resources in capabilities, and accordingly, in a positive performance (Ferreira and Azevedo, 2008). Various researchers have discussed the importance of innovation process in organization. Several phases of innovation have been recognized in innovation study. A clear innovation phase involved three levels namely; generation, development and implementation (Sundbo, 2001). An ultimate innovation impact can be measured through a last innovation process; the implementation phase. Implementation phase starts with application and adoption activities commenced for an innovation through previous phases which innovation is generated and developed, and then the implementation phase takes place involving transferring innovation to the operating locations, establishing the innovation into the market and reaching it to possible users (Angle and Van de Ven, 1989).

In this study, resource based view (RBV) and capability based theory (CBT) are used to explain the effect of organizational learning capability on the success of technological innovation implementation. Specifically, the study utilizes the assumptions of RBV in providing plausible explanation on how organizational learning capability is practiced among organizations. From innovation process perspective, this study will concentrate at implementation phase.

The study identifies organizational learning capability adopted in the manufacturing sector. Given the importance of learning, the study might contribute considerable knowledge to this area and provide a basis for future studies. This study identifies the factors or characteristics of organizational learning which influence the technological innovation implementation. This can add to the knowledge about how organizational learning diffuse among organizations. This knowledge can also enrich theories that deal with organizational learning such as resource based view theory. It will also provide insight into the role of knowledge complexity in moderating the relationship between organizational learning capability and technological innovation. This can add to knowledge about what enables or facilitates the success of technological innovation implementation.

CONCEPTUAL MODEL AND HYPOTHESES

Participative decision making and technological innovation implementation

Participative decision making is where employees have significant influence in the decision-making process (Cotton et al., 1988). Importantly, when a firm is experiencing a major technological change, the use of participative decision making is the main priority mechanism (Brown, 1979). To provide a better innovative solution, management needs to involve all related parties and it can be achieved by reducing bureaucratic problem in organization. The increase in participation during decision making will result in less resistance to change and better possibility for adoption of new technology (Wall and Lischeron, 1977). Bahrami and Evans (1987) assert that

successful high technology firms practice decentralized decision-making and high degree of participation by line managers in decision-making when dealing with changes in the environment. Furthermore, the ability to participate in decision making is a key process in enhancing innovation (West and Anderson, 1996). Participative decision making was most essential to technological innovation (Fadzil, 2001):

H_1: Participative decision making has a positive effect on technological innovation implementation.

Experimentation and technological innovation implementation

Experimentation deals with trying out new ideas, being curious about how things work or carrying out changes in work process (Nevis et al., 1995). Experimentation produces a flow of ideas or proposals that challenge the established order and is regarded as a manifestation of the creative environment (Alegre, 2003). Thomke (2001) asserts that experimentation lies at the heart of every company's ability to innovate. Management needs to encourage and support the freedom to conduct experiment with new work methods and innovative process (Senge, 1990; Garvin, 1993; Mcgill and Slocum, 1993). Organization can learn by analyzing the failure and then proceed with experimentation. A meaningful failure should be used as a learning process in organization. To optimize the learning process, team should "embrace failure" and systematically collect as many 'failures' as quickly as possible (Singer and Edmonson, 2006).

Thomke (1998) argue that to ensure that technological implementation works, it often requires experimentation, using trial and error to find solution. Companies that experiment novel technologies are better positioned to have a higher rate of innovation than firms that invest all their efforts in exploiting the existing, familiar technologies (Beerkens, 2004). Precipe (2000) mentions that to understand technological failure and to gain knowledge resulted from failure will be helpful for subsequent technology or product development. By experimenting with novel technologies, it permits an organization to evaluate the potential of technology in effective ways (Cohen and Levinthal, 1990). Through experimenting new technology, organization can acelerate its innovation in effective way especially in new technology:

H_2: Experimentation has a positive effect on technological innovation implementation interaction with external environment on technological innovation implementation.

Firms can learn from their external counterparts and use related information for organizational success. The external environment of an organization consists of those factors that are beyond the direct control of the organization, and include industrial agents such as competitors, the economic system, the social system, the monetary system and the political/legal system, among others (Alegre, 2004). Interacting with other companies such as customers and suppliers will promote companies to learn (Lundvall, 1988). Cyert and March (1963) argue that an organization needs to deal with external shocks, in turn, they must adapt and learn to cope with that situation in their whole life. External environment demands organization to be more cautious. Monitoring any changes of external environment contributes to learning by organization members. Additionally, it is important for organization to ensure the flow of relevant knowledge from both outside and inside organization so that it can be utilized in the innovation process (Savory, 2006).

Interacting with external sources can boost firms' knowledge about competitive trends and industry benchmark (Mu et al., 2008). Importantly, the affects of organizational learning process take place within a network of actors and importantly, within industrial system (Bagens and Araujo, 2002). Employees other than gatekeepers and technical staff are encouraged by firms to search for information related to technological and market trend then bring back to the firms (Matusik, 2002). In recent years, an escalating number of organizations are forming relationships with other organizations to enhance value through continuous knowledge management (Hagedoorn, 1993; Robertson and Yu, 2001). Organization need to establish relationship with external entities including customer, competitor or government agency, etc. Such collaboration will bring benefit to the firm including the latest changes or developments which affect firm competitiveness:

H₃: Interaction with external environment has a positive effect on technological innovation implementation

Risk taking and technological innovation implementation

Liles (1981) defines risk as the probability of an unconstructive result occurring from various courses of actions. Risk-taking is the organization's enthusiasm to break away from normal path and venture into unknown territory (Venkatraman, 1989; Wiklund and Shepherd, 2003). Risk-taking is also the extent to which managers are eager to make large and risky resource commitments (Miller and Friesen, 1978).

Kouzes and Posner (1987) argue that learning from successes and mistakes resulted from risk taking will lead to increasing business opportunities. Employees need support and collaboration among themselves to reduce fear and gain openness which encourages new risk taking (Hurley and Hult, 1998). When there are growths in new areas, there will be unfamiliarity with new

activities and management requires more efforts (Penrose, 1972) to deal with risk. Peter and Waterman (1982) suggest that companies that are able to manage risk taking properly in their industrial context will achieve excellence result. Saleh and Wang (1993) showed that innovative companies are more engaged in risk taking compare to less innovative companies. Rauch et al. (2004) found that the risk-taking is positively related to performance. Begley and Boyd (1987) found that relationship between firm's risk-taking and performance is at maximum level when risk taking is at medium level. Covin et al. (2006) found a positive significant relationship between risk-taking with business performance. The willingness to take risk will open great opportunity to firm in implementing technological innovation:

H₄: Risk taking has a positive effect on technological innovation implementation

Dialogue and technological innovation implementation

Isaacs (1993) defines dialogue as "a sustained collective inquiry into the processes, assumptions, and certainties that compose everyday experience". Dialogue is an interactive process of learning together, aims to achieve deeper levels of understanding between those participating (Ballantyne, 2004). Isaacs (1993) and Schein (1993) state that most scholars and practitioners of organizational learning see the process of dialogue as providing an avenue for communication and collaborative learning within and between groups and teams. Ganesan (1994) has established that the willingness to cooperate improves when partners always make constructive judgments about one another over time. It can be said that dialogue is part of organizational learning which encourages communication and tries to sharing the same conclusion between them. Thinking of each other's thoughts helps them to overcome the hurdles impeding their willingness to work with each other, and enables them to understand some of the difficult attitudes often held by various members (Muayyad Jabri, 2004). In organisational studies, dialogue has become important as an aspect of understanding the difficulties and possibilities of learning and change (Gear et al., 2003).

When team members communicate with each other frequently, an absorptive capacity is more likely to develop among them, enabling them to become more efficient in expanding and using information (Brown and Eisenhardt, 1995). Communicative interaction only takes place when the receiver derives some meaning from the message, which of course is less than what the sender intends (Ballantyne, 2004). Importantly, successful technological innovation is positively influenced by individuals' communication (Balthasar et al., 2000). The role of dialogue among organizational members can produce better understanding by sharing meaning on related issues. Organizational members can also reach mutual understanding and alleviate the speeding in sharing information:

H$_5$: Dialogue has a positive effect on technological innovation implementation.

MODERATING EFFECT OF KNOWLEDGE COMPLEXITY

Knowledge can be transmitted by affecting people, technology, or structure to the organization, or by changing people (for example, training), technology, and the structure of the beneficiary organization (Argote, 1999). For successful technological innovation, developing learning and knowledge management strategies has been considered effective and efficient (Martin and Matlay, 2003). Since innovation will strengthen a firm's competitive advantage, knowledge is the key element that combines organizational learning and innovative activities (Ju et al., 2006).

The concept of knowledge is complex and its relevance to organization theory has been insufficiently developed (Blackler, 1995). According to Vinekar (2008), the complexity of an organization's knowledge environment is the variety of knowledge that an organization needs. Knowledge complexity influences the way knowledge is transferred and integrated in organization. The higher levels of knowledge complexity result in more difficulties a company may encounter in the knowledge integration process (Ju et al., 2006). Complex knowledge mirrors the degree to which knowledge contains many different, unique and interdependent parts, for example, how one element works reveals little about how the different elements work together (McEvily and Chakravarthy, 2002). Thus, knowledge complexity raises an understanding from the types knowledge takes (tacit and explicit) and by the mean of which knowledge processes arise (McElroy, 2000).

In this study, knowledge complexity dimension is measured through codification and systems dependence as used by previous researchers (Hansen, 1999; Zandori, 2001). This is based on argument provided by Teece (1977) and Zander and Kogurt (1995), where difficulties happen in transferring non-codified and dependent knowledge. Simon (1962) also explained that complexity of system consists of many unique and interacting elements:

H$_6$: The relationship between organizational learning capability and technological innovation implementation will influence by knowledge complexity.

Level of codification

Winter (1987) and Zander and Kogut (1995) explained

that one dimension of complex knowledge is its level of codification. Hansen (1999) states codification is a degree to which the knowledge is fully documented or expressed in writing at the time of transfer between a subunit and a receiving subunit. Similarly, Zollo and Winter (2002) argue that codification is the process when individuals codify their understandings of the performance implications of internal routines in written tools, such as manuals, blueprints, spreadsheets, decision support systems, project management software. Importantly, knowledge with a low level of codification is closely related to the term of tacit knowledge which is difficult to be communicated or can only be obtained through experience (Polanyi, 1966; Nelson and Winter, 1982; Von Hippel, 1988). Tacit and explicit knowledge are comparable; tacit knowledge is more personal and explicit knowledge is more public (Kane et al., 2006). For tacit knowledge, it is difficult to be formalized and communicated to others (Nonaka and Takeuchi, 1995). Additionally, Polanyi (1966) stresses that two-way communication supported by strong ties is a key to assimilating the non-codified knowledge, because the recipient probably does not obtain the knowledge completely throughout the earliest interaction with the recipient but needs several opportunities to understand. The difficulty in transferring knowledge depends on its level of codification which is easy to understand or difficult to translate into meaningful meaning. Therefore, codification of knowledge consists of the elements of tacit and explicit knowledge, it depends on whether knowledge is hard or easy to be articulated by organizational members. Tacit knowledge creates difficulty in the process of selecting, moving and applying the knowledge (Grant, 1996; Hansen, 1999; Kogurt and Zander, 1992; Simonin, 1999). Besides, explicit knowledge can easily be transferred and it provides deep understanding compared to tacit knowledge which sometimes involves confusion and is difficult to understand. Therefore, tacit and explicit knowledge can be deliberated of as an end-to-end extreme on a range of all knowledge possibilities (Dixon, 2000). It is difficult to identify if knowledge is explicit or tacit in different organization. Every organization has its own experience, process and systems. Therefore, the identification of knowledge, either explicit or tacit, is complex:

H$_{6a}$: The relationship between organizational learning capability and technological innovation implementation will influence by level of codification

System dependence

Another knowledge complexity dimension is dependence, the level of knowledge to be transmitted or a component of a set of interdependent components (Teece, 1986; Winter, 1987). To perform the task better, individuals depend on knowledge from other units or departments. For example, production department depends on marketing department to know product demand for production planning.

If knowledge is easily acquired from others, firm operation is efficient and effective. If knowledge is difficult to be acquired from others, it will interrupt or delay the operation. Therefore, when knowledge is more complex, effective internal transfer is more complex and entails strong ties in the form of proper system and regular interaction (Hansen, 1999). If task knowledge is obtained from and dependent on a larger number of people, systems, or processes, then those looking for that knowledge have more possibility to search for knowledge from many diverse sources, more of which are possible to be people, rather than knowledge management system in organization (Bystrom, 2002).

The relationship between departments is crucial especially with regard to sharing different knowledge that is needed to perform tasks. Hansen (1999) considers knowledge sharing among people from different subunits as a dual problem of searching (looking for and identifying) and transferring (moving and incorporating) knowledge across organization subunits, taking into account the complexity of the knowledge that flows through inter-units relationship.

The interaction in organization involves people between units or departments. Most important activities performed by organization members need to involve knowledge from different units or departments. For example, production department needs information from marketing and finance department in operation activities, for example, cost and product acceptance. Marsh and Stock (2003) claim that gathering technological and marketing capabilities from past NPD projects and incorporating that knowledge in a systematic and purposeful manner into the development of future product increases project level performance.

Dependency on other units in an organization might be due to level of knowledge difficulty and how channel influences knowledge integration.

Organization knowledge created through different channels provides different interaction between tacit knowledge and explicit knowledge in organization (Nonaka, 1994). Sharing knowledge from other subunits creates duplication of efforts that can be avoided to increase the management role in handling technical problems (Teece, 1986). However, organization units that are not strongly connected to other units are more responsive because of fewer constrains in organization system (Weick, 1976). Previous research has revealed that access to information through network ties can facilitate performance outcomes (Tsai and Ghoshal, 1998; Tsai, 2001). Thus, in integrating knowledge, the process that is differently interpreted among units needs to be coordinated effectively. Interdependence between units may create divergent understanding. Organizations

need to identify the best method in coordinating knowledge that needs to be shared with other units:

H_{6b}: The relationship between organizational learning capability and technological innovation implementation will influence by system dependent.

CONCLUSION

Today, organizational learning issues receive increasing attention throughout a world. The proposed framework focused on examining organizational learning capability and technological innovation implementation relationship with moderating effect of knowledge complexity.

This study also emphasizes on the implementation phase of innovation process. The importance of learning and technological innovation must be emphasized by the organization, especially in knowledge-based industry. Without knowledge application, organizations would not be capable of fully taking advantage of the collective knowledge to achieve superior performance (Alavi and Leidner, 2001). Through organizational learning capability, firms learn how to improve or to change existing technology which contributes to organizational competitive advantage. By implementing latest technology, it will help organization to stay ahead of competitors. Failure to learn from change can lead to inability to survive (Garvin, 1993).

This study will identify factors that encourage organization to learn and provide insight into the role of knowledge complexity, thus, enhance the understanding of managers and policy makers on the influence of motivators on the outcomes of technological innovation. This understanding can help managers design appropriate policies for the technological innovation in organizations.

To sum up, this study highlighted two main issues emerged from the existing literature. First, the research has established that organizational learning capability is critical to success of innovation implementation. Secondly, it is important to manage knowledge in organization as a facilitator for technological innovation implementation.

REFERENCES

Aiman-Smith L, Green SG (2002). Implementing new manufacturing technology: The related effects of technology characteristics and user learning activities. J. Acad. Manag. 45(2):421-430.

Alavi M, Leidner DE (2001). Review: Knowledge management and knowledge management systems: Conceptual foundations and research issues. MIS Quart. 25(1):107-136.

Angle HL, Van de Ven AH (1989). Suggestions for managing the innovation journey. In: Van de Ven AH, Angle HL, Poole MS (eds.). Research on the Management of the Innovation Process: The Minnesota Studies. Harper and Row, New York.

Argote L (1999). Organizational Learning: Creating, Retaining, and Transferring Knowledge, Kluwer Academic, Boston, MA.

Arokiasamy S (2004). Critical success factor for successful implementation of enterprise resource planning systems in manufacturing organizations. Unpublished MBA thesis, School of Management, Universiti Sains Malaysia, Pulau Pinang.

Bagens L, Araujo L (2002). The Structures and Processes of Learning. A Case Study, J. Bus. Res. 55:571-581.

Balthasar A, Battig C, Wilhelm B (2000). Developers-key actors of the innovation process. Types of developers and their contacts to institution involved in research and development, continuing education and training, and transfer of technology, Technovation 14(2):269-523.

Ballantyne D (2004). Dialogue and its role in the development of relationship specific knowledge, J. Bus. Ind. Mark. 19(2):114-123.

Bessant J, Francis D (1998). Implementing the new product development process, Technovation 17(4):97-187.

Beerkens B (2004). External acquisition of technology: exploration and exploitation in international innovation. Eindhoven University Press, Unpublished Phd Thesis.

Beatty C (1992). Implementing advanced manufacturing technologies: Rules of the road. Sloan Manag. Rev. 33(4):49-60.

Begley TM, Boyd DP (1987). Psychological characteristics associated with performance in entrepreneurial firms and smaller businesses. J. Bus. Vent. 2(1):79-93.

Blackler F (1995). Knowledge, Knowledge Work and Organizations: An Overview and Interpretation. J. Organization Stud. 6(6):1021-1046.

Brown B (1979). Academic Libraries: an Operation Model for Participation. Can. Lib. J. 36:201-207.

Brown SL, Eisenhardt KM (1995). Product development: past research, present findings, and future direction, Acad. Manag. Rev. 20(2):343-378.

Bystrom K (2002) Information and information sources is task varying complexity. J. Am. Soc. Infor. Sci. Technol. 53(7):581-591.

Chiva R, Alegre J, Lapiedra R (2007). Measuring organisational learning capability among the workforce, Int. J. Manpow. 28(3/4):224-242.

Cohen WM, Levinthal DA (1990). Absorptive capacity: a new perspective on learning and innovation", Adm. Sci. Q. 35(1):128-152.

Cooper AC, Schendel D (1976). Strategic Responses to technological threats. Business Horizons pp.61-65.

Cottam A, Ensor J, Band C (2001). A benchmark study of strategic commitment to innovation, Eur. J. Innov. Manage. 4(2):88-94.

Cotton JL, Vollrath DA, Foggat KL, Lengnick-Hall ML, Jennings KR (1988). Employee participation: diverse forms and different outcomes, J. Acad. Manage. Rev. 13(1):8-22.

Covin JG, Green KM, Slevin DP (2006). Strategic process effects on the entrepreneurial orientation-sales growth rate relationship. Entrep. Theory. Pract. 30(1):57-81.

Cozijnsen AJ, Vrakking WJ, Ijzerloo MV (2000). Success and failure of 50 innovation projects in Dutch companies. Eur. J. Innov. Manage. 3(3):193-210.

Cyert RM, March JG (1963). A Behavioral Theory of the Firm. 2nd ed. Prentice Hall, Englewood Cliffs, NJ.

Day GS (1999). The market driven organization. J. Direct. Mark. 62(9):32-33.

Dixon NM (2000). Common knowledge: how companies thrive by sharing what they know. Boston: Harvard Business School Press.

Edmondson A, Moingeon B (1998). When to learn how and when to learn why: appropriate organisational learning processes as a source of competitive advantage. in Edmondson A, Moingeon B (Eds),Organisational Learning and Competitive Advantage, Sage, London pp.7-15.

Fadzil ANF (2001). Structural, cultural values and innovation, Unpublished MBA Theses, Schoool of Management, Universiti Sains Malaysia, Penang.

Ferreira J, Azevedo SG (2008). Entrepreneural orientation (EO) and growth of firms: Key lessons for managers and business professionals. J. Probl. Perspect. Manage. 6:81-87.

Galbraith C (1990). Transferring core manufacturing technologies in high-technology firms. Calif. Manage. Rev. 32(3):56-70.

Ganesan S (1994). Determinants of Long-Term Orientation in Buyer-Seller Relationships,' J. Mark. 58:1-19.

Garvin DA (1993). Building a learning organization, Harv. Bus. Rev. 71(4):78-91.

Gatignon H, Tushman ML, Smith W, Anderson P (2002). A structural approach to assessing innovation: Construct development of innovation locus, type, & characteristics. J. Manage. Sci. 48(9):1103-1122.

Gaynor GH (2002), Innovation by Design: What it Takes to Keep Your Company on The Cutting Edge, AMACOM American management association, New York, NY.

Gear T, Vince R, Read M, Minkes AL (2003). Group enquiry for collective learning in organisations. J. Manage. Dev. 22(2):88-102.

Glynn MA (1996). 'Innovative Genius: A Framework for Relating Individual and Organizational Intelligence to Innovation'. Acad. Manage. Rev. 2(1/4):1081-1111.

Goh S, Richards G (1997). "Benchmarking the learning capability of organizations", Eur. Manage. J. 15(5):575-583.

Gorton G, Schmid F (2000). Universal Banking and the Performance of German Firms. J. Fin. Econ. 58: 29-80.

Grant RM (1991). The resource-based theory of competitive advantage: Implications for strategy formulation. Calif. Manage. Rev. 33(3):114-135.

Grant RM (1996). Prospering in dynamically-competitive environments: Organizational capability as knowledge integration. Organ. Sci. 7(4):375-387.

Hagedoorn J (1993). Understanding the rationale of strategic technology partnering: inter-organizational modes of cooperation and sectoral differences. Strateg. Manage. J. 14:371-385.

Hansen MT (1999).The search-transfer problem: the role of weak ties in sharing knowledge across organization subunits, Adm. Sci. Q. 44(1):82-111.

Hayes JR (1996). A new model of cognition and affect in writing. In Levy CM and Ransdell S (Eds)., The science of writing. Hillsdale, NJ: Erlbaum pp.1-30.

Humphrey P, McAdam R, Leckey J (2005). Longitudinal evaluation of innovation implementation in SMEs, Eur. J. Innov. Manag.8(3):283-304.

Hurley RE, Hult GTM (1998). Innovation, market orientation and organizational learning: an integration and empirical examination, J. Mark. 62:42-54.

Isaacs W (1993). Dialogue, collective thinking, and organizational learning. Organ. Dyn. 22(2):24-39.

Johannessen JA, Olsen B, Olaisen H (1997). Organizing for Innovation. Long Range Plann. p.30.

Ju TL, Li C, Lee T (2006). A contingency model for knowledge management capability and innovation. J. Ind. Manage. Data Syst. 106(6):855-877.

Kane H, Ragsdell G, Oppenheim C (2006). Knowledge management methodologies. Electronic. J. Knowl. Manage. 4(2):141-152.

Kitchell S (1995). Corporate Culture, Environmental Adaptation, and Innovation Adoption: A Qualitative/Quantitative Approach, J. Acad. Mark. Sci. 23(3):195-205.

Kimberly JR (1981) In Handbook of Organization Design (Ed.) Starbuck, W., Oxford Press: New York.

Klein KJ, Sorra JS (1996). The challenge of innovation implementation. Acad. Manage. Rev. 21:1055-1080.

Kogurt B, Zander U (1992). Knowledge of the firm, combinative capabilities and the replication of technology. J. Organ. Sci. 3:383-397.

Kouzes JP, Posner BZ (1987). The Leadership Challenge: How to get extraordinary things done in organizations. Jossey-Bass, San Francisco.

Leonard-Barton D (1995). Wellsprings of knowledge. Boston: Harvard Business School Press.

Liles PR (1981). 'Who are the entrepreneurs?'. In P. Gorb, P. Dowell and P. Wilson (eds) Small Business Perspectives. London: Armstrong Pub.London Bus. Sch. Pp. 33–50.

Linton JD (2002). Implementation Research: State of the art and future directions. Technovation. 22(2):65-79.

Lipsey R (1996). Economic growth, technological change and Canadian economic policy. Toronto: C.D. Howe Institute.

Lukas BA (1996).Striving for quality: the key role of internal and external customers, J. Mark. Focused Manage. 1(2): 87-175.

Lundvall BÅ (1988). Innovation as an interactive process: from user-producer interaction to the national system of innovation. In: Dosi G, Freeman C, Nelson RR, Silverberg G, Soete L (Editors), Technical

Change and Economic Theory. Frances Pinter, London.

Mabey C, Salaman G (1995). Strategic Human Resource Management, Blackwell, Oxford.

Majchrzak A (1988). The human side of factory automation: Managerial and human resource strategies for making automation succeed. San Francisco: Jossey-Bass.

Marsh SJ, Stock GN (2003). "Building Dynamic Capabilities in New Product Development through Intertemporal Integration."J. Prod. Innov. Manage. 23:422-436.

Maskell BH (1991). Performance Measurement for World Class Manufacturing.Productivity Press. Cambridge. MA.

Martin LM, Matlay H (2003). Innovative use of the internet in established small firms; The impact of knowledge management and organizational learning in accessing new opportunities, J. Qualitative Market Res. 6(1):18-26.

McAdam R (2000).The implementation of reengineering in SMEs: a grounded study, Int. Small Bus. J. 18(72):29-45.

McElroy MW (2000). Integrating complexity theory, knowledge management and organizational learning, J. Knowl. Manage. 4(3):195-203.

McEvily SK, Chakravarthy B (2002). The persistence of knowledge-based advantage: An empirical test for product performance and technological knowledge. Strategic Manage. J. 23:285-305.

McGill ME, Slocum JW (1993). 'Unlearning the Organization', Organ. Dyn. 22:67-79.

Miller D, Friesen PH (1978). Archetypes of strategy formulation. Manage. Sci. 24: 921-933.

Mu J, Peng G, Love E (2008).Interfirm networks, social capital, and knowledge flow', J. Knowl. Manage. 12(4):86-100.

Muayyad J (2004). Team feedback based on dialogue: Implications for change management, J. Manage. Dev. 23(2): 141-151.

Narvekar RS, Jain K (2006). A new framework to understand the technological innovation process. J. Intellectual Capital. 7(2): 174-186.

Neely A, Gregory M, Platts K (2005). Performance measurement systemdesign. Int. J. Operations. Prod. Manage. 25(12):1228-1263.

Nelson RR, Winter SG (1982). An Evolutionary Theory of Economic Change. Harvard University Press: Cambridge, MA.

Newbert S (2007). Empirical research on the Resource-Based View of the firm: An assessment and suggestions for future research, J. Strategic Manage. 28:121-146.

Nonaka I (1994). A Dynamic Theory of Organizational Knowledge Creation,"Organization Sci. 5(1):14-37.

Nonaka I, Takeuchi H (1995). The Knowledge Creating Company: How Japanese Companies Create the Dynamics of Innovation, Oxford University Press, New York, NY.

Penrose E (1972). The theory of the growth of the firm. Basil Blackwell and Mott, Oxford, 5th edition.

Peters T, Waterman R (1982). In search of excellence: Lesson from America's best run companies. New York: Harper and Row.

Precipe A (2000). Breadth and depth of technological capabilities: in CoPS; The case of the Aircraft Engine Control System. J. Res. Policy. 29: 895-911.

Polanyi M (1966). The Tacit Dimension. New York: Anchor Day Books.

Ravichandran T (2000a). Redefining organizational innovation: towards theoretical advancements, J. High Technol. Manage. Res. 10(2):243-274.

Rauch A, Wiklund J, Freese M, Lumpkin GT (2004). Entrepreneurial orientation and business performance: Cumulative empirical evidence. Paper presented at the 23rd Babson College Entrepreneurship Research Conference. Glasgow, UK.

Robertson PL, Yu TF (2001). Firm strategy, innovation and consumer demand: A market process approach. Manag. Decis. Econ. 22:183-199.

Rogers EM (1995). Diffusion of innovations (4th ed.). New York: Free Press.

Savory C (2006). Translating knowledge to build technological competence. J. Manage. Decis. 44:8

Saleh SD, Wang CK (1993). The Management of Innovation: Strategy, Structure, and Organizational Climate. IEEE Trans. Eng. Manage. 40:13-21.

Saban K, Lanasa J, Lackman C, Pease G (2000). Organizational learning: a critical component to new product development, J. Prod. Brand Manage. 2:99-117.

Schein EH (1993). On dialogue, culture, and organizational learning, Organ. Dyn.22(2):40-51.

Senge P (1990). The leader's new work : Building learning organization. Sloan Manage. Rev. Fall. pp.7-23.

Simon HA (1962) "The architecture of complexity." Proceed. Am. Philos. Soc. 106:467-482.

Simonin BL (1999). Ambiguity and the process of knowledge transfer in strategic alliances. Strat. Manage. J. 20(7):595-623.

Singer SJ, Edmonson AC (2006) When learning and performance are odds: Confronting the tension, Working Paper, Harvard University, November.

Sinkula JM, Baker WE, Noordewier TA (2002). Framework for market-based organizational learning: Lin (2007king values, knowledge, and behavior. J. Acad. Mark. Sci. 25(4):18-305.

Stata R (1989). Organizational learning: the key to management innovation, Sloan Manage. Rev. 30:63-74.

Sundbo J (2001). The strategic management of innovation: A sociological and economic theory. Cheltenham UK: Edward Elgar.

Tang HK (2000). An Integrative Model of Innovation in Organizations. Technovation 18(5):297-309.

Teece DJ (1977). Technology transfer by multinational corporations: The resource cost of transferring technological knowhow. Econom. J. 87:242–261.

Teece DJ (1986). Profiting from technological innovation: implications for integration, collaboration, licensing, and public policy. Res. Policy 15:285-305.

Teece DJ, Pisano G, Shuen A (1997). Dynamic Capabilities and Strategic Management, J. Strat. Manage. 18(7):509-533.

Teece DJ (2007). 'Explicating Dynamic Capabilities: The Nature and Micro-foundations of (Sustainable) Enterprise Performance'. Strateg. Manage. J. 28(13): 1319–50.

Thomke S (1998). Managing experimentation in the design of new products. J. Manage. Sci. 44:743-762.

Thomke S (2001). Enlightened experimentation: The new imperative for innovation. Harv. Bus. Rev. 79:67-75.

Tidd J, Bessant J, Pavitt K (2001). Managing innovation: Integrating technological, market and organisational change. John Wiley, Chichester.

Tsai W, Ghoshal S (1998). Social Capital and Value Creation: The Role of Intrafirm Networks. Acad. Manage. J. 41:464-476.

Tsai W (2001). Knowledge transfer in intraorganizational networks:Effects of network positionand absorptive capacity on business unit innovation and performance. Acad. Manage. J. 44:996-1004.

Tyre M (1991). Managing the introduction of new process technology: International differences in a multi-plant network. Res. Policy 20:57-76.

Van de Ven AH (1993). Managing the process of organizational innovation. In G.P. Huber and W.H. Glick, eds., Organizational Change and Redesign, Oxford: Oxford University Press, pp.269-294.

Venkatraman N (1989) The concept of fit in strategy research: toward verbal and statistical correspondence, Acad. Manage. Rev. 9:513-525.

Vinekar V (2008). Strategies for learning: Reconceptualizing the strategy environment-performance relationship through a knowledge based perspectives www.decisionsciences.org/Proceedings/DSI2008/docs/554-2981.pdf Date 13/10/09.

Von Hippel E (1988). The Sources of Innovation. New York: Oxford University Press.

Wall TD, Lischeron JH (1977). Worker Participation: A Critique of the Literature and Some Fresh Evidence. Maidenhead, U.K.: McGraw-Hill.

Weick KE (1976). Educational organizations as loosely coupled systems. Adm. Sci. Q. 21:1-19.

West MA, Anderson NR (1996). `Innovation in top management teams'. J. Appl. Psychol. 81:680-693.

Wiklund J, Shepherd D (2003). Knowledge-Based Resources, Entrepreneurial Orientation, and the Performance of Small and Medium-Sized Businesses. Strat. Manage. J. 24:1307-1314.

Winter SG (1987). Knowledge and competence as strategic assets. In:

Teece DJ ed. The competitive challenge - strategies for industrial innovation and renewal, Ballinger Publ. Co, Cambridge, MA, pp.159-184.

Wolfe RA (1994). Organizational innovation: review, critique and suggested research directions', J. Manage. Stud. 31:405-431.

Zander U, Kogut B (1995). Knowledge and the speed of transfer and imitation of organizational capabilities: an empirical test, Organ. Sci. 6(91):76-92.

Zollo M, Winter SG (2002). Deliberate learning and the evolution of dynamic capabilities, Organ. Sci.13(3):339-351.

Zmund RW (1984). An examination of the "push-pull" theory applied to process innovation in knowledge work. Manage. Sci. 30(6):727-738.

10

Applying encryption schemed to supervisory control and data acquisition systems for security management

Tai-hoon Kim

GVSA and University of Tasmania, Australia.

Supervisory Control and Data Acquisition (SCADA) is the combination of telemetry and data acquisition. Supervisory Control and Data Acquisition system is compose of collecting of the information, transferring it to the central site, carrying out any necessary analysis and control and then displaying that information on the operator screens. Encryption Schemes are needed to secure communication in SCADA Systems. In the case of Symmetric key encryption, a secret key, which can be a number, a word, or just a string of random letters, is applied to the text of a message to change the content in a particular way. While in the case of Asymmetric Encryption, two keys are used. A public key is made freely available to anyone who might want to send you a message. A second, private key is kept secret, so that only you know it. These schemes can be integrated to SCADA communication for managing security level. In this paper, author compares Encryption Schemes as used in Communication between SCADA components to show the escalation of security level.

Key words: Supervisory Control and Data Acquisition, encryption, internet, communication, control system.

INTRODUCTION

Supervisory Control and Data Acquisition (SCADA) is an implementation of process control systems (PCS). Another common method is Distributed Control Systems (DCS). SCADA systems are typically spread over miles of distance and sometimes have their programmed control functions in the central host computer (Yardley, 2008; Hildick-Smith, 2005). SCADA systems provide automated control and remote human monitoring of real world processes. SCADA systems can be used to improve quality and efficiencies in processes such as beer brewing and snow making for ski resorts, but are traditionally used by utilities and industries in the areas of oil and natural gas, electric power, rail transportation, water and wastewater. SCADA systems provide near real time monitoring and control with time delays ranging between fractions of seconds to minutes. Depending on

the size and sophistication, SCADA systems can cost from tens of thousands of dollars to tens of millions of dollars (Hildick-Smith, 2005).

Because of the complexity of SCADA systems, vulnerabilities and threats often occur. SCADA control systems and protocols were often designed decades ago, when security was of little concern because of the closed nature of the communications networks and the general model of trusting the data on them. As these systems have been modernized, they have become inter-connected and have started running more modern services such as Web interfaces and interactive consoles and have implemented remote configuration protocols. Sadly, security has been lagging during the increased modernization of these systems (Yardley, 2008; Zhu et al., 2011; Abawajy and Robles, 2010).

Encryption in communication between SCADA components is very important. There are two widely used techniques for encrypting information: symmetric encryption which is also called secret key encryption and asymmetric encryption which is also called public key encryption. In the next sections, comparison between Encryption Schemes as used in Communication between SCADA Components is discussed.

RELATED LITERATURE

Supervisory control and data acquisition (SCADA)

Supervisory Control and Data Acquisition (SCADA) existed long time ago when control systems were introduced. SCADA systems that time use data acquisition by using strip chart recorders, panels of meters, and lights. Not similar to modern SCADA systems, there is an operator which manually operates various control knobs exercised supervisory control. These devices are still used to do supervisory control and data acquisition on power generating facilities, plants and factories (Robles et al., 2009; Kim, 2010).

Telemetry is automatic transmission and measurement of data from remote sources by wire or radio or other means. It is also used to send commands, programs and receives monitoring information from these remote locations. SCADA is the combination of telemetry and data acquisition. Supervisory Control and Data Acquisition system is compose of collecting of the information, transferring it to the central site, carrying out any necessary analysis and control and then displaying that information on the operator screens. The required control actions are then passed back to the process (Bailey and Wright, 2003).

The measurement and control system of SCADA has one master terminal unit (MTU) which could be called the brain of the system and one or more remote terminal units (RTU). The RTUs gather the data locally and send them to the MTU which then issues suitable commands to be executed on site. A system of either standard or customized software is used to collate, interpret and manage the data. Supervisory Control and Data Acquisition (SCADA) is conventionally set upped in a private network not connected to the internet (Figure 1). This is done for the purpose of isolating the confidential information as well as the control to the system itself (Kim, 2010).

Hardware

A SCADA system consists of a number of remote terminal units (RTUs) collecting field data and sending that data back to a master station, via a communication system (Hildick-Smith, 2005). The master station displays the acquired data and allows the operator to perform remote control tasks. The accurate and timely

data allows for optimization of the plant operation and process. Other benefits include more efficient, reliable and most importantly, safer operations. These results in a lower cost of operation compared to earlier non-automated systems (Kim, 2010).

Supervisory Control and Data Acquisition Systems usually have Distributed Control System components. PLCs or RTUs are also commonly used; they are capable of autonomously executing simple logic processes without a master computer controlling it. A functional block programming language, IEC 61131-3, is frequently used to create programs which run on these PLCs and RTUs. This allows SCADA system engineers to perform both the design and implementation of a program to be executed on an RTU or PLC. From 1998, major PLC manufacturers have offered integrated HMI /SCADA systems, many use open and non-proprietary communications protocols. Many third-party HMI/SCADA packages, offering built-in compatibility with most major PLCs, have also entered the market, allowing mechanical engineers, electrical engineers and technicians to configure HMIs themselves. Much other hardware are also basing its functionality to those of PLC's (NACS 2009).

The communications system provides the pathway for communication between the master station and the remote sites. This communication system can be wire, fiber optic, radio, telephone line, microwave and possibly even satellite. Specific protocols and error detection philosophies are used for efficient and optimum transfer of data. The master station (or sub-masters) gather data from the various RTUs and generally provide an operator interface for display of information and control of the remote sites. In large telemetry systems, sub-master sites gather information from remote sites and act as a relay back to the control master station (Kim, 2010).

Software

Supervisory Control and Data Acquisition software can be divided into proprietary type or open type. Proprietary software are developed and designed for the specific hardware and are usually sold together. The main problem with these systems is the overwhelming reliance on the supplier of the system. Open software systems are designed to communicate and control different types of hardware. It is popular because of the interoperability they bring to the system (Bailey and Wright, 2003). WonderWare and Citect are just two of the open software packages available in the market for SCADA systems. Some packages are now including asset management integrated within the SCADA system (Kim, 2010).

Human machine interface (HMI)

In SCADA and in the industrial design field of human-

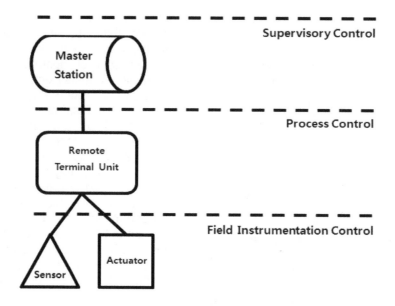

Figure 1. Conventional SCADA architecture.

machine interaction, the user interface is (a place) where interaction between humans and machines occurs. The goal of interaction between a human and a machine at the user interface is effective operation and control of the machine, and feedback from the machine which aids the operator in making operational decisions. Examples of this broad concept of user interfaces include the interactive aspects of computer operating systems, hand tools, heavy machinery operator controls and process controls (Kim, 2010).

The goal of human-machine interaction engineering is to produce a user interface which makes it easy, efficient, and enjoyable to operate a machine in the way which produces the desired result. This generally means that the operator needs to provide minimal input to achieve the desired output, and also that the machine minimizes undesired outputs to the human (Kim, 2010). Ever since the increased use of personal computers and the relative decline in societal awareness of heavy machinery, the term user interface has taken on overtones of the (graphical) user interface, while industrial control panel and machinery control design discussions more commonly refer to human-machine interfaces (Robles et al., 2009).

The design of a user interface affects the amount of effort the user must expend to provide input for the system and to interpret the output of the system, and how much effort it takes to learn how to do this. Usability is the degree to which the design of a particular user interface takes into account the human psychology and physiology of the users, and makes the process of using the system effective, efficient and satisfying. Usability is mainly a characteristic of the user interface, but is also associated with the functionalities of the product and the process to design it. It describes how well a product can

be used for its intended purpose by its target users with efficiency, effectiveness, and satisfaction (Kim, 2010).

SCADA system includes a user interface which is usually called Human Machine Interface (HMI). The HMI of a SCADA system is where data is processed and presented to be viewed and monitored by a human operator. This interface usually includes controls where the individual can interface with the SCADA system. HMI's are an easy way to standardize the facilitation of monitoring multiple RTU's or PLC's (programmable logic controllers). Usually RTU's or PLC's will run a pre programmed process, but monitoring each of them individually can be difficult, usually because they are spread out over the system. Because RTU's and PLC's historically had no standardized method to display or present data to an operator, the SCADA system communicates with PLC's throughout the system network and processes information that is easily disseminated by the HMI. HMI's can also be linked to a database, which can use data gathered from PLC's or RTU's to provide graphs on trends, logistic info, schematics for a specific sensor or machine or even make troubleshooting guides accessible. In the last decade, practically all SCADA systems include an integrated HMI and PLC device making it extremely easy to run and monitor a SCADA system (Kim, 2010).

The HMI package for the SCADA system typically includes a drawing program that the operators or system maintenance personnel use to change the way these points are represented in the interface. These representations can be as simple as an on-screen traffic light, which represents the state of an actual traffic light in the field, or as complex as a multi-projector display representing the position of all of the elevators in a skyscraper or all of the trains on a railway (Kim, 2010).

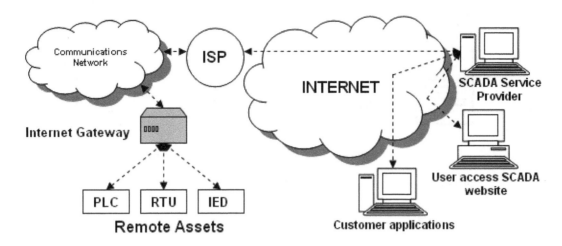

Figure 2. Internet SCADA architecture [Wallace, 2003].

Alarm handling is an important part of most SCADA implementations. The system monitors whether certain alarm conditions are satisfied, to determine when an alarm event has occurred. Once an alarm event has been detected, one or more actions are taken (such as the activation of one or more alarm indicators, and perhaps the generation of email or text messages so that management or remote SCADA operators are informed).

Internet SCADA or web SCADA

Conventional SCADA only have 4 components: The master station, plc/rtu, fieldbus and sensors (Figure 1). Internet SCADA replaces or extends the fieldbus to the internet. This means that the Master Station can be on a different network or location.

Figure 2 shows the architecture of SCADA which is connected through the internet. Like a normal SCADA, it has RTUs/PLCs/IEDs, The SCADA Service Provider or the Master Station. This also includes the user-access to SCADA website. This is for the smaller SCADA operators that can avail the services provided by the SCADA service provider. It can either be a company that uses SCADA exclusively. Another component of the internet SCADA is the Customer Application which allows report generation or billing. Along with the fieldbus, the internet is an extension. This is setup like a private network so that only the master station can have access to the remote assets. The master also has an extension that acts as a web server so that the SCADA users and customers can access the data through the SCADA provider website (Robles et al 2010).

AS the system evolves, SCADA systems are coming in line with standard networking technologies. Ethernet and TCP/IP based protocols are replacing the older proprietary standards. Although certain characteristics of frame-based network communication technology (deter-

minism, synchronization, protocol selection, environment suitability) have restricted the adoption of Ethernet in a few specialized applications, the vast majority of markets have accepted Ethernet networks for HMI/SCADA.

A few vendors have begun offering application specific SCADA systems hosted on remote platforms over the Internet. This removes the need to install and commission systems at the end-user's facility and takes advantage of security features already available in Internet technology, VPNs and SSL. Some concerns include security, (NACS, 2009) Internet connection reliability, and latency.

Symmetric encryption

Along with the advantages it brings, are security issues regarding wireless internet SCADA. In this section, we discuss internet SCADA, its connection through wireless communication and the security issues surrounding it. To answer the security issues, a symmetric-key encryption for wireless internet SCADA was proposed (Prasithsangaree and Krishnamurthy, 2003).

Utilization of symmetric key encryption

Symmetric-key algorithms are a class of algorithms for cryptography that use trivially related, often identical, cryptographic keys for both decryption and encryption (Figure 3). The encryption key is trivially related to the decryption key, in that they may be identical or there is a simple transform to go between the two keys. The keys, in practice, represent a shared secret between two or more parties that can be used to maintain a private information link (RSA Laboratories).

Symmetric-key algorithms can be divided into stream ciphers and block ciphers. Stream ciphers encrypt the bytes of the message one at a time, and block ciphers

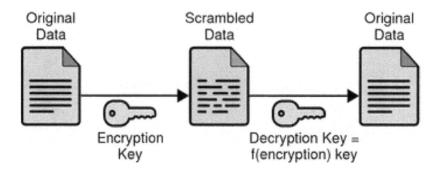

Figure 3. Symmetric key utilizing same key to encrypt and decrypt the data.

Figure 4. Asymmetric key encryption uses different keys for decryption and encryption.

take a number of bytes and encrypt them as a single unit. Blocks of 64 bits have been commonly used; the Advanced Encryption Standard algorithm approved by NIST in December 2001 uses 128-bit blocks (RSA Laboratories).

Asymmetric encryption

The internet SCADA facility has brought a lot of advantages in terms of control, data generation and viewing. With these advantages, come the security issues regarding web SCADA. In this section, web SCADA and its connectivity along with the issues regarding security will be discussed. A web SCADA security solution using asymmetric-key encryption will be explained.

Asymmetric-key encryption

Asymmetric key encryption uses different keys for decryption/encryption (Figure 4). These two keys are mathematically related and they form a key pair. One key is kept private, and is called private-key, and the other can be made public, called public-key. Hence this is also called Public Key Encryption. Public key can be sent by mail. A private key is typically used for encrypting the message-digest; in such an application private-key algorithm is called message-digest encryption algo-

rithm. A public key is typically used for encrypting the secret-key; in such a application private-key algorithm is called key encryption algorithm (Choi et al., 2009).

Popular private-key algorithms are RSA and DSA (Digital Signature Algorithm). While for an ordinary use of RSA, a key size of 768 can be used, but for corporate use a key size of 1024 and for extremely valuable information a key size of 2048 should be used. Asymmetric key encryption is much slower than symmetric key encryption and hence they are only used for key exchanges and digital signatures. RSA is an algorithm for public-key cryptography. It is the first algorithm known to be suitable for signing as well as encryption, and one of the first great advances in public key cryptography (Choi et al., 2009).

RSA is widely used in electronic commerce protocols, and is believed to be secure given sufficiently long keys and the use of up-to-date implementations. One of the most common digital signature mechanisms, the Digital Signature Algorithm (DSA) is the basis of the Digital Signature Standard (DSS), a U.S. Government document. As with other digital signature algorithms, DSA lets one person with a secret key "sign" a document, so that others with a matching public key can verify it must have been signed only by the holder of the secret key. Digital signatures depend on hash functions, which are one-way computations done on a message (Choi et al., 2009). They are called "one-way" because there is no known way (without infeasible amounts of computation) to find a

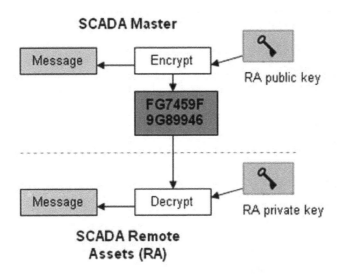

SCADA Master

SCADA Remote
Assets (RA)

Figure 5. Asymmetric-key encryption applied to internet SCADA.

message with a given hash value. In other words, a hash value can be determined for a given message, but it is not known to be possible to construct any message with a given hash value.

Hash functions are similar to the scrambling operations used in symmetric key encryption, except that there is no decryption key: the operation is irreversible. The result has a fixed length, which is 160 bits in the case of the Secure Hash Algorithm (SHA) used by DSA (Choi et al., 2009; Robles and Kim, 2011).

IMPLEMENTATION AND DISCUSSION

The following sub-sections discuss the implementation of the proposed solution. It contains the implementation of solutions like the Integration of Asymmetric-key Encryption to Internet SCADA; and Symmetric Key Encryption in SCADA Environment.

Integration of Asymmetric-key Encryption to Web SCADA

Authentication will be required to access the data and reports so that only users who have enough permission can access the information. Quality system administration techniques can make all the difference in security prevention (NACS, 2009). SCADA web server must always be secure since the data in it are very critical. Web server security software can also be added.

Communication from the customer or client will start with an http request to the master server. The client will be authenticated before the request will be completed. The SCADA master will then send back the requested information to the client. The information will also be encrypted using the same encryption that is proposed to be used between the SCADA master and the remote assets (Choi et al., 2009; Robles and Kim, 2011).

To test the usability of this scheme, it was tested using the web base Asymmetric-key Encryption simulator. Since there are many kinds of Asymmetric-key Encryption, in this simulator, RSA Cipher is used (Figure 6).

Table 1 shows the results of encrypted commands. The first column shows the command; the second column shows the key length; the third column shows the Modulo, the fourth column shows the key which is used for encrypting the command, the fifth column shows the encrypted data; the sixth column shows the key which is used to decrypt the data and the last column shows the actual command.

SCADA systems connected through the internet can provide access to real-time data display, alarming, trending, and reporting from remote equipment. But it also presents some vulnerabilities and security issues. In this section, the security issues in internet SCADA were pointed out. The utilization of asymmetric key encryption is suggested (Figure 5). It can provide security to the data that is transmitted from the SCADA master and the remote assets. Once a system is connected to the internet, it is not impossible for other internet users to have access to the system that is why encryption is very important (Choi et al., 2009; Stoica and Robles, 2010).

Symmetric key encryption in web SCADA

Symmetric cryptography uses the same key for both encryption and decryption. Using symmetric crypto-graphy, it is safe to send encrypted messages without fear of interception. This means only the SCADA master

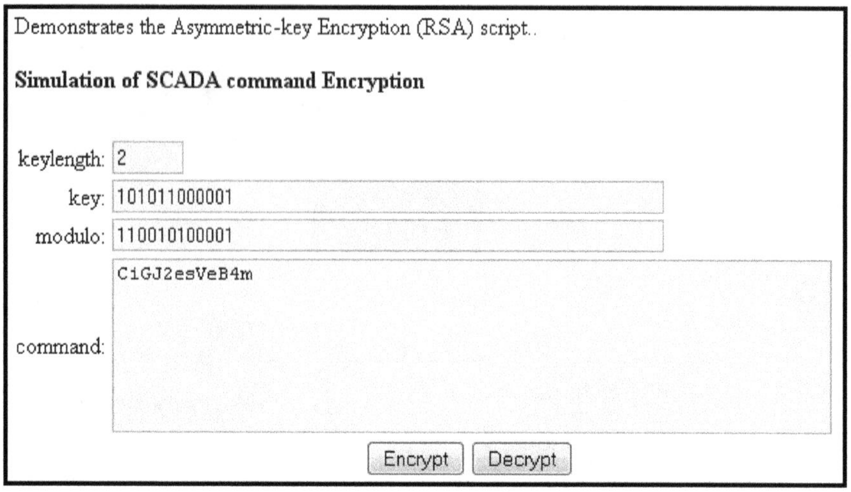

Demonstrates the Asymmetric-key Encryption (RSA) script..

Simulation of SCADA command Encryption

keylength: `2`

key: `101011000001`

modulo: `110010100001`

command:
`CiGJ2esVeB4m`

[Encrypt] [Decrypt]

Figure 6. Browser based RSA Cipher simulator.

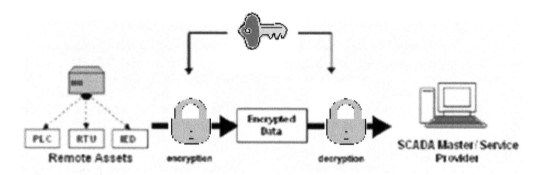

Figure 7. Symmetric cryptography between SCADA master station and remote components.

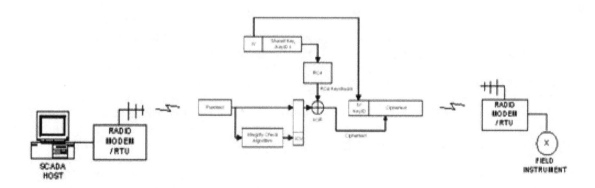

Figure 8. Standard WEP encryption in wireless SCADA environment.

and the remote assets can communicate with each other because of the said key (Figure 7).

WEP was included as the privacy of the original IEEE 802.11 standard. WEP uses the stream cipher RC4 for confidentiality, and the CRC-32 checksum for integrity. It can be implemented to wireless SCADA as it is implemented to other wireless systems. Messages between remote RTU's can be converted to ciphertext by utilizing this mechanism. Figure 8 shows how this is done.

The use of symmetric key encryption specifically the RC4 cipher is also applicable in a wireless Web-SCADA. It can provide security to the data that is transmitted from the SCADA master and the remote assets and also communication between remote RTU's. Once a system

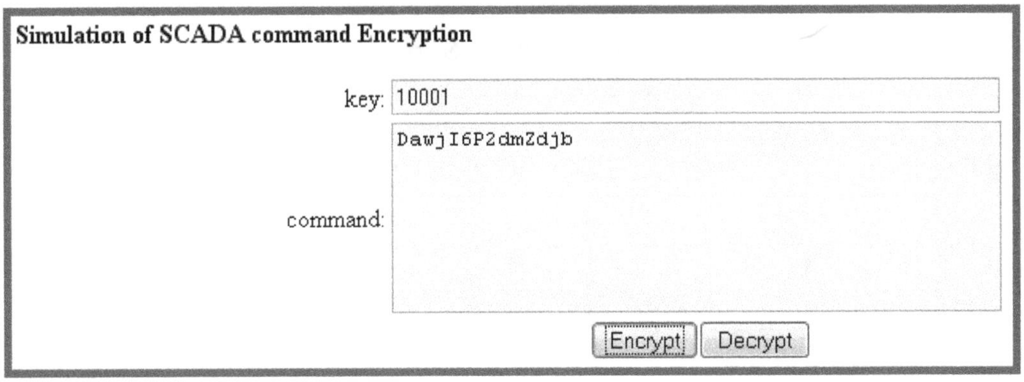

Figure 9. Browser based RC4 simulator.

Table 1. Asymmetric-key Encryption of SCADA commands.

Command	Key length	Modulo	Key 1	Encrypted data	Key 2	Decrypted data
Command 1	2 bytes	110010100001	10001	KAqm0dXhpbh6	101011000001	turn on
Command 2	2 bytes	110010100001	10001	9Ra8H"7TEXWLsc	101011000001	turn off
Command 3	2 bytes	110010100001	10001	qS70fd_L"ti	101011000001	connect
Command 4	2 bytes	110010100001	10001	bPWx5P_4o6JuC5B4	101011000001	disconnect
Command 5	2 bytes	110010100001	10001	JLaO2p5HZXTHLS_7	101011000001	open valve
Command 6	2 bytes	110010100001	10001	0XGvoFO4i7mIP3_M	101011000001	class valve
Command 7	2 bytes	110010100001	10001	MNG1pMdWdR3nG6g	101011000001	half open
Command 8	2 bytes	110010100001	10001	kRWKd7"nudFndww2	101011000001	half close

Table 2. Symmetric-key encryption of SCADA commands.

Command	Key 1	Encrypted data	Decrypted data
Command 1	10001	JqMgRYo7ca	turn on
Command 2	10001	JqMgRYo7kig	turn off
Command 3	10001	04NbRMk4ya	connect
Command 4	10001	ZG3gMoA7ce2dCb	disconnect
Command 5	10001	4ewdRYE9nGMgnb	open valve
Command 6	10001	003b2M6OAugaEXa	class valve
Command 7	10001	"ahbJYo7CeMa	half open
Command 8	10001	"ahbJYo4aS2hnb	half close

is connected to the internet especially wirelessly, it is not impossible for other internet users to have access to the system that is why encryption should be implemented. Data and report generation is also in demand so the internet SCADA is designed to have a web based report generation system through http. And to cut off the budget for communication lines, SCADA operators utilize the wireless based SCADA (NACS, 2009).

To test the usability of this scheme, it was tested using the web base Symmetric-key Encryption simulator. Since there are many kinds of Symmetric-key Encryption, in this simulator, RC4 is used (Figure 9). The simulator uses the following javascript function to encrypt the command:

```
function rc4encrypt() {
document.rc4.text.value=textToBase64(rc4(document.rc
4.key.value,document.rc4.text.value))
}
```

And the following javascript function is used to decrypt the command:

```
function rc4decrypt() {
document.rc4.text.value=(rc4(document.rc4.key.value,ba
se64ToText(document.rc4.text.value)))
}
```

Table 2 shows the results of encrypted commands. The

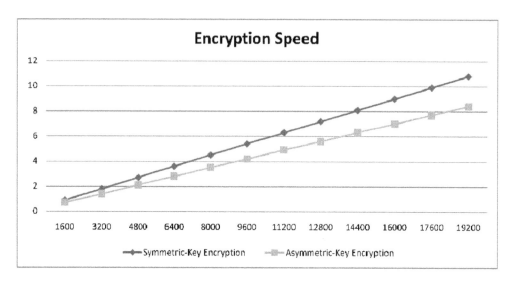

Figure 10. Encryption speed comparison.

first column shows the command; the second column shows the key which is used for encryption; the third column shows the encrypted data and the last column shows the actual command.

CONCLUSION

SCADA refers to the control system of the industry which is a computer system which controls and monitors a process. SCADA Communication is a core component of a SCADA Monitoring System. Common misconception regarding SCADA security was SCADA networks were isolated from all other networks and so attackers could not access the system. As the industry grows, the demand for more connectivity also increased. From a small range network, SCADA systems are sometimes connected to other networks like the internet. The open standards also make it very easy for attackers to gain in-depth knowledge about the working of these SCADA networks. Because of so many vulnerabilities encryption Schemes are applied to secure the communication between the components. This work compares different Encryption Schemes for Securing Internet SCADA Component Communication. And this work shows new method can manage the higher level in security.

An important thing to be considered is the Encryption Speed (Figure 10). Compared to Asymmetric Key Encryption, Symmetric Key Encryption appears to be slower. It's important to note right from the beginning that beyond some ridiculous point, it's not worth sacrificing speed for security. However, the measurements will still help us make certain decisions. It is also important to remember that SCADA Communication is a core component of a SCADA Monitoring System therefore it may not function properly without proper communication.

ACKNOWLEDGEMENTS

Author wishes to express special thanks to Dr. Rosslin John Robles and Dr. Maricel O. Balitanas who helped simulation. This work was done based on their endless passion.

REFERENCES

Abawajy J, Robles RJ (2010). "Secured Communication Scheme for SCADA in Smart Grid Environment". J. Sec. Eng. 7(6): 575:584

Bailey D, Wright E (2003). Practical SCADA for Industry, IDC Technologies, ISBN: 07506 58053.

Choi M, Robles RJ, Kim T (2009). "Application Possibility of Asymmetric-key Encryption to SCADA Security". J. Korean Inst. Info. Technol. 7(4): 208-217, ISSN: 1958-8619.

Hildick-Smith A (2005). "Security for Critical Infrastructure SCADA Systems", SANS Institute InfoSec Reading Room, http://www.sans.org/reading_room/whitepapers/warfare/security-critical-infrastructure-scada-systems_1644.

Kim T-h (2010). "Weather Condition Double Checking in Internet SCADA Environment", WSEAS TRANSACTIONS on SYSTEMS and CONTROL. 5(8): 623-634, ISSN: 1991-8763.

NACS (2009). "Client/Server Security Assessment and Awareness" Accessed: April 2009.

Prasithsangaree P, Krishnamurthy K (2003). "Analysis of Energy Consumption of RC4 and AES Algorithms in Wireless LANs", GLOBECOM 2003. pp. 1445-1449, 0-7803-7974-8.

"RC4", http://www.wisdom.weizmann.ac.il/~itsik/RC4/rc4.html. Accessed: June 2009.

Robles RJ, Choi M, Balitanas M, Sattarova F, Alisherov F, Kim N, Kim T (2009). "Vulnerabilities in Control Systems, Critical Infrastructure Systems and SCADA", Proceedings of the 8th KIIT IT based Convergence Service workshop & Summer Conference, Mokpo Maritime University (Mokpo, Korea), p.89, ISSN 2005-7334.

Robles RJ, Seo K, Kim T (2010). "Communication Security solution for internet SCADA", Korean Institute of Information Technology 2010 IT Convergence Technology - Summer workshops and Conference Proceedings 5:461-463.

Robles RJ, Kim T (2011). "Scheme to Secure Communication of SCADA Master Station and Remote HMI's through Smart Phones". J Sec. Eng. 8(3): 349-358.

RSA LAboratories "What is RC4?" http://www.rsa.com/rsalabs/node.asp?id=2250 Accessed: June 2009.

Stoica A, Robles RJ (2010). "Encryption Scheme for Control Systems through Web". J. Sec. Eng. 7(5): 511-520.

Wallace D (2003). "Control Engineering. How to put SCADA on the Internet", http://www.controleng.com/article/CA321065.html Accessed: January 2010.

Yardley T (2008). "SCADA: issues, vulnerabilities, and future directions", Systems and Internet Infrastructure Security Laboratory, http://www.usenix.org/publications/login/2008-12/pdfs/yardley.pdf. Accessed: March 2011.

Zhu B, Joseph A, Sastry S (2011). "A Taxonomy of Cyber Attacks on SCADA Systems", Internet of Things (iThings/CPSCom), 2011 International Conference on and 4th International Conference on Cyber, Physical and Social Computing. DOI: 10.1109/iThings/CPSCom.2011.34: 380-388.

11

The exploration on network behaviors by using the models of Theory of planned behaviors (TPB), Technology acceptance model (TAM) and C-TAM-TPB

Chih-Chung Chen

Department of Knowledge Management, Aletheia University (Matou campus), Taiwan, R.O.C.

This research mainly aims to explore the network behaviors of Web 2.0 users. The comparative analysis is also operated with the research models of Theory of planned behaviors (TPB), TAM and C-TAM-TPB. With network questionnaires, there are 638 valid replies received. The relations among different variables in this research are examined with the structural equation models. Additionally, it is found from research results, all hypotheses are established. Moreover, the explanatory power of planned behaviors is more acceptable than the technology acceptance model and C-TAM-TPB.

Key words: Theory of reasoned action (TRA), theory of innovation diffusion (TID), Theory of planned behaviors (TPB), TAM, C-TAM-TPB.

INTRODUCTION

The explanations on user behaviors to accept new technologies have been always a hot issue. The relevant researches on this issue are also widely known as one of the most mature research realms in the scientific lectures on modern information management. Therefore, from 1980 till now, by focusing on this issue, there are numerous models developed from information management science, sociology and psychology, inclusive of the theory of reasoned action (TRA), the theory of innovation diffusion (TID) (Rogers, 2003), the theory of planned behavior (TPB) (Ajzen,1985), the technology acceptance model (TAM) (Davis, 1989), combined TAM and TPB, C-TAM-TPB) (Taylor and Todd, 1995), etc. In view of the emphasis and prosperous development on the acceptance behavior theories for users to accept new technologies, the importance of researching technology acceptance behaviors for successful introduction can be clearly seen. However, among numerous theoretical models, there are different variables and causal relation-

ships included. Every theoretical model is vested with different influential variables and casual relationships due to different theoretical foundations and verification subjects. Therefore, in view of the applications for technology acceptance behaviors, there are many more empirical analysis required to discern various theoretical models and the applicability of variables to different industries.

It is found from past researches, TPB emphasizes behaviors (Timothy and Sulaiman, 2008), but TAM and C-TAM-TPB focus on the acceptance extents to new technology commodities (Marc and Christoph, 2008; Taylor and Todd, 1995). Based on the research results proposed by Davis (1989), as research results indicate, in view of the explanation on using information technologies, TAM shows stronger predicting power than that of TPB. However, as research results of Taylor and Todd (1995) indicated, TAM is added with social factors and control factors integrated into C-TAM-TPB with stronger exploration power to information technologies. Additionally, in view of theoretical convenience, TAM is superior to C-TAM-TPB. Taylor and Todd (1995) also contend to maintain the convenience to an excellent extent, the explanatory power to behaviors must be sacrificed in TAM (with social variables and control variables omitted). Unlike TPB, TAM is designed with different contents according to various situations. Additionally, there is no social variable and control variable included in TAM, because Davis (1989) contends social variables and control variables show no remarkable associations with behaviors like the effect caused by usefulness. However, Taylor and Todd (1995) indicate social variables and control variables cause direct associations with behaviors. Therefore, both TAM and TPB are integrated to develop a C-TAM-TPB model.

To sum up above mentions, this research is operated with 3 models, namely TPB, TAM and C-TAM-TPB for empirical exploration on their fitness.

LITERATURE AND HYPOTHESIS

Web 2.0

Web 2.0 is a new network trend firstly proposed by the founder and CEO of O'Reilly Media, Mr. Tim O'Reilly (2005). Web 2.0 means the new business management of websites gradually surfacing from the network bubbles since 2000. Web 2.0 is not an unchanged fixed model, but it means a concept with continuous progress and improvement. Furthermore, the increasing network surfing populations and the changes happening to users' life habits are also the important factors to make Web 2.0 appear. Because Web 2.0 in itself emerges from the interaction and cohesion among people, the increasing network surfing populations is one of the critical factors to the formation of Web 2.0 (Gong, 2006). Till 2010 Q4, the number of frequent network surfing populations locally has reached 10,790,000. Compared with 600,000 network surfing users in 1996, the growth pace is very fast (III FIND, 2011). With such a great number of network surfing populations, the fever of Web 2.0 network applications is formed currently. Regarding the researches on Web 2.0, most are applied to education activities with the platforms available to improve learning efficiency and shorten the digital divide (Gabriela, 2009; Gabriela and Carmen, 2010; James, 2010; Koong and Wu, 2010).

The Theory of Planned Behaviors (TPB)

In 1985, 1988 and 1991, the theory of planned behaviors was proposed by Ajzen. Because the theory was developed from the theory of reasoned action (TRA), both theories suppose behavioral intentions to be the

important factors to usage behaviors. Moreover, for other factors to possibly cause indirect influence on behaviors through intentions, there are 3 major dimensions to influence intentions including the internal factors whether individuals showing their own preference, attitude towards the behaviors (AT), whether some import others giving the supports to a certain behavior, the "subjective norms (SN)" and the factors coordinated with both opportunities and time, also, the difficulty extents for individuals to control themselves with some behaviors achieved, "perceived behavioral control (PBC)". The formation of attitude and subjective norms is identical to that of TRA. If the higher positive attitude of individuals is posed against a certain behavior perceiving much more pressure from important others and surrounding societies, the substantial control extents to such a behavior is perceived stronger; if the behavior control is easier, individuals show stronger intentions to conduct such a behavior. Regarding TPB researches, there are some applied to knowledge share (Johnny and Bolloju, 2005), breastfeeding attitudes (Melanie et al., 2007), piracy behaviors (Timothy and Sulaiman, 2008) and daily life behaviors of network administrators (Alma et al., 2010), etc.

It is found from past researches on TPB, behavioral attitudes and perceived behaviors cause positive influence and high explanatory power to behavioral intentions. Behavioral intentions cause positive influence on substantial usage behaviors. Therefore, there are some hypotheses proposed by this research:

H1: More positive attitudes posed by users against Web 2.0 can bring with stronger "behavioral intentions".
H2: More positive "subjective norms" posed by users against Web 2.0 can bring with stronger "behavioral intentions".
H3: More positive "perceived behavior control" posed by users against Web 2.0 can bring with stronger "behavioral intentions".
H4: More positive "behavioral intentions" posed by users against Web 2.0 can bring with stronger "substantial usage behaviors".

Technology Acceptance Model (TAM)

Technology Acceptance Model (TAM) was proposed by Davis in 1989. It is a model based on TRA especially focusing on the behaviors of using technologies. Till now, it is widely explained as the acceptance extents for users to accept new information technologies, namely, the associations formed by option faith and attitudes. It is meant to predict the acceptance extents of final users (Succi and Walter, 1999). Morris and Dillon (1997) contend no matter this system is actually applied, TAM provides researchers with a simpler and more cost-saving method to predict the extents of systematic success.

In the perspective of technology acceptance, Davis (1989) proposes perceived usefulness (PU) and perceived ease of use (PEU) are two major determining factors for attitudes. Through empirical verification, two dimensions of both perceived usefulness (PU) and perceived ease of use (PEU) cause influence on the attitudes of using technologies to further impact behavioral intentions. Furthermore, behavioral intentions impact usage behaviors. Regarding TAM researches, they are applied to BBS or website communities (Mathieson et al., 2001; Kwon and Wen, 2010), on-line games (Hsu and Lu, 2004), Internet banking (Rigopoulos and Askounis, 2007) and on-line learning systems (Liu et al., 2010), etc.

In view of past researches on TAM, it is found perceived ease of use causes positive influence on perceived usefulness. Both perceived usefulness and perceived ease of use cause positive influence on attitudes. Attitudes cause positive influence on behavioral intentions. Behavioral intentions cause positive influence on usage behaviors. Therefore, there are some hypotheses proposed in this research:

H5: "Perceived ease of use" causes positive influence on "perceived usefulness".

H6: "Perceived usefulness" causes positive influence on "attitudes".

H7: "Perceived ease of use" causes positive influence on "attitudes".

H8: "Attitudes" cause positive influence on "behavioral intentions".

H9: "Behavioral intentions" cause positive influence on "substantial usage behaviors".

Combined Technology Acceptance Models and the Theory of Planned Behaviors (Combined TAM and TPB, C-TAM-TPB)

Taylor and Todd (1995) contend TAM is meant to predict the behavioral intentions for using technologies among users and the capabilities of substantial usage behaviors. Although, it has been widely supported by a great number of scientific researches, yet there is no social factor and control factor integrated into the research model. The said two factors have been clearly verified by numerous empirical researches with remarkable influence on users' substantial usage behaviors for using technologies. The said two factors are also the key variables in TPB. Therefore, Taylor and Todd (1995) integrate both TAM and TPB further added with two control variables, subjective norms and perceived behavior control, in to the TAM model. The combined TAM and TPB, C-TAM-TPB is proposed. According to the research conducted by Taylor and Todd (1995), from the empirical results with students using the facilities of computing center resources, it is found the C-TAM-TPB

integrated by both TAM and TPB comes with excellently high fitness to explain user behaviors for using new technologies.

It is found from past C-TAM-TPB researches, perceived ease of use causes positive influence on perceived usefulness. Both perceived usefulness and perceived ease of use cause positive influence on attitudes. Attitudes, subjective norms and perceived behavior control cause positive influence on usage behaviors. Therefore, there are some hypotheses proposed in this research:

H10: "Perceived ease of use" causes positive influence on "perceived usefulness".

H11: "Perceived usefulness" causes positive influence on "attitudes".

H12: "Perceived ease of use" causes positive influence on "attitudes".

H13: More positive "attitudes" posed by users against Web 2.0 can bring with stronger "behavioral intentions".

H14: More positive "subjective norms" posed by users against Web 2.0 can bring with stronger "behavioral intentions".

H15: More positive "perceived behavior control" posed by users against Web 2.0 can bring with stronger "behavioral intentions".

H16: More positive "behavioral intentions" posed by users against Web 2.0 can bring with stronger "substantial usage behaviors".

RESEARCH METHODS

Measurements

Attitude: It means the intentional evaluation for individuals to use Web 2.0 websites. There are 7 questions totally with the question items proposed by Ajzen (1985), Johnny and Bolloju (2005).

Subjective norm: It means the Web 2.0 usage extents of important relevant persons perceived by users. There are totally 3 questions adopted from Ajzen (1985), Johnny and Bolloju (2005).

Perceived behavior control: It means the support extents provided by relevant infrastructures to use Web 2.0 websites perceived by users. There are totally 5 questions adopted from Ajzen (1985), Johnny and Bolloju (2005).

Perceived usefulness: It means the fruitful assistance to use Web 2.0 websites for more efficient communications and satisfaction perceived by users. There are totally 5 questions adopted from Davis (1989), Mathieson et al. (2001).

Perceived ease of use: It means the achieved intentions, effort spending and realizing functions to use Web 2.0 websites perceived by users. There are totally 6 questions adopted from Davis (1989), Mathieson et al. (2001).

Behavioral intention: It means the future intentions to use, recommend others to use and actively plans to use Web 2.0 websites perceived by users. There are totally 3 questions adopted from Ajzen (1985), Johnny and Bolloju (2005).

Substantial usage behavior: It means usage frequencies and durations of using Web 2.0 websites perceived by users. There are totally 3 questions adopted from Ajzen (1985), Johnny and Bolloju (2005).

The aforesaid scales are all designed with Likert 5-point scales. Respondents pose different extents of approvals (1: total disapproval, 5: total approval).

Demographic variable: There are totally 6 items, genders, marital status, education levels, durations to touch Internet, weekly average frequencies on internet surfing.

Subjects and sampling

This research is operated with internet questionnaires. It is because higher reliable questionnaire replies can be achieved by respondents through internet surfing environment (Hoffman and Novak, 1996). However, the most unconvincing factor of internet surveys is mainly because internet users are vested without population representativeness among samples. Such a situation is mainly because not every individual has internet facilities in hand (Couper, 2000). However, with the remarkably growing internet prevalence, convenience and usability recently, some researches reveal the compositions of internet surfers come with increasingly high heterogeneous users. Their difference to non-internet surfers is also dwindling gradually (Smith and Leigh, 1997; Hewson et al., 2003). Compared with traditional questionnaires, internet questionnaire surveys are merited with low cost and immediate response feedback. They can breakthrough the restrictions of time and space. They are featured with good anonymity and excellently independent replies to avoid the interference from others (Couper, 2000). Ilieva et al. (2002) contend the durations for internet surveys should last for 1 week at least. It is highly recommended the survey durations should last for 2 weeks roughly with sufficient time available for the survey involvement of respondents. Additionally, the number of samples should be larger than 150 just available for SEM analysis (Cheng et al., 2005).

The pre-tests are conducted on the student subjects from graduate schools and universities for questionnaire surveys. There are totally 67 valid replies received to evaluate the length and linguistic clearness of questionnaire contents. By using item analysis techniques, the questions with weaker influence can be realized for further deletion or correction to improve questionnaire quality. Finally, through the questionnaire surveys posted on the MY3Q website and various forums, respondents can directly reply questionnaires through the internet browser. The duration of questionnaire surveys is 3 months. There are totally 698 replies received with 60 invalid replies deleted. Therefore, there are totally 638 valid replies received.

Sample receipt and distribution

In view of gender distribution, males occupy 47.3% and females occupy 52.7%. Regarding the distribution of marital status, the unmarried samples occupy 64.8%. About gender distribution, most samples are young students aging from 20 to 30, occupying 41.7%. Regarding the distribution of education levels, most are university and college students, occupying 57.9%. In view of the durations of internet surfing, samples with 6 years of internet surfing experience occupy 54.3%. For average weekly internet surfing durations, samples with 30 more hours of internet surfing durations a week is a the largest proportion occupying 22.2%.

RESULTS

Reliability analysis and correlation analysis

From reliability analysis, it is found every dimensional Cronbach's α coefficient are rated above 0.7. Additionally, for TAM, TPB and C-TAM-TPB, the integral

Cronbach's α coefficients are separately rated at 0.84, 0.83 and 0.88. According to the suggestions from Guielford (1965), if Cronbach's α coefficients are rated above 0.70, it means high reliability. On the whole, the reliability levels of every variable are all rated above 0.7. It means this research is vested with very high reliability. The averages, standard deviations, correlation analysis and reliability analysis for every variable are shown as Table 1.

The analysis of structural equation modeling (SEM)

This research is operated with generally weighted least squares (WLS) as a method to examine parameter estimation and modal fitness. For the examination of modal fitness, this research refers to the opinions proposed by Bagozzi and Yi (1988). In 3 perspectives of preliminary fitness, overall modal fitness and internal structural fitness, the fitness for theoretical models and observed data is evaluated.

In view of preliminary fitness, in TPB, the measurement errors of Y variables (namely, $\varepsilon 1$, $\varepsilon 2 \sim \varepsilon 6$) and X variables ($\delta 1$, $\delta 2$, $\delta 3...\delta 15$), along with the residual errors of potential dependent variables ($\zeta 1...\zeta 2$) are all ranged between 0.17 and 0.4. There is no negative error found. Furthermore, all are rated above .05 to reach their significance levels. Factor loadings are ranged between 0.59 and 0.85. The standard errors of estimated parameters are ranged between 0.01 and 0.12 and there is no remarkable standard error found. To sum up above mentions, in view of preliminary fitness in models, TPB perfectly complies with the fitness criteria proposed by Bagozzi and Yi (1988). TPB paths established by this research show no specification error. Identically, TAM and C-TAM-TPB also satisfy this standard.

In view of overall fitness, in TPB, $\chi 2$ /DF is rated at 5 within the acceptable range. RMSEA is rated at 0.07. Although, the value is rated above the severe standard 0.05, P value is significant. It means theoretical models and observed data come with good fitness. Both GFI and AGFI indices are rated above 0.9 and 0.87. It reveals the theoretical models in this research are vested with excellently high explanatory power to variability and co-variables. NFI, CFI, IFI and RFI are orderly rated at 0.89, 0.91, 0.91 and 0.88. All of them are rated above or approached to the severe standard 0.90. It reveals the overall fitness for TPB established by this research and observed data can reach the ideal standard. PNFI and PGFI are orderly rated at 0.77 and 0.79 and both are rated above the standard .50. The AIC index achieved by this research is rated at 462.000 smaller than 1136.674 of the saturation model and 9238.336 of the independent model. It complies with the theoretical model requirement AIC shall be rated below the AIC standards of both the saturation model and the independent model. It reveals TPB established by this research is a streamlined model.

Table 1. Results of mean, sd, correlation and reliability analysis

	mean	sd	1	2	3	4	5	6	7
1 AT	3.78	.582	(0.92)						
2 SN	3.44	.713	0.5***	(0.81)					
3 PBC	3.61	.600	0.65***	0.62***	(0.78)				
4 BI	5.23	.694	0.42***	0.44***	0.5***	(0.81)			
5 B	3.54	.772	0.52***	0.45***	0.51***	0.45***	(0.91)		
6 PEU	3.54	.609	0.54***	0.55***	0.65***	0.52***	0.45***	(0.91)	
7 PU	3.60	.587	0.55***	0.55***	0.58***	0.57***	0.55***	0.65***	(0.82)

Note：*P＜0.05，**P＜0.01，***P＜0.000
Note： （ ）indicate reliability

Table 2. Results of three models

	TPB	TAM	C-TAM-TPB
Absolute fit measures			
Degrees of Freedom	183	246	457
Minimum Fit Function Chi-Square	1040.674(P=0.0)	1455.202(P=0.0)	2943.746(P=0.0)
Root Mean Square Error of Approximation(RMSEA)	0.07	0.07	0.08
P-Value for Test of Close Fit (RMSEA<0.05)	0.000	0.000	0.000
Goodness of Fit Index (GFI)	0.9	0.88	0.81
Adjusted Goodness of Fit Index (AGFI)	0.87	0.84	0.79
Incremental fit measures			
Normed Fit Index (NFI)	0.89	0.89	0.81
Comparative Fit Index (CFI)	0.91	0.9	0.83
Relative Fit Index (RFI)	0.88	0.88	0.79
Incremental Fit Index (IFI)	0.91	0.9	0.83
Parsimonious fit measures			
Independence AIC	9238.336	10976.634	3085.746
Model AIC	462.000	600.000	1056
Saturated AIC	1136.674	1563.202	14913.448
Parsimony Normed Fit Index (PNFI)	0.77	0.77	0.74
Parsimony Goodness of Fit Index (PGFI)	0.79	0.79	0.76

Identically, TAM and C-TAM-TPB also comply with this standard (Table 2).

In view of internal structural fitness, in TPB, all estimated factor loadings （λ values）reach their significant levels with t=2.41~27.20 and p<.05. It complies with the evaluation standard that factor loadings shall reach their significant levels（Bagozzi and Yi, 1988）. Secondly, the individual item reliability of 21 measurement indicators in TPB paths (Range values of X and Y measurement indicators predicted by potential variables) is ranged between 0.45 and 0.73. All values are rated above the standard .45, namely the ideally acceptable results. Thirdly, the 5 composite reliabilities of

potential variables in theoretical models are orderly rated at 0.89, 0.81, 0.84, 0.79 and 0.86. All values are rated above the evaluation standard .60. Fourthly, in view of extracted variances, the extracted variances of 5 potential variables in theoretical models (average extracted variances) are separately rated at 0.55, 0.57, 0.51, 0.57 and 0.68. All values are rated above the evaluation standard .50. Identically, TAM and C-TAM-TPB also satisfy the standard.

Additionally, in TPB, in the part of residual variances of internal potential variables (η), the residual variances (ξ1) of behavioral intentions are rated at 0.33; behavioral intentions are explained as 67% of the total variances of attitudes, subjective norms and perceived behavior

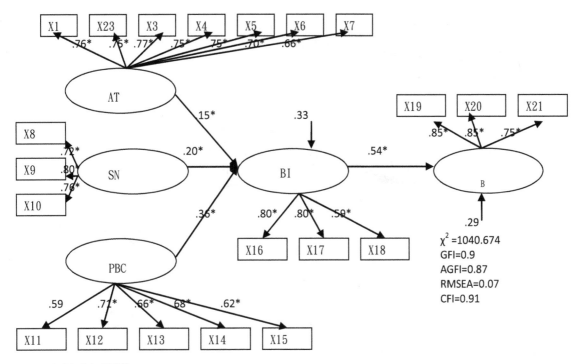

Figure 1. Model of TPB

control. The residual variance (ξ4) of substantial usage behaviors is rated at 0.29. The variance of substantial usage behaviors is explained as 71% of total variance by behavioral intentions (Figure 1).

TAM, for the part of residual variance from internal potential variables (η), the residual variance (ξ1) of perceived usefulness is rated at 0.54. Perceived usefulness is explained as 46% of total variance by perceived ease of use, the residual variance (ξ2) is 0.46, and attitudes are explained as 54% of total variance by both perceived usefulness and perceived ease of use. The residual variance (ξ3) of behavioral intentions is 0.31 behavioral intentions are explained as 69% of total variance by attitudes. The residual variance (ξ4) of substantial usage behaviors is 0.29 and substantial usage behaviors are explained as 71% of total variance by behavioral intentions (Figure 2).

In the C-TAM-TPB model, for the part of residual variance (η) of internal potential variables, the residual variance (ξ1) of perceived usefulness is 0.54; perceived usefulness is explained as 46% of total variance by perceived ease of use. The residual variance (ξ2) of attitudes is 0.43; attitudes are explained as 57% of total variance by both perceived usefulness and perceived ease of use. The residual variance (ξ3) of behavioral intentions is 0.53; behavioral intentions are explained as 47% of total variance by attitudes, subjective norms and perceived behavior control. The residual variance (ξ4) of substantial usage behaviors is 0.31 and substantial usage behaviors are explained as 69% of total variance by behavioral intentions (Figure 3).

Finally, in the analysis on model fitness and simplicity, in TPB, both GFI and AGFI values are rated at 0.9 and 0.87. In TAM, both GFI and AGFI values are rated at 0.88 and 0.84. In C-TAM-TPB, both GFI and AGFI values are rated at 0.81 and 0.79. To sum up above mentions, TPB values are superior to those of other models.

DISCUSSION AND CONCLUSION

Based on analysis results, all path coefficients reach their significant levels with all hypotheses well established. For the part of TPB (H1-H4), results reveal the attitudes, subjective norms and perceived behavior control of users can actually affect behavioral intentions. Also, behavioral intentions affect substantial usage behaviors. Additionally, it is found the attitudes toward Web 2.0 websites (3.78) show higher approval extents than those of behavior control to Web 2.0 websites (3.61) and subjective norms to websites (3.44). It reveals most users agree using Web 2.0 websites can save time. They are also functioned with much more resource to solve problems or give aids. Therefore, the upcoming usage intentions of users against Web 2.0 internet are enhanced.

For the part of TAM (H5-H9), results reveal perceived usefulness and perceived ease of use among users can affect the attitudes posed by users with subsequent influence on behavioral intentions and substantial behaviors. Among them, the approval extents of perceived usefulness (3.6) are higher than that of

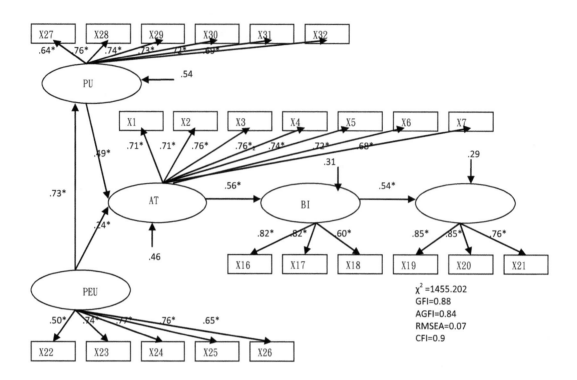

Figure 2. Model of TAM

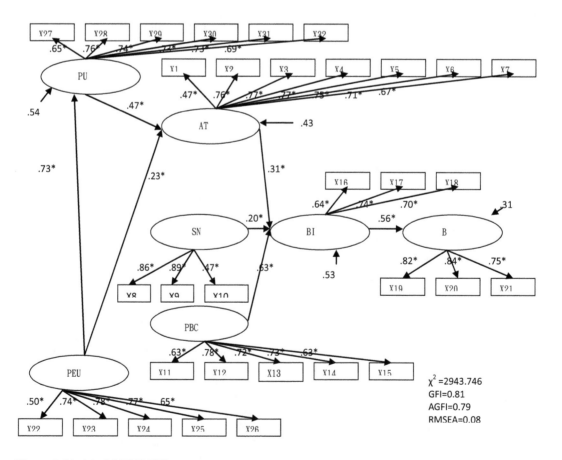

Figure 3. Model of C-TAM-TPB

perceived ease of use (3.54). It reveals most users agree that using Web 2.0 websites can enhance the convenience of daily life to satisfy information demands with pleasant emotion reachable.

For the part of C-TAM-TPB (H10-H16), results are identical to those of TPB and TAM. Among them, attitudes (3.78) show higher approval extents to perceived behavior control (3.61), subjective norms (3.44), perceived usefulness (3.6) and perceived ease of use (3.54). It reveals for users' behaviors, attitudes mean a very important influential factor.

Among the 3 modal comparison analysis mentioned in this research, for the overall modal fitness analysis among TPB, TAM and C-TAM-TPB, in TPB, both GFI and AGFI values are rated at 0.9 and 0.87; CFI and IFI values are 0.91 and 0.91 separately. It is better below two models. In TAM, both GFI and AGFI values are rated at 0.88 and 0.84; both CFI and IFI values are 0.9 and 0.9. In C-TAM-TPB, both GFI and AGFI are rated at 0.81 and 0.79; CFI and IFI are separately 0.83 and 0.83. For the part of path analysis, all the paths in TPB, TAM and C-TAM-TPB have been clearly examined in this research. For the part of explanatory power to variables, the explanatory powers of 3 models are all rated above the standard. For the part of substantial usage behaviors, the explanatory powers of both TPB and TAM (71%) are better than that of C-TAM-TPB (69%). To summarize above mentions, TPB shows its excellent fitness from the empirical analysis on user behaviors when they are using Web 2.0 websites.

It is known form the results in this research, 3 models are applicable to Web 2.0 websites. However, TPB shows higher applicability than those of TAM and C-TAM-TPB in this research. In this research, it is contended with the increasing prevalence of modern computer and information technologies, technological usefulness and ease of use have become one of the basic conditions. Also, accompanied with higher consumption power available, there is no obstacle for users to use technologies. Therefore, past research results are probably unsuitable for current researches on Web 2.0 websites. For past TPB researches, they emphasized usage behaviors (Timothy and Sulaiman, 2008). For TAM and C-TAM-TPB research models, they focused on the acceptance extents to new technology commodities (Marc and Christoph, 2008; Taylor and Todd, 1995). The results in this research are different from those of past researches. It is found research results users are deeper affected by external factors than internal factors to aggressively operate websites and users show higher operation frequencies of websites due to the factors from surrounding friends, relatives and individual facilities.

RESEARCH LIMITATION

In this research, the questionnaire messages are separately posted on internet relevant communities and forums, such as PTT and discussion forums, etc. With the aggressive propagation made by internet questionnaire respondents, samples are collected in a snowball way. Snowball sampling probably causes the issues of high homogeneity and restriction.

REFERENCES

Ajzen I (1985). From Intentions to Actions: a Theory of Planned Behavior. In J. Kuhl and J. Beckmann (eds.), Action Control: From Cognition to Behavior. New York: Springer Verlag, 11-39.

Alma M, Colette D, Geraldine G (2010). Work-life Balance Policy and Practice: Understanding Line Manager Attitudes and Behaviors, Hum. Resour. Manage. rev., 20(2): 158 - 167.

Bagozzi RP, Yi Y (1988). On the Evelution of Structure Equation Models. Acad. Mark. Sci., 16(1): 74 - 94.

Cheng ZC, Cheng BL, Cheng XF, Liu ZJ (2005). The Statistical Software Applications for Multivariate Analysis, Taipei: The Wunang Publisher.

Couper MP (2000). Web Surveys: A Review of Issues and Approaches. Public Opin Q. 64(4): 464 - 495.

Davis FD (1989). Perceived Usefulness, Perceived Ease of Use, and User Acceptance of Information Technology. MIS Q. 13(3):319 - 340.

Gabriela G (2009). To Use or Not to Use Web 2.0 in Higher Education? Soc Behav Sci. 1(1): 478 - 482

Gabriela G, Carmen H (2010). Microblogging Multimedia-Based Teaching Methods Best Practices with Cirip.eu. Social and Behavioral Sciences, 2(2): 2151 - 2155

Gong WR (2006). Earning Money and Creativities on Web 2.0, Institute for Information Industry, III.

Guielford JP (1965). Fundamental Statistics in Psychology and Education, 4th ed., New York: McGraw-Hill.

Hewson C, Yule P, Laurent D, Vogel C (2003). Internet Research Methods: A Practical Guide for the Social and Behavioral Sciences, Sage, London, UK.

Hoffman DL, Novak TP (1996). Marketing in Hypermedia Computer-Mediated Environments: Conceptual Foundations. J. Mark., 60(3):50 - 69.

Hsu CL, Lu HP (2004). Why Do People Play On-Line Games? an Extended TAM with Social Influences and Flow Experience. Inf. Manage., 41(7):853 - 868

III FIND (2011, March 16). Local Internet Surfing Population in Taiwan till December 2010, Retrieved May 26, 2011, from http://www.find.org.tw/find/home.aspx?page=many&id=282

Ilieva J, Baron S, Healy NM (2002). Online Surveys in Marketing Research: Pros and Cons. Int. J. Mark. Res., 44(3): 361 - 376

James PP (2010). The Changing Space of Research: Web 2.0 and the Integration of Research and Writing Environments. comput. compos., 27(1):48 - 58

Johnny CFS, Bolloju N (2005). Explaining the Intentions to Share and Reuse Knowledge in the Context of IT Service Operations. J. Knowl. Manage., 9(6):30 - 42

Koong CS, Wu CY (2010). An Interactive Item Sharing Website for Creating and Conducting On-Line Testing. Comput. Educ., 55(1):131 - 144

Kwon O, Wen Y (2010).An Empirical Study of the Factors Affecting Social Network Service Use.Comput. Human. Behav. 26(2):254 - 263

Liu IF, Chen MC, Sun YS, Wible D, Kuo CH (2010). Extending the TAM Model to Explore the Factors that Affect Intention to Use an Online Learning Community. Comput. Educ.,54(2):600 - 610

Marc F, Christoph L (2008). User Acceptance of Virtual Worlds. J. electron. commer. Res., 9(3): 231 - 242

Mathieson K, Peacock E, Chin WW(2001). Extending the Technology Acceptance Model: The Influence of Perceived User Resources. Database adv. inf. syst. , 32(3):86 - 113

Melanie G, Samantha C, Carol M, John M, Barbara SK, Marion W (2007). Measuring Young People's Attitudes to Breastfeeding Using the Theory of Planned Behaviour, J. Public Health., 29(1): 17 – 26

Morris MG, Dillon A (1997). How User Perceptions Influence Software Use. IEEE Softw., 14(4): 58 - 65.

Rigopoulos G, Askounis D (2007).A TAM Framework to Evaluate Users' Perception towards Online Electronic Payments. J. Internet Banking commer.,12(3): 1 - 6

Rogers EM (2003). Diffusion of Innovations, 5th ed., New York : Free Press.

Smith MA, Leigh B (1997). Virtual Subjects: Using the Internet as an Alternative Source of Subjects and Research Environment. behav. res. Methods., 29(4): 496 - 505.

Succi MJ, Walter ZD (1999). Theory of User Acceptance of Information Technologies: An Examination of Health Care Professionals, Systems sciences,HICSS-32, Proceedings of the 32nd Annual Hawaii International Conference, 1-6

Taylor S, Todd PA (1995). Understanding Information Technology Usage: a Test of Competing Models. inf. syst. Res., 6 (2):144 – 176.

Tim O'Reilly (2005, September 30). What-is-web-20: Design Patterns and Business Models for the Next Generation of Software, Retrieved May 25, 2011, from http://tim.oreilly.com/news/2005/09/30/what-is-web-20.html

Timothy PC, Sulaiman AR (2008). Factors that Influence the Intention to Pirate Software and Media. J. Bus. Ethics., 78(4): 527 – 545.

12

Accounting information system's barriers: Case of an emerging economy

Mahdi Salehi[1]* and Abdoreza Abdipour[2]

[1]Accounting, Ferdowsi University of Mashhad, Mashhad, Iran.
[2]Payame Noor University, Andimeshk Branch, Iran.

The current study aims to investigate the barriers of implementing accounting information system in Iran by postulating six hypotheses of accounting information system (middle managers, human resources, organizational structure, environmental factors, financial issues and organizational culture) in companies listed in Tehran Stock Exchange. In order to collect data, a questionnaire was designed and developed about the subject of the study. The statistical society includes all listed companies in Tehran Stock Exchange. Collected data were analyzed by parametric statistic tests. The results of the study confirmed the six postulated hypotheses. From the study, it can be concluded that giving reward to managers and staffs and encouraging staff to use the new system will help in justifying that the establishment of this system would be to their advantages; by the lever of reward, staff will be encouraged to compete in learning and work, which can therefore accelerate performance and system implementation. The main problems in data transferring were solved, and running instructions became clear.

Key words: Accounting information systems, corporate accounting system, financial system of average companies.

INTRODUCTION

Accounting information systems (AIS) are a tool, which when incorporated into the field of Information and Technology systems (IT), are designed to help in the management and control of topics related to firms' economic-financial area. However, the stunning advance in technology has opened up the possibility of generating and using accounting information from a strategic viewpoint. Since this is important for all firms, it is more important even for medium-sized and small ones that need this information to deal with a higher degree of uncertainty in the competitive market. The most important features of it are: high speed data processing, extremely high accuracy, high speed access to information, current, the possibility of electronic exchange of information, high quality, very cheap and declining price. On the other

hand, the study has the development of operation volume and complication of affairs. By considering these factors, there will be no need to justify the use of IT in today's world (Salehi et al., 2010a). In addition, accounting has to use and apply all or some of the new techniques in their services and obligations. So, providers of information especially accountants, should provide advanced and high-quality information so that their services can be bought in high prices. Otherwise, in the future they will not have any place (Sutton, 2000). AIS is developed between one or two or more units of a company to achieve a specific goal (Salehi et al., 2010b; Salehi and Alipour, 2010). It contains small sub-systems that support larger systems, and includes people, methods, infor-mation and software and information technology infrastructures (Lautier 2001). System consists of a set of incorporated components that are affiliated to achieve one or several particular goals in a way that, if one or more input can go into it, one or more output can exit

*Corresponding author. E-mail: mahdi_salehi54@yahoo.com.

(Frederick, 1984). AIS is a completely designed system for the production, collection, organization (processing), storage, retrieval and dissemination in an institution, organization or any other defined areas of society. AIS can help business units especially small and medium companies to solve short-term problems of managers in the areas of final price, cost and cash flow by providing information to support and supervise medium and active companies in a dynamic and competitive environment. It can also help in the integration of these companies and the operational considerations and strategic programs in the long term (Mitchell et al., 2000). Progress in the fields of accounting, information technology and information systems during the past two decades suggest conditions to consider the role of accounting information system. Examples include the evolution of active database technology, implementing new models, such as accounting resources and factors of planning resources and allowing accounting information to attract financial old data (Mauldin and Ruchala, 1999).

In another study by Bergeron et al. (2001), it was found that there is a relation between appropriate strategic orientation, organizational structure, management and administration of IT with company's performance. Available literatures show little evidence of developing AIS within medium companies. In fact, considerable evidences suggest that financial accountings in medium companies are the main source of information management (McMahon and Davies, 1994).

Advantages of JIT (just in time)

The advantages of the JIT philosophy are numerous. Giunipero et al. (2005) say that JIT has led to several benefits which include lower production cost, higher and faster throughputs, better product quality, reduced inventory costs and shorter lead times in purchasing. According to an American study of U.S. manufactures, companies can expect improved performance in lead times, quality levels, labour productivity, employee relations, inventory levels and manufacturing costs (White et al., 1999).

Fullerton and McWatters (2001) summarised benefits into five categories: quality benefits, time-based benefits, employee flexibility, accounting simplification and firm profitability. The increase in performance is usually attributable to a decrease in inventory levels, smoother production flow, lower storage cost and ultimately a decrease in average cost per unit. Callen et al. (2005) reported that JIT plants have significantly less WIP than non-JIT plants. JIT plants also store fewer finished products and have lower variable and total costs than the non-JIT equivalent. Callen et al. (2005) further found that JIT plants are significantly more profitable than non-JIT plants, but are neither successful at minimising WIP and costs nor maximising profits.

It is possible to observe that traditional performance measurement system is inconsistent with JIT system benefiting from technological innovations at a maximum level and also that it prevents or hides broad-based effectiveness of new production methods. In this sense, the restrictions of traditional measurement system in JIT environment might be listed as follows:

(a) Continuous development in production process is basic element in JIT manufacturing environment. To reach this aim easily, it is intended to make flow of production possible with minimal parties and decreasing stock levels to a minimum. Yet, production and productivity measures of traditional understanding have shown that productivity is low when small-lot production is made (Drury, 1990). For this reason, traditional accounting system suggests increasing batch capacity rather than decreasing lot size, which leads to raising stock levels, long supply process, increasing cost and declining customer's satisfaction (Mcnair et al., 1990).
(b) As in standard costing, appropriate operational control of traditional accounting system cannot be carried out in today's production environment (Allott, 2000; Cheatham and Cheatham, 1996; Ezzamel, 1992). Besides, due to the reliability and consistency of manufacturing processes in JIT environment, deviations do not exist or exist in quite low level and it leads to less use of deviation analyses.
(c) JIT manufacturing system changes will bring about changes in information requirements (Bowen et al., 2007). As it is known, normally, traditional performance reporting is prepared monthly or weekly and cannot detect on time real reasons of processes that are not realized as expected. Yet, in JIT production system there is a possibility of short production cycle; so it requires information for the problems coming out in accordance with one-day or "real time" principal.

Ahmad et al. (2004) presented potential benefits and performance improvements achieved through JIT implementation. Summary of the main benefits of JIT are listed as follows:

(i) reduced process time, setup time and lead time;
(ii) reduced raw material, WIP and finished goods inventory levels and lot size;
(iii) improved machinery and reduced machine breakdowns and downtimes;
(iv) minimised space requirement;
(v) improved flow of products;
(vi) lowered production costs;
(vii) simplified production processes;
(viii) improved quality;
(ix) improved flexibility, multifunctional ability, motivation and problem solving capability of employees;
(x) increased productivity and performance;
(xi) improved consistency of production scheduling and
(xii) increased emphasis on supplier integration.

THEORETICAL ISSUES AND REVIEW OF LITERATURE

IT is a company's key infrastructure that includes physical information technology infrastructures, information technology of human resources (technical and managerial skills) and technology of irreplaceable resources (Bharadwaj, 2000).

An important problem in management accounting and concern about AIS decision-making in organization regarding the need for information is communication and control of accounting information system. Computer system is based on a process that supports financial data for decision-making tasks of managers within the frame of coordination and control of company's activities, which have been analyzed in the researches of different models, between accounting information system with technology organization, organization's structure and organizational environment (Mia and Chenhall, 1994).

AIS is an important mechanism of an organization that is vital for effective management decision-making in controlling organization (Zimmerman, 1995). Generally, AIS is classified in two categories: a) Effective decision-making for information that is largely for control of organization and b) facilitation of information that is mainly used for coordination of organization in decision-making are used (Kren, 1992).

Effectiveness of AIS to increase system integration is to improve internal communications throughout the organization (Huber, 1990).

Top management team with various planning and management information system influences strategic performance (Gil, 2009).

Behavioral changes following Joint development show AIS support and participation of users that has been influencing accounting information system development and improving financial performance, which eventually lead to successful troubleshooting cost accounting system, are based activities.

The productivity of information technology within the information systems in public accounting is about a small number of respondents of the technology components who are aware of the major component of respondents' information technology data, and not the information system accounting. The development and effects of information system accounting on organization, human resources management and knowledge of technology and acceptance of data were evaluated (Mohdshaari, 2008).

Comparative advantage is a significant effective research model of value accounting information systems for scholars, and it represents the financial and human resources as the two basic pillars of research and development for supplement industry based on information systems, where absolute accounting superiority ensures business operations (Alles et al., 2008).

Management that stresses on critical factors of success for implementing organizational resources planning systems suggests that selecting appropriate time, completing project by one management, training personnel, superiority of project results to other projects, use of consultants, management interaction with users and use of project control committee bring about the difference between successful and unsuccessful projects (Bradley, 2008).

Test of textual factors and the impact of characteristics of technology on implementing auditing decisions are in such a way that the use of computer techniques by experienced auditors shows that companies which have experienced the ability of influencing implementation of new technology, using long-term budgets have assessed different courses through indirect control of the software (Curtis and Payne, 2008).

Intelligent business system and measuring of its effects alongside business processes and organizational performance is important, as information technology systems through specialized texts and literature is outstanding (Elbashir et al., 2008).

Testing the influence of international investors on the quality of accounting information demonstrates that the right choice of investment and increasing work quality of international investors have influenced Russian accounting companies (Bagaeva, 2008).

Current economic and the traditional model of accounting reports

Challenges and opportunities ahead of AIS researches prove that the economy in real condition can accelerate measurement and evaluation of business. Decision-making processes as a new business model result in decrease of internal and hidden processes. Therefore, AISs together with research literature have been successful in development of new models to accelerate accounting processes (Vasarhelyi and Alles, 2008).

Organizational determining factors acceptance and implementation of information technology in mean companies

Private and public companies show that limiting factors in the implementation and information technology include overhauling, reformation arrangement, changes, lack of qualified personnel to run the same technology and information systems.

Strategic planning of information systems

Case study in financial service companies in Germany represents that there is lack of scientific literature on implementation of strategic information systems planning, and data transfer is not mainly due to scientific literature.

Although scientific literature is inspiring, in practice to run strategic planning, information system is not included. Professional characters of management and different resources are of scientific characters. Thus, there is need for more experience in the role of management in the information technology practice through the opinions of staff (Teubner, 2007). More regulatory practices in information technology function of information technology organizations and business sector common understanding of the goals are associated with information technology. Examples include active participation in the committee information technology, trade balance, decisions regarding technology information and understanding of strategic policies and administrative information technology in successful exploitation of information technology projects.

Appropriate review between designing of AIS and performance of commercial units by analyzing strategies explains that high performance of commercial units depends on a wide range of accounting information systems (Boulianne, 2007).

In studying the integrated information system literatures of management accounting by considering its existing strengths, new integrated information system of accounting results in more development and understanding of theatrical frameworks in this regard. It identifies research gaps and suggests using research opportunities with different patterns and methods.

Ranking of AISs on performance of medium companies in Malaysia after studying of 310 companies through electronic questionnaire showed that, a significant and important part of medium companies in Malaysia were placed in high rank, and only a limited number of medium companies were in low level of accounting information systems because of low organizational performance (Azizi and King, 2005). Factors of users' concentration, measurement, report making, quality of management information provided and reviewing and checking group work of outcomes affect the quality of accounting information. To develop and spread AIS a special team should be organized for designing input and output concepts and processing stored information so that company's decisions for main outputs and comparing them with computer information be made possible and achievable.

Future development of AIS in investment shows that the successes in avoiding risking the capital of companies are of five categories: 1) Clear and bright offers; 2) Internal changes in institution's investment; 3) The variety of variables and repeating information change; 4) More use of information for supportive decisions support; 5) world-wide impacts on investment. These evidences are good reasons for the judge and future research in the development of AIS.

Mistry (2005) found that, though JIT has been widely implemented, interest in documenting its impact on financial performance and productivity was just generated

in the last few decades. For example, Inman and Mehra (1993) established the link between JIT benefits and bottom line financial measures. Olsen (2004, cited in Swamidass, 2007) stated, "lean/JIT firms tend to have better return on equity, since lean/JIT is associated with low inventories". However, according to Fullerton and McWatters (2001), the use of financial performance measurement under the present competitive market conditions appears unsustainable due to various reasons. Therefore, performance measurement system of a corporate body using JIT production system should support basic variations such as increasing product or service quality, continuous development and reducing losses (Hendricks, 1994) (Figure 1).

RESEARCH METHODOLOGY

The statistical society of this research is made up of the financial managers of the companies listed in Tehran Stock exchange (TSE). In order to determine the statistical society, the companies of TSE were listed on August 2010. For this purpose, a number of 442 companies were selected from TSE website. From the entire number of the selected companies, 36 companies were omitted from the list of listed companies of TSE following the session of Security Subscription Board. Eventually, the study was concentrated on 406 companies from 36 different industrial sectors.

The statistical community in this research could be all companies all over the country, but due to different directions, limitations of personal facilities and the study limited statistical community, 100 companies listed in TSE were selected.

Research data collection instrument is a questionnaire which has been standardized in the academic community; and in considering its validity, the opinions of specialized literatures and comments of expert managers in relevant areas were analyzed, and its validity was acceptable.

In order to determine the proper size of the specimen and calculate the Cronbach's Alpha coefficient a pre-testing process was conducted. The methodology of the process is as follows: A number of 13 questionnaires whose narration style had been confirmed were distributed by the researchers among the financial managers of the admitted companies of TSE, as an initial specimen. The original data showed that, on average, the affectivity of financial expense in order to establish an internet financial reporting was rated at 13.90, with standard deviation of 4 within the range of 5 to 25. In the society, in average comparison test, with the constant number of 15 (the middle point of the above range), and at least a number of 86 persons at 5% error rate provided 80.26% level of ability. In order to test the hypotheses, T-Test was employed in the study that fits the testing of the hypotheses.

Research objectives

The followings are the main objectives of the study:

1) Identify barriers in the establishment of AISs in companies.
2) Provide strategies for the establishment of AIS in obstacles companies listed in TSE.

Research hypotheses

First hypothesis: Middle managers prevent the establishment of AIS in financial units.

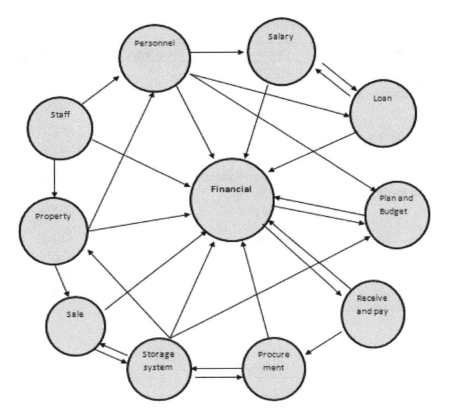

Figure 1. General plan of financial automation.

Second hypothesis: Organizational structure prevents the establishment of AIS in companies' financial units.
Third hypothesis: Organizational culture prevents the establishment of AIS in financial units.
Fourth hypothesis: Financial problems prevent the establishment of AIS in companies' financial units.
Fifth hypothesis: Labor prevents the establishment of AIS in financial units.
Sixth hypothesis: Environmental factors influencing AIS prevent the establishment of companies' financial units.

DATA ANALYSIS

In this section, demographic information of participants based on research experience, education, location, service and posting a separate organization is offered in Table 1.

Testing of hypotheses

First hypothesis: Middle managers prevent the establishment of information systems in companies' financial units.

SPSS software was used for the T-test of the above hypothesis. Confidence level of 0.95 is used and the results are demonstrated in Table 2.
H_0: M = 20)
(H_1: = M> 20

H_0: middle managers do not prevent the establishment of accounting information systems in financial units of companies.
H_1: middle managers prevent the establishment of accounting information systems in financial units of companies.

Information in Table 2 shows the level of significance to be 0.001, and since the significant level is less than 0.005, it means the hypothesis is accepted; so H0 is rejected and H1 is approved.

Second hypothesis: Organizational structure prevents the establishment of accounting information system in companies' financial units.

For the above hypothesis, single- sample T-test with confidence level of 0.95 is used and the results are given in Table 3.

H_0: M = 7)
(H_2: = M> 7

H_0: organizational structure does not prevent the establishment of accounting information system in financial units of companies.
H_2: organizational structure prevents the establishment of accounting information systems in financial units.

Table 1. General information of participants.

Item	Variable	Frequency	Percentage (%)
Educational background	Diploma	26	26.80
	B.A	59	60.80
	M.A	12	12.40
Field of the study	Accounting	59	60.80
	Management	38	39.20
Experience	Lee than 5 years	62	63.90
	6-10 years	28	28.80
	11-15 years	7	7.20
Designation	Manager	11	11.30
	Deputy	7	7.20
	Expert	41	42.30
	Clerk	38	39.20

Source: Research findings.

Table 2. The results of testing first hypothesis.

Test value = 20			
First hypothesis	D.f	T	Sig.
Middle managers	96	16.735	0.001

Source: Research findings.

Table 3. The results of second hypothesis.

Test value = 7			
The second hypothesis	D.f	T	Sig.
Organizational structure	96	15.550	0.001

Source: Research findings.

Information in the table shows that the level of significance is 0.001, and since the significant level is less than 0.005, the hypothesis is accepted; so H0 is rejected and H_2 is approved. Therefore, organizational structure is one of the barriers to the establishment of AIS in companies listed in TSE.

Third hypothesis: Organizational culture prevents the establishment of accounting information systems in financial units.
For the above hypothesis, single-sample T-test with confidence level of 0.095 is used and the results are given in Table 4.
H_0: M = 12)
(H_3: = M> 12

H_0: organizational culture does not prevent the establishment of AIS in financial units.
H_3: organizational culture system prevents the establishment of AIS in financial units.

Table 4. The results of testing third hypothesis.

Test value = 12			
The third hypothesis	D.f	T	Sig.
Organizational structure	96	68.246	0.001

Source: Research findings.

Information contained in Table 4 shows that the level of significance is 0.001, and since the significant level is less than 0.005, the hypothesis is accepted; so H_0 is rejected and H_3 is approved. Therefore, organizational culture prevents the establishment of AIS in companies' financial units.

Fourth hypothesis: Financial problems prevent the establishment of accounting information system in companies' financial units.

For the above hypothesis, single-sample T- test with confidence level of 0.95 is used and the results are given in Table 5.

H_0: M = 6)
(H_4: = M> 6

H_0: financial problems do not prevent the establishment of AIS in financial units.
H_4: Financial problems prevent the establishment of AIS in company's financial units.

Information contained in Table 5 shows that the level of significance is 0.001, and since the significant level is less than 0.005, H_0 is rejected; therefore, financial problems prevent the establishment of AIS in companies listed in TSE.

Table 5. The results of fourth hypothesis.

Test value = 6			
The fourth hypothesis	D.f	T	Sig.
Financial problems	96	28.426	0.001

Source: Research findings.

Table 6. The results of testing fifth hypothesis.

Test value = 17			
The fourth hypothesis	D.f	T	Sig.
Labors	96	67.887	0.001

Source: Research findings.

Table 7. Results of testing sixth hypothesis.

Test value = 12			
The sixth hypothesis	D.f	T	Sig.
Environmental factors	96	105.102	0.001

Source: Research findings.

Fifth hypothesis: Labor does not prevent the establishment of AIS in financial units.

For the above hypothesis, single- sample T-test with confidence level of 0.95 is used and the results are given in Table 6.

H_0: M = 17)
(H_5: = M> 17
H_0: Human resources do not prevent the establishment of accounting information system in companies' financial units.
H_5: Human resources prevent the establishment of accounting information system in companies' financial units.

Information contained in Table 6 shows that the level of significance is 0.001, and since the significant level is less than 0.005, H_0 is rejected and H_5 is approved. Hence, we can say that issues related to human resources are barriers to the establishment of accounting information system in companies found in stock exchange.

Sixth hypothesis: Environmental factors affecting accounting information system prevent the establishment of accounting information system in companies' financial units.

For the above hypothesis, single- sample T- test using SPSS software with confidence level of 0.95 is used and the results are given in Table 7.

H_0: M = 12)
(H_6: = M> 12

H_0: environmental factors affecting accounting information system do not prevent the establishment of AIS in companies' financial units.
H_6: Environmental factors affecting accounting information system prevent the establishment of AIS in companies' financial units.

Information contained in Table 7 shows that the level of significance is 0.001, and since the significant level is less than 0.005, the hypothesis is accepted; so H_0 is rejected and H_6 is approved. Hence, one can say that environmental factors can also be regarded as barriers to the establishment of accounting information system in companies listed in stock exchange.

DISCUSSION AND CONCLUSION

Middle managers prevent implementation of AIS in companies listed in TSE. Results of the above hypotheses using single-sample T-test with confidence level of 0.95 lead to the acceptance of these hypotheses of the research. It means that middle managers are barriers due to failure to implement accounting information system in the companies listed stock exchange. There is a meaningful relation between middle managers and implementation of accounting information system. Further, environmental factors prevent the implementation of AIS in listed companies in TSE. It shows that organizational structure is one of the barriers to the implementation of AIS in companies listed in TSE. There is a meaningful relation between organizational structure and implementation of AIS. By the way, the results reveal that organizational culture prevents the implementation of AIS in listed companies in TSE. The authors come to a conclusion, that are several barriers to the implementation of AIS in listed companies in TSE. In such a condition, it seems that without solving these problems the Iranian companies cannot enjoy the advantages of AIS, and may cause very big problems in near future. In order to solve these problems, everyone, from top managers to simple clerk should put their hand together and reduce at least these problems in this competitive world.

REFERENCES

Ahmad A, Mehra S, Pletcher M (2004). The perceived impact of JIT implementation on firms' financial/growth performance. J. Manuf. Technol. Manage. 15(2):118-130.
Alles GM, Kogan A, Vasarhelyi AM (2008). Exploits comparative advantage: A paradigm for value added research in accounting information systems. Int. J. Account. Inf. Syst. 9:202-215.
Allott A (2000). "Some Academics Say Management Accounting Has Not Changed in The Last 60 Years; Others Say It Has-Hugely Who's Right, Asks Anita Allott?" Manage. Account.: Mag. Chart. Manage. Account. 78(7):54-56.

Azizi NE, King M (2005). Firm performance and AIS alignment in Malaysian SME s. Int. J. Account. Inform. Syst. 6:241-259.

Bagaeva A (2008). An examination of the effect of international investors on accounting information quality in Russia. Adv. Account. 24:157-161.

Bergeron F, Raymond L, Rivard S (2001). Fit in strategic information technology management research: an empirical comparison of perspectives. OMEGA Int. J. Manage. Sci. 29:42-125.

Bharadwaj AS (2000). A resource-based perspective on information technology capability and firm performance: an empirical investigation. MIS Quart. 24(1):169-196.

Boulianne E (2007). Revisiting fit between AIS design and performance with the analyzer strategic-type. Int. J. Account. Inform. Syst. pp.1-16.

Bowen PL, Yin Decca Cheung M, Rohde FH (2007). Enhancing IT governance practices: A model and case study of organizations efforts. Int. J. Account. Inform. Syst. 8:191-221.

Bradley J (2008). Management based critical success factors in the implementation of enterprise resource planning systems. Int. J. Account. Inform. Syst. 9:175-200.

Callen JL, Morel M, Fader C (2005). Productivity Measurement and the Relationship between Plant Performance and JIT Intensity." Contemp. Account. Res. 22(2):271-309.

Cheatham CB, Cheatham LR (1996). "Redesigning Cost Systems: Is Standard Costing Obsolete?" Account. Horiz. 10(4):117-125.

Curtis MB, Payan A (2008). An examination of contextual factors and individual characteristics affecting technology implementation decisions in auditing. Int. J. Account. Inform. Syst. 9:104-121.

Drury C (1990). "Cost Control and Performance Measurement In an Amt Environment." Manage. Account. November pp.40-44.

Elbashir MZ, Collier PA, Davern MJ (2008). Measuring the effects of business intelligence systems: the relationship between business process and organizational performance. Int. J. Account. Inform. Syst. pp.135-153.

Ezzamel M (1992). Business Unit & Divisional Performance Measurement, CIMA, Academic Press, London.

Frederick HW (1984). Accounting information systems and practice, New York, Macgraw-Hill.

Fullerton RR, McWatters CS (2001). The production performance benefits from JIT implementation. J. Oper. Manage. 19(1):81-96.

Gil N (2009). Management information system and strategic performances: the role of top team composition. Int. J. Inform. Manage. 29:104-110.

Giunipero L, Pillai K, Chapman S, Clark R (2005). A longitudinal examination of JIT purchasing practices. Int. J. Logist. Manage. 16(1):51-70.

Hendricks JA (1994). Performance Measures For a JIT Manufacturer: The Role of The IE. Ind. Eng. January pp.24-32.

Huber GP (1990). A theory of the effects of advanced information technologies on organizational design, intelligence, and decision-making. Acad. Manage. Rev. 15:47-71.

Inman RA, Mehra S (1993). Financial justification of JIT implementation. Int. J. Oper. Prod. Manage. 13(4):32-39.

Kren L (1992). Budgetary participation and managerial performance: The impact of information and environmental volatility. Account Rev. 67:511-526.

Lautier W (2001). Accounting theory &practice, seventh edition England, Foundational times Prentices Hall.

Mauldin EG, Ruchala LV (1999). Towards a meta-theory of accounting information systems. Account. Organization Society 24:31-317.

McMahon RGP, Davies LG (1994). Financial reporting and analysis practices in small enterprises: Their association with growth rate and financial performance. J. Small Bus. Manage. 11:92-475.

Mcnair CJ, Lynch RL, Cross KF (1990). "Do Financial and Non-financial Performance Measures Have to Agree?" Manage. Account. November p.29.

Mia L, Chenhall RH (1994). The usefulness of management accounting systems, functional differentiation and managerial effectiveness. Account. Origination Society 19:1-13.

Mistry JJ (2005). Origins of profitability through JIT processes in the supply chain. Ind. Manage. Data Syst. 105(6):752-768.

Mitchell F, Reid G, Smith J (2000). Information system development in the small firm: the use of management accounting CIMA Publishing.

Mohdshaari A (2008). Utilization of data mining technology within the accounting information system in the public sector: a country study-Malaysia.

Noor Azizi, King M (2005). Firm performance and AIS alignment in Malaysian SMEs. Int. J. Account. Inform. Syst. 6:241-259.

Romeney B, Steinbart J (2003). Accounting information systems 9th edition, prentice hall business publishing.

Salehi M, Alipour M, Ramazani M (2010a). Impact of IT on Firms' Financial Performance: Some Iranian Evidence. Glob. J. Manage. Bus. Res. 10(4):21-29.

Salehi M, Alipour M (2010). E-banking in Emerging Economy: Empirical Evidence of Iran. Int. J. Econ. Financ. 2(1):201-209.

Salehi M, Moradi M, Ariyanpour A (2010b). A Study of the Integrity of Internet Financial Reporting: Empirical Evidence of Emerging Economy. Glob. J. Manage. Bus. Res. 10(1):148-158.

Sutton G (2000). The changing face of accounting in an information technology dominated world. Int. J. Account. Inform. Syst. pp. 1-8.

Swamidass PM (2007). The effect of TPS on US manufacturing during 1981-1998: Inventory increased or decreased as a function of plant performance. Int. J. Prod. Res. 45(16):3763-3778.

Teubner A (2007). Strategic information systems planning: a case study from the Financial services industry. J. Strateg. Inform. Syst. 16:105-125.

Vasarhelyi M, Alles G (2008). The "now" economy and the traditional accounting reporting model: opportunities and challenges for AIS research. Int. J. Account. Inform. Syst. 9:227-239.

White R, Pearson J, Wilson J (1999). JIT Manufacturing: A Survey of Implementations in Small and Large U.S. Manufacturers. Manage. Sci. 45(1):1-15.

Zimmerman JL (1995). Accounting for decision-making and control, Chicago: Irwin.

13

Adoption analysis of cloud computing services

Leonardo Rocha de Oliveira , Adriano JulioMurlick, Gabriela Viale Pereira and Rafael Vicentin

Pontifical University of Rio Grande do Sul, Brazil.

Making decisions for IT outsourcing is always a challenge for companies worldwide, and cloud computing has been growing as an alternative. This article analyzes the viewpoint of IT managers about the adoption of cloud computing services. It confronts the literature review on the main features of cloud computing with the opinion of sixteen managers responsible for IT departments in their companies. The interviews were conducted using a semi-structured questionnaire for collecting qualitative data. The results were divided into five main dimensions of analysis, which are: usability, scalability, service quality, security and cost. The results obtained in this study showed cloud computing as a subject present in the daily lives of IT managers. The main advantage pointed to cloud computing adoption was related to the scalability, especially due the ease and dynamism for adapting to variations of companies' IT needs. The results also show that security is a major concern among IT managers and crucial for CC adoption decisions. The possibility of paying only for the IT resources that are actually used makes cost attractive for cloud computing adopting decisions.

Key words: IT acceptance, cloud computing, IT management, IT outsourcing.

INTRODUCTION

The current dynamic and competitive economic market leads firms to face continuous challenges in their internal activities and external competitors. The ability to concentrate on their business core and quickly adapt to market changes are requirements for companies willing to survive and maintain their competitiveness (Babcock, 2010; Mansur, 2007). The growing role of Information Technology (IT) in a range of business aspects and the constant change in the way of using IT resources have required frequent and complex decisions from managers and executives (Weill and Ross, 2005). Cloud Computing (CC) is an example of IT resource, whose adoption in its various forms has challenged professionals from various levels of corporate hierarchies.

The success of companies is now increasingly dependent on the use of IT resources (Mansur, 2007). The agility to alter their ways of work and operate in dynamic business environments has been considered as a major factor for them to succeed (Fernandes and Abreu, 2009; IBM, 2010). Business agility in this work is related to the ability to quickly and successfully alter working and managerial processes to face external and internal challenges (Mansur, 2007). IT services that are traditionally managed by companies internally have been growing outsource to specialized firms, and they include systems backup, data warehousing, application development, technical support and information sharing. It is currently quite common to find companies deciding to outsource for IT resources operations in order to achieve better results in their core business activities (Fernandes and Abreu, 2009).

IT is a resource that requires strategic planning and management, as it may be decisive for the success or failure of a company. IT has currently a role that strongly impacts business activities, and one of the major management challenges for companies today is to align

IT resources with strategic business objectives (Weill and Ross, 2005). This alignment must occur in operational and strategic levels, leading to the establishment of mechanisms for managing IT services and resources (Armbrust et al., 2009; Weill and Ross, 2005). IT managers play an important role in this business scenario and are usually under constant pressure to ensure the provision of IT services and to work with limited budgets (Mansur, 2007).

CC offers an alternative to the provision of IT services by specialized companies with the capacity to cope with changes in business demands of its customers (Chorafas, 2011). IT services provided in the cloud have the potential to change the way that IT infrastructure and systems are used for supporting business objectives of organizations (Rittinghouse and Ransome, 2010). CC allows paying based on need and with an unlimited growing provision; thus allowing companies to innovate, even to start small and grow with time (Armbrust et al, 2009). CC seeks to provide easy access to IT services with low cost and offers features such as usability, scalability and security, thus challenging managers' decisions for adopting it in their companies. It also considers needs that are unique to each organization (Marks and Lozano, 2010; Sarna, 2011).

Like any other technology, the use of CC should be aligned with strategic business objectives and meet the needs of IT management contractors (Slabeva and Wozniak, 2010). Therefore, companies willing to adopt CC should conduct a detailed assessment of costs, benefits, cultural aspects, risks, corporate atmosphere, policies and compliance with legislation (Chorafas, 2011). Issues related to companies' existing IT resources and possible disposal must also be considered in this assessment.

CC contracts allow a range of service options and resources for contract, seeking to fulfill every customer's need (Marks and Lozano, 2010). Contractors may choose based on the offer of flexibility to scale up the IT service provision, as to meeting demand variations. Others may focus on business goals of IT outsourcing to specialized companies able to provide technical support, systems maintenance and infrastructure management. There is also the option of allowing contractors to focus on their key business objectives and outsourcing IT resources for specialized companies, such as CC suppliers (Marks and Lozano, 2010).

Among the reasons that can lead to adoption of CC, it should always be considered that results must meet objectives and guidelines portrayed by the contractors' strategic business plan (Armbrust et al., 2009; Rosenberg and Mateos, 2011). Hiring services of CC, it should be considered the specific needs for process operation and business strategic management, in compliance with corporate and industry policies and regulations. Contracts for hiring CC services may also pursue a hybrid approach, combining IT services provided inside the company with others provided by the cloud (Marks and Lozano, 2010).

CC has been seen as an option that will strongly impact the IT services providers market, as well as contractors' practices of IT management (Slabeva and Wozniak, 2010). CC providers have an opportunity for enlarging services deployment and optimizing IT resources and energy consumption (Armbrust et al., 2009). CC contractors foresee a possibility for hiring unlimited IT resources, though paying only for what has been actually consumed. Contractors may use a variety of devices for accessing IT services, such as desktop computers, laptops, smartphone and tablets as there are variety of options for contracting systems applications, data storage, platforms and operating systems for accessing CC services (Chorafas, 2011). Therefore, the market of IT devices manufacturers for accessing information and systems in the cloud will also be impacted (Chee and Franklin, 2010).

Making the right business decision for hiring CC services is a challenge faced by IT managers and business executives, which is the focus of this work, as it aims to analyze IT managers' acceptance for adopting CC services. Interviews were conducted with IT managers of companies in Porto Alegre (Brazil) and metropolitan area. Interview results show the viewpoint of professionals regarding various aspects of CC service, highlighting features such as usability, scalability, security, quality and cost.

Cloud computing (CC)

The term CC has historically been associated with World Wide Web (Web) systems and IT services that can be accessed from a remote location (Rittinghouse and Ransome, 2010). Web applications have always been linked to accessing virtual IT resources that sometimes are not even identifying the information source or destination. The concept of CC has been following the growth of web access (Slabeva and Wozniak, 2010). As far as in 1961 it was already suggested the possibility of sharing computer applications worldwide, though the term used to describe this kind of work was Utilitarian Computing (or Utility Computing) (Slabeva and Wozniak, 2010). That approach did not consider the growth of personal computers, but companies sharing IT resources from mainframes, with users accessing it remotely from a computer monitor and keyboard. Utilitarian computing practices were limited in their origin, due to technical aspects (limitations of bandwidth, disk space, cost of terminals for access and processing speed) and human (professional expertise and difficulty in realizing business usefulness). Although the IT infrastructure for this type of technology is almost obsolete, the use of leased mainframe processing has proven to be profitable for some time, both for contract and suppliers (Antonopoulos and Gillam, 2010).

Since 1990, there has been a growth in using personal computers, which are available everyday at lower cost and with higher processing power and data storage; they have reflected on the increasing amount of Web access, information sharing and CC services being offered (Babcock, 2010). The current status of CC services almost eliminates the needs of local information systems and database resources for running business applications, apart from the hardware devices required for accessing IT services in the cloud. Business objectives of CC service providers include allowing access to data, information and applications from anywhere in the world and at any time, regardless of the IT device (Slabeva and Wozniak, 2010).

CC involves a set of hardware, networking, storage, services and interfaces that enable the delivery of IT resources as a service. CC services include software delivery, infrastructure and data storage through the Web, in accordance to users' demand (Chee and Franklin, 2010). Accessing CC services requires only computers (or IT devices) with Internet access. All processing and computational resources are available on the Web and the client computer or device works just as hardware with Internet access (Buyya et al, 2011).

CC models

Companies' decisions for outsourcing IT resources in their business activities have been growing considering CC as an option, and there are four main different models as options for adoption: (i) Public, (ii) Private, (iii) Hybrid or (iv) Community (Chorafas, 2011; Antonopoulos and Gillam, 2010; Rittinghouse and Ransome, 2010):

1. Private Cloud - occurs when services are provided only for a unique client, who prefers to keep his data and systems in a specific IT infrastructure that is operated exclusively for the contractor. This option is usually taken by large companies or government institutions that require a high level of security, control and privacy for IT operations;
2. Public Cloud - is the most common model and it allows companies to share infrastructure resources and systems, while keeping data and information as a unique asset of each client. This model allows companies to outsource IT resources to specialized companies, and paying only for the services that are being used;
3. Community Cloud - the IT infrastructure is shared by a group of companies, usually with common characteristics, such as being part of the same production network, supply chain, government institution or companies' consortium. This model represents an attractive option for companies with similar needs for IT resources, such as website hosting, booking systems and financial controls for hotels of a similar tourist destination. In this

example, each client's data and information have privacy, but sharing costs of web hosting and systems development.
4. Hybrid Cloud – comprises using two or more models together (private, public and community), thus allowing that different business objectives could be aligned to the different characteristics of CC models, or even to have its own IT resources expanded in a public cloud. According to Goscinski and Brock (2010), this model is the most commonly adopted by companies that are just beginning to adopt CC services.

Although all four CC models are available for contracting, this work has the objective of analyzing the adoption of CC in any particular model. However, the results of the interviews have highlighted some characteristics of the different models that were considered by the respondents for adopting CC services in their companies.

CC services

There are different categories of IT services being offered by CC suppliers, which can be hired individually or combined. The main categories of CC services available are known as: (i) Infrastructure as a Service (IaaS), (ii) Platform as a Service (PaaS) and (iii) Software as a Service (SaaS). These services are provided and consumed in real time and are usually charged according to the amount of use (Buyya et al., 2011).

The category of (i) Infrastructure as a Service (IaaS) provides IT resources for processing, storage and group working, eliminating the need for acquisition and configuration of servers and network equipment (Buyya et al., 2011). Users are not supposed to manage the contracted IT resources, but should control such aspects as amount of data transactions, used storage space, applications and network access rates (Winkler, 2011).

The category (ii) Platform as a Service (PaaS) allows users to develop systems that are specific for the companies they work with, or even for their own interest (Buyya et al., 2011). PaaS offers to developers a programming environment to facilitate interaction and supporting the required scalability to run applications (Antonopoulos and Gillam, 2010). Developers have the benefits of developing applications in a cloud programming base that includes automatic sizing and load balancing, as well as integration with services as authentication, e-mail, users' interface and reports creation shared by all contractors (Winkler, 2011). Thus, much of the burden of developing applications is minimized and managed by the PaaS provider (Winkler, 2011).

The category (iii) Software as a Service (SaaS) is perhaps the most popular CC service (Sarna, 2011) and allows users to run their systems from a Web browser, paying only for the bandwidth consumed and data stored space. The category explores the use of systems from remote sessions in data centers, in which systems are deployed. SaaS is capable of adapting to demand variations of processing power and systems' memory, making contractors to avoid the need of investing on attending to IT using peak times (Rosenberg and Mateos, 2010). SaaS also allows reducing needs for hardware configuration requirements from client devices and it may be useful for easing the burden of software licensing and technical support (Sarna, 2011).

This work is not considering specific aspects of these three categories of CC services. The analysis in this work considers CC services as a whole, as the IT managers interview work in companies from different sectors and with different business goals and processes. However, results taken from the analysis are highlight some specific aspects from the different models and categories of CC services pointing out some barriers or justifying decisions for adopting CC.

CC characteristics

The aptitude for outsourcing IT resources by adopting CC services has been a growing interest for companies of all sectors (Rosenberg and Mateos, 2011). CC includes a number of features that may represent benefits for companies willing to improve the use of IT resources. These characteristics define the set of services and technologies involved in CC and it implies changes at working process of contracting companies. Therefore, companies willing to adopt CC services must consider impacts regarding human aspects, internal operations and strategic business activities (Rittinghouse and Ransome, 2010).

The literature review shows that the main characteristics to be considered by companies willing to adopt CC services are:

1. Scalability - this feature allows the contracted services to be customized and charged accordingly to contractors' business needs, and it includes aspects such as changes in bandwidth consumption, periodic (or seasonal) influence on data transactions amount, data storage space and even gradual upgrade for applications that become obsolete.

2. Usability- it impacts on how CC systems and resources will be integrated inside the contractors' companies and employees, whether they are business users or IT managers. CC services can be accessed by different types of computers and mobile devices with different operating systems. This feature has influence on users' policies and systems management, as it alters the way of working as well as eliminates geographic frontiers.

3. Quality of Service - it involves management aspects of CC service performance and the definition of roles, rights and responsibilities of all persons and companies involved with the contracting relationship. CC providers are responsible for service availability and should allow contractors to access from wherever and whenever they want, according to the quality levels established in the contract. Companies that carry out intensive amounts of data transactions need to assure that the CC service can sustain the expected performance, without excessive latency, even considering the existence of users who work outside the company or at locations with limited bandwidth.

4.Cost - contractors only pay for the services contracted for and consider the quality level agreed on as well as technical support; but it does not include infrastructure maintenance for running applications. Although contractors can save on hardware and software, there may be an increased cost due to network bandwidth demand, which may not be significant in cases of low data transactions rate. However, the bandwidth demand is expected to grow as more applications are hired and transferred to the cloud.

5. Security - this feature is a major concern for adopting CC services and involves various aspects of contractors and suppliers against attacks and vulnerabilities. Contractors' data and information are kept outside the realm and responsibility of internal staff, but users' policies and responsibilities must apply for both contractors and suppliers personnel.

Each one of these characteristics involves aspects that may influence decisions for adopting CC services. Although CC adoption may offer gains for contractors, especially for allowing business and IT personnel to work more on strategic activities, it is still a decision that involves many factors (Rittinghouse and Ransome, 2010). The following section shows the framework proposed in this work to help in understanding the factors involved in making decisions for CC adoption.

Adopting CC

For the analysis about the adoption of CC services proposed in this work, a literature review was carried out searching for previously developed models for evaluating results of IT adoption decisions, as well as for factors specifically related to adopting CC services. The aim at this stage is to identify a set of general factors to be considered for adopting CC, covering characteristics of workplaces and practices that may be unique for each company, users and business need (Klaus and Blanton, 2010; Petter et al., 2008).

One of the models mostly referred to in the literature for evaluating technology adoption is the TAM (Technology Acceptance Model) proposed by Davis (1989), which considers two principles relating to the perception of decision makers, which are (i) perceived usefulness and (ii) perceived ease of use. The TRI (Technology

Readiness Index) proposed by Parasuraman (2000) was also reviewed in this work and it considers two principles for IT adoption, which are (i) drivers (represented by optimism and innovation) and (ii) inhibitors (represented by discomfort and insecurity). It was also reviewed the EAOSS (Enterprise Adoption of Open Source Software) model proposed by Kwan and West (2005), which considers aspects of alignment between the system role to be adopted regarding companies' business strategies, covering such aspects as (i) strategy (competitive advantage and differentiation), (ii) critical mission (integration, reliability and risk), (iii) support (efficiency and cost), and (iv) laboratory (evolution and future benefits). Considering aspects of this work and its impact as a reference, the decision in this work was for taking the model UTAUT (Unified Theory of Acceptance and Use of Technology), which has been proposed by Venkatesh et al. (2003) and its applications are largely referenced in the literature. The UTAUT model indicates individual beliefs towards the four main determinants for analyzing the intent for IT adoption, which are:

1. Expected Performance – considers aspects regarding gains of performance in the workplace;
2. Effort Expectancy – involves issues related to the effort required for adopting the IT resource;
3. Social Influence – considers aspects from the users group regarding the IT adoption;
4. Facilitating Conditions – involve aspects of IT infrastructure and technical support present in the company for adopting the new technology.

The literature review on factors that may influence decisions for CC adoption shows a range of options, which may even be different when related to the model to be contracted (public, private, hybrid or community), as well as for the type of service (IaaS, PaaS, SaaS and their derivatives) (IBM, 2010; Rittinghouse and Ransome, 2010; Marks and Lozano, 2010; Babcock, 2010). Considering the factors listed in the literature review, this work considered the 5 characteristics of CC as dimensions for analyzing the intent for adopting CC services, which are (i) Scalability, (ii) Usability, (iii) Quality, (iv) Cost and (v) Security (see section 2.3).

Security related aspects were the most present in the literature review, which is not a surprise considering that CC is not different from any other emerging technology (Winkler, 2011). The cloud security must be part of the overall enterprise security strategy (Marks and Lozano, 2010). Most companies prioritize testing and monitoring threats on datacenter, buildings, people and information (Winkler, 2011). Security risks, threats and violations can come in many forms and from many places so that companies must adopt a comprehensive approach to managing IT security (Krutz and Vines, 2010).

Although the literature indicates that companies providing CC services offer good quality conditions of

security (physical, networking, operating system and application infrastructure), it is also the responsibility of the contractor to protect his applications, data and information (Krutz and Vines, 2010). Given the importance of security, CC suppliers offer a comprehensive set of terms in their contracts. However, most of these terms aim at protecting CC suppliers, thus requiring a careful understanding of contractors' responsibilities and rights (Krutz and Vines, 2010). From a technology standpoint, contractors should consider application rules for data security services of CC on the following instances (Winkler, 2011):

1. Stored data privacy, avoiding data that can be accessed or modified by unauthorized third parties (including the CC operator);
2. Runtime data privacy, preventing data from being seen and/or altered while in the clients' computer memory or in the service supplier machines;
3. Data transfer privacy, preventing access while in transfer to the CC provider, as well as in the contractors' intranet and suppliers' network;
4. Access data authentication, it considers rules and responsibilities of contractors to alter users' rights and include new ones.

In addition to technology solutions, business policies and legal guidelines can be used to ensure data security, providing terms and conditions for assuring the rights of all involved with the hiring and use of CC services, including penalties of financial compensation for cases of security breaches (Winkler, 2011). It is essential for companies willing to hire CC services to perform a detailed analysis of the impacts and risks regarding its adoption, especially if it involves a critical business activity. There are still plenty of room for the current state of the art of CC contracts to evolve, especially for considering specific contractors business needs, as the current reality is more related to protecting suppliers (Krutz and Vines, 2010).

The framework for analyzing the adoption of CC services has considered two viewpoints taken from the literature review, which are (i) the five main characteristics for adopting CC services, and (ii) the four factors present in the UTAUT model for IT adoption. The priority in this work was for identifying the most influencing characteristics for adopting CC services, thus offering a broad understanding on this issue. The framework was also used for understanding the relationship between the CC services characteristics with the IT adoption factors present in the UTAUT model. Therefore, the framework shown in Figure 1 was firstly drawn without the links between the analysis factors. However, the current version of the framework in Figure 1 shown in this work is already presenting the links taken as a result of the interviewing process.

The conceptual framework shown in Figure 1 was

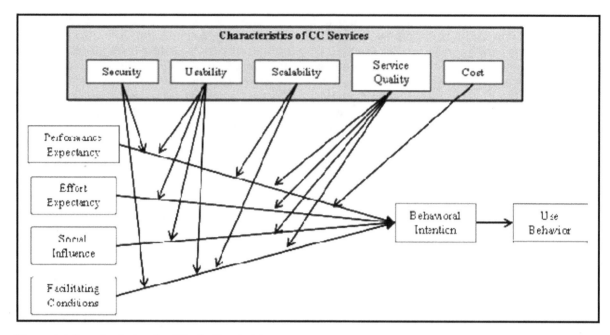

Figure 1. Influencing factors for CC adoption decisions.

subjected to the analysis of IT managers for understanding their viewpoints about the characteristics that mostlt influence decisions for adopting CC services. The framework was also used for identifying the interviewers' opinion in regard to the UTAUT determinants for analyzing the intent for IT adoption. Details regarding the research methodology and the interviewing process with the IT managers are presented as follows.

RESEARCH METHOD

This work presents an exploratory research that seeks for an understanding about the factors that influence IT managers' decisions for adopting CC services in their companies. This type of research is especially suited for cases in which there is neither a literature review specific to the area nor the researchers have an extensive knowledge on the matters in relation to the research problem (Cooper and Schindler, 2004). Although there are several literatures exploiting issues of CC services, this work focuses on the perception of IT managers about the main factors affecting the adoption of CC in the companies they work.

To deepen the understanding about the research objectives, qualitative interviews were carried out with IT managers experienced with CC adoption projects. The interviewing process was conducted based on a semi-structured instrument, which was firstly developed from the literature review, and represents the conceptual framework shown in Figure 1. The research instrument was designned with three sections. The first was for mapping respondents' profile and the companies they work for. The second aims at investigating respondents' opinions considering the relationships between the five characteristics for adopting CC services (Usability, Scalability, Service Quality, Security and Costs), each one in regard of the four determinants for IT adoption present in the UTAUT model (Expected Performance, Effort Expectancy, Social Influence and Facilitating Conditions). The last section of the instrument contains open questions for identifying general aspects of the

issues under study, such as standards that can be revealed or reasons for the respondents' positioning on certain research aspects (Cooper and Schindler, 2004).

The questions in the research instrument followed a guideline for identifying interviewers' opinions about all CC services characteristics. It means that there was neither time limit nor an expected standard for the contents of the answers. The interviewees' selection was based on convenience and considering the proximity to the researcher, though respecting the criteria of more than five years working experience as IT manager. A total of 16 IT managers of Brazilian and international companies from different sectors (retailing, manufacturing, services and IT) were interviewed, and all working at the southernmost state of Brazil.

The interviews were conducted face to face; focused and informal, allowing the interviewees to feel free to openly discuss the topics in the research instrument. This type of interview is often used for exploratory research, especially in cases where the researcher is dealing with unstructured knowledge (Cooper and Schindler, 2004). The interviews were conducted during May-July 2011 and confronting the IT managers' comments with the literature reviewed. The main advantage of a face to face interview is the opportunity to freely explore topics in depth, allowing the interviewer to feel comfortable for redirecting opinions and openly comment and justify their answers (Cooper and Schindler, 2004). However, the task of encouraging respondents to freely talk about the research topics belongs to the interviewer (Cooper and Schindler, 2004).

The interviews' content analysis was carried out for classifying, explaining and quantifying the respondents' understanding about the research context and CC aspects in the instrument. The content analysis applied thematic and categorical techniques, which are based on grouping the research issues into categories and explaining the context and application of the aspects present in the research instrument (Bardin, 2004; Cooper and Schindler, 2004). Though the interviews respected companies' policies and professionals' privacy, they were recorded for further analysis when allowed. The analysis proposed in this study can be repeated at a later date for comparing with the results obtained in this work, and thus evaluating changes in the IT managers' opinions.

Table 1. IT managers and companies' profile.

	1	2	3	4	5	6	7	8	9
M1	7	2	Software	Medium	IT	None	3	b	ii
M2	10	3	Financial	Big	Finance	MBA	1	a, b, d	i, ii, iii
M3	5	7	Services	Medium	IT	MBA	2	b	iii
M4	6	4	Services	Medium	Business	MBA	2	b	ii
M5	5	3	Software	Medium	IT	MBA	3	b	i, ii
M6	5	12	Financial	Big	Business	MBA	1	a	i, ii, iii
M7	9	6	Manufacturing	Big	Business	None	1	a, b	i, ii
M8	15	8	Bookstore	Big	IT	MBA	1	b, d	i, ii, iii
M9	9	3	Services	Big	Marketing	MBA	2	a, b	i, ii
M10	17	8	Manufacturing	Big	Business	MBA	2	a, b	i, ii, iii
M11	15	4	Retailing	Big	Business	MBA	2	b, d	i, iii
M12	20	9	Retailing	Big	Business	MBA	1	a, b	i, ii, iii
M13	15	6	Manufacturing	Medium	Engineer	MBA	2	b	i, iii
M14	16	7	Services	Big	Engineer	MBA	2	b, d	i, iii
M15	17	7	IT Hardware	Big	IT	Master	4	a	i, ii, iii
M16	19	9	IT Hardware	Big	Engineer	MBA	4	a, b	i, ii, iii

RESULT ANALYSES

The interviews carried out in this work took an average of 35 min conversation with each IT manager individually, and the result analysis present in this work starts by describing respondents' profile, and followed by showing aspects related to the five dimensions considered for CC services adoption decisions.

The research sought to capture the general perception of IT managers, regardless of market sector, business objectives and size of the company they work for. Table 1 shows the respondents' profile, considering aspects such as: (1) years of IT management experience, (2) years in the company, (3) company's business sector, (4) company's size, (5) academic undergraduate formation, (6) higher academic degree, (7) years of CC adopting experience, and (8) CC services adopted (a- Private Cloud; b- Public Cloud; c- Community Cloud; d- Hybrid Cloud), and (9) type of CC model adopted (i- Infrastructure as a Service; ii- Platform as a Service; iii Software as a Service). As solicited by some managers, their names and companies were preserved and only identified by a letter "M" followed by a number, according to the interviewing order (M1 to M16).

All respondents have academic degrees in areas related to the working activities they perform in their companies. In this work, it was not examined the relationship between the interviewees' profile and their point of view about the research objective of analyzing the acceptance for adopting CC services. Despite the differences of working time experience (5 to 20 years), all professionals built their formation in IT related areas, which is essential for this work, along with the time experience with CC services adoption (1 to 4 years). Although the there are differences in interviewees' profile, it does not seem to

have affected their opinions about CC services adoption, since most answers were justified based on technical aspects. Moreover, there was a consensus for answering the majority of the questions present in this work. Details of the answers provided for each of the five characteristics of CC services are described as follows.

Usability

Usability of CC in this work seeks to analyze whether the services being offered are aligned with business needs. The analysis considers users' experience with the companies' situation prior to adopting CC and the ability for adapting to the new technology, preferably with no great efforts for training, and perceiving advantages over the previous scenario (Antonopoulos and Gillam, 2010).

Managers' opinion highlighted that the mobility offered by CC is a strong motive for adopting (Performance Expectations). It was also indicated that Effort Expectancy for CC contracting firms must be analyzed from two perspectives: (i) from the point of view of IT professionals, who are responsible for managing CC services; as well as from (ii) the viewpoint of end users and managers of other business areas.

When asked to comment about (i) CC usability for IT managers, 10 of the 16 respondents agreed that this is not a problem since the interfaces for managing services are very similar to those they are used to. For instance, infrastructure management results provided by CC vendors are very similar to those currently used in their organizations. Moreover, they are transparent for contractors as well as for CC vendors. One respondent quoted that "I believe that the changes for IT managers are small compared to what they are accustomed to using, especially for web applications". The only barrier pointed by the respondents regarding the IT managers was Usability, quoted by M12, who said that "Some managers are very conservative and prefer to have privacy and full control over their information; they do not trust third party companies for providing IT services results; though I believe that it is something very personal and that has been losing ground".

Usability for (ii) end users was indicated by all respondents as a difficulty, and that cultural issues and changes on systems interfaces are obstacles for CC adoption. The Social Influence is a common barrier for most changes on current working situations, and IT projects are not an exception. M10 cited that "For some IT applications, end users may not even notice whether they using a local or a CC service". M11 reinforces it by saying that "Some applications require training, especially those that are 100% web based, but mostly those applications that will no longer have the same users".

The interviewees were also asked to point out the most important issues of Usability that they believe should merit attention for adopting CC services. M1, M3, M4 and M7 (4 of 16) referred to customizing CC services and applications for meeting specific business needs of contracting companies. M2, M6 and M9 (3 of 16) elected end users' training requirements as a major issue. M5, M8, M10, M11, M12, M13, M14, M15 and M16 (9 of 16) considered the adaptation of CC vendors for meeting specific business needs of contractors as the major Usability barrier. All agrees that training and a period for adapting to the CC supplier should be part of any CC migration project.

The Usability analysis carried out in this work shows that this characteristic should be considered, but it was not highlighted as a relevant barrier for adopting CC services. The interfaces provided by CC suppliers are similar to those used by IT managers as controlling consoles of IT resources. Though the respondents were instigated to talk openly about CC, there was no indication of concern regarding changes on working activities related to green IT and more efficiency on using energy. The major concern relies on selecting CC suppliers capable of offering a service that suits contractors' business needs. The analysis also shows that the Usability characteristic of CC influences aspects of Expected Performance, Effort Expectancy, Social Influence and Facilitating Conditions. Thus, Usability is a characteristic that influences all aspects of adopting new technologies of the UTAUT model.

Scalability

CC provides access to a wide range of IT services that are charged according to use in attending to contractors' demand variations (Rittinghouse and Ransome, 2010). CC has automated provisioning mechanisms to ensure that applications and services are continuously available and keeping the performance levels established in contracts (Antonopoulos and Gillam, 2010).

The respondents pointed out that Scalability is crucial as a Facilitating Condition for adopting CC services. They also consider its ability to adapt to contractors' demand variations as an important advantage of Performance Expectations. M5 cited that "the fact that there is a possibility to quickly add processing power for specific periods favors the current business agility demand". When asked specifically, all respondents mentioned that Scalability is an important factor for adopting CC services, but not the major. For instance, M8 said that "Scalability can be considered as the main advantage to certain companies, depending on the business area and technical expertise. In my particular case, I do not need to grow IT resources often". Actually, 10 of the 16 respondents quoted that they do not have large demand variations in their companies, though all mentioned to believe that CC vendors would meet their needs in case it is necessary. Respondents were asked to comment whether they had experienced with cases of increasing IT demands generated by business activities, in which CC Scalability was decisive. M1 cited that "Switching the company's e-mail to the cloud was one of the best decisions in terms of our infrastructure management, since we had a significant growth in our workforce and it was easily handled by the CC provider". M10 said that "since we began using CC we had a considerable growth on storage and processing power for meeting our project needs and we did not have any scalability problem". M12 also cited that "there are seasonal sales campaigns in my company that require IT services to grow significantly and CC has always supported our demand".

The Facilitating Condition of Scalability is a determinant factor for CC adoption. The ability to quickly acquire more computing resources, and in some cases automatically, and paying only for what is actually used was considered by 5 respondents as the main advantage of adopting CC. IT resources in CC can be purchased with varying amount and at any time, and all respondents had successful experiences with this ability to scale for meeting business needs.

The Scalability analysis carried out in this work shows that this characteristic influences aspects of Expected Performance and Facilitating Conditions for adopting new technologies present in the UTAUT model.

Service quality

Service Quality in CC aims to ensure that applications are being offered by attending to contractors' business demands and expectations, as agreed in the contract (Slabeva and Wozniak, 2010). Quality and utilization measurements of CC services must be available and transparent to contractors, as it also helps managers to rely on migrating their companies' IT applications (Rittinghouse and Ransome, 2010). As CC adoption involves becoming dependent on the supplier, it is necessary to ensure and manage service quality.

Respondents indicated that CC service quality should be managed based on the contract terms offered by suppliers. They also pointed that service quality is a CC characteristic that has influence over the four determinants for assessing Benefits Perception present in the UTAUT model (Performance Expectancy, Effort Expectancy, Social Influence and Facilitating Conditions). None of the respondents commented on having experienced difficulties related to contracted CC services quality. On the contrary, they indicated that CC vendors strive to ensure contractors' confidence by offering high service level agreements (SLA) and penalties for violations in the hiring contracts. Respondents M2, M3, M4, M7, M10, M12, M15 and M16 commented that they had excellent experiences adopting CC and achieved quality gains in comparison to the previous proprietary scenario in their companies. M4 cited that "my CC provider has been offering good quality on processing power, bandwidth, applications and technical support." M7 shares the same opinion and quoted that "we have been using our financial system and e-mail in the cloud for three years and yet no problems related to the CC supplier service quality. We had some problems, but mostly caused by our local network".

M1, M5, M6, M8 and M9 agreed in considering CC services quality as good, but with caveats. They heard of instabilities experienced by other companies and colleagues and quoted that this issue is closely tied to CC suppliers, and some still cannot assure the quality agreed in contract. The main restriction regarding CC quality was pointed by M11, who cited that some suppliers still need to evolve on providing better contracts and should go beyond the passive approach of just attending to contractors' demand and expectations.

When asked to comment on their experiences with CC service quality, the respondents said that, so far, there were no major disappointments. Concerns were most associated to bandwidth and technical support, which were indicated as crucial for evaluating CC services quality. M10 said that "There is no point on providing services with high processing power, storage space and technical support if the bandwidth is insufficient". M14 cited that "CC vendors sometimes are not providing technical support with the agility and quality I expected". M12 stated that "As applications are stored in the CC providers' infrastructure, it turns out that we became 100% dependent on their technical support for solving any problem that may happen". M11 was the only one to point out that they once had a quite serious problem, as the financial system was unavailable for 6 hours. M11 cited that "Although the financial system was not a business critical application, we did not take measures to end the contract with the CC supplier; but there was a lot

of inconvenience to our company".

Apart from some punctual restrictions, the respondents did not consider service quality as an obstacle for adopting CC. Although there were some caveats related specifically to some suppliers, bandwidth and technical support were pointed out as the most relevant aspects for evaluating CC service quality. Bandwidth can compromise the IT service continuity and technical support could somehow be the only option for returning the CC services. The analysis also shows that CC service quality has influences on all four determinants of adopting new technologies present in the UTAUT model, which are Expected Performance, Effort Expectancy, Social Influence and Facilitating Conditions.

Security

The literature review shows that security is considered as the major barrier for adopting CC (Minnear, 2011) and that was confirmed by the respondents in this work. Companies' expectation is to have protection, confidentiality, integrity, availability and access control over the IT resources and services, no matter if it is in the company or in a private or public cloud (Winkler, 2011). Safety measures and monitoring of IT resources should be kept consistent, based on CC (Krutz and Vines, 2010). Understanding the aspects that involve information security specifically related to adopting CC services is the issue focused on in this work.

The respondents indicated that Effort Expectancy and Social Influence do not apply as determinants for assessing the Benefits Perception for adopting CC services, as there are nothing specifically applied that is different from adopting any other IT resource. However, they pointed out that Performance Expectancy and Facilitating Conditions are determinants for adopting CC strongly related to CC security. Performance Expectancy was indicated as harshly related to the security terms present in the contract offered by CC suppliers. Moreover, the Facilitating Condition was directed as mostly dependent on the internal workplace and security matters from the contracting company. Part of the responsibility for protecting CC services goes to contracting firms, which also need to adapt for adopting CC. M1 says that "I consider CC safe because there are security mechanisms for assuring access and privacy of company's data and information."

The literature review shows that CC services can be provided with different models and contracts for adopting Public Cloud are the most common, allowing companies to share infrastructure and systems, but keeping data and information as a unique asset of each contractor. The respondents have not shown much concern for considering security as a barrier for adopting CC, even for Public Cloud contracts. They indicated that some security aspects can even be better provided by CC vendors, as they have the expertise for setting up, managing and updating IT infrastructure and applications. Only M6 and M15 quoted that they did not feel comfortable with hiring public CC services for security reasons and this specific reason leads them to hire a private CC service.

When asked about the security of information confidentiality, the respondents did not believe that it should be a barrier for CC adoption, as service providers have been dealing well with this issue. M8 said, "There are encryption techniques used by CC vendors that reduce this risk, and hence the restriction for adopting CC". M12 was the only one who showed some concern about information confidentiality and said, "No company would like to share information with another, especially with competitors, and it is difficult to assure that it is not happening with CC". M12 went further in this issue and stressed that confidentiality is a critical issue for adopting CC, and said, "This issue is even more critical when it comes to highly sensitive business information, such as financial results or product development projects, as leaks can cause losses that are hard to measure".

When questioned about the availability aspect of CC security, the respondents said that it is mostly related to bandwidth and CC suppliers have currently been capable of providing high level services. They recommended a prior detailed evaluation of suppliers and contract items, including issues of damage compensation that can be caused by service unavailability. Respondents also indicated that they are aware that Web accessing service does not need to be provided by CC suppliers, as it can be purchased from Internet Services Providers (ISP). M7 said, "bandwidth is my biggest concern and that may end up impacting directly on my company's business results". M7 also stressed that "Bandwidth is currently the most important constraint for information availability and it also requires attention in regard to the option of hiring from other than the CC supplier, as it may become difficult to know who is failing."

The accessibility aspect of security was pointed out by all respondents as a strong point for motivating the adoption of CC, as it deals with a wide variety of mobile and hardware devices for accessing services. The advantage due to the facility for accessing CC services from anywhere and anytime was well recognized by all respondents. M2 said that "The need and amount of integrated information for running business activities is increasingly every day and it must be readily available for everyone involved". M6 and M15 have shown concern on sharing IT resources with public clouds. M6 said that "I am worried about accessibility in Public Cloud contracts, as my company became dependent on security policies and management expertise of CC vendors". All other respondents pointed out that were comfortable with the current safety standards given by CC providers.

Security was considered as an important factor, but it was not considered as a major barrier for adopting CC services. Only two respondents showed some concern,

but it was specifically related to the adoption of Public Cloud services. The analysis also shows that CC security has influences only on two determinants for adopting new technologies from the UTAUT model, which are Expected Performance and Facilitating Conditions.

Cost

It is difficult for companies to precisely assess the real costs of IT resources or even for a particular application that runs internally using conventional datacenters. Thus, it is also difficult to compare costs for taking decisions to adopting CC services. CC can impact businesses of all types and companies, regardless of size and activity sector. CC also offers to micro, small, medium and big companies the opportunity to play as equals for accessing IT resources and making it as a competitive advantage (Antonopoulos and Gillam, 2010; Rittinghouse and Ransome, 2010; Rosenberg and Mateos, 2011). The fact is that CC services are available for hiring by any kind of company that could benefit from its adoption.

The respondents shared that although the expectation of reducing costs is real with CC adoption, it is very difficult for evaluating it precisely. There was also a consensus that the cost characteristic of CC is only related to the Expected Performance determinant of the UTAUT model. The opportunity for reducing fixed costs by paying only for the amount of the IT resources used was also pointed as a positive aspect for CC adoption. Beyond the cost of IT infrastructure, the adoption of CC also impacts aspects of systems licensing and personnel from technical areas that require expertize. Respondents agreed in considering that the cost for tech support is considered in CC suppliers' contracts. M10, M12 and M13 cited that although this cost may not be much smaller than by keeping personal into the company, professionals from CC suppliers are better trained and with higher expertise.

When asked about the prices charged by CC suppliers, the respondents commented that this issue is closely related to the type and amount of services hired. For instance, prices are very attractive for services that are considered simple, such as email, files exchanging and backup. However, services that are more complex and/or specifically customized for some companies' businesses have to be negotiated. M11 quoted that "Pricing for complex CC services are also dependent on the hiring context. The basic idea is that the more you hire from a vendor, the more you get as a whole". The general opinion is that prices are still high and the main reason indicated is that most CC vendors are outside of Brazil. M10 pointed that "As long as CC providers remain in Europe and US, the pricing for Brazilian companies would still be considered high".

Babcock (2010) cited that CC provides transferring IT resources cost from fixed to variable. It means that is

Table 2. CC characteristics vs. determinants for IT adoption.

Variable	Security (i) / (ii)	Usability (i) / (ii)	Scalability (i) / (ii)	Quality (i) / (ii)	Cost (i) / (ii)
Expected Performance	16 / 10	12 / 12	16 / 16	16 / 12	16 / 9
Effort Expectancy	2 / 2	15 / 13	1 / 2	14 / 2	2 / 5
Social Influence	3 / 1	16 / 10	2 / 2	13 / 4	1 / 2
Facilitating Conditions	16 / 11	12 / 12	15 / 15	13 / 10	2 / 2

possible to eliminate fixed cost of IT resources that are depreciated over time, such as servers, networking equipment and items related to datacenters. All respondents agreed that eliminating some IT infrastructure cost and having services charged according to the use are positive influences for adopting CC.

All respondents pointed out that cost is an essential characteristic for CC adoption, and it has to be evaluated from a short, medium and long term perspective. M6 commented that "The fact of no longer having to maintain a staff for this purpose and the rapid and frequent changes on operating systems, equipment and security measures should be considered for evaluating cost, though it is difficult for measuring".

The respondents did not consider cost as the main deciding factor for CC adoption. It was considered highly relevant and that should be carefully analyzed. Most respondents (14 of 16) indicated that decisions for adopting CC are already capable of providing cost reductions, though there are services that still could be cheaper when provided by IT legacy resources. They all believe that soon there should be a number of CC suppliers in Brazil, and it must lower the cost for adopting CC services. M16 cited that "Brazil is a country that shall soon be seen as an attractive option for CC suppliers, as electric energy is cheap and mostly provided by clean sustainable sources (hydroelectric dams)".

All respondents indicated that turning IT cost from fixed to variable is a positive influence for adopting CC. The analysis also shows that the cost characteristic influences only on the determinant of Expected Performance for adopting new technologies in the UTAUT model.

Consolidated results analysis

A quantitative summary of the results taken from the interviews is presented in Table 2 and it considers each one of the five main CC characteristics, in regard to (i) the influence and (ii) the perceived advantage over the four determinants for IT adoption in the UTAUT model. The first value in each cell (i) represents the amount of respondents that indicated a relationship between the CC characteristic with the UTAUT determinants for IT adoption. The second value (ii) in the cells shows the amount of respondents that indicated a perception of advantage in adopting CC services considering the CC characteristic

in regard to the UTAUT determinants for IT adoption.

The results in Table 2 were taken to build the relationships indicated by the connectors (arrows) in Figure 1. As shown in Table 2, Security was indicated by all 16 respondents as strongly associated with determinants such as Expected Performance (Winkler, 2011) and Facilitating Conditions (Winkler, 2011). However, only 10 respondents indicated that Security is perceived as an advantage that can be obtained by adopting CC in regard to Expected Performance (Kandukuri et al., 2009). Still, only 11 respondents indicated Security as an advantage related to the Facilitating Conditions that can be taken by adopting CC services (Gellman, 2009). However, Security was not an issue of concern regarding the adoption determinants of Effort Expectancy and Social Influence neither; it was not an influencing factor or perceived as having advantage over conventional computing services.

The CC characteristic of Usability was the one pointed out as the most capable of (i) influencing and (ii) providing advantages over the four determinants for IT adoption. Usability deals with the companies' ability to adapt to the new technology and involves training as well as advantages over the previous scenario of conventional computing (Antonopoulos and Gillam, 2010). Although the respondents were instigated to talk openly about all CC services issues, the reasons most related to Usability as capable of influencing all four determinants for IT adoption were users' interface, contract management and companies' policies.

The results for the CC characteristic of Scalability were very similar to Security. Though it was strongly considered as an advantage that can be taken from adopting CC services, it impacts only two determinants of IT adoption. For the determinant of Expected Performance, all 16 respondents pointed that Scalability represents an (i) influence (ii) and a perceived advantage over conventional computing. A similar result was shown for the Facilitating Conditions determinant for IT adoption, but only with 15 answers, as one of the respondents considered scalability as intrinsic for CC services and that it should not be considered as Facilitating, but only for Performance.

The results for Quality were highly evaluated as (i) influencing over all the four determinants for IT adoption. However, the (ii) perception of providing advantage over conventional computing was just related to the determinants of Expected Performance and Facilitating Conditions. Considering the interviews' contents as well as the respondents' position over the Quality characteristic of CC services, there has not been a concern for determinants of IT adoption as Effort Expectancy nor for Social Influence. Though Quality for CC services has been pointed as a concern in the literature review, mostly by the latency on accessing IT services from the cloud (Minnear, 2011), it is a major concern on aspects of how to be settled in contract and managed by contractors (Rittinghouse and Ransome, 2010)

Results in Table 2 also show that all 16 respondents pointed out that the cost of adopting CC is only and strongly (i) influencing the Expected Performance determinant. However, only 9 respondents indicated a perception of (ii) advantage in regard to the conventional IT services. Though it is not difficult to realize that Cost is not related to the other three determinants of IT adoption, it was expected in more than nine indications of a (ii) perception of providing advantages over conventional computing. The literature review shows that most end users are not satisfied with the current cost vs. IT services performance of conventional computing and that CC should help bridge this gap (Armbrust et al., 2009; Rittinghouse and Ransome, 2010; Chorafas, 2011).

Conclusion

CC is a growing business and represents an attractive opportunity for companies that operate with business objectives that are supported by IT resources and strive for keeping internal experts for support and maintenance. This work shows that CC is already present in the daily life of IT managers and it is considered as an option for most IT decisions in their companies. Constant needs for improving companies' business and IT resources as well as the continuous growth of CC services offered by suppliers are reasons that challenge IT managers for keeping up to date with this technology.

Scalability was pointed out in this work as the most positive characteristic that supports decisions for adopting CC services. The ability to scale an IT service and always cope with the demand, and paying according to what is actually used, represents an advantaged for CC adoption that was recognized by all interviewed. Although most managers believe that CC is safe, some expressed concern about this characteristic. Respondents indicated that they are aware that the CC architecture is designed to provide the highest possible level of security (considering reliability, availability, integrity and authenticity). However, there are different contracting options for hiring Private CC services that offer a higher security level.

The Cost for adopting CC services was only related to the Expected Performance determinant from the UTAUT model. The possibility of paying only for the amount of the CC services actually used was considered as a positive aspect for CC adoption. Cost also involves other aspects indicated as positive and related to depreciation and upgrade of IT infrastructure and systems update. Though these costs are in some ways considered by the hiring contracts, CC vendors have more expertise to making decisions for acquiring and updating IT resources, which can be shared between contractors, making the access cheaper as a whole.

Conclusions taken from the interviews showed that IT managers are satisfied with the service quality currently provided by CC suppliers. There is a growing number of IT services being offered as well as companies hiring CC resources. The most attractive CC services for hiring are currently those considered simple, such as email, web hosting and backup. It was also pointed out that most CC suppliers are outside Brazil and, though it may affect costs, it does not affect service quality. There was some concern with bandwidth, as well as with the terms for detailing the service level agreement in contracts, as they are more related to protecting CC vendors than assuring contractors' rights and penalties for failures.

Due to general difficulties with conventional IT resources, the interviewers quoted that hiring CC services shall soon to turn out to be a market standard for most companies. As some companies and business assets will keep running locally their IT resources, sharing IT services with CC is a close reality for such reasons as technical, strategic or personal.

As suggestion for future developments, the research carried out in this work should be applied to a larger number of IT managers for a quantitative evaluation of the relationships between the CC characteristics and the UTAUT determinants for IT adoption. It is also suggested to perform a specific research related to the costs of CC in comparison to conventional IT structures for companies with different sizes and business areas.

REFERENCES

Antonopoulos N, Gillam L (2010). Cloud Computing: Principles, Systems and Applications. Springer, London.

Armbrust M, Fox A, Griffith R, Joseph, AD, Katz RH, Konwinski A, Lee G, Patterson DA, Rabkin A, Stoica I, Zaharia, M (2009). Above the clouds: a Berkeley view of cloud computing, Technical Report UCB/EECS-2009. Department, University of California, Berkeley, Feb.

Babcock C (2010). Management Strategies for the Cloud Revolution.McGraw-Hill, New York.

Bardin L (2004). Análise de Conteúdo. Edições 70, Lisboa.

Buyya R, Broberg J, Goscinski A (2011). Cloud Computing: Principles and Paradigms. John Wiley & Sons, New Jersey.

Chee BJS, Franklin C (2010). Cloud Computing: Technologies and Strategies of the Ubiquitous Data Center. CRC Press, Boca Raton.

Chorafas DN (2011). Cloud Computing Strategies. CRC Press, Boca Raton.

Cooper DR, Schindler PS (2004). Business Research Methods. McGraw-Hill, New York.

Davis FD (1989). Perceived usefulness, perceived ease of use, and user acceptance of information technology. MIS Q. 13(3):319-341.

Fernandes AA, Abreu VF (2009). Implantando a Governança de TI da

Estratégia à Gestão de Processos e Serviços. Brasport, Rio de Janeiro.

Gellman R (2009). Privacy in the clouds: Risks to privacy and confidentiality from cloud computing, The World Privacy Forum, http://www.worldprivacyforum.org/pdf/WPF_Cloud_Privacy_Report.pdf.

Goscinski A, Brock M (2010). Toward dynamic and attribute based publication, discovery and selection for cloud computing. Future Gener. Comput. Syst. 26:947-70.

IBM (2010). Defining a Framework for Cloud Adoption.IBM Global Technology Services.Thought Leadership White Paper. USA, NY. Available at ftp://public.dhe.ibm.com/common/ssi/ecm/en/ciw03067usen/CIW03067USEN.PDF.Last accessed in 10/2011.

Kandukuri BR, Paturi RV, Rakshit A (2009). Cloud Security Issues. IEEE International Conference on Services Computing, Bangalore, India, September 21-25, 2009. In Proceedings of IEEE SCC'2009. pp.517-520, ISBN: 978-0-7695-3811-2.

Klaus T, Blanton JE (2010). User resistance determinants and the psychological contract in enterprise system implementations. Eur. J. Inform. Syst. 19:625-636.

Krutz RL, Vines RD (2010). Cloud Security: A Comprehensive Guide to Secure Cloud Computing. Wiley Publishing, Indianapolis.

Kwan S, West J (2005). A Conceptual Model for Enterprise Adoption of Open Source Software. In: BOLIN, S. (ed.), The Standards Edge: Open Season, Sheridan Books, pp.274-301, Ann Arbor.

Mansur R (2007). Governança de TI: Metodologias, frameworks e melhores práticas. Brasport, Rio de Janeiro.

Marks EA, Lozano B (2010). Executive´s Guide to Cloud Computing. John Wiley & Sons Inc., Hoboken.

Minnear R (2011). Latency: The Achilles Heel of Cloud Computing. Cloud Expo: Article, Cloud Computing Journal, March, http://cloudcomputing.sys-con.com/node/1745523.

Parasuraman A (2000). Technology Readiness Index (TRI): a multiple-item scale to measure readiness to embrace new technologies. J. Serv. Res. 2(4):307-320.

Petter S, DeLone, W, McLean E (2008). Measuring information system success: models dimensions, measures, and interrelationships. Eur. J. Inform. Syst. 17:236-263.

Rittinghouse JW, Ransome JF (2010). Cloud Computing: Implementation, Management and Security. Boca Raton, CRC Press.

Rosenberg J, Mateos A (2011). The Cloud at Your Service: The when, how, and why of enterprise cloud computing. Manning Publications, Greenwich.

Sarna DEY (2011). Implementing and Developing Cloud Computing Applications. CRC Press, New York.

Slabeva KS, Wozniak T (2010). Grid and Cloud Computing: A Business Perspective on Technology and Applications. Springer, New York.

Venkatesh V, Morris M, Davis G, Davis F (2003) User acceptance of information technology: toward a unified view.MIS Q. 27(3):425-478.

Weill P, Ross JW (2005). It Governance: How Top Performers Manage IT Decision Rights for Superior Results, Harvard Business School Press, Boston.

Winkler VJR (2011). Securing the Cloud Computer Security Techniques and Tactics. Elsevier, Waltham.

14

Reflecting on Information and Communication Technology (ICT) in marketing from a marketer's and student perspective

Deseré Kokt and Thakane Koelane

Faculty of Management Sciences, Central University of Technology, Free State, Bloemfontein, South Africa.

Information Communication Technology (ICT) has fundamentally changed the way in which global business is conducted. Of all the organisational functions, marketing has possibly been impacted the most by the emergence of ICT, as the array of available digital media presents a plethora of new ways in which goods and services could be marketed. Despite an increased emphasis on ICT deployment since the 1990s, marketers have struggled to fully embrace the integration of ICT in marketing. With this in mind, this investigation aimed to ascertain the extent to which ICT in marketing is embraced by marketers and the extent to which marketing students on a tertiary level are exposed to ICT in marketing, as part of their curriculum. The findings show that marketers are in a transition phase where ICT in marketing are increasingly used in conjunction with traditional marketing methods. It also highlights that marketing students need more specific exposure to ICT in marketing as part of their curriculum.

Key words: Information and Communication Technology (ICT) in marketing, marketers, marketing students.

INTRODUCTION

The technological innovation that characterised the late 20th century has led to significant development in a variety of new technologies – notably in the fields of biotechnology, new materials and product development, and computer and communications technology (Wange, 2007). Computer and communications technology, especially, has been subjected to great advancement in the past twenty years. The application and use of Information Technology (IT) has evolved to include various forms of microelectronic and telecommunications tools such as laptops and computers, the Internet (via optical fibres and wireless connections), mobile technology, iPads, digital television, palmtops, iPods and digital cameras/videos (Freeman and Hasnaoui, 2010). Furthermore, ICT is central to the acquisition, analysis, storage, retrieval, manipulation, management, control, movement, display, and transmission of data and information (Boritz, 2000).

These developments have indeed shaped the world into a global village, enabling communication and interaction irrespective of time and space. ICT has opened the world of marketing, giving marketers an array of new and innovative ways in which they can communicate with their customers. Acknowledging the importance of ICT in marketing has been highlighted by the Canadian Marke-ting Association as one of the seven key issues that marketers are facing currently (Gustavson, 2006). The 1990s were characterised by a burst of new technologies including the Internet and the World Wide Web (www) (Schultz and Patti, 2009: 76). Digitalisation brought along a large number of additional communication devices, products and services. First, fax machines and com-puters, then mobile phones, iPods, iPads, Blackberries, social networks, and the like.

While nearly all sectors and industries have been

greatly affected by advancements in technology, marketing has been most profoundly influenced by the development of ICT. It is thus imperative that marketing students, as the next generation of marketers, have sound operational knowledge of ICT to be able to properly position their organisations in the digital world (Lamont and Friedman, 2001). Since research (Mairead et al., 2008; Oshunloye, 2009; Zehrer and Grabmüller, 2012) indicates that marketers struggle to fully integrate ICT into their marketing strategies, this investigation aimed to ascertain the extent to which marketing professionals utilise ICT and to, by means of a case study, ascertain as to whether students at the Central University of Technology, Free State (CUT), are exposed to the various forms of ICT in marketing.

Research studies that focus on the integration of ICT in marketing are not abundant and most of them focuson the Internet as medium (Nothnagel, 2006; Oshunloye, 2009). Other studies include Brady et al. (2002, 2008) who investigated the integration of ICT into marketing practice and the role of ICT in contemporary marketing practice, respectively. In addition, Dye and Venter (2008) studied the rethinking of marketing curricula in the Internet age. There are also numerous studies that focus on ICT and its application in the tourism and hospitality industry (Qirici et al., 2011; Šeric and Gil-Saura 2012; Zehrer and Grabmüller, 2012; Burgess et al., 2011).

The contributory value of the current investigation lies in assessing the extent to which marketers use ICT in their marketing endeavours and whether students at the CUT, as a case study, are adequately exposed to ICT as part of their marketing course. The study was conducted in Bloemfontein, South Africa. The nature of the research problem necessitated a twofold approach and the study comprised both a qualitative and a quantitative research design. The qualitative section entailed semi-structured interviews with marketers in the Bloemfontein area, and the quantitative section involved administering a structured questionnaire to senior marketing students at the CUT.

The CUT is one of six so-called Universities of Technology (UoTs) in the South African context. The teaching and research aims of UoTs are distinct from that of other universities, as UoTs dove-tail theory and practice in providing business and industry with applicable workplace skills and innovation-oriented, applied research (Moraka and Hay, 2009). UoTs must therefore be attuned to the needs and requirements of business and industry.

EXPLAINING ICT IN MARKETING

ICT is a composite term that embodies three important concepts, namely" information", "communication" and "technology". "Information" in a scientific context canbe regarded as processed data that is obtained from, for example, business accounts and invoices. Information is an essential component of decision making and affects the management of knowledge in the organisational context. Though abstract, information can also be visualised as a commodity which can be bought or sold (Womboh and Abba, 2008). Furthermore, it can be defined as any communication or representation of knowledge such as facts or opinions in textual, numerical, graphic, cartographic, narrative or audio-visual forms.

"Communication" refers to the transfer or exchange of information from person to person or from one place to another. Communication is an integral part of human existence and implies the transfer of information, ideas, thoughts and messages (Womboh and Abba, 2008). "Technology" points to the use of scientific knowledge to facilitate the invention of tools that assist human beings in their efforts to overcome environmental hazards and impediments to comfort. In this regard, technology could refer to aspects such as computers, telephones (land lines), mobile phones, television, radio, and the like (Nchaka, 2009).

Tinio (2002) defines ICT as a set of technological tools or devices used by individuals to communicate, create, disseminate, store and manage information. Digital technology reflects hardware and software products, communication tools and products and/or services used to transmit information (Onunga and Shah, 2005; Pernia, 2008). This corresponds with the definition of Herselman and Britton (2002), who refers to ICT as comprising computers, software, networks, satellite links and related systems which allow people to access, analyse, create, exchange and use data, information and knowledge. On the other hand, ICT in marketing is described by Requena et al. (2007) as a tool that allows the development of strategies of differentiation based on product innovation, while Reinecke et al. (2009) define ICT as the application of technological tools and/or devices to differentiate products and services in an attempt to create value for customers.

ICT-RELATED MARKETING COMMUNICATION CHANNELS

Marketing involves a variety of activities to attract potential customers and aims, first and foremost, to generate interest in the products and services, and to stimulate repeat business. The digitally advanced and competitive environment in which modern organisations operate necessitates an ICT-integrated marketing approach, where new possibilities for the promotion of products and services could be exploited and where marketers can create stronger brand loyalties to ensure a sustainable competitive advantage for their organisations (Smith and ZeZook, 2011).

It should be emphasised that, although ICT opens up new markets and possibilities, the traditional forms of marketing is not diminishing in their importance (Winer,

2008). For example, radio is experiencing a resurgence with the advent of satellite and digital formats. Outdoor advertising is becoming more creative and, while newspapers and magazines have been negatively affected by ICT, they are still prominent marketing channels. Although this study focuses on ICT in marketing, traditional forms of marketing will inevitably form part of the discussion.

The Internet and the digitalisation of information have, together with the spread of the use of ICT devices, created the context of E-marketing. E-marketing has a broader meaning, as it includes not only digital media such as web, E-mail and wireless media, but also the management of digital customer data and electronic customer relationship management systems (E-CRM systems) (Cleofhas and Gibson, 2009). Within the broader E-marketing domain, this section aims to explain the main ICT-related marketing communication channels that should be considered in the overall design of an organisation's strategic marketing strategy. These channels include Internet marketing, social media marketing, digital marketing, mobile marketing and direct marketing.

Internet marketing

The Internet is often described as an engine of globalisation which knocks down borders and imposes market democracy on every nation. Indeed, the Internet has become integrated into the practices of businesses, governments and social movements and has changed the way modern individuals live and work. Hence, the Internet could be a powerful marketing tool if exploited by organisations (Yannopoulos, 2011). Besides being a new platform for buying and selling, the Internet has emerged as a new intermediary for companies to promote their businesses. Because of its characteristics and the high numbers of users, the Internet has become as powerful as traditional communication channels such as television, magazines and radio (Efendioglu and Igna, 2011).

The Internet enables Internet marketing, which aims to create, communicate and deliver value to customers. Internet marketing is defined as the process of building and maintaining customer relationships through online activities in order to facilitate the exchange of ideas, products and services that satisfy customer needs. Internet marketing can also be described as the process of using the Internet to achieve marketing objectives and to support the entire marketing process (Ngai, 2003). It is imperative that organisations have a user-friendly website in conjunction with online promotional techniques such as search engines, banner advertising, E-mails and direct links from own and other websites (Chaffey et al., 2006).

Social media marketing

The rise of social media is rapidly changing the way in

which organisations operate and communicate. According to Smith and ZeZook (2011), social media fulfils the fundamental human need of communication, and the emergence of social media could be regarded as the biggest development since the Industrial Revolution. Of all the different types of E-media, social media networking sites such as Facebook, MySpace, Twitter and YouTube have generated the most publicity. The term "social media" is the new buzz word in the communication and marketing industry. Tuomela (2010) asserts that social networking sites function by providing the platform for communication between the users. Consequently, social media marketing has grown in popularity and importance, for instance Facebook, a social networking site, which has enticed a wide variety of businesses to set up business profiles (Lewis, 2010).

Digital marketing

Urban (2004) suggests that digital marketing may use the Internet and IT to extend and improve traditional marketing functions. Digital marketing is defined as the practice of promoting products and services using digital distribution channels to reach consumers in a timely, relevant, personal and cost-effective manner (Merisavo, 2008). According to Chester and Montgomery (2008), venture capitalists are increasingly investing in the following three types of digital marketing, namely social networks (such as Facebook, Twitter and MySpace), mobile technology (such as Blackberry and iPhones) and online videos (such as YouTube). Other forms of digital marketing include podcasting, blogging, banner ads and video streams.

Mobile marketing

Mobile technology has catalysed information science on a mobile level, changing the pace of communication since the 1990s. The evolution from desktop to mobile communication is a key paradigm shift that has emerged prominently in the last decade. Twenty years ago individuals would not have imagined the endless connectivity made possible by mobile technology (Tetere, 2011). The Mobile Marketing Association (MMA, 2005) defines mobile marketing as any form of marketing, advertising or sales promotion aimed at influencing and informing consumers via a mobile channel. Mobile marketing connects businesses and customers with the right message at the right time and at the right place (Gregori, 2009). A number of products were introduced in 2010 that set the stage for an explosion of mobile marketing. Apple's iPhone, Google's introduction of Android, and Apple's launch of the iPad meant that smartphone adoption escalated. Mobile marketing can now move beyond mobile messaging to mobile E-mail and searching the Internet, which means that more potential marketing channels are opened to marketers (Bush, 2010). One critical factor that should be considered in mobile marketing is that the content must be relevant, informative and entertaining. Mobile channels are generally perceived to be more personal than traditional marketing channels (Heinonen and Strandvik, 2003), and meeting the needs of the target audience should be a main priority (Vatanparast and Butt, 2010).

Direct marketing

Direct marketing originated from mail-order services almost two centuries ago. This is in contrast to the claim that direct marketing is a new discipline (Tapp, 2008). In the last two decades, direct marketing has seen an enormous expansion, making it the fastest-growing marketing discipline worldwide. This is mainly because of the great benefits it offers to both buyers and sellers (Kotler and Armstrong, 2008). For buyers, direct marketing offers customers access to a wealth of individually designed products anywhere in the world. For sellers, it offers a lower-cost, rapid and efficient alternative for reaching their markets. According to Flici (2011), direct marketing is increasingly becoming part of key thinking regarding the development of strategic marketing strategies and the development of sustainable customer relationships.

This method targets specific customers with personalised advertising and promotional campaigns in order to increase higher returns on investments. Direct marketing is an interactive system that uses a variety of media to convey the marketing message. It applies marketing approaches that target specific individuals or groups of individuals by using both traditional and digital marketing methods such as mobile technology, E-mail (or spam), door-to-door selling, automated dialling machines and, more recently, automated SMS (Short Messaging Services) messages. Direct marketing is also used by charities (to secure donations), political parties and other social and welfare groups. Information obtained from marketing lists, public information (such as phone books or public registers) or information based on previous transactions supplies the sources that direct marketers use (Flici, 2011).

To summarise, the various forms of ICT in marketing should be considered when organisations contemplate their strategic marketing plans. The various ICT-based marketing methods should not be used in isolation, but should form part of the integrated approach where management considers the impact of the various types of channels on the overall marketing efforts of the organisation (Cleofhas and Gibson, 2009). In the context of contemporary business it is imperative that all organisations employ at least some form of ICT-based marketing communication as part of their overall marketing strategy. As consumers become more technologically inclined the prominence of ICT in marketing is likely to increase, leaving those behind who did not consider its prominence.

METHODOLOGY

The research problem emanated from the reported low levels of integration of ICT in marketing (Mairead et al., 2008; Oshunloye, 2009; Zehrer and Grabmüller, 2012). In addressing the problem, the investigation aimed to ascertain the extent to which marketers use ICT as part of their marketing endeavours and whether students at the CUT are adequately exposed to ICT in marketing as part of their curriculum. Both qualitative and quantitative research methodologies were applied in this investigation. The qualitative section involved semi-structured interviews that were conducted with marketers in the Bloemfontein area, and the quantitative section entailed administering a structured questionnaire to third- and fourth-year students at CUT.

The qualitative section

Qualitative research has its roots in social science and is more concerned with understanding human behaviour and the attitudes and beliefs of individuals. Salkind (2009) explains the primary goal of qualitative research as describing and understanding, as opposed to merely explaining, social action. The method of data collection applied to the qualitative section of the study was semi-structured interviews. Miller and Brewer (2003) assert that interviews are conversations with a purpose to collect detailed information about a specific topic or research question. These conversations do not just happen by chance, rather they are deliberately set up and follow certain rules and procedures.

Data were gathered from marketers about how and what type of ICT they apply in their work environment. The design of the semi-structured interview schedule was based on the themes which were identified in the literature and a similar interview schedule developed by Oshunloye (2009). For purposes of this investigation, snowball sampling was employed in selecting individuals for the interview. According to de Vos et al. (2005), snowball sampling is particularly useful in gaining access to individuals who are hard to reach. Marketers operate in numerous industries and positions, and the researcher used a few members from the target population to locate others. This process continued until a saturation point was reached.

Although a pilot study for qualitative research is less statistically correct, it should nevertheless be conducted (de Vos et al., 2005), as it enables the researcher to test the nature of the questions and to make rectifications where necessary. The interview schedule was piloted using one respondent, and the outcome indicated that all questions were clear and understandable. Interviews of about 15 min were scheduled with respondents. The researcher recorded all interviews and, after each interview, made notes on the general impression of the interview (Leedy and Ormrod, 2010). Any other open-ended discussions were also reflected upon after each interview. After the completion of each interview, the researcher consolidated the various responses and extracted the main themes that were identified by interviewees. Eight interviews were conducted. After the eighth interview, recurring responses were recorded, meaning the saturation point had been reached and no further interviews were deemed necessary.

The quantitative section

The quantitative section of the study consisted of a structured questionnaire that was administered to third- and fourth-year CUT

Table 1. Gender and racial profile of respondents.

Gender	Count	Percentage
Male	29	43
Female	38	57
Total	67	100

Race	Count	Percentage
African	62	92.54
Coloured	2	2.99
White	3	4.47
Total	67	100

students. Third- and fourth-year students were deliberately selected, as they have not only been exposed to marketing literature, but they have also participated in a service learning programme and completed a Work-Integrated Learning (WIL) module. Service learning is a pedagogical practice that integrates service and academic learning to promote increased understanding of course content, while helping students develop knowledge, skills and capacities to deal effectively with problems (Hurd, 2006). WIL is used as an umbrella term to describe curricular, pedagogic and assessment practices across a range of academic disciplines, as students are exposed to working in business and industry (CHE, 2010).

The population consisted of 117 individuals of which 67 were third-year and 50 were fourth-year students. The data collection tool employed in the quantitative section of the study was a structured questionnaire. One of the advantages of questionnaires is that they provide data amenable to quantification (de Vos et al., 2005). The primary purpose of the questionnaires was to gather and measure students' responses about their exposure to and application of ICT within the marketing programme. Moreover, the questionnaire enabled the capturing of responses about students' knowledge of ICT in the marketing field as well as their level of interaction with the various forms of ICT.

The questionnaire was based on constructs which were identified in the literature, and consisted of three sections: Section A captured the demographic data (gender, race and qualification enrolled for). Section B captured students' ICT access, usage and knowledge of ICT, which included how long respondents have been exposed to using computers and how many hours per week they use computers, where they have access to computers and how proficient they are with the various applications. It also captured respondents' knowledge of the various forms of traditional and E-marketing methods and whether they have been practically exposed to using these methods. Section C captured respondents' perceptions towards ICT.

Questionnaires were distributed to the marketing students during class time and were collected by the researchers. Of the 117 questionnaires distributed, 67 questionnaires were returned (N=67), yielding a response rate of 57%. Before the main study commenced, the questionnaire was piloted to five tourism and hospitality marketing students to ensure that it was clear and understandable to students. The pilot study confirmed that the questionnaire was clear and that it needed no further refinement.

DATA ANALYSIS AND RESLUTS

Analysing the qualitative results

The marketers interviewed were from a variety of industries (namely the hospitality industry, banking, telecommunications, pharmaceutical wholesalers and optical retailers) and were mostly marketing managers. The qualitative analysis of the findings showed that ICT in marketing is an important consideration for interviewees and that Internet marketing is pervasively used by those interviewed, followed by SMS, pamphlets and catalogues. It emerged from the interviews that an enormous amount of traditional marketing is still being utilised. Respondents further indicated that online visibility is crucial, especially having a user-friendly website and interacting on social media sites. Facebook and Twitter were indicated as prominent marketing tools used by respondents.

Analysing the quantitative results

Section A: Demographics

The gender and racial profile of respondents are displayed in Table 1. The majority of the respondents were female and African.

A total of 40.30% of respondents were enrolled for the National Diploma in Marketing and 59.70% were enrolled for Baccalareus Technologiae in Marketing.

Section B: ICT access, usage and knowledge

As computer literacy is imperative for accessing the various other forms of ICT, Graph 1 indicates how long respondents have been exposed to using computers.

Graph 1 shows that the majority of students have been using computers for three or more years. Graph 2 indicates how many hours per week respondents use computers.

Graph 2 shows that the majority of respondents use computers two to four hours per week. The majority of respondents were exposed to computers while in secondary school and have access to computers at the university and/or at home. The majority of respondents were acquainted with MS Word, MS Excel, MS Power Point and with using the Internet.

Table 2 indicates respondents' knowledge of the various forms of traditional and E-marketing methods and whether they have been practically exposed to using these methods.

It is clear from the responses captured in Table 2 that most respondents regard telephones (land lines and/or mobile phones) as the most effective method of marketing. This is followed by newspapers, Facebook, television, E-mail and SMS. The 'have used it and is most effective' column yielded low responses, apart from responses pertaining to Facebook and SMS. There is also a large number of missing values.

Table 2. Respondents' knowledge of the application of traditional and ICT marketing.

Internet, social media and other digital marketing	Most effective (%)	Have knowledge of using it (%)	Have used it and is most effective (%)	Missing values (%)	Totals
Television	29.85	2.99	-	67.16	100
Radio	17.91	5.97	4.48	71.64	100
Facebook	29.85	11.94	25.37	32.84	100
Twitter	7.46	4.48	-	88.06	100
MXit	5.97	8.96	1.49	83.58	100
Blogs	5.97	-	-	94.03	100
Direct and mobile marketing					
Newspaper	31.34	7.46	2.99	58.21	100
E-mail	25.37	11.94	7.46	55.23	100
SMS	26.87	14.93	10.45	47.76	100
MMS	2.99	2.99	-	94.02	100
Mobile phone	19.40	10.45	7.46	62.69.	100
Data marketing					
Mail/Post	16.42	14.93	1.49	67.16	100
Telephone – land line and mobile phone	40.30	19.40	8.96	31.34	100
SMS	10.45	25.37	11.94	52.24	100

Section C: Respondents' perceptions of ICT

In Section C respondents had to indicate whether they agree with statements on a four-point Likert scale. Cronbach's alpha coefficient test for reliability was performed on this question and yielded a score of 0.656793, which is close to the acceptable level of 0.7. The responses are captured in Table 3.

It is apparent from the responses captured in Table 3 that most respondents feel that computers enhance the quality of their assignments (Question 3.1) and that ICT makes the marketing course more interesting (Question 3.2). A total of 55.22% of respondents indicated that ICT can be helpful in group studies (Question 3.3), and 49.25% agreed and strongly agreed that ICT creates an interactive relationship between students and lecturers (Question 3.4). A total of 40.29% of respondents indicated that using ICT does not make classes more time consuming or learning more laborious (Questions 3.5 and 3.11). The majority of respondents agreed and strongly agreed that it is easy to obtain information via ICT (Question 3.6). Respondents also indicated that computers provide new learning experiences (Question 3.8) and that ICT improves note taking (Question 3.10).

FURTHER INTERPRETATION OF THE QUANTITATIVE RESEARCH RESULTS

Pearson's chi-square test (with a significance level of 0.05) was used to ascertain the correlation between how long students have been using computers and the qualification they are enrolled for. This yielded the following: Pearson's chi-square = 8.183123, df = 4; p = .08510, which implies that the time length of using computers is not related to the respondents' level of qualification. The relationship between the average hours per week that students access computers and the level of qualification they are enrolled for were also investigated using Pearson's chi-square test, which yielded Pearson's chi-square = 9.928560; df = 2; p = .00698. This implies that there is a relationship between the average number of hours per week and the level of qualification enrolled for.

Table 4 shows the correlation between the level of qualification (National Diploma versus Baccalareus Technologiae) students are enrolled for and their knowledge of the various types of ICT-related marketing (Internet/social media and other forms digital marketing, direct/mobile marketing and data marketing).

Table 4 points to a correlation between students' level of qualification enrolled for and their knowledge of the various forms of marketing-related ICT with relation to radio (Question 4.2), newspapers (Question 4.7), E-mail (Question 4.8), SMS (question 6.9) and telephones (land lines and mobile phones) (Question 4.13). This shows that respondents are acquainted with the more familiar types of marketing media.

Table 5 relates the perceptions of students towards ICT and correlates them to the level of qualification students

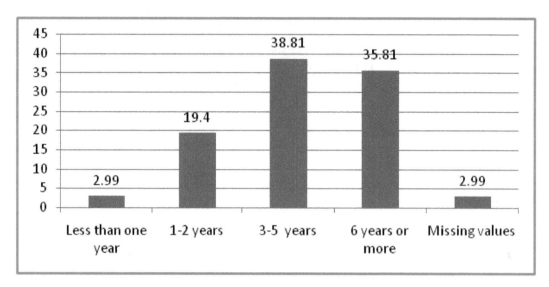

Graph 1. How long respondents have been using computers.

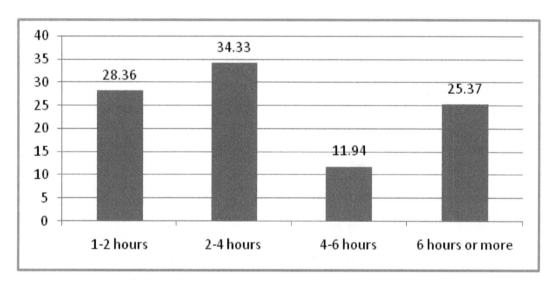

Graph 2. Hours per week respondents use computers.

are enrolled for.

The results of Table 5 point to a significant relationship only with regard to the level of qualification enrolled for and the existence of an interactive relationship between students and lecturers when using ICT (Question 5.4) and anxiousness and students' level of qualification (Question 5.7). This indicates that students need support and proper interaction when ICT integration is contemplated which may, in turn, have an impact on anxiousness on the part of students.

DISCUSSION

This investigation aimed to ascertain the extent to which

ICT integration has occurred in the marketing domain by focusing on the extent to which ICT in marketing has been embraced by marketers and how well marketing students at CUT are exposed to ICT in marketing, as part of their curriculum. This was achieved by employing both qualitative and quantitative research methodologies. To gather the qualitative data, snowball sampling was used in selecting participants (marketers in the Bloemfontein area) and semi-structured interviews were conducted with them. The quantitative data were gathered by means of a structured questionnaire administered to third- and fourth-year marketing students at the CUT.

It emanated from the interviews that the importance of using ICT in marketing is recognised by interviewees and that a combination of ICT and traditional marketing

Table 3. Respondents' perceptions of ICT.

Variable	Agree/Strongly agree (%)	Not sure (%)	Disagree/Strongly disagree (%)	Missing values %	Total
3.1 Computers enhance the quality of assignments.	85.07	8.96	5.97	–	100
3.2 Using ICT in the classroom can make the marketing course more interesting.	79.10	19.40	1.50	–	100
3.3 ICT is helpful in group studies.	55.22	19.40	20.89	4.49	100
3.4 The relationship between you and the lecturer should be interactive when using ICT.	49.25	31.34	17.91	1.50	100
3.5 Using computers in the classroom may be time consuming.	25.37	29.85	40.29	4.49	100
3.6 It is easy to obtain information via ICT.	91.04	4.48	1.49	2.99	100
3.7 Computers make me anxious.	23.88	22.39	49.25	4.48	100
3.8 Computers give me the opportunity to learn new things about marketing.	80.59	10.45	7.46	1.50	100
3.9 Only intelligent people can work with ICT.	4.47	20.90	74.63	–	100
3.10 Using ICT can make it easier to take notes (on paper or digitally).	79.10	10.45	8.95	1.50	100
3.11 Learning may take longer when ICT is used.	17.91	32.84	49.25	–	100

Table 4. Students' level of qualification and their knowledge of the various forms of ICT-related marketing.

Variable	Fisher's exact test
4.1 Level of qualification enrolled for and knowledge of television as digital marketing method.	$p = 0.3397$
4.2 Level of qualification enrolled for and knowledge of radio as digital marketing method.	$p = 0.0320*$
4.3 Level of qualification enrolled for and knowledge of Facebook as digital marketing method.	$p = 0.0755$
4.4 Level of qualification enrolled for and knowledge of Twitter as digital marketing method.	$p = 0.1685$
4.5 Level of qualification enrolled for and knowledge of MXit as digital marketing method.	$p = 0.2841$
4.6 Level of qualification enrolled for and blogs as digital marketing method.	$p = 0.1421$
4.7 Level of qualification enrolled for and knowledge of newspapers as direct marketing method.	$p = 0.0144*$
4.8 Level of qualification enrolled for and knowledge of E-mails as direct marketing method.	$p = 0.0029*$
4.9 Level of qualification enrolled for and knowledge of SMS as direct marketing method.	$p = 0.0093*$
4.10 Level of qualification enrolled for and knowledge of MMS as direct marketing method.	$p = 0.4138$
4.11 Level of qualification enrolled for and knowledge of mobile phones as direct marketing method.	$p = 0.3656$
4.12 Level of qualification enrolled for and knowledge of mail/post as data marketing method.	$p = 0.4699$
4.13 Level of qualification enrolled for and knowledge of telephones (land lines and mobile phones) as data marketing method.	$p = 0.0234*$
4.14 Level of qualification enrolled for and knowledge of SMS as data marketing method.	$p = 0.4429$

*Significance level of 0.05.

methods are employed by organisations. The Internet and social media marketing were recognised as a vital part of the marketing endeavours of interviewees. The importance of a user-friendly company website was reiterated by the interviewees as well as the use of social media networks. Furthermore, it emerged from the interviews that Facebook and Twitter were extensively used by respondents. Interviewees also acknowledged the continuous importance of social media, as a marketing tool, in the years to come. ICT offers a multitude of marketing possibilities and organisations need to, on a strategic level, decide which methods best suit their aims and objectives.

The interviews further confirmed that organisations still employ a great number of traditional marketing methods, supporting the notion that traditional marketing is not

Table 5. Students' perception of ICT versus the level of qualification enrolled for.

Variable	Fisher's exact test
5.1 Whether computers enhance the quality of assignments and student's level of qualification.	$p = 0.5868$
5.2 Whether ICT in the classroom makes the marketing course more interesting versus student's level of qualification.	$p = 0.9684$
5.3 Whether ICT is helpful in group studies and student's level of qualification.	$p = 0.1023$
5.4 Whether there is an interactive relationship between the students and lecturers when using ICT and student's level of qualification.	$p = 0.0451^*$
5.5 Whether using computers in the classroom is time consuming versus student's level of qualification.	$p = 0.2048$
5.6 Whether it is easy to obtain information via ICT and student's level of qualification.	$p = 0.8578$
5.7 Whether computers make students anxious and student's level of qualification.	$p = 0.0406^*$
5.8 Whether computers give students opportunities to learn new things about marketing and student's level of qualification.	$p = 0.8508$
5.9 Whether they feel only intelligent people can use ICT and student's level of qualification.	$p = 0.7837$
5.10 Whether using ICT improves taking notes, both on paper and digitally and student's level of qualification.	$p = 0.0958$
5.11 Whether students feel learning takes longer when using ICT versus student's level of qualification.	$p = 0.1531$

*Significance level of 0.05.

diminishing in its scope and importance (Winer, 2008). Traditional forms of marketing that are still being used include SMS, pamphlets and catalogues. The conclusions based on the quantitative part of the study show that the vast majority of the students (74.62%, Graph 1) have been using computers for three years or more. This indicates that students have been exposed to computers prior to the commencement of their studies, which is supported by the fact that the majority of students are acquainted with the various software packages such as MS Word, MS Excel and MS PowerPoint.

Respondents are further acquainted with the more familiar methods of marketing such as television and radio, as well as social media marketing, mobile marketing, SMS and E-mails. The fact that telephones (land lines and/or mobile phones) are regarded as the most effective method of marketing could be because most individuals have access to either land line telephones and/or mobile phones (Table 2). The large number of missing values in the 'have used it and is most effective' and 'missing values' column (Table 2) shows that respondents are not adequately informed as to how ICT could be applied in marketing. Although respondents are aware of the various ICT channels such as television, radio, social networks, MXit, blogs and even newspapers, they have not been exposed to using them in carrying out marketing actions. Very few respondents use E-mail and the vast majority did not answer the questions pertaining to the usage of MMS, telephone marketing and postal marketing. Interesting to note, although respondents are familiar with telephone marketing, they have not been exposed to using it in the context of marketing (as

indicated by Table 2, 'have used it and is most effective' column).

This also applies to the use of SMS, since a substantial number of respondents (47.76%) did not indicate whether they are acquainted with using SMS in the marketing context. The 'missing values' column of Table 2 confirms the finding that respondents are not acquainted with applying ICT in marketing. Although the marketing curriculum of the CUT has a sub-section dedicated to Internet marketing, it is evident that not enough emphasis is placed on how the various ICT methods should be applied in real-life marketing situations.

Regarding the attitudes of students, the majority agreed that computers enhance the quality of assignments and that it is an easy way to obtain information. The vast majority of respondents also indicated that the use of ICT will make the marketing course more interesting, stimulate new skills and assist in note taking. Furthermore, more than half of the respondents indicated that ICT could be useful in group studies. Respondents indicated the dominance of the Internet and social networks in the next five years and that marketer's should exploit these mechanisms.

Further interpretation of the research results indicates a relationship between the average number of hours respondents have been using computers per week and the level of qualification they are enrolled for. The results of Table 4 point to a significant relationship only with regard to the level of qualification and the existence of an interactive relationship between students and lecturers when using ICT and anxiousness and students' level of qualification. This indicates that students need support and proper interaction when ICT integration is contemplated.

CONCLUSIONS AND RECOMMENDATIONS

It could thus be concluded that marketers find themselves in a transition period – while ICT in marketing is strongly emerging, there is still a significant emphasis on using traditional marketing methods. It could also further be concluded that the students surveyed for this investigation need more direct exposure to applying ICT in marketing. The marketing programmes offered at especially UoTs, with their focus on vocational education and training, should adequately prepare students for the world of work. This does not only include the theoretical perspectives of ICT in marketing, but also exposing students to real-life simulations. The following recommendations can thus be proposed:

- Suitable laboratories should be established where marketing students could access the various types of ICT devices such as computers, iPads, iPods and digital cameras.
- Lecturers should be knowledgeable about ICT in marketing.
- Experts from business and industry should be utilised to instruct students on how to apply ICT in marketing.
- Practical assignments on applying ICT in marketing should be part of the curriculum of marketing students. This should not only include Internet marketing, but the entire bouquet of ICT tools and devices.

REFERENCES

Boritz JE (2000). The accounting curriculum and information technology. The Nigerian Accountant 33(2):26-34.

Brady M, Fellenz RM, Brookes R (2008). Researching the role of ICT in contemporary marketing practices. J. Bus. Ind. Market. 23(2):108-114.

Brady M, Saren M,Tzokas N(2002). Integrating information technology into marketing practice- the IT reality of contemporary marketing practice. J. Market. Manage. 18(5-6):555-578.

Burgess L, Parish B, Alcock C (2011). To what extent are regional tourism organisations (RTOs) in Australia leveraging the benefits of web technology for destination marketing and E-Commerce? Electronic Commerce Res.. 11(3):341-355.

Bush M (2010). 10 marketing trends for 2011.[Online].www. fifthgearanalytics.com (Accessed: 1 September 2011).

Chaffey D, Ellis-Chadwick F, Johnston, K, Mayer R (2006). Internet marketing: strategy, implementation and practice. 3rd ed.New Jersey: Pearson Education Limited.

CHE (Council on Higher Education) (2010).Kagisano No 7: Universities of Technology – deepening the debate. Auckland Park: Jacana Media.

Chester J, Montgomery K (2008). Digital marketing, interactive food and beverage marketing: targeting children and youth in the digital age. An update memo prepared for NPLAN/BMSG. Berkeley, CA. [Online]. http://ftc.gov/os/comments/foodmktgtokidspra-3/529477-00004.pdf (Accessed: 28 February 2013).

Cleofhas B, Gibson K (2009). Effects of IT in marketing of communication services. Case: Safaricom Kenya Ltd. Laurea

University of Applied Sciences, Vantaa, Finland.

De Vos AS, Strydom H, Fouché, CB, Delport CSL (2005). Research at grass roots. 2nd ed. Pretoria: Van Schaik Publishers.

Dye BAL, Venter PF (2008). Rethinking marketing curricula in the Internet age. S. Afr. J. Higher Educ. 22(3):538-555.

Efendioglu A, Igna F (2011). Attracting customers online: effectiveness of online marketing tools. Master's dissertation,Luleå University of Technology, Luleå, Sweden.

Flici A (2011). A conceptual framework for the direct marketing process using business intelligence. Doctoral thesis, Brunel University, London, United Kingdom.

Freeman I, Hasnaoui A (2010).Information communication technology: a tool to implement and drive corporate social responsibility (CSR). [Online].www.hal.archives-ouvertes.fr.docs/...aim2010-FreemanI-HasnaouiA.pdf (Accessed: 25 February 2013).

Gregori A (2009). Optimised mobile marketing as part of integrated marketing campaigns building quality leads.[Online].http://mobilemarketingwinners.com/resources/Presentations/08%20Alexander%20Gregori.pdf._(Accessed: 20 November 2012).

Gustavson J (2006). What keeps marketers awake?[Online].http://www.the-cma.org/about/blog/seven-key-issues-cause-of-insomnia-for-marketers. (Accessed: 28 August 2011).

Heinonen K, Strandvik T (2003).Consumer's responsiveness to mobile marketing. Paper presented at the Stockholm Mobility Roundtable, Stockholm Sweden, 22-23 May.[Online].http://citeseerx.ist.psu.edu/viewdoc/download?doi=10.1.1.102.3837&rep=rep1&type=pdf (Accessed: 28 February 2013).

Herselman M, Britton KG (2002). Analysing the role of ICT in bridging the digital divide amongst learners. S. Afr. J. Educ. 22(4):270-274.

Hurd CA (2006). Is service learning effective? A look at the current research.[Online].http://tilt.colostate.edu/sl/faculty/ls_Service-Learning_Effective.pdf(Accessed: 22 November 2012).

Kotler P, Armstrong G (2008). Principles of marketing.12th ed. New Jersey: Pearson PrenticeHall.

Lamont LM, Friedman K (2001). Meeting the challenges to undergraduate marketing education. J. Market. Educ. 19(3):17-30.

Leedy P, Ormrod J (2010). Practical research: planning and design. 7th ed. New Jersey: Merrill Prentice Hall.

Lewis BK (2010). Social media and strategic communication attitudes and perceptions among college students. Public Relat. J. 4(3):1-23.

Mairead B, FellenzMR, Brooks R(2008). Researching the role of information and communication technology (ICT) in contemporary marketing practices. J. Bus. Ind. Market. 23(2):108-114.

Merisavo M (2008). The interaction between digital marketing communication and customer loyalty. Master's dissertation, Helsinki School of Economics. Helsinki, Finland.

Miller RL, Brewer JD (2003). The a-z of social research. London: Sage Publication Ltd.

MMA (Mobile Marketing Association) (2005). Code for responsible mobile marketing. A code of conduct and guidelines to best practice. [Online].http://www.consumer-preference.com. (Accessed: 24 May 2012).

Moraka TS, Hay HR (2009). The implementation of a capacity development system for academic staff in higher education: The case of the Central University of Technology, Free State. J. New Gen. Sci. 7(2):218-233.

Nchaka M (2009). The Lesotho National Manpower development secretariat in the stakeholder century. An integrated marketing communication approach. Master's dissertation, University of the Free State, Bloemfontein, South Africa.

Ngai EWT (2003). Internet marketing research (1987-2000):A literature review and classification. Eur. J. Market. 37(1/2):24-49.

Nothnagel BL (2006). Internet marketing communications: a content analysis of the web sites of graded South African lodges. Master's dissertation. University of Pretoria, Pretoria, South Africa.

Onunga J, Shah A (2005). Computer studies: introduction to computers. 4thed. Nairobi: Mariwa Publishers.

Oshunloye AO (2009). ICT in marketing: a study of the use of Internet and mobile phones in five selected companies in Dublin. MBA dissertation. Blekinge Institute of Technology, Dublin, Ireland.

Pernia EE (2008). Strategy framework for promoting ICT literacy in the

Asia-Pacific region. Publication of UNESCO Bangkok Communication and Information Unit. Asia and Pacific Regional Bureau for Education, Bangkok, Thailand.[Online].http://www.unesco.org/new/en/communication-and-information/resources/publications-and-communication-materials/publications/full-list/strategy-framework-for-promoting-ict-literacy-in-the-asia-pacific-region/ (Accessed: 28 February 2013).

Qirici E, Theodhori O, Elmazi L (2011). E-marketing and ICT-supported tourist destination management: implications for tourism industry in global recession. Int. J. Manage. Cases 13(3):152-158.

Reinecke S, Tomczak T, Kub A (2009). Marketing planung. 6thed. Wiesbaden: GWV Fachverlage GmbH.

Requena JT, Sellens JT, Zarco AIJ (2007). ICT use in marketing as innovation success factor. Eur. J. Innov. Manage. 10(2):268-288.

Salkind NJ (2009). Exploring research. 7th ed. New Jersey: Pearson International Education.

Schultz DE, Patti CH (2009). The evolution of IMC: IMC in a customer driven marketplace. J. Market. Commun. 15(2-3):75-84.

Šeric M, Gil-Saura I (2012). ICT, IMC and brand equity in high quality hotels in Dalmatia: an analysis from guest perceptions. J. Hosp. Market. Manage. 21(8):821-851.

Smith PR, ZeZook (2011). Marketing communications: integrating offline and online with social media. How marketing has changed forever. 5th ed. London: Kogan Page.

Tapp A (2008). Principles of direct and database marketing. 4thed. London: Pearson Education Limited.

Tetere M (2011). Mobile marketing: brand performance and implications on brand identity: a case study of Adidas, Nike and Puma. Master's dissertation, Aarhus University, Aarhus, Denmark.

Tinio VL (2002). ICT in education. [Online].http://www.unesco.org/new/en/unesco/themes/icts/ (Accessed: 1 March 2013).

Tuomela S (2010). Marketing millennials in virtual community – SME perspective applied. Master's dissertation, AALTO University, Helsinki, Finland.

Urban GL (2004). Digital marketing strategy: text and cases. New Jersey: Pearson Prentice Hall.

Vatanparast R, Butt A (2010). An empirical study of factors affecting the use ofmobile advertising. Int. J. Mobile Market. 5(1):28-40.

Wange S (2007). African Economic Research Consortium (AERC). A review of methodology for assessing ICT impact on development and economic transformation. [Online].http://www.africaportal.org/dspace/articles/review-methodology-assessing-ict-impact-development-and-economic-transformation (Accessed: 28 February 2013).

Winer RS (2008). New communications approaches in marketing: issues and research directions. J. Interact. Market. 23(2):108-117.

Womboh BSH, Abba T (2008). The state of information and communication technology (ICT) in Nigerian university libraries: The experience of Ibrahim Babangida Library. [Online].http://digitalcommons.unl.edu/libphilprac/. (Accessed: 29 November 2012).

Yannopoulos P (2011). Impact of the internet on marketing strategy formulation. Brock University, Canada. Int. J. Bus. Soc. Sci. 2(18):1-7.

Zehrer A, Grabmüller A (2012). Social media marketing in tourism education: insights into the development and value of a social network site for a higher education institution in tourism. J. Vacat. Market. 18(3):221-228.

15

Designing a fuzzy model for decision support systems in the selection and recruitment process

Sabina Mirzaei Nobari[1] and Davood Hosein Zadeh[2]

[1]Azerbaijan National Academy of Sciences, Institute of Information Technologies 370141, Baku, Azerbaijan,
[2]Department of Psychology and Educational Sciences College, Islamic Azad University, Saveh Branch, Saveh, Iran.

Today, most companies require skilled and experienced staff in their firms, but they encounter problems in identifying the necessary personnel to recruit. However, there is lack of a system that has the capability of integrating the needs of organizations in this field. A case study is Iran Khodro Company, Iran's largest car maker which has always been faced with these problems. Based on this study, the head of the department of Human Resources of Iran Khodro Company Affairs was implemented as the deputy leader in their recruitment and selection plan. Acceptable performance results from this research are considered the most important achievement due to the study and it is application in other parts of the company by the deputy for recruitment and selection. The goal of this study is to introduce a model of fuzzy decision support systems that is in compliance with it; as such, Iran Khodro Company can improve their selection and hiring process. In this context, the absence of a model capable of compliance with specific restrictions on hiring decisions will be felt. The model can be developed to become a Decision Support System in the field of personnel selection. Therefore, the findings of this study can be used in making good decisions and senior managers can also assist in making comprehensive and scientific decisions. Also, according to environmental uncertainty, the research phase space can be near the amount of models to more realistic situations and can cause more aspects of the situation to decide on the actual model that gives the best expression.

Key words: Decision support system, fuzzy model, TOPSIS method, selection, recruitment.

INTRODUCTION

This pattern is suggested from widely used employment tests in the company that its overall framework includes five factors: medical, functional characteristics, behavioral and appearance characteristics, personality and psychological factors, and science and knowledge characteristics. Sub domain of each related factor has been extracted from employment tests, interviews with experts and selected documents studies.

Employed Applicants in Iran Khodro Company have been constantly evaluated by these criteria, but this assessment has never been integrated and systemic. Therefore, in this study, we intend to use existing models and experiences in organizations and offer a Decision Support Model for selection and employment. However,

considering the need and importance of human resource systems, each day, the last sub systems, particularly the recruitment and selection subsystem, need to develop human resources. Given that the importance of the organizations under the human resource systems have been realized (Boxall and Purcell, 2000). The importance of topic selection, recruitment, and hidden costs in an organization is required for human resources management system and operation, before any other action such as: planning and building subsystems and selection of personnel selection. The correct strategies for decisions are taken; nature of the modeling process to reduce the complexity of decision making can be a major role.

The criterions for this study were obtained from the

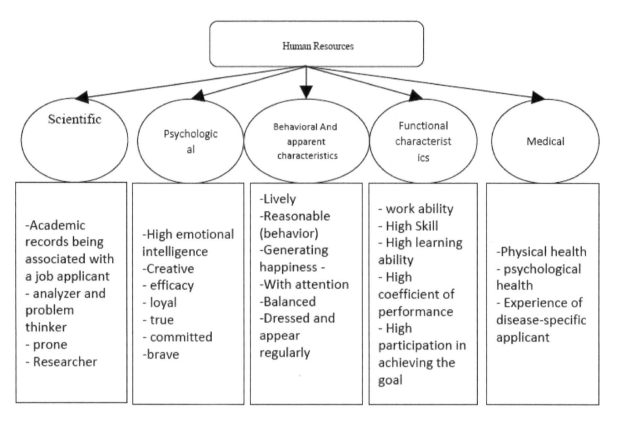

Figure 1. Part of total number of benchmark research of experts.

resources, experiences of Iran Khodro in selection and selection of field studies (observations of a researcher in the Department of resources and human cycles of selection and recruitment). Number of collected sub domain of factors is 34 criterions in the initial research phase that were classified into five key factors. The ultimate goal of this study is to provide appropriate and practical models to help identify risk factors in the recruitment and selection process (Figure 1).

The Fuzzy-TOPSIS method

Most researches on vendor selection problem consider crisp and exact data which are usually far from real-world situations. In the real-world, the rating values of alternatives as well as important weights of criteria usually have various types of vagueness, and we cannot always apply the classical decision-making techniques for these problems. Therefore, the fuzzy sets theory provides a precious tool for taking these realities into account. In a fuzzy multiple criteria decision making (FMCDM), linguistic variables were used to express the subjective and/or careless qualitative of a decision maker's assessments. A linguistic variable is a variable whose values are of linguistic terms (Kristof-Brown et al., 2005). Just a few researchers have applied the fuzzy sets theory into supplier selection problem. Cascio and Aguinis (2008) The TOPSIS method was first proposed by Hwang and Yoon (1981). The basic concept of this method is that the chosen alternative should have the shortest distance from the positive ideal solution and the farthest distance from a negative ideal solution (Feredrik, 2010).

For Fuzzy TOPSIS method, Feredrik (2010) introduced fuzzy

SMART approach for supplier selection. On the other hand, Kumar et al. (2006a) applied fuzzy programming approach for vendor selection, but they did not incorporate intangible criteria in the decision making process. In recent years, TOPSIS has been a favorable technique for solving MCDM problems. This is mainly for two reasons: Its concept is reasonable and easy to understand, and in comparison with other MCDM methods, like AHP, it requires less computational efforts, and therefore, can be easily applied. TOPSIS is based on the concept that the optimal alternative should have the shortest distance from the positive ideal solution (PIS) and the farthest distance from the negative ideal solution (NIS).

However, due to the advantages of TOPSIS method in this paper, a new fuzzy TOPSIS approach for vendor (supplier) selection problem was proposed. Cascio and Aguinis (2008) introduced fuzzy sets theory to supplier selection problem, but they only investigated a three-level hierarchy problem, that is, goal, criteria and alternatives. In this paper, to make a more detailed decision, we considered a four-level hierarchy problem- goal, criteria, sub-criteria and alternatives; furthermore, we used the canonical representation of multiplication operation on three trapezoidal fuzzy numbers (Ajzen and Fishbein, 1990) to evaluate and rank alternative suppliers and to select the most promising one.

A positive ideal solution is a solution that maximizes the benefit criteria and minimizes cost criteria; whereas, a negative ideal solution maximizes the cost criteria and minimizes the benefit criteria (Bennis, 1999). In the classical TOPSIS method, the weights of the criteria and the ratings of alternatives are precisely known and crisp values are applied for the evaluation process. However, under many conditions, crisp data are inadequate to model real-life decision problems. Therefore, the fuzzy TOPSIS method was proposed, in which the weights of criteria and ratings of alternatives were evaluated by linguistic variables represented by fuzzy numbers to deal with the deficiency in the traditional TOPSIS

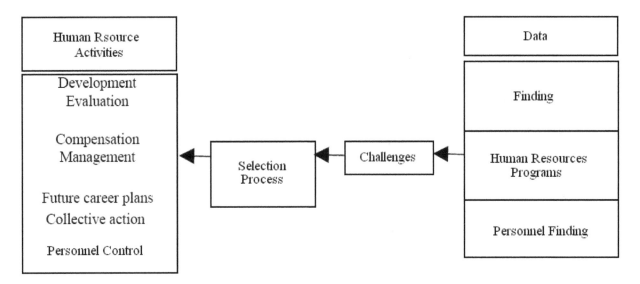

Figure 2. The selection operation.

(Pascal and Athos, 2001). The related algorithm can be described as follows (Guest, 2010; Waterman and Peters, 2002):

Step 1: A committee of the decision-makers is formed (Fuzzy rating of each decision maker).
Step 2: Criteria evaluation is determined.
Step 3: After that, appropriate linguistic variables are chosen for evaluating criteria and alternatives.
Step 4: The weight of criteria are aggregated.
Step 5: The fuzzy decision matrix is constructed.
Step 6: The above matrix is normalized.
Step 7: Considering the different weight of each criterion, the weighted normalized decision matrix is computed by multiplying the important weights of evaluation criteria and the values in the normalized fuzzy decision matrix.

Selection process

The selection process includes clear steps of decision about the selection process and hiring the best applicants from available applicants. This process provides job opening process that starts and ends with the hiring decision. However, in many cases, the final decision is with the selection and recruitment of a relevant supervisor or manager, but the role of the human resource units is to confirm applicants according to their potential merit. This process includes steps that require careful evaluation that adds time and complexity to the hiring process. At different steps, managers and human resources personnel employment units aligned the needs of the organization with each other. In many organizations, units combine finding and selection process and it is called employment operation. In large organizations, employment is one of the responsibilities of employment management, while in small organizations; it is the personnel management's task. Since the selection process is an important function in the department of human resources, therefore, employment is often a main focus of firms, and it would not be exaggerating to say that the selection process is considered on the basis of the organizations' successes or even a single organization's successes.

As seen in Figure 2, the selection operation is assisted by three factors that includes, job analysis information, which contains job description, person specification and performance standards in every job, the human resources' programs that identify empty jobs

and possible improvements to the selection in an effective way, and finding that creates a set of the applicants troubleshooting force and employees are selected from them. The employment is known as a source of other human resource management activities. Without employment process, the nature of human resource management as well as other activities will be at risk.

Population research and information provider

Population study of all managers and professionals in the Department of Human Resources is composed of Iran Khodro Company. Study population represents information including experts; managers are active in the field of human resources.

Data collection methods and tools

Human resource issues have different methods for gathering information, but the most important method of data collection methods, is interviews with experts and experienced people in this area. Also in this study, these tools and group interviews have been used to collect basic data. For completing the literature, we have tried to use library, related sites and areas of human resources-related magazines in systems that use appropriate recruitment and selection for its operation. Furthermore, using a field study (direct observation systems in the current selection and recruitment of human resources) we tried to know the influence of elements within the recruitment selection and employment tests.

Steps in problem solving based on fuzzy TOPSIS method

In this article, the priority of applicant is determined. Accordingly, in the main model, factors affecting recruitment and selection are in the first level; in the second level, criterions of research and in third level, applicants' research. In this model, weights and measures of factors is calculated by the geometric mean method that is one of the approximate methods in weight computing of hierarchical analysis.

Describing the Fuzzy- TOPSIS method, we require knowing some basic definitions of fuzzy sets, fuzzy numbers and linguistic

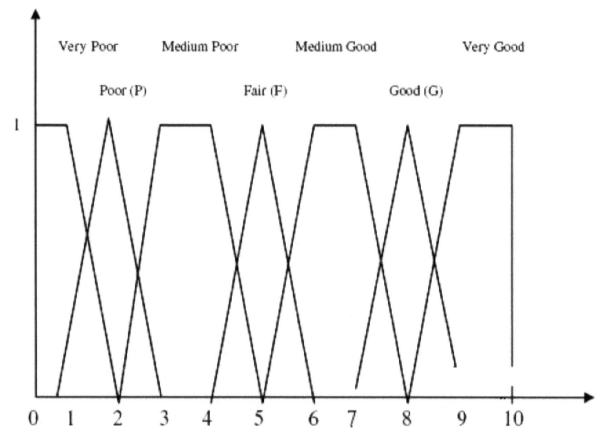

Figure 3. Fuzzy variables graph.

variables were checked. Ã fuzzy sets show that every x of X is in the numerical range of [0 1] when compared to a fuzzy subset of X. In Function (x), closing to 1 shows more belonging to x set. Therefore, fuzzy sets and membership functions are indicator functions and generalized definite set (Buckley, 1985):

relation 1:

$$\mu_{\tilde{n}}(x) = \begin{cases} 0, \\ \frac{x-n_1}{n_2-n_1}, \\ 1, \\ \frac{x-n_4}{n_3-n_4}, \\ 0 \end{cases}$$

In this study, each of the seven linguistic variables that have been used to convert linguistic variables to fuzzy numbers of the form as shown in Figure 3 and Table 1 is used.

RESULTS

In this study, we have applied only points of the Department of Human Resources' because it is the most important in the completion of paired comparisons questionnaire being experts to prevent diversion of results. Thus, for the first questionnaire, a sample of 40 experts in Human Resources Department of Iran Khodro Company and for the second questionnaire, sample size

is for very certified individuals of Human Resources Department. As mentioned earlier, three job applicants of the Department of Human Resources who had priority were evaluated by the four experts. Finally, with the help of the MATLAB program, software were prepared and run for determining priorities of different individuals that showed that both of their results are the same.

Weight of different criterions in Research shows that in order of personality, psychological, medical and scientific knowledge are functional and the appearance and behavior has been in priorities of Human Resources Department for Employment and selection (Table 2).

Although, weight of different criterions in each factor does not have a significant difference, but the relative priority of each criterion in each factor is caused by more attention of experts.

In medical factor, psychological criterion is in priority to physical health, whereas in the functional characteristics, high-skill has high-priority to physical health. In the behavior and appearance factor, being polite has a priority on balance in behavior. In psychological personality factors, criterions of creativity, integrity, emotional intelligence and being practical have a priority on order. In the science and knowledge factor, relevant education to the job has a priority for researcher.

As was explained previously, the final results of Topsis

Table 1. Corresponding values of trapezoidal fuzzy linguistic variables.

Row	Linguistic variable	A trapezoidal fuzzy number
1	Very good	(8, 9, 9, 10)
2	Good	(7, 8, 8, 9)
3	Somewhat good	(5, 6, 7, 8)
4	Average	(4, 5, 5, 6)
5	Somewhat weak	(2, 3, 4, 5)
6	Weak	(1, 2, 2, 3)
7	Very poor	(0, 1, 1, 2)

Table 2. Calculated weights.

Factor	Criterion	Factor weight	Criterion weight
Medical	Physical health	0.31	0.35
	Psychological health		0.65
Functional characteristics	Top skills	0.1	0.63
	High learning ability		0.37
Behavioral and morphological characteristics	With attention	0.08	0.53
	Balanced		0.47
Psychological character	Creative	0.4	0.32
	High emotional intelligence		0.22
	Honest		0.26
	Practical		0.2
Scientific knowledge	Researcher	0.11	0.46
	Academic records and relation between them and work		0.54

for fuzzy persons C, A and B, respectively were employed in preferences based on these results. Also, the output contents of C, A and B were the priorities that indicate equality in the TOPSIS programs.

SUGGESTIONS

Suggestions of research are from the results of this study, we hope that these suggestions will be used in Iran Khodro and other organizations. The suggestions are as follows:

1. More and more attention to employment testing and screening applicants, and determining minimum necessary for entry on the next steps of assessment.
2. Using linguistic variables and fuzzy logic in qualitative evaluation of individuals.
3. Enter values in the designed model in the MATLAB software.

4. Compare the results obtained by different people, and selection, and hiring the best of them

REFERENCES

Ajzen I, Fishbein M (1990). Understanding attitudes and predicting social behavior. Englewood Cliffs, NJ: Prentice-Hall.
Bennis W (1999). The leadership advantage, leader to leader. p.12.
Boxall P, Purcell J (2000). Strategic human resource management: Where have we come from and where should we be going? Int. J. Manag. Rev. 2(2):183-203.
Buckley JJ (1985). Fuzzy hierarchical analysis. Fuz. Set. Sys. 17:233-247.
Cascio WF, Aguinis H (2008). Research in Industrial and Organizational Psychology 1963-2007: Changes, Choices, and Trends. J. Appl. Psychol. 93(5):1062-1081.
Feredrik H (2010). Online at http://www.accelteam.com/human-relations/hrels_05_herzberg.html.
Guest H (2010). Guest's model of HRM, online at http://www.hrmguide.co.uk/introduction_to _hrm/guest-hrrm.htm.
Hwang CL, Yoon K (1981).Multiple attribute decision making:Methods and applications. Berlin: Springer.

Kristof-Brown AL, Zimmerman RD, Johnson EC (2005). Consequences of individuals' fit at work: A meta-analysis of person-job, person-organization, person-group, and person-supervisor fit. Pers. Psychol. 58(2):281-342.

Kumar M, Vrat P, Shankar R (2006a). A fuzzy programming approach for vendor selection problem in a supply chain. Int. J. Prod. Econ. 101(2):273-285.

Pascale RT, Athos AG (2001). The art of Japanese management, print hall. Inc

Waterman JR, Peters TJ (2002). In Search of Excellence: Lessons from Americas Best Run Companies, Print Hall. Inc.

16

Integration of Kano's model and SERVQUAL for enhancing standard hotel customer satisfaction

Li-Hsing Ho[1], Tien-Fu Peng[2], Shu-Yun Feng[2] and Tieh-Min Yen[1]

[1]Department of Technology Management, Chung-Hua University, 707, Sec. 2, WuFu Rd., HsinChu, Taiwan.
[2]Graduate Institute of Technology Management, Chung-Hua University, 707, Sec. 2, WuFu Rd., HsinChu, Taiwan.

The purpose of this study is to establish a new methodology for decision analysis. This is done by integrating Kano's model and SERVQUAL to help organizations identify core service quality attributes that will effectively enhance customers' satisfaction. SERVQUAL does not consider the non-linear impact of quality attributes and quality improvement effectiveness. Kano's model determines quality attributes by mode and ignores the cognition differences of quality attributes of different customers because it is unable to accurately analyze the priorities of quality improvement that results in wrong decisions. This study used the Kano's model of customer satisfaction improvement quantitative analysis integrated with SERVQUAL information on customers' expectation and perception. It used it to calculate the improvement ratio of expected service quality satisfaction improvement to determine improvement priorities. This study illustrated the methodology and effectiveness of integrating Kano's model and SERVQUAL.

Key words: Standard hotel, service quality, SERVQUAL, Kano's model, customer satisfaction, quality attribute.

INTRODUCTION

Gronroos (1984) suggested that service quality is the result of comparing customers' expectation and perception of service. Garvin (1983) indicated that service quality is user-oriented, that is, quality is determined by subjective perception of customers rather than objective assessment. Studies on the service quality of the hotel industry mainly use the SERVQUAL proposed by Parasuraman et al. (1988, 1991) (Eccles and Durand, 1997), and some have modified or developed specific SERVQUAL scales according to the attributes of the hotel industry (Akan, 1995; Juwaheer, 2004; Antony et al., 2004; Knutson et al., 1991, 1993; Getty and Thompson, 1994; Getty and Getty, 2003). Methods of literature review and experts' opinion can be used to obtain the service quality attributes, and questionnaire survey can determine the items of continuous improvement (Min and Min, 1997; Desombre and Eccles, 1998; Min et al., 2002; Tsang and

Qu, 2000; Wong et al., 1999). SERVQUAL studies focus on dimension, validity, reliability and weight (Carman, 1990; Cronin and Taylor, 1992; Llosa et al., 1998; Ladhari, 2008), research on the non-linear impact of quality attributes and effectiveness of quality improvement of customer satisfaction.

Regarding the studies on quality attribute and customers' satisfaction, Kano et al. (1984) proposed the two-dimension quality model (Kano's model) to establish the relationships between quality attributes and customer satisfaction according to preparedness. Kano et al. (1984) modified the two-dimension quality model developed from the dual factor theory proposed by Herzberg et al. (1959). The modified model can effectively assess and improve quality performance or develop new products and services to satisfy the needs and expectations of customers (Matzler and Hinterhuber, 1998; Lee et al.,

2008; Lee et al., 2009). Hence, Kano's model has been widely applied in various fields (Matzler et al., 1996; Eskildsen and Kristensen, 2006; Matzler and Hinterhuber, 1998; Xu et al., 2009; Nilsson-Witell and Fundin, 2005; Bayraktaroğlu and Özgen, 2008; Lee et al., 2008a; Lee et al., 2008b; Llinares and Page, 2011), and proved as a considerably useful tool for quality attribute classification and customer satisfaction enhancement (Lee et al., 2008a; Lee et al., 2009; Hu et al., 2009). Tan and Shen (2000), Lee et al. (2008; 2009) and Hu et al. (2009) respectively proposed the quantitative analysis model of Kano's model's to make improvement analysis and decision making more accurate. However, to determine quality attribute by mode the actual market information cannot be reflected and the quantitative analysis model of Kano's model has no reasonable comparison basis. Hence, this study proposed the methodology of decision analysis by integrating Kano's model with SERVQUAL.

LITERATURE REVIEW

The hotel industry refers to economic activities directly deriving from lodging accommodations. Hence, before discussing the hotel industry, it was necessary to briefly explore the concept of hotel and propose this study's considerations about the concept of hotel.

The term, hotel can be broadly interpreted as it can be called "hotel" or "restaurant" varying from different time periods. Li (2005) indicated that the definition of hotel should contain meanings in commercial, service, public, legal, even cultural and informational dimensions. Meanwhile, "hotel industry" should contain hotel attributes, the nature of industrial economy as well as comprehensive, diversified and multi-functional features.

According to the "Company and Firm Business Categorization Standards of the Republic of China", hotels are classified into tourist hotels including the international tourist hotel and general tourist hotel, and the standard hotels

Taiwan's hotel industry can be classified into the tourist hotel industry and the general hotel industry. According to sub-paragraph 7, Paragraph 1 of Article 2 of the current Regulations on Tourism Development, tourist hotel industry refers to international tourist hotels or general tourist hotels providing tourists with accommodations and related services for profits. According to the Industry Standard Classification of the Republic of China, businesses approved as "standard hotel" belong to the "hotel industry". Hence, this study defined standard hotels as profit making entities in the accommodation service industry to provide tourists with lodging, rest and other relevant businesses approved by the central competent authority except for the tourist hotel industry including international tourist hotels and general tourist hotels.

Parasuraman et al. (1985) proposed the conceptual model for service quality Gap analysis, suggesting that

five Gaps in service-providing process may affect service quality, and Gap 5 is the functional relationship from Gap 1 to Gap 4, namely, Gap5=f (Gap 1, Gap 2, Gap 3, Gap 4) where Gap 1, Gap 2, Gap 3, Gap 4 come from the service provider and are derived from organizational internal problems. Meanwhile, Gap 5 is determined by consumers and is derived from the gap between consumer expectations and actual perception. The Gap 5 must be reduced to get customer satisfaction. Parasuraman et al. (1988, 1991) proposed the SERVQUAL to compare the service quality of consumers' expectation (E) and perception (P) to assess service quality (Q) by Q=P-E. The proposal of SERVQUAL gave rise to many industrial applications and empirical studies (Ladhari, 2008) as well as comments and modifications of scholars (Carman, 1990; Cronin and Taylor, 1992; Llosa et al., 1998; Ladhari, 2008; Hu et al., 2010). Carman (1990) used the Q = W × (P - E) to assess service quality, with W representing weight. Cronin and Taylor (1992) proposed the SERVPERF model, suggesting that quality is the perceived satisfaction of customers toward the service. If considering the customer perception of quality attribute significance, then Q = W × P. Carrillat et al. (2007) pointed out that the advantage of SERVQUAL is to diagnose problems. SERVPERF focuses on simplification of scale and analysis of performance as purposes. Many studies have focused on the selection of SERVQUAL and SERVPERF, as well as the prediction results and discussions on general and specific scales. However, discussions on the impact of different quality attributes and the effect of quality improvement on customer satisfaction are inadequate.

Kano et al. (1984) proposed the quality attribute classification methodology to understand the quality attributes by the relationship between quality attribute preparedness and customer satisfaction. At the service design and planning stage, the service quality attributes are taken into consideration to satisfy customers' demands and expectations to create customer values. To understand the customer perception of service quality characteristics, the pairwise questionnaire design as shown in Table 1 is applied. It intends to determine the customer perception in the case of having quality attributes or not (Lee et al., 2009). From the answers of the customers, the service quality attributes as perceived by customers are shown in Table 2.

From Table 2, "A" represents "Attractive quality", "O" represents "One-dimensional quality", "M" represents "Must-be quality", "I" represents "Indifferent quality", "R" represents "Reversal quality", "Q" represents results with problems. Kano et al. (1984) classified the quality attributes affecting the customer satisfaction into five types:

1. M (Must-be quality): M is the basic indispensable quality attribute as the customer believes. The customer would be very dissatisfied if such needs were not met. Even if such needs were satisfied, the customer

Table 1. Functional and dysfunctional questions in the Kano's questionnaire.

If the standard hotel has room comfort and atmosphere (T1), how do you feel?	I like it that way. It must be that way. I am neutral. I can live with it that way. I dislike it that way.
If the standard hotel does not have room comfort and atmosphere (T1), how do you feel?	I like it that way. It must be that way. I am neutral. I can live with it that way. I dislike it that way.

Table 2. Kano's quality attributes classification matrix.

Service quality attributes		Dysfunctional form of the question				
		I like it that way	It must be that way	I am neutral	I can live with it that way	I dislike it that way
Functional form of the question	I like it that way.	Q	A	A	A	O
	It must be that way.	R	I	I	I	M
	I am neutral.	R	I	I	I	M
	I can live with it that way.	R	I	I	I	M
	I dislike it that way.	R	R	R	R	Q

Table 3. Results of Kano's quality attributes classification.

Quality attribute	A	O	M	I	R	Q	Total	Category
Guest room comfort and ambience (T1)	85	50	141	2	0	0	278	M
Decoration uniqueness (T2)	148	16	81	33	0	0	278	A
Good vision landscape (T3)	155	29	77	17	0	0	278	A

satisfaction would not increase. Matzler and Hinterhuber (1998) suggested that M is the basic factor of market competition.

2. O (One-dimensional quality): Customer satisfaction is proportional to the availability of quality attributes. Higher availability leads to higher customer satisfaction, and vice versa. Lee et al. (2009) indicated that O is the partition factor of market competition.

3. A (Attractive quality): The customer would feel considerably happy when the service has A attributes. The customer satisfaction would increase along with the availability of A attributes exponentially. Even if, the products do not have any A attribute, the customer would not feel unhappy about it. A is the key factor for developing differentiation and creating competitive advantage (Kano et al., 1984; Matzler et al., 1996; Lee et al., 2008a, 2009).

4. I (Indifferent quality): The availability of the quality attribute or not would never make the customer satisfied or dissatisfied. Kano (2001) suggested that the dynamic evolution sequence of quality attributes in the product life cycle is I, A, O, M, hence, I is the source of innovation.

5. R (Reversal quality): The availability of the quality attribute would lead to customer dissatisfaction and the absence of such quality attributes would make the customer satisfied.

The sum of the quality attributes as perceived by different customers and the one with highest number (mode) is the quality attribute, as shown in Table 3.

Kano's model uses the mode to determine quality attribute. When specific quality attributes cannot be clearly categorized, Matzler et al. (1996) proposed the simple classification decision making sequence as M > O > A > I. Berger et al. (1993) proposed to use the satisfaction increase indicator $Better = (A+O)/(A+O+M+I)$ and the dissatisfaction decrease indicator $Worse = (O+M)/(A+O+M+I) \times (-1)$ to decide the improvement sequence. As shown in Table 3, perception of quality attributes varies from customer to customer. The determination of quality attributes by using mode cannot reflect the actual customer perception and will overlook most meaningful statistical information. The study of Chen and Lee (2009), Lee and Huang (2009) and Lee et al. (2008b) also confirmed that the application of mode cannot determine quality attributes accurately.

Matzler et al. (1996) indicated that Kano's model provides a better method to understand the customer demands and market differentiation advantages. To reflect the cognitive differences of different customers, this study established a new methodology of decision analysis, namely, integrating the quantitative Kano's model and SERVQUAL to analyze the incremental ratio of satisfaction after quality improvement to determine the improvement priorities.

METHODOLOGY

Research subjects

Taiwan's standard hotel as the objects of service quality construction, this study helped the standard hotels to improve the current service quality to satisfy customer demands on accommodation quality and enhance industrial competitiveness. The research objects included: Hotels, guest house, hostels, motels, restaurants and inns.

Research method

The main purpose of this study is to establish the quantitative Kano's model and SERVQUAL methodology of decision analysis to consider the cognitive differences of quality attributes of different customers using the survey of Taiwan's standard hotel service quality, and to determine the improvement priorities according to the satisfaction increase ratio.

To establish the service quality attributes of standard hotels, this study referred to the literature of recent 20 years from the two databases of Emerald and Science Direct for literature review and summary, and discussed the service quality attributes by expert interview. This study conducted survey on the summarized service quality attributes by questionnaire. Then, random sampling was used according to the proportion of standard hotels around various regions. The collected data were analyzed by the decision analysis methodology integrating Kano's model and SERVQUAL to enhance customers' satisfaction in standard hotels.

Questionnaire design

Based on the five dimensions of the service quality proposed by Parasuraman et al. (1988, 1991), in this study service quality attributes were constructed by referring to the literature on hotel industry's service quality in recent 20 years. Then, by expert interview approach, a total of 12 experts from hotel-related industries, government officials and scholars were invited for interview; 38 service quality attributes of standard hotels were summarized as the questionnaire items.

The classification of service quality attributes followed the pairwise questionnaire of Kano's model to categorize the customer perception into five level: "I like it that way", "I must be that way", "I am neutral", "I can live with it that way", "I dislike it that way". The service quality performance assessment was made through the SERVQUAL questionnaire to understand the customer expectation and the actual perceived quality. The assessment of customer expectation (E) and perception (P) was measured by 5-point scale

with "1" representing "strongly disagree", and 5 representing "strongly agree".

Integration of Kano's model and SERVQUAL

By the parameter and equation approximation method, Tan and Shen (2000) proposed the quantitative Kano's model with relationship between customer satisfaction and quality attribute. Its functional relationship can be represented by $s = f(k, p)$, where s denotes customer satisfaction, k denotes Kano's model quality attribute classification parameter and p denotes quality attribute availability. The model proposed by Kano et al. (1984) suggested the influencing degree of quality attributes affecting customer satisfaction varies. When the quality availability level increases, the improvement effectiveness of A toward customer satisfaction is $\Delta s/s > \Delta p/p$, with Δs and Δp representing changes in customer satisfaction and quality attribute availability respectively. Similarly, O is $\Delta s/s = \Delta p/p$; and M is $\Delta s/s < \Delta p/p$. When quality attribute availability increases, the impact of A on satisfaction is greater than O, showing that the contribution of A to the increase of satisfaction is greater.

To simplify the relationship between satisfaction and quality performance, Tan and Shen (2000) assumed that $\Delta s/s$ and $\Delta p/p$ are linear and integrated the above three relationships by using parameter k into an equation $\Delta s/s = k(\Delta p/p)$, where parameter of A $k>1$; parameter of O $k=1$; parameter of M k ranging from 0 to 1. The equation can be converted into satisfaction and quality performance equation, $s = cp^k$, where c was a constant number.

To reflect the cognitive differences of different customers, for example, in Table 3, guest room comfort and ambience (T1), proportions of different customers with different cognitive differences about the service quality attribute are A 30.58%, O 17.99%, M 50.72%, I 0.72% and R 0.00%. Hence, it cannot reflect the actual customer satisfaction and cognition if mode is used to determine the quality attribute classification while losing the statistical significance as represented by questionnaire survey sampling. This study modified the functional relationship between satisfaction and service quality attribute as shown in equation (1):

$$s_i = c\left(\sum w_{ij}\overline{p}_i^k\right) \tag{1}$$

where, s_i is the i-th service quality attribute satisfaction ($i=1, 2,3,...,n$); w_{ij} is the weight of quality attribute (for example, Table 3 guest room comfort and ambience (T1), $w_{1A}=85/278=0.31$); $\overline{p}$ is the average service quality performance ; $j = $ A, O, M, I, R, k is a parameter between 0 and 1. The relationship between quality attribute availability and satisfaction constructed by Kano et al., (1984) is not suitable for quantitative analysis. Lee et al. (2009) proposed that quality attribute availability is determined by customer perception. Hence, scaled performance or customer perception can be used to represent quality attribute availability to facilitate quantitative analysis.

In Equation (1), service quality attribute improvement would generate different improvement efficiency due to differences in attribute, namely, the increase of satisfaction level would be different. This study adopted the SERVQUAL proposed by Parasuraman et al. (1988, 1991), expecting to compare the expected quality and the perceived quality to assess the service performance. Suppose customer satisfaction and performance of the i-th service quality as

s_i and $\overline{P}_i$, s_i' and $\overline{E}_i$ are the expected customer satisfaction and the expected performance. Suppose changes in satisfaction and performance would not change quality attribute classification and constant number, then the improvement coefficient of customer satisfaction level, IR, can serve as the basis for the improvement priority decision making as shown in equation (2):

$$IR_i = \frac{s_i'}{s_i} = \frac{c\left(\sum w_{ij} \times \overline{E}_i^k\right)}{c\left(\sum w_{ij} \times \overline{P}_i^k\right)} = \frac{\sum\left(w_{ij} \times \overline{E}_i^k\right)}{\sum\left(w_{ij} \times \overline{P}_i^k\right)} \qquad (2)$$

In Equation (2), if number of recollected questionnaires of I or R is very low (<5%), the influence on the increase of satisfaction level would be too small and can be ignored.

This study set the customer expectation E and perceived performance P at the range of [1,5] and used the value of k as proposed by Lee et al. (2009) to classify A, O, M, I and R as "2", "1", "1/2", "0" and "1". According to Equation (2), comparing the customer satisfaction before and after quality attribute improvement and the improvement coefficient IR of A, O, M, I and R can be obtained as the decision making basis for service quality attribute improvement priorities.

ANALYSIS AND RESULTS

This study constructed 38 standard hotel service quality attributes (Column 2; Table 4) by literature review and interviews with industrial representatives, governmental officials and scholars. The survey subjects were consumers of standard hotels in Taiwan. The questionnaires were distributed from March 31 to April 20, 2010. Random sampling was conducted according to the proportions of number of standard hotels in various regions. A total of 350 questionnaires were distributed, and 317 were retrieved, with a recovery rate of 90.571%. After eliminating 39 invalid samples, 278 valid questionnaires were obtained.

Kano's model and SERVQUAL analysis results

According to Kano's model questionnaire, the customer perception of the availability of standard hotel service quality attributes was collected and the quality attributes of the service items of standard hotel were analyzed by mode to get the results as shown in Table 4 (Cat.). Using guest room comfort and ambience (T1) as an example, as shown in Column 3-Column 5, $w_{1A}=0.31$, $w_{1O}=0.18$, $w_{1M}=0.51$, the service quality attribute was M. As shown in Table 4. there were 20 service quality assessment items of M. Such items were basic quality attributes of standard hotel as believed by customers, and were the definite market competition factors. Customers would consider such items, and they were basic items that consumers would think about before selecting the products and service. If the products had no such attributes, consumers would be not interested at all (Hu et al., 2009). There were 10 quality attributes of O; namely, customer satisfaction

and the service item availability were proportional. Generally, consumers would expressly demand for such quality attributes and compare (Hu et al., 2009). There were 6 quality attributes of A, which were factors to establish market competitive advantages (Hu et al., 2009) to bring rich business profits to the hotel. There were 2 quality attributes of I. The availability of such attributes would never affect customer satisfaction or dissatisfaction. However, such classification based on mode cannot actually reflect the consumer perceived quality attributes. For example, the booking procedure convenience (E1) $w_{28A}=0.31$, $w_{28O}=0.33$, $w_{28M}=0.33$ was classified as a quality attribute of M.

According to SERVQUAL questionnaire, this study analyzed the service quality customer expectation (E) and actual perception (P) and calculated by average number as shown in Column 10 to Column 11 (Table 4). With guest room comfort and ambience (T1) as an example, the average consumer perception ($\overline{P}$) was 3.77, the average consumer expectation ($\overline{E}$) was 4.47, Gap value G= 3.77-4.47=-0.7. The Gap values of various service quality for sequence were calculated and the one with bigger Gap value as priority was listed. The top five items to be improved were timely accomplishment of commitments to customers (REL4), cleanness (T4), lodging privacy (REL3), safety (REL1) and understanding the special needs of the customer (E11).

According to the average customer perception ($\overline{P}$) and expectation ($\overline{E}$), the improvement rate coefficient $IR_{(i)}$ can be calculated to enhance performance of the improvement target value. With guest room comfort and ambience (T1) as an example, the average customer perception $\overline{P}$ = 3.77, if the improvement target value was the average customer expectation $\overline{E}$ = 4.47, then the quality attribute was M (O), and the improvement rate coefficient proposed by Tan and Shen (2000) $IR_{(T1)}$ = (4.47 / 3.77)^{0.5} = 1.09 in the proximity of 1, showing that the improvement to target value contributed little to the increase of customer satisfaction. According to Column 3-Column 5 (Table 4) $w_{1A}=0.31$, $w_{1O}=0.18$, $w_{1M}=0.51$, representing the cognitive differences of customers regarding quality attributes and the improvement to average customer expectation ($\overline{E}$) had different impact on different customers. The improvement rate coefficient IR proposed by Tan and Shen (2000) and Lee and Chen (2009) did not consider the differences of different customers.

This study integrated the Kano's model and SERVQUAL methodology of decision analysis, taking into consideration the cognitive differences of different customers but also incorporating the information regarding the Gap value of customer perception and expectation. With guest room comfort and ambience (T1) as an example, the improvement rate coefficient $IR_{(T1)}$ can be calculated by equation (2).

Table 4. Kano's model and SERVQUAL analysis results.

Code	Dimensions of Service Quality	w_A	w_O	w_M	w_I	w_R	Q_r	Cat.	$\bar{P}$	$\bar{E}$	IR_i	Rank
T1	Guest room comfort and ambience	0.31	0.18	0.51	0.01	0.00	0.00	M	3.77	4.47	1.33	5
T2	Decoration uniqueness	0.53	0.06	0.29	0.12	0.00	0.00	A	3.48	3.84	1.20	31
T3	Good vision landscape	0.56	0.10	0.28	0.06	0.00	0.00	A	3.65	4.12	1.25	22
T4	Cleanness	0.13	0.58	0.26	0.02	0.00	0.01	O	3.96	4.83	1.32	11
T5	Good geographic and environmental location	0.36	0.08	0.44	0.13	0.00	0.00	M	3.65	4.00	1.17	33
T6	Big, numerous and highly convenient parking space	0.33	0.11	0.41	0.15	0.00	0.00	M	3.59	4.10	1.25	18
T7	Low consumption	0.47	0.16	0.29	0.08	0.00	0.00	A	3.60	4.17	1.30	14
T8	Clean dress and neat appearance of service personnel	0.33	0.13	0.44	0.10	0.00	0.01	M	3.76	3.95	1.08	37
T9	Modern facilities (Karaoke, TV, newspaper, journal, etc.)	0.42	0.06	0.35	0.16	0.00	0.00	A	3.59	3.83	1.12	36
T10	Facility diversity (swimming pool, air-conditioning, conference Room, sauna, Internet, etc.)	0.55	0.09	0.28	0.09	0.00	0.00	A	3.55	3.92	1.21	28
T11	Hotel marketing (advertising, website, etc.)	0.30	0.03	0.31	0.36	0.00	0.01	I	3.38	3.69	1.15	34
T12	Commodity sales (souvenir)	0.20	0.05	0.19	0.55	0.00	0.00	I	3.27	3.38	1.05	38
T13	Quiet guest house	0.13	0.54	0.28	0.04	0.00	0.01	O	3.89	4.57	1.25	19
REL1	Safety	0.11	0.59	0.26	0.04	0.00	0.00	O	3.81	4.59	1.28	15
REL2	Hotel with fame	0.41	0.06	0.28	0.24	0.00	0.00	A	3.44	3.84	1.21	26
REL3	Lodging privacy	0.13	0.58	0.24	0.05	0.00	0.00	O	3.82	4.68	1.33	10
REL4	Timely accomplishment of commitments to customers	0.21	0.51	0.21	0.06	0.00	0.01	O	3.70	4.59	1.39	1
RES1	Attentive service attitude of the staff	0.18	0.52	0.27	0.03	0.00	0.00	O	3.78	4.30	1.21	27
RES2	Service personnel are enthusiastic and willing to help and serve Customers	0.24	0.48	0.23	0.03	0.00	0.00	O	3.73	4.28	1.24	24
RES3	Service personnel's capabilities to solve consumer problems Timely	0.23	0.44	0.29	0.04	0.00	0.00	O	3.65	4.39	1.33	7
RES4	Provided service as expected by customer	0.32	0.34	0.29	0.05	0.00	0.00	O	3.64	4.22	1.28	16
A1	Service personnel can provide consumers with accurate information	0.23	0.22	0.51	0.04	0.00	0.00	M	3.65	4.10	1.19	29
A2	Service personnel is professional	0.23	0.26	0.46	0.05	0.00	0.00	M	3.65	4.10	1.20	30
A3	Service personnel is trustworthy	0.15	0.38	0.41	0.05	0.01	0.00	M	3.66	4.33	1.27	17
A4	Customer feel safe to interact with service personnel	0.17	0.32	0.46	0.05	0.00	0.00	M	3.75	4.35	1.24	21
A5	Service personnel can get proper support from the company to provide better service	0.26	0.29	0.38	0.06	0.00	0.00	M	3.71	4.18	1.21	25
A6	Service personnel can help each other to provide better services	0.26	0.31	0.38	0.06	0.00	0.00	M	3.69	4.01	1.14	35
E1	Room booking procedure convenience	0.31	0.33	0.33	0.03	0.00	0.00	M	3.81	4.52	1.33	6
E2	Convenience in lodging period	0.23	0.38	0.36	0.03	0.00	0.00	O	3.81	4.56	1.33	9
E3	Traffic convenience	0.26	0.31	0.40	0.04	0.00	0.00	M	3.79	4.34	1.24	23
E4	Providing tourism-related consultancy	0.28	0.13	0.48	0.10	0.00	0.00	M	3.53	4.04	1.24	20
E5	Barrier-free space and parent-child toilet	0.23	0.14	0.47	0.15	0.00	0.00	M	3.45	4.17	1.35	3
E6	Catering service	0.28	0.28	0.39	0.04	0.00	0.00	M	3.58	4.29	1.34	4
E7	Staffs can speak other languages	0.35	0.13	0.36	0.17	0.00	0.00	M	3.53	4.15	1.32	12
E8	Service personnel can give customers individual care	0.35	0.19	0.35	0.12	0.00	0.00	M	3.67	4.02	1.17	32
E9	Company considering customer rights as priority	0.26	0.36	0.36	0.02	0.00	0.00	M	3.65	4.37	1.33	8
E10	Service time can satisfy the needs of the customer	0.26	0.26	0.45	0.04	0.00	0.00	M	3.72	4.39	1.30	13
E11	Understand the special needs of the customer	0.33	0.26	0.35	0.06	0.00	0.00	M	3.64	4.40	1.37	2
Average value									3.66	4.21		

$$IR_1 = \frac{(0.31 \times 4.47^2 + 0.18 \times 4.47^{0.5} + 0.51 \times 4.47^1 + 0.01 \times 4.47^0 + 0.00 \times 4.47^1)}{(0.31 \times 3.77^2 + 0.18 \times 3.77^{0.5} + 0.51 \times 3.77^1 + 0.01 \times 3.77^0 + 0.00 \times 3.77^1)} = 1.33$$

above 1, indicating that improvement to target value contributed a great deal to the increase of customer satisfaction and can be listed as priority for improvement according to the needs of the organization. The improvement rate coefficient of various service quality attributes can be calculated by equation (2) with results as shown in Column 12 of Table 4 (IR_i).

This study used the methodology of decision analysis integrating Kano's model and SERVQUAL to find out service quality attributes of improvement priorities as follows: timely accomplishment of commitments to customers(REL4), understanding the special needs of the customer(E11), barrier-free space and parent-child toilet (E5), catering service (E6), room booking procedure convenience (E1), guest room comfort and ambience (T1), service personnel's capabilities to solve consumer problems timely (RES3), company considering customer rights as priority (E9), convenience in lodging period (E2) and lodging privacy (REL3).

DISCUSSION

Due to limited resources, standard hotels have to create competitive advantages with limited resources; hence, this study explored strategic development, continuous improvement and creative decision making according to the analysis results of the integration of Kano's model and SERVQUAL.

The A attributes of standard hotel service quality included decoration uniqueness(T2), good vision landscape(T3), low consumption (T7), modern equipment (T9), facility diversity(T10), hotel with fame(REL2). Table 4 illustrated that customer perception of differences can be obviously categorized into two groups of A and M. Meanwhile, when the Gap between customer perception and expectation was small, the service quality improvement was not significant. Kano (2001) indicated that many quality management personnel focus on the improvement of existing problems and overlooked the creative topics of A. Hence, customers regarding the attribute as belonging to A can be set as the target customer group. Ottenbacher and Harrington (2010) suggested that the attractiveness of target market and facilities are the sources of creativity of hotel services. Standard hotel can improve the service performance for the target market by taking differentiated policies to separate the market (Kano et al., 1984; Matzler et al. 1996; Lee et al., 2008a; Lee et al., 2009).

The O attributes of standard hotel service quality as the top 10 improvement performance items included timely accomplishment of commitments to customers (REL4), service personnel's capabilities to solve consumer problems timely (RES3), convenience in lodging period

(E2) and lodging privacy (REL3). Regarding such attributes of service quality w_{iA}=0.13~0.24, w_{iO}=0.44~0.58, w_{iM}=0.21~0.29, representing that about 50% customer perception as O and the service quality Gap value above G=1.33~1.39. Hence, the standard hotel owner should improve immediately (Lee et al., 2009; Yang, et al., 2011). Pfeffer (1994) suggested that the rising importance of human resources is due to the possibility of being copied regarding competitive advantages obtained from other resources. Ottenbacher and Harrington (2010) indicated that strategic human resources, authorization, education and training and performance assessment system based on service personnel behavior are the sources of hotel service creativity. Hence, the owners of standard hotels should immediately improve the frontline service personnel's capabilities to address the needs, problems and complaints of consumers by authorization, education and training, and assessment mechanism to win competitive advantages (Edgett, 1994; Chebat and Kollias, 2000; Ottenbacher and Harrington, 2010).

The top 10 items of high improvement effectiveness of M attributes of standard hotel service quality were understanding the special needs of the customer (E11), barrier-free space and parent-child toilet (E5), catering service (E6), room booking procedure convenience (E1), guest room comfort and ambience (T1) and company considering customer rights as priority (E9). Since the customer perception of such service quality attributes were obviously divided into two groups of A and M, and the Gap value of the customer perception and expectation G=1.33~1.37, representing that the service quality improvement increase was very high and the standard hotel owner should immediately improve them (Lee et al., 2009; Yang, et al., 2011). Customers regarding the attribute as belonging to A can be set as the target customer group. Standard hotels can enhance the service performance for the target market with high value contribution to consumers (Yang, et al., 2011). Differentiated strategies may be adopted to separate the market (Kano et al., 1984; Matzler et al. 1996; Lee et al., 2008a; Lee et al., 2009).

The I standard hotel service quality assessment items included hotel marketing (advertising, website) (T11) commodity selling (souvenir) (T12); since the Gap value of such standard hotel service quality attribute was small, it was not necessary to improve. Ottenbacher and Harrington (2010) suggested that the comprehensive capability of marketing is the source of the hotel service innovation. Kano (2001) indicated the dynamic evolution sequence of quality attributes in product life cycle is I, A, O, M. As a result, the standard hotel owner should pay attention to the evolution of customer perception for long term development as the source of service quality creativity and introduce relevant services timely to create competitive advantages.

Conclusion

This study integrated the Kano's model and SERVQUAL to develop a methodology of decision analysis. With Taiwan's standard hotels as the subjects of service quality construction survey and analysis, this study found the top 10 service quality attributes for improvement including timely accomplishment of commitments to customers (REL4), understanding the special needs of the customer (E11), barrier-free space and parent-child toilet (E5), catering service (E6), room booking procedure convenience (E1), guest room comfort and ambience (T1), service personnel's capabilities to solve consumer problems timely (RES3), company considering customer rights as priority (E9), convenience in lodging period (E2) and lodging privacy (REL3).

The contributions of this study are: Modify the quantitative analysis of Kano's model that does not consider the customer perception differences and the SERVQUAL that does not consider the impact of different quality attributes on customer satisfaction. Integration of Kano's model and SERVQUAL can provide an in-depth understanding of the service quality attributes, customer perception, expectation and satisfaction to help organizations to identify the core service quality attributes for continuous improvement in order to enhance customer satisfaction and create competitive advantages.

The limitation of this study was in the respect of methodology. This study applied the literature review and expert interview method, and confirmed consistency by consumer perception. The factor analysis methodology may be applied in the future for empirical study. In the respect of strategic analysis methodology, this study adopted the methodology of decision analysis integrating Kano's modeland SERVQUA. Future discussions may furthermore integrate the QFD method to more easily develop the creative services. Regarding the discussion subjects, this study was limited in the construction of Taiwan's standard hotel service quality attributes. In the future, it may be expanded to cover the overall hotel industry service quality to improve the service quality of Taiwan's hotel industry.

REFERENCES

Akan P (1995). Dimensions of service quality: a Study in Istanbul. Manag. Serv. Qual. 5(6):39-43.

Antony J, Antony FJ, Ghosh S (2004). Evaluating service quality in a UK hotel chain: a case study. Int. J. Contemp. Hosp. Manage. 16(6):380-384.

Bayraktaroğlu G, Özgen Ö (2008). Integrating the Kano model, AHP and planning matrix QFD application in library services. Lib. Manage. 29(4/5):327-351.

Berger C, Blauth R, Boger D, Burchill G, DuMouchel W, Pouliot F, Richter R, Rubinoff A, Shen D, Timko M, Walden D (1993). Kano's

Methods for Understanding Customer-Defined Quality. Center Qual. Manage. J. 2(4):3-36.

Carman JM (1990). Consumer perceptions of service quality: an assessment of the SERVQUAL dimensions. J. Retail. 66(1):33-55.

Carrillat FA, Jaramillo F, Mulki JP (2007). The validity of the SERVQUAL and SERVPERF scales A meta-analytic view of 17 years of research across five continents. Int. J. Serv. Ind. Manage. 18(5):472-490.

Chebat JC, Kollias P (2000). The impact of empowerment on customer contact employees' roles in service organizations. Journal of Service Research. 3(1):66-81.

Chen JK, Lee YC (2009). A new method to identify the category of quality attribute. Total Qual. Manage. 20(10):1139-1152.

Cronin JJ, Taylor SA (1992). Measuring service quality: a reexamination and extension. J. Market. 56(3):55-68.

Desombre T, Eccles G (1998). Improving service quality in NHS trust hospitals: lessons from the hotel sector. Int. J. Health Care Qual. 11(1):21-26.

Eccles G, Durand P (1997). Improving service quality: lessons and practice from the hotel sector. Manag. Serv. Qual. 7(5):224-226.

Edgett SJ (1994). The traits of successful new service development. J. Serv. Market. 8(3):40-49.

Eskildsen JK, Kristensen K (2006). Enhancing Importance-performance Analysis. Int. J. Prod. Perform. Manage. 55(1/2):40-60.

Garvin DA (1983). Quality on the line. Harv. Bus. Rev. 61:65-73.

Getty JM, Getty RL (2003). Lodging quality index (LQI): asseeeing customers' perceptions of quality delivery. Int. J. Contemp. Hosp. Manage. 15(2):94-104.

Getty JM, Thomson KN (1994). A procedure for scaling perceptions of lodging quality. Hosp. Res. J. 18(2):75-96.

Gronroos C (1984). A service quality model and its marketing implications. Eur. J. Market. 18(4):36-44.

Herzberg F, Mausner B, Snyderman BB (1959). The motivation to work, New York: Wiley.

Hu HY, Lee YC, Yen TM (2009). Amend importance-performance analysis method with Kano's model and DEMATEL. J. Appl. Sci. 9(10):1833-1846.

Hu HY, Lee YC, Yen TM (2010). Service quality gaps analysis based on Fuzzy linguistic SERVQUAL with a case study in hospital out-patient services. TQM J. 22(5):499-515.

Juwaheer TD (2004). Exploring international tourist's perceptions of hotel operations by using a modified SERVQUAL approach – a case study of Mauritius. Manag. Serv. Qual. 14(5):350-364.

Kano N (2001). Life cycle and creation of attractive quality. Paper presented at the 4th international QMOD Conference Quality Management and Organizational Development. Linköpings Universitet, Sweden.

Kano N, Seraku N, Takanashi F, Tsjui S (1984). Attractive Quality and Must-be Quality. J. Jpn. Soc. Qual. Control 14(2):39-48.

Knutson B, Stevens P, Patton M, Thompson C (1993). Consumers' expectation for service quality in economy, mid-price and luxury hotels. J. Hosp. Leisure Market. 1(2):27-43.

Knutson B, Stevens P, Wullaert C, Patton M, Yokoyama F (1991). Lodgserv a service quality index for the lodging industry. Hosp. Res. J. 14(3):277-284.

Ladhari R (2008). Alternative measures of service quality: a review, Meas. Serv. Qual. 18(1):65-86.

Lee YC, Chen JK (2009). A new service development integrated model. Service Ind. J. 29(12):1669-1686.

Lee YC, Cheng CC, Yen TM (2009). Integrate Kano's model and IPA to Improve Order-Winner Criteria: A Study of Computer Industry. J. Appl. Sci. 9(1):38-48.

Lee YC, Hu HY, Yen TM, Tsai CH (2008a). Kano's model and Decision Making Trial and Evaluation Laboratory Applied to Order-Winners and Qualifiers Improvement: A Study of Computer Industry. Inform. Technol. J. 7(5):702-714.

Lee YC, Huang SY (2009). A new fuzzy concept approach for Kano's model. Expert Syst. Appl. 36:4479-4484.

Lee YC, Sheu LC, Tsou YG (2008b). Quality function deployment implementation based on Fuzzy Kano model: An application in PLM system. Comput. Ind. Eng. 55:48-63.

Llinares G, Page AF (2011). Kano's model in Kansei Engineering to evaluate subjective real estate consumer preferences. Int. J. Ind.

Ergon. 41:233-246.

Llosa S, Chandon J, Orsingher C (1998). An empirical study of SERVQUAL's dimensionality. Serv. Ind. J. 18 (1):16-44.

Matzler K, Hinterhuber HH (1998). How to Make Product Development Projects More Successful by Integrating Kano's model into Quality Function Deployment. Technovation 18(1):25-38.

Matzler K, Hinterhuber HH, Bailon F, Sauerwein E (1996). How to Delight Your Customers. J. Prod. Brand Manage. 5(2):6-18.

Min H, Min H (1997). Benchmarking the quality of hotel services: managerial perspectives. Int. J. Qual. Reliab. Manage. 14(6):582-597.

Min H, Min H, Chung K (2002). Dynamic benchmarking of hotel service quality. J. Serv. Market. 16(4):302-321.

Nilsson-Witell L, Fundin A (2005). Dynamics of service attributes: A test of Kano's theory of attractive quality. Int. J. Serv. Ind. Manage. 16(2):152-168.

Ottenbacher MC, Harrington RJ (2010). Strategies for achieving success for innovative versus incremental new service. J. Serv. Market. 24(1):3-15.

Parasuraman A, Zethaml VA, Berry LL (1985). A conceptual model of service quality and its implications for future research. J. Market. 49(4):41-50.

Parasuraman A, Zeithaml VA, Berry LL (1988). SERVQUAL: a multi-item scale of measuring consumer perceptions of service quality. J. Retail. 64:12-41.

Parasuraman A, Zeithaml V, Berry LL (1991). Refinement and Reassessment of the SERVQUAL Scale. J. Retail. 67(4):420-450.

Pfeffer J (1994). Competitive advantage through people: Unleashing the power of the work force. Harvard Business School Press, Boston, MA.

Tan KC, Shen XX (2000). Integrating Kano's model in Planning Matrix of Quality Function Deployment. Total Qual. Manage. 11(8):1141-1151.

Tsang N, Qu H (2000). Service quality in China's hotel industry: a perspective from tourist and hotel managers. Int. J. Contemp. Hosp. Manage. 12(5):316-326.

Wong AOM, Dean AM, White CJ (1999). Analyzing service quality in the hospitality industry. Meas. Serv. Qual. 9(2):136-143.

Xu Q, Jiao RJ, Yang X, Helander M (2009). An analytical Kano model for customer need analysis. Design Stud. 30(1):87-110.

Yang CC, Jou YT, Cheng LY (2011). Using integrated quality assessment for hotel service quality. Qual. Quant. 45:349-364.

17

Evaluating advance efficiency of Bangladeshi online banks using stochastic frontier analysis

Azizul Baten[1] and Anton Abdulbasah Kamil[2]

[1]Department of Statistics, School of Physical Sciences, ShahJalal University of Science and Technology, Sylhet-3114, Bangladesh.
[2]School of Distance Education, Universiti Sains Malaysia, 11800 USM, Penang, Malaysia.

Online bank advance efficiency and various factors causing the efficiency level of banks are investigated using stochastic frontier technique for the period 2001-2007. A sample of 20 banks are used following four different groups like NBs (National Banks), ISBs (Islamic Banks), FBs (Foreign Banks), and PBs (Private Banks). A group wise, year wise, and individual banks with their efficiency scores are compared in this study. The significant variations of advance efficiency of banks during this reference period were observed. The year wise average efficiency of banks was estimated (0.516) from the advance frontier model while group wise average technical efficiency was 0.592. Nationalized Commercial Bank had the highest advances producing group compared to others; Private Banks are at the lowest level in producing advances. ISBs, FBs, and PBs are observed inefficient in producing advances. The most efficient banks are found to be government owned Sonali and Janata Bank with efficiency score (0.94) while lowest efficient bank was experienced by Shahajalal Islamic Bank with efficiency score of 0.34.

Key words: Advance efficiency, translog production function, stochastic frontier analysis.

INTRODUCTION

There has been a widespread discussion on lack of sufficient technical efficiency of banks in developing countries compared to their counterparts in the developing world (Das, 1997; Shanmugan and Lakshmanasamy, 2001; Kumar and Verma, 2003; Kumbhakara and Sarkar, 2003; De, 2004; Mohan and Ray, 2004; Das et al., 2005). Even some works have been done for Bangladesh banking sector (Raihan, 1998; Choudhury et al., 1999; Choudhury 2002). No attempt has been made to check the performance and efficiency measure of the commercial banks with advance output. Again, question arises how successfully the nationalized private commercial banks are serving the country, how far they have achieved their desired goals. Studies on online Bangladeshi banks will give answer to such questions. This study intends to reveal the overall performance of commercial banks with loan default and measuring technical advance efficiency of banks in Bangladesh.

Stochastic production frontier model proposed by Battese and Coelli (1995) is used in this paper to measure advance efficiency of banks individually and in accordance with four groups namely NBs, IBs, FBs, and PBs in Bangladesh. To determine the important factors causing advance efficiency differential on banking industry in Bangladesh is also of interest in this study. The remainder of the paper is organized as follows. Section two begins with a formulation of stochastic Translog production frontier model with its functional form. Likelihood ratio (L-R) test statistic is explained here for the purpose of testing null hypotheses. A detailed description of variables, sources and different types of data used are discussed in this paper. In section three, we have analyzed advance frontier model in measuring efficiency for different banks of Bangladesh. The last section contains concluding remarks.

MATERIALS AND METHODS

Bank efficiency based on stochastic frontier analysis

The stochastic frontier model proposed by Battese and Coelli (1995) can be expressed as:

$$\ln(Y_{it}) = \beta X_{it} + (V_{it} - U_{it}), \ i = 1, 2, \ldots\ldots\ldots, N; \ t = 1, 2, \ldots\ldots, T \ \ldots\ldots\ldots(1)$$

where Y_{it} is the output of the ith bank in t^{th} period; X_{it} is a vector of input quantities; β_i's are unknown parameters to be estimated; V_{it}'s random variables which are assumed to be i.i.d., $N(0, \sigma_v^2)$ and independent of U_{it}; U_{it}'s are non-negative random variables which are assumed to account for technical inefficiency in output and to be independently distributed as truncations at zero of the $N(\mu, \sigma_u^2)$ distribution; where $U_{it} = Z_{it}\delta$; where; Z_{it} is a $(1 \times p)$ vector of variables which may influence the inefficiency of bank industry and δ is a $(p \times 1)$ vector of parameters to be estimated. The impact of the inefficiency term, as measured by the contribution of its variance to overall variance, is denoted by $\gamma = \sigma_u^2 / (\sigma_u^2 + \sigma_v^2)$. The technical

inefficiency effect U_{it} in the stochastic frontier model is specified as follows;

$$U_{it} = Z_{it}\delta + W_{it} \ \ldots\ldots\ldots(2),$$

where, the random variable, W_{it} follows truncated normal distribution with mean zero and variance σ^2, such that the point of truncation is $-Z_{it}\delta$. After obtaining the estimates of U_{it} the technical efficiency of the i-th bank industry at t-th time period is given by:

$$TE_{it} = \exp(-U_{it}) = \exp(-Z_{it}\delta - W_{it}) \ \ldots\ldots\ldots(3).$$

In the present study the functional form of Translog advance frontier production is considered as:

$$\ln(Y_{it}) = \beta_0 + \beta_1 \ln K_{it} + \beta_2 \ln M_{it} + \beta_3 \ln L_{it} + \beta_4 T$$
$$+ \frac{1}{2}\left(\beta_{11} \ln K_{it}^2 + \beta_{22} \ln M_{it}^2 + \beta_{33} \ln L_{it}^2 + \beta_{44} T^2\right)$$
$$+ \beta_{12} \ln K_{it} * \ln M_{it} + \beta_{13} \ln K_{it} * \ln L_{it} + \beta_{14} \ln K_{it} * T + \beta_{23} \ln M_{it} * \ln L_{it} + \beta_{24} \ln M_{it} * T$$
$$+ \beta_{34} \ln L_{it} * T + V_{it} - U_{it} \ldots\ldots\ldots(4),$$

where, the subscripts i and t represent the i-th online bank industry and the t-th year of observation, respectively; $i = 1, 2, \ldots, 20$; $t = 1, 2, \ldots, 7$; Y_{it} denotes the output variables (advance) of the ith online bank industry in the t-th period in values (taka); K_{it} denotes capital (fixed assets of a online bank in a year which also adds premises, furniture and fixture) of i-th online bank industry in the t-th period; M_{it} represents materials (the sum of expenditure on printing and stationeries and postage, telegrams and telephones etc) of i-th online bank industry in the t-th period; L_{it} represents labor (the total number of employees which include officers, sub-ordinates and clerks) of i-th online bank industry in the t-th period; T represents year of observation; "ln" refers to the natural logarithm.
Further the technical inefficiency effects are the function of some explanatory variables defined as follows:

$$U_{it} = \delta_0 + \delta_1 TA + \delta_2 HI + \delta_3 NB + \delta_4 ISB + \delta_5 FB + \delta_6 PB + W_{it} \ \ldots\ldots\ldots(5),$$

where δ_0 is the intercept term and δ_j $(j = 1, 2, 3, 4, 5, 6)$ is the parameter for the j-th explanatory variable, TA=Total Assets, HI=Herfindahl Index.
NB is the dummy variable for Nationalized Commercial Banks: NB=1 if an observation involves a Nationalized Commercial Bank,

zero otherwise.
ISB is the dummy variable for Islamic banks: ISB=1 if an observation involves an Islamic bank, zero otherwise.
FB is dummy variable for Foreign Banks: FB=1 if an observation involves a Foreign Bank, zero otherwise.
PB is dummy variable for Private Banks: PB=1 if an observation involves a Private Bank, zero otherwise.

Likelihood ratio tests and hypothesis

The likelihood ratio test is used to determine whether Translog production function is better. The hypotheses require testing with the generalized likelihood ratio test statistic defined by

$$\lambda = -2\{\ln[L(H_0)/L(H_1)]\} = -2\{\ln[L(H_0)] - \ln[L(H_1)]\} \ \cdots\cdots(6)$$

where $L(H_0)$ and $L(H_1)$ are the value of the likelihood function for the advance frontier model under the null and alternative hypotheses. Under the null hypothesis, this test statistic is assumed to be asymptotically distributed as mixture of chi-square distribution with degree of freedom equal to the number of restrictions involved. The restrictions imposed by the null hypothesis are rejected when λ exceeds the critical value (Taymaz and Saatci, 1997).
The following null hypotheses will be tested:

$H_0 : \beta_{ij} = 0,$ the null hypothesis that identifies an appropriate functional form either the restrictive Cobb-Douglas or Translog production function.

$H_0 : \gamma = 0,$ the null hypothesis specifies that the technical inefficiency effects in online banks are zero. If the null hypothesis is accepted this would indicate that σ_u^2 is zero and hence that the U_{it} term should be removed from the model, leaving a specification with parameters that can be consistently estimated using ordinary least square (OLS).

Further $H_0 : \eta = 0,$ the null hypothesis that the technical inefficiency effects are time invariant i.e., there is no change in the technical inefficiency effects over time. If the null hypothesis is true, the generalized likelihood ratio statistic λ is asymptotically distributed as a chi-square (or mixed chi-square) random variable.

Data set

We have used data for the period of 2001-2007 from 20 commercial banks of Bangladesh. Banks are grouped into four categories: (i) National Banks (NBs), (ii) Islamic Banks (ISBs), (iii) Foreign Banks (FBs), (iv) Private Banks (PBs). Most of the data are collected from the annual reports of the specific banks of Bangladesh and the rest of them are collected from annual accounts of Scheduled Commercial Banks published by Bangladesh Bank, the Central Bank of Bangladesh.

All nominal values are converted on real by deflating with GDP deflator and all values are in their natural logarithms.

Dependent variables

Advance (Y): Advances are used as output and equal to total loans and advances. These values are also deflated by relevant consumer price index (CPI).

Independent variables

Capital (X_1): Capital is the input variable used to represent the fixed assets of a bank in a year which also adds premises, furniture and fixture. Capital figures are deflated by capital price index.
Labor (X_2): Labor is the inputs to measure the productivity of a firm. Here labor means number of employee and is measured as the total number of employees which include officers, sub-ordinates and clerks.
Material (X_3): Material is used as the sum of expenditure on printing and stationeries and postage, telegrams and telephones etc. Material prices are deflated by non-food price index.
Time (X_4): To find the productive efficiency of a bank over time is used as the input variable. Data used in this study for seven years from 2001 to 2007 and considered 1 for year 2001, 2 for 2002 and so on.

Explanatory variables

Total Asset (Z_1): Total asset is used as the influencing variable and it is the sum of all assets and courses of their book value.
Herfindahl Index (Z_2): Herfindahl index is known as measure of competition which is measured as the sum of squared of the output share of each of bank in the output of considered total banks in Bangladesh.

NB, ISB, FB, and PB are bank group specific dummies for National Bank, Islamic Bank, Foreign Bank, and Private Bank respectfully. The dummy variables can take either 1 or 0 depending on data availability or not respectively.

RESULTS

Estimation of advances efficiency model

Ordinary Least Square Estimates (OLS) and Maximum Likelihood Estimates (MLE) estimates of the parameters of Translog frontier production function are reported in Tables 1 - 3. First, by grid search the ordinary least square estimates of parameters are obtained and then OLS estimates are used to estimate the maximum likelihood estimates of the parameters in the context of Translog production function.

Hypothesis tests of advances frontier model

The results of various hypothesis tests of the advances frontier model are presented in Table 4.

Since the hypothesis $H_0 : \gamma = 0$ is rejected, so we can conclude that there is a technical inefficiency effect in the model. From the outcome it is observed that the null hypothesis $H_0 : \beta_{ij} = 0$ is rejected and so Translog production function is more favorable. The null hypothesis $H_0 : \eta = 0$ is rejected indicating that the technical inefficiency effect differs significantly over time (Table 5).

DISCUSSION

All the coefficients of the first order parameters are found statistically significant at 1 percent level of significance but the second order coefficients of material and time are insignificant. The significant result indicated that these input variables importantly affect the level of producing bank advances.

The maximum likelihood estimates of the parameters of advances frontier model using Translog production function are mentioned in Table 3. We observe that all the first-order coefficients except labor and second-order coefficients are found significant excluding interaction variables material and labor, material and time, labor and time. In case of producing advances we can infer that the number of labor is not an affecting variable. Hence, to uphill the advances productivity the bank authority needs to improve the skill of employees. The most significant variable is capital which includes all physical value of fixed assets to increase efficiency of a bank. In both OLS and MLE we have observed that the coefficient of labor holds negative sign which is not surprising but indicating that some banks may be still overstaffed even after many years of reforms.

Table 1. OLS estimates of translog advances frontier production function.

Variables	Parameters	Coefficients	S.E	t-value
Constant	β_0	8.922[*]	0.727	12.273
Capital	β_1	-0.634[*]	0.264	-2.397
Material	β_2	1.219[*]	0.384	3.175
Labor	β_3	-0.863[*]	0.201	-4.297
Time	β_4	0.533[*]	0.079	6.784
Capital*Capital	β_{11}	0.628[*]	0.104	6.052
Material*Material	β_{22}	-0.099[@]	0.157	-0.630
Labor*Labor	β_{33}	0.486[*]	0.073	6.630
Time*Time	β_{44}	-0.004[@]	0.011	-0.339
Capital*Material	β_{12}	0.021[@]	0.095	0.220
Capital*Labor	β_{13}	-0.365[*]	0.067	-5.446
Capital*Time	β_{14}	-0.106[*]	0.021	-5.029
Material*Labor	β_{23}	-0.080[@]	0.086	-0.926
Material*Time	β_{24}	-0.005[@]	0.028	-0.189
Labor*Time	β_{34}	0.031[**]	0.016	1.999
Sigma-squared		0.047		
Log likelihood function		23.857		

[*], [**], [***] Significance level at 1,5, 10% consecutively. [@] means insignificant, S.E = standard error.

Table 2. Maximum-likelihood estimates of translog advances frontier production function and inefficiency effects model.

Variables	Parameters	Coefficients	S.E	t-value
Constant	β_0	8.952[*]	0.819	10.936
Capital	β_1	-0.857[*]	0.216	-3.965
Material	β_2	0.701[**]	0.393	1.785
Labor	β_3	-0.062[@]	0.193	-0.323
Time	β_4	0.563[*]	0.031	18.278
Capital*Capital	β_{11}	0.497[*]	0.083	6.010
Material*Material	β_{22}	-0.189[@]	0.177	-1.067
Labor*Labor	β_{33}	0.348[*]	0.047	7.356
Time*Time	β_{44}	-0.016[*]	0.006	-2.724
Capital*Material	β_{12}	0.160[***]	0.103	1.550
Capital*Labor	β_{13}	-0.330[*]	0.049	-6.691
Capital*Time	β_{14}	-0.083[*]	0.005	-15.816
Material*Labor	β_{23}	-0.078[@]	0.085	-0.920
Material*Time	β_{24}	0.006[@]	0.016	0.398
Labor*Time	β_{34}	0.011[@]	0.013	0.887

Total assets and Herphindahl index gives negative sign in advances inefficiency model indicating that both total assets and Herphindahl index reduce inefficiency. Here the important thing is that the competition among the bank decreases the advances inefficiency. From the coefficients of the dummy variables it is observed that ISB, FB, and PB dummies are significant at 5 percent level and all of them are positive sign indicating that they are highly inefficient.

The year wise average advances efficiency of 20 banks are delineated in Figure 1. From the analysis it is observed that in the year 2001 the technical efficiency is

Table 3. Inefficiency effects of model estimates.

Variables	Parameters	Coefficients	S.E	t-value
Constant	δ_0	2.357[*]	0.514	4.585
Total Assets	δ_1	-0.240[*]	0.036	-6.582
Herpindahl Index	δ_2	-0.025[@]	0.032	-0.787
NB Dummy	δ_3	0.044[@]	0.499	0.087
ISB Dummy	δ_4	0.743[**]	0.444	1.674
FB Dummy	δ_5	0.770[**]	0.441	1.744
PB Dummy	δ_6	0.801[**]	0.438	1.830
Sigma-squared		0.031[*]	0.004	8.054
Gamma		.98711[*]	0.000054	66947.359

*,**,*** Significance level at 1, 5, 10% consecutively. @ means insignificant, S.E = standard error.

Table 4. Likelihood-ratio test of hypothesis of the stochastic advances frontier production function.

Null hypothesis	Log-likelihood function	Test statistic	Critical value	Decision
$H_0 : \gamma = 0$	23.85	78.04	3.38	Reject H_0
$H_0 : \beta_{ij} = 0$	-30.86	133.46	19.35	Reject H_0
$H_0 : \eta = 0$	23.86	100.88	3.38	Reject H_0

Notes: All critical values are at 5% level of significance.

Table 5. Advance efficiency of banks in Bangladesh.

Bank's name	2001	2002	2003	2004	2005	2006	2007	Mean efficiency
Sonali Bank	0.99	0.99	0.83	0.82	1.00	0.96	1.00	0.941
Janata Bank	0.87	1.00	0.91	0.91	0.97	0.96	0.99	0.943
Islami Bank	0.67	0.67	0.74	0.77	0.72	0.76	0.98	0.759
Shahajal Islami Bank	0.38	0.36	0.27	0.29	0.33	0.36	0.39	0.341
Al Arafah Bank	0.30	0.40	0.37	0.36	0.41	0.44	0.42	0.385
Bank Asia	0.35	0.46	0.48	0.49	0.57	0.52	0.53	0.486
The city Bank	0.48	0.45	0.44	0.45	0.52	0.50	0.36	0.457
National Bank	0.52	0.52	0.47	0.44	0.40	0.44	0.45	0.462
Prime Bank	0.50	0.52	0.51	0.57	0.60	0.69	0.66	0.579
Uttara Bank	0.62	0.52	0.37	0.33	0.34	0.35	0.37	0.412
One Bank	0.46	0.41	0.32	0.37	0.33	0.37	0.34	0.370
UCB Bank	0.49	0.42	0.42	0.41	0.42	0.41	0.47	0.434
Pubali Bank	0.53	0.51	0.44	0.41	0.39	0.48	0.54	0.472
Premier Bank	0.25	0.36	0.38	0.46	0.42	0.36	0.36	0.371
Mutual Bank	0.29	0.33	0.41	0.57	0.54	0.57	0.51	0.462
South East Bank	0.44	0.51	0.62	0.66	0.59	0.50	0.48	0.543
Eastern Bank	0.62	0.51	0.48	0.50	0.37	0.39	0.32	0.457
AB Bank	0.78	0.74	0.64	0.41	0.46	0.53	0.37	0.562
Dhaka Bank	0.60	0.47	0.37	0.38	0.40	0.50	0.50	0.459
DBBI	0.48	0.41	0.43	0.43	0.42	0.48	0.31	0.424

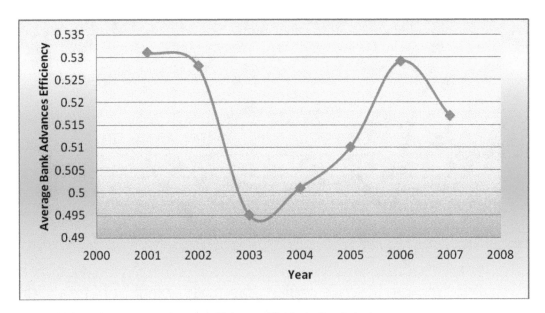

Figure 1. Year wise average advances efficiency of Banks in Bangladesh.

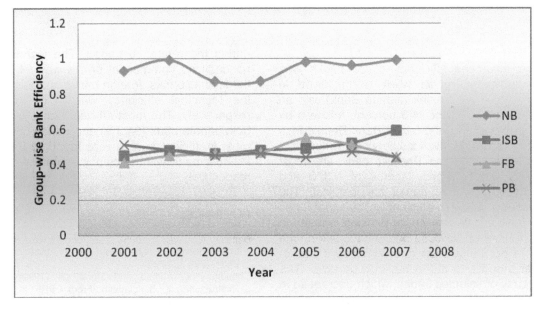

Figure 2. Group-wise bank advances efficiency.

highest with 53.1 percent and in the year 2003 it is lowest; although year wise bank's advances efficiency is almost around 50 percent. Hence from this result it is inferred that all banks excluding NBs have a wide chance to increase their advances efficiency through proper utilizing their total assets and labor.

The group wise bank efficiency has been revealed in Figure 2. The average advances efficiency of the banks during the study period is 0.516. This means that on an average Bangladeshi banks are 51.6 percent efficient in producing advances relative to the best practicing bank

during the study period. It is very interesting that Nationalized Commercial Banks are highest advances producing group over the sample period 2001-2007 compared to their counterparts and on the other hand private banks are at the lowest level in producing advances. The estimated efficiency of NBs is 94.2% and ISBs, FBs, and PBs are 49.5, 47.1, and 46.2%, respectively. Hence huge gap is observed between NBs and others that support the findings of Mahesh and Rajeev (2006). But it is matter of hope that the advances efficiency levels are almost stable over the sample

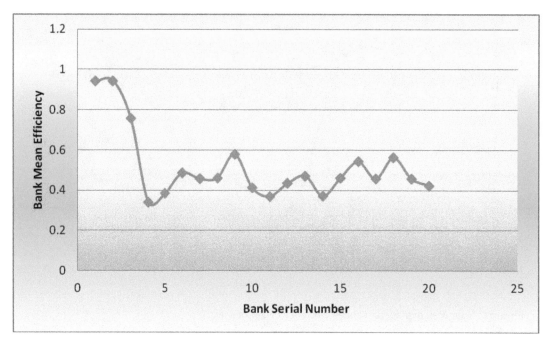

Figure 3. Advance efficiency of Banks in Bangladesh.

period.

The average advances efficiency of 20 banks was estimated for advances model which is displayed in Figure 3. The most efficient bank (Janata Bank) with an average technical efficiency of 94.3 percent, followed by Sonali Bank (94.1 percent) and Islami Bank Bangladesh ltd. (75.9 percent) showed advances services. Among the private banks, one bank and Premier bank are most inefficient banks with efficiency scores of 0.370 and 0.371, respectively. All other banks are identical. The temporal behavior of advance efficiency shows that it has declined marginally for the maximum banking industry in the year 2003; it may be because banks have taken time to adjust to the new regulation and competitive frame-work. However this differs at the bank group level. The advance efficiency of selected banks, which decreased in the year 2003 and increased for the remaining study period but the advance efficiency of Sonali Bank and Janata Bank are found almost stable.

Conclusion

This paper studied the development of online bank advance efficiency in Bangladesh and it applied the Stochastic Frontier Approach in evaluating the efficiency, to a sample of 20 banks during the period of 2001-2007. The findings showed that the average efficiency of the overall considered banks has increased after the year 2003 while the average efficiency trend has been decreased during the period, 2001 to 2003. The results suggested that the mean technical efficiency improved

during the reference period. The technical efficiency of nationalized commercial banks was 94.2%, higher than the Islamic banks, foreign banks and private banks where the technical efficiency was 49.5, 47.1 and 46.2%, respectively. The most efficient banks were observed for both Janata bank (94.3%) and Sonali bank (94.1%) while most inefficient banks were found to be One bank and Premier bank with efficiency scores of 0.370 and 0.371 respectively.

REFERENCES

Battese GE, Coelli T (1995). A Model for Technical Inefficiency Effects in a Stochastic Frontier Production Function for Panel Data. Emp. Econ. (20): 325-332.

Choudhury T, Ahmed and Moral LH (1999). Commercial Bank Restructuring in Bangladesh: From FSRP to BRC/ CBRP, Bank Parikrama. 22-31.

Chowdhury A (2002). Politics, society and financial sector reform in Bangladesh. Inter. J. Social Econo. 29(12): 963-988.

Coelli T (1996). A Guide to FRONTIER Version 4.1: A Computer Program for Stochastic Frontier Production and Cost Function Estimation, CEPA Working Paper, University of New England, Armidale (Australia).

Das A, Ashok N, Subhash R (2005). Liberalisation, Ownership and Efficiency in Indian Banking: A Nonparametric Analysis. Econ. Poli. Weekly. 19(12).

Das A (1997). Technical, Allocative and Scale Efficiency of Public Sector Banks in India. RBI Occasional Papers,18(2&3).

De PK (2004). Technical Efficiency, Ownership and Reforms: An Econometric Study of Indian Banking Industry. Indian Econ. Rev. XXXIX(1: 261-294.

Kumbhakar SC, Subrata S (2003). Deregulation, Ownership, and Productivity Growth in the Banking Industry: Evidence from India, J. Money, Credit and Banking. 35(3).

Kumar S, Satish V (2003). Technical Efficiency, Benchmarking and Targets: A Case Study of Indian Public Sector Banks. Prajnan.

XXI(4): 275-311.

Mohan TTR, Ray S (2004). Comparing Performance of Public and Private Sector Banks: A Revenue Maximization Approach. Econ. Poli. Weekly. 20: 1271-75.

Raihan A (1998). Status of Banking Technology in Bangladesh: Problems and Prospects. Keynote paper presented in the Round Table on "Status of Information technology in Bangladesh", held in BIBM, July 29.

Shanmugan KR, Lakshmanasamy T (2001). Production Frontier Efficiency and Measures: An Analysis of the Banking Sector in India. Asia Afr. J. Econ. Economet. 1(2).

Taymaz E, Saatci (1997). Technical Change and Efficiency in Turkish Manufacturing Industries. J. Prod. Ana. 8: 474.

Appendix

Banks name	Serial number	Banks name	Serial number
Sonali Bank	1	One Bank	11
Janata Bank	2	UCB Bank	12
Islami Bank	3	Pubali Bank	13
Shahajal Islami Bank	4	Premier Bank	14
Al Arafah Bank	5	Mutual Bank	15
Bank Asia	6	South East Bank	16
The city Bank	7	Eastern Bank	17
National Bank	8	AB Bank	18
Prime Bank	9	Dhaka Bank	19
Uttara Bank	10	DBBl	20

18

Web 2.0 usage and security practices of online users at a South African university

Riaan Rudman and Len Steenkamp

Stellenbosch University, Department of Accounting, Private Bag X1, Matieland, 7602, South-Africa.

The proliferation of Web 2.0 technologies and the increasing number of risks that exist online have resulted in more emphasis being placed on creating awareness in users on the use of Web 2.0 technologies and related risks. South-African university students are taught about the risks and related security controls that exist within Web 2.0 technologies. The question arises as to whether they change their online behaviour, in terms of the nature and amount of information they disclose online when using Web 2.0 technologies in light of the fact that they are taught about the risks that exist within Web 2.0 technologies. Against this background, a survey was conducted of South-African university students to determine which online practices they employed when using Web 2.0 technologies. 660 students completed the survey resulting in a response rate of 22.4%. The respondents indicated they accessed Web 2.0 at least once a week and that social networking sites were accessed more frequently. Nearly half of the respondents indicated that they amended and submitted content frequently. The respondents indicated that they were aware of the risks; however, this did not influence their online activities or they implemented safeguards in a haphazard manner. It may appear that educating users on the risks that exist in Web 2.0 technologies is being flogged to death in the popular press, but reality shows that this is taken too lightly.

Key words: Web 2.0, social media, controls, risks, user's behaviour.

INTRODUCTION

Recently, online business-to-business collaboration has been on the increase, where business functionality is supported through virtual applications, often driven by Web 2.0 technologies (referred to as 'Web 2.0' hence forth). This makes it necessary for business users to have greater access to the Internet as part of their normal business day, even in South-Africa with low internet penetration. This trend, which is expected to continue, is driven by the new generation of Internet users entering the workforce from university and bringing with them the familiarity of Web 2.0 (Hampton et al., 2012). As users are more comfortable with Web 2.0 in their personal lives, they also demand this in their business lives. With the

growth and widespread use of Web 2.0, much of the focus has been on ensuring that users gain access to data and resources, with less thought being given to whether users should have access or how they gain access and how that access is controlled. Many organisations are now becoming more worried about the impact of Web 2.0 on security, productivity and privacy. The publicity resulting from the increasing number of Internet incidences has caused more emphasis to be placed on advising users on the use of Web 2.0. The question now arises as to which practices online Web 2.0 users employ when managing their online identity and to what extent do users protect their privacy when submitting information online in light of their education and the increase in publicity around Web 2.0 use, risks and consequences. The research objective can be broken down into two parts:

To assess which practices online students employ when using Web 2.0.
To evaluate whether the students' behaviour is influenced by the acceptable online practices they are taught in lectures.

University students are used as a proxy for educated users.

It is important to understand how Web 2.0 users manage their identity, as Web 2.0 is a new, poorly understood technology and, with the growing mobility of users, the potential threat increases (D'Agostino, 2006). The study also considers the popularity of these sites to determine the scale of the potential threat to corporate security, since university students, who are future business IT users, are the most connected Internet users because all of them have access to computer facilities on campus and are the early adopters of technology. In many instances they are the ones responsible for introducing new technologies to businesses. They are also the main users (Clearswift, 2008).

The results of this study will help business determine strategies to aid in the adoption and diffusion of Web 2.0.

Literature Review

Web 2.0

The traditional Internet hosted mostly static, one-way websites. Users visited these sites passively, mostly to retrieve information. Web 2.0 operates differently. Users are able to actively update websites in real-time and can collaborate with others in order to contribute content online (referred to as the "*read-write web*"). Although numerous definitions exist for the term 'Web 2.0', it is not well defined (Radcliff, 2007). The debate around defining Web 2.0 falls outside of the scope of this research. On 20 January, 2012, Wikipedia (2012) defined Web 2.0 as *Web applications that facilitate participatory information sharing, interoperability, user-centred design, and collaboration on the World Wide Web. A Web 2.0 site allows users to interact and collaborate with each other in a social media dialogue as creators of user-generated content in a virtual community, in contrast to websites where users are limited to the passive viewing of content that was created for them.*

The definition of Web 2.0 is continuously evolving. Three components or shared values have been identified:

1. Community and social: This allows users to change

and improve content and to simultaneously redistribute it in modified form.
2. Technology and architecture: These are web-based applications with a rich interface that run in a web browser technology and do not require specific software installation, device or platform.
3. Business and process: It involves resources on a network made available as independent services that can be accessed without knowledge of their underlying platforms. Software is being delivered as a service rather than an installed product, freeing users from a specific platform.

Web 2.0 constitutes a paradigm shift in the manner in which existing technology is used. It is the evolution of the static browser to a dynamic, asynchronous interface, building on the knowledge and skills of the users. Some examples of Web 2.0 include the following: content generation (examples, Blogs, Wiki, Really Simple Syndication feeds), building social networks and communicating information (via applications such as Facebook, MySpace, LinkedIn, Twitter), sharing video and audio recordings (Podcasts and via applications such as YouTube, MySpace), trading products (eBay), and even living in virtual worlds such as Second Life.

Historical review of prior research

As the popularity of Web 2.0 services grew, the popular media published various articles on, for example, security risks relating to Web 2.0 services, while others focused mainly on business risks (D'Agostino, 2006; Fanning, 2007; Mitchell, 2007). Popular media publications in almost every industry have published some kind of article outlining how Web 2.0 has impacted that specific industry.

Most research relating to Web 2.0 has been conducted by private organisations such as Gartner, Clearswift, Pew Internet and American Life Project and KPMG, amongst others, with limited academic peer-reviewed research being performed (Shin, 2008). Initially, research focused on understanding the technology, its benefits, uses in a business environment and potential challenges (Clearswift, 2007a; 2007b). Other research studies focused on the areas of privacy (Cavoukian and Tapscott, 2006), collaboration (Lee and Lan, 2007), usage and users' behaviour patterns (Horrigan, 2007; Lenhart and Madden, 2007a, b; Shin, 2008; Smith, 2011). Various attempts have been made to develop an organisational framework to help businesses to understand and address Web 2.0 risks and to generate business value for enterprises using Web 2.0. The most widely used frameworks were developed by Dawson (2008). Rudman (2010a) developed a framework to identify and manage Web 2.0 risks in a particular company. Before frameworks for risk or value evaluation can be implemented, users' behaviour needs to be understood.

Prior research studies covering online users' behaviour

Much work has been conducted on users' behaviour, what information users disclose and how users manage their privacy. The Pew Internet and American Life Project has conducted a series of studies on Internet users' behaviour and related topics such as privacy trust online, identity management and protection. These focused on various user groups ranging from teens to established employees. Earlier studies by Fox et al. (2000) focused on the use of the Internet. These authors concluded that there is a presumption of privacy when users go online and that many users are uneducated about how to manage their identities and the risks they expose themselves too. Early in 2007, when the focus changed to Web 2.0, Lenhart and Madden (2007a) conducted a national survey of young people between the ages of 12 and 17 across the United States. The study focused on which sites were used, the reasons for using these sites and how they were used, as well methods to mitigate any potential threats. During April 2007 another study was conducted that focused specifically on the information teens share, on assessing how teens evaluated vulnerabilities and relationships online. Researchers found that most teens protect themselves by limiting the information they share and to whom, yet rely very little on automated protection (Lenhart and Madden, 2007b).

Guess (2007) reported on a study that investigated how college students were using information technology and its impact on improving the learning experience. Researchers found that students spent significant amount of time on the Internet, mainly accessing it via mobile technology. They also noted a change in the reasons why students were using the Internet, as well as the tools being used. Engineering and business students relied more on spreadsheets and graphics editing tools on the Internet. This confirmed comments by Horrigan (2007).

Other research focused on business users' behaviour in general, as well as industry-specific business users. Clearswift (2007a) investigated the impact of Web 2.0 on security, and while conducting the study also investigated usage patterns and management of identity of employees in the world's two most developed countries. Researchers focused on the type of service most frequently used, the time spent, as well as most prominent risks and related safeguards to mitigate any risks. Another study conducted by Clearswift in 2008, investigated the attitude of human resources (HR) professionals to Web 2.0 and how they had adapted Web 2.0 to their organisations. Authors found that organisations perceived risks in allowing employees uncontrolled access to Web 2.0, and although many sites have security features, many users were unaware of the features or did not enable these features. Rudman (2010b) wrote a paper on the incremental risks in Web 2.0.

These studies highlight the importance of identity management and risks in an international mature context. In this research, there is an implied assumption that the users are informed and aware of the risks and safeguards relating to Web 2.0. However, a similar study taking users' knowledge explicitly into account has not been conducted.

Research Methodology and Target Population

A literature review was undertaken to identify existing research on online users' behaviour. A web-based survey was conducted among students in the Faculty of Economic and Management Sciences at a South African university to assess the practices they employed when using Web 2.0. The questionnaire contained questions relating to three areas:

- To determine how the students manage their Web 2.0 identity and their usage patterns;
- To evaluate the users' awareness of the risks relating to Web 2.0 and how they manage these risks.

Particular consideration was given to the risks and safeguards the students are taught in class. The questions contained in the research questionnaire were based on questionnaires used in other research studies. The research question is available on request. Before the questionnaire was distributed to the target population, the questionnaire was reviewed by lecturers in both the field of auditing and information systems, a statistician and ten volunteers from the target student population. They considered the questionnaire in terms of logic and intelligibility. Minor amendments were made on the basis of their feedback. Thereafter, the questionnaire was distributed to students enrolled in a number of courses from first year to honours year courses, all in the field of economic and management sciences. These students are taught the risks related to Internet, as well as safeguards, either in their Information Technology or their Auditing and Governance courses. The following study aids were used in lectures to illustrate the risks and mitigating controls:

- Textbooks examples outlining the risks and related controls;
- Screenshots showing pictures of the controls;
- Illustrations of walk through tests;
- Class examples and homework assignment questions which students were required to complete; and
- The students were assessed using a theoretical company.

The students were not only taught by means of examples, they were also taught using a principled based approach which would allow them to identify any risks and controls irrespective of the technology. The study aids covered the following:

- Detailed examples of risks and controls, as well as examples of what can go wrong in systems and controls are not implemented;
- Do's and don'ts of users' behaviour;
- Examples of general, as well as application controls;
- The importance of governance; and
- The importance of using a framework or structured approach for identifying risks and controls.

In selecting the students, the researchers were able to identify whether users apply better practices as they become more technology literate and aware of the dangers of Web 2.0, as opposed to other potentially less computer aware users. In total, 2 944 invitations to participate in the study were sent to students. Altogether 660 students completed the questionnaire. The response rate of 22.4% is considered sufficient to arrive at the necessary conclusions. All the responses from the target population were scrutinised to eliminate instances where respondents clearly did not attempt to answer the questions. The answers to the open-ended questions were analysed and summarised in similar categories.

FINDINGS

The respondents were questioned about the nature of Internet use before specific consideration was given to Web 2.0 related matters.

Respondents' profile and internet activity

The 660 respondents comprised 54% male and 46% female students, of whom 71% were white, 24%, black (5% preferred not to indicate ethnicity). The demographic profile is not as important as the respondents' connectivity, because all respondents have access to the same resources at university. The majority (52.5%) of the respondents indicated that, other than using their cell phones, they accessed the Internet from their place of residence, while the remainder (43.4%) used the university's computer facilities. The source of access had a direct impact on the frequency at which the respondents accessed the Internet and the time spent on the Internet: 76% of the respondents indicated that they accessed Web 2.0 at least once a week, clearly indicating that this was a favoured activity. The nature of the most frequently visited sites is presented in Table 1. It is interesting to note that the sites with a direct communication component are used more often than content driven services. It can be surmised that the open communication platform usage is under estimated, because mobile access is not considered. Many South-African students access social media from their cell phones.

Awareness and utilisation of Web 2.0 services

Although a wide range of services was used, many of these users were not aware of the nature of the service they used. Those respondents that were able to identify Web 2.0 listed the differentiating characteristics of these sites as interactive, constantly changing, personal information sharing and user-orientated. This is important because the changes in technology give rise to new risks, which need to be controlled by new safeguards (Rudman, 2010a). One of the primary characteristics of Web 2.0 is the interactivity of the sites and the multiple features.

More than half of the respondents (53.3%) indicated that they mainly view content on the Internet: 15.0 and 8.4% of the respondents indicated that they submitted and amended information online, respectively, while 23.3% used online applications. These results are summarised in Figure 1 and concur with the findings by Guess (2007) and Horrigan (2007).

The influence of Web 2.0

Web 2.0 technologies are more resource-intensive and consequently could have a greater negative influence on organisations, compared to traditional Web 1.0 websites. Therefore, a number of questions were asked to gauge the respondents' awareness of the effect of Web 2.0 on them and others. Of the respondents, 30.5% were of the opinion that Web 2.0 usage did not influence university resources. But interestingly, 57.4% were of the opinion that the time spent on Web 2.0 sites influenced other users. This might be because 43.4% of the respondents used the university's computer facilities to access the Internet. Similarly, 46% of the respondents stated that they believed that Web 2.0 use influences students' studies. This, in light of the fact that the respondents mainly used Web 2.0 for non-academic purposes may indicate that the effect will be predominantly negative. It also potentially takes time away from academic endeavours. Additionally, 48.2% believed that Web 2.0 influenced their social life and the ways in which they interact socially.

Risks and consequences

Unproductive time and resources constitute but only one risk. Overall (65.3%) the respondents were not aware of the risks posed specifically by Web 2.0, although the students were taught in class that the same vulnerabilities that affect traditional web applications also impact new technologies such as Web 2.0. New threats have been developed specifically to target Web 2.0, but Web 2.0 did not change the risks; it changed the manner in which the threats are delivered. A detailed list of all risks and safeguards is contained in Rudman (2010b).

The respondents were required to rate seven potential risks, where '1' was the most significant risk and '7' was the least significant risk. Table 2 contains the average ratings for the risks. The most significant risk identified was electronic intrusion. Phishing attacks, a real risk which could be based on socially engineered information, was rated second. Unproductive time and unavailability for services were rated low, confirming earlier findings. This is a contradiction to what the students are taught in class. The students rated the risks that according to the textbooks are the easiest to control, the highest and the risk that has the greatest business impact, as the least

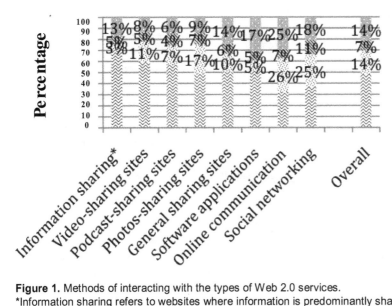

Figure 1. Methods of interacting with the types of Web 2.0 services.
*Information sharing refers to websites where information is predominantly shared by way of text.

Table 1. Most frequently visited types of sites.

Type of sites	Percentage
Personal communication	
Closed one-on-one communication such as webmail and Instant messaging	40.7
Open communication such as social networking sites	27.8
Information source	
Passive interaction information sources	15.9
Active interaction information sources	4.2
Sharing sites	8.9
Online applications, services and worlds	2.6

risky.

Inappropriate disclosure of information

Many of the risks presented in the previous section arise from sharing too much information. Approximately, 80% of the respondents believed that sharing too much information could lead to attacks. Two types of personal information could be posted online, either by means of creating a profile or through sharing personal information. Of the respondents, 80.6% indicated that they created online profiles on Web 2.0 sites, being most likely to share personal information (such as first name [94.5%]; last name [87.5%]), followed by information about where they reside (university name [77.2%]; residence [70.2%]), followed by contact information. They were least likely to share content that is resource intensive to upload or stream video (13.8%) or audio (6.0%) files. They would

share personal information regardless of whether it would make them vulnerable to social engineered attacks: 61.7% of respondents acknowledge that a motivated Internet user would be able to identify them from their Internet profiles. In light of the responses above, the respondents were asked which types of information they disclosed on Web 2.0 sites other than when creating their profile (Table 3).

Respondents would be willing to share biographical and personal information such as their religious affiliation, relationship status, and less likely to share all types of contact information. The lower willingness to share information could be attributed to the fact that students do not want to share their personal information because of the fear of being unnecessarily contacted, rather than because of security concerns. Most (53%) would also disclose their e-mail addresses. One quarter of the respondents would provide their cell phone numbers and 13% would knowingly provide other information that

Table 2. Average ranking of risks by respondents.

Risk	Average	Reality	Theory
Electronic intrusion (worms, zombie bots) embedded in downloads	1.96	Most significant	Easiest controlled
Phishing attacks, including spam.	2.63		Easiest controlled
Breach of security of the controls on the website	2.64		Greatest business and audit impact
Information leakage and brand damage	2.92		Small or no audit impact
Unproductive time	3.38		Small or no audit impact
Content errors on websites	3.40		Small or no business impact
Denial of service	3.59	Least significant	Greatest business impact

Table 3. Nature of information shared on Web 2.0.

Type of information	Yes (%)	No (%)	Maybe (%)
Biographical information	53	35	12
Contact information	33	54	13
Personal information	43	43	14

might allow someone to find them easily, such as address, and home phone number. 12% would provide their passwords online and 10% would share personal identification information such as identity numbers, or medical information.

Safeguards to mitigate risk

In order to limit the risks, safeguards could be implemented, by limiting use, self-protection, or policy implementation. The majority (44.2%) indicated that they would at least limit their activities, if they knew they were being monitored, while 11.6% indicated that they would stop using the Internet. Another 4.3% felt that with the large volume of online activity, it would be impossible for someone to effectively monitor activities and, consequently, they would not act. Of the respondents, 39.9% felt that their activities did not expose them to risks requiring them to change their Internet behaviour, irrespective of the fact that they were taught the risks relating to Web 2.0 in class.

While the respondents may have been unaware of the risks, 60.6% of the respondents did take some steps to protect themselves online ---63.4% made use of the security settings, while 25% were not sure whether they did. Altogether 56.3% made their information only available to their friends. One fifth of the respondents made their profiles visible to anyone, while 10.3% did not know to whom their profiles were visible. Other methods that respondents used to restrict access to their profiles were: giving as little personal information as possible (50.4%), password protection (59.5%) and disclosing information to known friends (37.1%). This confirms findings by Fox et al. (2000) and Lenhart and Madden

(2007b).

Many organisations have Internet policies that govern the use of company resources. The majority of the respondents (82.8%) indicated that they would comply with such a policy, if they were aware of it, while 14.2% would probably ignore the policy in their use of the Internet. Alternatively, access could be blocked; however, 68% of the respondents felt that access should not be blocked, even though nearly half (47.2%) stated that Web 2.0 related risks may impact on the security of the organisation. In addition, 37% of the respondents indicated that employees should be entitled to access Web 2.0 content from their work computer for personal reasons, irrespective of the risks. Based on the findings, Table 4 lists the controls the students were taught in class compared to the extent that they would implement the controls.

Discussion and Conclusion

Internet security and privacy is a concern for most businesses. With the growing use of Web 2.0, the potential risk related to Web 2.0 will not abate in the future. Against this background, a study was conducted to determine which practices university students employed when using Web 2.0. The respondents indicated that two thirds of them accessed Web 2.0 at least once a week and that social networking sites were accessed frequently. Nearly half of the respondents indicated that they fully engaged with Web 2.0 through amending and submitting content. The respondents were aware of the risks. However, this did not influence their online activities. Most respondents indicated that they did take some measures to protect themselves, but they implemented safeguards in a haphazard manner. The results of this study, therefore, indicate that Web 2.0 is used widely; and that although students are educated on the risks and controls in class, they do not necessarily implement safeguards to address the risks. Considerations should be given to blocking access to popular Web 2.0 and implementing strict controls that do not rely on user implementation, since potential safeguards would, in all probability, be ignored even by informed

Table 4. Extent to which safeguards are implemented in practice.

Theoretical safeguard	Ignored	Unaware	Effective
Block access to designated websites, file types and utilities			X
Implement a next generation reputation based filtering			X
Utilise deep-scanning behavioural anti-malware programs			X
Monitor, review and investigate resource activity	X	X	
Ensure that all network and software up-to-date		X	
Utilise browser security and configure browser correctly		X	
Utilise security features and configure correctly		X	
Implement a robust policy		X	
Educate users on Web 2.0 risks and related safeguards	X		

users or not used. This also says a lot about the manner in which students study and are able to apply theory to practice. When teaching information security, greater emphasis should be placed on practical examples, identification of risks and the real-life implementation of controls. Moreover, organizations cannot rely only on users to employ proper controls. It may seem as if educating users on the risks posed by the Internet is being flogged to death in the popular press. Yet this study has indicated that this process can never be taken too lightly, especially in protecting businesses' most important resource: information.

Acknowledgements

This paper has been presented at the *International Conference on Information Communication Technologies in Education (ICICTE)* held in Rhodes, Greece on 5-7 July 2012. The organising committee granted permission that the article may be published.

REFERENCES

Cavoukian A, Tapscott D (2006). Privacy and the Enterprise 2.0.New Paradigm Learning Corporation. [Online]. Available fromhttp://newparadigm.com/media/Privacy_and_the_Enterprise_2.0.pdf[Accessed on 15 February 2012].

Clearswift (2007a). Content security 2.0: The impact of Web 2.0 on corporate security. [Online]. Available from http://resources. clearswift.com/Externalcontent/Features/Clearswift/9586/200704Surv eyReport_US_1063233.pdf[Accessed on 23 February 2012].

Clearswift (2007b). Demystifying Web 2.0.[Online].Available fromhttp://resources.clearswift.com/ExternalContent/C12CUST/Clear swift/9514/200707 DemystifyingWeb21.0_US_1062190.pdf [Accessed on 15 February 2012].

Clearswift (2008). Content security 2.0: The role of HR and IT in effectively managing the business benefits and risks of Web 2.0. [Online]. Available fromhttp://resources.clearswift.com/main/pages/ Clearswift/RSRCCTR/ContentDisplay.aspx?sid=3230&yid=2711[Acc essed on 23 February 2012].

D'Agostino D (Winter 2006). Security in the world of Web 2.0.CIO Insight, pp. 12-15.

Dawson R (2008). An enterprise 2.0 Governance Framework-looking for input! [Online].Available fromhttp://rossdawsonblog.com/weblog/ archives/2008/2/an_enterprise_2.html[Accessed on 23 February 2012].

Fanning E (2007).Security for Web 2.0.Computerworld, 3 September, 44.

Fox S, Rainie L, Horrigan J, Lenhart A, Spooner T, Carter C (2000). Trust and privacy online: Why Americans want to rewrite the rules.Pew Internet & American Life Project: Washington D.C. [Online]. Available fromhttp://pewinternet.org/Reports/2000/Trust- and-Privacy-Online.aspx[Accessed on 19 February 2012].

Guess A (2007) Students' 'evolving' use of technology. Inside Higher ED. [Online].Available from http://www.insidehighered.com/ news/2007/09/17/it[Accessed on 20 February 2012].

Hampton K, Goulet LS, Marlow C, Rainie L (2012). Why most Facebook users get more than they give. Pew Internet & American Life Project: Washington, D.C. [Online]. Available from http://www. pewinternet.org/Reports/2012/Facebook-users.aspx [Accessed on 19 February 2012].

Horrigan J (2007). A typology of information and communication users.Pew Internet & American life Project. [Online].Available fromhttp://www.pewInternet.org/pdfs/PIP_ICT_Typology.pdf[Accesse d on 15 February 2012].

Lee M, Lan Y (2007). From Web 2.0 to conversational knowledge management: Towards collaborative intelligence. J. Entrep. Res. 2(2):47-62.

Lenhart A, Madden M (2007a). Social networking websites and teens: An overview. Pew Internet & American life Project, [Online]. Available from http://www.pewinternet.org/~/media//Files/ Reports/2007/ PIP_SNS_Data_Memo_Jan_2007.pdf [Accessed on 19 February 2012].

Lenhart A, Madden M (2007b). Teens, privacy, and online social networks.Pew Internet & American life Project.[Online].Available fromhttp://www.pewInternet.org/pdfs/PIPTeensPrivacySNSReport.pdf [Accessed on 15 February 2012].

Mitchell R (2007). Web 2.0 users open a box of security risks. Computer world, 26 March, p.32.

Radcliff D (2007). Are you watching? SC Magazine, September, pp.40- 43.

Rudman R (2010a). Framework to identify and manage risks in Web 2.0 applications. Afr. J. Bus. Manage. 4(13):3251-3264.

Rudman R (2010b). Incremental risks in Web 2.0 applications. Elec. Lib. 28(2):210-230.

Shin D (2008). Understanding purchasing behaviour in a virtual economy: Consumer behaviour involving currency in Web 2.0 communities. Interact. Comput. 20:433-446.

Smith A (2011).Why Americans use social media.Pew Internet & American life Project.[Online]. Available fromhttp://pewinternet.org/~/ media//Files/Reports/2011/WhyAmericansUseSocialMedia.pdf[Acces sed on 20 February 2012].

Wikipedia (2012). Web 2.0.Wikipedia.[Online].Available fromhttp:// en.wikipedia.org/wiki/Web_2[Accessed on 19 February 2012].

19

The relationship between information system (IS) innovation and innovation among Iranian small and medium enterprises (SMEs)

Aminreza Kamalian [1], Maryam Rashki [1]* and Mah Lagha Arbabi[2]

[1]Department of Management and Accounting, Zahedan University of Sistan and Baluchestan, Zahedan, Iran.
[2]Management department of International University of Chabahar, Chabahar, Iran.

Information system (IS) innovation is one of the most important types of innovation. IS innovations frequently demand the fashioning and incorporation of new roles, responsibilities, relationships, lines of authority, control mechanisms, work processes and work flows-in short, new organizational designs. The survival and growth of business enterprises increasingly depends on their ability to respond to globalization and rapidly changing in market demands, technologies and consumer expectations. Small and Medium enterprises (SMEs) constitute 94% of Iranian firms. According to Iran statistic website the value added of 94% of Iranian firms is just about 10% of the whole value added in country. This study assumes the lag of IS and innovation is the reason of uncompetitive nature of Iranian SMEs. This paper reports on the results of a study that examined Information system (IS) innovation among a sample of 86 managers of small and medium-sized enterprises (SMEs) in Iran. As the survey results show that the most information resource is clients, customers and acquisition of external knowledge has a positive and significant effect on innovation. Iranian SMEs are not collaborating with universities and higher education institutions; they do not see university as a main source of information.

Keywords: IS innovation, innovation, SMEs.

INTRODUCTION

Small and medium enterprises (SMEs) are integral sources of revenue, employment and product innovation for the economic growth of a country. SMEs are generally characterized by a smaller workforce and lower turnover. Information system and Communication Technologies can help SMEs create business opportunities and combat pressures from competition (Levy and Powell, 2005; Kotelnikov, 2007). This study focuses on SMEs because they are important to economic development in developing countries such as Iran. A commitment to innovation has long been considered to be important to

the success of entrepreneurial ventures and small firms (Fiol, 1996). Research has shown that innovation stimulates ventures' growth (Wolff and Pett, 2006) and also provides a key source of competitive advantage in the absence of scale economies (Lewis et al., 2002). Considered from the resource-based view of the firm (Barney, 1991), successful innovation may be dependent on the presence of other organization-specific skills and capabilities. For example, substantial evidence has begun to accumulate that suggests that appropriate strategic employment of IS (Figure 1) may be essential in translating strategies (for example, innovation) into enhanced firm performance (Ray et al., 2005; Sakaguchi et al., 2004). A direct linkage between IS and firm performance was established by Powell and Dent-Micallef (1997). There are many good reasons for paying attention to SMEs. They constitute the 94% of Iranian firms (amar.org), they are a main source of employment,

---

*Corresponding author. E-mail: maream_rashki@yahoo.com.

Abbreviations: SMEs, Small and medium enterprises; **IS,** information system; **IT,** information technology.

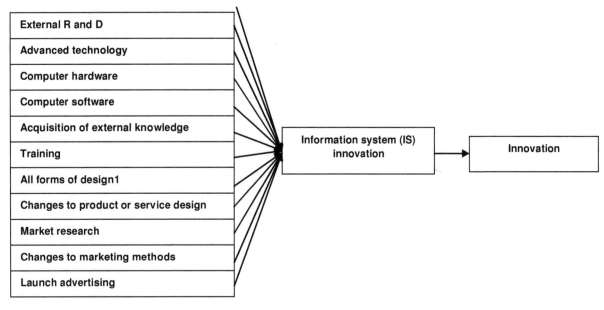

Figure 1. Research model.

and they are flexible. Iran defines SMEs as independent businesses that employ less than 250 people (Iranian Commission, 2003). SMEs can be split up in micro, SMEs. The research will be conducted in the Sistan and Baluchestan region of Iran. The lag in innovation among the region firms relative to those of other countries in eastern countries could result in reduced competitive capacity of the Sistan and Baluchestan firms. Iranian manufacturing and services are not able to compete with others in the world and this study assumes the lag of IS and innovation is the reason of uncompetitive nature of Iranian firms.

REVIEW OF LITERATURE

Innovation and its importance for organizations

New technologies had a great impact on all aspects of innovation and are a pre-requisite for any successful organization. That does not necessarily mean that product innovation lead many leading organizations to achieve success according to how they run their business, not by inventing a better product or service. To achieve success over a long period of time, all organizations need to embrace innovation. An interesting point about innovation was found in Windrum (2006) "Innovation begets further innovation". He argued that through organizational innovation, managers gain a more specific view of the different activities of the firm, and see the potential creative opportunities that arise through breaking down 'departmental silos' and creating novel synergistic activities. McAdam and McConvery (2004) concluded that SMEs exhibit resistance to innovation.

Weak management commitment, which can be a signal that the organizational culture does not support innovation. Employees and innovators often question the value of a strategy that embraces innovation (Storey, 2000). Some of this resistance has been found to be consistent with a direct management style, in some cases further compounded by an owner-manager relationship (Mosey et al., 2002). Several studies have emphasized the role of employee resistance to innovation based on issues such as poor communication, existing corporate norms, weak human resources practices and lack of commitment of top management (Zwick, 2002; Osterman, 2000; Kane et al., 1999).

A result of organizational cultures being unreceptive to innovation is the risk of failure to seize new approaches to pursuing market opportunities (Roper and Hofmann, 1993). Adoption of innovation requires employee commitment and effort (Acemoglu and Pishke, 1999). Constraints arising from weak management support are an innovation choke point because innovation can disrupt established routines and schedules (Shanteau and Rohrbaugh, 2000). Baldwin and Lin (2002) recognized that resistance to change, some of which results from inadequate training or poor employee skills, is an important organizational challenge. Hausman (2005) pointed out that small business managers often lack the types of education and training that have been linked with a successful innovation strategy. Freel (2000) also emphasized that firms are constrained in their ability to attract, train and retrain managers who are qualified to effectively incorporate innovation into business strategy. The firm's external environment includes a variety of influences, such as global competition, government policy and economic uncertainty. These challenges require that firms effectively communicate to managers the importance of innovation as a core firm strategy that will help maintain market competitiveness (Frishammar and Horte, 2005). Porter (1985) noted that competitive pressures often force firms to adopt new technologies so as to become differentiated from competitors or gain a cost advantage. Katila and Shane (2005), Souitaris (2002) Khan and Manopichetwattana (1989) found a positive relationship between external economic uncertainty and the rate of innovation; firms in more turbulent external environments have higher potential for innovation, because turbulent environments trigger firms to incorporate innovation into their business strategy in order to remain competitive and ultimately survive (Miller 1987). Information about a firm's external environment, such as market opportunities, changes in technology, and government policy, impact managers' adoption of innovation as a strategy to better meet customer needs and to help make the firm more competitive. Information about technology, markets and government policy initiatives can reinforce the importance and potential advantages of becoming more innovative (Galia and Legros, 2004). Lack of information, however, can become another obstacle to innovation (Frenkel, 2003; Hadjimanolis, 1999), and uncertainty about government policy, especially in European countries, can become a significant barrier to innovation. Piatier (1984) found that lack of government assistance was the third most important barrier to innovation in European countries.

Information system (IS) role for organizations

Miles et al. (1978) based is work on the idea that IS can enhance an organization's ability to respond to these demands, adapting its product and service offerings. Developments in information technology increasingly offer organizations the opportunity to adopt or create new innovative products, work processes and market strategies (Sambamurthy and Zmud, 2000). These IS capabilities are formulated in both technologies and human resources and provide the ability to employ resources in ways that enable delivery of new products and services (Bharadwaj, 2000). Attention of IS vendors has moved recently to SMEs offering them a vast range of solutions, which were formerly adopted by large firms only (Ramdani and Kawalek, 2007b). Most small firms still under-utilise the potential value of IS innovations by only restricting them to administrative tasks (Brock, 2000). The Unites Kingdom Department of Trade and Industry (DTI) literature claims that IS adoption and implementation is crucial to the survival and growth of the economy in general and small business sector in particular (Martin and Matlay, 2001). Without a better understanding of the complex processes and the differentiating factors that affect IS adoption level, the drive of IS adoption and development will not success-

fully contribute to SMEs' competitiveness (Martin and Matlay, 2001). Lack of (or substantially less sophisticated) information system management (Kagan et al., 1990); Frequent concentration of information-gathering responsibilities into one or two individuals, rather than the specialization of scanning activities among top executives (Hambrick, 1981); Lower levels of resource available for information-gathering; and quantity and quality of available environmental information (Pearceet al., 1982).

New technologies provide SMEs with opportunities that are largely unexploited (Brock, 2000; Corso et al., 2001). It is hard nowadays to imagine SMEs operating without some use of IS. However, SMEs differ in the level of IS usage (Blackburn and McClure, 1998). Southern and Tilley (2000) identifies three categories of small firms with different attitude to IS: SMEs with low-end IS use, medium-level IS users and high-end IS users. According to Brock (2000), there are various research streams influencing research concerning IS adoption in small firms ranging from computer science, behavioral science, decision science, organizational science, social science and management science to economic and political science. He classified the key research streams that have developed over time to four main groups which are:

1). Adoption research: research interested in the determinants of organizational adoption of IS [for example: Thong and Yap (1995) Fink (1998)].
2). Implementation research: research interested in the post-adoption processes [for example: Cooper and Zmud (1990) Saga and Zmud (1994)].
3). Strategic management research: research interested in the potential strategic value of IS for organizations [for example: Sethi and King (1994); Elliot and Melhuish (1995)].
4). Impact research: research interested in the various effects of an IS on the operations of individuals, work groups or the whole organization [for example: Delone and McLean (1992) Hitt and Brynjolfsson (1996)]. Furthermore, Southern and Tilley (2000) identifies three alternative research perspectives:

i).Technological: this type of work has arguably dominated the field and has generally used an IS perspective and mainly concerned with examining factors leading to IS success within a firm [for example: Naylor and Williams (1994); Cragg and King (1993); Raymond and Pare (1992)].
ii).Organizational: work in this category is concerned with understanding the small firm's strategic approach to using IS and the capabilities and structures of SMEs to use the technology [for example: Doherty and King (1998); Swatz and Boaden (1997); Thong and Yap (1995)].
iii). Small firms: this approach aims to develop an understanding of the domain from the perspective of the owner/manager of a small firm [for example: Blackburn

Table 1. Proportion of enterprises in the population covered by the survey.

Manufacturing and services	Number of employees		
	1_10	10_100	101_1000
Percentages of all respondents	28.6	57.1	14.3

and McClure (1998); Fuller (1996); Fuller and Southern (1999)].

Another classification of research in IS implementation in SMEs has been introduced by Premkumar (2003). The five major domains in his framework are individual, task, innovation/ technology, organization and environment. He explains that the domains can be considered as different layers of the environment that influences the design and use of information technology. He argues that the core of the framework includes individuals and task because the primary purpose of IS in an organization is to enable people to complete work-related tasks. At the next layer, technology domain provides the tools and information to aid the individual in his or her task. Technology is implemented in an organization, which is presented as a different layer. The overarching layer represents the external environment.

Research questions

1) Which type of Innovation-active is dominated on SMEs?
2) Is there any relationship between dimension of information system innovation and innovation?
3) What are the most important dimensions of information system innovation from point view of owner of SMEs?
4) What is the most important information resource from point view of owner of SMEs?

Description of sampling

Data for this study were collected by questionnaires of information system and innovation that contained 18 items. From the 86 distributed questionnaires that was respondent by management of SEMs of the Sistan and Baluchestan province of Iran, 50 were completed and returned for the response rate 58.13%. Cronbach α for this scale was 0.91. Data analysis was carried out by using the statistical program packages SPSS. Innovation takes place through a wide variety of business practices, and a range of indicators can be used to measure its level within the enterprise or in the economy as a whole. These include the levels of effort employed (measured through resources allocated to innovation) and of achievement (the introduction of new or improved products and processes). This section reports on the types and levels of innovation activity over the three-year period 2008 to 2010. Innovation activity is defined here as where enterprises were engaged in any of the following:

1). Introduction of a new or significantly improved product (goods or

service) or process.
2). Engagement in innovation projects not yet complete or abandoned.
3). Expenditure in areas such as internal research and development, training, acquisition of external knowledge, or machinery and equipment linked to innovation activities.

The proportion of enterprises (Table 1) having participated in some innovation-related activity (64%) shows that SMEs recognize the need to assign resources to innovation. Around 17.6% of SMEs report abandoned projects. The Pearson correlation for the study variable is given in Table 3. IS Innovation and dimensions were correlated with innovation? Dimensions of is innovation were significantly related to innovation and the results of Table 3 illustrates that there are positive relationship between some items. The Table 4 is illustrating model summery of regression of constraining factors innovate and innovate. As seen, the signification predictor (Acquisition of external knowledge) has determined 16.8% variance of innovation. As it was expected to predict creating depending on IS innovation and dimensions, p-variable regression was applied and IS innovation as predictor variable and innovation as depended variable were analyzed. Data of Table 5 illustrated that IS innovation and its dimensions predicts on the innovation. Eventually each increase or decrease in dimensions of IS innovation reason same change in innovation. As seen, acquisition of external knowledge has satisfied the entrance criterion or the regression and entered as a first important predictor (Beta=0.410). Another result provides that acquisition of external knowledge have a positive and significant effect on the innovation propensity.

Information sources of innovation

Respondents were asked to rank a number of potential information sources on a scale from 'no relationship' to 'high importance'. The mean and standard deviation of each category (information source) is shown in Table 6. Internal from within the enterprise itself or other enterprises within the enterprise group. Market from suppliers, customers, clients, consultants, competitors, commercial laboratories or research and development enterprises. Institutional from the public sector such as government research organizations and universities or private research institutes and other from conferences, trade fairs and exhibitions; scientific journals, trade/technical publications; professional and industry associations; technical industry or service standards. The results show that client or customers were cited as the most important source of information by Sistan and Baluchestan SMEs and it is followed by suppliers of equipments. Universities and other higher education institutes were seen as the least important source of information.

Analysis

The results were initially summarized using statistics to provide a better understanding of the respondents and characteristics of the responding companies (Table 7).

Table 2. Innovation-active enterprises: by type of activity, 2008 to 2010 percentages.

Innovation -activities	64
Product(good/service) innovator	50
Process innovator	64
Abandoned activities	17.6

Table 3. Person correlation coefficient between IS innovation and innovation (n=50).

Variable	Innovate
Internal R and D	0.351
External R and D	0.184
Advanced Technology	0.402
Computer hardware	0.131
Computer software	0.086
Acquisition of external knowledge	0.410
Training	0.344
All forms of design	0.187
Changes to product or service design	0.186
Market research	0.187
Changes to marketing methods	0.280
Launch advertising	0.188
IS innovate ion	0.375

Correlation is significant at the 0.05 level (2-tailed).

From the 86 distributed questionnaires, 50 were completed and returned for the response rate 58.13 and 80% of Sistan and Baluchestan SMEs operate at a regional level, about 44% at Iran level and 0% worldwide. Just under a quarter (20%) of businesses reported any exports for the years 2008 to 2010. Innovation takes place through a wide variety of business practices, and a range of indicators can be used to measure its level within the enterprise or in the economy as a whole. These include internal R and D, External R and D, Acquisition of machinery equipment and software and hardware, acquisition of external knowledge, training and all forms of design, changes to product or service design, market research and changes to marketing methods, launch advertising. According to Table 2. Overall, 64% of enterprises were classed as being innovation-active during 2008 to 2010. The proportion of enterprises having participated in some innovation-related activity (64%) shows that firms recognize the need to assign resources to innovation. The most commonly reported activities were in advanced technology, followed by internal R and D and computer hardware.

The internationalization of Rand D seems to be a useful instrument to mitigate the effects of innovation often faced by SMEs (Tiwari and Buse, 2007). During 2008 to 2010, acquisition of external knowledge. As the range of technologies necessitated for innovation has spread out

and technologies have become more complex, companies can no longer cover all relevant disciplines. Many key developments draw on a wide range of scientific and commercial knowledge, so that the need for co-operation among participants in different fields of expertise has become greater in order to reduce uncertainty, share costs and knowledge and bring innovative products and services to the market (OECD, 2000). The results of the survey on Sistan and Baluchestan province of Iran shows that in Iranian SMEs the most frequent partners for co-operation were suppliers (76% of enterprises with co-operation agreements) and other business in their enterprise (72%). Around 44% of collaborators included universities amongst their partners. Information system was reported as the least important to innovation. Innovation is not wholly about the development or use of technology or other forms of product (goods and services) and process change. Enterprises can also change their organizational structure, marketing strategy, corporate strategy and advanced management techniques to make the more competitive. 63.6% of Iranian SMEs made changes to their management strategy during 2008 to 2010. As would be expected, great proportion of SMEs engaged in one or more of these changes. Advanced management techniques was most commonly reported, with the introduction implementing new organizational structures being least frequent? Table 8 is designed to examine in what extent the findings of the survey is related to information system innovation.

CONCLUSION

Successful firms adopt IS as part of a system or cluster of mutually reinforcing organizational changes. IS use is correlated with workers skills suggesting that firms that use high levels of IS also employ more knowledge workers. IS use is also found to be correlated with organizational innovations in production and efficiency practices, HRM practices and product/service quality related practices, supporting the view that IS and organizational changes are complements. This paper examines IS innovation and innovation, among a sample of 86 Iranian manufacturing SMEs located in the Sistan and Baluchestan province of Iran. The Sistan and Baluchestan province economic situation is interesting due to the need to increase the investment in innovation by manufacturing SMEs. This need is because recent regional Gross Domestic Product has not been growth in compare with three years ago. In the selected case (Sistan and Baluchestan SMEs), an in-depth study of IS innovation were done through distributing questionnaire. This study addressed analyzing innovation practices in SMEs of Iran. The survey results indicate that innovation is also becoming increasingly popular among SMEs. After all, SMEs often lack resources to develop and commercialize new product in house and as a result are

Table 4. Model summery of regression of IS innovation and innovation (n=50).

R	R square	Adjusted R square	Std. Error of the estimate	F Change
0.410[a]	0.168	0.150	0.358	9.49

a. Predictors: (constant), q (acquisition of external knowledge).

Table 5. Regression analysis to predict constraining factors innovates on the innovate (n=50).

Predictor Variable	B	Std. error	Beta	T	Sig
(Constant)	0.379	0.68		5.704	0.00
Acquisition of external knowledge	0.321	0.104	0.410	3.081	0.003

a. Dependent variable: q (innovation).

Table 6. Ranks of Information resources.

Variable	Mean rank
Within your enterprise group	6.84
Suppliers of equipment	7.92
Clients or customers	8.36
Competitors or other enterprises within your industry	7.34
Consultants, commercial labs or private R and D institutes	5.24
Universities or other higher education institutes	4.40
Government or public research institutes	5.22
Conferences, trade fairs and exhibitions	3.92
Scientific journals and trade/technical publications	5.24
Professional and industry associations	5.10
Technical, industry or service standards	6.42

Table 7. Test statistics[a].

N	Chi-square	df	Asymp sig
50	146.532	10	0.000

a. Friedman test.

more often inclined to collaborate with other enterprises in their own business. Innovation activity is most important type of activity (64%) from point view of owner of SMEs. Around 17.6% of SMEs report abandoned projects.

The survey results indicate that Iranian SMEs prefer to engage more in acquisition of external knowledge, followed by a considerable investment in advanced technology and external R and D. According to Morton (1971) Zaltman et al. (1973) Organizations facilitate innovation through project teams or R and D departments. But there is evidence that Iranian SMEs do not concentrate on R and D investment as one of the main innovation activities. Enterprises engage with external sources of technology and other innovation-related knowledge and information. Enterprises reported market and internal sources as most important for information on innovation. This suggests that enterprises tend to rely on their own experience and knowledge coupled with information from customers and clients, suppliers. The survey results show that Iranian SMEs are not collaborating with universities and higher education institutions nevertheless our expectation is based on the literature. It could be argued that the long-term solution to fostering innovation within information technology (IT) lies not with industry but the school system and higher education. Van de Ven (1986) argues that as individuals have access to more information about available innovations and are more globally informed

Table 8. The degree of importance of different points of IS innovation on Sistan and Baluchestan province.

Important points in IS development/innovation according to literature	Evidence of the survey
Reducing cost as a driving force of IS innovation	Reported as the forth important factor
Creating new or different products that no one else produces as a driving force to IS innovation	Reported as important by 47% of SMEs
Better products than competitors as a driving force to IS innovation	Reported as the most important factor by 64% of SMEs
Locking suppliers or customers in to the organization's products or services as a driving force to IS innovation (improving flexibility of production)	Reported as least important motivational factor to innovation
See university as a main partner for enterprises	Reported as the sixth important partner Between seven partners that are defined in the survey
See university as a main source of information for enterprises	Reported as the tenth source of information among the twelfth information sources
See R and D department as one of the main departments in organization	Reported as the ninth important activity in the enterprises among thirteenth defined activity
Complexity of the software development process (lack of information on technology) as a constrain to IS innovation	Reported as an important barrier by less than of half
Lack of adequate resources(financial resources) as a barrier to IS innovation	Reported as the second important constraint to innovation
Poor project management skills and Shortage of IT skills and lack of senior manager (lack of qualified personnel) as a barrier to IS innovation	Reported as important factor by half of the firms

about the implications of innovative ideas, they are better able to relate the "parts to the whole." In general, individuals with a broader awareness of the consequences and implications of innovative ideas facilitate the process of organizational innovation. But according to the survey SMEs in Sistan and Baluchestan do not concern to one of the most important factors in IS innovation.

REFRENCES

Baldwin J, Lin Z (2002). "Impediments to Advanced Technology Adoption for Canadian Manufacturers", Research Paper No. 11F0019MPE No 173, Statistics Canada, downloads from http://www.statcan.ca/, other version: Res. Policy 31:1-28.

Barney J (1991). "Firm Resources and Sustained Competitive Advantage," J. Manage. 17:99-120.

Bharadwaj AS (2000). A resource-based perspective on information technology capability and firm performance: An empirical investigation". MIS Q. 24(1):169-196.

Blackburn R, McClure R (1998). The use of information and communication technologies (ICTs) in small business service firms: Report to Midland Bank". Small Business Research Centre, Kingston Business School, UK.

Brock JK (2000). "Information and Communication Technology in the Small Firm". In Jones-Evans D & Carter S (Eds.), Enterprise and small business: Principles, practice and policy (pp. 384-408). Harlow, England: FT - Prentice Hall.

Cooper RB, Zmud RW (1990). "Information Technology Implementation Research: A Technological Diffusion Approach," Manage. Sci. 36(2): 123-139.

Corso M, Martini A, Paolucci E, Pellegrini L (2001). "Information and communication technologies in product innovation within SMEs – The role of product complexity". Enterprise Innov. Manage. Stud. 2:35.

Cragg PB, King M (1993). "Small-firm computing: Motivators and inhibitors". MIS Q. 17(1):47-60.

Delone WH, McLean ER (1992). "Information systems success: The quest for the dependent Variable". Inform. Syst. Res. 3:60-95.

Doherty NF, King M (1998). The consideration of organizational issues during the systems development process: An empirical analysis". Behav. Inform. Technol. 17:41-51.

Elliot AJ, Melhunish P (1995)." A methodology for the evaluation of IT for strategic implementation". J. Inform. Technol. 10(2):87-100.

Fink D (1998). "Guidelines for the successful adoption of information technology in small and medium Enterprises". Int. J. Inform. Manage. 18(4):243-253.

Fiol CM (1996). "Squeezing Harder Doesn't Always Work: Continuing the Search for Consistency in Innovation Research," Acad. Manage. Rev. 21:1012-1021.

Freel M (2000). "Barriers to Product Innovation in Small Manufacturing Firms," Int. Small Bus. J., 18(2): 60-79.

Frenkel A (2003). "Barriers and Limitations in the Development of Industrial Innovation in the Region", Eur. Plan. Stud. 11: 115-137.

Frishammar J, Hörte SÅ (2005). Managing External Information in Manufacturing Firms: The Impact on Innovation Performance2. J. Prod. Inno. Manage. 22(3): 251-266.

Fuller EC, Southern A (1999). "Small firms and information and communication technologies: Policy issues and some words of caution". Environment and Planning C: Govern. Policy 17(3): 287-302.

Fuller T (1996). "Fulfilling IT needs in small businesses; a recursive learning model". Int. Small Bus. J. 14(4):25-44.

Galia F, Legros D, (2004). Complementarities between obstacles to innovation: evidence from France. Res. Policy. 33(8): 1185-1199.

Hadjimanolis A (1999). "Barriers to innovation for SMEs in a small less developed country (Cyprus)". Technovation, 19: 561-570.

Hambrick DC (1981). Specialization of environmental scanning activities among upper level executives. J. Manage. Stud. 18(3):299-320.

Hausman A (2005). Innovativeness Among Small Businesses: Theory and Propositions for Future Research. Ind. Marke. Manage. 34(8): 773-182

Hitt LM, Brynjolfsson E (1996). Productivity, business profitability, and consumer surplus: Three Different measures of information technology value. MIS Q. 121-142.

Kagan A, Lau K, Nusgart KR (1990). "Information system usage within small business firms". Entrepreneurship: Theory Practice 14(3):25-37.

Katila R, Shane S (2005). When does lack of resources make new firms innovative? Acad. Manage. J. 48(5): 814–829.

Khan A, Manopichetwattana V (1989). Models for distinguishing innovative and non innovative small firms. J. Bus. Ventur. 4(3): 187-196

Kotelnikov V (2007). Small and Medium Enterprises and ICT. Asia-Pacific Development. Information Programme.

Levy M, Powell P, Worrall L (2005). "Strategic intent and e-business in SMEs: Enablers and inhibitors". Information Resources Manage. J. 18(4): 1-20.

Lewis MW, Welsh MA, Dehler GE, Green SG (2002). "Product Development Tensions: Exploring Contrasting Styles of Project Management," Acad. Manage. J. 45(3):546-564.

Martin LM, Matlay H (2001). "Blanket" approaches to promoting ICT in small firms: Some lessons from the DTI ladder adoption model in the UK. Internet Research: Electronic Netw. Appl. Policy 11(5):399-410.

McAdam R, McConvery T, Armstrong G (2004). Barriers to innovation within small firms in a peripheral location. Inter J. Entre. Behav Res. 10(3): 206-221

Miles RE, Snow CC, Meyer AD, Coleman Jr HJ (1978). "Organizational Strategy, Structure, and Process," Acad. Manage. Rev. 3(3):545-562.

Miller D (1987). Strategy making and structure: Analysis and implications for performance. Acad. Manage. J. 30: 7-32.

Morton JA (1971). Organizing for Innovation, New York: McGraw-Hill.

Naylor JB, Williams J (1994). The successful use of IT in SMEs on Merseyside. Eur. J. Inform. Syst. 3(1):48-56.

OECD (2000). "A New Economy? The changing Role of Innovation and Information technology in Growth", Organization for Economic Co-operation and Development, Paris.

Pearce IJA, Chapman BL, David FR (1982). Environmental scanning for small and growing Firms. J. Small Bus. Manage. 20(3):27-34.

Piatier A (1984). Barriers to Innovation, London: Frances Pinter

Powell TC, Dent-Micallef A (1997). "Information Technology as Competitive Advantage:The Role of Human, Business, and Technology Resources," Strategic Manage. J. 18(5):375-405.

Premkumar G (2003). A meta-analysis of research on information technology implementation in small Business. J. Organ. Comput. Electronic Commerce 13(2):91-121.

Ramdani B, Kawalek P (2007b). SME adoption of enterprise systems in the northwest of England: An environmental, technological and organizational perspective. In T. McMaster, D. Wastell, E. Ferneley & J. I. DeGross (Eds.), IFIP - The International Federation for Information Processing, Volume 235, Organizational Dynamics of Technology-Based Innovation: Diversifying the Research Agenda (pp. 409-430). Boston: Springer.

Ray G, Muhanna WA, Barney JB (2005). "Information Technology and the Performance of the Customer Service Process: A Resource-Based Analysis," MIS Q. 29:625-651.

Raymond L, Pare G (1992). Measurement of information technology sophistication in small manufacturing firms. Inform. Resour. Manage. J. PP 1-13.

Saga VL, Zmud RW (1994, 11-13 October 1993). The nature and determinants of IT acceptance, Routinization and infusion. In: Levine L (Ed.). Diffusion, transfer and implementation of information technology. Paper presented at the Proceedings of the IFIP TC8 Working Conference, Pittsburgh.

Sakaguchi T, Nicovich S, Dibrell C (2004). "Empirical Evaluation of an Integrated Supply Chain Model for Small and Medium Sized Firms," Inform. Resour. Manage. J. 17(3):1-19.

Sambamurthy V, Zmud RW (2000). Research commentary: the organizing logic for an enterprise IT activities in the digital era – a prognosis of practice and a call for research. Inform. Syst. Res. 11(2):105-114

Sethi V, King WR (1994). Development of measures to assess the extent to which an information Technology application provides competitive advantage. Manage. Sci. 40(12):1601-1627.

Souitaris V (2002). Technological trajectories as moderators of firm-level determinants of innovation. Res. Policy 31: 877–898.

Southern A, Tilley F (2000). Small firms and information and communication technologies (ICTs): Toward a typology of ICTs usage. New Technology, Work Employment 15(2):138-154.

Storey J (2000). "The Management of Innovation Problem," Int. J. Innov. Manage. 4(3):347-369.

Swartz E, Boaden R (1997). A methodology for researching the process of information management in small firms. Int. J. Entrepre. Behav. Res. 3(1): 53-65

Tiwari R, Buse S (2007). Barriers to Innovation in SMEs: Can the Internationalization of R&D Mitigate Their Effects? Paper presented at the Proceedings of the First European Conference on Knowledge for Growth: Role and Dynamics of Corporate R&D (CONCORD 2007). Seville, Spain.

Thong JYL, Yap CS (1995). CEO characteristics, organizational characteristics and information Technology adoption in small businesses. Omega – Int. J. Manage. Sci. 23(4): 429-442.

Van de Ven AH (1986). Central Problems in the management of innovation. Manage. Sci. 32:590-608.

Windrum P (2006). Heterogeneous preferences and new innovation cycles in mature industries: the amateur camera industry 1955-1974, Ind. Corp. Change 14(6):1043-1074.

Wolff JA, Pett TL (2006). "Small-Firm Performance: Modeling the Role of Product and Process Improvements," J. Small Bus. Manage. 44(2):268-284.

Zaltman G, Duncan R, Holbek J (1973). Innovations and Organizations, Wiley, New York.

20

A hybrid tabu search algorithm for the vehicle routing problem with simultaneous pickup and delivery and maximum tour time length

Milad Keshvari Fard and M. Reza Akbari

Department of Industrial Engineering, Sharif University of Technology, Tehran, Iran.

The vehicle routing problem with simultaneous pick-up and delivery (VRPSPD) and maximum time limit for traversing of each tour is a variant of the classical vehicle routing problem (VRP) where customers require simultaneous delivery and pick-up. Delivery loads are taken from a single depot at the beginning of the vehicle's service, while pick-up loads are delivered to the same depot at the end of the service. Also traversing time of each route should not encroach the specified limit. In this research, the aforesaid problem was introduced and a mixed integer programming model was developed for it. Because of being NP-Hard and the impossibility of solving it in the large instances, a hybrid tabu search algorithm was developed to handle the problem. For producing the initial solution for this algorithm, two methods were built. Furthermore, five procedures for improving the solution were developed, which three of them are being used for inter-route and the other two for intra-route improvement. Computational results were reported for 26 produced test problems of the size between 5 to 200 customers.

Key words: Vehicle routing problem, simultaneous pickup and delivery, maximum tour time length, heuristic, hybrid tabu search.

INTRODUCTION

The vehicle routing problem (VRP) is a general name for a large group of problems for determining vehicle routes, in which each vehicle departs from a specified depot, serves some customers and returns back to the depot at the end of its service. There is a variety of services in the real world, but physical delivery of goods is the most common type of it.

VRP in its ordinary mode consists of a depot, a fleet of homogenous vehicles placed in the depot and a set of customers who need delivery of goods from the depot. The goal of the problem in its simplest status is to minimize the total routing cost subject to the capacity of vehicles. Beside the basic VRP, there is a vast variety of related problems. Toth and Vigo (2002) provided comprehensive details of these problems.

One extension of the basic VRP is the vehicle routing problem with simultaneous pickup and delivery (VRPSPD). In this problem that first was introduced by Min (1989), not only customers require delivery of goods, but also they need a simultaneous pickup of goods that should be sent to the depot.

From the practical point of view, many situations need simultaneously pickup and delivery; for example in soft drink industry not only full bottles should be delivered to the customers, but also empty ones must be picked up and sent back to the depot. Reverse logistics is another area in which planning for vehicle routes is a kind of VRPSPD. This is a very important issue, especially in countries that companies are obliged for taking the responsibility of their products during the life cycle. Managing the returned goods can also take the form of VRPSPD in some problems. Furthermore VRPSPD may be seen in many other real world problems; for example Galvao and Guimaraes formulated the problem of transporting the individuals between the continent and oil exploration and

---
*Corresponding author. E-mail: milad.keshvarifard@essec.edu.

production platforms located in the Campos Basin in the state of Rio de Janeiro, in which transportation was carried out by helicopters based on the continent (Montané and Galvao, 2006).

The main contribution of this research is that we have added the maximum tour time length constraint to the original VRPSPD. This constraint can be found in many other vehicle routing problems, but according to our best knowledge it has not been considered in the VRPSPDs.

The main application of this constraint is in problems that the loads are spoilable and the travel time should not exceed a specified amount. As a good example we can mention transporting the comestibles (meat, fruits, vegetables, etc.) through ships. Another application is when there is a necessity for fleets' planning in different times without transforming the problem to a dynamic problem. In this case we can be assured about the upper limit of the time each customer are being served and also availability of a vehicle after a specific time; therefore we will be able to plan in a more efficient way for our fleet.

It should be said that maximum tour time length constraint resembles to the maximum distance travelled restriction. As the costs are presented by either distance or time between the customers, these two problems are very similar, however in our problem, unlike the problems with maximum distance traveled, service time in the customers' place has been considered too. Since this time is not a tiny amount in many cases such as loading and unloading the ships, considering it makes the problem more realistic. Furthermore these two problems have some differences in their essences.

In the current problem, all vehicles are similar and there is just one depot. These assumptions have been considered in all of the VRPSPD researches in the literature. Also to make the problem more realistic, the travel's time matrix between customers is assumed to be asymmetric. The aim of the problem originally is to minimize the travel time of all vehicles, but there can be one more goal of minimizing the vehicles' number in addition to the previous one in the proposed Hybrid algorithm. In this method that first was proposed by Casco et al. (1988), a penalty factor is added to every arc connected to the depot. Moreover, by removing maximum tour time constraint or equating pickup or delivery demands of customers to zero, the problem can be changed to eight more different vehicle routing problems.

The reminder of this paper is organized as follows. A brief literature review of VRPSPD is presented. Also, we present mathematical formulation of the problem, and therefore explain our proposed algorithm for solving the problem. This is then followed by computational results and conclusion.

RELATED WORKS

The VRPSPD was first introduced by Min (1989) which was a real life problem concerning the distribution of books among libraries by two vehicles. To solve this problem, he proposed a two-step procedure in which customers first were clustered into groups according to their positions, and then in each cluster, a TSP is solved by using branch-and-price technique. The resulting infeasible arcs were penalized by setting their lengths to infinity, and the TSPs were solved again. After Min's (1989) research, there was a gap of more than 10 years without any published work on this problem. Salhi and Nagy (1999) introduced a comprehensive classification of different types of vehicle routing problem with pickup and delivery (VRPPD) and separated VRPSPDs from vehicle routing problem with mixed backhaul (VRPMB). They developed four insertion-based heuristics to solve VRPSPD which first generated partial routes for the customers and then inserted the remaining customers into these routes. Dethloff (2001) introduced a cheapest insertion algorithm according to the remaining vehicle's capacity and the least possible increasing of the total length. Nagy and Salhi (2005) added three new methods to their previous work and also presented some methods to refine solutions as well as more complex functions on nodes. Crispim and Brandao (2005) solved VRPSPD by a hybrid algorithm of tabu search and variable neighborhood descent. Chen and Wu (2006) developed a solution that in its first step, the initial solution was made by a cheapest insertion algorithm and then was improved by a hybrid algorithm of tabu search and record-to-record travel. Dell'Amico et al. (2006) presented the first published work on exact method for this problem by a branch-and-price algorithm. Montané and Galvao (2006) considered the problem with maximum tour length assumption. Initial solutions were found using a number of methodologies (sweep, tour partitioning, and extensions of the TSPPD heuristics) and then acted as inputs for the next step which was a tabu search algorithm. Bianchessi and Righini (2007) proposed some constructive algorithms, local search, and tabu search methods for this problem and concluded that using tabu search with complex neighborhoods produces better solutions. Wassan et al. (2008) used a reactive tabu search which utilized modified sweep algorithm for generating initial solutions. Gajpal and Abad (2009a) proposed a saving based algorithm for the problem. In the same year they also proposed a hybrid algorithm of Ant colony system and two local search schemes for it (Gajpal and Abad, 2009a). Subramanian et al. (2010) suggested a parallel metaheuristic algorithm consist of random neighborhood ordering and iterated local search using a constructive algorithm to generate initial solution for this problem. Zachariadis et al. (2009) proposed a hybrid algorithm of tabu search and guided local search that used a construction heuristic based on cost saving to get an initial point. Karlaftis et al. (2009) used a genetic algorithm to solve the problem of ship routing between some ports in Greece. This problem also included the time windows assumption. Ai and Kachitvichyanukul (2009) proposed a particle swarm optimization for this problem. Zachariadis et al. (2010) developed a metaheuristic algorithm based on adaptive memory which used different aspects of the good solutions to make better ones. Catay (2010) proposed a hybrid algorithm of ant colony and local search which made initial solution by the nearest neighborhood heuristic. Mingyong and Erbao (2010) added time windows and maximum distance traveled constraints to the original VRPSPD and solved it by a differential evolution algorithm. Gutiérrez-Jarpa et al. (2010) developed another branch and price algorithm for the problem considering the assumption of time windows. Their algorithm was capable of solving the sample sizes up to 50 customers. Fan (2011) considered VRPSPD problem with time windows and defined customer satisfaction according to the time which customer is being visited and its requested time windows. He used a Tabu search algorithm and solved problem up to the size of 50 customers. Subramanian et al. (2011) proposed a branch and cut algorithm which was able to find better lower and upper bounds for the VRPSPD problems for problems with size up to 200 customers. Zachariadis and Kiranoudis (2011) proposed a local search heuristic which used aspiration criteria of Tabu search for diversification. They tested their algorithm on data with maximum size of 400 customers. Tasan and Gen (2012) presented a genetic algorithm for VRPSPD. Wang and Chen (2012) also considered the problem with time windows constraints and proposed a genetic algorithm for it. Their algorithm was able to solve problems with up to 100 customers. Goksal et al. (2012) used a hybrid algorithm of particle swarm and simulated annealing to solve VRPSPD. Cruz et al. (2012) proposed a hybrid heuristic of variable neighborhood descent, tabu search, and path relinking for VRPSPD. Zhang et al. (2012) were the first who consider VRPSPD with stochastic travel time and solved it using scatter search algorithm. They solved problems with at most 400 customers.

MATHEMATICAL FORMULATION FOR VRPSPD

Suppose G = (V, A) is a directed graph where $V = \{v_0, v_1, ..., v_n\}$ is the vertex set and $A = \{(v_i, v_j) : v_i, v_j \in V, i \neq j\}$ is the arc set. Also vertex v_0 represents the depot. The other parameters and variables are as the following.

n: total number of customers; n=|V|-1

t_{ij}: time to traverse distance from customer i to j

p_j: pickup demand of customer j; j=1,...,n

d_j: delivery demand of customer j; j=1,...,n

s_j: service time of customer j; j=1,...,n

Q: vehicle's capacity

T: maximum allowed time for each route

$\bar{k}$: maximum number of available vehicles

Decision variables

x_{ij}^k: is 1 if arc (i, j) belongs to the route operated by vehicle k, otherwise is 0;

y_{ij}: demand picked-up in customers routed up to node i (including node i) and transported in arc (i, j);

z_{ij}: demand to be delivered to customers routed after node i and transported in arc (i, j);

The corresponding mathematical formulation is given by

$$Min \sum_{k=1}^{\bar{k}} \sum_{i=0}^{n} \sum_{j=0}^{n} t_{ij} x_{ijk} \tag{1}$$

St:

$$\sum_{i=0}^{n} \sum_{k=1}^{\bar{k}} x_{ijk} = 1 \qquad j = 1,...,n \tag{2}$$

$$\sum_{i=0}^{n} x_{ijk} - \sum_{l=0}^{n} x_{jlk} = 0 \qquad \begin{array}{l} j = 0,...,n \\ k = 1,...,\bar{k} \end{array} \tag{3}$$

$$\sum_{j=1}^{n} x_{0jk} \leq 1 \qquad k = 1,...,\bar{k} \tag{4}$$

$$\sum_{i=0}^{n} y_{ji} - \sum_{l=0}^{n} y_{lj} = p_j \qquad j = 1,...,n \tag{5}$$

$$\sum_{i=0}^{n} z_{ji} - \sum_{l=0}^{n} z_{lj} = -d_j \qquad j = 1,...,n \tag{6}$$

$$y_{ij} + z_{ij} \leq \sum_{k=1}^{\bar{k}} Q x_{ijk} \qquad i = j = 0,...,n \tag{7}$$

$$\sum_{i=0}^{n} \sum_{j=0}^{n} x_{ijk} (s_i + t_{ij}) \leq T \qquad k = 1,...,\bar{k} \tag{8}$$

$$x_{ijk} \in \{0,1\} \tag{9}$$

$$y_{ij}, z_{ij} \geq 0 \tag{10}$$

In this model that is an extension of the proposed model by Montané and Galvao (2006), the objective function seeks to minimize total distance traveled. Constraints (2) ensure that each customer is visited by exactly one vehicle while constraints (3) guarantee that the same vehicle arrives and departs from each customer it serves.

Constraints (4) show the maximum number of vehicles that can be used. Restrictions (5) and (6) are flow equations for pickup and delivery demands, respectively; they guarantee that both demands are satisfied for each customer. Constraints (7) establish that pickup and delivery demands will only be transported using arcs included in the solution; they further impose an upper limit on the total load transported by a vehicle in any given section of the route. Restrictions (8) clarify that traversing time of each route should not exceed the specified limit. Finally constraints (9) and (10) define the nature of the decision variables.

In short the set of aforementioned constraints ensures that each vehicle departs the depot with a load equal to the sum of delivery demand of customers in its route and comes back to the depot with a load equal to the sum of pickup demand of customers in the same route; while there is no violation on vehicle's capacity and maximum tour time. Toth and Vigo (2002) showed that capacitated vehicle routing problem (CVRP) is NP-Hard, and hence the current problem is a generalization of CVRP (by equating traverse time to infinity and equating pickup demands of customers to zero), it is a NP-Hard problem too. Because of this, we should seek heuristic and metaheuristic methods for solving it.

SOLUTION ALGORITHM

Tabu search that was first introduced by Glover (1976), is one of the most famous improving metaheuristic algorithms which is widely used in the literature. It uses an initial solution as a starting basis for seeking improved solutions. We start by describing two constructive heuristics that were used to generate this initial solution, proceed with discussing different neighborhoods, then talking about our tabu search algorithm and its characteristics (short-term memory, tabu tenure, long-term memory and etc.), and finally describe the general framework of the proposed tabu search algorithm for the current problem.

Initial solution

In this research we used two methods to generate initial solution as a starting point to the hybrid algorithm that are as follows.

Initial algorithm 1

In this algorithm, first an initial complete tour starting from the depot which consists of all of the customers is built by solving a TSP problem through a greedy heuristic algorithm. Then the customers, according to their position in this initial tour, are added to the end of routes -just before the depot- which starts from depot and ends to it. Afterwards, it is examined whether there is any violation of vehicle's capacity and maximum tour time length or not. In case of trespassing from each of these constraints, the current route would close and the customer is added to the next route; this will continue until all of customers have been assigned to routes. Then this work is repeated for different starting points in the primary TSP tour. After that, the primary TSP tour is reversed (It is traversed in the opposite direction) and all of the operations above will be repeated for it. Therefore this algorithm recurs for 2n times and at last the best solution is reported as the initial solution.

Initial algorithm 2

This method is actually a constructive heuristic that a TSP sub-problem is solved for producing a route. In this method we choose among customers that still have not been assigned to any route; the one that is the nearest to the last placed customer in the current route, is chosen for the last position in the route (in case that current route is still null, the nearest customer to the depot), and by supposing of existence the depot at the beginning and the end of this route, we check the feasibility of maximum tour time and vehicle's capacity for that route. In case of violating, this customer is removed from current route, the route is closed and the customer is added to a new route from depot to depot. To get an initial solution, both methods are executed and the better answer is caught as the initial solution; thus initial solution is chosen among 2n+1 solutions.

Improvement procedures

Five common improving functions are used in order to enhance solution's quality. As we know, due to the fluctuation of vehicle's load in a route, by adding or substituting a new customer into a route, all of the customers must be reassessed to ensure that vehicle's capacity is not violated. Since this study is based on a complete neighborhood's search, by increasing the problem size, computing time increases exponentially; so some algorithms are developed for these operators to decrease computational operations. Since these algorithms deal with vehicle's capacity, they can be used in other VRPSPDs. Figure 1 shows the function of these improving operators.

Shift

This operator searches to find the best place for each customer in the other routes. Also it may assign a new (empty) route to a customer or removes a route (if it contains just one customer). It should be said that the mechanism for feasibility test is according to the proposed algorithm by Wassan et al. (2008). Also because it is faster to check tour time constraint, it is checked first. To reduce the calculations in each iteration, only the best feasible place is saved for each customer. Then the best replacement is chosen among at most, n, found neighborhoods.

Interchange

This function switches two customers in different routes. It checks all of the possible attitudes for each two different routes and each two customers in these routes, and chooses the best feasible move according to the solution's value and tabu degree of that move. To reduce the huge amount of calculations, at the beginning of each implementation of this procedure, a function calculates the vehicle's load after visiting each of the customers in the route for all of the routes, and identifies customer(s) in each route that the vehicle's load becomes maximum after visiting them.

Also to hasten implementation of this operator, a procedure for reducing the calculations related to vehicle's capacity was developed. For each of the two routes, suppose that the customer which is going to be removed, is X and the customer that is planned to be inserted, is Y. Moreover delivery and pickup demands of X are p_x and d_x. Vehicle's capacity is Cap and maximum load of the vehicle during its current path is maxload. There are two possibilities for X:

1) The position of customer X on its current route is equal or greater than the position of the last maxload on that route. This path would be feasible after switching the two customers if the two conditions below are valid.

- $d_Y - d_X + \max load \leq Cap$
- For all the customers in the route whose positions are between X's position (consist of X) to the last customer in the route:

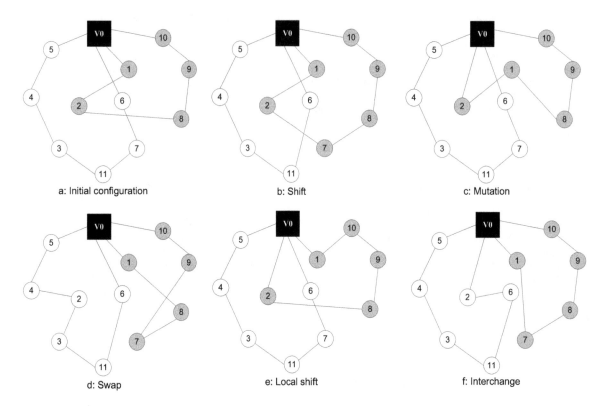

Figure 1. Improving operators.

Vehicle's load after visiting the customer $+ p_Y - p_X \le Cap$

If both conditions are true, then this substitution is feasible.
2) The position of customer X on its current route is less than the position of the first maxload on that route. This path would be feasible after substitution if two conditions below are valid.

- $\qquad p_Y - p_X + \max load \le Cap$
- For all the customers in the route from the beginning of the route until X's position: Vehicle's load after visiting the customer + $d_Y - d_X \le Cap$

If both conditions be true, then this substitution is feasible.

Therefore we will have four special situations (according to two customers' positions in their current routes) and in the case of none of those (the position of X is between two maxloads), the algorithm would check the whole route for feasibility of vehicle's capacity. This algorithm is caught according to this fact that by adding (removing) customer X, vehicle's load would increase by p_x for the customers after X, and decrease by d_x for those before X. Using this method, checking the vehicle's capacity feasibility is done for almost half of the route and therefore computing time decreases a huge amount. This procedure would give better results in cases that vehicle's capacity is considerable in comparison with each customer's demand (more than 8 times).

Mutation

This function switches the places of two customers within a route. The algorithm that is used in this function to deal with vehicle's capacity constraint for reducing the amount of calculations, is that if

the position of the two customers are simultaneously less than the position of the first maxload or simultaneously equal or greater than the position of the last maxload in that route, this switching is feasible for vehicle's capacity; otherwise feasibility of capacity must be examined in a normal way. Also at the beginning of this algorithm, another function should identify customer(s) in each route, which maxload occurs after visiting them.

The logic in this algorithm is that if both customers be at one side of the maxload's position, none of their pickup or delivery loads would affect on maxload and hence, no violation of vehicle's capacity would occur. Using this method caused almost halving the computational operations related to capacity feasibility test of this function. Like Interchange, the performance of this function will increase by having more spacious vehicles.

Swap

This function acts like interchange; it takes different pairs of routes; in each pair chooses pairs of customers and moves each of the two customers simultaneously to the best possible place in the other's route.

Before each iteration of this operator, by a separate function, algorithm finds vehicle's load after visiting each of the customers in a route and the maxload of that route in the case of removing each of the customers of that route, and does it for all of the routes. Also by splitting each part of the algorithm and changing some orders during implementation, computation time decreases more than fifty percent. Because of the numerous steps of the algorithm, we skip it here.

Local shift

This function catches a customer and moves it to the best place on its route. This work is done for all routes and all customers in each route. In this function, the method introduced in Mutation is used in order to decrease the number of needed computations for vehicle's capacity constraint. Also to restrain storing of bad neighborhoods, this function uses the foresaid method in Shift.

The Tabu Search strategy in neighborhood's searching

Each of the five mentioned improving operators act as below in the framework of tabu search.

1. Start;
2. For current solution survey all of the possible neighborhoods and identify their value and tabu degree and save them;
3. Let $x_{n+1} = x_n$ in cases of no feasible solution and go to step 6, otherwise go to step 4;
4. Find the solution with best value (x'); if it is better than x^* (The best solution found) let $x^* = x_{n+1} = x'$ and go to step 6, otherwise go to 5;
5. Choose the solution that first has the least tabu degree and second has the least value (x'') and let $x_{n+1} = x''$;
6. End.

The aforementioned procedure is used has more authorization to move in tabu areas in comparison with the customary procedure of tabu search. The reason for this work is the little number of feasible neighborhoods in each iteration, even by doing a complete search in neighborhood; it is caused by the nature of the problem and constraints. It can be leaded to entrap the search into a local optimum and to prohibit moving to other promising areas especially by progressing the problem and tightening the routes. Hence the mentioned procedure was used to deal with this issue.

Tabu list: In vehicle routing problems, this list is usually about the arcs or nodes that is added or removed from a route. In this paper after each movement, all of the inserted and removed arcs are added to the tabu list.

Tabu tenure: The number of iterations that one arc remains tabu should be higher for deleted arcs than the inserted ones; it is because that inserted arcs are promising and is better to have more freedom. To find the best values for tabu tenure, several values were tested. Unlike many papers that believed tabu tenure should be a percent of the number of customers, best values of this factor were founded in relation to the root of n. In fact, large values for tabu tenure make the search random. Also choosing tabu tenure from an interval showed better results than using constant values.

Tabu tenure for deleted arcs: $\begin{cases} [2,3] & n \le 6 \\ [3,4] & 7 \le n \le 12 \\ [[0.9\sqrt{n}],[1.3\sqrt{n}]] & n \ge 13 \end{cases}$

Tabu tenure for inserted arcs: $\begin{cases} [2,2] & n \le 6 \\ [2,3] & 7 \le n \le 12 \\ [[0.6\sqrt{n}],[0.9\sqrt{n}]] & n \ge 13 \end{cases}$

Long term memory: Two diversification and intensification phases were used in order to improve the solution quality. The method is exactly the one that was used by Montané and Galvao (2006).

Hybrid tabu search algorithm framework

Step 0: Generate an initial solution by two mentioned procedures.
Step 1: Perform normal tabu search by starting from the initial solution for I1 iterations.
Step 2:
1- Equate the tabu list values to zero.
Halve intervals of tabu tenure.
Perform intensification phase by starting from the best found solution in the previous step for I2 iterations.
Step 3: Performing diversification phase for I3 iterations.
Step 4:
Return tabu tenure values to its original state.
Perform normal tabu search for I4 iterations.
Step 5: Perform local search phase by starting from the best solution found in previous steps for I5 iterations.

Although the stopping condition is finishing of all the above steps, but steps 1 and 4 will finish if there is no change in the best found solution for I6 iterations. The values of I1 to I6 are follows. They decrease by increasing the problem's size in such way to catch the best balance between solution's quality and time.

$I1 = [4000/\sqrt{n}]$;
$I2 = [I1/6]$;
$I3 = [I1/8]$;
$I4 = [\frac{2}{5} I1]$;
$I5 = 10$;
$I6 = [7000/\sqrt{n}]$;

In steps 1, 4 and 5, in each iteration, three improving operators of Shift, Swap and Local shift are done successively. Also five improving operators of Shift, Swap, Local shift, Interchange and Mutation act in a sequential manner in each iteration of intensification and diversification phases.

COMPUTATIONAL RESULTS

For implementing the proposed algorithm, instances with number of customers equal to 5,6,7,8,9,10,11,12,20,50, 100,150 and 200 are created. 12, was the problem with the maximum number of customers which could be solved by exact method in less than 30 min.

Three instances for each of the scales with 50 customers or more for better assessing were used. As the problem was introduced for the first time, no match benchmark data were available and hence our data is generated by distributions (as follow) that are adopted from CMT problems of Salhi and Nagy (1999).

- X coordinate of customers and depot: UNI [0-71]
- Y coordinate of customers and depot: UNI [0-71]
- Pickup demand of each customer: UNI [0-41]
- Delivery demand of each customer: UNI [0-41]

Also service time to each customer was caught from UNI [1-12], vehicle's capacity considered to be 100 and the total tour time was equated to 330.

The proposed hybrid tabu search algorithm was implemented in MATLAB and the exact method was

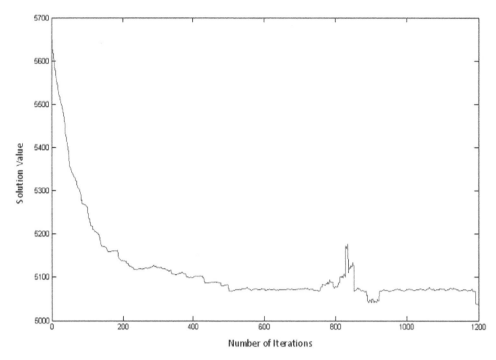

Figure 2. Convergence of hybrid tabu search algorithm in problem 200-3.

executed by CPLEX 12. Both codes ran on an INTEL Core 2 Quad (using just a single core) with 2.4 GHz, 4 GB RAM, and operating system of Windows 7.

Comparison between initial solution algorithms

As earlier mentioned, two methods were used to generate initial solutions. In Table 1, required time for each method to be performed, number of routes generated by that method and cost of the proposed solution are presented.

From observation, solutions quality in initial algorithm 1 is better or equal to initial algorithm 2 and hence it is identified as the starting point of search by the tabu search algorithm. However initial algorithm 2 in most cases produced acceptable solutions (3.27% difference with initial algorithm 1) and the two problems generated the best initial solution; but the strength point of this algorithm is in its very small computing times as well as a linear increase in them by enhancing the problem's size unlike the other method.

An evidence for the power of these two algorithms is the small difference of the accepted initial solution with the global optimum found by exact method (4.64%) in 8 small problems (problems 5 to 12). They also directly produced the global optimum for problems 5 and 9.

Computational results of the hybrid tabu search algorithm

In Table 2, information about solving time, the number of produced routes and objective functions are presented for both of the hybrid algorithm and exact method.

As it can be seen, for all of small problems except problem 8, the solution found is equal to the solution of exact algorithm. This reveals the power of the hybrid algorithm. Figure 2 demonstrates the convergence of this algorithm during the implementation. In this figure the effect of each step is obvious.

Both in this problem or other problems solved by this algorithm, the Tabu search algorithm starts with a steep decrease in the objective function and after a while it reaches to a steady state. Then, intensification phase is started and we observed some decrease (between 0.1% to 1.2%) in the best solutions found in previous phase; these solutions had very little deviance from those of previous phase by the general position of the customers in the routes. After that, diversification phase makes some turmoil in the solutions, and in near half of the cases, it could generate improvements up to 0.9% in the solution. The fourth phase gave improvement just in 4 problems; none of them were higher than 1%. Finally, the local search phase which was started from the best solution found in previous phases, almost in all cases provided improvements at most equal to 0.7%.

The proposed Hybrid algorithm was able to create a total decrease of 10.5% to more than 17% (12.5% in average) to the initial solution in medium and large size problems. The algorithm also provided an average of 17.3% decrease in the number of required routes from the best initial solution. The latter improvement has a high importance, since it determines the number of required vehicles and has a high weight in determining the total

Table 1. Comparison between methods of generating initial solution.

Problem	Initial algorithm 1			Initial algorithm 2		
	Time(s)	No. of routes	Value	Time (s)	No. of routes	Value
5	0.00376	2	272.1	0.00083	2	277.6
6	0.00505	2	355	0.00099	3	367.8
7	0.00841	2	307.8	0.00099	2	307.8
8	0.00801	3	378.3	0.00103	3	468.4
9	0.0091	2	380.2	0.00108	2	386
10	0.02013	4	413.5	0.00189	4	436.7
11	0.02105	3	501.9	0.00121	3	513.6
12	0.01708	4	457.3	0.00132	4	486.2
20	0.04229	7	734.2	0.00181	7	734.2
50-1	0.17155	12	1661.9	0.00224	13	1697.2
50-2	0.18598	14	1509.1	0.00225	15	1524.3
50-3	0.16843	15	1631.4	0.00225	15	1702.6
100-1	0.58481	28	3377.1	0.00425	29	3474.9
100-2	0.61825	29	3111	0.00434	29	3132.2
100-3	0.57716	26	2759.9	0.00422	26	2818.2
150-1	1.33166	42	4285.8	0.00636	42	4311.7
150-2	1.33994	44	4959.2	0.00641	47	5257.3
150-3	1.36214	45	5047.3	0.00641	45	5076.8
200-1	2.39265	61	6679.2	0.00833	61	6810.1
200-2	2.3817	61	6270.2	0.0086	62	6303.2
200-3	2.33211	54	5657.7	0.00847	53	5699.9

Table 2. Results for the hybrid tabu search and the exact method.

Problem	Initial solution		Hybrid tabu search			Exact method		
	No. of routes	Value	Time (s)	No. of routes	Value	Time (s)	No. of routes	Value
5	2	272.1	0.6	2	272.1	0.01	2	272.1
6	2	355.0	0.7	2	331.0	0.19	2	331.0
7	2	307.8	1.5	2	302.1	1.31	2	302.1
8	3	378.3	3.7	2	357.5	2.06	3	344.5
9	2	380.2	1.6	2	380.2	7.05	2	380.2
10	4	413.5	1.2	4	376.1	19.34	4	376.1
11	4	501.9	1.5	3	468.3	24.14	3	468.3
12	4	457.3	1.7	4	439.9	210.60	4	439.9
20	7	734.2	30.7	6	637.0	-	-	-
50-1	12	1661.9	35.5	11	1476.8	-	-	-
50-2	14	1509.1	45.3	12	1308.9	-	-	-
50-3	15	1631.4	46.3	13	1460.3	-	-	-
100-1	28	3377.1	76.0	22	2802.7	-	-	-
100-2	29	3111.0	94.5	23	2730.8	-	-	-
100-3	26	2759.9	86.9	22	2491.6	-	-	-
150-1	42	4285.8	169.1	35	3766.4	-	-	-
150-2	44	4959.2	147.3	36	4413.2	-	-	-
150-3	45	5047.3	180.3	37	4403.2	-	-	-
200-1	61	6679.2	311.1	47	5640.2	-	-	-
200-2	61	6270.2	376.8	48	5416.5	-	-	-
200-3	54	5657.7	364.3	45	5037.0	-	-	-

cost.

Conclusion

VRPSPD has been receiving growing attention due to the increasing importance of the reserve logistic activities in the past few years. In this paper the vehicle routing problem with simultaneous pickup and delivery and maximum tour time length constraint was introduced for the first time to cope with the subset of such problems in which the total time of each trip (consist of travel time as well as loading and unloading time) should not exceed a specified amount. Then a mathematical formulation was developed for the problem. Since this problem is NP-Hard, exact methods cannot deal with it in large scale instances, and hence using heuristic methods to solve it is inevitable.

For this purpose, first, two procedures for generating the initial solution were developed. Although solution's values which were produced by initial algorithm 1 were slightly better than those of the initial algorithm 2, but the computational time of the latter algorithm was significantly better than the time needed by initial algorithm 1.

Then a number of the most famous improving functions were developed to be compatible with current problem. Also by doing some changes in their algorithms, needed operations and therefore their computational time were decreased considerably. Hence these modifies were about vehicle's capacity, those algorithms with some little changes would be applicable for the other VRPSPDs. So in addition to developing a new problem in the field of VRPSPD, the second contribution of this paper is defined as developing new procedures for some famous improving methods in VRPSPDs for reducing calculation-time, which are practical in other VRPSPDs.

Then, a hybrid algorithm of tabu search and local search was developed to improve the initial solution through the improving procedures. It was implemented on test problems from 5 to 200 customers. This algorithm could find global optimum in 88% of small problems and showed to be a time effective algorithm since the maximum time it spent was 376 s.

In terms of future research directions, the proposed algorithm can be tested on VRPSPD without tour time constraint to show its strength in comparison with the other algorithms developed for it. Moreover this algorithm can be combined with other heuristics to reach better results. Other algorithms which have been verified to be powerful in dealing with VRPSPDs like ACS can be developed for this problem. Finally adding multiple depots assumption makes the problem more realistic.

REFERENCES

Ai T, Kachitvichyanukul V (2009). "A particle swarm optimization for the vehicle routing problem with simultaneous pickup and delivery" Comput. Oper. Res. 36:1693-1702.

Bianchessi N, Righini G (2007). "Heuristic algorithms for the vehicle routing problem with simultaneous pick-up and delivery", Comput. Oper. Res. 34:578-594.

Casco D, Golden B, Wasil E (1988). "Vehicle routing with backhauls: models algorithms and case studies", In: Golden B, Assad A (Eds.), Vehicle Routing: Methods and Studies. North-Holland, Amsterdam pp.127-147.

Catay B (2010). "A new saving-based ant algorithm for the Vehicle Routing Problem with Simultaneous Pickup and Delivery", Expert Syst. Appl. 37(10):6809-6817.

Chen J, Wu T (2006). "Vehicle routing problem with simultaneous deliveries and pickups", J. Oper. Res. Soc. 57(5):579-587.

Crispim J, Brandao J (2005). "Metaheuristics applied to mixed and simultaneous extensions of vehicle routing problems with backhauls", J. Oper. Res. Soc. 56(11):1296-1302.

Cruz R, Silva T, Souza M, Coelho V, Mine M, Martins A (2012). "GENVNS-TS-CL-PR: A heuristic approach for solving the vehicle routing problem with simultaneous pickup and delivery", Electron. Notes Discrete Math. 39:217-224 .

Dell'Amico M, Righini G, Salani M (2006). "A branch-and-price approach to the vehicle routing problem with simultaneous distribution and collection", Transp. Sci. 40(2):235-247.

Dethloff J (2001). "Vehicle routing and reverse logistics: The vehicle routing problem with simultaneous delivery and pick-up", OR Spektrum 23:79-96.

Fan J (2011). "The Vehicle Routing Problem with Simultaneous Pickup and Delivery Based on Customer Satisfaction", Procedia Eng. 15:5284-5289

Gajpal Y, Abad P (2009a). "An ant colony system (ACS) for vehicle routing problem with simultaneous delivery and pickup", Comput. Oper. Res. 36(12):3215-3223.

Gajpal Y, Abad P (2009b). "Saving-based algorithms for vehicle routing problem with simultaneous pickup and delivery", J. Oper. Res. Soc. 61:1498-1509.

Goksal F, Karaoglanb I, Altiparmak F (2012). "A hybrid discrete particle swarm optimization for vehicle routing problem with simultaneous pickup and delivery", Comput. Ind. Eng. (In Press).

Gutiérrez-Jarpa G, Desaulniers G, Laporte G, Marianov V (2010). "A branch-and-price algorithm for the Vehicle Routing Problem with Deliveries, Selective Pickups and Time Windows", Eur. J. Oper. Res. 206:341-349.

Karlaftis M, Kepaptsoglou K, Sambracos E (2009). "Containership routing with time deadlines and simultaneous deliveries and pick-ups", Transp. Res. 45(1):210-221.

Min H (1989). "The multiple vehicle routing problem with simultaneous delivery and pickup points", Transp. Res. A 23(5):377-386

Mingyong L, Erbao C (2010). "An improved differential evolution algorithm for vehicle routing problem with simultaneous pickups and deliveries and time windows", Eng. Appl. Artif. Intell. 23(2):188-195.

Montané F, Galvao R (2006). "A tabu search algorithm for the vehicle routing problem with simultaneous pick-up and delivery service", Comput. Operat. Res. 33(3):595-619.

Nagy G, Salhi S (2005). "Heuristic algorithms for single and multiple depot vehicle routing problems with pickups and deliveries", Eur. J. Oper. Res. 162(1):126-141.

Salhi S, Nagy G (1999). "A cluster insertion heuristic for single and multiple depot vehicle routing problems with backhauling", J. Oper. Res. Soc. 50(10):1034-1042.

Subramanian A, Drummonda L, Bentes C, Ochi L, Farias R (2010). "A parallel heuristic for the Vehicle Routing Problem with Simultaneous Pickup and Delivery", Comput. Oper. Res. 37(11):1899-1911.

Subramanian A, Uchoac E, Pessoa A, Ochi L (2011). "Branch-and-cut with lazy separation for the vehicle routing problem with simultaneous pickup and delivery", Oper. Res. Lett. (In press).

Tasan AS, Gen M (2012). "A genetic algorithm based approach to vehicle routing problem with simultaneous pick-up and deliveries", Comput. Ind. Eng. 62(3):755-761.

Toth P, Vigo D (2002). "The vehicle routing problem", Philadelphia, PA: SIAM Philadelphia.

Wang H, Chen Y (2012). "A genetic algorithm for the simultaneous delivery and pickup problems with time window", Comput. Ind. Eng. pp.84-95.

Wassan N, Wassan A, Nagy G (2008). "A reactive tabu search algorithm for the vehicle routing problem with simultaneous pickups and deliveries", J. Comb. Optim. 15(4):368-386.

Zachariadis E, Kiranoudis C (2011). "A local search metaheuristic algorithm for the vehicle routing problem with simultaneous pick-ups and deliveries", Expert. Syst. Appl. 38(3):2717-2726.

Zachariadis E, Tarantilis C, Kiranoudis C (2009). "A hybrid metaheuristic algorithm for the vehicle routing problem with simultaneous delivery and pick-up service", Expert Syst. Appl. 36(2):1070-1081.

Zachariadis E, Tarantilis C, Kiranoudis C (2010). "An adaptive memory methodology for the vehicle routing problem with simultaneous pick-ups and deliveries", Eur. J. Oper. Res. 202(2):401-411.

Zhang T, Chaovalitwongse W, Zhang Y (2012). "Scatter search for the stochastic travel-time vehicle routing problem with simultaneous pick-ups and deliveries", Comput. Oper. Res. 39(10):2277-2290.

21

Towards sustainable green ship technology

O. Sulaiman[1]*, A. H. Saharuddin[1], and A. S. A. Kader[2]

[1]Faculty of Maritime Studies and Marine Science, Universiti Malaysia Terengganu, 21030 UMT, Kuala Terengganu, Terengganu, Malaysia.
[2]Faculty of Mechanical Engineering, Department of Marine Technology, Universiti Technologi Malaysia, 81300 Skudai, Johor, Malaysia.

Man live in two worlds, the biosphere and the techno sphere world over the years, time needs, growth, speed, and knowledge and competition have created demand that necessitated man to build complex institution. Ship design is not left out in this process. Inland water, are under treat from untreated waste that can feed bacteria and algae, which in turn exhaust the oxygen. The ocean cover 70% of the globe, many think that everything that run into it is infinite, the ocean is providing the source of freshening winds and current that are far more vulnerable to polluting activities that have run off into them too many poisons, that the ocean may cease to serve more purpose if care is not taking to prevent pollution. This issue of environment becomes so sensitive in recently and most are linked to infrastructure development work. Most especially in maritime industry polluting activities from oil bilge to ballast pumping that has turned into poison has advert effect on water resources. Some have choked too much estuarine water where there is fish spawn. In a nutshell, the two worlds we live are currently out of balance and in potential conflict. Man is in the middle, and since the treat are mostly water related, ship is in the middle too. Historical records of number of calamity that has resulted to heavy lost and pollution call for environmentally sound ship. This has led to a number of regulations today that will subsequently affect policies change and procedures interaction with the system. The current situation has affected the design of new ships and modification of existing ships. This paper review and discuss green technology emanating from regulations and highlight new system design being driven by marine pollution prevention and, protection and control regulation.

Key words: Sustainability, ship, design, environment, safety, mitigation, impact, control.

INTRODUCTION

Human civilization from stone age to industrial, computer, and information to multimedia innovative technological era, work has been mostly about building and forgetting the inherited biosphere environment world that support planetary life. Today human sensitivity is aggressively defining age as an age of sensitivity, safety and environment. Human developmental works for years during this era of transition have been built with oblivion or lack of consciousness to the environment. The term "environmental issues" usually implies one of two interpretations: 1) Wind, waves, tides, sediment characteristics and or other environmental factors involved in

development work 2) Environmental protection in the sense of reducing the negative impact on water, air, soil quality, infrastructure, health and coastal habitat. In the first sense of the term, all concern need to agree that methods for predicting and reporting environmental conditions have greatly improved, especially in the dimension of scientific analysis. This can provide directions to connect necessary dots. In shipping and associated industries, ship protection and marine pollution are respectively interlinked in terms of safety and environment, conventionally ship safety is being dealt with as its occurrence causes environmental problem.

Pollution from maritime industry seems to be small; currently it is approximated to be 3%, especially considering green house gas (GHG) emission. Today

*Corresponding author. E-mail: o.sulaiman@umt.edu.my.

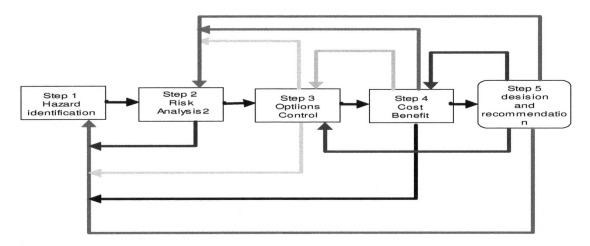

Figure 1. Risk approach.

considering volume of ships in the world ocean, pollution from shipping can be considered to be exponentially rising. Culmination of oversight regarding emission has lead to point form pollution that has contributed to the impact of ozone layer depletion, incessant flooding, global warming and more unknown calamity whose source is hard to be determined seem to be increasing if caution is not exercise in the current ways of doing things. Shipping is not left behind in this, in fact, maritime world seem to be the most to get hit by next big environmental revolt. Pollutions is about accident and accident is about pollution, because, the later is the cause of the former. This paper addresses environmental impacts to ship design with respect to human, safety, ship, reliability, channel, maneuverability factors and marine environment. The paper also emphasizes on the need to incorporate in the ship design spiral, the design process regarding the afore-mentioned enumerated factors, for example environmental issues were never part of the ship design spiral (Erik, 2009; Intertanko, 1998; NMD, 2008).

REVIEW APPROACH

This review paper collected information and used a risk based approach to analyze environmental issue, ship system, current practice and regulatory analysis to deduce prospect green technology and practice for ship. Figure 1 describes the qualitative process of examination of the issue under examination, which involve matching system requirement with regulation to deduce gap and technological requirement. The issue of green ship concept is addressed by analyzing evolving technology. In respect to the afore-mentioned, current situation is examined, policy, demand, mitigation and way to move forward green ship is addressed. Also addressed is importance of simulation and scientific system based risk

analysis, especially for ship complex and dynamic system design, and channel accommodation of large ship movement in port as well as the introduction of marine environment awareness in maritime curriculum. Need to incorporate as much of cybernetic technology in navigational and maritime operations for sustainable and efficient performance is stressed. Actionable marine environment mitigation measure, recommendation for strategies to achieve safe, cost marine ship efficient navigation and protection of the marine environment cost effective state of art sustainable of ship design at planning stage is advised (Intertanko, 1998). Risk based design is advised to be incorporated in decision leading adopting new green technology, the process should include determination of high goal based objectives from gap between system compatibility with compliance couple with hazard identification, this is followed by risk analysis and risk control option, then reliability, system complexity and uncertainty analysis and lastly cost benefit, and sustainability analysis. Figure 1 shows risk approach to process for green ship technology.

Less attention is also given to ship life cycle, material properties, variable and frequency matching with the environment. A situation that has led to unbearable condition like corrosion and other unseen environmental degradation that accumulate into painful catastrophically loses or abrupt system failure. Also in the long run, ship scraping and what happen to the environment after ship scraping is another issue of environment under discussion in International Maritime Organisation (IMO). In ship recycling little or no attention is given to the residual material that finds their ways to pollute the sea (IMO, 1980; Bian et al., 2000). Other areas of concern in the ship design process are consideration for channel design criteria, ships controllability and maneuverability in dredged channels due to rapid erosion. All in all, incorporating preventive and control sensible measures in ship design can only be optimize method and give us confidence reliability on our for environment environmental conservation. Focal areas that need revolutionary changes in ship design that is being identified in this paper (Tarrason et al., 2003) include issue relating to material selection to withstand structural, weight, economical lifecycle anticorrosion and fouling, incorporating ship simulation at early stage of ship design as well as structural scantly to withstand structural function, reliability, integrity, weight and economical lifecycle. Also discussed is incorporation maneuvering ship simulation at early stage of design iteration, incorporate new close loop environmental disposal technology system to make new ships environmental safe towards achieving low pollutions and efficiency ship system.

ENVIRONMENTAL ISSUE AND IMPACT AREAS

Environmental issue becomes a blessing through opening new window of green technology opportunity for conservation, recycling, miniaturization, system integration and management of resources. It is important to start to implement clean ships initiative for ship design, this include optimal choice require to design shipboard pollution control system that will allow waste or hazard treat or process on board or allow integration of such system in existing ship. Most especially, it is necessary to incorporate such system in earlier ship design process through forming basic concept to set aside enough space on board for scalable, efficient proactive and sustainable system (Watson, 1998). There is need to design system that will allow waste to be destroyed on board the ship and those that cannot be destroyed would be treated to level where discharge is harmless. Advert environmental occurrence and impact of recent days, is evolving sensitivity leading to new policies for pollution control and more seem to be coming (WHO, 2003). For example, NOx emission limit compliance and SOx sulfur emission control area (SECA) in the Baltic is an example of best practice that is being implemented. If actions are not taken now, the repercussion could include similitude of inconvenience of discharge regulation, possible more MARPOL special discharge areas and augmentation of confusion caused by waste signature (advert of floating of debris).

Considering the beneficent part of this contemporary issue, environmentally sound ship with self contained pollution control system, can be independent of shore facilities for shipboard waste management and will end up reducing logistic requirement and costs. Time has seen how in economical and inconvenience it is for ships pumping liquid waste to pier side reception facilities, offload solid waste and excess hazardous material for disposal. Where vessels are astronomically being charge substantial costs by private contractors to dispose generated wastes. With this, green ship will nonetheless give the following beneficial business advantages to

maritime industry green ship certification (Karma and Morgan, 1975). With green ship credential, the ships will be among the significant ship of tomorrow, they will be the ship with good pride and public image that will provide leadership definition to shipping companies of tomorrow. They will be safer, environmental friendly (everything around them including marine recourses will be safe). Also, the ship will maintain good relationship with legislation and environmental agencies (hence minimizes the risk of fines and litigation). Green ship will helps in the control of operational pollution, ship movement in waterways, minimizing the risk of an environmental incident and enables companies to demonstrate a proactive approach to environmental protection. Green ship concept will also helps companies to gain recognition of investment in pollution control technology as well as improves operational efficiency will provides confidence that environmental risk is being managed effectively. High levels of environmental performance can create competitive advantage

In today environmentally conscious world, there is already so much pressure on ship owners to minimize the impact of their operations on the environment. More regulations are likely to be enforced; luckily, human civilization is enjoying an age of environmental based innovation and development. Advancement in transportation, information and technology has involved dynamic and complex activities that manage speed, safety, reliability, miniaturization, cost, mobility and networking in most industries efficiently. This poweress of human civilization is evidence that technology that is required to developed efficient low pollution and environmental friendly technology are available. It is matter of exercising more creativity and culture of sharing, complementation available resources within limited time and employing them to meet requirement of sustainable system equity law (safety, cost, speed, efficiency, low pollution etc) (Landsburg et al., 1983).

Major environmental impact areas

Environmental protection is considered a design constraint when evaluating cost, schedule, and performance of systems under development, and product improvement. The engineer need to consider the environmental impact of proposed actions, and mitigation plan required to supports unrestricted operations. This can be achieved by developing, producing, installing, and managing all shipboard equipment, systems, and procedures require reducing and managing shipboard wastes in compliance with existing and anticipated environmental worldwide restrictions. Table 1 shows Global warming potential for from marine activities. This should be done without jeopardizing the ship mission, survivability, or habitability. The major effects of ships environmental effects that must be prevented, protected or control can be in the

Table 1. Global worming potential (GWP) of various compound (RINA. 2007).

Compound	GWP (100 Year ITH)	Inclusion
Cox	1	
NOx	296	Natural occurring compounds
CHX	23	
HFC-134a	1,300	
HFC-227ea	3,500	HFC`s
HFC-c-23a	12,000	
CF	1	Novec 1230 Fire protection fluid

following form of intentional and unintentional discharge from ship (oil, garbage, antifouling paint, and transfer of indigenous species from ballast water), or environmental damage and pollution due to port activities, or disturbance of marine environmental (collision and noise) or intentional and unintentional (emission from energy equipments as well as from scraping of ships at the end of their life cycle) (IMO, 1998; Slocombe, 1993).

Risk associated with environmental issue in ship design (MSA, 1995) involve i) accidental risk: that includes marine accident that could result to that oil spills which then end up degrading the environment. Group of Expert on Scientific Aspect of Marine Environmental Protection (GESAMP) reported that 300 to 400 thousands of oil that entered the world ocean according to (GESAMP, 1993) was caused by collision with marine mammal, which then cause propeller injuries, hence more economic losses. ii) Operational risks: socio economic impacts to marine ecology, habitat, and coastal infrastructures are affected through operational activities that result to oil spill, emission, ballast water, garbage, dredge contamination, and antifouling. Other accident risk are vessel, channel and maneuverability risk: in the context of ship design, the impacts areas are related to shipping trends, channel design criteria, ship maneuverability, ship controllability, and use of simulators in channel studies. Since World War II many nations built port but forget about maintaining them according to larger ships being produced by shipyards. Physical dimension and ratio of ships to channel that have impact in today's ship controllability design include Increase in ship beam expansion where as channel width is not, length/beam (L/B) ratio; Radius of turns and turning areas-radius of turns is directly related to navigation safety and protection of the marine environment, large rudder angles are needed to navigate small radius turns rudder size, this is hardly critically taken into consideration in ship design work; Power/tonnage ratio and minimum bare steerage speed and windage;

Over the last decade, each passing years has been augmented with concerned about issue of environment. The issue touch all area of human endeavors, in maritime technology this include design, construction, operation and beneficial disposal of marine articraft. The non renewable energy source that has driven past technology has ended up with increasing the resources of the planet, but depleting components of environment that support life. This has accumulated to production that demands long term sustainability of the earth. Precipitated point form pollution effect over the year is currently calling for public awareness and it translating into impacts of the following areas described (Barry, 1993):

i) Commercial forces: this include situation of company or product that operate in unenvironmental friendly way, people are prone to spurn the company's products and service. This has impact on company return on investment.

ii) Regulations: public pressure on governmental and non-governmental organization regulating environmental impacts due to untold stories of disaster and impact. The public is very concerned about quality of life of people and the need for it is to be sustained. To meet their requirement and need of the future generation, then the environment must be protected. Conspicuous issue, expertise and new finding on multidimensional uncertainty make them to go extra length on unseen issue. Contrasting between the first two, commercial force action on can become forth problems.

iii) Water, air and soil pollution: Water volume that support the planet, scarcity of land, Global warming and health impacts.

iv) Ship concept design: is very important in shipping and it account for 80% of failure, therefore compliance and making of optimal design at concept stage has a great impact in ship whole life cycle. The impact of environment in ship design is very difficult because of large numbers of associated uncertainties within the phases of design process.

Environmental impact that need to be taken into considerations in concept design that take into consideration (IMO, 2000) construction and associated elements of pollution, this comes into picture when multidirectional thinking give wisdom on what happen during transportation, material handling and what is being released to the nearby rivers. Operations considering limiting life cycle of ships at estimate of 20 years, issues relating to operation are equally not easy to quantify in design work. Even thus a lot of research effort has been set on to move on this. But the call of the day requires allowable clearance and solution to be given to accidental, ballast waste, fouling and biodiversification. Disposal: issue of disposal that cover waste and emission and as well as what to do with the ship at the end of her life cycle. And finally energy and environment: The case of air pollution, global warming, ozone depletion and climate change.

i) Commercial forces: this include situation of company or product that operate in unenvironmental friendly way, people are prone to spurn the company's products and service. This has impact on company return on investment.

ii) Regulations: public pressure on governmental and non-governmental organization regulating environmental impacts due to untold stories of disaster and impact. The public is very concerned about quality of life of people and the need for it is to be sustained. To meet their requirement and need of the future generation, then the environment must be protected. Conspicuous issue, expertise and new finding on multidimensional uncertainty make them to go extra length on unseen issue. Contrasting between the first two, commercial force action on can become forth problems.

iii) Water, air and soil pollution: Water volume that support the planet, scarcity of land, Global warming and health impacts.

iv) Ship concept design: is very important in shipping and it account for 80 percent of failure, therefore compliance and making of optimal design at concept stage has a great impact in ship whole life cycle. The impact of environment in ship design is very difficult because of large numbers of associated uncertainties within the phases of design process. Environmental impact that need to be taken into considerations in concept design can be classified into the following (IMO, 2000):

a) Construction: this involve pollution, this comes into picture when multidirectional thinking give wisdom on what happen during transportation, material handling and what is being released to the nearby rivers.

b) Operations: considering limiting life cycle of ships at estimate of 20 years, issues relating to operation are equally not easy to quantify in design work. Even thus a lot of research effort has been set on move on this. But the call of the day requires allowable clearance and solution to be given to accidental, ballast waste, fouling and bio-diversification.

c) Disposal: issue of disposal that cover waste and emission and as well as what to do with the ship at the end of her life cycle.

d) Energy and environment: The case of air pollution, global warming, ozone depletion and climate change

International Maritime Organization (IMO) gets serious

Evidence about the volume of the water planetary percentile, how significant this is to the safeguard of the planet and conversely the volume of ships that ply every day the ocean of the world put pressure from land based environmental organization to sea based regulatory governor (IMO, 2000; De Leeuw et al., 2001).

Important IMO Conventions (http://www.imo.org/About/Conventions/ListOfConventions)

i) International Convention for the Safety of Life at Sea (SOLAS), 1974, as amended
ii) International Convention for the Prevention of Pollution from Ships, 1973, as modified by the Protocol of 1978 relating thereto and by the Protocol of 1997(MARPOL)
iii) International Convention on Standards of Training, Certification and Watch keeping for Seafarers (STCW) as amended, including the 1995 and 2010 Manila Amendments.

Other conventions relating to maritime safety and security and ship/port interface

i) Convention on the International Regulations for Preventing Collisions at Sea (COLREG), 1972
ii) Convention on Facilitation of International Maritime Traffic (FAL), 1965
iii) International Convention on Load Lines (LL), 1966
iv) International Convention on Maritime Search and Rescue (SAR), 1979
v) Convention for the Suppression of Unlawful Acts Against the Safety of Maritime Navigation (SUA), 1988, and Protocol for the Suppression of Unlawful Acts Against the Safety of Fixed Platforms located on the Continental Shelf (and the 2005 Protocols)
International Convention for Safe Containers (CSC), 1972
Convention on the International Maritime Satellite Organization (IMSO C), 1976
The Torremolinos International Convention for the Safety of Fishing Vessels (SFV), 1977
vi) International Convention on Standards of Training, Certification and Watchkeeping for Fishing Vessel Personnel (STCW-F), 1995
Special Trade Passenger Ships Agreement (STP), 1971 and Protocol on Space Requirements for Special Trade Passenger Ships, 1973
vii) Other conventions relating to prevention of marine pollution

Table 2. MARPOL Coverage.

MARPOL (Annex)	Coverage
I	Oil
II	Noxious liquid chemicals
III	Harmful Goods (package)
III	Sewage
III	Garbage
VI	Emission and air pollution -SOx, NOx and green house gas Green House Gas (GHG), emission of ozone depletion gas (ODG)Ozone Depletion Gas (ODG)

viii) International Convention Relating to Intervention on the High Seas in Cases of Oil Pollution Casualties (INTERVENTION), 1969

Convention on the Prevention of Marine Pollution by Dumping of Wastes and Other Matter (LC), 1972 (and the 1996 London Protocol)

ix) International Convention on Oil Pollution Preparedness, Response and Co-operation (OPRC), 1990

Protocol on Preparedness, Response and Co-operation to pollution Incidents by Hazardous and Noxious Substances, 2000 (OPRC-HNS Protocol)

x) International Convention on the Control of Harmful Anti-fouling Systems on Ships (AFS), 2001

International Convention for the Control and Management of Ships' Ballast Water and Sediments, 2004

The Hong Kong International Convention for the Safe and Environmentally Sound Recycling of Ships, 2009

xi) Conventions covering liability and compensation

xii) International Convention on Civil Liability for Oil Pollution Damage (CLC), 1969,

1992 Protocol to the International Convention on the Establishment of an International Fund for Compensation for Oil Pollution Damage (FUND 1992)

Convention relating to Civil Liability in the Field of Maritime Carriage of Nuclear Material (NUCLEAR), 1971

Athens Convention relating to the Carriage of Passengers and their Luggage by Sea (PAL), 1974

Convention on Limitation of Liability for Maritime Claims (LLMC), 1976

International Convention on Liability and Compensation for Damage in Connection with the Carriage of Hazardous and Noxious Substances by Sea (HNS), 1996 (and its 2010 Protocol)

International Convention on Civil Liability for Bunker Oil Pollution Damage, 2001

Nairobi International Convention on the Removal of Wrecks, 2007

Other subjects convention

i) International Convention on Tonnage Measurement of Ships (TONNAGE), 1969

ii) International Convention on Salvage (SALVAGE), 1989

Policies and procedures build-up: Pollution / emission prevention and control

The earlier pollution regulation by IMO work under International convention for the prevention of pollution from ships involves (MARPOL) 1973. It covers accidental and operational oil pollution as well as pollution by chemicals, goods in packaged form, sewage, and garbage. Its adoption was later modified to follow tacit procedure by protocol of 1978 relating thereto (MARPOL 1973, 1978) because of urgency of implementation, (Table 2). New annex to MARPOL have been introduced in diplomatic conference because of need of the time. Especially annex VI was quickly adopted, but allowances are given for independent adoption and implementation because of environmental geographical differences, resources availability and also because lack of enough evidence of data (IMO, 2008).

Other areas where IMO focus on are process and facilitation and system base framework like the use of formal safety assessment and International Safety Management (ISM) check list and, documentation, and provision of International safety management. Annex is the latest that is attracting more scurrility like oxide of nitrogen (NOx) limit for new design, collection of air pollution data by al ports, sulfur emission control area. Table 2 illustrates MARPOL (1973, 1978). New Annex to MARPOL covers i) control and management of ballast water to minimize transfer of harmful foreign species EMS, 2000). ii) Global prohibition of Tributyltin (TBT) in antifouling coating - phase out in 2008. iii) Control and management of emission from ship combustion machineries (Annex VI). Other areas IMO gets serious are: i) Marine environmental protection committee (MEPC), IMO technical committee forming subcommittee on specific issue to implement regulation towards necessary mitigation. ii) International Convention on oil Pollution, Response and Cooperation (OPRC), 1990: policy to combat major incidents or threats of marine pollution through port state control (PSC) to prevent mitigates or eliminates danger to the coastline from a maritime casualty. Protocol under this convention covers marine pollution by hazardous and noxious substance (HNS Protocol). ii) The IMO proposal to regulate the use of TBT-based antifouling paints. A ban on application of

TBT-based paints in 2003 and a total ban in 2008 is suggested. In anticipation of new regulations, the marine paint industry has developed alternatives to tributyltin self-polishing copolymers (TBT-SPCs). iii) IMO establishment of safety management system (SMS). and This is a part of the requirement for obtaining and maintaining ISM certification.

As a result of this, international environmental organizations are seriously encouraging all concerned parties to galvanize their community by setting up panels, collaborating with scientists and technical bodies, to encourage the use of existing scientific bodies and research centers for global observation systems. This includes the taping of the informal sources of information related to early warning as part of the solution to deal with the problem of sharing data among countries, as well using human capacity and the rapid spread of internet as a tool for information compilation, discussions and news dissemination. Some of the land and sea based regulations that have been passed are IMO (1997), Murphy (1996), Ronald (1997): i) MARPOL (1978): Cover Annex I, includes Oil, Annex II - Noxious liquid chemicals, Annex III - Harmful Goods (package), Annex IV - Sewage, Annex V - Ballast water. ii) Adoption of control and prevention measures in 2003 by IMO, as well as problems associated with the transfer of harmful aquatic organisms in ships' ballast water to address greenhouse gas emissions. iii) IMO also passed the MARPOL Annex VI during a diplomatic conference and bypassed the usual tacit procedure. Whereby Annex VI - emission and air pollution SOx, NOx and green house gas, emission of ozone depletion gas (ODG). iv) Adopt the convention in 2004 to support the International Convention on the Control of Harmful Anti-fouling Systems on Ships 2001. The diplomatic conference also addressed the implementation of the International Convention on Oil Pollution Preparedness, Response and Co-operation 1990. vi) Global prohibition of TBT in antifouling coating - phase out scheduled for 2008. vii) International convention on oil pollution response and cooperation (OPRC) (1990). viii) Policy to combat major accidents or threats, control to prevent, mitigate or eliminate the danger of marine pollution from the port to its coastline from a maritime casualty. ix) Protocol on the carriage of hazardous and noxious substances (HNS). x) Oil Spills Protocol: Protocol Concerning Specially Protected Areas and Wildlife (SPAW Protocol). xii) Protocol Concerning Pollution from Land-based Sources and Activities (LBS Protocol). xii) Agenda 21 debut on sustainable development.

Maritime work and regulation has always been a top down set-up, as a result of IMO seriousness on environmental issue various maritime organization follow suite, some of the development that follows IMO actions leads to classification societies to aggressively building service on environment protection, notation, and various performance indicators to get all concern committed to running an environmentally sound ships. This include Lloyds through risk assessment holistic method deduce effects and framework for clean ship the benchmark standard and DnV has equally lunched Environmental Ballast Water Management Assessment (EMBLA) database integrated project that will manage discharge of ballast water. Other institution that take beyond compliance measure include the European Union, recently the European Union has embarked on multinational project call On Board Treatment of Ballast Water (MARTOB) ballast water. Also Montreal Protocol was passed, where some 110 governments attended Parties to the Montreal Protocol, in September 1997 where several important decisions were reached, including the tightening of restrictions on several destructive chemicals. Others global organization measure include the export of hazardous waste from Organization for Economic Cooperation and Development (OECD) countries to non-OECD countries is banned under the convention; this ban entered into force in 1998 in the EU countries. Local involve Nordic tanker, where, Trim optimization by NORDEN/Green Steam and Nordic Tankers was introduced. Effort by company involves real-time analysis of bunker quality and emissions by A. P. Møller and automated engine monitoring by Man and A. P. Møller

Policies and procedures build-up for collision preventions and control measures

Although ships may spend 90 to 98% of their operational lives underway at sea speed in deep water, it is during the mandatory beginning and end of every voyage when the risk of collisions and groundings are highest. Ensuring the ability to maintain complete and positive control of a ship's movement during these segments of a voyage is absolutely vital if that risk of navigation safety and protection of the marine environment is to be reduced. According to Intertanko's (1996) on port and putting bigger and bigger ships (and more of them) into the same old channel has been going on for a long time, to mitigate collision whose occurrence lead to environmental problem. The design recommended limit for trim by the stern for a tanker is 0.015L in accordance with Regulation 13 of MARPOL (1973, 1978), Annex I. This information, which is based on tests conducted in deepwater, includes a turning circle diagram as well as tables showing time and distance to stop the vessel from full and half-speed. IMO Resolution A601 (15), which was adopted in 1987, contains recommendations for ensuring maneuvering information is available on board the ship, furthermore, The 1995 Seafarers' Training, Certification and Watch keeping STCW Code, Section A-VIII/2 part 3-1, and article 49 require the master and pilot to "exchange information regarding navigation procedures, local conditions and the ship's characteristics." Also, Marine Board study assessed the use of numerical

Table 3. Parameters demand and Impact.

Environmental parameters	Environmental Demand	Impact areas
Ship design,	Need for longer safe life cycle	New limit definition, correct material selection, Material technology, quality control of safety and environment
Construction	High worker safety standards, low energy input	Improved hull hydrodynamic,
Emission	Minimum pollution and emission, Minimum SOx, NOx and green house gas-zero discharge	Advance close loop process on board, waste recycling equipment, improve training
Scrapping	Zero harmful emission	Beneficial disposal
Operations waste,	Efficient maneuverability	Improve maneuverability

simulation technology to train mariners and concluded that while modeling accuracy is sufficient for deep-water operations; modeling requires refinement to provide the accuracy needed for shallow and restricted water operations (Kågeson, 1999; Huey, 1997).

Ship design policy build-up

In 1971, IMO adopted Resolution A.209 (VII) establishing recommendations regarding posting maneuvering regulation II-1/29.3.2 of SOLAS requires rudder movement from 35° on either side to 35° to the other side within 28 s or less. IMO approved circular MSC/Circ.389 in 1985 establish interim guidelines for estimating the maneuverability. This include rudder size and effectiveness, ability to transit at slow forward speed, propulsion and propeller characteristics, number of available engine reversals, adequate horsepower for control, extra reserve rudder angle needed to allow for ship crabbing from wind forces or moored ship suction, visibility from bridge and bridge arrangement, hull form squat (trim and sink age) characteristics and also, effect of bank forces on moorings and passing ships, air draft, emergency anchoring ability, amount of tow line leads and line access (MARPOL, 1978).

Current ship design practice

Existing design tools cannot, at least with any degree of reliability is required to be used to design a vessel and ensure that it will ensure environmental reliability and adequate maneuverability in shallow or restricted waters. Neither can it be used to satisfy demand need by clean ships. In part this is because of the extreme on-linearity of hull and propulsion characteristics under these conditions. In general, naval architects and marine engineers are to be educated and equipped with knowledge, skills, and design processes that permit continuous checking and balancing of constraints and design tradeoffs of

vessel capabilities as the design progresses. The intended result of the design process is the best design given the basic requirements of speed, payload, and endurance to achieve sustainable system design. Also, ship design focus is not placed on how the channels and waterways are designed. Even more importantly, there is a general lack of understanding of the operational scenario regarding piloting of vessels in constrained waterways. Only recently has there been a real attempt to fully integrate human operational practices with vessel design. The involvement of human beings on board vessels both extends and restricts the inherent vessel maneuvering capabilities. This also complicates the necessary methodology for assuring safe and efficient operations.

Taking waste, pollution issue and restricted waterway maneuverability as an important part of ship design spiral would be a necessary step to enabling proper tradeoffs in vessel design. The reality is that maneuverability and pollution protection is still not an important consideration in ship design of many merchant ships. The result is that design decisions that can compromise environment and collision are decided in favor of other factors. Consideration for full range of ship, channel design, environment, maneuverability, technology and human factors relationships offer opportunity to achieve high efficient and safe environmental friendly sustainable marine transportation. The new challenge of environment is also a reminder for need to squeeze in more stuff in the design spiral. Table 3 shows demand and impact parameters for technological signature.

Environmental mitigation toward green technology (pollution prevention protection and control measure)

Shipboard waste and emission prevention, protection and control

Treatment and elimination -pollution prevention or pollution control (P^2C) is backbone of the thrust in achieving

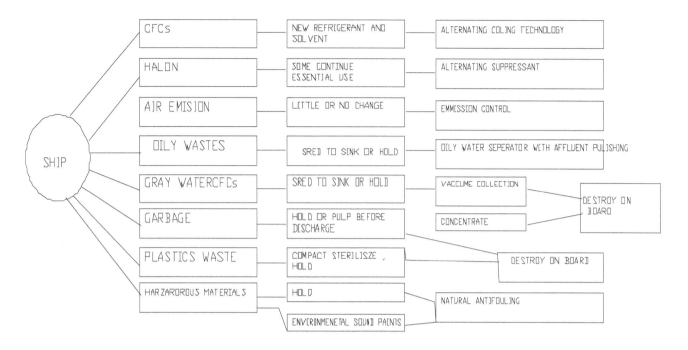

Figure 2. Strategies for green ship technology.

clean ship system and technology. Pollution prevention uses fewer environmentally harmful sub-stances and generates less waste on board. Pollution control: involve increase treatment, processing, or destruction of wastes on board. The basic of P²C prin-ciples follows elimination of the use of environmentally harmful chemicals, such as ozone-depleting substance (ODSs), toxic antifouling hull coatings, and other hazardous materials, through the best approach for dealing with some potential problems. Reducing the amount of waste being generated on board is often better than treating it on board. For example, reducing the amount of plastics and other packaging materials taken aboard can simplify solid and plastics waste management. Similarly, reducing the volume of liquid wastes generated (such as gray water) may simplify onboard liquid-waste treatment system and ope-ration. Figure 2 shows strategies for green ship techno-logy. Table 4 shows environmental impact and response. Table 5 describes reduction potential from research conducted in Europe (NRL, 2008).

For the wastes and hazardous materials that cannot be prevented, it is important to develop pollution-control strategies and technologies categories, other technical mitigation measures are:

1) Antifouling: Toxic approach uses other metals such copper and zinc, or agrochemicals for example, triazines. Fouling release is confronted by the use physical properties of low surface energy coating that cause the very weak attachment of fouling organisms. For example, silicone based coating. Fouling deterrence marine organism not known for fouling like corals are use. Mobile hull cleaning is also being use operationally

2) Ballast water discharge: On board treatment of chemical (chlorination), physical treatment (Ultra violet light, heat treatment), filtration and cyclonic separation, shore base treatment is sometime being used but not common. Operational mitigation based on information of biological difference between coastal ocean water where ballasting and deballasting is done accordingly.

3) Air emission: Sulfur reduction in bunker fuel. Nitrogen reduction to choice of propulsion system (retrofit). On board emission control retrofitting system like, water injection, emulsion operationally speed reduction and use of shore power connection can be implemented

a) Ship to be scrap may contain on-board consumables hazardous wastes. Unless subjected to prior cleaning, these substances will follow the vessel to the ship breaking facility. Most ship dismantling occurs in developing countries. The Basel Convention controls the trans-boundary movements and disposal of hazardous wastes. Up to now dismantling sites have been chosen by ship owners on a commercial basis. This has resulted in ship dismantling activities today being mainly per-formed in a few developing countries (India, Bangladesh and Pakistan with increasing interest in China, Vietnam and the Philippines) where there is little or no alternative employment for the workforce and where safety, health and environment regulations applicable in most of the developed countries are not applied. The dismantling procedures used can result in hazardous conditions for

Table 4. Environmental impact and response (EU, 2002).

Environmental impact	Mitigation science	Mitigation response
More energy and power means more emission	Maximum fuel efficiency	environmental friendly retrofit and hybrid design, use of alternative energy
Antifouling	Harmless	Biocide free technology
Ballast water	Zero biological invasion or transfer of alien species	Segregated ballast tanks, improved ballast water tank design, ballast water treatment, ballast water data base
Sea mamma Interaction	Maneuverability capability	Safer ship structure design, Improve maneuvering capability, Navigation aid, misinformation, exchange, reeducation
Accident	Able officer, Ship structure, Integrity	New monitoring through port sate control
Fire	Harmless	Halon phase out
Wave wash of high speed marine craft	Zero inundation and spray ashore	Moderation of hydrodynamic force

the workforce and both local and global pollution of the environment. This issue concern related to ship dismantling has been raised in the UN, and the potential for improvements in ship dismantling is believed to be significant and important environmental aspects for ship at the end of their life. Methods used at present in the ship demolition industry to recover the values represented by scrap materials themselves create contamination and pollution. The discharge of gases from cutting and burn-off operations presents a threat to the environment as well as to the individuals exposed. Important environmental aspects of concern with ship breaking are Cathodic protection (Al, Zn), Batteries (Pb, Cd, Ni and sulphuric acid) Coatings and paint (PCB, Cu, Zn, Cl and TBT), Fire fighting agents, Refrigerants dichlorodifluoromethane (Freon-12), and chlorodi-fluormethane (R22), Thermal insulation (asbestos, PCB), The hull and large steel structures (Fe), Electrical system (Cu, PVC, PCB, Pb, Hg), m. Hydrocarbons and cargo residues.

Ship collision prevention (safety and environmental prevention, protection and control measure)

Most accident is attributed to a flagrant controllability problem. They remain the classic impetus necessary to make improvements to safety and environmental protection. There is need to ensure adequate vessel maneuverability perhaps better matching of vessel, channel, and operational practices.

1) Ship maneuverability as major iterative element of design spiral: Ship maneuverability is not considered

particularly important during the design process. Because owners generally do not include maneuverability require-ments as part of the design specification; Firm deep- and shallow/restricted water maneuvering standards that can be applied during the design process should be established.

2) Modeling and simulation: Collection of data using dual frequency differential global positioning system (DGPS) receivers and proper analysis needs to be supported to enable unlocking understanding of restricted water operations.

Antifouling

a) Toxic approach uses other metals such copper and zinc, or agrochemicals for example, triazines
b) Fouling release is confronted by the use physical properties of low surface energy coating that cause the very weak attachment of fouling organisms. For example, silicone based coating
c) Fouling deterrence marine organism not know for fouling like corals are use
d) Mobile hull cleaning is also being use operationally

Ballast water discharge

a) On board treatment of chemical (chlorination), physical treatment (Ultra violet light, heat treatment), filtration and cyclonic separation, shore base treatment is sometime being used but not common.
b) Operational mitigation based on information of

Table 5. Reduction potentials (NTNU, 2005).

Primary measures:	Secondary measures:	Operationally	Retrofitting for existing engines	For new engines
1. Use of low sulfur fuel – (less than 6 g/kwh)	1. Exhaust gas cleaning system or technology Sox for SECA (Emission Control Area) & Fuel change over.	1. On board Catalytic system like: Converter, water injection Emulsion	1. Use of NOx injectors.	1. Engine certification
2. HFO sulfur content - Need for oil company to change their equipment for low sulfur oil production-> ship-owner will face high cost, additive solution has been expensive so far	2. Nitrogen reduction through choice of propulsion system	2. speed reduction (10 to 20%).	2. Retarding injection timing	2. Pre-certification,
3. Reduction of NOx, SOx, + cost saving through boiled off gas reuse.	3. Sulfur reduction -in bunker fuel	3. Use of shore power connection	3. Temperature control of the charge air.	3. Technical file clarification on engine family and group,
	4. Reliquification plants for Liquified Natural Gas (LNG)/Liquified Petroleum Gas(LPG) carriers	4. Dual fuel option for low sulfur restricted areas (1.5-4.5), this comes with need for additional tanks.	4. Exhaust gas recirculation (EGR)	4. Final certification
	5. Use of Turbo generator plant –> Paticulate matter (PM)- SAC volume is the void space in the fuel valve downstream of the closing face	5. The content of hydrocarbons in the exhaust gas from large diesel engines depends on the type of fuel, the engine adjustment and design.	5. Fuel / water emulsion	5. Alfa Lubricator system
			6. Water injection	6. Reduction in cylinder oil consumption-> reduction in particulate emission
			7. Humid air motor (HAM) technique- addition of wet steam to the engine 50% reduction	7. Electronic control engine Programmed fuel injection for exhaust valve emission reduction
			8. Selective catalytic reduction (SCR)	8. Use of high efficiency air flow for power take off reduces fuel and reduction of emission.

biological difference between coastal ocean water where ballasting and deballasting is done accordingly.

Air emission

a) Sulfur reduction in bunker fuel
b) Nitrogen reduction to choice of propulsion system (retrofit)
c) On board emission control retrofitting system

like, water injection, emulsion
d) Operationally speed reduction and use of shore power connection can be implemented

Ship to be scrap may contain on-board consumables may hazardous wastes

Unless subjected to prior cleaning, these substances will follow the vessel to the ship breaking facility. Most ship dismantling occurs in

developing countries. The Basel Convention controls the transboundary movements and disposal of hazardous wastes. Up to now dismantling sites have been chosen by ship owners on a commercial basis. This has resulted in ship dismantling activities today being mainly performed in a few developing countries (India, Bangladesh and Pakistan with increasing interest in China, Vietnam and the Philippines) where there is little or no alternative employment for the workforce and where safety, health and

Table 6. Development coalition control services model (Pedersen, 1992).

Model	Environmental performance
Kutsuro Kijima	Showed a modeling approach that permitted analysis of passing situations of vessels in waterways that would help set procedural standards for safe passing vessels in port.
IanDand	Reported on the development of models for ship squat model those have shown very good accuracy over the years.
Larry Daggett	Described the advent of dual frequency DGPS receivers and their role in gathering full-scale ship trial data. In addition to the excellent horizontal accuracy of the normal DGPS receiver, these receivers provide vertical location with an accuracy measured in centimeters.

environment regulations applicable in most of the developed countries are not applied.

The dismantling procedures used can result in hazardous conditions for the workforce and both local and global pollution of the environment. This issue concern that is related to ship dismantling has been raised in the UN, and the potential for improvements in ship dismantling is believed to be significant. Important environmental aspects for ship at the end of their life. Methods used at present in the ship demolition industry to recover the values represented by scrap materials themselves create contamination and pollution. The discharge of gases from cutting and burn-off operations presents a threat to the environment as well as to the individuals exposed. Important environmental aspects of concern with ship breaking are:

a) Cathodic protection (Al, Zn)
b) Batteries (Pb, Cd, Ni and sulphuric acid)
c) Coatings and paint (PCB, Cu, Zn, Cl and TBT)
d) Fire fighting agents
e) Refrigerants dichlorodifluoromethane (Freon-12), and chlorodifluormethane (R22)
f) Thermal insulation (asbestos, PCB)
g) The hull and large steel structures (Fe)
h) Electrical system (Cu, PVC, PCB, Pb, Hg)
i) Hydrocarbons and cargo residues

MAJOR FINDING AND BEST PRACTICE GREEN SHIP TECHNOLOGY

Environmental technology also becomes a serious issue of environment represent start of another revolution in human history. Today environmental technology product and services are booming. The major environmental aspects related to maintaining machinery and auxiliary systems are oil (additives), coolants, gases, electrical/electronic waste, seals, insulation, and scrap-metals. The maintenance system shall design targets strategies that provide continuous improvement of existing procedures and routines. Improvements in maintenance are mainly motivated by cost reduction, and increased operational reliability and safety conside-rations, but often have positive environmental conse-quence in addition. Table 5, 6 and 7 shows some resent environmental performance products. A number of promising developments that exist today are shown in Figures 3 and 4. For green ship project, conventional wastes and emissions must be control according to the present strategy for treating or eliminating these wastes using the aforementioned principle behavior of system (Pedersen et al., 1992).

Green house emission green technology

Recent critical environmental revolt such as the issue of the rising sea levels and floods has brought about a sense of awareness with regards to environmental degradation. There is an increased awareness that everything on this planet is interconnected. Water will flow to the rivers through the ground and eventually end up in the sea. This makes the management of the quality of water and air, the balance of their purity and the prevention of the substance running into them a crucial point in protecting the environment from further deterioration (IMO, 2000). High pressure associated with air pollution due to the rapid climate change, led IMO diplomatic conferences to the new Annex VI, Chapter III which deals with the requirements for the control of emissions from ships including (IMO, 2000):

i) Regulation 12: Ozone depletion substances
ii) Regulation 13: NOx
iii) Regulation 14: SOx
iv) Regulation 15: Volatile organic compounds
v) Regulation 16: Shipboard incinerator
vi) Regulation 17: Reception facilities
vii) Regulation 18: Fuel oil requirement
viii) Regulation 19: Requirement for platform and drilling rigs.

Table 7. Environmental performance technology (NREL, 2008).

Product	Target	Environmental performance
200-Ton air-conditioning plant conversion kit	Ozone safe substances:	The CG-47and DDG-51 plants have been successfully converted to the ozone-friendly refrigerant HFC-236fa where conversion kit has been established by Naval Surface Warfare Center, Carderock Division (NSWCCD).
Waste pulpers	Solid waste: Solid	The pulper is the machine into which you dump tremendous quantities of paper, cardboard, or food waste. The waste mixes with seawater to form slurry, which is then discharged overboard. Studies show an immediate 100,000-to-1 dilution when discharged into the wake of a ship. Ships equipped with a pulper can dispose of their paper, cardboard, and food waste just about anywhere and at anytime at sea including MARPOL areas.
OWS oil water separator (OWS) and Bilge water Polishers	Liquid waste	These bilge cleaners the US Navy uses, it contain long-lasting emulsifying agents, which produce stable oil-in-water emulsions that shipboard OWSs cannot effectively process.
Valve gauge		Valve gauge assembly developed by NSWCCD the ring-gauge isolator to improve the reliability of sanitary waste system sewage transfer-pump suction and discharge gauges [8]. Figure 2 shows the valve gauge assembly.
Integrated liquid discharge system	Therma destruction	NRL plan for concept where ultrafiltration membrane systems would concentrate bilgewater, graywater, and sewage (as previously described); the clean effluents would be discharged; and the concentrates would be evaporated/incinerated in a thermal-destruction system (Figure 3)

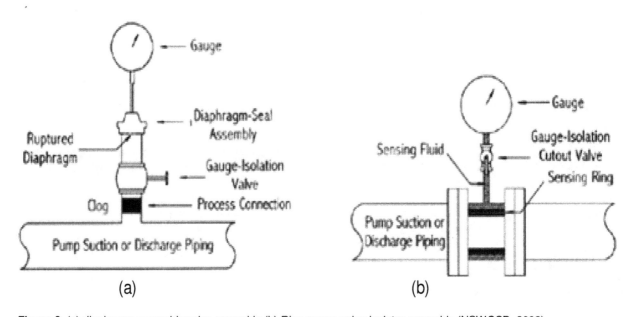

Figure 3. (a) diaphragm assembly valve assemble (b) Ring gauge valve isolator assembly (NSWCCD, 2008).

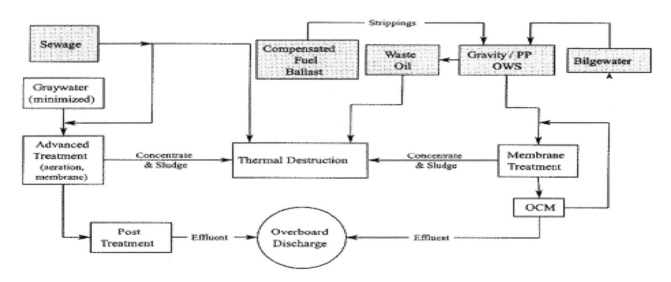

Figure 4. Integrated liquid discharge system concept (NREL, 2008).

Table 8. Emission and reduction measures (NTNU, 2007).

Category	Components	Sources	Current method of reduction
Emission to air	COx	Machineries/incinerator/boiler	Operational and energy efficiency measures
	SOx	Machineries/incinerator/boiler	Low sulfur fuel exhaust washing
	NOx	Machineries/incinerator/boiler	Exhaust cleaning, engine modification, or input media
	HC	Machineries/incinerator/boiler	Exhaust gas recirculation
	Noise	Machineries/cargo operations	Insulation
	Particles	Machineries/incinerator/boiler	Electronics lubrication and injection
	HFC/Halon	Fire extinguisher / refrigeration system	vapor return, recovery plant
	VOC	Cargo operation	Sequential loading

Fossil fuel is considered as the single largest contributor to emissions. Apart from the NOx and SOx regulation which has been introduced, COx smoke emission is likely to be regulated. To facilitate the adoption to emission regulations, operators, officers, engine builders, yards and ship-owners are doubling their efforts to adopt new technologies to make this earth a better place to live in. However of late, the issue became increasingly serious with the Marine Environment Protection Committee (MEPC) in its 60th session on 22 to 26 March, 2010 concluding that more work needs to be done before it could finalized the proposed mandatory application of technical and operational measures which was designed to regulate and reduce the emission of greenhouse gases (GHGs) from international shipping. IMO has been waiting for the outcome of the COP 15 before they hit the industry with the new emission regulations where unilateral options for the maritime industry were being considered. The technical and operational measures which was adopted includes the interim guideline on the methods of calculation and the voluntary verification of

the Energy Efficiency Design Index (EEDI) for new ships, which will stimulate innovation and the technical development of all the elements influencing the energy efficiency of a ship, as well as the guidance on the development of a Ship Energy Efficiency Management Plan for all ships in operation. Table 8 shows potential achieve-ment to implementation of the technology (IMO, 1997; Psaraftis, 2009).

The main area to meet emission reduction targets, Machinery WHR, scrubbers, EGR, etc.

i) Propulsion: Propellers, rudders, trim optimization, etc.
ii) Operations: Route planning, performance monitoring, etc.
iii) Logistics: Better interaction between transport forms, envelopment development /modification of existing ship types etc.

Tables 8 and 9 show strategies to reduce air pollution from ship. In respect to operations, companies have used

Table 9. Machineries.

Waste heat recovery system	A. P. Møller – MAN, Aalborg Industries, Odense Lindø Shipyard		6. Use main engine exhaust gas heat that contains hot energy that is transformed to steam. The steam can be used for cargo and fuel heating power generation - 7-14% of fuel can be saved from heat recovery system (Hinrich, 2004)
Exhaust Gas Recirculation system	MAN, A.P. Møller	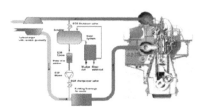	NOx is formed at high temperature; therefore, its formulation can be reduced by lowering the temperature in the system. Exhaust gas can be recirculated, where some is mixed scavenge air to reduce the oxygen content, and consequential reduction in temperature in the system. The technology has potential to reduce Nox by 80%.
Water in fuel emulsion (WIF)	MAN and A. P. Møller		Reduction of 30 to 35% NOx can be achieved by adding water to the fuel before injection
Scrubbers	Aalborg Industries and DFDS		This technology can be used to control future regulation of SOx release. The scrubber use water to wash the sulfur out of the exhaust gas. Testing of the system has shown SOx reduction of 98% and simultaneous reduction of harmful particle late matter are reduced by 80%.
Optimization of pump system and cooling systems	DESMI, APV, Odense Lindø, Grontmij Carl-Bro		20% electrical power generation reduction can be achieved by using optimized cooling water system. Also 90% power saving, can be achieved can be reduced through reduction in pump resistance. Pump size can also be reduced via this technology
LNG for aux. engines and gas turbines	Mols-Linen and DTU		Most diesel engine in harbor run in diesel, by using switching to LNG to run auxiliary engine under fuel arrangement, 20% of Cox35% of NOx can be achieved
Selective Catalytic Reduction	Dansk Teknologi and Danish Navy		
Turbo charging with variable nozzles	MAN and ABB	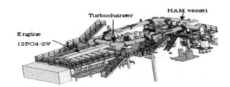	

Figure 5. Maersk line.

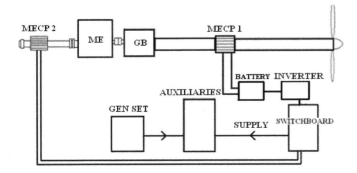

Figure 6. Magneto electric system model (UMT, 2010).

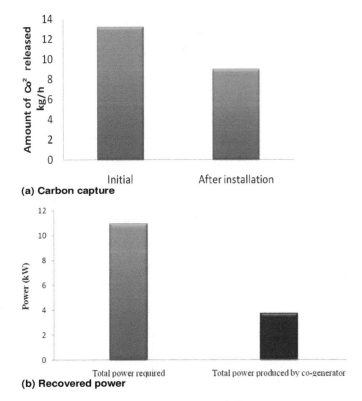

(a) Carbon capture

(b) Recovered power

Figure 7. Magneto electric model result (UMT, 2010).

voyage planning, •marine Institution established student forum that focus on green ship technologies, other arrangement at sea include introduction of 'Green shipping' in the working procedures onboard and implementation of constant focus on energy saving possibilities on the ships. In respect to logistics better transport planning, better tools for evaluation of the most, energy efficient transport forms and better cooperation between the transport providers are current practice that are working to reduce pollution (Murphy, 1996).

i) Another best practice is the case of MASRK ship a 8500 TEU container vessel, optimised with (Figure 5) waste heat recovery exhaust boilers, power and steam turbine technology
ii) Water in fuel technology (WIF), exhaust gas recycling (EGR), exhaust gas scrubber extra costs 30 mill USD (approx 10% of new building costs).
iii) Waste heat recovery exhaust boilers
iv) Power and steam turbine technology
v) Water in fuel technology (WIF)
vi) Exhaust gas recycling (EGR)
vii) Exhaust gas scrubber extra costs 30 mill USD (approx 10% of new building costs)

The goals were to have -30% reductions of CO_2 emissions, achieved result include 11 to 14 to 90% reduction of NOx emissions-achieved 80 to 90% reduction of SOx emissions-achieved 90%. Figure 6 shows a magto-electric waste energy recovery system modeled numerically at UMT, while Figure 7 shows the amount of additional energy which can be produced from the system (Sulaiman, 2009).

The system offers flexibility in optimizing plant operations to minimize operation costs or maximize propulsion power. The use of these sets is considerably reduced thereby providing a further potential to reduce operating costs.

Regulatory prediction process

Figure 1 shows risk based process for system regulatory requirement. However, based on risk analysis outcome, regulation influence can be predicted and quantified by assigning a numerical weighting value to each link between factors. Future system will require design based on risk that matches system functionality with requirement. The ship design spiral shown in Figure 8 does not include most of the process described earlier, and some will require mandatory insertion in the spiral. Figure 9 show expected regulatory compliance for standards acceptability IMO model. Figure 10 shows cost benefit analyses that can be deduced from potential consequence in risk of do nothing.

In estimation of regulation, the concordant process require expert rating which is translated into the weighing factors, this weighting can be placed on factors at a lower

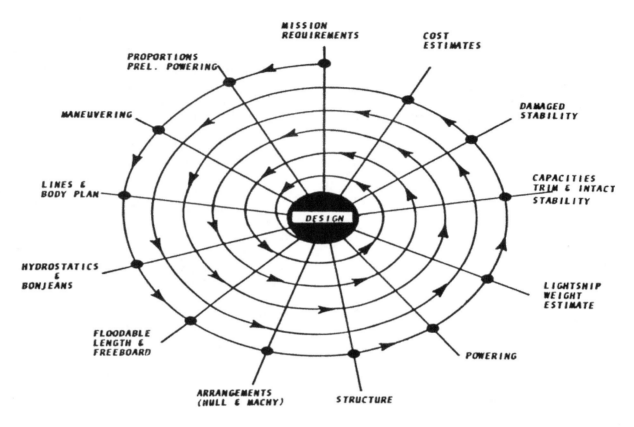

Figure 8. Ship design spiral (NRL, 2008).

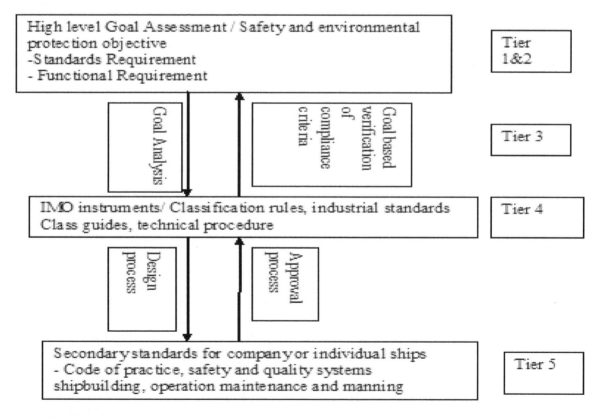

Figure 9. High Level goal standard assessment.

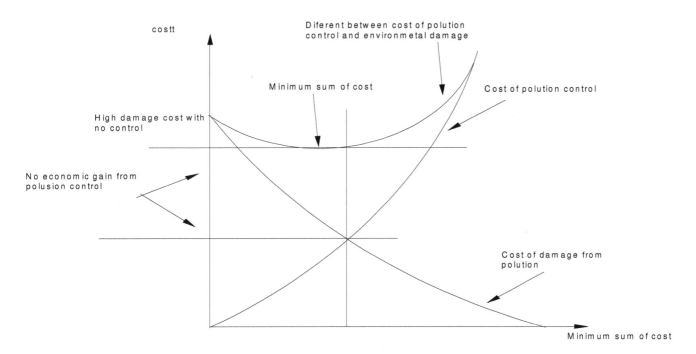

Figure 10. Cost and sustainability components.

level in the diagram, factors at a higher level that are influenced by that lower level factor, and also by assigning a numerical "rating" value to every factor. The weighting values between factors quantify the relative importance of the influence of lower level factors upon higher level factors. Weighting values are assigned as percentages on a scale of zero to 100%, such that for any factor at a higher level, the sum of the weightings of all the lower level factors which influence the higher level factor is 100%. This is otherwise described as Concordia principle.

$$W1 + W2 + W3 + W4 = 100\% \qquad (1)$$

Where W1, W2, W3, & W4 are the weightings linking factor E1, E2, E3, & E4 to factor P1. Consider the environmental level factors which link with the first policy level factor, P1. Say these environmental level factors are E1, E2 and E4. Let the weightings of these environmental factors on the first policy level factor be W (E1, P1), W (E2, P1) and W (E4, P1) respectively. Furthermore, let the respective ratings of these factors be R (E1), R (E2) and R (E4. W (E1, P1) W (E3, P1) W (E2, P1). A calculated rating value for factor P1 is derived as being: Figure 8 shows the regulatory requirement to achieve design goal.

$$R(P1c) = R(E1) \times W(E1,P1) + R(E2) \times W(E2,P1) + R(E4) \times W(E4,P1) \qquad (2)$$

Figure 10 shows cost and sustainability analyses instrument graph. The way forward

Recent safety and environmental strategic focus on developing metrics to measure and evaluate progress, the key to issues and actions are is to be incorporated in the clean ship concept. Ships owner and operators must understand the need to include wastes stream management in mission requirement in the design stages, with the goal of ships being in compliance. Ship designer must pursue technologies to reduce or eliminate waste streams. The metrics use to monitor progress towards achieving environmentally sound ships will focus on shipboard pollution control equipment installations, specifically the planned versus actual installations. Each waste stream or environmental pollutant, equipment installations, the percentage of total installations completed versus the planned percentage, will be used as a measure of progress for that waste stream. For waste streams and contaminants for which no equipment has been approved or anticipated, the metric will born many R&D for necessary findings. There is need for effectively integration of pollution prevention and safety into the design and life cycle of our ships, systems, ordnance into the execution of our processes, and into the operation. Managing the whole process is another thing; environmental management can be optimizing by incorporating the following concept in our system. Table 10 shows potential marine technology research are for waterborne transportation, this include Total cost minimization concept, innovative safety and environmental strategy management and integration planning for uncertainty and risk, use of probabilistic and holistic methods, education

Table 10. Propulsion.

New paint systems	Hempel		Choosing right antifouling paint with low water friction is beneficial to reduce ship resistance and subsequencial saving of fuel of 3 to 8%, hence proportional reduction of emission.
Advance Rudder and propeller system	MAN and ABB		Modern ruder design that combine propeller with asymmetric ruder called costa bulb, efficient propeller design provide smooth slipstream from the proper to the rudder, and asymmetry rudder rotational energy is utilized more efficiently.
Speed nozzle	MAN and ABB		Nozzle are used to improve the bollard pull on tugs, supply vessel, fishing boats and other vessel which need high pulling power at low speed. Speed nozzle are modern nozzle with improve propulsion power at service speed. The technology has reduction capability up to 5%

Table 11. Marin technology and research areas for waterborne transportation.

Marine technology areas	Need	Technology platforms
Efficient, safe and environmentally friendly ships and vessels of the future	Improvement of concepts of multi-site design, engineering or environmental kindliness production	fast vessels for passengers, cars and cargo; - deep-sea ships for passengers and unit cargo; - deep-sea floating structures for production storage and off-loading of gas; - unmanned, autonomous and remotely operated survey vehicles; and - new concepts for short-sea operations and polar shipping.
Maximizing interoperability, transshipment and vessel performance	Improvement of port infrastructures, reducing operating costs, improving maneuverability of ships in restricted waters and ports and efficient cargo handling and transshipment.	Research is focusing on integrating advanced concepts for unitised cargo and for ship types operating in coastal, restricted and limited waters. The strategic aim is to demonstrate concepts for multimodal cargo units and reinforcing intermodal links to ease improve and facilitate cargo flows between inland waterways and the sea.
Innovative technologies for monitoring, exploration and sustainable exploitation of the sea	Development unmanned surveying, in-situ monitoring and industrial operation.	
Competitive shipbuilding	Hull design to reduce environmental impact from loss of structural integrity, fuel consumption through hull form optimization, wave / wash generation, corrosion noise and vibration and use of new material.	Research is helping to demonstrate streamlined and seamless vessel development processes and systems, and support advanced production systems which improve customer response, product quality and manufacturing process flexibility and control

and training.

CONCLUSION

Working better by working together

This paper discussed environmental technology issue and potential research direction for green technology for ship. Beside miniaturization, use of nature and system integration will be next in line in the process for system to work efficiently. Even thus, the environment has naturally integrated everything in this planet between air, water and soil. The same apply to maritime industry on the issue of safety and marine environmental impact control and protection. Environmental issue has become so sensitive because it is more or less of evidence that nature has exercise enough patience, impact has reach flash point and those who are knowledgeable about the behavior of matter and environment have been giving predictive data about potential of contagious chain reaction of climate change and potential consequential heavy calamity damage and lost. Existing engine and future engines will be forced to adapt new technologies presented in this paper in the near future. Green technology highlighted in this paper will be a major catalyst to ignite a series of research activities to solve the current energy and environmental problems. Data collected from such research will be utilized to enforce relevant climate change control and compliance laws. The data can be used for simulation purposes and support the deployment of new systems. The evolving technology discussed could help meet the current demand by IMO for the implementation of Energy Efficiency Design Index (EEDI), Ship Energy Efficient Management Plan (SEEMP) and Ship Energy Efficiency Operational Indicator (SEEOI) rules which was launched recently towards global warming, climate change and ozone depletion in the maritime industry. The following are recommended for future technological compliance to regulation:

1. It is important for the main players in marine time industry (pilots, regulators, channel designers, simulator experts and ship operators) to share experience regarding differences in rules and design requirement for clean system.
2. Among regulators it is important to review rules that are taken too light, most of which are currently being implemented unilaterally because of variability in environment.
3. Naval architects and ship handlers alike should take the importance of GHG, green ship issue, risk based design and ship maneuvering unrestricted in ship design process. It is important o integrate design requirement related to this in ship design spiral.
4. Tackling the issue of environment equally required hybridizations of all the methodology we have been using

reactive process. The use of proactive approach that consider sensitivity of area, degrees of hazard for various ship types, and of course employment holistic institutionalized risk based system design method that compare and consider trend analysis of every elements of the new sustainable technology system development is recommended.

The political will for green technology is a wakeup call for all ship owners to be ready for new regulatory regime that will dictate technology for ship. Green ship technology will also be main factors for shipper and ship charters and insurance company look looking for in order to make decision for future business deal. Adoption of green ship technology will define significant ship, award winning vessel and qualification of green passport of next generation ship. That ship will be able to go anywhere and will face no delay in their transportation activities.

REFERENCES

Barry A (1993). Wade and Denise Forrest Improving Company Profitability and Public Image - The Money Index #370. pp.25-29.

Bian H, Mario D, Ivar K, Anik MF (2000). Technologies for reduced environmental impact of ships. Shipbuilding, maintenance and dismantling, Proc. ENSUS`2000, UK. pp.2-24.

De Leeuw F, Moussiopoulos, N, Bartanova A, Sahm P, Pulles, T, Visschedijk A (2001). Air quality in larger cities in the European Union. A contribution to the Auto-Oil II programme. Topic report 3/2001.European Environment Agency, Copenhagen, Denmark. (www.eea.eu.int).

Environmental Management Systems (EMS) (2000) Policy and Strategy Working Group "Major Country" Research Report (CWIP/CR3) 4/1/

Erik.Ranheim. Shipping and the Environment GHG Emissions from Ships the Industry's Perspective. The European Maritime Day. Cyprus 2009

EU (1996). Eco-Management and Audit Regulation – Roszell Hunter,

GESAMP (1993). Impact of oil and related chemicals and wastes on marine environment. GEAMP reports and studies No50 joint group of expert of marine pollution. Available at: http://www.gesamp.imo.org/no65/

Hinrich S (2004). Less Emission through Waste Heat Recovery, Wartisilla Switzerland Ltd.

Huey DJ (1997). Green Plans Greenprint for Sustainability.

IMO (1997). International Convention on the Prevention of Pollution at sea, 1973, consolidated edition, IMO London. Report of the Commissioner of the Environment and Sustainable Development. (1999) Canada

IMO (1980). International Convention for the Prevention of Pollution from Ships) and Protocol MARPOL 73/78 (1978). See especially Annex I, Regulation 10: Special Areas, and Regulation Reception Facilities.

IMO (1998). Annex VI of MARPOL 73/78: Regulations for the prevention of air pollution from ships and NOx technical code. Publication IMO-664E. London,UK.

IMO (1998). Guidelines for the Designation of Special Areas under Marpol 73/78 andGuidelines for the Identification and Designation of Particularly Sensitive Sea Areas. Assembly Resolution A.927(22).

IMO (2000). Marine Environmental Protection Committee" 44th session available at: http: www.imo.org/meeting/44.html. IMO (1998a), MARPOL Focus on IMO.

Intertanko (1998). Reception facilities for tankers. Intertanko. Oslo.

Kågeson P (1999). Economic instruments for reducing emissions from sea transport. The Swedish NGO Secretariat on Acid Rain, European Federation for Transport and Environment and European Environmental Bureau, Brussels

Karma RA, Morgan KZ (1975). Energy and environment cost–benefit analysis: Supplement o an international journal. Georgia Institute of Technology. London pp.491-507.

Landsburg AC, Card JC, Crane JC, Iman PRA, Bertsche WR, Boyleston JW, Eda H, McCallum VF, Miller IR, Taplin A (1983). Design and Verification for Adequate Ship Maneuverability. SNAME Transactions. p.91.

MARPOL. International Convention for the Prevention of Marine Pollution from Ships (73/78). .Naval Research Lab news. Available at http://www.navyseic.com/solid/solid.htm. accessed in 2008

MSA (1995). Project 366: Formal Safety Assessment: Draft Stage 1 Report. Marine Safety Agencies. Southampton. February. 2002.

Murphy (1996). Variable speed drives for marine electric propulsion, Trans IMarE 108(2):97-107.

Norwegian Maritime Directory (NMD). (2008). Rules and Regulations, Standards and Guidelines

Pedersen C, Nielsen JA, Riber JP, Madsen HO, Krenk S (1992). Reliability based inspection planning for the TYRA fields. Proc. 11th International Conference-OMAE II:255-263

Psaraftis HN, Kontovas CA (2009), Ship Emissions: Logistics and Other Tradeoffs," International Marine Design Conference (IMDC 2009), Trondheim, Norway.

Ronald Begley. Value of ISO 14000 (1997). Management Systems Put to the Test. Environmental Science and Technology News 31:8.

Slocombe NDS (1993). Environmental planning, ecosystem science, and ecosystem approaches for integrating environment and development. Environmental Management.

Sulaiman O, Fakrudeen W (2010). Manoelectric Recycle Energy for Sustainable Marine Power Plant. University Malaysia Terengganu.

Tarrason L, Klein S, Benedictow V Rigler E, Posch S (2003). Transboundary acidification, eutrophication and ground-level ozone in Europe. Status Report. EMEP. Part III. By Oslo, Norway. (www.emep.int).

Watson DGM (1998).Practical Ship Design". Elsevier. NewYork

WHO (2003). Health aspects of air pollution with particulate matter, ozone and nitrogen Dioxide. Reporton a WHO Working Group, January 2003. WHO.

Appendix. IMO Conventions.

1. Convention on the International Maritime Organization (IMO CONVENTION) (in force);
2. 1991 Amendments to the IMO Convention which were adopted by the Assembly of the Organization on 7 November 1991 by resolution A.724 (17) (IMO AMENDS -91) (in force);
3. 1993 Amendments to the IMO Convention which were adopted by the Assembly of the Organization on 4 November 1993 by resolution A.735 (18) (IMO AMENDS-93) (in force);
4. International Convention for the Safety of Life at Sea, 1974, as amended (SOLAS 1974) (in force);
5. Protocol of 1978 relating to the International Convention for the Safety of Life at Sea, 1974, as amended (SOLAS PROT 1978) (in force);
6. Protocol of 1988 relating to the International Convention for the Safety of Life at Sea, 1974 (SOLAS PROT 1988) (in force);
7. Agreement concerning specific stability requirements for Ro-Ro passenger ships undertaking regular scheduled international voyages between or to or from designated ports in North West Europe and the Baltic Sea (SOLAS AGR 1996) (in force);
8. Convention on the International Regulations for Preventing Collisions at Sea, 1972, as amended (COLREG 1972) (in force);
9. Protocol of 1978 relating to the International Convention for the Prevention of Pollution from Ships, 1973, as amended (MARPOL 73/78)
10. Annex III to MARPOL 73/78 (in force);
11. Annex IV to MARPOL 73/78 (in force);
12. Annex V to MARPOL 73/78 (in force);
13. Protocol of 1997 to amend the International Convention for the Prevention of Pollution from Ships, 1973, as modified by the Protocol of 1978 relating thereto (MARPOL PROT 1997) (in force);
14. Convention on Facilitation of International Maritime Traffic, 1965, as amended (FAL, 1965) (in force);
15. International Convention on Load Lines, 1966 (LL 1966) (in force);
16. Protocol of 1988 relating to the International Convention on Load Lines, 1966 (LL PROT 1988) (in force);
17. International Convention on Tonnage Measurement of Ships, 1969 (TONNAGE 1969) (in force);
18. International Convention Relating to Intervention on the High Seas in Cases of Oil Pollution Casualties, 1969 (INTERVENTION 1969) (in force);
19. Protocol relating to Intervention on the High Seas in Cases of Pollution by Substances other than Oil, 1973, as amended (INTERVENTION PROT 1973) (in force);
20. International Convention on Civil Liability for Oil Pollution Damage, 1969 (CLC 1969) (in force);
21. Protocol to the International Convention on Civil Liability for Oil Pollution Damage, 1969 (CLC PROT 1976) (in force);
22. Protocol of 1992 to amend the International Convention on Civil Liability for Oil Pollution Damage, 1969 (CLC PROT 1992) (in force);
23. Special Trade Passenger Ships Agreement, 1971 (STP 1971) (in force);
24. Protocol on Space Requirements for Special Trade Passenger Ships, 1973 (SPACE STP 1973) (in force);
25. Convention relating to Civil Liability in the Field of Maritime Carriage of Nuclear Material, 1971 (NUCLEAR 1971) (in force);
26. Protocol of 1992 to amend the International Convention on the Establishment of an International Fund for Compensation for Oil Pollution Damage, 1971 (FUND PROT 1992) (in force);
27. Protocol of 2000 to the International Convention on the Establishment of an International Fund for Compensation for Oil Pollution Damage, 1972 (FUND PROT 2000) (in force);
28. Protocol of 2003 to the International Convention on the Establishment of an International Fund for Compensation for Oil Pollution Damage, 1992 (FUND PROT 2003) (in force);
29. International Convention for Safe Containers (CSC), 1972, as amended (CSC 1972) (in force);
30. Athens Convention relating to the Carriage of Passengers and their Luggage by Sea, 1974 (PAL 1974) (in force);
31. Protocol to the Athens Convention relating to the Carriage of Passengers and their Luggage by Sea, 1974 (PAL PROT 1976) (in force);
32. Protocol of 1990 to amend the Athens Convention relating to the Carriage of Passengers and their Luggage by Sea, 1974 (PAL PROT 1990) (not yet in force);
33. Protocol of 2002 to the Athens Convention relating to the Carriage of Passengers and their Luggage by Sea, 1974 (PAL PROT 2002) (not yet in force);
34. Convention on the International Mobile Satellite Organization (Inmarsat), as amended (INMARSAT C) (in force);
35. Operating Agreement on the International Mobile Satellite Organization (Inmarsat), as amended (INMARSAT OA) (in force);
36. Convention on Limitation of Liability for Maritime Claims, 1976 (LLMC 1976) (in force);
37. Protocol of 1996 to amend the Convention on Limitation of Liability for Maritime Claims, 1976 (LLMC PROT 1996) (in force);
38. International Convention on Standards of Training, Certification and Watch-keeping for Seafarers, 1978, as amended (STCW 1978) (in force);
39. International Convention on Standards of Training, Certification and Watch-keeping for Fishing Vessel Personnel, 1995 (STCW-F 1995) (not yet in force);
40. International Convention on Maritime Search and Rescue, 1979 (SAR 1979) (in force);
41. Convention for the Suppression of Unlawful Acts

against the Safety of Maritime Navigation (SUA) (in force);

42. Protocol for the Suppression of Unlawful Acts against the Safety of Fixed Platforms Located on the Continental Shelf (SUA PROT) (in force);

43. Protocol of 2005 to the Convention for the Suppression of Unlawful Acts against the Safety of Maritime Navigation (SUA 2005) (not yet in force);

44. Protocol of 2005 to the Protocol for the Suppression of Unlawful Acts against the Safety of Fixed Platforms Located on the Continental Shelf (SUA PROT 2005) (not yet in force);

45. The International COSPAS-SARSAT Programme Agreement (COS-SAR 1988) (in force);

46. International Convention on Salvage, 1989 (SALVAGE 1989) (in force);

47. International Convention on Oil Pollution Preparedness, Response and Co-operation, 1990 (OPRC 1990) (in force);

48. Protocol on Preparedness, Response and Co-operation to Pollution Incidents by Hazardous and Noxious Substances, 2000 (OPRC-HNS 2000) (in force);

49. Torremolinos Protocol of 1993 relating to the Torremolinos International Convention for the Safety of Fishing Vessels, 1977 (SFV PROT 1993) (not yet in force);

50. International Convention on Liability and Compensation for Damage in connection with the Carriage of Hazardous and Noxious Substances by Sea, 1996 (HNS 1996) (not yet in force);

51. International Convention on Civil Liability for Bunker Oil Pollution Damage, 2001 (BUNKERS 2001) (in force);

52. International Convention on the Control of Harmful Anti-fouling Systems on Ships, 2001 (AFS 2001) (in force);

53. International Convention for the Control and Management of Ships' Ballast Water and Sediments, 2004 (BWM 2004) (not yet in force);

54. Convention on the Prevention of Marine Pollution by Dumping of Wastes and Other Matter, 1972, as amended (LC 1972) (in force);

55. 1996 Protocol to the Convention on the Prevention of Marine Pollution by Dumping of Wastes and Other Matter, 1972 (LC PROT 1996) (in force);

56. Nairobi International Convention on the Removal of Wrecks, 2007 (NAIROBI WRC 2007) (not yet in force).

Instruments which are in force or applicable but which are no longer fully operational because they have been superseded by later instruments[1]

1. International Convention for the Safety of Life at Sea, 1948 (SOLAS 1948)

2. International Convention for the Prevention of Pollution of the Sea by Oil, 1954, as amended (OILPOL 1954)

3. International Convention for the Safety of Life at Sea, 1960 (SOLAS 1960)

4. International Regulations for Preventing Collisions at Sea, 1960 (COLREG 1960)

5. International Convention on the Establishment of an International Fund for Compensation for Oil Pollution Damage, 1971 (FUND 1971)

6. Protocol to the International Convention on the Establishment of an International Fund for Compensation for Oil Pollution Damage, 1971 (FUND PROT 1976).

Instruments not yet in force and not intended to enter into force

1. International Convention for the Prevention of Pollution from Ships, 1973 (MARPOL 1973)

2. Torremolinos International Convention for the Safety of Fishing Vessels, 1977 (SFV 1977)

3. Protocol of 1984 to amend the International Convention on Civil Liability for Oil Pollution Damage, 1969 (CLC PROT 1984)

4. Protocol of 1984 to amend the International Convention on the Establishment of an International Fund for Compensation for Oil Pollution Damage, 1971 (FUND PROT 1984).

22

A causal relationship between trade, FDI, exchange rates and economic growth of Pakistan

M. Azeem Naseer

Commerce and Finance, Superior University Lahore, Pakistan.

This study aims to do an empirical investigation of the causal relationship among FDI (foreign direct investment), trade, real effective exchange rates and economic growth. Economic growth attracts FDI and enhances trade as explained in some literatures. The present study focuses on Pakistan during the period 1980 to 2012. The Johansson co-integration analysis shows the long term relationship between the Trade, FDI, real effective exchange rate and economic growth of Pakistan. The results of ECM suggest that there is a significant relationship between the variables. The findings of this study suggest that foreign income, foreign direct investment, GDP, trade and real effective exchange rate significantly affect trade. The Granger causality test shows that export causes increase in economic growth and economic growth attracts the inflow of FDI.

Key word: Investigation, enhancement, significance, economic growth, inflows.

INTRODUCTION

In developing countries, FDI is a key factor that enhances exports as well as economic growth. FDI plays a pivotal role in enhancing employment levels, increases productivity of host countries, improves exports and ultimately enhances transfer of technology. The exports of developing countries like Pakistan have received substantial foreign direct investment in the past (Arshad, 2008 cited in Falki (2009)). The World Development Indicator shows that in Pakistan, the amount of FDI inflow increased from $ 0.24 billion in 1990 to $ 55 billion in 2011.

In FY04-06, Pakistan cumulatively attracted $8 billion FDI. Of this amount, 26.5% was from proceeds generated from sales of public assets and 49.2% from FDI, with the remaining coming from foreign portfolio investment. These foreign inflows were ploughed into banking, telecom and oil and gas sectors primarily. Prospects are that Pakistan will attract about US$6.0 billion in FY07 – an all time high annual flow since the advent of de-regulation, privatization and liberalization policies initiated at the end of the 1980s.

The host country receiving FDI has as advantage the creation of employment opportunities, use of modern technology and increase in productivity. Previous inflows of FDI into Pakistan were meager, accounting for only 0.2% of its overall economic growth and less than one percent of Asian's subtotal each year in the 90s. Among the major challenges that led to this situation were urban violence, inconsistent economic policies and government bureaucracy. Corrective measures were therefore essential.

The economic growth of Pakistan however improved significantly from 2.8% in 1986 to 6% in 1988. But due to the collapse of the Soviet Union and European countries, Pakistan's economic growth rate lowered again to an average of 4.4 % in the late 80s. The country's economic growth rate was again recorded in 1995 and 1996 as 9% which is a significant improvement. As the economic crisis hit the Asian continent however, it affected Pakistan's growth rate by 5.8% in 1998. The country's economic growth rate was 4.8% in1990, which is the lowest ever recorded in the 90s. Pakistan's economy has however recovered from the economic crisis of Asia and it maintains an average economic growth of 7.48% from 2001 – 2005.

During the period 1980 to 2008, the average annual growth rate of Pakistan's exports was nearly 20%. The exports value index increased 41 times from $0.80 billions to almost $32 billions in 2005. Pakistan's exports contribution to total trade increased from 32% in 1980 to 46% during the period 2001 to 2005.

Results obtained from previous studies suggest that the causal relationship among FDI trades; growth and exchange rates are mixed. Some reviewed studies indicate a positive relationship while others indicate otherwise. However the degree of relationship among these variables is not clear. This ambiguity is due to the fact that trade stimulates growth and, to some degree, growth in turn leads to trade. Every country has its level of technology, labor and similar endowments. And so, the rate of economic growth will vary from country to country depending on the availability of these factors. However, fiscal and monetary policies can have negative side effects on a country's economic growth_(Melina et al., 2004).

LITERATURE REVIEW

The economic growth of India has been affected by FDI and exports. However, Indian's high or low economic growth has no effect in the presence of FDI and exports of India. The economic growth, FDI and trade have no reciprocal causality relationship among them.

Wai et al. (2008) used an annual data (1970-2005) of the Malaysian economy by employing simple ordinary least square (OLS) regression method to reveal the relationship between foreign direct investment and economic growth. They concluded that a positive relationship exists between foreign direct investment and economic growth.

Zhang (2005) discovered the relationship between FDI and exports of china. The results show that there is a great influence of FDI at the industry level in china.

By using the data of 126 developing countries from 1985-2002 to find the effect of foreign direct investment and portfolio investment on economic growth, Vita and Kyaw (2009) concluded that the effect of foreign direct investment on economic growth is positive in developing countries with lower-middle and upper-middle income but negative in low income countries. On the whole, the findings suggest that to achieve positive results, developing countries have to reach a minimum level of development and absorption capacity.

Pacheco-Lopez (2005) used the granger causality test to discover the causal relationship between FDI and export. They discovered that there is bi-directional relationship between FDI and export performance of Mexico.

Using the Moroccan data, Baliamoune and Lutz (2004) analyzed that there is two causal relationships among FDI, economic growth and exports by the aid of the Granger causality test.

Melina et al. (2004) analyzed that there is long term relationship among FDI, economic growth and exports in Greece by using the co integration test. Their study period for the country spanned the years 1960-2002. Based on their results, they concluded that there was a causal relationship among these variables as the Granger causality test employed pointed out.

Alici and Ucal (2003) investigated the causal relationship among FDI, exports and economic growth of turkey by using the Granger causality test. They found out that there was no link between FDI–led exports growth during the period 1987 to 2002.

Liu et al. (2002) used the Granger causality test and found a two way causal relationships among internal foreign direct investment, trade and the economic growth of China. For this purpose, the country's data at aggregate level was used from 1981-1997.

Khan and Leng (1997) examined the economic growth, FDI and exports of three countries, viz Singapore, South Korea and Taiwan. The data was examined at aggregate levels from the period 1965 to 1995. By using the Granger causality test, they discovered that no causal relationship exist among FDI, exports and economic growth of the observed countries.

Duttaray et al. (2008) used the data of 66 developing countries to find the causal relationship between foreign direct investment (FDI) and economic growth. Their findings show that FDI affects growth in 29 countries; while growth does not affect FDI at all. A reverse causal relationship from FDI, exports, productivity or growth is present in 30 of the 66 countries. This suggests that a close correlation between growth and FDI does not in any way imply that FDI causes growth, exports or productivity change.

Chakraborty and Basu (2002) used the method developed by Johansen and Juselius to find out the co integration among FDI, real GDP and the other variable unit cost of labor. They found out that there is a long term relationship among these variables. They equally found the relationship among FDI, real GDP and import duties of India, in addition to the relationship between GDP and unit cost of labor in India.

More so, by using the Granger causality test, they found a unidirectional relationship between FDI and ral GDP of India.

Liu et al. (2001) examined data from China and other 19 economies that traded with China during the period 1984-1998. They applied the Granger causality test to find the relationship between FDI and foreign trade. An increase in internal FDI was discovered to be due to increase in the imports of China.

Chowdhury and Mavrotas (2006) analyzed data from three countries – Chile, Malaysia and Thailand from 1969 to 2000. They employed an innovative methodology for testing the causal direction between FDI and growth. They concluded that GDP causes FDI in Chile and not vice versa. And a bi-directional causal relationship between GDP and FDI exist in Malaysia and Thailand.

Ericsson and Irandoust (2001) investigated the relationship between the real GDP per capita and the inflows of FDI for the four countries - Sweden, Denmark, Norway and Finland. They found out that there is no causal relationship between the variables of FDI and GDP per capita in Denmark and Finland. However, they discovered that there is a bi-directional causal link between FDI and GDP per capita in Sweden. The causal link between the FDI and GDP per capita in Norway was found to be present.

By using the data of five Asian countries namely, Malaysia, Indonesia, Singapore, Thailand and Philippines, from 1970-2007, Pradhan (2009) concluded that there exists a long term relationship between foreign direct investment (FDI) and economic growth. The variables are co-integrated at panel levels. Except for Malaysia, they discovered that a bi-directional causal relationship exist between the variables both at individual and panel level.

METHODOLOGY

$LEX = \beta_0 + \beta_1\ LGDP + \beta_2\ LFDI + \beta_3\ LREER + \epsilon_t$
LEX = log of value of export
LGDP = log of Gross Domestic Product
LFDI = log of Foreign Direct Investment
LREER = Log of real effective exchange rate.
ϵ_t = Error Term

Definition of the variables

Gross domestic product (GDP)

GDP of purchaser's prices is the sum of gross value added by all resident producers in the economy, plus any product taxes; and minus any subsidies not included in the value of the products. It is calculated without making deductions from depreciated fabricated assets or from depleted and degraded natural resources. Data are in current U.S. dollars. Dollar figures for GDP are converted from domestic currencies using single year official exchange rates. For a few countries where the official exchange rate does not reflect, the rate is effectively applied to actual foreign exchange transactions and an alternative conversion factor is used.

Real effective exchange rate (REER)

Real effective exchange rate is the nominal effective exchange rate (a measure of the value of a currency against a weighted average of several foreign currencies) divided by a price deflator or index of costs.

Foreign direct investment (FDI)

Foreign direct investment is the net inflows of investment to acquire a lasting management interest (10% or more of voting stock) in an enterprise operating in an economy other than that of the investor. It is the sum of equity capital, reinvestment of earnings, other long-term capital, and short-term capital as shown in the balance of payments. This series shows net inflows in the reporting economy. Data is in current U.S. dollars.

Value of exports

Export values are from UNCTAD's value indexes or from current values of merchandise exports of Pakistan.

Econometric methodology

Unit root tests

Unit root test has been conducted to check the stationary and non stationary of the variables. If the macroeconomic variables are not stationary, they can exhibit a stochastic or deterministic trend. In order to check the order of integration of the selected variables, the Augmented Dickey Fuller (ADF) test is conducted.

Lag order selection

The distribution of lag order selection can be sensitive in the selection of lag order. Appropriate selection of lag order gives the reliable results of the analysis. On the other hand, if the selection of the lag order is not appropriate, then the results of ant study will be biased and the residual can serially be correlated. In this paper, the Schwartz test was used to overcome the problem of the lag order. This procedure removes arbitrariness in choosing the lag length in test of causality.

Co integration test

After the selection of the lag orders and stationary of the variables, the co integration of the variables is checked. Johansen co integration test is conducted in order to check whether the selected variables are co integrated. The following VAR model is formulated for the Johansen co integration test.:

$$Y_t = \Gamma_1\ (L)\ Y_{t-1} + \Gamma_2\ (L)\ Y_{t-1} + \ldots\ldots\ldots\ldots\ldots\ \Gamma_p\ (L)\ Y_{t-1} + \epsilon_{t-p}$$

Where,
$Y_t = [$ LEX, LGDP, LGDI, LREER$]$ is a column vector and $\Gamma_i\ (L)$ with $I = 1\ \ldots\ldots.p$ is lag operator. ϵ is white noise residual of zero mean and constant variance. The order of the model p must be determined in advance using the SIC (Schwartz Information Criterion) The null hypothesis that there is r or fewer co integration vectors can be tested using the following two test statistics.

A causality test

The Granger causality test is conducted for determining whether one time series is useful in forecasting another. The causality of the selected variables under study are value of exports (EX), Gross Domestic Product (GDP), FDI and Real effective exchange rates is checked in this study.

Collection of data

Annual data from world development bank (WDI 2012) have been collected for the selected variables, Value of trade, FDI, GDP and

Table 1. ADF unit root test: level series.

Variables	ADF	C.V.(5%)
LEX	0.041585	-2.971853
LFDI	-0.155049	-2.971853
LGDP	1.211986	-2.971853
LREER	-1.574096	-3.580623

Note: ADF shows that there is unit root in the series.

Table 2. ADF unit root test: 1st difference series.

Variables	ADF	C.V.(5%)
ΔLEX	-6.001442	-3.587527
ΔLFDI	-4.949822	-3.587527
ΔLGDP	-5.345549	-3.587527
ΔREER	-5.649235	-3.587527

Note: ADF shows that the series are stationary.

the real rate of exchange. The data is collected in US dollars of these variables.

RESULT

Testing for stationary

The first step is to check whether the variables under consideration are stationary or not. A univariate analysis is carried out to check the stationary of the data. Table 1 represents the results of Augmented Dickey Fuller Test (ADF) for the log levels and first difference of the logs of all the variables. According to the results shown in Table 1, augmented dickey fuller test indicates that the level of the series contains unit root. In order to make the data stationary, unit root test is run again by taking first differences of all the series. Table 2 shows that first difference series are stationary.

Null hypothesis is not rejected at 5% level of significance.

Testing for co integration

After identifying that all the variables in the study are integrated in order of one, that is, I (1), the second step is to test whether the variables are co integrated or not. For this purpose Johansen and Juselius' (1990) co integration tests are employed.

The results of Johansen co integration test are reported in Table 3. Both the tests (Trace tests and Maximum Eigen Value) show the existence of unique co integration among the variables at 5% level of significance. This indicates that the variables under consideration are

driven by at least one common trend. This implies that the relationship between the variables is not spurious and that they move together.

Error correction model

The results of error correction model are presented in Table 4. The error correction term is negative and signifycant, which is an indication that there exists a relationship between the variables. The sign of the error term is negative, which means that it is convergent towards equilibrium and its magnitude shows that 25% adjustment are done in first period. The probability is less than 5%, which means that the relationship is significant. The value of Durbin-Watson statistics is 2.176915, which indicates that there is no autocorrelation between the variables.

Granger causality test

The results in Table 4 show that there is co integration between the selected variables. The next step is to check the causality direction by applying the Granger Causality Test. Table 5 shows the causality between the LEX, LFDI, LGDP and LREER. . There is no causal relationship present except among the LEX and LGDP, LGDP and LFDI variables in the Granger Causality Test. However, there is causality effect present between the value of exports (LEX) and the foreign direct investment LFDI and this causality is unidirectional in nature. Value of exports (LEX) also causes (LGDP) Gross Domestic Product and this causality is also unidirectional with only exports causing the GDP. It suggest that the exports have been playing a key role in the development of Pakistan as it was clear in the literature There is also a causal relationship between the LGDP and LFDI. It suggests therefore that economic growth has attracted foreign direct investment for Pakistan.

Conclusion

The objective of this study is to investigate empirically the short term and long term causal relationship between trade, FDI growth and real effective exchange rate of Pakistan during the period 1980 to 2012.

By applying the Johansen's co integration test, it was discovered that the selected variables for the study are integrated in I (1) co integrated, implying a long term relationship among these variables. According to the results of the study, there is no reciprocal causal relationship among these variables in Pakistan. The direction of the short term and long term relationship is determined by using the Granger Causality relationship. The results indicate that the direction of causality from export to FDI causality exists between GDP and FDI. It can therefore be concluded that exports of Pakistan help in increasing

Table 3. Johansen co integration test variable/series: LGDP, LFDI, LCF, LFCE.

Variable	Hypothesized No. of CE(s)	Eigen value	Trace statistic	5% critical value	Max-Eigen statistics	5% critical value
LEX	None*	0.672667	51.0336	47.85613	30.15297	27.58434
LFDI	At Most 1	0.440842	20.8807	29.79707	15.69574	21.13162
LGDP	At Most 2	0.161638	5.18492	15.49471	4.760231	14.26460
LREER	At Most 3	0.015606	0.42469	3.841466	0.424687	3.841466

Table 4. Dependent variable Δlex.

Variables	Coefficient	Std. error	t-Statistic	Prob.
ΔFDI	0.123677	0.060112	2.057437	0.0529
ΔGDP	0.463915	0.208227	2.227930	0.0375
ΔREER	-0.697905	0.231822	-3.010518	0.0069
EC(-1)	-0.928933	0.254732	-3.646708	0.0016

Table 5. Granger causality test.

Null hypothesis	F –Statistic	Probability
LFDI does not Granger Cause LEX	0.70109	0.50679
LEX does not Granger Cause LFDI	8.25651	0.00211
LGDP does not Granger Cause LEX	0.83138	0.44867
LEX does not Granger Cause LGDP	5.12724	0.01486
LREER does not Granger Cause LEX	0.37806	0.68956
LEX does not Granger Cause LREER	1.20165	0.31968
LGDP does not Granger Cause LFDI	5.86895	0.00906
LFDI does not Granger Cause LGDP	0.73260	0.49202
LREER does not Granger Cause LFDI	1.50160	0.24474
LFDI does not Granger Cause LREER	0.36750	0.69664
LREER does not Granger Cause LGDP	0.33630	0.71802
LGDP does not Granger Cause LREER	0.23004	0.79639

economic growth, and economic growth will in turn lead to the ultimate survival of the economy. If the costs of production and export incentives are given to the various manufacturing industries, there can be increase in exports. Moreover, FDI and trade are two important factors that enhance the effect of economic growth in Pakistan.

REFRENCES

Alici AA, Ucal MS (2003). "Foreign direct investment, exports and output growth of Turkey: Causality Analysis", Paper presented at the European Trade Study Group (ETSG) fifth annual conference, Madrid, 11-13, Sept.

Baliamoune-Lutz MN (2004). "Doest FDI contributes to economic growth? Knowledge about the effects of FDI improves negotiating positions and reduces risk for firms investing in developing countries", Bus. Econ. 39(2):49-56.

Chakraborty C, Basu P (2002). "Foreign Direct Investment and growth in India a Co integration approach", Appl. Econ. 34:1061-1073.

Chowdhury A, Mavrotas D (2006). FDI and Growth? What causes what? United Nations University.

Duttaray M, Dutt A, Mukhopadhyay K (2008). Foreign direct investment and economic growth in less developed countries: an empirical study of causality and mechanisms Appl. Econ. Lett. 40:1927-1939

Ericsson J, Irandoust M (2001). "On the causality between foreign direct investment and output: a comparative study", Int. Trade J. 15:1-26.

Falki N (2009). Impact of Foreign Direct Investment on Economic Growth in Pakistan. International Review of Business Research Papers Vol. 5 No. 5 September 2009 Pp. 110-120

Granger CWJ (1969). "Investigating causal relations by econometric models and cross-spectral methods". Econometric 37(3):424- Duttaray 438.

Khan K, Leng K (1997), "Foreign Direct Investment, exports and Economic growth", Singapore Econ. Rev. 42(2):40-60.

Liu XM, Wang CG, Wei YQ (2001). "Causal links between foreign direct investment and trade in China", China Econ. Rev. 12:190-202.

Liu X, Burridge P, Sinclair PJN (2002). "Relationship between economic growth, foreign direct investment and trade: evidence from China", Appl. Econ. 34:1433-1440.

Melina D, Chaido D, Antonios A (2004). "A Causal Relationship between Trade, Foreign Direct Investment and Economic Growth for Greece", Am. J. Appl. Sci. 1(3):230-235.

Pacheco-Lopez P (2005). "Foreign Direct Investment, Exports and Imports in Mexico", the World Economy 28(8):1157-1172.

Pradhan RP (2009). The FDI-Led-Growth in ASEAN-5 Countries: Evidence From Co integrated Panel Analysis. Int. J. Bus. Manage. 4(12).

Vita GD, Kyaw KS (2009). Growth effects of FDI and portfolio investment flows to developing countries: a disaggregated analysis by income levels. Appl. Econ. Lett. 16:277-283.

Wai HM, Teo KL, Yee KM (2008). FDI and Economic Growth Relationship: An Empirical Study on Malaysia. Int. Bus. Res. 01/2009

23

Mobile technology interaction to e-Commerce in promising of u-Commerce

George S. Oreku

Research Development, Faculty of Economic Sciences and Information Technology, North-West University, Vaal Triangle Campus, P. O. Box 1174, Vanderbijlpark 1900, Gauteng, South Africa. E-mail: george.oreku@gmail.com.

Mobile technology interaction is gaining increasing acceptance. The need for mobility is a primary driving force behind mobile banking, mobile entertainment and mobile marketing, and is supported by an ever increasing convergence of computers and mobile telecommunication devices. This article examines the conceptual background and existing experience of another wave of change that provides the ultimate form of ubiquitous networks and universal devices. It presents understanding of another form of commerce, a form that goes over above and beyond traditional commerce, simply "u-commerce", in order to make consumers and service-providers aware of new business opportunities arising out of this convergence.

Key words: Knowledge management, mobile technology, unified communication, U-commerce.

INTRODUCTION

After the emergence of E-Commerce in the late 90's, we reached a new milestone in the evolution of how goods and services are exchanged between producer and consumer. Businesses all over the world need to be ready for the next big step, a full integration of traditional commerce, E-commerce, mobile commerce and even television commerce.

Mobile commerce, also known as M-Commerce is the ability to conduct commerce using a mobile device, such as a mobile phone, a PDA (personal digital assistant), or using other emerging mobile equipment such as dashtop mobile devices and smartphone. However mobile commerce has been defined differently with different authors but according to Tiwari and Buse (2007), they have defined mobile commerce as any transaction involving the transfer of ownership or rights to use goods and services, which is initiated and/or completed by using mobile access to computer-mediated networks with the help of an electronic device.

According to comScore, up to November 2011, 38% of smartphone owners have used their phone to make a purchase at least once.

The convergence of industry, technology and communications has plunged us into a dynamic economic environment. New E-Commerce and mobile commerce capabilities are bringing us closer together and empowering individuals as never before. These changes are heralding the emergence of "U-commerce" – universal or ubiquitous commerce, where the traditional barriers of time, geography, currency and access have ceased to exist.

Mobile technology is faced with the pressing issue of managing the access to, the demand for, and the concerns about sharing information. Barely before Internet-facilitated E-Commerce has begun to take hold, a new wave of technology-driven commerce has started mobile (m-) commerce. Fuelled by the increasing saturation of mobile technology, such as phones and PDAs, m-Commerce promises to inject considerable change into the way certain activities are conducted. Some issues are becoming more complex like video creation and sharing rapidly move to higher bandwidth and mobile platforms. With a focus on unified communications capabilities, firms are trying to deal with how to best present and position their products and services in a world where video access and sharing are becoming pervasive. We however, reports from a primarily business application oriented aspect in particular E-Commerce and mobile technology to the promising future of U-commerce. Equipped with micro-browsers and other mobile applications, the new range of mobile technologies offer the internet 'in your pocket' for which the consumer possibilities are endless, including banking, booking or buying tickets, shopping and real-time news. Drawing on some of the key factors that may influence the take-up of M-Commerce including technological and other issues the chapter also provides predictions regarding outcome of all these as future "U-commerce". The rise of mobile technology in video and the organizational responses to it are examined within the theoretical contexts of its applications.

U-Commerce is not a trend that will occur some time far off in the future. It is a real-time change that is happening today. U-Commerce is the natural evolution of E-Commerce and mobile commerce from "point of sale" to "point of convenience" whether a transaction occurs in a store, in your home, on the street or even on an airplane.

The way that consumers access the internet and shop online is changing. Desktop computers, laptops, mobile internet devices, and mobile phones are converging into a larger category of Internet enabled devices. Millions of new users and new shoppers comes online daily.

By way of example, last year eMarketer estimated that by 2013 74.9% of all Canadians would be internet users. Put another way, essentially every Canadian between the age of 5 and 65 will have web access within a few years. In the U.S. there were an estimated 234.4 million internet users at the end of last year or about 76.3% of the total population.

Meanwhile, TechCrunch has reported that mobile internet use in North America grew 110% in 2009 according to Quantcast. That number would be impressive except it trails worldwide mobile internet growth, which was pegged at 148% in 2009.

The rest of the paper is organized as follow; U-Commerce concept is discussed. Mobile technology integrations to commercial applications specifically focusing on U-commerce, and promising issues concerning U-Commerce are presented. Our critical analysis on mobile and E-Commerce use situation are discussed. Finally, the paper is concluded.

UNDERSTANDING - U-COMMERCE

Geographic Commerce ⇨ Electronic Commerce ⇨ Mobile Commerce ⇨ U-Commerce

U-Commerce or universal commerce covers these newly arising opportunities and challenges that companies are facing by defining four fundamental constructs: ubiquity, uniqueness, universality, and unison.

- *Ubiquity* allows users to access networks from anywhere at any time, and in turn, to be reachable at any place and any time.
- *Uniqueness* allows users to be uniquely identified not only in terms of their identity and associated preferences, but also in terms of their geographical position.

- *Universality* means mobile devices are universally usable and multi-functional. Currently, for instance, U.S. cell phones are unlikely to work in Europe because of different standards and network frequencies, and vice versa.
- *Unison* covers the idea of integrated data across multiple applications so that users have a consistent view on their information-irrespective of the device used.

Thus, we define U-Commerce as "the use of ubiquitous networks to support personalized and uninterrupted communications and transactions between a firm and its various stakeholders to provide a level of value over, above, and beyond traditional commerce" (Watson et al., 2002).

In the past few years, E-Commerce has joined the vocabulary of many languages. Many organizations talk of "I-commerce" or the use of intranet technologies (internal corporate internets) to pursue internal marketing strategies. Already, m-Commerce (mobile commerce) is gaining currency as cell phone owners acquire access to mobile services such as Delta Airlines' arrival and departure information service for mobile phones and PDAs. Marketing practitioners will be very concerned with the impacts that these technologies will have on their organizations and on their relationships with customers. Marketing scholars will need to study how these technologies will affect the discipline to determine whether existing theories will explain the phenomena adequately or whether new theories will be needed. Likewise, marketing teachers will want to keep their students at all levels abreast of events and developments, for they will be better equipped to deal with turbulent work environments if they at least have a point of view where we are ultimately headed.

We believe that in the next few years, we will see the emergence of a multifaceted *u-commerce*, where the *u* stands for ubiquitous, universal, unique, and unison. We can think of it as *Über*-commerce - over, above, and beyond traditional commerce. Thus, we define u-Commerce as the use of ubiquitous networks to support personalized and uninterrupted communications and transactions between a firm and its various stakeholders to provide a level of value over, above, and beyond traditional commerce.

U-Commerce plays a key role in the long-term vision for the payments industry and integrating business anywhere. It is built on several global phenomena that will only accelerate as we go forward. Developments in mobile technology and information management technologies have resulted in efficiency division such as: V-commerce: - Using voice commands to do Transactions, P - commerce: - Proximity commerce uses bluetooth or infrared technology and so on. E-commerce: - Most popular, doing transaction on internet conducting business online. Selling goods, in the traditional sense, is possible to do electronically because of certain software programs that run the main functions of an E-Commerce website, including product display, online ordering, and inventory management. The software resides on a commerce server and works in conjunction with online payment systems to process payments. Since these servers and data lines make up the backbone of the Internet, in a broad sense, e-Commerce means doing business over interconnected networks. The definition of e-Commerce includes business activities that are business-to-business (B2B), business-to-consumer (B2C), extended enterprise computing (also known as "newly emerging value chains"), d-commerce, and m-commerce. E-Commerce is a major factor in the U.S. economy because it assists companies with many levels of current business transactions, as well as creating new online business opportunities that are global in nature.

M-commerce: - Business transactions through mobile. M-Commerce (mobile commerce) is the buying and selling of goods and services through wireless handheld devices such as cellular telephone (PDAs). Known as next-generation e-commerce, m-Commerce enables users to access the internet without needing to find a place to plug in. The emerging technology behind m-commerce, which is based on the wireless application protocol (WAP), has made far greater strides in Europe, where mobile devices equipped with web-ready micro-browsers are much more common than in the United T -commerce: - Use Television set - top box to do commercial transactions \ T-commerce encompasses all revenues that are generated through the television set. It allows the purchase of goods and services that are seen on the TV set. It is a subset of interactive TV. According to this definition, T-commerce comprises the following sub-markets: That is TV shopping, direct response TV, Travel shopping, Interactive TV applications.

The defined terminologies (u-Commerce, m-Commerce and t-Commerce) have a higher payoff in the form of more efficient processes, lower costs and potentially greater profits. They both address these processes, as well as a technology infrastructure of databases, application servers, security tools, systems management and legacy systems. And both involve the creation of new value chains between a company and its customers and suppliers, as well as within the company itself. However they do have differences whereby mobile commerce main purpose is to do both financial and promotional activities, e-Commerce involves in online shopping to do only financial activities within the help of internet. Similarly, it is different from u-Commerce which is fully integrated with the content management system which enables one to create beautifully designed stores, and enabling also the back office capabilities to configure and customize the store of one's liking.

MOBILE APPLICATION AND EARLY U-COMMERCE INDICATORS

The first mobile commerce discussion was held at the University of Oxford in 2003, with Tomi Ahonen and Steve Jones lecturing. As of 2008, UCL Computer Science and Peter J. Bentley demonstrated the potential for medical applications on mobile devices. Ahonen and Jones (2003).

Since the launch of the iPhone, mobile commerce has moved away from SMS systems and into actual applications. SMS has significant security vulnerabilities and congestion problems, even though it is widely available and accessible.

The applications have been extended to Mobile ticketing technology where mobile are being used for the distribution of vouchers, coupons, and loyalty cards. These items are represented by a virtual token that is sent to the mobile phone. Stores may send coupons to customers using location-based services to determine when the customer is nearby; this can be sited from www.mobilestarterstore.com

The reinvention of the mobile phone as a touch sensitive handheld computer has for the first time made mobile commerce practically feasible. 'According to ABI Research, mobile is going to get a lot bigger in the ecommerce market. The research firm is predicting that in 2015, $119bn worth of goods and services will be purchased via a mobile phone.'

Mobile devices are heavily used in South Korea to conduct mobile commerce. Mobile companies in South Korea believed that mobile technology would become synonymous with youth life style, based on their experience with previous generations of South Koreans. "Profitability for device vendors and carriers hinges on high-end mobile devices and the accompanying killer applications (Harden, 2012).

In California, Illinois and other states in the U.S., transit agencies are distributing electronic bridge toll devices (which leverage credit and debit payment functions) and have the ability to be used in other "proximity" environments, such as service stations or fast-food drive-through. Individually, these are all powerful and innovative examples of new ways to pay and new ways to *leverage* payments. But they are just early steps in realizing the full potential of u-commerce.

U-commerce, by definition, implies the continued existence of traditional payment forms such as cash and checks, which may always exist. But in the u-Commerce environment, cash and checks will become increasingly marginalized because they provide diminished value and utility. It is also important to note that in the world of u-commerce, "traditional" credit and debit card payments (face-to-face transactions at point-of-sale) will always play a dominant role.

There is still huge growth potential for traditional credit and debit products worldwide, particularly in emerging markets. Extending the scope and scale of these core payment products, in addition to the development of new products and channels, is part of the u-Commerce growth equation. We believe there are tremendous benefits from u-Commerce for individual buyers and sellers. But we believe there are also significant macroeconomic benefits. Payments are the lifeblood of economies. By facilitating the exchange of goods and services, they enable the different components of an economy to interact with one another. Removing friction from this process which u-Commerce is all about – can help economies to operate more fluidly and efficiently.

Sensemaking depends upon the ability to find relevant reference resources. For media this means providing knowledge management mechanisms that provide efficient search and retrieval of relevant content. Video files, including employee-generated videos, must be cataloged and indexed so that employees can use enterprise and/or mobile search engines to ask for and secure video content meeting user-specified criteria. This means that sensemaking requires providing the capability for retrieving a list of enterprise videos that match user search criteria and which is sorted with respect to some measure of relevance. Use of search engines may provide a secondary benefit of promoting greater access to enterprise video content and increased viewing activity. For example, when YouTube videos was acquired by Google and then subsequently included on the Google Video Search Index, YouTube's site visits rose immediately by 18.5% (Tancer, 2007).

Image and video content upload systems typically rely on simple techniques like asking the user to file the image under a category, or to click a set of checkboxes of descriptive tags, or to type in a one-sentence description that can later be automatically parsed by the system to generate detailed metadata. These requests for metadata can overburden users when they are uploading megabytes of images and video information.

However, innovative approaches are emerging to improve this process. Google, for example, has created Google Image Labeler that automatically pairs video content users and asks them to add as many labels to as many images as possible in a 90-second period. The more images and labels that are added, the more point the participants receive and the site lists that day's and the all-time top-point winners. There is no prize except the satisfaction that you are helping Google deliver more relevant search results.

However, as more users capture and share cellphone images at low cost, the potential for new and innovative search labeling services becomes essential. According to study done by Nokia, it was estimated that cameraphones will be able to capture 100 billion images by the year 2011 alone (Pepus, 2007). This fact argues that if a company is participating in this market as a manufacturer, a service provider, or a content supplier, content-based image and video search capabilities should be made more efficient.

To that end PiXlogic has developed the most advanced commercially available enterprise search engines for images and videos. It is based on automatic indexing of the contents of the image, without the need for any manually input textual metadata. PiXlogic uses a concept called "notions" that are interpreted understandings about the context of the image and the objects in it and it has created a contextually rich and accurate search environment that exploits this. To catalog a repository of images or videos, the user points PiXlogic's piXserve application software to that repository (or uses a web crawler to collect images) and it automatically indexes the content of those files. Through a browser, users can then search using an image and/or point to one or more items in the image that are of interest to them. The software can also see and recognize any text that may appear anywhere in the field of view of the image (for example, picking out names of recruitment candidates, knowledge videos and experts, and other online video resources). Where most image and video search technologies work by trying to match image signatures that are based on simple concepts such as textual labels, color histograms, texture, or edges, for example, piXserve "sees" the image as being composed of man objects, creates a representation describing the objects, and stores them in a database (Pepus, 2007).

Internet audio and video streaming technology is getting more and more sophisticated. All you have to do is look around you and you will see people watching videos and listening to music with their I-pods, MP3 and MP4 players. Incidentally, the best sources for their audio and video needs can be found on the internet. So, imagine all the audio/video data streaming, downloading and uploading around in the internet, and you will have a good idea of just how measly a 10 s video is in terms of today's technology.

As discussed, the use of audio/video streaming on the internet is a powerful marketing tool. However, the technology for it has matured enough in that audio and video files use more space from storage devices such as hard drives and I-pods. Already, hard drives of computers have transcended the megabyte barrier and are now storing gigabytes, terabytes, petabyte, exabyte and zettabyte of data (one zettabyte = 10^{21} or one sextillion bytes).

In the context of mobile commerce, mobile marketing refers to marketing sent to mobile devices. Companies have reported that they see better response from mobile marketing campaigns than from traditional campaigns. Mobile campaigns must be based on the global content generation or what is called Generation C and four other 'C's: Creativity, Casual Collapse, Control, and Celebrity. A brief introduction... Creativity: let's face it, we're all creatives, if not artists! (Notice we didn't mean talented artists ;-). And as creativity normally leads to content, the link with GENERATION C is obvious. Which then brings us to Casual Collapse: the ongoing demise of many beliefs, rituals, formal requirements and laws modern societies have held dear, which continue to 'collapse' without causing the apocalyptic aftermath often predicted by conservative minds. From women's rights to gay marriage to not wearing a tie to work if you don't feel like it (http://youpark.com/)

Research demonstrates that consumers of mobile and wireline markets represent two distinct groups who are driven by different values and behaviors, and who exhibit dissimilar psychographic and demographic profiles (Schejter et al., 2010). As a result, successful mobile commerce requires the development of marketing campaigns targeted to this particular market segment.

THE PROMISING U-COMMERCE

Newer technologies, empowered customers, and highly competitive market place make it imperative for businesses to invest into ways of improving the overall business performance. "The internet has introduced a significant wave of change. We expect – indeed, it seems virtually certain – that these new network resources will, especially in combination, stimulate a new generation of personalized applications and services. These massively joined technologies will form "dynamic ecosystems", immersed in computerized ambient environments, and growing and adapting themselves to the evolving needs of individual users and communities.

A 4G system is expected to provide a comprehensive and secure all-IP based mobile broadband solution to laptop computer wireless modems, smartphones, and other mobile devices. Facilities such as ultra-broadband internet access, IP telephony, gaming services, and streamed multimedia may be provided to users. IMT-Advanced compliant versions of LTE and WiMAX are under development and called "LTE Advanced" and "WirelessMAN-Advanced" respectively. ITU has decided that LTE Advanced and WirelessMAN-Advanced should be accorded the official designation of IMT-Advanced. On December 6, 2010, ITU recognized that current versions of LTE, WiMax and other evolved 3G technologies that do not fulfill "IMT-Advanced" requirements could nevertheless be considered "4G", provided they represent forerunners to IMT-Advanced and "a substantial level of improvement in performance and capabilities with respect to the initial third generation systems now deployed (ITU, 2010).

Our communication patterns have changed. We have become dependent on email. We interact with firms via web sites, e-Commerce for example, plays a catalytic role in poverty alleviation to some places where well applied and manage by enormous quantities of business information that are generated in the internet for modeling the living (Bourguignon, 2003; GoT, 2001; IMF, 2004). The World Development Report (2000/01): Attacking poverty identifies three priority areas for reducing poverty: increasing opportunity, enhancing empowerment, and improving people's life (http://web.worldbank.org). Opportunity makes markets work for the poor and expands poor people's assets. Empowerment and technology makes state institutions work better for poor people and removes social barriers. The next wave introduced through wireless technology is about to change our lives even more. The increase in transmission capacity of wireless devices lays the foundation for communication unrestricted by physical locations. We can surf the internet decoupled from landline computers. The emergence and evolution of eCommerce has proved to be a highly successful and profitable venture for companies of different sizes and origin.

We are now shifted to do business in virtual space rather only proving ourselves in geographical space (Jay, 2004). The new technologies will have significant effects in our lives and this will definitely lead to a re-defining a lot of what we call today general concepts. For example, the whole issue of who is a buyer and seller may change.

The projection indicates that STAMFORD, Conn., November 18, 2009, Gartner, Inc. has identified the top 10 consumer mobile applications for 2012 (Pettey and Stevens, 2012).

Gartner listed applications based on their impact on consumers and industry players, considering revenue, loyalty, business model, consumer value and estimated market penetration. These included;

No. 1: Money transfer

This service allows people to send money to others using Short Message Service (SMS). Its lower costs, faster speed and convenience compared with traditional transfer services have strong appeal to users in developing markets, and most services signed up several million users within their first year.

No. 2: Location-based services

Location-based services (LBS) form part of context-aware services, a service that Gartner expects will be one of the most disruptive in the next few years. Gartner predicts that the LBS user base will grow globally from 96 million in 2009 to more than 526 million in 2012. LBS is ranked No. 2 in Gartner's top 10 because of its perceived high user value and its influence on user loyalty.

No. 3: Mobile search

The ultimate purpose of mobile search is to drive sales and marketing opportunities on the mobile phone. To achieve this, the industry first needs to improve the user experience of mobile search so that people will come back again. Mobile search is ranked No. 3 because of its high impact on technology innovation and industry revenue.

No. 4: Mobile browsing

Mobile browsing is a widely available technology present on more than 60% of handsets shipped in 2009, a percentage Gartner expects to rise to approximately 80% in 2013. Gartner has ranked mobile browsing No. 4 because of its broad appeal to all businesses. Mobile Web systems have the potential to offer a good return on investment.

No. 5: Mobile health monitoring

Mobile health monitoring is the use of IT and mobile telecommunications to monitor patients remotely, and could help governments, care delivery organizations (CDOs) and healthcare payers reduce costs related to chronic diseases and improve the quality of life of their patients. In developing markets, the mobility aspect is key as mobile network coverage is superior to fixed network in the majority of developing countries. Currently, mobile health monitoring is at an early stage of market maturity and implementation, and project rollouts have so far been limited to pilot projects.

No. 6: Mobile payment

Mobile payment usually serves three purposes. First, it is a way of making payment when few alternatives are available. Second, it is an extension of online payment for easy access and convenience. Third, it is an additional factor of authentication for enhanced security. Mobile payment made Gartner's top 10 list because of the number of parties it affects including mobile carriers, banks, merchants, device vendors, regulators and consumers and the rising interest from both developing and developed markets. Because of the many choices of technologies and business models, as well as regulatory requirements and local conditions, mobile payment will be a highly fragmented market. There will not be standard practices of deployment, so parties will need to find a working solution on a case-by-case basis.

No. 7: Near field communication services

Near field communication (NFC) allows contactless data transfer between compatible devices by placing them close to each other, within ten centimeters. The technology can be used, for example, for retail purchases, transportation, personal identification and loyalty cards. NFC is ranked No. 7 in Gartner's top ten because it can increase user loyalty for all service providers, and it will have a big impact on carriers' business models. However, its biggest challenge is reaching business agreement between mobile carriers and service providers, such as

banks and transportation companies.

No. 8: Mobile advertising

Mobile advertising in all regions is continuing to grow through the economic downturn, driven by interest from advertisers in this new opportunity and by the increased use of smartphones and the wireless internet. Total spending on mobile advertising in 2008 was $530.2 million, which Gartner expects will grow to $7.5 billion in 2012. Mobile advertising makes the top 10 list because it will be an important way to monetize content on the mobile internet, offering free applications and services to end users. The mobile channel will be used as part of larger advertising campaigns in various media, including TV, radio, print and outdoors.

No. 9: Mobile instant messaging

Price and usability problems have historically held back adoption of mobile instant messaging (IM), while commercial barriers and uncertain business models have precluded widespread carrier deployment and promotion. Mobile IM is on Gartner's top 10 list because of latent user demand and market conditions that are conducive to its future adoption. It has a particular appeal to users in developing markets that may rely on mobile phones as their only connectivity device. Mobile IM presents an opportunity for mobile advertising and social networking, which have been built into some of the more advanced mobile IM clients.

No. 10: Mobile music

Mobile music so far has been disappointing - except for ring tones and ring-back tones, which have turned into a multibillion-dollar service. On the other hand, it is unfair to dismiss the value of mobile music, as consumers want music on their phones and to carry it around. We see efforts by various players in coming up with innovative models, such as device or service bundles, to address pricing and usability issues. iTunes makes people pay for music, which shows that a superior user experience does make a difference.

"Consumer mobile applications and services are no longer the prerogative of mobile carriers," said Sandy Shen, research director at Gartner. "The increasing consumer interest in smartphones, the participation of internet players in the mobile space, and the emergence of application stores and cross-industry services are reducing the dominance of mobile carriers. Each player will influence how the application is delivered and experienced by consumers, who ultimately vote with their attention and spending power."

"The ultimate competition between industry players is for control of the 'ecosystem' and user experience, and the owner of the ecosystem will benefit the most in terms of revenue and user loyalty," Ms. Shen said. "We predict that most users will use no more than five mobile applications at a time and most future opportunities will come from niche market 'killer applications'."

U-Commerce enables dramatic improvements in m-payment as well as in CRM processes. From Gartner's list of application it is vividly proven that u-Commerce creates an economy that is more flexible, interconnected and more efficient. However from our finding u-Commerce technology is already available in transition economies to countries in Africa (www.ystats.com/uploads/report_abstracts/939.pdf). Major research issue is to which extend u-Commerce penetrated in these countries economy which will be the next step for our future research. Further research should also focus on enablers and drivers of u-Commerce adoption by African enterprises and public services providers. Another possible research avenue could be implementation of u-Commerce applications in various marketing contexts. Therefore we hypothesized our finding as follows:

H1: African countries large enterprises are familiar with u-Commerce technologies.
H2: African countries large enterprises are using u-Commerce technologies as enabler in marketing and sales activities.
H3: African countries large cities are implementing u-City concept.

From the research presented u-Commerce is being implemented in services sector, particularly in travel, entertainment and tourism Industry in many African countries (www.ystats.com/uploads/report_abstracts/939.pdf?phpsessid). The findings considered the u-Commerce as new distribution channel for financial services industry. There is growing enthusiasm about the increasing number of mobile phones in the developing world and the potential of the mobile platform in helping to address the needs of individuals and small businesses (UNCTAD, 2012).

Unified communication

Businesses are faced with a proliferation of communications tools and firms must find ways to link them. Rather than trying to maintain multiple separate communications channels, the goal is to integrate and manage e-mail, phone calls, instant messaging video conferencing and other forms of communication to allow workers to communicate more quickly and easily and to work faster even when they are mobile. Guth (2007) notes that in its simplest form, unification might allow a

user to click on a phone number in an e-mail to place a call from a PC. In its more advanced form, the technology might offer the ability to use a PC or cellular phone to determine if a person is online, on a cellphone or a desk phone, and to call them or launch a conference call by clicking on an icon or button.

One key question about unified communication for organizations will be where best to apply the technology. Mobile workers and those who routinely need timely information from an assortment of others would appear to benefit most from this technology. Early adopters of unified communication include companies that are geographically dispersed or businesses that depend on rapid communication to compete such as financial institutions. However, unified communication may be less suited to those businesses where workers do not have to interact with a host of other people or who mainly interact with the same group (Guth, 2007).

Since unified communications cross organizational boundaries they are complex in nature. They demand management that can navigate organizational politics, train people of diverse backgrounds, and deal with multiple vendors each of whom is supplying a subset of the technology infrastructure, applications, and channels. Unified communications can create regulatory issues because electronic attachments and mobile communications might need to be archived (for example, to meet Sarbanes-Oxley requirements).

Unified communications are important because of the demand of workers and students for communication devices that minimize the need for channel-dependent hardware. Where cellphones, text messaging, and instant messaging eclipsed e-mail as the preferred means to communicate, video creation and exchange now provide another viable and potentially critical need for mobile users.

The worldwide market for online video content grew tenfold by 2010, growing from about 13 million households during 2005 to more than 131 million households by 2010, becoming an $11 billion annual business by 2011 (Carvajal, 2007). Of all broadband households today, 12.8% are already regularly viewing professional content via online content aggregators. The number of broadband households is expected to double between 2005 and 2010, to more than 413 million.

On See Me TV, a service offered by European provider 3, users can shoot video on the mobile phones, bypass video sites like YouTube, or Yahoo, and post them to a gallery where the videos can be watched by others on their phones. And to spur usage, people who contribute video clips get paid for it, getting 10% of the revenue generated when others download their clip. See Me TV and several services like it are among the first to offer cellphone users the same kind of interactive, self-generated content that is offered to PC users (Abboud, 2007).

AT&T's Video Share allows its users to send live or

recorded videos to others while they are talking to them on their cellphones. The one-way video streaming service is available on AT&T's high-speed 3G UMTS/HSDPA network. Two people can view a video when they are in a two-way cellular connection. Video Share is the first application for AT&T's emerging internet protocol multimedia subsystem (IMS) platform, which will eventually be used as the vehicle for delivering IP services over wireless and wired network connections (Gardner, 2007).

Demand for more social networking bandwidth will also push unified communications. Mobile users want access to entertaining sites such as YouTube, ifilm, MySpace, Vimeo, Eyespot, Jumpcut, Ourmedia, vSocial, Google video, Grouper, Revver, VideoEgg, and Yahoo! And as is the case with other mobile platforms having network access there will be supply and demand for substantive video content on cellular devices. FORA.tv, for example, delivers discourse, discussions and debates on political, social and cultural issues, and enables viewers to join the conversation. It provides deep, unfiltered content, tools for self-expression, and a place for the interactive community to gather online.

Research Channel is a consortium of major universities that puts presentations by their top researchers on its web site, ResearchChannel.org. It has a video library of more than 3,000 titles with topics that include business and economics, computer science and engineering, health and medicine, and the sciences. Princeton University's University Channel focuses on public and international affairs videos, while www.Research-TV.com emphasizes work at U.K. colleges and universities. There are niche-oriented "smart" video sites that focus on such topics as energy policy (for example, EnergyPolicy TV.com), technology, entertainment, business, science, and culture (for example, ted.com).

Corporate personnel recruitment is another obvious opportunity for mobile cellular communications that will push the requirement for unified communications. Von Bergen (2007) notes that while job seekers have been putting videos online for some time employers are now taking the same route. Online videos are being created to recruit workers. Organizations realize that they can reach potential employees where they are, and younger job candidates prefer YouTube and sites like it.

Many corporations have been delivering their own video content to potential recruits, employees, customers, or other important constituencies across time and place. What has become different and important now is getting the content moved to cellular devices. Companies can create and publish the videos themselves or outsource all or part of the process. Firms like uVuMobile, Inc. (uVuMobile.com) provide organizations with mobility software and services that offer content providers, carriers, and entertainment brands a full suite of products to deliver their video and audio content to mobile handsets. Companies like uVuMobile can provide

platforms that are seamlessly integrated with a robust set of applications supported by a suite of enablers that include mobile marketing, reporting, content aggregation, e-Commerce options, advertising and other professional services.

Unique integrated solutions can be developed for mobile markets, providing scalable mobile technology to create and manage mobile initiatives, including hosting services, marketing, media solutions and mobile content distribution.

There are a number of start-up companies that offer new ways for cellphone users to access internet video content previously controlled by their cellphone carrier. These companies allow users to view a wider array of internet video clips without a subscription and without having to use a specific phone model.

Users of these services can view online videos on any standard video-enabled phone and the videos can be wirelessly downloaded to a handset for viewing later, or streamed over cellular networks to be viewed in real time. While the quality of the video content is rarely as crisp as users are accustomed to online, and viewing can be limited by the amount of storage on the phone, the services are generally free, powered by advertising, and independent of particular carriers. Several of the new companies offering these services (for example, Cellfish Media, MyWaves, and 3Guppies) have already attracted nearly a million users and are attracting tens of thousands more a day (Vascellaro, 2007a). These new services are part of a broad sweep of mobile companies trying to get consumers to translate their fanaticism for online video watching to smaller screens. But have these services caught on? According to the research firm M:Metrics Inc., of the nearly seven million who watch movie or TV video from their phones every month, the vast majority watch video clips sent to them from family or friends, rather than video prepackaged by a carrier. And Telephis Inc. reports that only 3.6% of US cellphone users subscribed to a mobile video service in the first quarter of 2007, up from 1.6% in the year-earlier period. Inhibiting the growth is consumer concerns about cellphone storage and lag time and delays when downloading the video content (Vascellaro, 2007b). A "Future and Emerging Technologies" activity could act as the development pathfinder and as a structured foresight service for future communications tools. By supporting upfront collaborative basic research at the frontier of knowledge in core mobile technology, e-Commerce and in their combination with other relevant disciplines, could continue identifying emerging mobile related research domains and exploring options in mobile R&D roadmaps where road blocks are anticipated and where "no known solutions" are available. e-Commerce could pursue its mission of nurturing many "novel ideas" for core technologies and radically new uses, up to their blooming into the first proof of concept and of narrowing down options that would lead to the industrial solutions of tomorrow.

Integrated approach to business

An integrated approach is the key. A type of commerce where a commercial transaction can be performed securely, any time, anywhere in the world, from any equipment, whether wired or wireless, using Internet technologies. "U-Commerce is a dynamic convergence of the physical and the digital, the interface of brick-and-mortar commerce with Web-based wireless and other next-generation technologies in ways that will create new levels of convenience and value for buyers and sellers (Jay, 2004).

A term u-Commerce has been created in the Internet world that refers to commerce that can be conducted anywhere and any time in that it is a fusion of e-commerce, m-Commerce (mobile commerce), t-commerce (television commerce) and bricks and mortar. It means seamless movement for consumers. U-Commerce means that customers can come from all angles - today they may be in a showroom, tomorrow they may come at you via a website, cellular telephone phone or interactive television thanks to mobile technology (Jay, 2004). On-Line There are four Fundamental dimensions of u-Commerce as described by Watson, Richard T., Leyland F. 1. Ubiquity, 2. Uniqueness, 3. Universality and 4. Unison.

Ubiquity allows users to access networks from anywhere at any time, and in turn, to be reachable at any place and any time. Computer will be useful everywhere. Basically we can say chip will be embedded in our daily life so as to be benefited by Internet and wireless technology supported by intelligent systems. For example, Payment technology is becoming ubiquitous, shattering past constraints of location and functionality. It can now connect the smallest rural community, enabling it to conduct commerce with the rest of the world.

Uniqueness allows users to be uniquely identified—not only in terms of their identity and associated preferences, but also in terms of their geographical position. Avail only services what you want. Every program will be customization of your needs. It will be according to your roles in daily life. Download songs to make your mood or transfer sales records to your business data server on the spot of sale. Everything is unique and customized.

Universality means devices are universally usable and multi-functional. Due to Internet and satellites your desktop, laptop, cell phone, or PDA will avail free mobility and lots of information at any time.

Unison covers the idea of integrated data across multiple applications so that users have a consistent view on their information-irrespective of the device used. Consistency means if I change an address in my phone book it should reflect changes in my cellphone, calendar and PDA simultaneously.

In December 2001 a group of researchers met in Berlin, Germany to analyse these events and discuss future prospects for ecommerce. They concluded that e-Commerce was not dead, but had moved on from its overly hyped beginning (Nathalie, 2001).

This accelerated integration of many mobile technology fields, in which eCommerce will be playing a primary role, will be at the origin of a coming composite revolution that will be driving the emergence of a whole range of new technologies and disciplines (from meta-materials and nanotechnologies, to bio-informatics, bio-computing, bio-sensors and direct neural interfaces, etc). In particular, it is expected that the fundamental models of information, computing and communication will soon be revisited to address an emerging post-Turing and post-Shannon e-Commerce era.

Market drivers

The pervasiveness of technology

History has clearly demonstrated that technology, properly applied, drives efficiencies, productivity, and value. As technology becomes more pervasive think of the explosive growth of nanotechnology as well as ongoing capital investments in technology at the enterprise level there is a larger platform on which to leverage innovation and new applications.

The growth of wireless

One of the fastest growing distributed bases of new technology is wireless, with up to one billion mobile phones alone was expected to be in use by 2003 As wireless networks have expanded around the globe, mobile phone usage and new applications have exploded. To that end, an eye opening study conducted by experience revealed that there were 2.7 billion mobile phones in use by year 2010. The study also revealed that about two thirds of mobile phone users were "active users of SMS text messaging. Approximately 1.8 billion people actively texting today 2010 (Michael, 2008).

One of the most successful new applications was DoCoMo's iMode service in Japan, which allowed its 20 million subscribers to download music, shop and send instant messages. Americans and Europeans were also excited by the possibilities. In a survey conducted by Accenture, 40% of wireless phone users in the U.S. and Europe found the idea of shopping with their phones an appealing concept (Schapp and Cornelius, 2002). The potential of wireless is not limited to consumer applications. In some developing countries, for example, ATMs, one of the signal innovations of the retail banking industry, are now running off wireless GSM networks.

Increasing bandwidth and connectivity

Bandwidth has been doubling every nine months or roughly at twice the growth rate of computing power. It is not hard to imagine a world where IPv6 potential and promise may come to be realized and interactivity is possible in appliances as ubiquitous as televisions, medicine cabinets and refrigerators. Increasing bandwidth will lead to the creation of what is being called the "evernet," where billions of devices will be connected to the hyperspeed, broadband, multiformat Web 2.0. In the future, the Internet will always be "on." These are very powerful and far-reaching phenomena that can clearly drive all sorts of business models (as they did in the dotcom explosion of the late 90s). But to paraphrase Peter Drucker, every great idea eventually degenerates into work. Realizing the full vision of u-Commerce commerce that is universal, seamless, and secure will require a great deal of effort in a number of key areas.

ANALYSES OF MOBILE AND E-COMMERCE USE SITUATION

In mobile commerce context, several studies have examined the adoption of mobile technologies and services, suggesting the Technological Acceptance Model (TAM) and innovation diffusion theories providing relevant means for explaining mobile services adoption and use (Hung et al., 2003; Han et al., 2004; Kleijnen et al., 2004; Lee et al., 2003; Teo and Pok, 2003). In this section, we analyze on the technology, with emphasis on studies on mobile and ecommerce services.

Early stage research on mobile banking adoption in UK confirms that relative advantage over existing services, compatibility of mobile banking with consumer needs and lifestyle, and the ability to test a new service and observe the successful outcomes of other users increased positive attitudes towards adopting, whereas perceived complexity and risks had a negative effect on the attitudes towards adoption (Lee et al., 2003).

The most significant feature of mobile technology is the mobility *per se*: ability to access services ubiquitously, on the move, and through wireless networks and various devices, such as, PDAs and mobile phones (Coursaris and Hassanein, 2002; Lyytinen and Yoo, 2002). Compared with traditional electronic commerce, where transactions are commonly conducted through stationary desktop and laptop computers, mobile computing provides users with more freedom, as they can access information and services without having to find a physical space, such as, an office or an Internet café for internet connection (May, 2001). Kleinrock (1996) labeled the benefits provided by mobile technologies as "anytime and anywhere computing" and outlined the two most common dimensions of mobility – independence of time and place. The spatial and temporal dimensions of mobility extend computing and allow, in principle, anytime and anywhere

access to information, communication, and services. Kakihara and Sørensen (2001) expanded the concept of mobility into three dimensions of human interaction; spatial, temporal and contextual mobility. The spatial and temporal dimensions correspond to those of Kleinrock's anytime and anywhere computing, whereas the contextual dimension extends the definition further.

Contexts in which people reside continuously frame their interaction with others, including people's cultural background, particular situation or mood, and degree of mutual recognition (Kakihara and Sørensen, 2001).

Perry et al. (2001) discuss restrictions that use situations pose to the ubiquitous computing. Specifically, the anytime and anywhere access is dependent on technological and social conditions of the use environment; not all places provide the needed technological infrastructure such as network connections required for ubiquitous computing, and not all social situations are adequate for mobile computing (Perry et al., 2001). The potential of mobile technology for the retail sector is endless. Advances in Internet and network technology and the rapidly growing number of mobile personal devices result in the fast growth of Mobile e-Commerce, m-Commerce and eventually u-Commerce. Many retailers are already using SMS to alert customers of special events and offers and Bluetooth technology could lead to customers receiving sales messages the minute they walk into stores.

CONCLUSION

Our preliminary study is focusing on recognition of u-Commerce concept in realizing the promising of u-commerce. This paper is presenting preliminary results and announcing deeper second wave survey which should provide empirical evidence to support hypothesis that African enterprises and public services providers are following global trend of increasing u-Commerce technologies international importance and penetration.

Now that mobile penetration in many parts of the world has reached a plateau, new growth depends, to a large extent, on generating revenue from new services. And advances in the devices that customers use to access cellular networks often can help enable those new services. Recognizing that, the fact that wireless device sales outpaced market forecasts for 2005 is a very positive sign.

We are in a transitional phase of the global commerce. Some of the assumptions and early tenets of the "new commerce" are being challenged. To us, the labels "old business" and "new business" are, in fact, a false distinction. The evolution we are witnessing and want to help drive is the evolution of the "smart commerce." This is a commerce that is more flexible, fluid, interconnected, efficient and resilient. We believe u-Commerce will be both a driver and an outcome of the smart commerce with the mobile technology growth. The smart commerce is poised to grow explosively, with many players from multiple industries all vying for the customer's attention. These players will be offering new services, new payment tools, and a host of new ways to get access to goods and services anytime, anywhere, and any way due to mobile technology. We expect competition to be fierce among players in the payments chain, with the advantage going to those who recognize a few fundamental rules about this emerging environment.

U-commerce represents the next step in digitization as true ubiquity has profound implications. Thus, marketing and other scholars need to be preparing for this final destination and recognize that e-Commerce and m-Commerce are way stations on the path. They are signposts on the road from somewhere to everywhere. To traverse this path, marketing scholars need to investigate several significant issues.

REFERENCES

Abboud L (2007). Cellphones' coming attraction: You! Wall St. J. B1.

Africa Internet & B2C E-Commerce Report 2012, RESEARCH ON INTERNATIONAL MARKETS accessed in October 2012from www.ystats.com/uploads/report_abstracts/939.pdf?PHPSESSID.

Ahonen A, Jones S (2003). iStethoscope in Medical Journal.http://apps.peterjbentley.com/Blog/?e=53483&d=08/29/2010&s=iStethoscope%20Pro%20in%20a%20medical%20journal. Retrieved November 23, 2010).

Bergen J (2007). Recruiters: You, too, can YouTube. The Philadelphia Inquirer. C1-C8.

Bourguignon F (2003). The Growth Elasticity of Poverty Reduction in T. Eicher and S. Turnovsky (eds.): Inequality of Growth, Cambridge, MA: The MIT Press.

Carvajal D (2007). Sneak preview of Europe's Internet video market. International Herald Tribune. http//www.iht.com/articles/2007/02/11/business/video12.php.

Coursaris C, Hassanein K (2002). Understanding m-Commerce a consumer centric model, Quarterly journal of electronic commerce, 3, 3, 247-271.

Gardner W (2007). AT&T debuts video share, but not for iPhone. http://www.informationweek.com/internet/showArticle.jhtml;jsessionid=UJ2SS3E2OQWVQQSNDLQCKHSCJUNN2JVN?articleID=201200463&articleID=201200463.

GoT (2001). Poverty Reduction Strategy Paper. Progress Report 2000/01, Dar es Salaam: Government of Tanzania, August ComScore: 38 Percent Of Smartphone Owners Have Used A Mobile Device To Make A Purchase". http://techcrunch.com/2011/12/05/comscore-38-percent-of-smartphone-owners-have-used-a-mobile-device-to-make-a purchase/?utm_source=feedburner&utm_medium=feed&utm_campaign=Feed%3A+Techcrunch+%28TechCrunch%29. Retrieved December 6, 2011.

Guth R (2007). Let's get together. Wall St. J. R9.

Han S, Harkke V, Mustonen P, Seppänen M, Kallio M (2004). Mobilizing medical information and knowledge: some insights from a survey. In 12th European Conference on Information Systems. Turku, Finland.

Harden T (2012).Mobile marketing methods that get results Mobile Marketing Trends. http://www.bobiznow.com. Retrieved February 2012.

http://citeseerx.ist.psu.edu/viewdoc/download?doi=10.1.1.94.46&rep=rep1&type=pdf. Retrieved August 23, 2010.

http://web.worldbank.org/WBSITE/EXTERNAL/TOPICS/EXTPOVERTY/0,contentMDK:20195989~pagePK:148956~piPK:2166 18~theSitePK:336992, 00.html cited on May 2007.

Hung SY, Ku CY, Chang CM (2003). Critical Factors of WAP Services Adoption: an Empirical Study. Electronic Commer. Res. Appl. 2(1):42-60.

IMF (2004). Joint Staff Assessment of the Poverty Reduction Strategy Paper Progress Report, IMF Country Report No. 04/283, Washington DC: International Monetary Fund.

ITU World Radiocommunication Seminar highlights future communication technologies". http://www.itu.int/net/pressoffice/press_releases/2010/48.aspx.

Jay CU (2004). Commerce Integrating business anywhere sited on 7 June 2008 at http://www.buzzle.com/editorials/3-16-2004-51736.asp.

Kakihara M, Sørensen C (2001). Expanding the Mobility' Concept. ACM SIGGROUP Bull. 22(3):33-37.

Kleijnen M, Wetzels M, de Ruyter K (2004). Consumer acceptance of wireless finance. J. Financial Serv. Mark. 8(3):206-217.

Kleinrock L (1996). Nomadicity: anytime, anywhere in a disconnected world. Mob. Netw. Appl. 1(4):351-357.

Lee MSY, McGoldrick PJ, Keeling KA, Doherty J (2003). Using ZMET to explore barriers to the adoption of 3G mobile banking services", Int. J. Retail Distrib. Manage. 31(6):340-348.

Lyytinen K, Yoo Y (2002). Research Commentary: The Next Wave of Nomadic Computing". Information Syst. Res. 13(4):377-388.

May P (2001). Mobile Commerce: Opportunities, Applications, and Technologies of Wireless Business: Cambridge University Press.

Michael (2008). Mobile Growth is Exceeding Expectations Globally Mobile Marketing http://www.mobilemarketingwatch.com/mobile-growth-is-exceeding-expectations-globally-2/ sited 21/August/2008.

Mobile Store front. Mobile Commerce News. http://www.mobilestarterstore.com/index.php?option=com_content&view=category&layout=blog&id=1&Itemid=50 Retrieved November 2011.

Nathalie S (2001). Book Review Benoît DANARD & Rémy LE CHAMPION In a group of researchers met in Berlin, Germany to analyse these events and discuss future prospects for e-commerce p.123.

Pepus G (2007). Smart image and video search. KMWorld 16(6) 6-8.

Perry M, O'hara K, Sellen A, Brown B, Harper R (2001). Dealing with Mobility: Understanding Access Anytime, Anywhere. ACM Trans. Comput. Hum. Interact. 8(4):323-347.

Pettey C, Stevens H (2012). Gartner Identifies the Top 10 Consumer Mobile Applications for 2012, The report is available on Gartner's website at http://www.gartner.com/resId=1205513.Retrived Retrieved January 2012.

Schapp S, Cornelius R D (2000). A white paper U-Commerce Leading the New World of Payments.

Schejter A, Serenko A, Turel O, Zahaf M (2010). Policy implications of market segmentation as a determinant of fixed-mobile service substitution: What it means for carriers and policy makers". Telematics Inform. 27(1):90-102.

Tancer W (2007). YouTube and Google: Quantifying the Synergy.http://weblogs.hitwise.com/billtancer/2007/01/youtube_and_google_quantifying.htmlVon.

Teo, TSH, Pok SH (2003). Adoption of WAP-enabled Mobile Phones Among Internet Users". Omega 31(6):483-498.

Tiwari R, Buse S (2007). The Mobile Commerce Prospects: A strategic analysis of opportunities in the banking sector (PDF). Hamburg: Hamburg University Press. p. 33. ISBN 978-3-937816-31-9.

UNCTAD (2012). Mobile Money for Business Development in the east African community, A Comparative Study of Existing Platforms and Regulations United nations Conference on Trade and Development, access on October 2012 from http://unctad.org/en/PublicationsLibrary/dtlstict2012d2_en.pdf.

Vascellaro J (2007a). What's a Cellphone for. Wall St. J. B5.

Vascellaro J (2007b). Calling all videos. Wall St. J. D1-2.

Watson RT, Pitt LF, Berthon P, Zinkhan GM (2002). "U-Commerce: Extending the Universe of Marketing," J. Acad. Market. Sci. 30((4):329-343.

World Bank (2001). Social Development in Europe and Central Asia Region: Issues and Directions. Environmentally and Socially Sustainable Development, Social Development Team, Europe and Central Asia, World Bank.

24

Accounting information systems in the fast food industry: A valuable tool for small business survival

Thembelihle Allah, Puleng August, Siphamandla Bhaza, Tinashe Chigovanyika, Unathi Dyan, Tinashe Muteweye, Mandisi Ngcoza, Neliswa Tshiwula, Vuyiseka Qambela, Yanga Vooi and Juan-Pierré Bruwer

Faculty of Business, Cape Peninsula University of Technology, PO Box 625, Cape Town, 8000, South Africa.

Prior research has shown that small businesses make limited use of financial information which has a distinct and direct effect on the performance, profitability and overall success of these entities holistically. It has been reported that up to 90% of small businesses fail within a period of 5 years. It is also evident that over 60% of small medium and micro enterprises (SMMEs) make use of financial information systems which have to be updated manually on a periodic basis. From this dispensation, the perception was formulated by the authors that small businesses are success adverse as a result of making inadequate use of accounting information systems. The main aim of this study was to determine to what extent small businesses make use of accounting information systems. In essence, this empirical research which fell within the positivistic research paradigm and responses were gleaned from 30 owners and/or managers of small businesses, operating in the fast food industry. Furthermore these entities also operated in the Cape Metropole and were targeted by means of purposive sampling. All respondents were assured of confidentiality and anonymity, and all responses were of a voluntary nature. Descriptive research was utilised to extract relevant findings, which were followed by relevant conclusions.

Key words: SMME, accounting information systems, success, profitability, sustainability.

INTRODUCTION

Small businesses and small business success

Small businesses in South Africa account for more than 56% of private sector's employment and 36% of the national Gross Domestic Product according to DTI (2008). According to Shah and Khedkar (2006), SMMEs play a catalytic role in the development of any country as they are described as the 'engines of growth' in developing and transition economies, accounting for a significant proportion in manufacturing, exports and employment, and are deemed as major contributors to the national GDP. Despite the aforementioned, Brink et al. (2003) express the view that the survival rate of small businesses is fairly low in South Africa as less than 50% of newly established businesses survive beyond five years.

Various factors are perceived to contribute to the high failure rate of these enterprises, including limited financing opportunities, legislation, inflation, interest rates and market fluctuations. Among this list of factors is the inadequate utilisation of Accounting Information Systems (hereafter referred to as AIS). By adequately using AIS it is possible to assess the risk of some operations and/or predict probable future earnings with sophisticated statistical software applications with the main intention to enhance business operations. Deloitte Touch Tohmatsu Limited (2007) conducted a study whereby the power of AIS has been tested and tried in larger companies with great success. In essence it was found that the AIS generated information which, in turn, benefited management in making proper decisions to enhance their firm's

---

*Corresponding author. E-mail: BruwerJP@cput.ac.za.

overall survival. The same AIS, according to the previous authors, could be implemented in SMMEs.

AIS are also to record financial transactions of an organisation by means of combining methodologies, controls and accounting techniques with relevant technologies (Berisha-Namani, 2009). This type of system is used to track transactions and provides internal reporting data, external reporting data, financial statements, and respective trend analysis for specific 'time-intervals' (information for relevant decision-making). Small businesses require effective information systems to support and to deliver information to the different internal users to make the correct business decisions, but more often than not a limited number of these entities actually make use of such a system (Bruwer and Watkins, 2010).

LITERATURE REVIEW

Small business success

Small businesses play an important role in the stimulation of the economy through means of creating jobs and eliminating the poverty (Joubert et al., 1999). According to Luiz (2002), small business survival can be considered as a vital indicator of economic prosperity as these entities have a remarkable capacity to absorb labour; absorbing well over 50% of the South Africa's total employment. Bloom (2009) further states that unfortunately small businesses survival in South Africa leaves much to be desired. The latter is affirmed by Baron (2000) when stating that an estimated 70 to 80% of start-up small businesses in South Africa fail with their first five years of existence.

Du Plooy et al. (2005) explains that the survival (and business success in essence) of small businesses can be measured by means of performance measures which include: financial performance measures (for example, profitability, liquidity, solvency, etc.) and non-financial performance measures (for example, customer base-size, employee satisfaction and customer satisfaction, etc.). The term 'business success' has different meanings to different people as it can also be viewed in the light of a business owner achieving his/her personal objective(s) through means of a business, delivering superior customer service or having a sound atmosphere within the respective business venture (Femsa, 2007). Unfortunately, it is Adeniran and Johnston (2012:3089) who state that South African SMMEs have limited capabilities in terms of business success and are adversely affected by competitive forces of micro economic factors among other factors.

Factors affecting small business success

Prior research has shown that factors affecting SMME

survival and success pertain to that of macro-economic factors and micro-economic-factors. Economic factors influence the state of the economy and have both long-term and short-term effects thereon. According to Mohr and Fourie (2004:11-12) economic factors can be sub-categorised as follows: macro economic factors and micro economic factors. These sub-categories are briefly expanded upon.

Macro economic factors: Mohr and Fourie (2004:11-12) explain that macro-economic factors are external factors around a business that affects it directly. Businesses have limited/no control over such factors. Popular macro economic factors, that affect business survival (of both large and small entities) to a great extent, include crime, currency, fluctuating market conditions, political changes, unemployment, interest rates and exchange rates.

The global financial crisis can be regarded as a macro economic factor which adversely affected the economic landscapes of South Africa, and Germany during from 2010 onwards. Essentially other macro economic factors to the likes of inflation rates and unemployment rates, among other, were largely affected by one major macro economic factor, namely that of the global economic crisis.

Micro economic factors: Mohr and Fourie (2004:11-12) explain that micro-economic factors are internal factors inside a business, which affects it. Popular micro economic factors, that affect business survival (and business success) to a great extent include, management skills, business skills, financial management skills, business knowledge, accounting skills, financial difficulties and overhead costs.

Brink et al. (2003) make mention that other micro economic factors which influenced the survival and success of small businesses include financial problems, the lack of funding, insufficient bookkeeping skills, expensive operating expenditure, poor cash flow management and bad debts. Jooste (2008) is of the opinion that small business survival is also adversely affected as a result of monetary issues, limited exposure, lack of sales, lack of competent staff and the negligence of financial performance measures.

All in all these economic factors need to be managed effectively as they influence business decisions. To ensure that a well-informed business decision is made by management of small businesses, it is recommended that Accounting Information Systems are deployed.

Business decisions, AIS and its importance

Sharkas (1974) is of the opinion that majority of small businesses fail due to inappropriate business decisions being made. In fundamental nature business decisions should be made with information (pertaining to the relevant business venture) which is accurate, reliable, and valid. One way to ensure that adequate business decisions are made is through means of utilising AIS. Femsa (2007) further states that AIS are capable of analysing and interpreting financial data to produce important information for decision-making. From a technological dispensation, AIS is available for use in an electronic format, which can provide all relevant stakeholders with 'real-time-information' on demand.

AIS are regarded as tools which, when incorporated into business process, help in the management and control of business related activities in the firms' economic and financial areas, by providing information for better decision-making. Sharkas (1974) explains that AIS should be simple, flexible, self-explanatory, based upon conventional accounting practices and capable of monitoring information for control as well as arrangements for planning and budgeting. In essence AIS should also provide an affordable, comprehensive solution for managing an entire business from sales and customer relationships to financials and operations. Rootman and Kruger (2010) collaborate the importance of AIS in the following extract:

"SMMEs need to be familiar with their business functions as these functions are essential towards a firm's overall performance measured by sales, profits, rates of return, customer satisfaction and customer retention. It is this important for a firm's owners and managers to be able to adjust and manage these functions when global economic changes occur".

Rootman and Kruger (2010) further make mention that the lack of such systems can lead to high lead times in the business process, high cycle times in business transactions and poor utilisation of business resources. With AIS, small businesses can streamline operations, act on timely and complete information, and accelerate profitable growth. Briggs et al. (2003) raise the opinion that AIS should provide solutions (information which will lead to better decision-making) that are custom-made for small businesses, which should allow them to operate efficiently and to save on costs by managing more effectively. This is done by recording all transaction in a common database that is used by users throughout a business, by means of providing performance indicators to make the best possible business decisions. In essence, all accounting systems are designed with the main intention to provide information to decision-makers to assist them in their decision making (Sowden-Service, 2006).

RESEARCH DESIGN

This research was empirical in nature as it involved a practical involvement with specific research subjects as predetermined by the authors. Moreover, this research was deemed as a descriptive research as it describes a specific phenomenon at hand (Collis and Hussey, 2009). This research study also fell within the positivistic research paradigm as the research was quantitative in nature.

Data collection

Data were collected through means of questionnaires by taking into consideration a sample size of owner-managers of small businesses that operated in the fast-food industry within the Cape Metropole. Apart from the latter, SMMEs targeted also had to adhere to the following delineation criteria:

1. SMMEs should have been in existence for at least 1 year.
2. SMMEs owner and/or manager must be actively involved in business operations.

As the actual size of the population was unknown, an attempt was made to gather information on the identified research problem. For this reason a total sample size of 30 SMMEs was chosen for this study.

The study required authors to make use of non-probability sampling (purposive sampling), with the intention to glean rich data for data analysis purposes. The data collection tool used was that of a questionnaire which consisted mostly of close-ended questions, and Likert-scale questions. All data collected were analysed accordingly through means of descriptive statistics

RESEARCH FINDINGS AND DISCUSSION

Respondents were specifically asked which AIS they make use of on a regular basis. Approximately 28% of respondents revealed that they make use of technological AIS, despite the fact that the phenomenon of information technology has been in existence for over 10 years. The collaborated view of respondents, pertaining to the afore-going question, is evident in Table 1.

It is clear from Table 1 that the bulk of respondents made use of manual systems, meaning that all relevant information stemming from accounting data (to make effective decisions) had to be calculated on a manual, periodic basis as opposed to having real time information at their disposal.

Respondents were further asked what information they normally glean from using their current AIS (be it manual or automatic). The summary of responses is evident as shown in Table 2.

As accounting information generally stems from past events, it was interesting to note that accounting information is mostly used for predictive purposes in the sense of budgets (79.17%). The second most important reason why accounting information were used, was for controlling purposes in the sense of controlling stock (77.5%) and cash flow (74.17%)

When respondents were asked how their AIS add value to their business, the following dispensation emerged in Table 3.

From Table 3, it is evident that the accounting information at the disposal of management's fingertips is of some value (on average 66.53%) to their respective businesses.

Table 1. The utilisation of AIS by respondents.

IAS used	Make use of (%)
Pastel	6.5
SAP	0.5
MRP Software	2.0
Quick Books	11.5
Vision Point 2000	4.0
Business Version 32	2.0
e-Business Suite	2.0
MS Office (Excel)	18.5
Manuel System	53.0

Table 2. Uses of AIS in respondents' businesses.

System used for	Frequency (%)
Billing	69.17
Stock control	77.50
Production planning	65.00
Budgeting	79.17
Cash flow	74.17
Calculating taxation	71.67

Table 3. How AIS add value to respondents' businesses.

Add value by means of	Frequency (%)
Feedback on the status of an order	64.17
Saving time (doing books)	63.33
Helps circulate information better	63.33
Measure business growth	67.50
Consolidate financial statements better	71.67
Helps with accurate re-ordering level	69.17

LIMITATIONS OF THE RESEARCH

This research only took into consideration the perception of small business enterprise owners and/or managers which operated in the fast moving consumer goods industry in the Cape Metro pole. In essence, the respondents also had to adhere to a predetermined set of delineation criteria. Both time and monetary constraints played an imperative role in the formulation of this research study as quantitative data had to be collected in a relatively short period of time (2 months).

ETHICAL CONSIDERATIONS

All respondents were assured of confidentiality and anonymity and all respondents were assured safety from any harm. Furthermore, all responses were voluntary in nature and respondents were informed that they could withdraw from the study any time so they wished.

Conclusion

Despite the improvement and advancement in the field of information technology, it is clear that small businesses are reluctant to adapt to new technology as the bulk of SMMEs still make use of manual accounting information systems. AIS are perceived as critical in establishing 'solid ground' in the business realm however these entities lag behind in the implementation of these systems compared to large companies (Deloitte Touch Tohmatsu Limited, 2007).

The afore-mentioned situation is largely attributed to economic factors, both macro and micro as the ability of small businesses to realise their goals depends on how well they acquire, interpret, synthesise, evaluate and understand accounting information at their disposal, in order to manage and/or control these economic factors.

REFERENCES

Adeniran T, Johnston K (2012). Investigating the dynamic capabilities and competitive advantage of South African SMEs. Afr. J. Bus. Manage. 6(11) pp. 4088-4099.
Baron C (2000). Brilliant ideas but spectacular flops. Sunday Times Business Times: 1, 9 Apr.
Berisha-Namani M (2009). The Role of Information Technology in Small and Medium Sized Enterprises in Kosova. Fulbright Academy 2009 Conference.
Bloom K (2009). South Africa: Advancing or inhibiting entrepreneurs. Entrepreneur, 36:62, July.
Briggs R, De Vreede G, Nunamaker J (2003). Special Issue: Information Systems Success. J. Manag. Inf. Syst. 19(4):5-8.
Brink A, Cant M, Ligthelm A (2003). Problems experiences by small businesses is South Africa. Paper presented at the Annual conference of Small Enterprise Association of Australia and New Zealand, University of Ballarat, Australia.
Bruwer J, Watkins J (2010). Sustainability of South African FMCG SMME retail businesses in the Cape Peninsula. Afr. J. Bus. Manage. 4(16):3550-3555.
Collis J, Hussey R (2009). Business Research: A practical guide for undergraduate and post graduate students. Hampshire: Palgrave Macmillan.
Deloitte Touch Tohmatsu Limited (2007). *In the Dark II: What many boards and executives STILL don't know about the health of their businesses - a survey by Deloitte in co-operation with The Economist Intelligence Unit.* Deloitte Touch Tohmatsu Limited. New York: DTT Global Office Creative Studio.
DTI (2008). Department of Trade and Industry – Annual Report [Online]. Available from: http://www.info.gov.za/view/DownloadFileAction?id=111951 [Accessed on 08/10/2012].
Du Plooy S, Goodey H, Lötter W, Nortjé D, Meyer C (2005). X-Kit Undergraduate – Financial Accounting. Cape Town: Maskew Miller Longman (Pty) Ltd.
Femsa (2007). How do we build a successful business model? [**Online**]. Available from http://www.femsa.com/en/assets/006/17646.pdf [Accessed on 08/10/2012].
Jooste B (2008). SMEs are feeling the pinch. Available from: http://www.iol.co.za/news/south-africa/smes-are-feeling-the-pinch-1.419931 397975 [Accessed: 08/10/2012].

Joubert C, Schoeman N, Blignaut J (1999). Small, Medium and MicroSized Enterprises (SMMEs) and the Housing Construction Industry: A Possible Solution to South Africa's Socio-Economic Problems. South Afr. J. Econ. Manage. Sci. 2(1):21.

Luiz J (2002). Small business development, entrepreneurship and expanding the business sector in a developing economy: the case of South Africa. J. Appl. Bus. Res. 8(2):53–68.

Mohr P, Fourie L (2004). Ekonomie vir Suid-Afrikaanse studente. Pretoria: Van Schaik Publishers.

Rootman C, Kruger J (2010). Adapting SMME Business Functions During Economic Turmoil. Acta Commercial 2010.

Shah T, Khedkar A (2006). Case on successful SME financing – SIDBI. Indian Institute of Planning and Management (IIPM), Ahmedabad.

Sharkas W (1974). The mini information system – an aid to small business survival. J. Small Bus. Manage. 1974, pp. 39-41.

Sowden-Service C (2006). Gripping GAAP. Durban: CSS Publishers.

25

Calculating the best cut off point using logistic regression and neural network on credit scoring problem- A case study of a commercial bank

Mehrnaz Heidari Soureshjani and Ali Mohammad Kimiagari

Department of Industrial Engineering, Amirkabir University of Technology, Tehran, Iran.

Credit scoring is a method used to estimate the probability of default or becoming delinquent of a loan applicant or existing borrower. There are several methods used for scoring, such as traditional statistics models like probit and logistic regression, data mining approaches and also artificial intelligence algorithms. In this paper, two high-usage methods on real data of legal customers of a commercial were used, and also their performance have been compared. It was found that logistic regression as a statistic model can estimate a good econometrics model which is able to calculate the probability of defaulting, and also neural networks is a very high performance black box method which can be used in credit scoring problems. Also the best cut off point in both logistic regression and neural network is calculated by these methods which have minimum errors on the available data.

Key words: Credit scoring, logistic regression, goodness of fitness, cut off point, neural network.

INTRODUCTION

Devoting capital and asset to economic activities is accomplished through financial market, in which banking is the main part. This is done through lending to the bank's customers. Credit risk means the probability of default or becoming delinquent of a loan applicant or existing borrower. Reducing and controlling this risk is one of the main parameters which resulted to better lending approaches and performance improvement of the banks.

There are several methods used to solve the problem of credits scoring. These different useful techniques, known as the credit scoring models, have been developed by the banks and researchers in order to solve the problems involved during the evaluation process. The objective of credit scoring models is to assign credit applicants to either a "good credit" group that is likely to repay financial obligation or a "bad credit" group who has high possibility of defaulting on the financial obligation. Therefore, credit scoring problems are basically in the scope of the more general and widely discussed classification problems (Lu and Chen, 2009).

As a legal customer applied to obtain a loan, the bank should assess the applicant and decide whether to approve the loan request or not. This is done through human analysis on the main characteristics of the customer. But accepting the characteristics remarked by customer itself may mislead the decision maker. So the bank must make the decision based on real, trustworthy and documented information. In order to handle these information altogether, the bank need to automate the credit evaluation process.

As a result, customers with high probability of default accounts can be monitored and necessary proceedings can be taken in order to prevent the account defaulting. In response, the statistical methods, non-parametric statistical methods, and artificial intelligence approaches have been proposed to support the credit approval decision process.

Credit scoring models are commonly structured along the lines of Altman's (1968) Z-score model using historical loan and borrower data to identify which borrower characteristics are able to distinguish between defaulted and non defaulted loans. Other general introductions to credit scoring are proposed by Mays (1998), Hand and Henley (1997), Mester (1997), Viganò (1993), and Lewis (1990). A *credit-scoring* model is a formula that puts weight on different characteristics of a borrower, lender, and loan (Nanni and Lumini, 2009).

Among several methods used for credit scoring, discriminant analysis and logistic regression are two most commonly used data mining techniques to construct credit scoring models. However, linear discriminant analysis (LDA) has often been criticized because of its assumption about the categorical nature of the data and the fact that the covariance matrices of different classes are unlikely to be equal. In addition to the LDA approach, logistic regression is an alternative to an alternative way to set down credit scoring. Basically, the logistic regression model emerged as the technique in predicting dichotomous outcomes. A number of logistic regression models for credit scoring applications have been reported in the literature. Harrell and Lee (1985) found out that logistic regression is as efficient as LDA (Lee et al., 2006).

In addition to LDA and logistic regression, credit scoring also lends itself to a recent development of neural networks approach. Neural networks provide an alternative way for LDA and logistic regression, particularly in situations where the dependent and independent variables exhibit complex nonlinear relationships. Even though neural networks have been reported to have better credit scoring capability than LDA and logistic regression (Desai et al., 1996; Jensen, 1992; Piramuthu, 1999), they are, however, also being criticized for their long training process in designing the optimal network's topology and inability to identify the relative importance of potential input variables, as a result of which they have limited its applicability in handling credit scoring problems (Piramuthu, 1999).

Beside these methods, there are several data mining methodologies used in previous years, such as classification and decision trees (CART), multi-adaptive regression splines (MARS) and bootstrap aggregation (Bagging) (Hothorn and Lausen, 2003).

Data mining approaches are becoming a common alternative for making credit scoring models due to their associated memory characteristic, generalization capability, and outstanding credit scoring capability, but these approaches are also being criticized for their long training process, inability to identify the relative importance of potential input variables, and certain interpretative difficulties (Lee et al., 2006).

There are two main scoring types: External scoring and internal scoring. Some international committees have published standard scoring methods based on probability of default, such as Basel committee, Fitch, S&P and other committees (Basel, 2000). Scoring based on these standards usually is named as external scoring. But each bank in its own country, area of activity and capability can have a special scoring model, which will be its scoring model. This is usually called internal scoring.

Purpose of this study

In this article we tried to find a special model for calculating the probability of default of legal customers in a commercial bank using two approaches which have generally been used for credit risk problems, logistic regression and neural network.

Every modeling method may have errors, and especially in credit risk modeling, there are two types of errors: Error type 1 which means reporting a bad credit as a good one, and Error type 2 which means reporting a good credit as a bad one. Error type 1 may cause losing the loan, losing the loan's profit and also pursuit costs but error type 2 may cause losing a good opportunity for bank. Finding a model which can minimize both error type 1 and 2, is the goal of this article.

METHODOLOGY

As mentioned earlier, two main approaches to calculate probability of default in this article are logistic regression and neural network. The case study contains 127 legal customer's data of a commercial bank. These customers have borrowed a loan and 21 of them did not repay their loan. These historical data have been gathered and some variables have been calculated based on their balance sheet information at the moment of applying for the loan.

There are 4 main financial ratios which are liquidity ratios, leveraging ratios, activity ratios, and profitability ratios. Liquidity ratios measure the availability of cash to pay debt. Leveraging ratios or Debt ratios measure the firm's ability to repay long-term debt. Activity ratios measure the effectiveness of the firm's use of resources. Profitability ratios measure the company's use of its assets and control of its expenses to generate an acceptable rate of return (Williams et al., 2008).

These ratios are the main financial information which a bank can used to calculate the probability of default of a customer. Other information such as management measures, Characteristics and perspectives of the products and competitions are also important (Jiao et al., 2007). But this information can be kept in view as this information was not in the scope of this article.

Logistic regression

Distribution of the credit information data is usually non-normal and in this case a suitable extension is a generalized linear model known as logistic regression or logit model. Given a vector of application characteristics x, the probability of default p is related to vector x by the following equation:

$$logit(p) = \ln \frac{p}{1-p} = w_0 + w_1 x_1 + w_2 x_2 + \cdots + w_k x_k$$

Logistic regression provides a method for modeling a binary response variable, which takes values 1 and 0 by mapping the data on a logit curve (Figure 1).

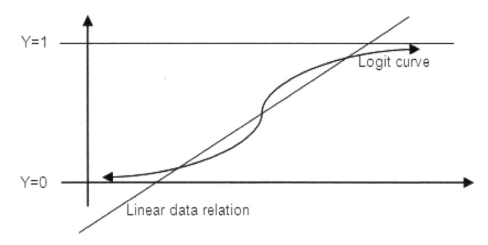

Figure 1. Logit curve.

The response variable here is 1 for those customers who have defaulted, and 0 for those repaid their loan at regular time. The vector x is the vector of characteristics which are actually the financial ratios for each customer in the moment of applying for debt. The vector w is calculated through maximum likelihood estimation. In this method, a function is defined based on the probability and w, named likelihood function. Maximizing the logarithm of the likelihood function will maximize the prediction rate of the model.

To evaluate the illustrated logit model, there are four main tests, (a) overall model evaluation, (b) statistical tests of individual predictors, (c) goodness-of-fit statistics, and (d) validations of predicted probabilities (Ying et al., 2002).

A logistic model is said to provide a better fit to the data if it demonstrates an improvement over the intercept-only model (also called the null model). An improvement over this baseline is examined using the LR or -2lnL(null)- 2lnL(model), which lnL(model) is maximum likelihood as the estimated variables are meaningful in the model, and lnL(null) is likelihood with assuming zero for all variables.

The statistical significance of individual regression coefficients is tested using the Wald chi-square statistic. If the statistic is less than 0.05, then the variable merely should be included in the model.

Goodness-of-fit statistics assess the fit of a logistic model against actual outcomes. The inferential goodness-of-fit test is the Hosmer–Lemeshow (H–L) test. This statistic tests H_0 hypothesis of

$$H_0 : E[Y] = \frac{exp(x'w)}{1+exp(x'w)}$$ using chi-square, and if becomes

more than 0.05, shows that the model fits well to data.

Logistic regression predicts the logit of an event outcome from a set of predictors, and it can be transformed back to the probability scale:

$$p = \frac{exp(x'w)}{1 + exp(x'w)} = \frac{e^{(w_0+w_1x_1+\cdots+w_kx_k)}}{1 + e^{(w_0+w_1x_1+\cdots+w_kx_k)}}$$

The resultant predicted probabilities can then be revalidated with the actual outcome to determine if high probabilities are indeed associated with events and low probabilities with nonevents. The degree to which predicted probabilities agree with actual outcomes is expressed as either a measure of association or a classification table.

As the study use classification table for assessing the logit

model, the cut-off point should be considered. In a classification table, if the predicted probability of default for a customer becomes more than cut off point, we can report the customer as a "bad" customer, and if this probability becomes less than the cut-off point, we can report the customer as a "good" one. The pre-defined cut off point value in statistical and econometrics software such as *Eviews* and *SPSS*, is usually 0.5. But what is the best cut off point?

As mentioned earlier, the best model for a bank is the one that minimizes both type 1 and 2 errors. Selecting the best cut off point is done by minimizing these errors.

Neural network

Neural networks are artificial intelligence algorithms that allow for some learning through experience to discern the relationship between borrower characteristics and the probability of default and to determine which characteristics are most important in predicting default (Mester, 1997).

Research into neural networks began in 1943 with the publication written by MCCULLOCH and PITT. According to the proclaimed principle, a mathematical model had to be developed that could simulate the natural operation of the neuron. For us, the important parts of a neuron are the dendrites, through which the neuron receives signals, and the axons, which help to forward processed information to other neurons. Synapses play a significant part in processing information. It is through them that axons connect to the dendrites of other neurons (Ferenc, 2003). The operation of the mathematical neuron model is similar to human's brain. Using a given function, they process the information received from dendrites, and if the incoming signal exceeds a so-called stimulus threshold, they forward the information via axons. The most important property of the neuron is that it is continuously changing its operation (that is, its internal function) based on the data received – it is 'learning'. Synapses play an important role in this learning process, as they are able to amplify or subdue the signals coming from other neurons. In the learning process, signal amplification factors change on synapses (referred to as 'weights' in the model in light of their function). In the neuron model, the change or modification of these weights means learning.

Characteristics of the customers are input variables in neural network for credit scoring problem. The output variable is the actual condition of the customers, either they have defaulted or not.

To assess a neural network, there are 3 main indicators that show whether the network can estimate the outputs or not (Ravi et

Table 1. Variables in the survey to find effective variables.

Category	Name	Formula	Variable name
Liquidity ratios	Current ratio (working capital ratio)	Current asset/ current liabilities	X_1
	Quick ratio	Current asset – (Inventories+ prepayments)/ current liabilities	X_2
Leveraging ratios	Debt ratio	Total liabilities/ total assets	X_3
	Debt to equity ratio	Long term debt+ value of leases/ average shareholder equity	X_4
Activity ratios	Asset turnover	Net sales/ total assets	X_5
	Receivable turnover ratio	Net sales/ average net receivables	X_6
	Stock turnover ratio	Cost of goods sold/ average inventory	X_7
Profitability ratios	Return on assets	Net income/ total assets	X_8
	Return on equity	Net income/ average shareholder equity	X_9
	Profit margin	Net profit/ net sales	X_{10}

al., 2002). These indicators are PR, RMSE and MAPE. PR means the amount of outputs predicted correctly (F) on the amount of total predicted outputs (N):

$$PR = \frac{F}{N}$$

root mean square (RMS) is calculated from the following equation, which O_m^i is the predicted output from neural network and O_a^i is the actual amount of output.

$$RMS = \sqrt{\frac{\sum_{i=1}^{n}\left(O_a^i - O_m^i\right)^2}{n}}$$

MAPE means the average of absolute error:

$$MAPE = \frac{1}{N} \sum_{i=1}^{n} \frac{|actual_i - forecast_i|}{actual_i}$$

The best learned neural network is that which can predict outputs more correctly. More PR and less RMS and less MAPE can show this. But the meaning of PR is closely related to the cut-off point we define in calculating error, or what we say "correct prediction". So in this article, besides calculating RMS and choosing the best neural network, the study also check different cut off points to find the best for calculating credit risk. The amount of MAPE can't be calculated, because there are zeros as denominator.

RESULTS

The two main approaches used in this article have been briefly discussed before. In this article, the study have used the approaches and illustrated model to specify variables influencing default of the customers. Almost 1000 data of legal customers of a commercial bank gathered and because the data base has had several missing data, filtered. As mentioned, the data of 127 legal customers were finally selected and taken into account for illustrating the logit model.

The main variables which were in the survey were financial ratios which are listed in Table 1. The variables entered into the model illustration process one by one, and the best model which has got the characteristics mentioned earlier selected as final logit model. The Eviews output window for illustrating the model is shown in Table 2. The final equation which models the default of these 127 customers is:

$$logit(p) = ln\frac{p}{1-p}$$
$$= -7.233126173 - 4.814803512 * X_1 + 13.63992793 * X_3$$
$$- 22.78927478 * X_8$$

This result shows that 3 main variables affect the default of a customer which are current ratio, debt ratio and return on assets. As it is shown in Table 2, the model's LR amount is 81.35 and the statistic is almost $0<0.05$, so the hypothesis of being zero for all variables is not true, so the logit model is truly illustrated. Also the chi-square statistic for each variable is less than 0.05 and shows that these variables merely should be included in the model.

As shown in Table 3, the probability of chi-square statistic in Hosmer-Lemeshow goodness of fitness test shows that the model fits data very well.

To calculate the default probability of customers using logit model, we can use the following equation:

$$p = \frac{e^{(-7.233126173 - 4.814803512 * X_1 + 13.63992793 * X_3 - 22.78927478 * X_8)}}{1 + e^{(-7.233126173 - 4.814803512 * X_1 + 13.63992793 * X_3 - 22.78927478 * X_8)}}$$

Calculating the probability for each customer and comparing the estimated probability with actual position

Table 2. Output window for final illustrated model.

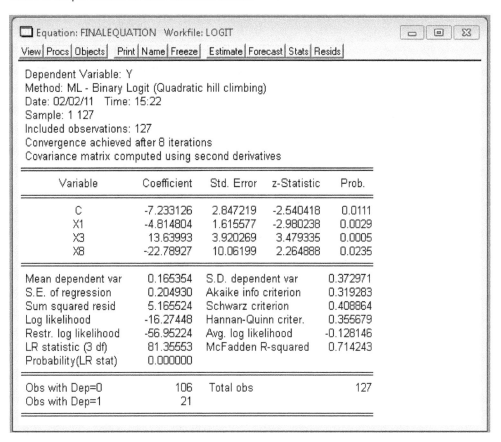

```
Equation: FINALEQUATION  Workfile: LOGIT                    [ _ ][ □ ][ ✕ ]
View Procs Objects  Print Name Freeze  Estimate Forecast Stats Resids

Dependent Variable: Y
Method: ML - Binary Logit (Quadratic hill climbing)
Date: 02/02/11   Time: 15:22
Sample: 1 127
Included observations: 127
Convergence achieved after 8 iterations
Covariance matrix computed using second derivatives
```

Variable	Coefficient	Std. Error	z-Statistic	Prob.
C	-7.233126	2.847219	-2.540418	0.0111
X1	-4.814804	1.615577	-2.980238	0.0029
X3	13.63993	3.920269	3.479335	0.0005
X8	-22.78927	10.06199	2.264888	0.0235

Mean dependent var	0.165354	S.D. dependent var	0.372971
S.E. of regression	0.204930	Akaike info criterion	0.319283
Sum squared resid	5.165524	Schwarz criterion	0.408864
Log likelihood	-16.27448	Hannan-Quinn criter.	0.355679
Restr. log likelihood	-56.95224	Avg. log likelihood	-0.128146
LR statistic (3 df)	81.35553	McFadden R-squared	0.714243
Probability(LR stat)	0.000000		

Obs with Dep=0	106	Total obs	127
Obs with Dep=1	21		

Table 3. Hosmer-Lemeshow goodness of fitness test.

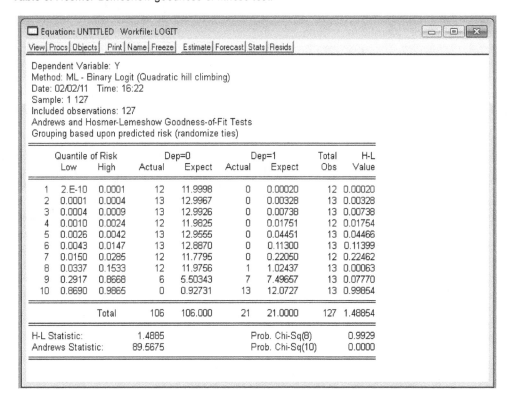

```
Equation: UNTITLED  Workfile: LOGIT                         [ _ ][ □ ][ ✕ ]
View Procs Objects  Print Name Freeze  Estimate Forecast Stats Resids

Dependent Variable: Y
Method: ML - Binary Logit (Quadratic hill climbing)
Date: 02/02/11   Time: 16:22
Sample: 1 127
Included observations: 127
Andrews and Hosmer-Lemeshow Goodness-of-Fit Tests
Grouping based upon predicted risk (randomize ties)
```

	Quantile of Risk Low	High	Dep=0 Actual	Expect	Dep=1 Actual	Expect	Total Obs	H-L Value
1	2.E-10	0.0001	12	11.9998	0	0.00020	12	0.00020
2	0.0001	0.0004	13	12.9967	0	0.00328	13	0.00328
3	0.0004	0.0009	13	12.9926	0	0.00738	13	0.00738
4	0.0010	0.0024	12	11.9825	0	0.01751	12	0.01754
5	0.0026	0.0042	13	12.9555	0	0.04451	13	0.04466
6	0.0043	0.0147	13	12.8870	0	0.11300	13	0.11399
7	0.0150	0.0285	12	11.7795	0	0.22050	12	0.22462
8	0.0337	0.1533	12	11.9756	1	1.02437	13	0.00063
9	0.2917	0.8668	6	5.50343	7	7.49657	13	0.07770
10	0.8690	0.9865	0	0.92731	13	12.0727	13	0.99854

	Total	Actual	Expect	Actual	Expect	Total Obs	H-L Value
	Total	106	106.000	21	21.0000	127	1.48854

H-L Statistic:	1.4885	Prob. Chi-Sq(8)	0.9929
Andrews Statistic:	89.5675	Prob. Chi-Sq(10)	0.0000

Table 4. Classification table, with cut off point equal to 0.5.

	Observed		Predicted		Percentage correct
			y		
			.00	1.00	
Step 1	y	0.00	103	3	97.2
		1.00	5	16	76.2
	Overall percentage				93.7

Table 5. Sensitivity and specifity of model with different cut off points.

Cut off point	Specifity	Sensitivity	Sum
0.01	69.7	100	169.7
0.1	90.6	95.2	185.8
0.2	94.3	95.2	189.5
0.3	95.3	95.2	190.5
0.4	97.2	90.5	187.7
0.5	97.2	76.2	173.4
0.6	97.2	71.4	168.6
0.7	97.2	71.4	168.6
0.8	97.2	71.4	168.6
0.9	100	33.3	133.3
0.99	100	0	100

of customers, either have defaulted or not, the study have classified customers in Table 4, with cut off point equal to 0.5.

The two error types are clear in the classification table. For cut-off point equal to 0.5, the Type 1 error is 23.8% and the Type 2 error is 2.8.

To minimize the overall error, Korsholm proved that if one of 4 main situations occurs, the amount of overall error will be minimized (Korsholm, 2004). If the proportion of defaulted customer's output variable was named (y=1) correctly predicted as "sensitivity of the model" and the proportion of non-defaulted customer's output variable (y=0) correctly predicted as "specifity of the model", these 4 situations are:

1) Sum of sensitivity and specifity degree of the model becomes maximal
2) If the sensitivity becomes more than 80%, then sum of sensitivity and specifity degree of the model becomes maximal
3) The minimum amount between sensitivity and specifity degree of the model, becomes maximal
4) If the type1 error is x multifold important than type 2 error for the bank, then the amount of (x* sensitivity + specifity) becomes maximal.

It is notable that sensitivity degree equals to 1- error type 1 and specifity degree equals to 1- error type 2. Using different cut off points and calculation the classification tables, error type 1 and error type 2 and

sensitivity and specifity degree of the model for each cut off point, the best cut off point will be 0.3, as is summarized in Table 5 and is shown in Figure 2.

Another point that can confirm the result of logit modeling is relative operating characteristic (ROC) curve, which shows a receiver operating characteristics and used for evaluating the logit model as well. The ROC plot is merely the graph of points defined by sensitivity and (1 – specificity). Customarily, sensitivity takes the y axis and (1 – specificity) takes the x axis. If the area under the curve becomes maximum amount, then the model fits data well. The curve is shown in Figure 3.

To evaluate the overall illustrated model, the study can compare the results of logit model with the results of neural network. For this purpose, the study take 112 data as learning data and 15 data as test data. And the 3 variables that finally illustrate the logit model used as input data and the actual position of customers as output data. It used a feed-forward network-error back propagation algorithm with 3 neurons in hidden layer. The RMS of test data was 0.151 and the study calculated the prediction rate (PR), with two amounts of 0.5 as a default probability cut off point and then 0.3 which is the best cut off point in logit modeling. The results are shown in Table 6.

Conclusion

In this article we calculated the best cut off point which

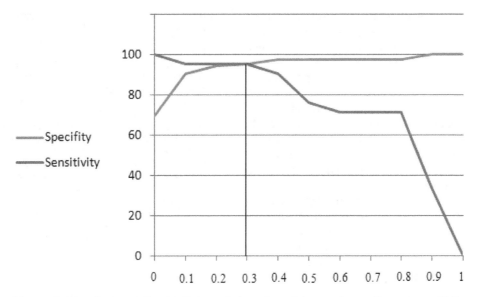

Figure 2. Best find cut off point that maximizes the minimum of specifity and sensitivity degree.

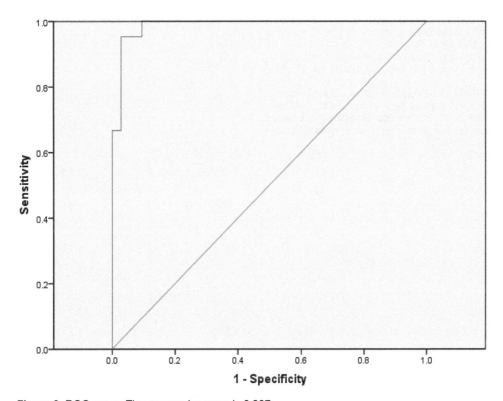

Figure 3. ROC curve- The area under curve is 0.987.

Table 6. RMS and PR using neural network.

Input data: 3 variables (current ratio, debt ratio, return on assets)			
RMS	PR- cut off point equal to 0.3	PR- cut off point equal to 0.5	Neurons of hidden layer
0.151	124/127=0.97	124/127=0.97	3

minimizes the overall error of modeling credit risk, both with logistic regression and neural network methods which are two most used methodologies in credit risk analysis.

The best amount of cut off point for every bank is the amount that minimizes the overall error of illustrated model. In logistic regression modeling, the cut-off point is the point that the decision maker decides whether to accept the loan application or not. If the probability becomes more than the cut-off point, the customer will be in the class of "bad customers", otherwise will be in the class of "good customers".

In neural network, for calculating the prediction rate of the network, we should use a threshold of correct prediction on incorrect one which is similar to the cut-off point in logit modeling. Using the neural network shows that the calculated best cut off point via logit modeling is also good for neural network.

REFERENCES

Basel (2000). Committee on Banking Supervision, Principal for Management of Credit Risk, September.
Desai VS, Crook JN, Overstreet Jr. GA (1996). "A Comparison of Neural Networks and Linear Scoring Models in the Credit Union Environment". Eur. J. Oper. Res. 95:24-37
Ferenc (2003). Credit scoring process from a knowledge management perspective. Periodical Polytechnic Ser. Soc.Manag.Sci. (11/1):95-110.
Harrell FE, Lee KL (1985). A comparison of the discrimination of discriminant analysis and logistic regression under multivariate normality. In P. K. Sen (Ed.): Biostatistics: Statistics in Biomedical, Public Health and Environmental Sciences. North-Holland: Elsevier Science Publishers pp.333-343.
Hothorn T, Lausen B (2003). Double-bagging: combining classifiers by bootstrap aggregation. Pattern Recognit. 36:1303-1309.
Jensen HL (1992). "Using Neural Networks for Credit Scoring", Manag. Financ. 18:15-26
Jiao Y, Syau YR, Lee ES (2007). Modeling credit rating by fuzzy adaptive network. Math. Comput. Model. 45:717-731.
Korsholm L (2004). Analysis Of Diagnostic Studies, Sensitivity and specificity positive and negative predicted values ROC curves tests based on logistic regression, Department Of Statistics And Demography, University Of Southern Denmark.
Lee TS, Chiu CC, Chou YC, Lu CJ (2006). Mining the customer credit using classification and regression tree and multivariate adaptive regression splines, Comput. Stat. Data Anal. 50:1113-1130.
Lu CL, Chen TC (2009). A study of applying data mining approach to the information disclosure for Taiwan's stock market investors. Expert Syst. Appl. 36:3536-3542
Mester L (1997). What's the point of the credit scoring? Business Review-Federal Reserve Bank of Philadelphia
Nanni L, Lumini A (2009). An experimental comparison of ensemble of classifiers for bankruptcy prediction and credit scoring. Expert Syst. Appl. 36:1-4.
Piramuthu S (1999). Financial Credit-Risk Evaluation with Neural and Neuro-fuzzy Systems. Eur. J. Oper. Res. 112:310-321.
Ravi BS, Warren FW, Jos LGAM (2002). Modelling and Evaluating Quality Measurement using Neural Networks. Int. J. Oper. Prod. Manage. 22(10):1162-11855.
Williams JR, Haka FS, Bettner MS, Carcello JV (2008). Financial and Managerial Accounting. McGraw-Hill Irwin.
Ying CH, Peng J, Lee KL, Ingersoll GM (2002). An Introduction to Logistic Regression Analysis and Reporting. J. Educ. Res. 96:1.

26

Dedicated Business Intelligence System for SMEs Consortium

Katarzyna Rostek

Warsaw University of Technology, Faculty of Management, ul.Narbutta 85, 02-524 Warsaw, Poland.

The paper proposes a new methodological approach to the organization and implementation of Business Intelligence in the SME sector. It is based on the assumption that SMEs do not have sufficient knowledge, skills and organizational, personnel and financial resources to make independent implementation of solutions of this class. On the other hand, such tools could have a significant impact on a growth of their competitiveness and strengthen their position in a competitive market. In this context, a new solution is proposed for design, implementation and deployment of the BI system, supporting the competitiveness management of SMEs.

Key words: SMEs, Business Intelligence, competitiveness, benchmarking, outsourcing, cloud computing, supporting of management decisions.

INTRODUCTION

The market of small and medium-sized enterprises (SMEs) plays a key role in shaping and developing the economy worldwide. Studies have shown that the SME sector is essential for the proper development of any economy because:

- Six out of ten new jobs are created in the SME sector;
- SMEs pave the way for the transformation of traditional forms of production into advanced technologies (Audretsch, 2001; Dibrell et al., 2008; Freel, 2003);
- SMEs play a key role in the development of innovations designed to improve market competitiveness (Audretsch, 2001; Low and Chapman, 2007):
- SMEs contribute to the development of the global market (Acedo and Florin, 2006; Karaganni and Labriandis, 2001; Lituchy and Rail, 2000; Salvato et al., 2007).

SMEs need to have strong competencies in order to survive in a changing environment and a growing competition (Teece et al., 1997; Tenai et al., 2009; Blackburn and Jarvis, 2010). In this respect, the possibility of consciously shaping the competitiveness of SMEs to ensure a stable market position becomes the key issue of management in this sector. The basic requirement that must be met in order to improve the management efficiency in the area of an enterprise's competitiveness is access to timely, complete and useful management information and the ability to effectively support decision making. These requirements can be best met through the deployment of Business Intelligence (BI) technology.

In the context of management, BI is a system or an IT solution based on production processes implemented in the enterprise and optimized for the flow of information between organizational units involved in the implementtation of these processes. In terms of technology, BI is a specialized analytical and reporting software with a graphical user interface for processing and visualization of information for management decision support.

The implementation of a BI system entails compliance

with other organizational and technological requirements and the commitment of resources. It can also lead to changes in the business management model. SMEs need support in each of these areas because they do not have the required: knowledge, trained personnel or financial resources that are sufficient for an independent and effective implementation of this type of solution. The present paper identifies SME constraints in the implementation of BI and proposes a methodological approach which will have a significant impact on these constraints.

Regarding the aforementioned obligations, the structure of the paper seeks to answer the following research questions:

RQ1: What are the needs of SMEs in the area of the Business Intelligence functionalities?
RQ2: What are the conditions precedent SMEs must meet in order to implement a Business Intelligence technology?
RQ3: What are the measurable effects of the implementation of a Business Intelligence system for SMEs?

In this context, the needs of SMEs in supporting managerial decision making (related to RQ1) is discussed. Also, we explore the conditions needed for the implementation of BI technology and the associated restrictions of SME sector (related to RQ2). The following section discusses the methodological approach to the design, the implementation and the deployment of a BI solution dedicated to SMEs (response to RQ1 and RQ2). And reports on a sample test of the method in a group of medical clinics (related to RQ3) are presented. Finally, the paper presents summary of the findings and then conclusions.

THE NEEDS OF SMES IN THE AREA OF MANAGEMENT SUPPORT SYSTEMS

In today's economy, competitiveness is considered an important determinant of business growth and is used for assessing the enterprise's market performance. Competition in a market economy consists of activities through which market participants present customers with more favorable offers to buy more attractive goods or services sold at more favorable prices, more powerful promotions than others, so as to meet their interests and the performance gains (Porter, 1998). Competition is recognized as the most important mechanism for promoting the most favorable solutions from the viewpoint of the economic criteria. It leads also to the development of an economy through unleashing the creativity of competing market operators (Garengo et al., 2005).

The above statements are particularly important due to the ongoing global crisis that has not left Poland and its business sector unaffected. This crisis is likely to last for

years causing problems such as weak consumer demand and strong fluctuations in the financial market. This is why both new investments and changes to strengthen long-term competitiveness in relation to domestic and foreign rivals will be necessary for survival. Of particular importance will be the ability to combine these two components that is to invest in projects that would contribute to enhanced competitiveness. This is the main subject of this article.

However, Polish SMEs have serious problems developing and implementing strategic plans and short-term management aspects dominate over the long-term ones, as shown in research conducted by PARP[1] for many years. Future growth of competitiveness in the Polish SME sector is largely associated with the elimination of barriers limiting and sometimes even preventing their development (Żołnierski, 2009; Wilmańska, 2010; Brussa and Tarnawa, 2011; Tarnawa and Zadura-Lichota, 2012). The basic division of barriers to SME development can be either internal (dependent on the company) or external (influenced by market and global factors). Here are some barriers:

- Knowledge barriers leading to problems experience in strategic and operational management;
- Financial barriers resulting in investment and development issues;
- Personnel barriers leading to problems in productivity and quality of work.

External barriers may include:

- Economic barriers involving the problems that arise from general economic conditions and the legislative issues;
- Market barriers resulting in the problems of frequent changes to competition levels in the market.

The support of government organizations can be of paramount importance in the case of external barriers. Governments in many countries recognize the importance and impact of SMEs on the economy and so create organizations that support the development and the operation of this sector (Di Giacomo, 2004; Secrieru and Vigneault, 2004; Mason and Harrison, 2004; Cumming and MacIntosh, 2002). However, in the case of internal barriers companies should largely rely on their internal resources to address their own problems. Access to new technologies and modern management techniques to remove or reduce the impact of market barriers methods of management support for eliminating (or at least reducing the negative impacts) of the market barriers while taking into account the constraints posed by the financial and the personnel barriers. Researchers from

---

[1] PARP (pol. Polska Agencja Rozwoju Przedsiębiorczości) – Polish Agency for Enterprise Development.

PARP (Żołnierski, 2009; Wilmańska, 2010; Brussa and Tarnawa, 2011; Tarnawa and Zadura-Lichota, 2012) highlight the importance of implementing new IT technologies that will support enterprise management and help to obtain information that supports decision-making in the competitiveness development process. Therefore, the use of Business Intelligence technology seems to be the right solution as it will effectively support the development of a competitive SME sector. This leads to the formulation of the research question:

RQ1: What are the needs of SMEs in the area of Business Intelligence functionalities?

In order to answer RQ1, a quantitative research program was developed which was aimed at identifying the needs and capabilities of a selected group of SMEs in supporting managerial decision making. The test population included 150 dental clinics interviewed using the computer aided personal interview (CAPI) technique. The study was conducted in November 2009[2].

The total population of private dental practices in Poland amounted to 3,693 in 2009. The sufficient sample size for this set was determined under the following assumptions:

- Confidence level (1-α) = 95%;
- Confidence interval t = 1.96;
- Estimation of the population fraction has got analyzed characteristic p = 50%;
- Estimation of the population fraction has not got analyzed characteristic (1-p) = 50%,
- Maximum allowable error margin d = 8%.

The assumptions made it possible to determine the minimum size of the research group:

$$n = \frac{t^2 p(1-p)}{d^2} = \frac{1.96^2 * 0.5 * 0.5}{0.08^2} = 150.0625$$

The selection of respondents was carried out using a purposeful random method. Purposeful (arbitrary) sample was based on knowledge of the research population and the specific research goals.

The clinics included in the sample had to meet the following criteria:

- SME status; that is they must employ 2 to 250 people and generate an annual revenue of less than PLN 210 million;
- Provision of dental services: they employ 2 to 21 dentists;
- IT infrastructure in place: – own 1 to 60 computers;
- Located in 10 major Polish cities: Gdansk (11 surveys), Gdynia (5 surveys), Katowice (11 surveys), Krakow (9

surveys), Lublin (13 surveys), Lodz (9 surveys), Poznan (21 surveys), Sopot (1 survey), Warsaw (50 surveys) and Wroclaw (20 surveys).

Based on the aforementioned criteria, 150 dental clinics were sampled on a random basis. The sample was tested using CAPI (Computer-Aided Personal Interview). The aim of this study was to determine the needs of the research group in the field of support of decision making process. The following interview questions were clustered in four sections:

1. General information: the characteristics of the enterprises, the type and scope of the services offered, the level of IT in the company;
2. Decision making process: methods supporting the process of decision making, tools supporting this process, issues and challenges of the decision making process;
3. Data analysis: the level of willingness to be included in benchmarking, commitment to company analysis, , the readiness to incur costs of implementing and using IT analytics;
4. Business intelligence: existing knowledge of Business intelligence solutions, the level of commitment to BI, the readiness to use BI technology in business management.

The overall response to the second group of questions reveal that dental clinics largely rely on experience and intuition in their decisions making. Specifically, it is usually the experience of dentists who own the clinics that matters the most. Consulting external experts, market research and analytics, financial policy, legal and political conditions, incidents and random events scored much lower. On the one hand, the respondents the majority of whom were clinic managers, did not notice any deficits in up-to-date and complete information for their decision making processes. Yet, the very same people emphasize the need for a better access to information and efficient communication within the company. This suggests a problem in this area.

Similarly, in the third and fourth group of questions most respondents admitted using IT and analytical tools only to a limited extent. Most of them did not understand the term Business Intelligence or interpreted it as referring to the intelligence and level of education of managers. They do not see much sense in investing expensive IT solutions to support management decision-making.

The results obtained in the group of Polish dental clinics reflect the general level of knowledge and awareness in the SME sector in Poland. Strategically managed solely relying on in-house expertise and intuition, a few of the clinics actually went bankrupt within two months of this research project. However, there was a group of managers (about 35% of respondents) who argued that the management process would be much more effective if there were opportunities, time and skills

---

[2] Research funded from public sources in 2009-2011 as research project No. 0078/B/H03/2009/37.

to use additional information and knowledge gathered from the available data sources in the clinic. In this case a major condition is the availability of an IT tool that would be cheap and intuitive to deploy and use, and quite sufficient for the existing analytical needs. This was a strong premise for a need of building and implementing a Dedicated Business Intelligence system (DBI) for the SME sector and the input restriction for the RQ2 research question.

MAIN CONDITIONS TO IMPLEMENTING BI IN SMES

BI systems belong to the category of Decision Support Systems (DSS). They are information systems supporting business and organizational activities in the area of managerial decision making (Power, 2007; Finlay, 1994). Additionally, thanks to being adaptable, flexible, inter-active and intuitive, BI is user-friendly and allows freedom and creativity of action (Turban, 1995).

The Business Intelligence term was first used by Luhn (1958) to describe the possibility of showing interrelations between analyzed facts in such a way as to facilitate the decision-maker achieving the intended business goals. Gartner Group[3] defines Business Intelligence as a user-oriented process of collecting, exploring, interpreting and analyzing data to streamline and rationalize the decision making process. Business Intelligence is also a computer system that uses a structured sequence of transfor-mations of data collected by the enterprise to increase the efficiency of the decision making process by reducing the three types of delays resulting from the need to: prepare data for analysis, perform the analysis and deliver analysis results to the decision maker.

According to IDC[4] research, the Business Intelligence market is now the fastest growing IT sector and one of the few that have experienced growth in own value during crisis years. According to IDG[5] and SAS Institute[6] (Żółcińska, 2009) the reason for this that enterprises see in this category of IT solutions as an opportunity to gain competitive advantage (80% of surveyed companies) and overcome the effects of economic slowdown (70% of surveyed companies).

The SAS research mentioned earlier was conducted in over 80 medium-size and large Polish companies in 2009. It showed that the most important effects of the implementation of Business Intelligence system are

(Żółcińska, 2009): better quality and availability of management information (62% of respondents), the opportunity to optimize and improve efficiency of business processes (60% of respondents), support reasonable reduction in operating costs (44%), increase management efficiency (40% of respondents), increase revenues (20% of respondents), improve customer relationships (16% of respondents), increase financial transparency within the enterprise (10%). The surveyed entrepreneurs use Business Intelligence tools in the management of (Żółcińska, 2009): finance (56%), strategy (38%), customer relationships (38%), supply chain (16% of respondents), production (16% respon-dents), marketing (12% of respondents), human resources (8% of respondents).

Although the survey was conducted among medium and large enterprises, Business Intelligence solutions vendors claim that SMEs buy them more and more often for the same reasons (DiS[7], 2010). This is possible because software vendors begin to see the needs of SMEs and their products are becoming more financially and organizationally available for this sector. However, there are still several necessary requirements associated with the implementation of BI systems in the SME sector that must be met. The following research question addresses these requirements:

RQ2: What are conditions precedent SMEs must meet in order to implement Business Intelligence technology?
  Some of the conditions include:

- Process approach to business management;
- Business process reorganization to improve workflow;
- Acquisition of a sufficient amount of operational data necessary in the analytical processing;
- Developing the correct structure of the analytical database enabling in-depth, multi-dimensional analysis of operational data at the appropriate level of detail;
- Development of multi-dimensional analytical models for OLAP and data mining analysis to ensure the efficient acquisition of management information from their operational data;
- Providing a flexible distribution of analytical results in time, form and the most appropriate response to management decision makers.

However, as shown in survey results conducted among 150 dental clinics in the SME sector (in detail described in previous section), the most important restrictions on the use of IT tools in supporting decision-making are:

- Lack of technical expertise in the field of IT solutions for decision-making support;
- Lack of trained personnel, which could be addressed by implementing and maintaining such solutions;

---

[3]Gartner Group - international company with a global reputation in the area of the information technology analysis and consultancy.

[4]IDC (International Data Corporation) - one of the biggest ICT market research companies. It is involved in sectoral research and offers strategic advice in ICT projects. It focuses on identifying current and future trends in in the individual sectors of the ICT market.

[5]IDG (International Data Group) – An international provider of multimedia and marketing services, organization of conferences and meetings, scientific publishing, market research, consultancy of design and implementation and the dissemination of knowledge about modern IT technologies.

[6]SAS Institute – international IT Corporation classified as a Business Intelligence market leader.

---

[7]DiS - Polish Market Research Institute.

Table 1. Comparison of requirements and restrictions of SMEs with the capabilities of Business Intelligence technology (Source: own).

SMEs requirements for BI technology	Threat to implementation of requirement	Capabilities of BI system
BI system integration with the applied process management model	- Limited knowledge of business management (management based on intuition and experience) - Lack of trained personnel who could deal with the implementation and maintain such a solution	Requirement can be met provided the BI system is well designed and implemented
Automation of the key analytical and decision-making areas	- Limited knowledge of business analysis - Lack of expertise in the field of decision support systems	Requirement can be met if architecture well selected a BI system
Information and advisory support in the decision making process	- Limited knowledge of business management (management based on intuition and experience) - Limited amount of data collected, limited resources for BI technology financing	Requirement difficult to meet without consulting support
Price and technological availability of the proposed solution without sacrificing the expected functionalities	- Limited options to finance BI technology - IT departments in SMEs do not have a strong understanding of decision support systems - Lack of trained personnel who could deal with the implementation and maintain such a solution	Requirement difficult to meet without consulting support

- Limited knowledge among business management (management too often rely on intuition and past experience);
- Limited financial resources;
- Limited and often insufficient amount of operational data to feed into multidimensional analyses.

A comparison of the aforementioned restrictions with the requirements of the implementation of a Business Intelligence system, as defined in the introduction and presented capabilities of a classical Business Intelligence concept, is presented in Table 1.

While analyzing the results of Table 1 it can be noted that a conventional concept of Business Intelligence is not sufficient in relation to the requirements and constraints of SMEs. Therefore, it becomes reasonable to refer to the research conducted in the area of BI solutions. The following aspects exist for BI implementation which were addressed in existing research literature:

- BI integration into existing business processes;
- Development of the BI system architecture;
- Development of analytical methods and techniques used in BI;
- Development of approach to the design and implementation of the BI system.

The integration of Business Intelligence into existing business processes arises from the need to support not only the strategic, but also the operational management with one technology. BI decision support at the operational level must be preceded by the introduction of a process approach to business management and the availability of business process management on the system platform. The integration of the Business Process Management system (BPM) with BI creates an opportunity to use any data and information collected within company which are essential in making management decisions (Curko et al., 2007; Tan et al., 2008). On the other hand, a combination of Business Process Management with Business Intelligence enables optimization of the results of process implementation. This leads to an increase in management effectiveness across the enterprise (Marjanovic, 2007, 2010).

Increasing the requirements for a range of supported data and the time horizon of their acquisition from source systems enforces the development of the data collection layer of BI. In order to ensure the integration of BPM and BI systems there is a need to create an analytical data repository which will collect, select, integrate and transform operational data, collected in real time. This function can be provided by a data warehouse and this is another subject of research work designed to: reduce the time of project creation and implementation of solutions (Inmon et al., 2008), optimize data and metadata model for speed, flexibility and accessibility of solutions (Zepeda and Celma, 2006; Zhang and Pan, 2010; Pan and Pan, 2010), and broaden the scope of its functionality, e.g. collecting spatial data (Malinowski and Zimanyi, 2007).

Operational data management and real time data processing also require changes in the organizational architecture of the BI system which are becoming as a multi-agent solution (Chunxu and Li, 2010), lowering the cost of implementation and maintenance of BI (Venkatadri et al., 2010; Feng et al., 2010). Another technological and organizational solution aimed at lowering the costs of implementing and maintaining the system is SaaS BI (Hongfeng and Liya, 2009; Bitterer, 2011). SaaS BI means Software-as-a-Service Business Intelligence, also called On-Demand BI. Its main advantage is a pay-as-you-go system (e.g. you may choose to only pay for analytical) and there is no need to install and maintain your own IT solution. An extension of the BI service offer is provided by Cloud Business Intelligence, where services can cover each component of the system (Goel, 2010; Chadha and Iyer, 2010).

Architectural design is also accompanied by changes in methods and analytical techniques which has a significant impact on the design of BI solution. The development of BI analytical environment has recently shifted towards integration with Knowledge Management (KM) systems (Campbell, 2006). The layer of analytical data processing uses methods such as: fuzzy sets theory (Chen and Wang, 2010; Thomas et al., 2006) or the cognitive systems theory (Niu et al., 2007). A significant area of BI analytics development is the acquisition, processing, organizing and sharing of network information, based on the use of text mining (Chung et al., 2003; Zhou et al., 2007) and web mining (Tiwari et al., 2011).

The effectiveness of Business Intelligence is closely related to the scope of its functionality and the management area that it covers with its operation. In their twenty-year history analytical and reporting systems have developed a wide diversity of analytical tools, repositories, and areas covered by the analysis. Consequently, it is difficult to develop a cross-sectional report, involving more than one aspect of business management. It is also difficult to manage the quality and consistency of data stored in dispersed analytical repositories. The BI SOA architecture aims to address these issues by integrating a variety of analytical solutions and transforming them into a common BI structure (Wu et al., 2007; Javanmard et al., 2011; Ganapathy and Vaidehi, 2011). Then the BI environment development can be supervised by a competence center, which consists of representatives from various departments, and thus represents various areas, perspectives and approaches to management. This provides a deeper integration of the analytical environment in the area of the entire enterprise and a common BI development policy (Miller, 2005; Bogza and Zaharie, 2008).

In the longer term, with increased awareness and needs of the management, the Business Intelligence system evolves into a comprehensive Corporate Performance Management (CPM) system, which is used to support the overall management of the enterprise (Andonov-Acev et al., 2008; Shi and Lu, 2010). This type of comprehensive solutions are based on Active Data Warehouses functioning like operating systems which process operational data and provide information in real time (Brobst and Morris, 2002; Polyzotis et al., 2007, 2008; Qin, 2009). The concept of Corporate Performance Management was introduced by the Gartner Group in 2001, defining it as processes, methodologies, indicators and technologies used by the company for measuring, monitoring and business performance management (Wade and Recardo, 2001). The task of CPM is to integrate the previously used methods and management techniques, such as: managerial control, measures and measurements of results, management information systems or Balanced Scorecard. CPM integrates the various areas of management, optimizing their performance from the standpoint of the strategy implemented throughout the company, not just its individual departments. The basic functionalities of CPM solutions were defined by the Gartner Group, and should include (Paladino, 2007): planning and budgeting, profitability modeling, financial consolidation, reporting, applications that support the balanced scorecard, forecasting and optimization. With such a wide functionality, the CPM system allows instant access to the picture of the entire enterprise. It allows online evaluation of the quality of decisions, and use their results to plan and possibly correct current operations. Its purpose is to create a common management platform where conflict would be resolved and irregularities eliminated, resulting from the natural differences between the objectives of the various areas of management.

As can be noted, the research project is aimed at developing the BI technology through the development of system architecture, extending the area of possible applications and the use of an increasing number of available techniques and analytical methods. These studies however do not translate to the scope of applicability of analytical tools in Polish enterprises. According to research of IDC conducted in 2008, 75% of companies surveyed said they faced the phenomenon of information overload and that only 50% of the information available was really useful in making decisions. Sixty six per cent of these enterprises manually scour their IT systems to find the needed information and make the decisions without the support of data analysis. In the case of the SME sector, the percentage of companies using analytical tools is even smaller and according to research by IDG conducted in 2007 it was only 10% of the population. The reasons for this may include:

- Lack of awareness of the need to use tools to support the decision-making process;
- Organizational, human and financial limitations for the implementation of tools supporting the decision-making process;
- Uncertainty about the effectiveness of the results of the implementation of tools supporting the decision-making process.
- These obstacles can be overcome the applicability of BI

Table 2. Limitations of the BI technology for SME sector vs. the DBI System Concept (Source: own research).

Limitations of BI technology in SME sector	DBI
Lack of expertise in the area of possible management decision support systems	Shipped as the complete solution/ no need for high IT expertise
Limited expertise in modern business management methods and models	Architecture and structure of data model based on predefined model of key competitiveness factors dedicated to a specific group of enterprises
Lack of in-house capacity to implement/maintain a BI system	Implemented and delivered as a service (e.g. outsourcing, cloud computing)
Limited IT b budgets	Implemented, maintained and funded as a product shared by a group of enterprises rather than a solution for a single organization
Limited/insufficient amount of source data collected	Supports a whole group of comparable and competing enterprises by using their data and sharing all findings

technologies in the SME sector can be increased if the implementation process and adequate tools are mobilized so that they:

- Provide growth of competitiveness of the enterprise within the scope of implementation;
- Would are available in terms of organization, human resources and finances for the SME sector within the implementation, maintenance and development of the system environment.

The proposed methodological approach is designed to meet the needs of SMEs in supporting management decision making, also taking into account the restrictions on the use Business Intelligence technology in the SME sector.

NEW ORGANIZATION OF BI SYSTEM FOR A CONSORTIUM OF SMES

The proposed concept of DBI (Dedicated Business Intelligence System) is based on the assumption that SMEs receives a ready-to-use product which actively supports the development of its competitive strategy. This has a direct impact on the scope of the functionality of the BI tool but is necessary due to the low awareness of management and thus also to the lack of skills to use computer applications supporting the decision making process. This problem does not only concern the SME sector but all uses of advanced analytical systems which are not properly operated after implementation and consequently do not bring expected economic and performance outcomes. The proposed the BI solution has predefined modules equipped with a complete set of analyses and reports (dedicated to specific industry or business) and a data warehouse which integrates data collected from a group of enterprises.

With the adoption of a common DBI solution for a group of comparable and mutually competing enterprises a new, so far unknown functionality become available:. benchmarking. It is possible to determine the mutual competitive position of several organizations in one industry and use the experience of the group leaders while defining the individual strategy for competitiveness. Specific limitations defined in Section 2, in relation to the solutions proposed in the DBI system, are presented in Table 2.

The DBI system model is presented on Figure 1. A group of DBI users periodically supply their performance data. The data are integrated in a common repository, then processed analytically and shared with users in the form of ready-made analytical results, statistical summaries and reports. The data model and the analytical layer of the DBI system are dedicated to the needs of its users. In addition, the DBI system is delivered as a service, so the burden of managing the system is not on the users but on the provider. The whole solution is focused on minimizing costs and maximizing effectiveness.

Declarations contained in Table 2 and Figure 1 result from the design, implementation and exploitation requirements of DBI. A method of building such a solution is presented in Figure 2.

Stage 1 – Needs assessment and DBI feasibility study

Step 1.1 – Setting business objectives of the project

The complexity of BI system design requires detailed definition of business objectives and scope of the project. The purpose of implementing DBI is to support decision-making processes in managing competitiveness. Use of DBI for this purpose will result in:
- The ability to determine the current competitive position

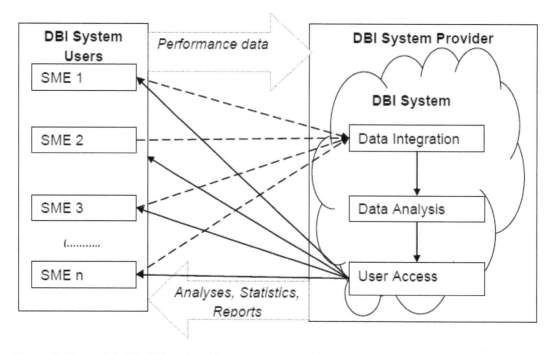

Figure 1. The model of the DBI system (Source: own research).

of the enterprise;
- The alignment of the competitiveness strategy to reach the target competitive position.

Step 1.2 – Analysis of the project feasibility

Estimating the risks and costs in relation to measurable and immeasurable benefits of implementing the DBI system. The analysis of project feasibility at this stage should lead to the identification of problems and limitations in such areas as current access to management information, business objectives and funding sources of the project, readiness to implement the solution, costs of designing, implementing and maintaining the system, and the expected return on investment period (ROI). The summary of the project feasibility study should provide objective answers to the following questions:

- Is the project necessary? Is it justified by potential benefits? What are the estimated losses if the project is not implemented?
- Is the project feasible? Is it financially and/or logistically possible to implement a complete DBI system in the enterprise?

If the answer to any of the above questions is negative the BI project should be postponed or cancelled. The enterprise may find it challenging if the question about the advisability of implementing a BI system is answered positively and the feasibility question is answered

negatively. This is a typical situation in the SME sector. Meanwhile the author proposes such approach to the organization of the BI system (called DBI), which requires only a positive answer to the first question and then seek appropriate provider of BI solution in the cloud.

Stage 2 – Select BI vendors and DBI contractors

Step 2.1 – Select BI solution provider and method of DBI implementation

Based on the needs assessment in Stage 1, it is possible to look for a BI solution that would be available as a service and would be financially and logistically feasible to the enterprise. The use of outsourcing services implies that an external company would take the responsibility for maintaining and protecting all or part of implemented system infrastructure. There are several different ways of outsourcing services in the BI systems (Baars et al., 2007):

- Reporting service - outsourcing of tools to build analytical reports *via* the internet based solely on local data of the user;
- OLAP service - outsourcing of multi-dimensional analytic structure built on the basis of market data, which can be expanded on user's own data and integrated with its analytical system;
- Data mining and visualization of data service - the client uses an external service of professionals in the implementation and the presentation of results based on the

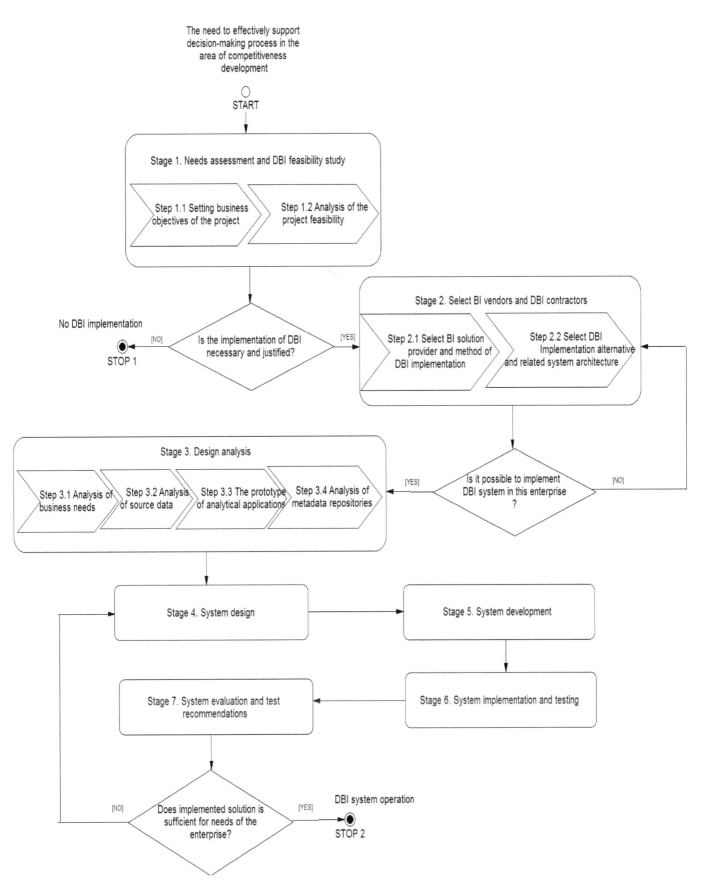

Figure 2. The method of implementing the DBI system (Source: own research).

resources of own collected data;
- Data warehouse and ETL service– supplying data into the data warehouse and maintaining its resources done exclusively by the equipment provider.

It is clear that these types of outsourcing services can be combined, e.g. data warehouse and ETL service with data mining and data visualization service. The type of the DBI system will have a direct impact on its architecture.

Step 2.2 – Select DBI implementation alternative and related system architecture

The choice of the implementation type of the DBI system offered as a service will have a direct impact on its architecture and the user competence in providing and maintaining system infrastructure, which includes:

- Technical infrastructure: hardware, software, network cabling, peripherals, database systems, operating systems, network components, metadata repositories, user applications etc.;
- Non-technical infrastructure: metadata standards, data mining standards, logical database model, methodology, manuals, test protocols, procedures for change control, change management procedures etc.

The choice of the DBI system implementation alternative is determined by answers to three basic questions:

- What parts of the DBI system can the enterprise maintain independently and what parts will it have to outsource?
- What data are available for analysis (quantity, quality and scope) and what is their level of confidentiality?
- How much is enterprise ready to pay for the implementation and maintenance of the DBI system?

The answers to these questions allow the selection of a package of internally implemented and outsourced services. The rights and responsibilities of the provider and the recipient must be carefully considered with respect to the management of the DBI architecture which needs to be kept up-to-date. With the dominating model of outsourcing most or all of the services, SMEs can also consider the DBI in the cloud option.

Cloud computing solutions are available in four versions of implementation: public, social, private and hybrid. From the perspective of maintenance costs the cheapest solution is a public cloud. From the perspective of safety and confidentiality of data processed the best solution is a private cloud. From the perspective of making benchmarking analysis in a group of enterprises which ensuring confidentiality and safety of data processed, the social cloud is the most recommended option. It is clear that the selection of implementation type

should be based on the size of the budget and the needs for processing and analyzing data in the DBI system.

Stage 3 – Design analysis

Step 3.1 – Analysis of business needs

Whether outsourced or in a cloud, a set of system functionalities must be defined by the enterprise to meet the needs of users. Furthermore, the enterprise must be capable of ensuring that the system is well maintained (e.g. it must be prepared to pay a monthly maintenance fee).

It is suggested that the DBI system implementation should be preceded by the construction of a reference model of key competitiveness factors. The main goal of the model is to determine the competitive position occupied by the enterprise in the analyzed group. The model allows both: to conduct internal analysis of the enterprise's competitiveness and to compare its situation with respect to the competitive environment or other co-users of the DBI system. The results provide managers with the knowledge about the importance and the impact of the key identified competitiveness factors on the competitive position, which is then reflected in the strategy and results in an increase the efficiency of competitiveness development management. The reference model of key competitiveness factors helps the DBI system project develop into a sustainable and relevant decision-making and analytical tool.

Step 3.2 – Analysis of source data

Analyses are conducted in terms of: accessibility, quality and size of resource data collected by the enterprise. This leads to the development of the model of storage, processing and sharing of data through provider of the DBI solutions. The size and analytical power of data resources in the DBI system is greatly enhanced compared to single data resources through the integration of multiple external sources, derived from multiple SME users. This concept is consistent with the approach proposed by analysts of Gartner Group (Vijayan, 2011), who at Gartner BI Summit Conference in May 2011 proposed the output with BI system outside the enterprise by using not only internal but also external data sources. This postulate was seen as useful but very difficult to pursue. The proposed solution demonstrates how it can be achieved in practice.

Step 3.3 – The prototype of analytical applications

The analytical system which will operate under the project can be successfully achieved using the prototyping method. This is a combination of analytical applications and IT tools oriented at well-defined analytical needs of the user.

Step 3.4 – Analysis of metadata repositories

As in the case of source data, the metadata will also be stored by the supplier's DBI solution. It should be also nuanced model of their storage and sharing. This model will condition the degree of independence of DBI users in a relation to possible changes in the individual layers of the system.

Stage 4 – System design

The system design is the responsibility of the solution provider and it is not a burden for the recipient of services. The design will consist of the following parts: analytical repository, ETL process, analytical applications, presentation layer and metadata repository. Using predefined industry-specific BI models can significantly accelerate and facility the DBI system design and implementation. Such type of solutions, very popular with data warehouse vendors, have now been increasingly offered by BI vendors. Each solution is customized but the time needed for needs assessment and system design is much shorter with each new implementation - it takes several weeks rather than several months.

Stage 5 – System development

The development of the system to be delivered as a service includes ensuring user access to the required set of functionalities and applications. The provider of the DBI system must develop the system in accordance with the design approved by the user.

Stage 6 – System implementation and testing

At this stage, the functionalities of the system are made available *via* a web browser and intuitive applications that do not require long and complicated training or IT skills. The whole solution is focused on minimizing implementation and training time and to run the system for the user as soon as possible.

Users of services provided also have the guarantee that their software will be constantly updated and any technical problems will be solved by the service provider. The enterprise pays for the use of specific application package or functionalities of these applications, as well as for maintaining and sharing the data collected. Yet, it does not have to bear the costs of maintenance, updating and servicing the system, which represents a significant fixed operating cost in any BI solution.

Stage 7 – System evaluation and test recommendations

The use of DBI system always leads to improved management awareness of the possibilities of using IT solutions in decision making process. Analytical and reporting needs of users are changing and they usually grow while the system is in place. If the system is supplied as a service its development is possible and available at any time at the request of the user. The provider takes the responsibility for delivering the expected modifications and all the customer is expected to do is to pay a potentially higher monthly fee.

The proposed approach to a DBI system offered as a service with a predefined analytical module and the database structure adapted to this module appears to be both affordable and feasible for SME customers. Tangible and intangible benefits from using that system are described in the next section.

BENEFITS FROM THE IMPLEMENTATION OF THE DBI SYSTEM IN A CONSORTIUM OF SMES

The implementation of such a complex project as the DBI system requires an assessment of the anticipated benefits from the implementation, which can be captured in the following research question:

RQ3: What are the measurable effects of the implementation of the DBI system for SMEs?

Every component of the system architecture has measurable and immeasurable impacts on the implementation of the DBI solution. The expected range of effects of the DBI implementation is shown in Table 3.

As seen in Table 3, if properly implemented and effectively used the DBI system will result in time savings, rationalization of costs and the optimization of management efficiency. The proposed system architecture also allows the enrichment of management experience by exposure to the experience of competing enterprises in the common market, according to good practices and ethical code of benchmarking.

The utility of the proposed solution was tested in a research experiment involving 10 dental clinics of the original group of 150 (covered by survey research). The data collected from these clinics were used to build the DBI system. The purpose of using the system was to determine the competitive position of each clinic in the group. A reference model of key competitiveness factors was developed as the structure of:

- Three identified areas of measurable effects (E1 - modernity and quality of medical services, E2 - the ability to meet the needs of patients, E3 - results of sales);
- Group of key competitiveness factors (C1- technological level, C2 – the quality of services, C3 - timeliness of

Table 3. Effects of the implementation of the DBI system for a Consortium of SMEs (Source: own research).

DBI feature	Measurable effects	Immeasurable effects
Analysis of competitive position of the enterprise	Maximization of profit, rationalization of costs	Support for setting goals and guiding the development of competitive strategy
Benchmarking results between co-users the DBI system	Maximization of profit, rationalization of costs	Competitive strategy driven by experiences of DBI co-users
Analytics and reporting	Budgeting	Less uncertainty the management decision process
Predictive analysis	Rationalization of costs of competitive growth	Fewer operational risk in the management decision process
Analytical data repository, data warehouse	Instant access to management information	Improved availability of analytical data for a wider range of users in any place and at any time
Multidimensional data processing tools	Queries and analyses less time consuming	Improved availability of analytics for a wider range of users in any place and at any time
Visualization tools, presentation and distribution of information	Instant reporting and dissemination	Improved availability of management information for a wider range of users in any place and at any time
ETL tools	Improved data quality also in transactional systems	Data standardization across the enterprise for all co-users the DBI system

service delivery, C4 - lasting relationships with customers, C5 - sales, C6 - costs and expenses, C7 - the utilization of fixed assets, C8 – the staff productivity) defined value of the competitive position CP for each enterprise in analyzed group.

Then benchmarking of the obtained results allowed for matching the strategy of competitive development to this competitive position which the clinic intends to take in this group in the future.

The results of the experiment confirmed the utility of the proposed DBI concept. The DBI system enhanced by the reference model of key competitiveness factors was more understandable, friendly and helpful to users than the IT solution equipped only with analytical and reporting tools. Users in the dental clinics could adjust their strategic plans and activities to their expected competitive position. Examples of practical applications of this solution and its effects were described in detail in (Rostek, 2012). The following assessment was carried out to provide evidence for the cost-effectiveness and efficiently of the DBI implementation.

It assumed that the payback period of a properly implemented and effectively used BI system should 3 years. Based on the results of an assessment of 180 systems (Burns, 2009) and Pentaho (Madsen, 2010) it can be concluded that the costs of implementation and maintenance of BI within the first three years of use are

at a level of US$30,000 to 100,000 in small companies and US$ 30,000 to 400,000 in medium-sized companies. Referring to the cost of financial performance of the SME sector in Poland it can be said that the implementation of the BI system and maintaining it in its first year of life is a burden of 3.5 to 25.5% of annual earnings of a small company and 2.8 to 30% of average annual earnings a medium-size company. During the estimated 3 years of the payback period this load is 3.4 to 12% of 3-year earnings of a small company and 1 to13.5% of 3-year earnings of medium-size company. The upper limits of these ranges are a barrier to implementing a BI in SMEs.

By adopting the proposed DBI solution for a group of 12 small SMEs (total number of users is 25), the load in the first year of the system is less than 10% of the earnings of each company, and in the 3-year period below 3.5% of 3-year earnings of each of them (Table 4). Thus, for each of the project implementation, knowing the estimated costs as defined by the software vendor and the service provider, you can determine the optimal size of the DBI system user group the, which will reduce costs and increase the efficiency of its implementation.

Considering the effects of the use DBI solution in the research group a change in results is observed after using analytics and reports in 2008 to 2009 and their impact on the results of 2010 (Table 5).

Over 2-month periods of 2010 compared to the years 2008 to 2009 gross sales grew by an average of PLN

Table 4. The share of the DBI system cost in the financial results of the group of 12 small enterprises about 25 users (Source: own research).

Software vendor	Solution name	System cost / Financial result [%]	
		1st year of the system life	Within 3 years of the system life
Microsoft	SQL Server 2008 R2 Enterprise Edition	0.86	0.29
QlikTech	QlikView	1.36	0.69
Pentaho (Open source solution)	Pentaho Business Intelligence Gold Edition	0.86	0.86
SAP	SAP BusinessObjects Edge Professional Edition	4.54	2.05
MicroStrategy	MicroStrategy 9	6.28	2.85
IBM	Cognos 8 Business Intelligence	6.72	3.16
Oracle	Oracle Business Intelligence Suite Enterprise Edition Plus	9.17	4.16

Table 5. The DBI system efficiency in 2010 (Source: own research).

Period of analysis		Number of patients	Gross sales	Profit	Number of patient visits
2008-2009	On average within 2 months [PLN ,000]	4,714	319.00	28.00	2,011
	Per one patient visit [PLN]		158.64	13.73	
2010	On average within 2 months [PLN ,000]	18,742	603.00	97.00	3,760
	Per one patient visit [PLN]		160.28	25.68	
The difference: 2010-(2008/2009)	On average within 2 months [PLN ,000]	14,028	284.00	69.00	1,749
	Per one patient visit [PLN]		1.64	11.95	

284, 000 and profits earned in that period grew by PLN 69,000. Assuming that about 50% of this profit is a result of the use of prepared analyses and reports in the management process and that this trend will be permanent, it becomes possible to calculate the rate of return on investment ROI in one-year and three-year periods (Table 6).

Table 6 shows that clinics that act alone could implement only the cheapest solutions - Microsoft, QlikTech or Pentaho. However, as a group of 10 clinics, using a shared DBI system they can choose any vendor, even the most expensive in the market. In this situation the determinant of used technology does not have limited financial resources, but the actual analytical and information needs of an enterprise. This confirms the validity of the concept of group system implementation for the SME sector.

SUMMARY

The paper presents research results which reveal that Polish SMEs have not been heavy users of IT tools to support their management decision making. There is evidence, however, that suggests that the use of Business Intelligence solutions can significantly increase the quality of management decisions and reduce management risks.

The implementation of a typical integrated BI solution with development and maintenance cost borne by the enterprise seems too big a technical, logistical and financial burden for individual SMEs. One additional constraint is the low IT awareness of managers in the SME sector who have limited understanding and the advanced methods of data analysis. Further, companies do not collect insufficient amount of data. Therefore, an alternative approach is proposed to the development of a DBI solution:

- DBI system offered as a shared service for a group of SMEs;
- All DBI users supply their data into the system thus increasing informational and analytical system strength;
- The DBI system is based on predefined components

Table 6. ROI on the implementation of DBI by a single vs. a group of 10 clinics (Source: own research).

Software vendor	Solution name	ROI (1year) for single clinic (%)	ROI (1 year) for a group of 10 clinics (%)	ROI (3 years) for single clinic (%)	ROI (3 years) for a group of 10 clinics (%)
Microsoft	SQL Server 2008 R2 Enterprise Edition	35.64	1256.38	306.91	3969.13
QlikTech	QlikView	-14.49	755.11	68.58	1585.78
Pentaho (open source solution)	Pentaho Business Intelligence Gold Edition	35.64	1256.38	35.64	1256.38
SAP	SAP BusinessObjects Edge Professional Edition	-74.46	155.42	-43.54	464.62
MicroStrategy	MicroStrategy 9	-81.53	84.67	-59.31	306.91
IBM	Cognos 8 Business Intelligence	-82.75	72.52	-63.24	267.62
Oracle	Oracle Business Intelligence Suite Enterprise Edition Plus	-87.35	26.48	-72.10	178.97

with the key role played by a reference model of competitiveness factors dedicated to a specific group of SMEs;
- DBI offering an intuitive capability with predefined analytics and reports scenarios.

As seen earlier, a proper implementation and an effective use of the DBI system will result in time savings, rationalization of costs and the optimization of management efficiency. The proposed system architecture also allows the enrichment of own management experience by experiences of competing enterprises in the common market, according to good practices and ethical code of benchmarking. The proposed concept of The DBI system, as demonstrated by the results of the experiment, can efficiently support the development of strategies shaping competitiveness in SMEs. Therefore it is the prospect of develop BI technology and the possibility of its wider use in enterprises of all business sectors.

REFERENCES

Acedo F, Florin J (2006). An entrepreneurial cognition perspective on the internationalization of SMEs. J. Int. Entrep. 4(1):49-67.
Andonov-Acev D, Buckovska A, Blagojevic Z, Kraljevski V (2008). Enterprise performance monitoring. Information Technology Interfaces (ITI 2008), 30th International Conference pp.185-190.
Audretsch D (2001). Research issues relating to structure, competition, and performance of small technology-based firms. Small Bus. Econ. 16(1):37-51.
Baars H, Horakh T, Kemper H (2007). Business Intelligence outsourcing a framework, Proceedings of the 15th European Conference on Information Systems (ECIS2007), St. Gallen (Switzerland) pp.1155-1166.
Bitterer A (2011) - Hype Cycle for Business Intelligence. Gartner Report, Gartner Inc., Stamford, CT.
Blackburn R, Jarvis R (2010). The Role of Small and Medium Practices in Providing Business Support to Small- and Medium-sized Enterprises. Information paper. International Federation of Accounts, New York, 2010.
Bogza RM, Zaharie D (2008). Business intelligence as a competitive differentiator. Automation, Quality and Testing, Robotics. AQTR 2008. IEEE International Conference 1:146-151.
Brobst S, Morris M (2002). An advanced I/O architecture for supporting mixed workloads in an active data warehouse environment. Database and Expert Systems Applications. Proceedings. 13th International Workshop pp.779-784.
Burns M (2009). BI/CPM survey 2009. Using technology to improve the way you do business. CA Magazine. December 2009, Canada.
Campbell H (2006).The role of organizational knowledge management strategies in the quest for business intelligence. Engineering Management Conference, 2006 IEEE International, Bahia pp.231-236.
Chadha B, Iyer M (2010). BI in a Cloud: Defining the Architecture for Quick Wins. SetLabs Briefings, vol. 8, no. 1, Infosys Limited.
Chen M, Wang S (2010). The use of a hybrid fuzzy-Delphi-AHP approach to develop global business intelligence for information service firms. Expert Syst. Appl. 37:7394-7407.
Chung W, Chen H, Nunamaker JF (2003). Business intelligence explorer: a knowledge map framework for discovering business intelligence on the Web. System Sciences. Proceedings of the 36th Annual Hawaii International Conference pp.6-10.
Chunxu JH, Li WJ (2010). Research on EDA based Right-Time Business Intelligence System. Information Management and Engineering (ICIME), The 2nd IEEE International Conference, Chengdu pp.476-479.
Cumming D, MacIntosh J (2006). Crowding out private equity: Canadian evidence. J. Bus. Venturing 21(5):569-609.
Curko K, Bach MP, Radonic G (2007). Business Intelligence and Business Process Management in Banking Operations. Information Technology Interfaces 2007 (ITI 2007), 29th International Conference pp.57-62.
Di Giacomo M (2004). Public support to entrepreneurial firms. J. Private Equity 8(1):22-38.
Dibrell C, Davis P, Craig J (2008). Fuelling innovation through

information technology in SMEs. J. Small Bus. Manage. 46(2):203-218.

Feng Y, Liu Y, Li X, Gao C, Xu H (2010). Design of the Low-cost Business Intelligence System Based on Multi-agent. Information Science and Management Engineering (ISME), 2010 International Conference, Xi'an pp.291-294.

Finlay PN (1994). Introducing decision support systems. Oxford, UK Cambridge, Mass., NCC Blackwell; Blackwell Publishers.

Freel M (2003). Sectoral patterns of small firm innovation, networking and proximity. Res. Policy 32(3):751-770.

Ganapathy K, Vaidehi V (2011). Medical intelligence for quality improvement in Service Oriented Architecture. Recent Trends in Information Technology (ICRTIT), International Conference pp.161-166.

Garengo P, Biazzo S, Bitici US (2005). Performance measurement systems in SMEs: a review for a research agenda. Int. J. Manage. Rev. 7(1):25-47.

Goel M (2010). Cloud ready business intelligence with Oracle Business Intelligence 11g. Oracle Corporation, Redwood Shores, CA.

Hongfeng X, Liya Y (2009). Research Standardization for Business Intelligence Systems Integration based on SaaS. Networking and Digital Society. ICNDS '09. International Conference, Guiyang, Guizhou 2:242-246.

Inmon WH, Strauss D, Neushloss G (2008). DW 2.0: The Architecture for the Next Generation of Data Warehousing. Morgan Kaufmann, San Francisco.

Javanmard J, Moaven S, Habibi J (2011). Introducing a framework to use SOA in business intelligence for real-time environments. Software Engineering and Service Science (ICSESS), IEEE 2nd International Conference on 2011, pp. 94-99.

Karaganni S., Labriandis L (2001) - The pros and cons of SME going international. East. Europ. Econ. 39(2):5-29.

Lituchy T, Rail A (2000). Bed and breakfasts, Small Inns, and the Internet: The impact of technology on the globalization of small businesses. J. Int. Market. 8(2):86-97.

Low D, Chapman R (2007). Inter-relationships between innovation and market orientation of SMEs. Manage. Res. News 30(12):878-891.

Luhn HP (1958). A Business Intelligence system. IBM J. 2(4).

Madsen M (2010). Lowering the Cost of Business Intelligence With Open Source. Third Nature, Rogue River, USA.

Malinowski E, Zimanyi E (2007). Spatial DataWarehouses: Some Solutions and Unresolved Problems. Databases for Next Generation Researchers (SWOD 2007), IEEE International Workshop pp.1-6.

Marjanovic O (2007). The Next Stage of Operational Business Intelligence: Creating New Challenges for Business Process Management. System Sciences 2007 (HICSS 2007), 40th Annual Hawaii International Conference, s.1-10.

Marjanovic O (2010). Business Value Creation through Business Processes Management and Operational Business Intelligence Integration. System Sciences 2010 (HICSS 2010), 43rd Hawaii International Conference pp.1-10.

Mason C, Harrison R (2004). Improving access to early stage venture capital in regional economies: A new approach to investment readiness. Local Economy 19(2):159-173.

Miller GJ (ed.) (2005). The Business Intelligence Competency Center: a SAS Aproach. SAS Institute Inc., Cary, North Carolina.

Niu L, Lu J, Chew E, Zhang G (2007). An Exploratory Cognitive Business Intelligence System. In: Proceedings of Web Intelligence pp.812-815.

Paladino B (2007). Five Key Principles of Corporate Performance Management. Wiley, Hoboken, NJ.

Pan D, Pan Y (2010). Metadata versioning for DW2.0 architecture. 29th Control Conference (CCC), Chinese pp.5106-5109.

Polyzotis N, Skiadopoulos S, Vassiliadis P, Simitsis A, Frantzell NE (2007). Supporting Streaming Updates in an Active Data Warehouse. Data Engineering (ICDE 2007). IEEE 23rd International Conference on 2007 pp.476-485.

Polyzotis N, Skiadopoulos S, Vassiliadis P, Simitsis A, Frantzell N (2008). Meshing Streaming Updates with Persistent Data in an Active Data Warehouse. Knowledge and Data Engineering, IEEE Transactions 20(7):976-991.

Porter ME (1998). Competitive Strategy: Techniques for Analyzing

Industries and Competitors. Free Press.

Power DJ (2007). A Brief History of Decision Support Systems. DSSResources.COM, World Wide Web, ver. 4.0. http://DSSResources.COM/history/dsshistory.html (read on 16-03-2012).

Rostek K (2012). The reference model of competitiveness factors for SME medical sector. Econ. Model. 29(2012):2039-2048.

Qin D (2009). Design of Medical Insurance Supervision System Based on Active Data Warehouse and SOA. Computer Science and Information Engineering, WRI World Congress 3:45-49.

Salvato C, Lassini U, Wiklund J (2007). Dynamics of external growth in SMEs: Process of model acquisition capabilities emergence. Schmalebach Bus. Rev. 59(3):282-305.

Secrieru O, Vigneault M (2004). Public venture capital, occupational choice, and entrepreneurship. Top. Econ. Anal. Policy 4(1):1-22.

Shi Y, Lu X (2010). The Role of Business Intelligence in Business Performance Management. Information Management, Innovation Management and Industrial Engineering (ICIII), International Conference 4:184-186.

Tan W, Shen W, Xu L, Zhou B, Li L (2008). A Business Process Intelligence System for Enterprise Process Performance Management. Systems, Man, and Cybernetics, Part C: Applications and Reviews. IEEE Transactions 38(6):745-756.

Teece DJ, Pisano G, Shuen A (1997). Dynamic Capabilities and Strategic Management. In: Strateg. Manage. J. 18(7):509-533.

Tenai JK, Bitok JK, Cheruiyot TK, Maru LC (2009). Moderating Variables On SME's Strategies And Competitiveness For International Trade: A Survey of Horticultural Traders in Urban and Peri-Urban Areas in Kenya. Int. Bus. Econ. Res. J. 8(12):105-114.

Thomas O, Adam O, Leyking K, Loos P (2006). A Fuzzy Paradigm Approach for Business Process Intelligence. IEEE Joint Conference on E-Commerce Technology (CEC 2006) and Enterprise Computing, IEEE Computer Society Press pp.206-213.

Tiwari S, Razdan D, Richariya P, Tomar S (2011). A web usage mining framework for business intelligence. Communication Software and Networks (ICCSN), IEEE 3rd International Conference, pp.731-734.

Turban E (1995). Decision support and expert systems: management support systems. Englewood Cliffs, N.J., Prentice Hall.

Venkatadri M, Hanumat GS, Manjunath G (2010). A Novel Business Intelligence System Framework. Universal Journal of Computer Science and Engineering Technology 2:112-116.

Vijayan J (2011). BI must become part of broad IT strategy. Computerworld, Los Angeles, http://www.computerworld.com/s/article/9216450/BI_must_become_part_of_ broad_IT_strategy (read on 16-09-2012).

Wade D, Recardo R (2001). Corporate Performance Management. Wyd. Butterworth-Heinemann, Massatchussetts.

Wu L, Barash G, Bartolini C (2007). A Service-oriented Architecture for Business Intelligence. Service-Oriented Computing and Applications. SOCA '07. IEEE International Conference pp.279-285.

Zepeda L, Celma M (2006). A model driven approach for data warehouse conceptual design. Databases and Information Systems, 7th International Baltic Conference, pp.114-121.

Zhang R, Pan D (2010). Metadata management based on Lifecycle for DW 2.0. Intelligent Control and Automation (WCICA), 8th World Congress, pp.5154-5157.

Zhou N, Cheng H, Chen H, Xiao S (2007). The Framework of Text-Driven Business Intelligence. Wireless Communications, Networking and Mobile Computing. WiCom 2007. International Conference pp.5468-5471.

Polish Special Reports

Brussa A, Tarnawa A eds. (2011) - The report on the state of the sector of small and medium-sized enterprises in Poland in 2009–2010. PARP, Warsaw.

DiS (2010). BI market in Poland in 2005-2012. Monitor IT, 14(2):321.

Tarnawa A, Zadura-Lichota P eds. (2012). The report on the state of the sector of small and medium-sized enterprises in Poland in 2010–2011. PARP, Warsaw.

Wilmańska A ed. (2010). The report on the state of the sector of small and medium-sized enterprises in Poland in 2008–2009. PARP,

Warsaw.

Żółcińska W (2009). What Polish companies expect from BI? CIO Magazine of IT Directors, International Data Group Poland, No. 07/2009, Warszawa.

Żołnierski A ed. (2009). The report on the state of the sector of small and medium-sized enterprises in Poland in 2007-2008. PARP, Warsaw.

Permissions

The contributors of this book come from diverse backgrounds, making this book a truly international effort. This book will bring forth new frontiers with its revolutionizing research information and detailed analysis of the nascent developments around the world.

We would like to thank all the contributing authors for lending their expertise to make the book truly unique. They have played a crucial role in the development of this book. Without their invaluable contributions this book wouldn't have been possible. They have made vital efforts to compile up to date information on the varied aspects of this subject to make this book a valuable addition to the collection of many professionals and students.

This book was conceptualized with the vision of imparting up-to-date information and advanced data in this field. To ensure the same, a matchless editorial board was set up. Every individual on the board went through rigorous rounds of assessment to prove their worth. After which they invested a large part of their time researching and compiling the most relevant data for our readers.

The editorial board has been involved in producing this book since its inception. They have spent rigorous hours researching and exploring the diverse topics which have resulted in the successful publishing of this book. They have passed on their knowledge of decades through this book. To expedite this challenging task, the publisher supported the team at every step. A small team of assistant editors was also appointed to further simplify the editing procedure and attain best results for the readers.

Apart from the editorial board, the designing team has also invested a significant amount of their time in understanding the subject and creating the most relevant covers. They scrutinized every image to scout for the most suitable representation of the subject and create an appropriate cover for the book.

The publishing team has been an ardent support to the editorial, designing and production team. Their endless efforts to recruit the best for this project, has resulted in the accomplishment of this book. They are a veteran in the field of academics and their pool of knowledge is as vast as their experience in printing. Their expertise and guidance has proved useful at every step. Their uncompromising quality standards have made this book an exceptional effort. Their encouragement from time to time has been an inspiration for everyone.

The publisher and the editorial board hope that this book will prove to be a valuable piece of knowledge for researchers, students, practitioners and scholars across the globe.

List of Contributors

Hui-Ming Teng
Department of Business Administration, Chihlee Institute of Technology, No. 313, Sec. 1, Wunhua Road, Banciao City, Taipei County 220, Taiwan

Marcelo Seido Nagano
Department of Production Engineering, School of Engineering, São Carlos, University of São Paulo Av. Trabalhador Sãocarlense, 400, São Carlos – SP, 13566-590, Brazil

Marcelo Botelho da Costa Moraes
Department of Production Engineering, School of Engineering, São Carlos, University of São Paulo Av. Trabalhador Sãocarlense, 400, São Carlos – SP, 13566-590, Brazil

Elahe Shariatmadari Serkani
Department of Industrial Engineering, Science and Research Branch, Islamic Azad University, Tehran, Iran

Mostafa Mardi
Department of Management, Islamic Azad University, Tehran Central Branch, Iran

Esmaeel Najafi
Department of Management and Economics, Islamic Azad University, Science and Research Branch, Tehran, Iran

Khadijeh Jahanian
Department of Management and Economics, Islamic Azad University, Science and Research Branch, Tehran, Iran

Ali Taghizadeh Herat
Department of Management and Economics, Islamic Azad University, Science and Research Branch, Tehran, Iran

Taghizadeh Houshang
Islamic Azad University - Tabriz Branch, - Yaghchian-Tohid Street- Mosque Square- Saba Alley- West Sixth alley- No. 229- Second Floor, Tabriz, Iran

Honarpour Amir
University Teknology Malaysia, 33c-30-1, Villa Puteri Condo, Jalan Tun Ismail, Kuala Lumpur, Malaysia

Rahul Hakhu
Rayat Institute of Management, Rayat Technology Centre of Excellence, RailMajra, District. S.B.S. Nagar, Punjab, INDIA-144 533

Ravi Kiran
School of Management and Social Sciences, Thapar University, Patiala, Punjab, INDIA – 147 004

D. P. Goyal
Management Development Institute, Gurgaon, INDIA - 122 007

Omonijo, Dare Ojo
Department of Student Affairs, Covenant University, P. M. B. 1023 Ota, Nigeria

Nnedum, Obiajulu Anthony Ugochukwu
Department of Psychology, Nnamdi Azikiwe University, P. M. B. 5025 Awka, Nigeria

Fadugba, Akinrole Olumuyiwa
Department of Business Management, Covenant University, P. M. B. 1023 Ota, Nigeria

Uche, Onyekwere Chizaram Oliver
Department of Religion and Human Relations, Nnamdi Azikiwe University, P. M. B. 5025, Awka, Nigeria

Biereenu-Nnabugwu, Makodi
Department of Political Science, Nnamdi Azikiwe University, P. M. B. 5025, Awka, Nigeria

Eduardo Scherer Rücker
Production and System Engineering Program – UNISINOS, Research Group on Modeling for Learning – GMAP, Av. Unisinos, 950 – São Leopoldo – Rio Grande do Sul – Brasil

Luis Henrique Rodrigues
Production and System Engineering Program – UNISINOS, Research Group on Modeling for Learning – GMAP, Av. Unisinos, 950 – São Leopoldo – Rio Grande do Sul – Brasil

Daniel Pacheco Lacerda
Production and System Engineering Program – UNISINOS, Research Group on Modeling for Learning – GMAP, Av. Unisinos, 950 – São Leopoldo – Rio Grande do Sul – Brasil

Ricardo Augusto Cassel
Production Engineering Program – UFRGS, Av. Osvaldo Aranha, 99 – 5°. Andar – Porto Alegre – Rio Grande do Sul – Brasil

Mohd Noor Azli Ali Khan
Department of Management, Faculty of Management and Human Resource Development, Universiti Teknologi Malaysia, Johor Bahru, Johor, Malaysia

Noor Azizi Ismail
College of Business, Universiti Utara Malaysia, Sintok, Kedah, Malaysia

Norhayati Zakuan
Department of Management, Faculty of Management and Human Resource Development, Universiti Teknologi Malaysia, Johor Bahru, Johor, Malaysia

Adam Mat
Faculty of Business Management, Universiti Teknologi MARA (UiTM), Malaysia

Razli Che Razak
Centre for International Affairs and Cooperation (CIAC), Universiti Utara Malaysia (UUM), Sintok, Kedah, Malaysia

Tai-hoon Kim
GVSA and University of Tasmania, Australia

Chih-Chung Chen
Department of Knowledge Management, Aletheia University (Matou campus), Taiwan, R.O.C

Mahdi Salehi
Accounting, Ferdowsi University of Mashhad, Mashhad, Iran

Abdoreza Abdipour
Payame Noor University, Andimeshk Branch, Iran

Leonardo Rocha de Oliveira
Pontifical University of Rio Grande do Sul, Brazil

Adriano JulioMurlick
Pontifical University of Rio Grande do Sul, Brazil

Gabriela Viale Pereira
Pontifical University of Rio Grande do Sul, Brazil

Rafael Vicentin
Pontifical University of Rio Grande do Sul, Brazil

Deseré Kokt
Faculty of Management Sciences, Central University of Technology, Free State, Bloemfontein, South Africa

Thakane Koelane
Faculty of Management Sciences, Central University of Technology, Free State, Bloemfontein, South Africa

Sabina Mirzaei Nobari
Azerbaijan National Academy of Sciences, Institute of Information Technologies 370141, Baku, Azerbaijan

Davood Hosein Zadeh
Department of Psychology and Educational Sciences College, Islamic Azad University, Saveh Branch, Saveh, Iran

Li-Hsing Ho
Department of Technology Management, Chung-Hua University, 707, Sec. 2, WuFu Rd., HsinChu, Taiwan

Tien-Fu Peng
Graduate Institute of Technology Management, Chung-Hua University, 707, Sec. 2, WuFu Rd., HsinChu, Taiwan

Shu-Yun Feng
Graduate Institute of Technology Management, Chung-Hua University, 707, Sec. 2, WuFu Rd., HsinChu, Taiwan

Tieh-Min Yen
Department of Technology Management, Chung-Hua University, 707, Sec. 2, WuFu Rd., HsinChu, Taiwan

Azizul Baten
Department of Statistics, School of Physical Sciences, ShahJalal University of Science and Technology, Sylhet-3114, Bangladesh

Anton Abdulbasah Kamil
School of Distance Education, Universiti Sains Malaysia, 11800 USM, Penang, Malaysia

Riaan Rudman
Stellenbosch University, Department of Accounting, Private Bag X1, Matieland, 7602, South-Africa

Len Steenkamp
Stellenbosch University, Department of Accounting, Private Bag X1, Matieland, 7602, South-Africa

Aminreza Kamalian
Department of Management and Accounting, Zahedan University of Sistan and Baluchestan, Zahedan, Iran

Maryam Rashki
Department of Management and Accounting, Zahedan University of Sistan and Baluchestan, Zahedan, Iran

Mah Lagha Arbabi
Management department of International University of Chabahar, Chabahar, Iran

Milad Keshvari Fard
Department of Industrial Engineering, Sharif University of Technology, Tehran, Iran

M. Reza Akbari
Department of Industrial Engineering, Sharif University of Technology, Tehran, Iran

O. Sulaiman
Faculty of Maritime Studies and Marine Science, Universiti Malaysia Terengganu, 21030 UMT, Kuala Terengganu, Terengganu, Malaysia

A. H. Saharuddin
Faculty of Maritime Studies and Marine Science, Universiti Malaysia Terengganu, 21030 UMT, Kuala Terengganu, Terengganu, Malaysia

A. S. A. Kader
Faculty of Mechanical Engineering, Department of Marine Technology, Universiti Technologi Malaysia, 81300 Skudai, Johor, Malaysia

M. Azeem Naseer
Commerce and Finance, Superior University Lahore, Pakistan

George S. Oreku
Research Development, Faculty of Economic Sciences and Information Technology, North-West University, Vaal Triangle Campus, P. O. Box 1174, Vanderbijlpark 1900, Gauteng, South Africa

Thembelihle Allah
Faculty of Business, Cape Peninsula University of Technology, PO Box 625, Cape Town, 8000, South Africa

Puleng August
Faculty of Business, Cape Peninsula University of Technology, PO Box 625, Cape Town, 8000, South Africa

Siphamandla Bhaza
Faculty of Business, Cape Peninsula University of Technology, PO Box 625, Cape Town, 8000, South Africa

Tinashe Chigovanyika
Faculty of Business, Cape Peninsula University of Technology, PO Box 625, Cape Town, 8000, South Africa

Unathi Dyan
Faculty of Business, Cape Peninsula University of Technology, PO Box 625, Cape Town, 8000, South Africa

Tinashe Muteweye
Faculty of Business, Cape Peninsula University of Technology, PO Box 625, Cape Town, 8000, South Africa

Mandisi Ngcoza
Faculty of Business, Cape Peninsula University of Technology, PO Box 625, Cape Town, 8000, South Africa

Neliswa Tshiwula
Faculty of Business, Cape Peninsula University of Technology, PO Box 625, Cape Town, 8000, South Africa

Vuyiseka Qambela
Faculty of Business, Cape Peninsula University of Technology, PO Box 625, Cape Town, 8000, South Africa

Yanga Vooi
Faculty of Business, Cape Peninsula University of Technology, PO Box 625, Cape Town, 8000, South Africa

Juan-Pierré Bruwer
Faculty of Business, Cape Peninsula University of Technology, PO Box 625, Cape Town, 8000, South Africa

Mehrnaz Heidari Soureshjani
Department of Industrial Engineering, Amirkabir University of Technology, Tehran, Iran

Ali Mohammad Kimiagari
Department of Industrial Engineering, Amirkabir University of Technology, Tehran, Iran

Katarzyna Rostek
Warsaw University of Technology, Faculty of Management, ul.Narbutta 85, 02-524 Warsaw, Poland

Printed in the USA
CPSIA information can be obtained
at www.ICGtesting.com
JSHW051429221024
72173JS00006B/1414